33

MAR 1 4 2006

■ The Japanese Voter

The

Japanese

Voter

Scott C. Flanagan, Shinsaku Kohei,

Ichiro Miyake, Bradley M. Richardson,

and Joji Watanuki

with a Foreword by Warren E. Miller

Yale University Press

New Haven and London

The costs of publishing this book have been defrayed in part by an award from the Books on Japan Fund in respect of *The Formation of Science in Japan*, by James Bartholomew, published by Yale University Press. The Fund is financed by the Japan Foundation from funds contributed generously by Japanese companies.

Designed by James J. Johnson and set in Times Roman by The Composing Room of Michigan, Inc.
Printed in the United States of America by Vail-Ballou Press, Binghamton, New York.

Library of Congress Cataloging-in-Publication Data

The Japanese voter / Scott C. Flanagan . . . [et al.].
    p.   cm.
    Includes bibliographical references and index.
    ISBN 0-300-04780-0 (cloth)
    1. Elections—Japan.   2. Voting—Japan.   3. Japan—Politics and government—1945–   4. Japan—Social conditions—1945–   I. Flanagan, Scott C.
JQ1692.J37   1991
324.952′04—dc20   91-8348
                                              CIP

The paper in this book meets the guidelines for permanence and durability of the Committee on Production Guidelines for Book Longevity of the Council on Library Resources.

10   9   8   7   6   5   4   3   2   1

■ Contents

Part III Short-term Influences on Voting Behavior

Part IV Conclusions

■ Tables

■ Figures

■ Foreword

Volumes like *The Japanese Voter* are unique in their contribution to scholarship well beyond their manifest contribution to a specific body of knowledge. Books like *Political Action, Political Change in Britain,* or *The American Voter*—the avowed model for *The Japanese Voter*—come into existence because of commitments to ideas that go beyond the range of most individual, personal scholarly efforts. For this genre it is not just the challenge of opening a new intellectual domain but also the acceptance of obligations to fellow investigators that veritably create a new collegial institution engaged in an extended undertaking of great organizational complexity and intellectual difficulty. Research activities directly relevant to this book span a full quarter of a century. Support for data collection and analysis was provided by a host of institutions, both Japanese and American. And the end product exists because the several authors gave priorities to their common endeavor over and above the unremitting pressures of more local and personal needs.

The accomplishments of the authors of *The Japanese Voter* are the more extraordinary as they bridge a formidable and heretofore virtually unsurmountable cultural gap. They eliminate a language barrier that has long deprived most occidental scholars of more than journalistic accounts of Japanese electoral behavior. Even more crucial to the internationalization of our scholarship, they successfully bring Japanese political research into the intellectual mainstream in a comprehensive treatment commensurate with the established tradition of the national election studies of the Atlantic community. The emphasis that earlier case studies of Japanese voting behavior gave to social networks and interpersonal influences reappears in *The Japanese Voter*. The treatment is no longer ideographic, however; instead, this book translates many of the culturally unique patterns of influence to compatibility with those streams of Western thought that both separate and integrate the personal and the political along with the short term and the long term. It is doubly important that this happen at a time when the growing complexity of Japanese party politics commands increasing attention throughout the world.

The authors bear gracefully the burden of representing their mentors and a variety of scholarly traditions with their own creative integration of what they themselves have learned over three decades of study. *The Japanese Voter* takes its place along with *Political Action, Political Representation in France, The Civic Culture, The Labyrinth of Democracy, Political Change in Britain,* and *The American Voter*—all major collaborative works long in the making—as evidence that apparently still waters of scholarship are often running deep.

Warren E. Miller

■ Preface

The Japanese Voter is the first comprehensive study of voting behavior in Japan to appear in English. As such, it has self-consciously drawn its inspiration from works like *The American Voter* and *Political Change in Britain*. While the reader will have to decide whether our effort should be mentioned with such august company, it was our intention to perform the same kind of initial, inclusive survey of the variety of influences that impinge upon the voting decision. In pursuing this objective we have tried to present a model of Japanese voting behavior that is both familiar to and interpretable by Western scholars. Heretofore most of the readily available English-language books on Japanese parties, elections, and political behavior have followed a case-study approach that adopts an anthropological style of analysis. These studies frequently stress cultural categories and explanations, drawing our attention to unique patterns that have no close cognates in the West. Unfortunately, these studies have simply reinforced a widespread impression among Western behaviorists that Japan remains a largely inaccessible, exceptional case. (Japan specialists have been moving away from cultural and other kinds of unique explanations of political behavior in Japan, and a growing emphasis on comparative conceptual categories in their work can be seen. There has been a lag in the diffusion of this shifting perspective among non-Japan specialists, however; this is perhaps most true in the case of Western behaviorists, who have often found little in the standard nonquantitative treatments of Japanese political behavior to which they can relate.) We have tried to cut through this exceptionalism by presenting an analysis of Japanese voting behavior in terms that are readily familiar to Western behaviorists. At the same time we draw the reader's attention to contrasts between Japanese and Western voting behavior. While Japan is not unique, there are nevertheless a number of intriguing differences in the patterns of influence that impact upon the decision of the Japanese voter.

This book is the fruition of a long-term research effort that provided extensive interaction among the five project members. The careers of all of our team members have been deeply immersed in the study of Japanese voting behavior, but this work goes well beyond presenting simply a survey and summary of previous findings in the extant literature. Rather, each chapter is based on the respective author's original research, yielding in many cases new findings and innovative conceptualizations. Moreover, despite the fact that most chapters are the work of a single author, the book stands as a team effort rather than a collection of individual contributions. This team product resulted first from our adoption of a tightly organized design. The introductory chapter lays out the variety of kinds of influences affecting voting decisions that have been identified in the comparative literature and previous Japanese research. Chapters 2 through 9 address successively one or two of these influences, which are presented in the following sequence: long-term social influences, long-term political influences, short-term political influences, and short-term social influences. The concluding section is divided into two chapters. The first integrates all these variables into a common model, assesses their relative influence at one point in time, 1976, and in summarizing the study's major conclusions emphasizes the stable aspects of Japanese voting behavior. The second focuses on the ways voting behavior has been changing in Japan over time through an analysis of the 1989 and 1990 elections and the identification of the growing and waning influences of different sets of variables.

Beyond our common design, we worked toward a more coherent and integrated product through an extensive cross-fertilization and editing process. We all learned from each other's findings and perspectives and benefited from each other's comments and criticisms. Moreover, many of the key concepts introduced in the book were group rather than individual creations. For example, the concepts of affective and cognitive partisanship introduced in chapters 6 and 10 were hatched through Ichiro Miyake and Bradley Richardson's innovative and distinct approaches to operationalizing partisanship and my efforts as editor to integrate them. Throughout the book, the relevant findings from other chapters are carefully cross-referenced.

Voting research in Japan has been hampered by the absence of an institutionalized national election survey project (like the National Election Studies in the United States), and more important, the lack of any central data archive or a tradition of sharing data. Therefore, while many election surveys are conducted in Japan, most of these efforts are not available for secondary analysis. This has meant that there is no standard set of time series data available for research. Much of the electoral research in Japan is in fact conducted by the media and hence serves their circumscribed, short-term, and changing concerns. Even academically oriented surveys in Japan have tended to be limited by culturally imposed time constraints regarding the acceptable length of interviews, and hence they tend to be rather short and restricted in their scope and design. This book stands apart from those research traditions in that it is based primarily on our 1976 JABISS survey, a major nationwide panel survey containing nearly four hundred items. In this regard it represents the omnibus approach to electoral research in Japan, as pioneered by the 1967 Japanese Election Study conducted by Robert Ward and Akira Kubota and extended by the 1983 JES study conducted by Joji Watanuki, Ichiro Miyake, Takashi Inoguchi, and Ikuo Kabashima. Most of the members of our team have been intimately involved with the primary or secondary analysis of at least two of these three major surveys, providing our work with a time perspective. Our study has also been informed by the data and findings of the election studies of the Akarui Senkyo Suishin Kyokai, which extend from the 1950s up through 1990. Finally, where appropriate, we have drawn on the findings of numerous other surveys, including those by NHK and the Tokei Suri Kenkyujo.

Our early interest in electoral research was derived from a variety of influences. Ichiro Miyake was invited to the University of Michigan for study by Robert Ward and during his stay was influenced by his interactions with Angus Campbell, Philip Converse, Warren Miller, and Donald Stokes. Joji Watanuki's involvement with Japanese electoral research can be traced to his long association with the surveys of the Society for the Promotion of Clean Elections (Akarui Senkyo Suishin Kyokai, formerly the Kommei Senkyo Renmei), while Shinsaku Kohei's interest was derived from his extended role as a principal investigator with the NHK Public Opinion Research Institute's election studies. Bradley Richardson and I were in graduate school at Berkeley and Stanford in the 1960s when the behavioral revolution was on the rise, and we were deeply influenced not only by leading examples of this new wave of research, such as *The American Voter,* but through our personal interactions with such key figures in the revolution as Heinz Eulau and Gabriel Almond. And in the mid-1960s we both found ourselves involved in local election studies in Japan. Bradley pursued his dissertation research in Kanagawa and Shimane under the direction of Robert Scalapino, and I worked in Miyagi prefecture. We appreciate the grants from the Social Science Research Council and the Japan Foundation that brought the two of us together and to Japan in 1974–75, where we became involved with the Japanese members of our team and designed our project. We are most grateful to the National Science Foundation and the Hoso Bunka Foundation for the support to collect and analyze our data. Finally, I am personally indebted to the four other members of our team for their patience, encouragement, and assistance in bringing this project to completion.

Scott C. Flanagan
Editor

■ Abbreviations

CGP	Clean Government Party or Komeito
DSP	Democratic Socialist Party
HC	House of Councillors
HR	House of Representatives
JABISS	1976 Japanese Election Study conducted by *J*. Watanuki, *B*. Richardson, *I*. Miyake, *S*. Kohei, and *S*. Flanagan
JCP	Japan Communist Party
JSP	Japan Socialist Party
LDP	Liberal Democratic Party
NHK	Japan Broadcasting Corporation
NLC	New Liberal Club
SDF	Social Democratic Federation

Part I ■ Introduction

One ■ Japanese Voting Behavior in
Comparative Perspective

BRADLEY M. RICHARDSON

Japan's post–World War II electoral experience is a history of paradoxes. On the one hand, Japan's conservative party movement dominated the polls from 1947 through the present by winning majorities or pluralities in all general elections held during this period, with the single exception of the 1989 House of Councillors election. Relatedly, from 1948 through 1955 conservative party coalitions held Diet majorities, while, since its formation in 1955, the main party in the conservative camp, the Liberal Democratic Party (LDP), has consistently held majorities in the Japanese parliament's more important House of Representatives.[1] This continuity in conservative rule and the relative stability of Japan's one-party dominant system can be seen in the national vote totals from House of Representatives (HR) elections up through 1990 as shown in table 1.1. Although interelection changes in conservative strength reached the fairly high figure of 9 percent in the fluid early postwar era, in general elections from 1952 on, shifts in conservative support between elections averaged under 3 percent of the total vote.

The first paradox of the postwar Japanese experience is that the conservative movement, though it maintained its dominant role for four decades, experienced a slow, steady decline at the polls from 1953 through 1976. Paralleling the slow decline of conservative fortunes during much of the postwar era was a steady secular increase in the electoral successes of Japan's opposition parties.

1. This dominance extended to the upper house up until the 1989 election. Throughout this book our main concern is with Japanese voters' responses to national politics. Our focus is on electoral attitudes identified in the context of the House of Representatives elections. The House of Representatives is the "lower" and more powerful of Japan's two parliamentary bodies. Importantly, voting trends described here for the lower house are reasonably similar to those in elections for Japan's upper house, the House of Councillors in most years. Finally, we tend to emphasize electoral responses to Japan's five most important parties since the mid-1960s—the Liberal Democratic Party, the Japan Socialist Party, the Democratic Socialist Party, the Clean Government Party, and the Japan Communist Party. In addition to their lesser real-world importance, supporters of minor groups constitute too small a category of survey respondents to permit meaningful statistical analysis.

Table 1.1 Percentages of Vote by Party in House of Representatives Elections, 1946–90

	1946	'47	'49	'52	'53	'55	'58	'60	'63	'67	'69	'72	'76	'79	'80	'83	'86	'90
Right																		
LDP[a]	43	52	60	66	66	63	58	58	55	49	48	47	42	45	48	46	49	46
Center																		
NLC[b]	—	—	—	—	—	—	—	—	—	—	—	—	4	3	3	3	2	—
DSP	—	—	—	—	—	—	—	9	7	7	8	7	6	7	7	7	6	5
CGP	—	—	—	—	—	—	—	—	—	5	11	8	11	10	9	10	9	8
Left																		
JSP[c]	18	26	14	21	27	29	33	28	29	28	21	22	21	20	19	19	17	24
JCP	4	4	10	3	2	2	3	3	4	5	7	11	10	10	10	9	9	8

Source: All data are from the Home Ministry.

Note: All figures are percentages of total vote in each election; totals do not equal 100 percent owing to the presence of some minor parties and independent candidates.

[a] Up through 1955, the LDP vote represents the combined vote of the conservative parties (the Progressive or Democratic Party and the Liberal Party) that ultimately joined together to form the Liberal Democratic Party in 1955. The other party abbreviations in the table are as follows: NLC—New Liberal Club; DSP—Democratic Socialist Party; CGP—Clean Government Party; JSP—Japan Socialist Party; and JCP—Japan Communist Party.

[b] Dashes represent election years in which the NLC and the other center parties did not exist and hence did not put up candidates for election.

[c] Includes both left and right wings of the socialist movement in relevant years.

From the early 1950s through 1958 this trend favored the Japan Socialist Party (JSP), which was and remains the largest party in the opposition camp. However, the fortunes of the Japan Socialists began to falter after the party's right wing defected in 1959 to form a second socialist party, the Democratic Socialists (DSP), and they more or less declined since that time, until the unusual spurt in Socialist fortunes in the 1989 House of Councillors election. This upward movement in JSP support was carried over to some degree in the 1990 lower house election, but it is too early to tell if these 1989–90 results represent a reversal in the Socialists' long-term downward trend (see chapter 11).

Related to this declining trend in JSP strength since the late 1950s, and as a further paradox within a paradox, the opposition parties experienced two decades of fragmentation beginning in 1959. In addition to the Democratic Socialists' formation of a viable second socialist party, which has gained between 5 to 8 percent of the vote in HR elections since 1960, the Japan Communist Party (JCP) increased its support from three percent of the House of Representatives vote in 1960 to 11 percent in 1972, and that support has ranged from 8 to 10 percent of the vote in every election since then. Moreover, the Clean Government Party (CGP), which developed out of and maintains close ties with the Soka Gakkai religious movement, began to run candidates in HR elections in 1967 and quickly increased its vote share to 11 percent in the 1969 election, leveling off at the 8 to 11 percent range thereafter. Finally the New Liberal Club (NLC) emerged through defections from the LDP in the context of the Lockheed scandal in 1976, but after gaining 4 percent of the national vote that year NLC steadily declined thereafter until it was reabsorbed in the ruling party following the 1986 election. As a result of these combined movements in electoral support between the conservatives and the opposition and within the opposition camp, the Japanese party system in the 1970s came to resemble the multiparty configurations of some European party systems, a sharp contrast with the simple "one-and-a-half" party system of the 1950s.[2]

2. Because the Liberal Democrats commanded roughly two-thirds of the votes and seats in the HR elections in the 1950s, while the JSP as the major opposition party was receiving about one-third of the votes and seats, the term "one-and-a-half party," originally coined to characterize postwar West German party patterns, was used as a label for the Japanese system (Scalapino and Masumi, 1962).

While there have been other mini-parties that have appeared in the 1980s to compete in the upper house national constituency races, the only other party that is regularly mentioned in the Japanese press is the Social Democratic Federation (SDF). The SDF emerged as a result of defections from the JSP in 1977 and 1978, but it has never received even 1 percent of the national vote and will therefore be ignored in our analysis.

We often follow Japanese practice by distinguishing between the conservative camp and the "opposition." This should not be read as implying that all opposition parties have been leftist in political orientation. The contemporary Democratic Socialists and Clean Government Party are often characterized as middle-of-the-road groupings, while the Japan Socialist Party and Japan Communist Party are seen appropriately as leftist groupings.

The paradoxes of simultaneously fairly high levels of stability amidst secular shifts in opposition and conservative camp support, further accompanied by a trend toward fragmentation within the opposition, were paralleled by interesting discontinuities in recent decades in electoral trends at the constituency level (Nishihira, 1972; Richardson, 1977; Flanagan, 1980b). In certain rural constituencies, support for the Liberal Democratic Party was remarkably stable in recent decades, even in the presence of national trends of conservative decline. Elsewhere, there was actually intense change and volatility at the constituency level in many urban and suburban districts beginning in the late 1960s and continuing into the 1970s.

We have used the term "paradox" in describing recent Japanese electoral trends simply because elements of both remarkable stability and substantial volatility could be seen, depending on which aspect of electoral trends were examined. Explanations advanced for these tendencies in the aggregate vote in Japanese lower house elections have themselves sought to show alternatively sources of stability and forces promoting change, depending on their timing and focus. Stability in the conservative vote has been argued to reflect the ruling party's continued successful electoral mobilization efforts in Japan's rural and provincial city sector, supplemented by the effects of an electoral system that has typically overrepresented the rural and small city electorate in many districts and thus delayed the political impact of the dwindling of the rural electorate that has been rather dramatic since the early 1950s.[3] Some stability in the opposition camp probably also accrued from the socialist parties' ties with Japan's labor union movement. High economic growth under conservative rule in the late 1950s and 1960s, which was accompanied by spreading affluence among Japan's citizens, might be another source of stable patterns in electoral support, or at least could have acted as a brake on forces of change. Overall, the "anchoring" effects of the organization of the vote through rural community

3. The movement of the population from the farms to the cities over the first three and a half decades after the end of World War II is clearly of great importance to Japanese electoral politics, as we shall emphasize at many points. Just after World War II, nearly half of Japan's people lived on farms, partly because of dire conditions in the cities at that time. The early and mid-postwar era witnessed a steady erosion of the proportions of persons living in rural districts and employed in agriculture. Farm interests still touch a substantial proportion of the population, however, because of the extensive amount of part-time farming that exists in Japan. As explained in chapter 2, note 9, if we count all those living in households engaged in even part-time farming, then the farm population in Japan in 1980 was still over 18 percent of the total population.

Further enhancing the political power of farm interests is the fact that Japan's electoral laws dramatically overrepresent the vote of persons living in the rural parts of the country. Although a few new districts have been created since the late 1960s to reflect population growth in the cities and surrounding areas, no adjustments have been made in rural districts to promote electoral balance between the large cities and the rural periphery.

social networks and urban secondary organizations have been seen as the major factors in many explanations of electoral stability. Indeed, while other factors such as issues could have played some role, they have usually been assessed as being of lesser importance in the Japanese context.

Meanwhile, an explosive shift in Japan's population to the cities and suburban districts surrounding the major cities in recent decades has been seen as a major factor in electoral change, even given the unfavorable treatment of urban voters in Japan's current election laws. The move to the cities is believed to have removed people from the influences of traditional methods of electoral mobilization in Japan's rural districts and to have exposed them to new political climates and the mobilizing efforts of unions and leftist parties (Scalapino and Masumi, 1962). Relatedly, problems that grew out of Japan's high economic growth and rapid urbanization—such as overcrowding, dramatic environmental pollution, and some other kinds of deterioration in the quality of city life—may have contributed to the fairly massive decline in the Liberal Democratic vote noted in metropolitan districts in the 1960s and 1970s. Thus, issues can count in Japanese elections even if they are not a dominant factor in many individual contests.

■ The Focus of This Study

This book is a study of the forces that have affected the political attitudes and vote choices of the Japanese electorate across the post–World War II period. While several of the subsequent chapters will draw on data from the 1950s through the 1980s, the bulk of our analysis will be based on a large nationwide panel survey of Japanese citizens conducted before and after the December 1976 House of Representatives election.[4] Although synchronic research such as ours cannot fully explain the diachronic patterns of electoral performance we have just described, we hasten to add that this is not a study of one particular Japanese election. Indeed, we are not particularly interested in explaining the specific electoral outcome in 1976 in terms of the rise and fall in party fortunes. Nor will we endeavor to explain the behavior of politicians, their campaign strategies, or their use of issues in the specific context of the 1976 election. Rather, what we will try to explain is how *the Japanese voter* reaches an electoral decision. We will be looking, then, at the various kinds of influences that bear on voters' decisions, from party and candidate images and media exposure to voters' social status, values, and social networks.

4. The 1976 JABISS Japanese Election Study is a large pre- and postelection panel study including over three hundres items. This study was supported by funds received from the National Science Foundation of the United States and the Hoso Bunka Foundation of Japan.

There are a variety of influences that go into the decisions of Japanese voters, and these *types* of influences tend to remain the same even while the particular stimuli—candidates, issues and events—change. Moreover, individual voters are likely to rely on the same kinds of influences from election to election, unless they themselves undergo change as a result of rising levels of education, a new social or occupational environment, or other alterations in attributes or circumstances. All the relevant kinds of influences that bear upon a voter's decision, therefore, can be observed and studied in any election. While the proportions of voters who are persuaded by one or another type or category of influence may be changing between elections and over time, those changes tend in most instances to be either marginal or gradual.

We do not want to overstate the generalizability of our findings. Certainly some of the discrete events of the 1976 election were not necessarily linked with the forces that anchored or moved the electorate in the preceding two decades, just as some parameters have changed since that time. Still, there were many elements of that specific electoral environment that did reflect the presence of more durable forces than the particular events of the 1976 campaign. By looking for attitudes among the electorate that reflect responses to political objects which were themselves part of a longer temporal frame of reference, we can discover some of the influences that have structured Japanese voters' preferences over time. Moreover, the enterprise we are most interested in is not assessing the precise relative influences of a variety of factors on the voting decision, an exercise which may yield varying results across elections, but rather determining which influences are and which are not of great importance in the Japanese electoral context and how these influences—from social structure, social networks, and values to partisanship, issues, and the media—operate within that context.

Our efforts to generalize beyond the 1976 election are enhanced by several factors peculiar to the Japanese setting. The first of these is the enormous stability in Japanese voting patterns. This can be seen in the small election-to-election shifts in party vote shares (punctuated only rarely by more than modest swings in the vote, of which the 1989 upper house election was the most extreme example). This steadying factor has been reinforced by the arresting of the LDP's long-term secular decline in the 1970s and the stabilization of party vote shares across the last two decades. The Lockheed scandal produced a short-lived downward blip in LDP electoral support, which reached an all time low of 42 percent in the 1976 election. This short-term effect will be addressed in chapters 7 and 8. If we exclude this election, however, the LDP vote share fluctuated between 47 to 49 percent during the previous decade, going back to 1967, and varied from 45 to 49 percent in the following decade and a half going up through 1990. Even including the 1976 election, the average vote shift in LDP support between contiguous elections for the nine elections across these decades averaged 2.5 percentage points. These averages were substantially lower for all the other parties as can be seen from table 1.1 above. Clearly there are strong, enduring influences that are anchoring Japanese voting decisions and yielding only small shifts in party vote shares across elections. As will be noted in chapter 11, even the startling events of the 1989 House of Councillors election fit into patterns of mobilization, response, and motivation observable in other contests.

A second factor that enhances the durability of explanations of how voters behave is found in the manner in which the realignment took place in Japan across the 1950s and 1960s. Scott Flanagan (1984) has argued that rather than a sectoral realignment—a change in the base of support for one or more parties— what we found in Japan was an ecological realignment—a change in the relative size of one or more social groups or economic strata. Specifically the decline in the LDP vote is directly related to declines in the proportions of farmers and other occupations within the old middle class, of highly bound and integrated communities, and of adherents of traditional values. In their place emerged greater numbers of the new middle class, unionized blue- and white-collar workers, unbound and transient communities, and adherents of modern values. Therefore it is not so much that the kinds of influences found in Japanese electoral contexts were changing but that the proportions of voter that were subject to certain partisan influences and appeals were changing.

A third factor that strengthens the lasting relevance of voting explanations in Japan is the unusual strength of long-term compared to short-term factors in understanding voting decisions. For example, in the Japanese context both the media and issues play an unusually weak direct role in voting behavior, at least in the short time span of most parliamentary elections. Thus, in the case of issues, the most important of these are long-term, domestic and foreign policy issue alternatives that have differentiated the parties since the early 1950s. Because the major political parties have made what must appear to the voting public to be only minor adjustments in their positions on long-standing issues of defense and security, while positions on constitutional issues are even more rigidly defined, these aspects of the electorate's response are more or less frozen around earlier axes of cleavage.

■ Models of Voting Choice and Partisanship

Some Western studies of Japanese politics and of Japan in general have emphasized the presence of what were viewed as unique and idiosyncratic features of the Japanese setting. Typically these studies have simply failed to look at Japan from a comparative perspective. Research by Japanese on their own society and political system has often had a similar emphasis. By ignoring what is comparable in the Japanese experience or how specific features of the Japanese environment are related to counterparts elsewhere, important opportunities for scholarly inquiry were lost. By emphasizing uniqueness and the differences between Japan and other societies or political systems, such studies perpetuated a view that Japanese culture and behavior are somehow exotic and removed from the experiences of other societies and particularly those in the Western industrialized category.

Our own emphasis in the study of Japanese voting is comparative in perspective. Through such an approach we hope to understand Japan better and to relate the Japanese experience to a larger body of electoral research and findings. In so doing we will take advantage of models of voting choice and partisanship that have been widely used in empirical research in North America, Europe, India, and other contexts where democratic institutions permit regularized mass participation in elections. As we will find, most of these models have important applications for the analysis of Japanese attitudes and behavior.

A Sociological Model of Voting

Until recently the most popular comparative approach to mass political behavior analysis was the "sociological" paradigm of voting behavior. The sociological approach, while owing a great deal to Marxian theories of social conflict and its assumed base in class differences, developed first and foremost as a scholarly response to the emergence of nineteenth- and twentieth-century European party systems in environments of often intense conflict between supporters of different religions, members of different social strata, and persons within different ethnic, micronational, or regional subcultures. Thus, the development of modern European party systems was seen as the eruption into politics of long-standing social cleavages, with these party systems taking shape around the dominant social issues that the cleavages produced.

At the macrohistorical level, primal social cleavages were seen as having produced the major divisive issues of European politics from the middle of the nineteenth century on if not earlier. As parties came into being as parliamentary groups and later as organizations seeking support in elections, both the parties themselves and their appeals to emerging electorates were shaped around basic social issues and the rhetoric of conflict among a society's major social groupings. And as electorates grew many European political parties became "frozen" in position as articulators of social group interests and manipulators of group members' votes. The history of modern party system development, according to the sociological approach, is the organization and institutionalization of party systems and party competition around the major divisive issues within a society—typically issues of religion, class, and ethnicity (Lipset, 1960; Lipset and Rokkan, 1967).

The macrosocietal perspective of sociologists concerned with broad historical patterns in the emergence and perpetuation of contemporary European party systems was reflected in the microsocietal or individual-focused research of political sociology beginning in the 1930s and gaining momentum after World War II.[5] It thus became conventional to analyze party support and voting choices in terms of people's social status, religious attachments, ethnicity, and even their sex and age, even though these variables were not always indicators of membership in a social cleavage group. Social affiliations and positions were thus seen as the basis for attraction to particular political parties, both in the cleavage-dominated European settings as well as in the more complexly structured American system (Rossi, 1959). They also became the basis of analyses of the Japanese electorate beginning in the 1950s.

Many of these microsociological studies presented their analyses of the social basis of the vote without attention to the assumed dynamic that linked groups and their individual members to particular parties. But some sociological studies speculated about this linkage and, inter alia, argued that members of particular social groups or strata had common interests which they perceived to be supported by a particular party (Lipset, 1960). Alternatively, people were seen as being socialized by common group experiences, or it was postulated that their vote was mobilized through membership in secondary organizations such as particular religious sects or trade unions.

The Social Psychological Approach

A second and alternative approach to the analysis of mass electoral behavior developed in the United States in the early postwar years. Closely identified with the University of Michigan's Survey Research Center, this approach to voting behavior, which was strongly influenced by social psychology, saw the political attitudes of the individual voter as the central determinants of his choices at the polls and, for that matter, his initial decision to participate in elections.[6] The early Michigan studies (Campbell, Gurin, and Miller, 1954; and Campbell, Converse, Miller, and Stokes, 1960) formulated a model of

5. Actually, the earliest political sociological cum geographical studies were conducted in the early part of this century (Siegfried, 1913) and like their successors up until the postwar era, these early efforts were based on the analysis of aggregate election results. After World War II, however, most research of a sociological persuasion was based on analysis of mass surveys.

6. There is a link between the sociological approach and the more recent social psychological concerns in that the presence of attitudes such as those emphasized by the social psychological school was often inferred by political sociologists.

individual choice and attitude development that continues to this day with only minor modifications as the central organizing paradigm of most American voting behavior studies. Voters were seen as influenced by primarily three basic kinds of attitudes—loyalties to political parties, evaluation of candidates, and attitudes on current issues—and their choices in particular elections were believed to represent the net sum of these differential forces operating on individual electoral decisions.

Reflecting their social psychological orientations, the leading members of the Michigan school saw these three basic attitudes as products of small-group experiences and exposure to campaign communications. Party loyalties, known as party identifications, were believed to develop primarily through early formative experiences and exposure to partisan symbols within the parental family.[7] In contrast, issue attitudes were believed to develop mainly from experiences and communications exposure at the time of a specific election campaign or, in the case of some issues of longer duration, stimuli that were sustained over the period of several campaigns. Candidate evaluations were viewed themselves as mainly products of exposure to the appeals of specific campaigns, given the assumption that candidates were fairly temporary phenomena and salient mainly during the months prior to the election. The focus of American research on presidential elections, where candidates are highly visible and candidate incumbency is limited to at most two elections, encouraged such a view.

Thus, party identification came to be seen as a long-term component of the vote while issue attitudes were characterized as either middle-term or short-term responses from the perspective of their assumed genesis and durability, and candidate attitudes were viewed as being mainly of a short-term duration (Campbell et al., 1960; Converse, 1975). Broad social group memberships and social status were relegated to very long-term, antecedent status although they were not completely neglected by the architects of the social psychological approach (Campbell et al., 1960). Indeed, components of the sociological paradigm became in many instances integral variables in social psychological studies of voting behavior, even despite the primary emphasis on attitudes that were seen as more closely linked to specific political experiences over an

---

There are many definitions of attitude; probably the most relevant conceptualizations for purposes of voting research are those that see attitudes as either orientations toward external objects or predispositions toward certain kinds of behavior (McGuire, 1968).

7. McClosky and Dahlgren (1959) also found adult friendship groups to be characterized by considerable partisan homogeneity, although they could not clearly determine whether groups influenced their members' partisanship or whether persons chose their friends on the basis of partisan considerations.

individual's life span or exposure to the events and appeals of particular election campaigns.

Within the spectrum of concerns of the social psychological approach, party identification early assumed an importance beyond that of other attitudes. Party identifications were believed to have certain basic properties, including the aforementioned transmittability across generations. The idea that party loyalties were commonly acquired early in life through exposure to the partisan environment within the family was supported by empirical findings when Campbell and his associates (1960) demonstrated high levels of congruence between respondents' partisanship and their memories of the partisan preferences of their parents during their childhood. And because recall findings were supported by existing political socialization research (for example, Hyman, 1959), the Michigan group felt comfortable with the idea that a high proportion of American adults had inherited their partisanship via processes much like those involved in the intergenerational transmission of religious affiliations.

Party identification was also seen as an attitude that tended to be stable over time and that intensified over the life span of the typical citizen as an attachment formed in the preadult years was enhanced by periodic behavioral reinforcement in the form of electoral choices for the favored party. Party loyalties were nevertheless seen as independent from the voting choices made in particular elections. Stability was inferred from recall evidence on the consistency of partisanship in the memories of voters interviewed at the time of the 1956 United States presidential election.

As a result of these findings, partisanship was believed to remain intact over the entire life span for most people. Some persons might defect from party ties acquired early in life as the result of personal influences such as marriage to a partisan of another party and progress through the life cycle, or broad social and political forces such as the polarization of opinion on particular issues and exposure to national crises like the Great Depression, but stability of partisan identifications was believed to be the norm (Campbell et al., 1960). The impression that partisanship also "grew" across the life spans of typical citizens was gained from observations of the patterns of affiliation and intensities of party identifications among 1956 partisans in different age groups within the population (Campbell et al., 1960), wherein the ratio of the population manifesting partisan ties and strong rather than weak loyalties was much higher among successively older age cohorts.

In addition to its stability over time and tendency toward intensification, party identification was seen also as influencing other voter political attitudes. correlations between party attachments and attitudes toward ies. Party loyalties were consequently seen as a force favoring consistency in responses to the complex and ambiguous world of politics and elections. Party identification was also shown to be a major influence on the voting decision and was shown to promote consistency in voting over time. Finally, attachments to parties tended to encourage feelings of political involvement, although there was some question about the direction of causality between these two kinds of attitudes; relatedly, partisan ties led people to go out to vote rather than abstain in elections (Campbell et al., 1960).

In sum, party identification, reflecting ideas from reference group theory in social psychology, was seen as a long-term affective attachment to a particular party. Moreover, this attachment was viewed as displaying properties of independence (shown by deviations from party loyalties in response to short-term forces in particular election situations), stability, and intensification. Finally, party identifications were believed to influence both other kinds of attitude formation and various kinds of political behavior.

■ Applying the Sociological Model

The above two "traditional" models of sociological and social psychological influences on mass electoral behavior will serve as the main theoretical reference points in our study of the Japanese voter. However, our study is not simply an application of these models to the Japanese case in some simplistic, mechanical sense. In our analysis of Japanese behavior, there has been a natural interaction between the foreign and comparative models of behavior and our own appraisals of the forces that appear to be major determinants of how Japanese citizens respond to politics and make choices at election time. In this and following sections, we will indicate both some of the adaptations that have been made over time in the two traditional voting behavior models in research outside Japan and our own conceptualizations of how these models and subsequent refinements can best be integrated with credible portrayals of the reality of mass political behavior in Japan.

Applications of the Sociological Approach Outside Japan
The sociological approach has had great appeal to students of European politics, and hundreds of studies have examined the social origins of party alignments in the European context in varying degrees of complexity. Through this scholarship it is well established that religion is the dominant social basis of contemporary party affiliations and voting choices in the majority of European countries where social cleavages are still a central and consistent force linked with political behavior at the mass level (Rose, 1974; Rose and Urwin, 1969; Lipjhart, 1979). Class is the second most important cleavage in European

systems. Class is particularly salient as an influence on partisanship in societies like the Scandinavian countries (and Britain in a more restricted sense), where a single religion is dominant and neither secular-religious cleavages, of the scale found in some predominantly Catholic societies such as Italy, nor Catholic-Protestant antagonisms, which divide or have divided populations in countries like the Netherlands or prewar Germany, are important. Language, ethnic, or regional differences, while extremely influential on political behavior in societies like Belgium or Spain, are only third in importance in Europe in general.[8]

Numerous studies consequently demonstrate the "power" of the sociological approach in the European case, in the sense that cleavages dividing broad population groups since the middle part of the nineteenth century or earlier are reflected in the partisan preferences of persons in different social groups or social strata, even in the face of major social change. There have been important controversies within political sociology over the ways in which social cleavages translate into party support (Sartori, 1969; Sani, 1974a), and important qualifications to sociological hypotheses as societies have become more mobile (Butler and Stokes, 1969; LoPreato, 1971; Miller and Stouthard, 1975) and more affluent (Hamilton, 1967; Goldthorpe, 1968; Inglehart, 1971, 1977; Dalton, Flanagan, and Beck, 1984). But the sociological explanation of popular political preferences remains a potent force in political behavior analysis in many countries (for example, Crewe and Denver, 1985). Britain is an instructive case: despite gradual declines in the potency of social class as a voting cue, social strata divisions still remain relevant for the political choices of large numbers of citizens (Heath, Jowell, and Curtice, 1985; Rose and McAllister, 1986).

The Sociology of the Vote in Japan

Almost all the existing studies of Japanese partisanship conducted by either Japanese or foreign scholars have had a sociological component. Inclusion of a "sociological dimension" has reflected more than anything else a reaction to the presence in Japan of fairly stable urban-rural differences in patterns of party

---

8. Sex and age, while often employed in sociological analyses of partisanship in a meaningful way, are still not usually seen as the basis of society-wide cleavages, even though at times particular political generations assume special importance and/or sex- and age-related issues may achieve great prominence in political debate. Thus, generational conflict has been a central latent theme in Inglehart's work (see below) and in various analyses of student activism in the 1960s in both Europe and the United States. More recently, a "gender gap" has been identified in press coverage of American elections and in the findings of related opinion polls, reflecting visible differences between the sexes, particularly those involving the preferences of females who are single and family heads compared with women in other categories.

support, as well as the presence of some other important social group differences with regard to voting. Yet, as several studies have shown, Japan lacks the basic religious, ethnic, and, in recent times, regional cleavages that have been so important in the structuring of party alignments in Europe (Watanuki, 1967b; Flanagan and Richardson, 1977). Moreover, the potential for a class cleavage, which exists in Japan as in other industrial societies, has been only partially realized in Japan because of potent forces which have tended to blur the link between social class and party preferences (Dore, 1958; Watanuki, 1967b).

Nevertheless, relationships between demographic characteristics and voting choices can be seen in Japan, and it is to both the charting of these relationships across time and their explanation that Joji Watanuki dedicates his efforts in chapter 2. In so doing, Watanuki pays special attention to what he terms the *matrix* patterns of party support among social groups in Japan. This notion of a matrix rather than a cleavage model of voting highlights the increasingly complex relationships between occupational status and other social characteristics and patterns in party support. At the same time, age and urban-rural residence remain potent factors in the partisan proclivities of contemporary Japanese. In his treatment of the complexities of parties' social bases in Japan, Watanuki repeatedly calls our attention to the importance of elite coalitions and group and party mobilization, just as the research outside Japan has done in many instances. Thus Japan becomes another case that confirms the basic importance of electoral mobilization as a critical link in sociological explanations of party preferences. Even in the absence of European-type cleavage politics, there is still a parallel in the importance of political mobilization between the Japanese and the European examples.

Social Networks and Contextual Effects

Watanuki's analysis of the importance of electoral mobilization in Japanese politics underscores one of the major themes of our book. Many studies (for example, Watanuki, 1967b; Curtis, 1971) note that Japanese parties and candidates organize political support through appeals to local elites, community and group endorsements, and the manipulation of social networks. Just as Watanuki emphasizes the importance of these patterns to the sociology of the vote, we will return to them repeatedly as they relate to other aspects of Japanese political behavior.

Indeed, the prominence placed in this study on social network and organizational context and their effects on the vote in Japan can be seen from the fact that these approaches form the dominant or major themes in chapters 3, 4, 5, and 9. This emphasis draws both on our earlier work on Japan (Richardson, 1967b; Flanagan, 1968; Flanagan and Richardson, 1977; Flanagan 1980b) and on a renewed interest in this long-neglected research agenda in the West (Sheingold, 1973; Weatherford, 1982; Huckfeldt, 1986; Eulau and Rothenberg, 1986; Huckfeldt and Sprague, 1987). As is pointed out in the chapters below, there are a number of reasons for expecting that social context and social network models of voting should be even more relevant to the study of electoral behavior in Japan than they are in the West.

Studies of contextual influences investigate how a respondent's vote can be structured or guided by location in different kinds of social settings. In chapter 3, Scott Flanagan analyzes the effects of certain kinds of residential and occupational environments on voting preferences, while in chapter 5 Ichiro Miyake investigates the impact of these kinds of settings and movement from one to another of them on partisan socialization and partisan change. Social network explanations look inside these contexts at the patterns of interpersonal contacts and flow of influence communications within the formal and informal groups with which the individual is involved. The expectation is that long-standing groups based on close interpersonal ties will tend to develop fairly homogeneous and stable political attitudes over time and induce high levels of uniformity in their members' voting choices. In chapter 4, Flanagan conceptualizes several distinct mechanisms or means through which social networks can influence a voter's decision. This typology differentiates between long- and short-term effects and influence communications that are high and low in political content, yielding a fourfold classification including assimilation, opinion leader, reference group, and mobilization effects. That chapter introduces the reader to many of the special characteristics of the Japanese electoral setting and analyzes the relevance of each type of social network influence to an explanation of Japanese voting behavior. Chapter 9 also includes discussion of the short-term effects of social networks on voting decisions.

Value Cleavages

The voting tendencies within different social groups in Japan reflect an additional dimension of Japanese political life that is of substantial comparative importance. In earlier work on the sociology of the vote in Japan, Watanuki (1967b) argued that the basic cleavage in Japanese politics between urban and rural voters, between unionists and farmers, while in part reflecting different patterns of sociopolitical mobilization, was also linked with profound value differences that were influencing partisan orientations. The presence of such a value cleavage between the holders of *traditional* and *modern* values represented the electorate's response to the "cultural" politics of the 1950s, which had involved among other things a long debate over the legitimacy of Japan's postwar constitution and the style of postwar politics.

The existence and impact of different value systems is investigated in detail here by Flanagan in chapter 3. Following his earlier work on this subject (Flanagan, 1979, 1980c, 1982, 1987), Flanagan explores the content or nature of the politically relevant value cleavages that divide Japanese society along the lines of age and education, and he explores how and why these values have been changing in Japan across the post–World War II period. In this effort, he presents a theory of value change with ramifications that go well beyond the Japanese case and have obvious relevance for Ronald Inglehart's (1977) arguments linking value change with voter realignments in the West. Flanagan outlines the fundamental changes in the basic conditions of life that have been stimulating important changes in the value preferences of large portions of the electorates in the industrialized democracies. Importantly, Flanagan deals with a value cleavage that has been well documented over the past three decades in Japan (see Hayashi et al., 1982), thus escaping the criticism leveled at analyses linking social, value, and partisan change in Europe, where some shifts in values were believed to be potentially lacking in durability. Once establishing how and why values are changing in Japan, the analysis turns to an elaboration of the linkages between values and partisanship to explain the strong associations found in Japan between traditional and modern value types and voting choices across the entire postwar period. The differences found between Japan and the West in the timing and content of a politically salient postwar value cleavage inform the value change theory in both settings.

■ Party Identification: Contemporary Trends and the Japanese Case

Political parties are a universal phenomenon in democratic political systems. They occupy the center of attention in elite and legislative politics and play major roles in popular elections. People's attitudes toward political parties are also central in their assortment of feelings toward politics, according to the Michigan social psychological school of voting behavior studies. Yet the status of party identification has been questioned more than once by students of comparative politics, who see departures from the basic Michigan model in their studies of partisanship in countries outside of the United States. And even on its home ground the concept has received some critical scrutiny, as findings that qualify some traditional assumptions begin to accumulate. The recent comparative and American political behavior literatures have focused on variations between nations or across time in levels of aggregate party identification and have also presented new evidence about the "performance" of party loyalties, with special emphasis on the role of party loyalties in explaining voting decisions, the extent to which identifications and the vote are interdependent, and the degree of stability of partisanship across time. Because party identification appears to function somewhat differently in different settings and recent research has sometimes produced results that conflict with traditional conceptualizations, both the concept of party identification and related measurement strategies have been questioned.

Levels of Party Identification

Several studies have shown that aggregate frequencies of party identification among persons in different countries vary substantially (Converse and Dupeux, 1962; Eldersveld, 1973; Richardson, 1975). Party loyalties are apparently more common among the British and Americans than among citizens of most other countries. Around 90 percent of the persons surveyed in the 1960s in the United States and Great Britain reported psychological ties to political parties, while the percentages of persons reporting party ties were as low as 65 percent in other countries. There were also major discrepancies in the frequencies of *strong* identifiers in different countries, with the highest levels being observed in India (70 percent) and Britain (43 percent) and the lowest shares of strong identifiers being found in Japan (12 percent). More recent data presented in table 1.2 indicate much the same profile of differences across nations.[9] Even though cross-cultural measurement problems might account for some discrepancies in national configurations of party loyalties, the differences discovered in studies conducted in different national settings were still usually sufficiently great to encourage looking beyond measurement strategies alone for explanations.

One of the most promising explanations for country differences in levels of partisanship hypothesized that party loyalties in the postwar era could reflect the results of past differences in national party system development in different countries. On the one hand, both the United States and Britain had histories of relatively stable party system development, even though there had been a major realignment among British voters over the first half of the twentieth century (Butler and Stokes, 1969). In contrast, nations like Germany, Italy, and Japan had undergone disruptions of varying duration in their experience with democratic party systems. Philip Converse (1969) explored the plausible effects of differing party system histories in different nations on party loyalties in more

9. There are still some differences in the relative rankings of certain countries between the different time points when surveys were conducted that are attributable to both differences in the political context surrounding the surveys and some variations in question wording that resulted in lower levels of reported party loyalties in the findings of the more recent studies.

Table 1.2   Party Identification in Six Countries for Selected Years (In Percentages)

Japan	United States	United Kingdom	Germany	Italy	Netherlands
1967	1968	1966	1972	1968	1970
66[a]	88[b]	95[c]	77[d]	78[e]	44[f]
1976	1974	1973	1974	1975	1974
59[g]	82[b]	81[e]	63[e]	73[e]	83[e]

Note: All figures are percentages of total sample based on analysis of marginal distributions in relevant ICPSR and the 1976 Japan study codebooks. Superscript letters refer to critical variations in question wording, as follows:

[a] Which party do you like?

[b] Generally speaking do you consider yourself as a Republican, Democrat, Independent, or what? (Follow-up item: Do you think of yourself as closer to the Democratic or Republican party?)

[c] Generally speaking do you think of yourself as Conservative, Labour, Liberal, or what?

[d] Do you lean toward a political party?

[e] To which party do you usually feel closest? (In Germany: Do you in general lean toward a particular party?)

[f] Do you usually think of yourself as an adherent of a certain party or not?

[g] Is there some party that you ordinarily like?

Where follow-up questions were asked, the answers indicating a party "leaning" were included in the percentages of persons having a party identification.

recent periods and concluded that party system histories were indeed an important explanation of cross-national variations in partisanship in the postwar era. In the same study, Converse projected on the basis of his model of aggregate learning processes in "normal" systems that higher levels of partisanship would emerge over time even in countries that had experienced major discontinuities. In other studies of aggregate trends in party loyalties, Richardson (1975) and Zohlnhofer (1969) examined age cohorts and concluded that the relatively low levels of party identifiers in these countries could be attributed to the effects of earlier disruptions in party system development, supplemented by the delayed acquisition of the franchise by women in the Japanese case.

Notably, the studies we have just cited assumed that the processes of intergenerational transmission of party loyalties observed in the American case constituted a norm with regard to which tendencies in other countries could be meaningfully compared and analyzed. Converse and Dupeux's (1962) analysis of French and American socialization experiences and partisanship made the same assumption and concluded that the lower visibility of partisan cues in parent-child communications in France helped explain the remarkably lower levels of partisanship found in France compared with the United States.

In contrast to these early comparative studies, some recent research on movements of aggregate levels of party loyalties across time has produced a more qualified view of the importance and role of families in partisanship learning processes. Cameron (1972–73) reported that the fairly dramatic increases in aggregate levels of French partisanship observed between 1958 and 1968 could be explained in part by the mobilizing effects of the Gaullist movement among certain population groups, notably women. In discussing the implications of his work for assumptions about the importance of families in the transmission of party identifications, Cameron hypothesized that considerable adult learning had occurred between the two points in time as the result of the increase over one decade in the popularity of the Gaullist appeal. Meanwhile, recent research in the United States (Dennis, 1975; Pomper, 1972; Nie, Verba, and Petrocik, 1976; Wattenberg, 1981) has uncovered a significant trend of partisan dealignment, part of which could be attributed to breakdowns in the intergenerational transmission of party preferences. Among the various patterns observable across time in the United States was a loosening of party ties among young people, roughly half of whom in the late 1960s had specifically abandoned the parties of their parents. Apparently, under the disturbing effects of new issue cleavages and greater political cynicism, disruption of family learning processes may occur in even stable party systems. Significantly, there was also some erosion of party ties among long-standing partisans in the 1960s, according to recent American studies, although this phenomenon was nowhere nearly as pronounced as the "abandonment" of family partisan traditions among young voters.

In summary, both comparative and American research on party identification indicates important variations in levels of partisanship in different countries and times as a response to breakdowns in intergenerational partisanship transmission processes in changing and less stable environments. At the same time, there are other sources of partisan learning besides childhood socialization that affect general levels of party support and are important in their own right. Moreover, the French experience reported by Cameron (1972–73) would suggest that alternative learning experiences among adults can exist, as a result of dynamic mobilizing forces operating in a context where familial partisan learning processes are apparently weak. Relatedly, Eldersveld (1973) adds to our appreciation of the apparent diversity of partisan learning processes by identifying a high level of mobilization of partisan loyalties in India that could not be explained by a family socialization model, given the youth of the Indian system at the time of his research. The most recent European research, notably Rose and McAllister's (1986) discussion of Britain's "open electorate," also assumes that learning is a lifelong process and that many individuals' political orientations are influenced by experiences occurring after acquisition of the franchise.

The "Performance" of Party Identification

The basic model of party identification postulated in the 1950s was that partisanship was a stable attitude independent from the voting act. Recent studies have examined patterns of short-term stability and change in party identification and have raised some doubts about the conclusions of the research on early party loyalties. Several comparative studies have noted higher short-term volatility in party loyalties outside the United States than seem to have been anticipated in the traditional American model or were identified in the early American findings (for example, Butler and Stokes, 1969; Kaase, 1970). Comparative scholarship's findings that party loyalties are not always as stable as implied in the traditional social psychological model are interestingly paralleled by the concerns of several American studies (Dobson and St. Angelo, 1975; Brody, 1977; Howell, 1981), which indicate that party loyalties in the United States are less stable than was assumed in earlier research and that the observed volatility can be attributed to the influence of major political events and short-term forces. One interpretation of American voting behavior (Fiorina, 1981) even goes to the extreme of seeing party identification as a running tally of evaluations of political performance.

Recent studies emphasizing that party identification is less stable than had been assumed raise important questions. However, as a study of stability and change in party identification in West Germany pointed out (Norpoth, 1978), 80 percent of respondents to a three-wave panel conducted during the 1972 Bundestag election remained constant in their partisan loyalties; what movement could be discerned in party loyalties occurred between the nonpartisan category and that of possession of party affiliations rather than from an identification with one party to a tie with a different party. So levels of stability outside the United States can still be fairly high, at least in some cases. Also, party loyalties are still comparatively stable in the American setting, even if there are some qualifications to older expectations.

Some examinations of short-term stability and instability in partisanship abroad have looked specifically at the relationship between partisanship, vote intention, and actual vote. These studies have produced results that raise questions about the independence of the concept of a party identification—which is supposed to be tapping a stable, long-term attachment—from a short-term voting preference (Butler and Stokes, 1969; Thomassen, 1976; Radtke, 1972; Borre and Katz, 1973; Norpoth, 1978; LeDuc, 1981). For example, several of these analyses have discovered parallel movements of volatility between party vote and party loyalties at different times in several countries. Specifically, the party identifications of voters in several electorates changed after particular elections as an apparent response to immediately prior voting decisions. That pattern of change violates the American concept of party identification and raises the question of whether the standard party ID questions may, in some countries for some undeterminate proportions of their samples, be measuring a short-term voting intention rather than a long-term party attachment.

These findings have led scholars to challenge the earlier American assumption that party identification and the vote are independent. When it was also observed, in marked contrast to the American case, that there was consistently a very strong relationship between party loyalties, as measured by survey questions, and actual partisan vote choices, a number of scholars raised questions about the meaning to respondents of the party identification questions. Some critics felt that the European short ballot and parliamentary elections, as compared with the American long ballot and presidential elections, rendered the distinction between a short-term voting choice and a long-term party loyalty much less meaningful in the European context. As a result, these scholars contend, respondents fail to distinguish between these two concepts and reply to the party identification item with an answer reflecting their current voting intention. Relatedly, some scholars questioned the utility of party loyalties as an interesting variable in voting behavior analysis by suggesting that party identification and voting choices stand too "close" to each other in the stream of important causal influences affecting behavior. This criticism argues that the high levels of convergence between these two variables endows the party ID concept with great predictive power but little theoretical interest. These scholars contend that voting research should focus on more theoretically interesting variables to explain the long-term anchoring of the vote, such as the social cleavages long studied in political sociology (Budge et al., 1976) or more recently the political "principles" that are seen to guide political behavior across time (Rose and McAllister, 1986).

Party Identification and the Japanese Case

Many of the issues raised in the comparative and American party identification literature are important in the Japanese setting. Analysis of aggregate levels of partisanship in Japan has interested both Japanese and foreign scholars, because of the possible effects on partisanship of the break between pre–World War II and postwar party systems and the presence of other features of Japanese experience or political culture that could potentially affect the development of party loyalties.

Leftist parties appeared as viable contestants in Japanese elections only after the end of the war; their emergence is one major discontinuity between pre- and postwar partisan alternatives. There were also important changes in party labels within the conservative movement between these two periods.[10] The fact that women did not receive the franchise in Japan until 1946 could also affect patterns of party identifications in Japan to some degree, even though we would anticipate from Converse's (1969) projections that normal levels of party identifications might have emerged in Japan by the time of our survey, other things being equal. However, the earlier elements of discontinuity in Japan were actually supplemented by patterns of party development in the postwar era. Factional feuding resulted in quite a few further changes in party names and alignments between 1946 and 1955 within the conservative camp, while the socialist movement split into two parties for several years during this period. Finally, as noted above, several new minor parties emerged in Japan in the 1960s and 1970s.

The fact that Japan has lower levels of aggregate party loyalties than many Western democracies certainly may reflect the effects on political learning of the kinds of system discontinuities we have just outlined. In addition to the potentially disruptive effects of political experience, the lower levels of contemporary partisanship in Japan could be linked with tendencies in Japan's political culture. Japanese are more critical and distrustful of politics than persons in a number of Western countries, as shown in table 1.3; these cynical attitudes could lead to a rejection of political parties.[11] Japanese are also less emotionally involved in political affairs and less interested in national politics

10. In addition, the postwar occupation purges of wartime political elites removed many key figures in the prewar parties from the political scene.

11. Obviously, the patterns of pessimism in different countries reflect different kinds of reactions to the questions in different political contexts or nuances peculiar to language differences. In some senses, construction of an index for use in our comparisons would be more satisfactory, since such an effort would involve use of several measures for the same concept. But in view of the inconsistencies in the marginals, it is not clear that such a strategy would necessarily improve equivalence across cultures. Moreover, our main point here is that there are cross-cultural differences which might affect how party loyalties develop and how the linkages forecast in the traditional social psychological approach between party identification and other attitudes might develop. For example, can we expect intensities of party loyalties to have the same meaning and relationships to other variables in political systems where involvement is lower and pessimism is common, as in more politicized and less cynical environments? These and many other transmutations of the party identification model might occur where cultural parameters change the centrality of parties (Converse, 1975) and the frame of reference in which the parties are evaluated.

The data we report in table 1.3 on involvement and levels of neutrality in responses to thermometer questions about feelings toward political parties are a little problematical, since they cannot be seen as causally independent from party identification (Campbell et al., 1960). Still, as has been argued elsewhere (Richardson, 1975), these political culture traits could have developed before the emergence of the contemporary party system and thus be partially independent from contemporary patterns of partisanship. Interestingly, such an argument is enhanced in the case of the patterns in affective neutrality, since these are quite stable across both contemporary partisan objects and a variety of other referents, such as various social groups, according to our findings.

Table 1.3   Engagement in Politics across Seven Political Cultures
(In Percentages)

	Japan	Britain	Germany	Netherlands	Austria	United States	Italy
Interest in politics[a]	49	45	63	58	54	69	21
Trust in politics[b]	27	45	69	58	71	31	22
Personal efficacy[c]	27	37	27	44	28	59	28
Neutral affect[d]	43	18	16	22	19	14	25

Source: 1976 Japan survey and ICPSR "Political Action" study codebook.

[a]Respondents answering they were interested in politics "all of the time" or "sometimes"; missing data are excluded from calculations.

[b]Respondents answering that "the people" rather than "big interests" run politics.

[c]Respondents answering that people have a "say" in what government does.

[d]Respondents who indicated neutrality or responded "don't know" to thermometer questions about affective feelings toward the major right and left groups and organizations in each country.

than Americans, all of which could imply lower levels of political mobilization than occur in some other democratic political systems.

Ichiro Miyake's detailed analysis of partisanship and related political socialization processes in chapters 5 and 6 is set within the parameters of comparative research traditions, such as those we have mentioned above, and the parameters of Japanese political culture and history. In chapter 5, the analysis parallels recent research themes of adult socialization. Miyake shows how Japanese voters, whose lives have been characterized by social and/or geographic mobility, tend to abandon the partisan traditions of their parents unusually easily and completely and adopt the party ties of persons in their new social environment.

In chapter 6, Miyake approaches the problem of the poor fit between the Michigan party identification concept and partisanship in Japan by presenting a fourfold classification of different partisan types. In this effort he is building on an earlier approach developed by Flanagan and McDonald (1979). That analysis identified in Japan disturbingly high proportions of self-professed identifiers who failed to meet the expectations of the party ID concept, especially in regard to cross-time stability. The deviating categories included volatile partisans (who switched parties over relatively short periods of time), sporadic partisans (who failed to identify any preferred party half the time they were asked), tautological partisans (who changed their short-term voting intentions and partisanship in tandem, and negative partisans (persons who had no positive affect for their preferred party). Flanagan and McDonald argued that from the perspective of the Michigan concept these identifiers were misspecified, because their identifications failed to exhibit the stability, independence, or level of commitment implied by that concept. Moreover, the levels of these misspecified identifiers were found to be so much higher in Japan than the United States as to suggest that as many as half of the self-professed Japanese partisans might not qualify as party identifiers in the Michigan sense of the term.

Miyake's approach employs a much more sophisticated set of procedures to identify different types of partisan. Using an extensive battery of measures of attitudes toward political parties—in itself an innovative departure from the frequent dependence of party identification research on fairly simple measurement strategies—Miyake develops a fourfold classification of Japanese partisans; party loyalists, negative partisans, the uncommitted, and the uninformed. These types of partisans behave in different ways with regard to basic political involvement, the stability of their partisan attitudes, issue opinions, and voting behavior. It is worth noting that only Miyake's concept of party loyalists conforms to the full set of connotations and attributes associated with the Michigan notion of a party identification. While many of those who fall into his uncommitted or uninformed types might be viewed from the American perspective as independent or apathetic nonpartisans, the negative partisans represent an important new concept of the partisan who is neutral or negative in party affect but high in political cognitions.

Miyake thus addresses the concerns of comparative political behavior in a way that shows how a more complex conceptualization of partisanship, one that goes well beyond the concept of party ID, could help explain troubling issues of short-term instability and concept validity in European research. In Miyake's view, a partisan preference does not mean the same thing for all people, and these four types of partisans exhibit different kinds of voting behavior in terms of turnout, level of commitment, and stability. Moreover, the prevailing cynicism of substantial portions of the electorate contributes to the unusual prominence in Japan of negative partisans. The concept of negative partisans, persons who continue to support a particular party without any positive affect toward that party, is certainly a major departure from the original party identification concept.

A different approach to the problem of conceptualizing partisanship in Japan is presented in chapter 10 below. The solution offered there emerges from a long but essentially disconnected literature on party images (Matthews and Prothro, 1966; Trilling, 1976; Butler and Stokes, 1969; Baker, Dalton, and Hildebrandt, 1981; Wattenberg, 1981) and more recent developments in the study of political cognitions, specifically efforts to identify partisan and candidate schema (Miller, Wattenberg, and Malanchuk, 1986; Lau, 1986; Lodge and Hamill, 1986). By asking a different kind of question—not whether all self-identified partisans meet the required attributes of the Michigan party ID concept but whether all of the large percentages of nonidentifiers found in Japan are really completely volatile in their voting patterns, without any anchoring party preferences—a different perspective on the nature of partisanship in Japan is provided. Despite the high levels of negative affect or cynicism toward parties in Japan, voters may still have images and evaluations of the parties that guide their voting decisions. While these party images may not be as stable as party identifications in the Michigan sense, insomuch as they lack a visible emotional tie, they are still likely to be fairly durable. After all, parties are rather stable political objects. Certainly they are much more enduring than candidates and far more visible to the average voter. Party policy positions, internal leadership disputes, and other party actions both in and out of the Diet are constantly reported in the media. Thus it would be difficult for the average voter not to have some images and evaluations of at least some of the parties.

For many voters in Japan, therefore, it may be more appropriate to speak of party images rather than party identifications. Miyake's negative partisans, for example, are clearly not motivated to support a party by positive affective attachments to that party. Rather, their partisan preference may be comprised of a combination of stronger dislikes of other parties and relative evaluations of the different parties' performance capabilities that favor their preferred party. This conceptualization of partisanship as a current preference based on a running account of accumulated and recent images and evaluations may better fit the experience of many or even most Japanese voters than does the Michigan concept. Moreover, a view of partisanship as a running tally of images is consistent with the most recent theoretical formulation of party identification in American research (Fiorina, 1981). One advantage this conceptualization has is that it helps to explain why partisanship changes so dramatically in Japan when one's socializing environment changes, or when specific issues have become unusually salient, as, for example, when LDP partisans, according to Yomiuri polls, dropped from over 50 percent of the electorate in September 1988 to 26 percent in May 1989 (see chapter 11). If we think of partisanship for many Japanese as a set of images that guide voting decisions rather than a positive emotional attachment, the potential impact of the social environment becomes much greater. When this environment communicates alternative party cues, partisan change does not require the breaking down of an internalized affective bond but rather the reshaping os images and evaluations of political objects that, for most citizens, are rather remote and disconnected with their daily life.

■ Short-Term Influences on the Vote in Japan

The early social psychological studies of voting behavior assumed that some attitudes were more durable than others. People's identifications with political parties were seen as long-term attitudes while attitudes toward candidates and issues were viewed as of fairly short-term duration. This distinction continues today and is buttressed by empirical evidence. Research in the United States has shown that cross-panel consistency is much higher for respondents' party loyalties than for issue attitudes (Converse, 1966; Converse and Markus, 1979). Comparable tendencies can be seen in Britain; only some 30 percent of panel respondents held stable opinions about major political issues across a two- or three-year time span in the early 1960s (Butler and Stokes, 1969), in contrast with 75 percent who displayed consistent ties to parties. We are encouraged, therefore, to continue usage of the traditional distal-proximal temporal distinctions in our conceptualization of the attitudinal bases of electoral choice in Japan. At the same time, this long-term/short-term dichotomy should be qualified in the Japanese case by the fact that many important issue attitudes and most party images need to be seen as of at least intermediate-term duration.

Issue Attitudes

While many scholars agree on the relatively shorter duration of popular attitudes about issues relative to feelings toward parties, determination of the effect of issue attitudes on voting choices and of their causal status relative to other attitudes has long troubled students of political behavior. Early research (Campbell et al., 1960) was fairly pessimistic in its assessment of the effects on behavior of issue attitudes, given findings of low levels of citizen issue familiarity and frequent failure to report any perceptions of governmental performance or awareness of party differences on a broad range of issue alternatives believed to be salient in the mid-1950s.[12] The same pioneer study was even more pessimistic about the degree to which underlying belief systems could be identified which might integrate issue positions and generally guide voters in their response to party appeals and government performance.

Later research criticized these first major findings, first on methodological grounds and later on the basis of believed changes in the American issue environment. Repass (1971) found higher levels of issue awareness and linkage between issue opinions and partisan preferences in the case of issues that

12. According to Campbell et al. (1960), two requirements had to be met for issues to influence voting behavior: people had to be aware of issues and take positions on them, and they had to perceive party differences on the same issue dimensions. Butler and Stokes (1969) added a requirement that opinions on an issue must be skewed for that issue to make an appreciable difference to the vote.

members of the electorate felt were salient. Meanwhile, various studies conducted in the United States during the 1960s reported increased voter issue competence and greater citizen ability clearly to differentiate the parties' issue positions relative to the patterns observed in the 1952 and 1956 electorates upon which earlier research was based (Nie and Andersen, 1974; Nie, Verba, and Petrocik, 1976; Pomper, 1972). Further study of the role of issues has provided additional information on the issue–party choice linkage: convergence between peoples' issue opinions and their partisan attitudes or choices is improved in the case of "easy" issues, that is, issues in regard to which information costs are negligible, in contrast with "hard" issues about which the public does not easily acquire information (Carmines and Stimson, 1980). Rabinowitz, Prothro, and Jacoby (1982) push the distinction between the electorate's responses to different kinds of issues even further by denoting comparatively higher levels of issue voting where issues are *both* salient and easy.

Determination of the direction of causal flow between issues and other attitudes has remained a hard task for voting behavior research, even while sophistication about determinants of issue familiarity and linkage has grown over time. The earliest American research assumed that issue attitudes, while mainly a short-term component of voting choices, could alternatively be influenced by long-term partisan preferences or could be a disturbing factor leading to deviations from traditional partisanship in some elections or even to widespread partisan change if popular feelings on a particular issue became polarized or reached crisis proportions (Campbell et al., 1960).[13] Subsequent thinking about the causal status of issue attitudes led to an awareness of areas of considerable ambiguity, since there are several plausible ways by which issue positions and other attitudes including candidate evaluations can become congruent (Brody and Page, 1972). Prior issue attitudes could lead voters to prefer candidates perceived to have similar positions; support for a candidate could lead to endorsement of the candidate's perceived issue position; or perceptions of favored candidates' positions could be adjusted to fit the voters' own preferences. Reflecting growing awareness of the potentially complex interdependence between party identification, issue attitudes, and candidate evaluations, American research (Jackson, 1975; Page and Jones, 1979; Markus and Converse, 1979) has begun to explore the contribution of reciprocal relationships among different attitudes to resolve some of the inherent ambiguities in individual attitude formation processes.[14]

13. Small-scale changes in party support could result from the impact on adults' party identifications of increasing polarization on issues, while in times of crisis, in addition to some plausible adult change, many apolitical persons were believed to be mobilized into new party affiliations.

14. The analysis of Markus and Converse (1979) is especially persuasive because they use

Research outside of the United States has until fairly recently paid relatively scant attention to issue attitudes, probably because of a preoccupation with political sociology questions about the effects of social cleavages on party preferences. Still, convergence of issue positions with left-right self-identifications (Barnes, 1971; Barnes and Pierce, 1971; Klingemann, 1972) and with partisanship (Campbell and Valen, 1961; Converse and Dupeux, 1962) have provided useful indications of levels of issue differentiation among population sub-groups and party identifiers in European electorates. When compared with Americans, European partisans tend to have more distinctive issue opinions, reflecting the mobilizing effects of the better organized European parties or the distinctiveness of the European parties' own issue stands. Issues have also been seen as having some weight in voting decisions, specifically in Britain (Butler and Stokes, 1969; Studlar and Welch, 1981), even in the face of findings that the British electorate was cognitively impoverished. Creative uses of issue attitudes in studies of intra-campaign opinion change (Klingemann and Pappi, 1970) and voting choices (Klingemann, 1973; Baker, Dalton, and Hildebrandt, 1981) can also be found in German research, as well as in a stimulating study of the apparent partial collapse of long-term political cleavages in Denmark in the early 1970s (Rusk and Borre, 1974). In the most recent decade, however, issues have reached new prominence, most visibly in British research, which has seen some issues as having long-term prominence for many voters in their function as structuring "principles" (Rose and McAllister, 1986).

A substantial number of Japanese studies (for example, Miyake, 1970; Kohei, 1972, 1974) have shown that issue cleavages not unlike those seen as focused on political principles in Britain exist in Japan and are linked with party support or partisan vote choices.[15] However, Japanese research has also shown that there is a substantial discrepancy between people's positions on some issues and their partisanship, as well as a considerable lack of familiarity with issues among the electorate. The lack of convergence displayed by some partisans with regard to issue opinions may reflect the effects of other forces believed to influence attitudes and behavior in the Japanese setting, such as the prominent role often given candidate attachments and electoral mobilization in some scholarly studies (for example, Curtis, 1971; Richardson, 1967b; Flanagan, 1968).[16] But the nature of Japanese party competition may also play

---

panel data from the 1972 and 1976 elections in their research, which permits examination of possible causal relationships across the critical dimension of time.

15. Some of the Japanese research omitted party identification, thereby showing substantial direct effects of issues on voting.

16. The Japanese press also gives great attention to candidates' efforts to mobilize the vote in different constituencies in each national election, and perusal of their often detailed accounts

some role as well: co-optation of opposition issue positions by the long-dominant Liberal Democratic Party may have confused the electorate with regard to interparty differences in many cases, and intraparty issue conflicts on some issues may have had similar effects by presenting potentially conflictual or confusing stimuli to the electorate. Finally, even the most cursory look at arrays of partisans and their positions on many issues at different times in the past three decades makes it clear that the dominant Liberal Democrats' policies are not endorsed by many LDP followers. Partisanship in Japan has normally been based more on representation of interests and mobilization, and related imagery coupled with the 1950s set of issue commitments, than on feelings about transitory issues.

As Shinsaku Kohei, Ichiro Miyake, and Joji Watanuki demonstrate in chapter 7, there have been several issues in Japanese politics that were salient in the years prior to the 1976 election. In some cases, the positions of the different parties and camps were also clearly differentiated, so as to produce fairly clear cues to the electorate. Some party issue differences, notably those related to Japan's international security and defense policies, had been durable fixtures in the Japanese political landscape across the entire postwar period. Even though these issues were changing in both form and salience by the 1970s, their durability could have encouraged greater familiarity among voters than in the case of more recent issues. Certain issues, such as welfare, taxes, and major corruption scandals, have also been highly visible components of the short-term political landscape in some campaigns, including that of 1976. Given the presence of both lasting issue cleavages and highly visible short-term issues, issue attitudes could be a viable force in mass political behavior in Japan, either as "structural" correlates of party support (thereby encouraging stability in voting patterns) or as short-term influences encouraging volatility in voting behavior relative to existing or past party loyalties.

The emergence of a newer set of quality-of-life issues in the late 1960s amidst the decline of aggregate party identifications might also suggest that issue attitudes could be of increasing importance in Japanese voters' electoral choices. Indeed, the increasing salience of these issues in the late 1960s and early 1970s could have contributed to the shifts in voting patterns noted at the beginning of this chapter. However, by 1974 the salience of this newer set of quality-of-life issues was at least temporarily overshadowed in the public mind by the energy crisis. Moreover, given the ruling party's belated but serious response to pollution, welfare, and other urban issues in the early 1970s, the

---

provides fascinating reading on the techniques used in vote gathering in different districts in any given election.

quality-of-life issues were not associated with clearly perceived party divisions by the time of the 1976 campaign.

In summary, there are good reasons to examine the character and effects of issue attitudes on Japanese voting behavior in 1976, even though past research has indicated that issues may play a fairly limited role for many voters in Japan. In chapter 7, special attention is given to the Japanese electorate's reactions both to several long-standing "traditional" issues and to certain political questions of high visibility in the mid-1970s, such as the Lockheed bribery scandal and political corruption. Issue saliency and familiarity are examined and the important links between self, issues, and parties are shown through analytical models familiar to students of American and British political behavior. Perhaps one of the most interesting and paradoxical findings is that it was the long-standing set of 1950s *cultural politics* issues that continued to exhibit by far the strongest correlations with the vote, despite the fact that by the mid-1970s these issues had declined greatly in importance and indeed were among the lowest in salience among all the surveyed issues.

Media Effects

In chapter 8, Flanagan explores a broad range of questions about media exposure and media trust in ways that parallel or augment traditional and current concerns for media effects on political behavior in the American setting (Berelson, Lazarsfeld, and McPhee, 1954; Converse, 1966; MacKuen and Coombs, 1981). Certainly the media seem to be playing an increasingly prominent role in American elections, and recent research (for example Iyengar, Peters, and Kinder, 1982) suggests that media treatments of election campaigns may be influencing voting behavior in important ways, such as by setting "issue agendas" and "priming" specific kinds of responses. In the Japanese case, however, the media seem to play a rather modest role, due in large part to the more restrained and restricted use of the media in Japanese election campaigns. The greatest effects of the media would appear to be not in influencing election outcomes but in raising the levels of citizen competence, psychological involvement, and political participation. The media are also arguably of great importance in determining longer-term images of the political parties, and in certain situations, such as the 1989 upper house election, may play a dominant role in setting voters' agendas.

Nevertheless, findings are presented that demonstrate that the media do exert some influence on voting outcomes, both indirectly through shaping long-term attitudes and party images and directly through diffusing popular or unpopular candidate images and setting the issue agenda. Specifically there is evidence that media exposure in Japan diffuses modern values and increases cynicism, attitudes that are themselves related to partisan preferences. Moreover, in certain kinds of elections, such as gubernatorial contests in large urban prefectures that command wide media coverage, the media are found not only to shape and propagate candidate images but substantially to heighten the importance of these images relative to party and issues preferences in voting decisions.

Perhaps the most important direct media effect on the 1976 election outcome that is demonstrated in chapter 8 is derived from the media's ability to reorder the relative salience of various kinds of political issues in a context in which different issues favor different parties. This is, of course, the precise representation in Japan of the agenda setting function identified in American research. In this case the Lockheed scandal was featured prominently and continuously in media coverage of Japanese politics for nearly an entire year prior to the 1976 election. Here the effect is limited in that it is restricted to a rather narrow segment of the electorate. Among that segment, however, the effect was rather dramatic, revealing both the potential for and limitations of media effects on election outcomes.

Candidate Images

Candidate evaluations or perceptions have played a large role in social psychological models of voting choice. In the traditional Michigan approach candidate images were seen as one of the important short-term influences on the vote, an assumption which seemed highly plausible in the context of American presidential contests where candidates typically have very high visibility. Initially, candidate images were seen as one of a triad of influences, along with party identification and issue attitudes, central to American voting choices (Campbell et al., 1960; Converse, 1975). In a manner similar to the role assigned to issue positions, candidate images were thought to be influenced by presumably more durable party identifications as well as to provide the basis for short-term deviations from long-term partisanship as a response to the climate of a particular election and the attraction of specific candidates. More recent studies of American presidential elections have given candidate images an even more central role in voting choices by postulating that candidate evaluations interact with partisanship and issue preferences in a reciprocal fashion while also serving as the main linkage between these attitudes and current vote preferences (Markus and Converse, 1979; Page and Jones, 1979). Similarly, candidate evaluations are seen as the immediate determinant of the vote in recent studies of American congressional elections (Mann and Wolfinger, 1980; Asher, 1982).

Despite the emphasis given to candidate images in models of voting choice in the American literature, little has been done to examine the processes by which candidate evaluations develop (Asher, 1982). Moreover, with the exception of the possibility that candidate familiarity, particularly in a presidential campaign, may be substantially lower in cost than issue familiarity, many of the ambiguities present in portrayals of the causal priority and contribution of issue opinions are also present in consideration of the role of candidate evaluations.

Interestingly, with only a few exceptions (Butler and Stokes, 1969; Winham and Cunningham, 1970; Klingemann and Taylor, 1978; Norpoth, 1977), students of European political behavior have shown little interest until very recently in candidate images. According to one account (Baker, Dalton, and Hildebrandt, 1981), the absence of scholarly concern for the role of candidate evaluations abroad is a reflection of evidence showing that even images of party leaders have little consequence for voting choices in parliamentary elections in countries like Germany. Evaluations of ordinary parliamentary candidates can also be assumed to have only a limited influence on voting decisions in European parliamentary elections, given the deemphasis on candidates in elections where the general presence of proportional representation formulae place primary importance on party labels. Evaluations of party leaders have been important in a few instances in European elections, as research in Britain has shown (Butler and Stokes, 1969). In recent years British research has indicated distinctive effects for leader popularity as a voting determinant (Graetz and McAllister, 1987; Mughan, 1989). However, the role of party leaders in most European countries still fails to attract research attention, perhaps because of a lack of the high visibility accruing to American presidential candidates. Thus the British example appears to be an exception to the more general rule that candidate images are of fairly small importance in Western European elections.

Concerning the potential importance of candidate images, Japan is quite a different political setting from Europe. While Japan also has a parliamentary system, the electoral system is radically different from those found in continental Europe. Rather than leading to a central role for parties, the presence of multimember constituencies in Japanese elections, coupled with limited voting and the absence of proportional representation formulae, typically forces competition between candidates of the same party, at least in the case of the LDP and often the JSP in districts where these parties can potentially elect more than one Diet representative. In comparison with European electoral systems, therefore, the Japanese system actually increases the visibility of candidates.[17] As a result

17. As a result of a revision of the election law in 1982, however, elections in the national constituency of House of Councillors beginning in 1983 have been decided through a proportional representation formula. This change may enhance the saliency of parties relative to that of candidates in upper house contests.

of these electoral arrangements, voting choices also potentially involve two dimensions, since people must often choose both between parties and between candidates from the party of their choice.

As a general rule, individual candidates in Japan also directly mobilize support independently from the campaigns of the parties with which they are affiliated.[18] As some have argued (Richardson, 1974), the effects of the electoral system, which places a high priority on candidates' personal qualities, are reinforced by a cultural expectation that politicians will assume the roles of district benefactor and personal intermediary in disputes with private citizens and public officials. Whatever the specific combination of causes, candidate evaluations undoubtedly play an important role in the electoral decisions of Japanese voters. As reported in table 1.4, this is reflected by the dominance of "candidate" over "party" in self-assessed voting motivations in HR elections up until the late 1960s and the continued importance of "candidate" in self-assessments of reasons for selections in national, prefectural, and local elections even today (Akarui Senkyo Suishin Kyokai, 1979, 1980a, 1980b).[19]

As I demonstrate in chapter 9, the levels of familiarity with constituency candidates are quite high in Japan. One reason for these high levels of candidate familiarity may be found in the high incumbency rates of members of parliament. In the 1976 HR election, 49 percent of the candidates were incumbents, while another 7 percent were former members of the lower house, that is, they had been members in earlier terms even though they were not incumbents in 1976. An overwhelming 88 percent of those elected were incumbents or former members. (More impressively, this high level of incumbent success was achieved in an election that, owing to a major scandal, was noted for the high numbers of elected "new faces.") This means that the same men face the electorate again and again, a factor which enhances their visibility to many voters.

Despite the fact that candidates are in the forefront in Japanese elections, and therefore candidate attitudes are worthy of attention, we shall report at a later point that the interplay between party and candidate attitudes in voting is actually very complex. The importance of the candidate as a voting consideration relative to party is shown clearly by the data in table 1.4. But "party" is also important. Our own survey echoes the findings from other research by showing that 32 percent of the 1976 electorate reported having emphasized "candidate"

18. Dating back to Dore's (1956) early analysis, observers have typically found that conservative candidates mentioned district issues and personal accomplishments much more often than their parties' positions on national issues.

19. "Candidate" is now less important than party in national elections for both houses, but "candidate" remains the dominant concern in prefectural and local election choices.

Table 1.4 Salience of "Candidate" versus "Party" in House of
Representatives Elections (In Percentages)

	Candidate	Party	Both[a]	Don't Know	N
1958[b]	45	32	10	13	(2,157)
1960[c]	43	33	19	5	(2,228)
1963[d]	51	31	14	3	(2,107)
1969[e]	33	48	13	5	(2,043)
1972[f]	38	48	12	2	(2,151)
1976[f]	40	46	12	2	(2,048)
1979[f]	46	41	12	1	(2,003)
1983[f]	42	47	10	1	(1,978)
1986[f]	39	49	10	2	(2,026)
1990[f]	37	51	10	2	(2,031)

Notes: All figures are percentages of total sample. Surveys were conducted at the time of House of Representatives elections.

[a] Wording was changed to "cannot say" in 1963.

[b] Jichisho Senkyokyoku, *Sosenkyo no Jittai* (Tokyo: 1958).

[c] Komei Senkyo Renmei, *Sosenkyo no Jittai* (Tokyo: 1961).

[d] Komei Senkyo Renmei, *Sosenkyo no Jittai* (Tokyo: 1964).

[e] Komei Senkyo Renmei, *Shugiin Giin Sosenkyo no Jittai* (Tokyo: 1970).

[f] Akarui Senkyo Suishin Kyokai, *Shugiin Giin Sosenkyo no Jittai* (Tokyo: 1972, 1977, 1980, 1984, 1986, 1990, respective years).

in their voting decision while 26 percent stressed party, and a full 37 percent indicated that they had considered "both" candidate and party. An evaluation of the relative influence of party versus candidate images in voting decisions will be further addressed in chapter 10, where measurements of the saliency of both attitudes will be evaluated. At this point, however, we will caution the reader to assume that the relationship between candidate and party images and vote choice is a rather complex one, which varies with different kinds of voters. The presence in Japanese HR elections of a two-dimensional or, for some voters, possibly a two-stage decision process (choice of which party and then which candidate of that party) presents substantial problems for construction of adequate models of the forces influencing the vote and the linkages among them.

Social Networks

To this complexity must be added still another important feature of Japanese elections that has direct implications for the role of candidate images in voting decisions. As has been cited earlier in our discussion, a substantial amount of mobilization of social networks and organizational ties is believed to accompany many candidates' efforts to gain office in Japanese elections, including those for the House of Representatives. Although traditionally believed more prevalent in the rural districts of Japan, direct efforts to mobilize the vote apparently occur throughout the country. The prevalence of direct efforts at influencing the vote using existing social institutions and informal networks seemed to us to be an additional short-term influence of sufficient magnitude that measurement of their incidence and impact through a battery of specially designed questions was one of our research priorities. That the presence of fairly widespread efforts by candidates to influence the vote in their own favor could lead to a reported emphasis on "candidate" in the absence of extensive candidate familiarity and favorable feelings should also be obvious.

Given the high potential for overlapping effects of efforts to mobilize support for candidates and people's own perceptions of the candidates, we decided to combine an analysis of candidate images with probes into the nature of the "influence communications" that surrounded candidates' efforts to seek election. This combined analysis is found in chapter 9, where I explore sequentially the frequency, demographic correlates, and impact of influence communications and then compare the effects of efforts at voter manipulation through social networks and organizational channels with the summed effects of favorable candidate images and the relative weight of party identification on the candidate and partisan components of the voting decision.

■ Paradigms and General Issues

In this chapter I have discussed the development of the sociological and social psychological approaches to voting behavior and their application to Japan. I emphasized the difference between long-term and short-term attitudes and influences on voting behavior. These distinctions are reflected in the organization of this book, as well as constituting part of the initial central intellectual structure of our work.

Figure 1.1 shows the main properties of these different influences on the voting decision graphically. It is a four-cell representation of the interaction of the dimensions of time and focus in conceptualizations of the forces influencing the vote and is presented here as a visual summary of my earlier discussions. Social and value cleavages are perhaps the longest of the long-term forces believed to affect mass political behavior, and they appropriately appear in the cell in figure 1.1 that represents *long-term* attitudes concerning *social* affiliations and relationships. Partisanship is also a *long-term* attitude, and this fact plus its focus on *political* objects is reflected in the diagram. Issue preferences and candidate images are generally seen as *short-term* forces, and since the

Figure 1.1   Long- and Short-term Influences on Voting Behavior

	Long-term	Short-term
Political	Partisanship	Issue attitudes Media effects Candidate images
Social	Social & value cleavages Contextual effects Social networks	Social networks

objects that form the focus of these attitudes are *political,* these influences are found in the cell formed by the intersection of the political and short-term dimensions.[20]

The Japanese Voter as a Mobilized Voter

It is important that we examine how voting behavior in Japan is affected by exposure to the political content of social network and small-group communications. Social networks and small-group relationships are believed especially important in people's lives in Japanese society (Fukutake, 1967; Nakane, 1970). Looking at the political effects of social networks and small groups will help us better understand such diverse phenomena as political mobilization within different occupational groups, the development of a cultural cleavage in Japan, alternative socialization patterns to family influences in the learning of party loyalties, variations in exposure to political information in the news media, differential familiarity with political issues, and, direct mobilization of electoral support through "influence communications" targeted at individual voters. Both the social and social psychological approaches to voting behavior research have stressed the effects of groups and social relationships on learning and behavior. However, we examine their impact in greater detail than most

20. At various points I have hinted that some issue attitudes and candidate attitudes may be of intermediate- or even long-term status. With regard to issue attitudes, at least one qualification is in order. What will be called later in this book the "1950s" or cultural politics set of issue attitudes was still alive in the 1970s, a fact which might encourage us to see these issue attitudes as more durable than others. Still, we must quickly observe that the context in which the relevant issues first emerged and that of the 1970s were quite different. There were new parties, and old parties had adopted new positions, while the intensity of traditional issue conflicts had declined. Thus, we cannot assume a constancy of nuance and saliency even though the attitudes on these issues have some superficial appearance of fairly long-term durability.

studies conducted in other countries or previously in Japan and use a variety of direct perceptual measures of these phenomena not used in earlier research. Because of the importance we assign to an analysis of the effects of people's social relationships and group environment on their political socialization and behavior, and owing to the different time frames through which network influences operate in our analyses, "social networks" are included as a dimension in both the long- and short-term social forces categories in figure 1.1.

In further recognition of the importance of social networks and social context in general, and of the function which these play in electoral campaigns in particular in Japan, we present our concluding findings in a conceptual framework in which we single out mobilization and repeated mobilization as a special category for analysis. We further see repeated mobilization, and the resulting repeated behavior, as important in the conversion processes of attitude/image nurture and reinforcement. Repeated mobilization also provides cues in the processes by which people develop cognitive images of parties and candidates. This framework marries the externally oriented properties of political sociological concepts with the internally oriented terms of social psychology, a function we find especially apt in the Japanese setting. In placing so much emphasis on mobilization and related processes of individual response, we are not abandoning the long- and short-term distinction so useful to understanding the roots of electoral stability and volatility. At the same time, we hope that by calling attention to the socializing effects of repeated mobilization in specific elections over considerable time spans, the deep importance of this feature of Japanese elections will be better appreciated. A somewhat similar argument that links cumulative media effects to frequently repeated information is also presented.

Elements of Stability and Volatility

At the outset of this chapter, I indicated that this book will explore Japan's somewhat paradoxical features of simultaneously substantial electoral stability and volatility. In considering the effects of different kinds of attitudes and social forces on voting behavior I have tried to show how each might affect behavior to promote stability or encourage change. Since electoral stability and change are so central to the concerns of this book, I will reiterate the possible effects of the different kinds of attitudes and social ties. Sociopolitical cleavages, which form the first of our sequential concerns with different forces affecting voting behavior, have long been seen as a source of electoral and party system stability in Europe. However, rapid social change in European societies in recent years has also encouraged the view that social change is a factor leading to changes in party support. Much the same is true for Japan: the rural-urban and generational patterns that have been a dominant factor in postwar political affiliations are augmented by what Joji Watanuki calls an emerging "matrix" pattern of social mobilization, reflecting the complex effects of population changes and new partisan initiatives.

Partisanship is also seen as a stabilizing force in electoral patterns (Converse and Dupeux, 1962), if sufficient levels of party attachments are present to anchor citizens' behavior. For this reason, much of Ichiro Miyake's detailed attention to measurement questions, concept elaboration, and the effects of contemporary partisan loyalties on other attitudes and behavior addresses the point of whether a distinction should be made between the concept of party identification as developed in the Michigan model and partisanship as we find it in Japan. Miyake shows how a more complex elaboration of the concept of partisanship could help explain troubling issues of short-term instability and concept validity (such as are embodied in the voting consistency-independence discussions in European research), as well as showing how some types of partisanship still contribute to stability. At the same time, Miyake presents evidence suggesting that partisan stability in Japan is to an unusual degree dependent on reinforcing influences in the adult socializing environment. To a remarkable degree, Japanese voters are found to abandon the partisan traditions of their parents and adopt the party ties of persons in their new social environment when they experience geographic or occupational mobility. As noted above, these findings suggest that chapter 10's concept of a cognitive and evaluative party *image,* rather than an affective party *identification,* may more accurately describe the long-term anchoring effect of partisanship on the voting behavior of many Japanese.

Issue preferences and candidate images can also have alternately stabilizing and destabilizing effects. If issue attitudes and candidate loyalties are highly congruent with durable party loyalties, they can be a reinforcing element to the anchoring effects of partisanship. But if citizens often deviate from the issue positions of the parties they habitually support or are vulnerable to appeals from candidates from other parties, these short-term forces may encourage electoral volatility or even defection from existing party affiliations. The effects of exposure to political communications within social networks are similarly ambiguous: discussions of politics and solicitations of a vote for a particular candidate and party may occur between copartisans or between supporters of different parties. Thus, informal communications may supplement or reinforce people's existing partisan loyalties, or they may be a source of learning and behavior that deviates from traditional attachments.[21] As we examine the

21. Actually, some interpretations of the effects of population movements in Japan have assumed that, by moving, people removed themselves from the influence of some social networks and were in turn involved in new relationships, with the obvious possibility that the candidate focus

effects on voting behavior of social and value cleavages, social contexts, partisanship, issue attitudes, media exposure, candidate images, and social networks in the chapters that follow, their various possible consequences for electoral stability and change should be kept in mind. Generally, more of the attitudes and politically relevant social factors we examine favor stability than volatility. But there are still ample examples of sources of change and instability as well, as are highlighted perhaps most clearly in chapter 11's analysis of the 1989 and 1990 general elections.

■ Research Design and Method

The research findings reported in this book are based in large part on the analysis of a nationwide survey of the Japanese electorate conducted before and after the 1976 House of Representatives election. The survey was based on a stratified, randomly drawn sample of the total electorate, in which sampling points were selected to represent urban-rural variations in types of election districts, while individuals within sampling points were selected at random. With only certain minor distortions the survey sample is representative of the demographic composition of the total electorate in the fall of 1976.[22] The survey incorporated a panel design, in that both preelection and postelection interviews were conducted with the same persons wherever possible. Out of a total sample of 2,500 persons, 1,921 were interviewed during the first wave of interviews, which was conducted in late November, 1976; in the second wave of the survey conducted in mid-December, 1,564 persons were interviewed; while 1,332 persons were queried in both panel waves.[23]

The interview schedule used in the 1976 survey contained a maximum possible total of slightly over three hundred basic and follow-up items. Roughly 60 percent of the questions were approximately equivalent in substance and format to questions asked repeatedly in the University of Michigan Center for Political Studies national election studies or questions used in the comparative "Political Action Study" project (see Barnes and Kaase, 1979). The remaining

would change and partisan stimuli might change as well. Indeed, we might assume that under certain conditions the mobilizing effects of social networks might be extremely fragile, and that as a consequence the Japanese system may have some built-in potential for sudden volatility such as was observed in the Netherlands and Denmark in the early 1970s. In those cases, the mobilizing effects of long-standing social cleavages suddenly crumbled for many people. We will return to this point in a discussion of the events surrounding the 1989 upper house elections.

22. There were, however, slightly more female respondents proportionately in our sample than in the general population.

23. The second wave included people who were added from the randomly selected names pool to enhance the representativeness of the second-wave interviews, even though they were not interviewed before the election in the first panel wave.

40 percent of the questions—items such as direct efforts to solicit voters' support, group memberships and political orientations, and respondents' evaluations of parties and candidates—were based on either prior Japanese political survey practice or our own response to long-standing issues in Japanese voting behavior research. Many of the questions were designed to explore parts of Japanese electoral behavior hitherto untapped by survey research.

Certain difficulties stand out as particularly important in our survey effort, as they do in survey research in general and in Japanese survey research in particular. These include the problem of measurement validity and the related question of comparative measurement equivalence, and, a problem which has existed in political behavior research in Japan over some time, the question of the size and substantive meaning and implications of the significant number of respondents who answer "don't know" to many questions.

All survey research incurs the risk of measurement biases and errors. Variations in wording of questions about partisanship in Japan, for example, like those elsewhere, have produced substantial differences in the proportions of persons who manifest a partisan tie. The Asahi newspaper's long-standing question that solicits party "likes" is a case in point. As many as 90 percent of the electorate usually indicate some kind of party tie in response to either this question or a related follow-up item that tries to simply force a choice—"If you had to choose, which party would you pick?" (Asahi Shimbunsha, 1976). In contrast, a question used by the Jiji press services which asks about party "support" results in much lower levels of reported partisanship (Jiji Tsushinsha, 1981).[24] Furthermore, both of these polling groups supply respondents with lists of parties, and there is no prior question asking whether or not a respondent likes or supports *any* party. Where surveys were formulated so as to question the very existence of party ties, as was the case in various Clean Election League studies, levels of expressed partisanship fell to as low as the 40 percentile range, obviously a vast difference from the 80 to 90 percent support ranges identified in the Asahi polls.[25]

These differences in response frequencies reflect differing levels of commitment. The Asahi forced choice approach is obviously picking up many respondents who have some discriminating images of the parties but not necessarily any strong affective attachments. As we move successively to question

24. As indicated, the Asahi figures cited in the text reflect the inclusion from 1953 on of a follow-up probe to the initial question about party "likes" stating, "Liking or disliking aside, if you had to choose, which party would you prefer?" Although the Jiji and Asahi results have varied slightly at different points in time, inclusion of this probe in the Asahi surveys has resulted usually in gaps of 20 to 25 percent between party support levels identified by Jiji and party preferences reported by Asahi.

25. One example of this question format can be found in Oita, 1962.

wordings that imply higher and higher levels of commitment or affiliation, fewer "partisans" are identified. Which wording is preferable depends on one's purposes. We selected the most widely used version of the partisanship question in Japan—namely, "Which party do you support?"—as a kind of compromise between the high and low threshold alternatives. This approach, however, tends to lump together many different kinds of partisans, as Miyake so clearly points out.

Thus we have identified two distinct approaches to resolving the perplexing issues of who are the partisans in Japan and what are the behavioral implications of their partisanship. The party image approach is similar to the Asahi forced-choice alternative in that it presents respondents with the lowest possible threshold of inclusion—holding some kind of image of at least one party. This approach has the advantages of being easily and unambiguously measured, of excluding few respondents, and still yielding strong predictions of short-term voting decisions. The disadvantage it has is that it fails to separate out which respondents have long-term commitments to their preferred party, which hold only volatile or nominal attachments, and which are simply temporarily throwing their support to the lesser of evils while waiting for a better alternative to emerge. From this latter perspective, the more complex Miyake multitype classification approach to conceptualizing partisanship is clearly superior.

As this discussion suggests, care must be exercised in question construction to try to obtain maximum fit between concepts and measurement strategy. In general, our response to this issue was similar to that of other research scholars concerned with measurement validity. We introduced multiple measures relating to the same concept wherever possible, to avoid the distorting effects that single measures might have. To tap party loyalties more effectively we augmented a "traditional" party identification question adapted to the Japanese context with other kinds of measures, such as thermometer questions that tapped feelings toward parties and questions about parties which the respondent would never support. The format of these additional items was designed to validate both the directionality of our basic party identification question and the intensity of partisan commitment, which is typically tapped in the customary party identification batteries. To validate the basic measure further we asked a hypothetical question regarding the possibility that the respondent might defect to another party in the future. Similar employment of multiple items to try to measure important concepts validly can be seen in questions about traditional and modern values, community integration, political trust, and political involvement. Utilization of these measurement strategies is documented at many points in our discussions of particular substantive findings.

Measurement validity is an especially troubling problem in comparative research, and, since we did want to relate our work to scholarship in other countries where it seemed reasonable to do so, great attention was paid to seeking Japanese formulations of questions that approximated our understanding of concepts and questions employed in research outside Japan. The collective judgment of the research team was the ultimate criterion in this exercise, as has been the case in other comparatively oriented studies. But we did perform some informal back translation in our lengthy discussions of question formulation as one accepted procedure to minimize loss of comparability. However, as Converse and Dupeux (1962) and others have observed, since we must rely on functional equivalence we are necessarily more confident when comparing relationships between variables than we are in simple comparisons of frequencies of amounts and levels of particular attitudes across nations and cultures.

The sizable proportion of "don't know" answers to some kinds of questions is a troubling methodological problem facing scholars who conduct political behavior research in Japan, as it is to researchers in most other countries, albeit in different degrees. Even use of multiple measures for different concepts, which can be a corrective for reducing the excessive loss of cases, does not fully resolve the problem. There is simply a portion of the Japanese electorate that is not sufficiently politicized to feel comfortable with some questions about politics and therefore indicates an inability to respond to questions. Importantly, there were sizable variations in levels of "don't know" answers depending on the type of question. Levels of self-reported ignorance are very low with regard to individuals' own political involvement and participation in political activities or exposure to the media. In contrast, fairly high levels of "don't know" answers are found in replies to questions about such abstract and remote aspects of politics as foreign policy and even some domestic policy issues, queries about evaluations of personal competence and system responsiveness, and, interestingly, items soliciting knowledge of parental political interest and partisanship. We have shown some of these differences in table 1.5, where "don't know" levels in 1976 are compared across different kinds of questions and between Japanese and American respondents.[26]

26. We made comparisons with American respondents' "don't know" levels as a way to emphasize the nature of our problem. We do not assume that the American patterns are a norm among Western industrialized societies. Although some European surveys have shown fairly high levels of "don't knows" at times in comparison with the American case, patterns in "don't know" answers between European electorates and the American public are fairly similar in the Political Action Study findings, which represent a fairly recent example of cross-national survey research employing standardized questions. However, to try to establish a comparative norm would lie beyond the object of this research.

It should also be clear that neither here nor elsewhere do we make any value judgements about the requisite levels of a particular kind of political attitude. Different nations simply have had different experiences, and mixes of "good" and "bad" attitudes relative to any particular value objective can most likely by found in most political cultures.

Table 1.5 Proportions of "Don't Know" Answers in Japan and the United States

	Japan	United States
Party identification	4–6	1
Father's interest in politics	26	7
Mother's interest in politics	32	5
Father's party identification	47	10
Mother's party identification	56	12
Respondent's interest in politics	2–3	1
Respondent's political efficacy	15–34	2–4
Respondent's political trust	7–17	3–10
Domestic issue opinions	10–22	2–31
Foreign policy issue opinions	24–39	6–11

Sources: 1976 Japan survey codebook and 1972 United States election codebook (ICPR; CPS 1972 American National Election Study).

Note: All figures are percentages of total sample. Where more than one number is given, figures refer to ranges of "don't know" answers to several questions in the relevant substance areas.

Presumably these variations in levels of reported ignorance in response to different kinds of questions reflect a complex combination of the effects of political socialization patterns, a cultural reticence to express clear and unambiguous preferences where opinions rather than information are sought, and the nature of political stimuli in the Japanese setting. The presence of these sometimes sizable arrays of "don't know" responses does not hamper our analyses of the replies of persons who do answer questions. Moreover, "don't know" answers are much more common among people who did not vote than among people who did participate in the 1976 election, the targeted population in our analysis. Still, high levels of "don't know" answers on some items do mean that there is an untapped section of the electorate whose attitudes on some dimensions remain unknown. While the presence of such a group is a limiting factor in the inferences we can draw about the total population from our analysis, there is no reason to believe that these frequent "don't know" respondents behave any differently from those respondents for whom we do have information that have similar attributes, such as low occupational status or low interest in politics. There is always the possibility that the "Don't Know" category may bring an element of extreme volatility to elections when these respondents decide to vote, however.

The Japanese Voter is the first major comprehensive study of the attitudes and voting choices of the Japanese electorate in any Western language. We have endeavored to identify the critical dimensions of the Japanese electorate's responses to politics and to portray the nature of the long- and short-term forces that have been influencing voting behavior in Japan over the last three decades. Throughout our effort we have tried to integrate comparative concepts and hypotheses with formulations derived from Japanese research in a realistic and balanced way, and through so doing contribute both to new knowledge about Japan and a greater understanding of the tendencies in political behavior across nations.

Part II ■ Long-term Influences on Voting Behavior

Two ■ Social Structure and Voting Behavior

JOJI WATANUKI

I will begin with an overview of the relation between social-structure variables and the nature of partisan cleavages in prewar Japan. My starting point will be 1890, since that was the date of Japan's first general election with the opening of the Diet under the Meiji constitution. Of the four types of social cleavages usually associated with voting behavior—regional or ethnic divisions, religious divisions, agrarian-industrial divisions, and class divisions (Lipset and Rokkan, 1967:14)—Japan was basically exempt from the first two and has been so throughout the modern period (Flanagan and Richardson, 1977:15–18).[1] Ethnic and religious homogeneity, in fact, has been utilized by the ruling group as a powerful instrument through which to cope with other cleavages. For example, in prewar Japan, the quasi-religious indoctrination into emperor worship and the ultranationalist ideology of racial superiority were exploited to diffuse the challenge of potential class cleavages (Maruyama, 1963).

Conditions were present, however, that might have fostered the development of the Japanese party system around the third type of social cleavage—the agrarian-industrial division. In 1868 when Japan began to build a modern nation, the society was predominantly agrarian, with more than 80 percent of the population engaged in agriculture. The new Meiji government, which was led by ex-samurai political leaders primarily from the two major domains (*han*) of Satsuma and Choshu, was determined to promote industrialization and to build a modern nation with a strong centralized bureaucracy at the expense of agriculture and the traditional privileges of the various local feudal fiefs. Opposed to this program, there emerged in the 1870s and 1880s a powerful movement that criticized the government and demanded recognition of people's rights; this was the Freedom and People's Rights Movement. This move-

---

1. As is mentioned later, Japan is not completely homogeneous in terms of religion. Different religions in Japan are mutually overlapping and mutually tolerant, however, a situation not conducive to the formation of religious cleavages.

ment, which was based in rural areas, was led by wealthy, independent farmers and manufacturers. What the movement revealed was a cleavage between the national leadership core of ex-samurai groups from certain former feudal domains (*han-batsu*) and landed interests in local areas. The national core was quick to accommodate at least partially the demands of the landed interests, however. A national parliament and a constitution were promised in 1881 and actualized in 1889 as a response to the rights movement.

Subsequent to the establishment of parliamentary government, the first ten years of the Japanese Imperial Diet's operation were ones of confrontation between the government bureaucracy and Diet members elected from agrarian-based local notables, thus continuing the cleavage that predated establishment of a parliament. However, such a cleavage was not a major threat and the government could survive and function even with an opposition House of Representatives, because, under the Meiji Constitution, the cabinet was not based on majority support in the parliament. Rather, the House of Representatives, which was the elected branch of the parliament, was simply one of the organs designed to assist imperial rule. In the meantime, the government succeeded in building modern civil and military bureaucracies and a modern educational system. The government also drew upon various indigenous cultural elements in putting together a new ideological orthodoxy, into which it proceeded to indoctrinate the population. In this orthodox ideology, the traditional values of village communal life, the Confucian ethic of deference, and the samurai concept of loyalty to one's lord were linked to worship of the emperor. The 1890 Imperial Rescript on Education, which incorporated these ideas, became the central document of moral indoctrination in this period and remained so up until Japan's defeat in World War II.

From around 1900, the Meiji government made another effort at rapprochement with the elected political forces in the House of Representatives. In 1898, two important members of the House, who both had once been leaders of the Freedom and People's Rights Movement and who also were founders and leaders respectively of major political parties in the House, were requested jointly to organize a cabinet. This cabinet lasted for only four months, however. This opening to the parties was followed in 1900 by a more enduring move when one of the central leaders of the Meiji government, Hirobumi Itoh, decided to organize a new "catch-all" political party.[2] By drawing together party politicians in the House of Representatives, notables in rural areas, bureaucrats in the government, and newly emerging business leaders, Itoh formed the Seiyukai political party, which in time became one of the two parties that

---

2. Itoh had started as a lower-ranking samurai in Choshu before the Meiji Restoration and served as a key figure in the Restoration and subsequent nation-building efforts.

dominated the prewar Japanese political scene. Later, a Seiyukai politician, Takashi Hara, skillfully developed the party as a link between national and local interests (Mitani, 1977); Hara also became president of the party and, finally, became prime minister. Hara's formation of a cabinet in 1918 based on a majority in the House of Representatives has been regarded as marking the beginning of the period of Taisho Democracy.[3] During the subsequent period, from 1918 to 1932, the House of Representatives and the parties were the de facto supreme bodies of government, despite the extremely weak basis of power provided to the elected lower house and its representatives by the Meiji constitution.

Another major prewar party, the Minseito, was subsequently formed by a broad coalition of local notables, businessmen, and bureaucrats. The Minseito also succeeded in building vote-getting machinery throughout the nation using methods similar to those of the Seiyukai (Masumi, 1965–79, 5: chap. 14). The Minseito subsequently competed with the Seiyukai in elections and was successful at mobilizing electoral majorities in some general elections, with the result that the Minseito and Seiyukai alternated in forming cabinets during this period.

In short, between 1900 and 1932, agrarian and industrial cleavages were skillfully avoided by creating two major catch-all parties, both of which aggregated and accommodated agrarian landed interests, businessmen, and bureaucratic interests. These interest coalitions in turn participated in government leadership through the granting of de facto power to the parliamentary majority party between 1918 and 1932. Thus, even though the constitution did not call for parliamentary rule, this principle was implemented in practice.

The amalgamation of landed and business interests after 1900 was facilitated by the accelerating pace of industrialization whereby local landed notables often became businessmen, joining together to establish private corporations in such fields as banking and railways. While such persons consequently often lived in cities at some distance from their native place, they still usually retained close ties with their tenant farmers, relatives, and members of branch families engaged in farming (Masumi, 1965–79, 4: chap. 10). At the top level of political party power stood the prewar family financial and industrial conglomerates, the *zaibatsu,* who provided large sums of money as political funds to the Seiyukai and Minseito (Masumi, 1965–79, 5:274–75).

Thus, the prewar Japanese political system did not reflect an agrarian-

3. "Taisho" is the reign period of the Taisho emperor (1912–26). During this era, a democratic movement emerged and certain democratic reforms were achieved under the Meiji constitution. This movement, known as "Taisho Democracy," began with the appointment of the Hara Cabinet in 1918. The democratic practices associated with this period were maintained throughout the 1920s.

industrial cleavage, even though the social basis for such a cleavage existed. Instead of the emergence of a genuine agrarian party or an urban liberal party, what we find in Japan is a party system dominated by two conservative catch-all parties that mirrored each other in social base composition, each representing a coalition of agrarian and industrial interests.

This leaves us with only the fourth and final type of social cleavage—class divisions. Since in many Western nations the conflict between workers and employers emerged as the most important social cleavage accompanying the industrialization process, the question arises as to how strongly this cleavage was manifested in the prewar Japanese party system. With the progress of industrialization, initiated and sponsored by the Meiji government, the non-agricultural population in Japan had grown rapidly. By around 1900, the non-agricultural population had already reached one-third of the total of gainfully employed persons. By 1920, the population was almost equally divided be-tween the agricultural and nonagricultural sectors. At this time, however, the ratio of "workers" employed in modern industry was much lower. Takafusa Nakamura (1971) estimates that in the period 1916–20 less than one-fourth of the nonagriculturally engaged population could be regarded as workers in modern industries. Other persons within the nonagricultural population were engaged in commerce, manufacturing, or other activities as small company owners or family workers, or as apprentices bound by traditional ties to their communities or by trade-association or master-apprentice relationships. In real numbers, it is estimated that about three million people were engaged in mod-ern industry. According to other statistics, two million were blue-collar workers in modern factories; within this group an estimated 300,000 were union mem-bers by the 1920s (Masumi, 1965–79, 5:355–56).

With the emergence of a "working class" and efforts to organize this class into a union movement, the 1920s witnessed the rise of various socialist parties. Beginning in 1928, when universal manhood suffrage was first introduced in elections for the House of Representatives, a small number of candidates from various socialist parties were elected to this lower house. These leftist parties also experienced some growth across the remaining prewar elections, with eight socialist members elected in 1928, five in 1930 and 1932, twenty-two in 1936, and forty in 1937. The number of votes cast for socialist candidates was 460,000 in 1928, 510,000 in 1930, 260,000 in 1932, 620,000 in 1936, and 1,030,000 in 1937. Even at its high point in 1937, however, the socialist vote represented only 10 percent of the total vote.

Despite the importance of the emergence on the Japanese political scene of a nascent socialist movement, in the period during which the House of Repre-sentatives and the political parties held meaningful power in Japanese politics—that is, up until 1932—the socialists remained a tiny minority. Throughout the period of party governments, the two dominant conservative parties—the Seiyukai and the Minseito—accounted for about 90 percent of the popular vote and 95 percent of the seats in the House of Representatives. The decline of the House of Representatives and the political parties, which commenced in the early 1930s, was accompanied by the complete suppression of the communists and left-wing socialists. Only after these developments were moderate socialists able to capture even as much as 10 percent of the vote. Moreover, some of these so-called socialists acted more like "state socialists" and supported the ascendancy of the bureaucracy.

Thus, in prewar Japan, a class cleavage failed to affect the partisan alignment of the Diet significantly. There were several reasons for this failure. First of all, despite large-scale industrialization beginning in the 1920s and the adoption in 1925 of universal manhood suffrage, genuine "workers," in the modern industrial sense, were still a small voting minority. Moreover, most of the expanding urban population continued to be under the influence of urban notables (Masumi, 1965–79, 5:358), and, as a result, supported the two major conservative parties. In the rural districts, a comparable situation prevailed. Despite the fact that the majority of peasants were tenants (69.3 percent in 1920), these lower-class persons were hemmed in by various relationships—community, kinship, and extended family ties—as well as by the internalized, traditional value of deference. As a result, poor rural people found it difficult to join the tenants' unions led by the leftists, and at its peak in 1925, the Japan Farmers' Union was only able to organize around seventy thousand of the nation's farmers, or about 1.2 percent of the 5.5 million farming households. The weakness of the tenant union movement, in turn, meant that the political potential of class relationships in the rural areas was never realized.

Another factor inhibiting the emergence of working class parties was political suppression. Communists and all left-wing socialists suspected of having ties with the communists were the targets of ruthless suppression by the police as early as the 1920s. Communist ideology was regarded as particularly dangerous in prewar Japan. Communism was totally antagonistic to the worship of the emperor, and emperor worship had been a key factor in the governing elites' nation-building programs of socialization and indoctrination since the Meiji period. Introduction of universal manhood suffrage in 1925 was accompanied by the legislation of the Peace Preservation Law, which imposed severe penalties for any attempt to overthrow the kokutai (the principle of the Japanese state), which was the official philosophical rationalization for the emperor system. In 1928, that law was revised with the maximum penalty becoming the death penalty. The Marxist ideology of class war was regarded as a grave threat to the existing political, social, and moral order of Japanese society, upon which the two dominant political parties were based. Because these conservative parties relied on local notables for votes in both the rural and urban sectors, encouragement of class conflict posed a major threat to the status quo. Japan's leaders were not hesitant to suppress the spread of such a dangerous set of ideas. The leaders of the two parties were, after all, not liberals but conservatives.

After the 1932 assassination of Prime Minister Tsuyoshi Inukai, leader of the Minseito (which had emerged victorious in the February general election of that year), the process of cabinet formation in Japan returned to the older pattern where cabinets were not based on a majority in the House of Representatives. Cabinets were formed, as before, on the advice of the *genro* (senior advisors to the emperor), but with increased pressure from the army. In the latter half of the 1930s, the influence of the House of Representatives and the political parties in the Japanese political system increasingly declined, while the power of the army and the bureaucracy increased. Finally, in 1940, all political parties, including the moderate socialists, were dissolved in order to form a unitary political association to "assist" imperial rule. With that event, parliamentary democracy and political party activity in prewar Japan came to an end.[4]

■ Postwar Democracy: The Emergence of "Cultural Politics" in the 1950s

The defeat in World War II and subsequent occupation of Japan opened a new era in Japanese politics. A number of reforms were introduced under the Occupation, among them the creation of a new constitution, land reform, reform of family law, legal recognition of labor unions, extension of the suffrage to women, and guarantees for freedom of speech and association. On the other hand, the Occupation was an indirect occupation, meaning that the existing government apparatus was allowed to function on its own, subject to the directives of the Supreme Commander of Allied Powers, General Douglas McArthur, and the General Headquarters. Therefore, a high degree of formal continuity was maintained with the prewar period, despite the many changes that occurred in this period.

The Diet, consisting of the House of Representatives whose members were

---

4. It is appropriate to mention, however, that in April 1942, in the midst of World War II, a general election for the House of Representatives was held. The election was abnormal by democratic standards, in the sense that no political party was allowed except the unitary association for assisting Imperial Rule, and that association recommended all officially preferred candidates. Still, unrecommended candidates were permitted to run, and eighty-five were elected despite various obstructions by the government.

elected in 1942 and the prewar House of Peers, continued to exist and reopened sessions in the autumn of 1945. Those sessions discussed and passed a revision of the election law that extended the suffrage to women. The House of Representatives was later dissolved in order to hold a general election before the expiration of the terms of the members elected in 1942.[5] Politicians with prewar roots, that is, those whose parties had been dissolved in 1940, were quick to reestablish themselves in their former organizations, believing or hoping not only that they were immune to responsibility for the war but that they were needed for the proposed reconstruction of Japan along the democratic lines encouraged by the Occupation.

In November 1945, the Japan Liberal Party (Nihon Jiyuto) was established by allegedly liberal factions of the prewar Seiyukai under the leadership of Ichiro Hatoyama. In December of the same year, the Japan Progressive Party (Nihon Shimpoto) was organized by politicians who had been committed in 1940 to the Imperial Rule Assistance Association (later, in 1945, the Greater Japan Political Association). These politicians were able to claim loyalty to parliamentary democracy despite their membership in the Association because they had been completely ignored in government decision making during the war. The Japan Progressive Party was a mixture of politicians and factions identified with the prewar Seiyukai and Minseito parties. The socialists, whose fortunes had basically been poor before the war, formed the Japan Socialist Party in November 1945. In addition, the communists, who had never had a legal organization in the prewar period, emerged as a formal party in December 1945. Two of the conservative parties—the Japan Liberal Party and the Japan Progressive Party—were the predecessors of the present-day Liberal Democratic Party, which has consistently held power since its formation in 1955. This particular political lineage demonstrates the tenacity of the Japanese conservative parties even after the trauma of defeat in World War II and subsequent occupation.

Conservative continuity in Japan is all the more impressive in view of the fact that before the first postwar general election was actually held in April 1946, a severe purge of prewar political leaders was carried out under a directive of the General Headquarters. In January 1946, 260 of the Japan Progressive Party's 274 Diet members and 30 of the Japan Liberal Party's 43 members were purged (Tominomori, 1977:10). The two conservative parties thus faced the

5. This election was officially designated as the 22nd General Election, and indeed it has been the practice of the Secretariat of the House of Representatives throughout the postwar period to count general elections of the House of Representatives beginning with that held in 1890, without regard for the Occupation in 1945 or subsequent changes made in the constitution in 1947. This numbering system has been widely adopted in official documents and by the mass media.

first general election after the war with an added disadvantage. Still, the results of the general election were not totally discouraging for the conservatives. Out of 464 seats, the Japan Liberal Party and Japan Progressive Party together won 234 seats, far outnumbering the Japan Socialist Party's 92 seats and the Japan Communist Party's five seats.

The next general election, April 1947, was held to meet the provisions of the new constitution, which was coming into effect in May, for an altered national legislature. Under the provisions of this new basic law, the Diet, composed of the House of Representatives and a newly created House of Councillors, became the "highest organ of state power," and the House of Representatives was given superior decision-making power. In the 1947 election and successive general elections held in 1949 and 1952, the conservatives, consisting of two or three parties with changing names, increased their share of seats in the Diet along with their share of the popular vote. This was accomplished mainly by absorbing other minor parties and independent candidates. In the 1952 general election, the two conservative parties at that time won 325 out of 466 seats (70 percent) and 66.1 percent of the total votes cast—the highest postwar figure for the conservatives—while the total share of three socialist parties was 115 seats (25 percent) and 21.9 percent of the vote. The communists gained no seats and received only 2.7 percent of the popular vote.

There were several reasons for the success of the conservatives during this period. First, a coalition government led by Socialists had failed dismally in 1947. Second, a change in United States occupation policy, caused by the intensification of the Cold War and the outbreak of the Korean conflict, favored the conservatives by allowing for the early return of those purged conservative politicians. At the same time, the conservatives' leftist opposition was weakened by a "counterpurge" of communist leaders. In addition, the main social-structural basis for conservative strength in the postwar era, Japan's rural districts, was consolidated. Because of damage to modern industry by the war, demobilization of millions from the armed forces, and the repatriation of overseas Japanese, the agrarian population grew in this period to 45.5 percent of the total gainfully engaged population, which was the highest proportion registered since the 1920s (Fukutake, 1972:22). Immediately after the war, there had been signs of rural unrest. Membership in the Japan Farmer's Union, which began its history as the guardian of tenant farmer interests in the 1920s, grew explosively from the prewar peak of 70,000 to 1,200,000 in 1948. However, the land reform conducted from 1946 to 1950 under pressure from the Occupation and in cooperation with Japanese agricultural bureaucrats was highly successful in transferring land to tenants and creating many small, independent farmers.

Implementation of land reform was a major factor undermining the conditions favorable to the growth of conflict and class sentiments in the countryside. The ratio of tenant-farmer land to total agricultural land dropped from 50 percent before the war to less than 10 percent after the land reform, while farmers who rented all of their land dropped from the prewar level of 30 percent to a mere 3 percent by 1950 (Fukutake, 1972:18). This brought with it the sudden decline of the Japan Farmer's Union and the reemergence of conservative dominance in rural areas.

Another source of conservative strength in the early postwar era was the support of older voters. Age is thus another significant factor in Japanese mass political attitudes. Despite defeat in the war and the introduction of various political freedoms, older people retained an emotional attachment to the emperor and remained attached to traditional values, such as deference and group solidarity. As a result of their value preferences, older people tended to support the conservative parties on the basis of their pledges to uphold the emperor system and arguments for the preservation of prewar virtues. Table 2.1 shows clearly the kinds of associations that existed in this period between age and partisanship relative to the effects of other "sociological" variables such as occupation, education, and sex.

In the 1950s, although conservative hegemony was well established, there was a trend favoring the Socialists, as manifested in the general elections of 1953, 1955, and 1958. The Socialists, who had split into three parties, increased their seats and share of the popular vote from 115 and 21.9 percent in the 1952 general election to 143 and 27.6 percent in 1953, and to 160 and 31.2 percent in 1955. Finally, campaigning as a unified party after 1955, the Japan Socialist Party reached the postwar peak level of their electoral strength by garnering 166 seats and 32.9 percent of the popular vote in 1958. Paralleling this increase in Socialist support, the conservatives stagnated and began to decline slightly in this period, moving from 325 seats and a 66.1 percent share of the vote in 1952 to 287 seats and 57.8 percent of the vote in 1958.

Contributing to this shift in the fortunes of the two main political camps was a noticeable change in social structure. The agricultural population shrank, and white-collar and blue-collar workers increased as a result of the Korean War boom of the early 1950s and high economic growth centering on the heavy and chemical industries in the late 1950s. Census figures show that the agricultural population declined from 45.2 percent of the total gainfully engaged population in 1950 to 30 percent in 1960, or a decrease of four million farmers in only ten years. A more important factor explaining the change of partisan support in this period, however, was a change in the party preferences of various social strata.

Table 2.1   Partisanship of Japanese Voters in 1952

	Conservatives[a]	Socialists[b]	Communists	Others	Total
Occupation					
Salaried employees	56	43	0	2	101%
Industrial workers	46	52	2	0	100%
Self-employed merchants and manufacturers	73	27	0	0	100%
Farmers and fishermen	77	21	0	2	100%
Age					
20–29	57	43	0	0	100%
30–39	60	37	2	2	101%
40–49	72	25	2	2	101%
50–59	75	23	0	2	100%
Over 60	81	19	0	0	100%
Education					
0–9 years	70	30	0	0	100%
10–12 years	64	33	2	2	101%
Over 13 years	51	49	0	0	100%
Sex					
Male	64	33	2	2	101%
Female	68	32	0	0	100%

Source: Calculated from an opinion poll on party support conducted in September 1952 by the *Asahi Shimbun*, based on the assumption that "no party to support" or "DK" people would either not vote at all or vote according to the proportion of those who support a party (*Asahi Shimbun*, 1976:96). Although the number of cases is not indicated in each table reported in this chapter, the *Asahi Shimbun*'s standard opinion polls are designed with a nationwide stratified random sample of 3,000, which typically yields a return rate of 80 percent. Percentages may not equal 100 owing to rounding error.

[a]Liberty Party (Jiyuto) and Reformist Party (Kaishinto).

[b]Right-wing socialists and left-wing socialists are grouped together.

As we can see from a comparison of the figures in tables 2.1 and 2.2, this period witnessed a radicalization—that is, an increase of support for the Socialists in various social strata—among women, youths, white-collar workers, and the highly educated.

The success of the Socialists and especially the left-wing Socialists in developing support among various strata was due to their posture as guardians of the ideals of "peace and democracy" embodied in the 1947 constitution. The conservatives were eager to revise the constitution and to amend the "excessive" portions of it, that is, those portions referring to the symbolic status of the

Table 2.2   Partisanship of Japanese Voters in 1958

	Conservatives	Socialists	Communists	Total
Occupation				
Salaried employees	43	56	1	100%
Industrial workers	41	58	1	100%
Self-employed merchants and manufacturers	69	30	1	100%
Farmers and fishermen	70	30	0	100%
Age				
20–29	44	55	1	100%
30–39	49	51	0	100%
40–49	65	33	2	100%
50–59	70	29	1	100%
Over 60	77	23	0	100%
Education				
0–6 years	64	36	0	100%
7–9 years	58	41	1	100%
10–12 years	54	46	0	100%
Over 13 years	43	52	5	100%
Sex				
Male	57	42	1	100%
Female	56	42	1	99%

Source: Calculated from an opinion poll on party support conducted in September 1958 by the *Asahi Shimbun*, based on the same methods noted in table 2.1 (*Asahi Shimbun*, 1976:111).

emperor, recognition of labor unions, equality of the sexes, unconditional guarantee of basic human rights, and, of course, article 9, which prohibited Japan from having armed forces or waging war. In short, the conservatives sought to reverse the postwar occupation reforms by revising the constitution and reverting to a social order more like that of the prewar period. The Socialists, who fiercely opposed the conservatives' position on these issues, succeeded in gradually increasing their seats in both houses, and finally in the February 1955 general election surpassed one-third of the total seats in the House of Representatives, thus making it impossible to initiate a move to revise the constitution.[6]

In this confrontation between the conservatives and the leftists, the issue was neither capitalism nor socialism; nor was the underlying cleavage deter-

6. The postwar constitution stipulates that its amendment can only be achieved by securing the agreement of more than two-thirds of the memberships of both houses, followed by a majority popular vote in a referendum.

mined by class. Rather, the differences arose from a conflict between the traditional values of emperor worship, emphasis on hierarchy and harmony, and belief in a militarily strong nation—all of which were strongly supported in the prewar era—and the "modern" values of the postwar era of individualism, equality, and fear of military buildup and war. Thus, the central cleavage was basically a cleavage of values that were unrelated to class conflict but rooted in differences between age cohorts and persons with different levels of education. The younger and the more highly educated tended to support modern, postwar values, and, consequently, to support the socialists. I have introduced the label "cultural politics" to represent the pattern of partisanship and voting based on this kind of value cleavage (Watanuki, 1967b).

As will be shown below and in chapter 3, value cleavages remain an important factor in determining partisan choice in Japan even today. However, in the 1960s and 1970s, the salience of the original cultural politics issues lost considerable weight compared to their role in the 1950s.

■ Diversification of the Social Structure and LDP and JSP Decline in the 1960s

The 1960s was a decade of sustained high economic growth in which the gross national product increased in real terms at a rate of more than 10 percent annually. Relatedly, the agricultural population, which had already begun to decrease in the latter half of the 1950s, continued to shrink throughout the decade, declining from 13 million in 1960 to 9.3 million in 1970. In contrast, the nonagricultural population increased by 12.5 million owing to the huge supply of industrial and service jobs created by high economic growth. Rather than going into agriculture, millions of sons and daughters of farmers moved out of the villages and into the cities and towns to take nonagricultural jobs, on a seasonal or temporary basis or on a full-time basis.

This process, however, did not result in the formation of a simple social structure dominated by the nonagricultural working class. Although the decrease in predominantly self-employed farmers caused the ratio of self-employed people in the total working population to drop from 46.0 percent in 1960 to 35.7 percent in 1970, this latter figure was still considerably higher than for other industrialized nations. Moreover, a considerable increase in the number of self-employed and family workers could be seen in the nonagricultural realm in industries such as commerce, service, manufacturing, and construction. Despite high economic growth, the social group of self-employed entrepreneurs, which has been variously labeled as "merchants and manufacturers," "small business," or the "old middle class" in the breakdowns of survey data, remained a solid and important feature of the Japanese social structure.

The trends in other social categories were similarly complex. For example, company employees jumped from 54 percent of the total working population in 1960 to 64.2 percent in 1970. However, this shift did not simply mean an increase in "industrial workers" in large unionized factories. If we look at the increase of employees broken down by industry and size of factory or shop, we find that the increase was generally spread evenly, meaning that both unionized workers in large factories and nonunionized workers in small factories increased in importance while sales as well as industrial workers grew in numbers. Actually, the *ratio* of unionization among employees remained almost the same throughout this decade.

Meanwhile, as shown in table 2.3, the increase in the number of sales workers (persons employed in the wholesale and retail industries) was slightly higher than that of other industries, with the result that the size of this group became considerable. In fact, sales workers numbered 6.2 million in 1970, making them the second largest group of employees, surpassed only by those in manufacturing. Sales workers in turn constituted the employee group with the lowest level of unionization and the highest ratio of employment in small enterprises, in comparison with other categories of the work force. Reflecting

Table 2.3 Change in Labor Force by Industry and Employment Status between 1960 and 1970
(In Thousands)

Industry	Self-Employed and Family Workers	Employed	Total
Agriculture, fishing, and forestry	−3863	−300	−4163
Mining	−6	−318	−324
Construction	+358	+898	+1256
Manufacturing	+845	+3285	+4130
Wholesale and retail sales	+658	+2517	+3175
Finance, insurance, and real estate	+79	+516	+595
Transport, communications, and other public utilities	+46	+981	+1027
Service	+489	+1970	+2459
Public service	—	+391	+391

Source: 1960 and 1970 census.

the importance of this trend, both scholars and journalists began from the middle of the 1960s to treat "sales workers" or "sales and service workers" as a group distinct from either "blue-collar workers" or "white-collar workers" (Watanuki, 1967a and Asahi Shimbunsha, 1976:190).

We may conclude that despite high economic growth and seemingly drastic changes in the employment structure in Japan in the 1960s, the combined size of the occupational groups that had been the voting base for the conservatives in previous years and remained so in the 1960s—namely, self-employed farmers, merchants and manufacturers, and employees in small enterprises—was, as a whole, not drastically reduced. On the other hand, these changes were not without significance for the fortunes of the Liberal Democratic Party at the polls for two reasons. First, table 2.3 reveals that there was a net decline in the self-employed of nearly 1.4 million during the decade. Second, during the 1960s the levels of support for the conservatives continued at very high levels among farmers but declined somewhat among the other traditionally conservative occupational categories.[7] Thus the redistribution of the population from farming to other conservative occupational categories also yielded a net negative effect on LDP support and contributed to the continuing erosion of its vote across the decade, falling from 58 percent in 1960 to 48 percent in 1969 (refer to table 1.1).

The trends in this period in the occupational groups that included "professionals" and "managers and administrators" were important out of proportion to their size, even though their contribution to political change only became clear at a later point in time. During the 1960s, professionals increased from 2 million, or 4.9 percent of the total gainfully employed population, to 3.4 million, or 6.6 percent, and "managers and administrators" grew from 1 million, or 2.3 percent of employed persons, to 2 million or 3.9 percent. The political predispositions of these groups are not easy to summarize, but their increased size added complications to the relationships between the social-structure variables and partisanship.

Whatever the reservations suggested by the complex trends in occupational categories, an increase of 10 million employees should have meant favorable conditions for the Socialists. Yet in the 1960s, they failed to take advantage of this apparent opportunity. The Japan Socialist Party actually stagnated throughout the decade in terms of both vote shares and Diet seats. Usually the Socialists' decline is explained by two factors. One is the weakening salience of the "cultural politics" issues that were powerful forces favoring the Socialists in the

7. For example, the 1967 Japanese Election Study survey findings reveal that 76 percent of the farmers compared to only 62 percent of the merchants, managers, and manufacturers voted LDP in that election (Flanagan and Richardson, 1977).

1950s. After 1960, the conservatives under the leadership of Prime Minister Hayato Ikeda (1960–64) avoided political confrontation with the Socialists by adopting a "low posture," that is, a conciliatory stance, while simultaneously emphasizing policies focusing on the economy, such as the well-known "income-doubling plan." Subsequently, all segments of the population, including big business, labor unions, and farmers, became relatively satisfied with the conditions achieved under sustained economic growth, especially given the comparatively fair distribution of its fruits (Takayama, 1980: chap. 1; Tominaga, 1979:43–44). Many voters, and notably those with higher education, gradually ceased to base their partisan support on the cultural politics issues of the 1950s and deserted the Socialists in favor of other parties. Young people began to think of the status quo as given and natural and were polarized into either a conservative mood or a radical criticism of the status quo such as is characterized by a communist or New Left bent.

The second factor that explains the socialist decline is the rise of minor parties. This development became important in the 1960s as a number of minor parties, taking advantage of the diversification and deintensification of the 1950s value cleavage, began to emerge and gain strength. First of all, the Democratic Socialist Party split off from the Japan Socialist Party in 1960. The electoral performance of the DSP has not been particularly impressive, but its political initiatives have still been important. The DSP over time has received around 3.6 million votes, or roughly 7 percent of the total vote in various general elections and between 19 and 35 Diet seats. Despite its relative weakness at the polls, the new party's existence contributed to the development of a second major national federation of labor unions (Domei) closely linked with the party, which, in the private sector, became bigger and stronger than the older federation of unions under Sohyo's banner, which was traditionally linked to the Japan Socialist Party. Although Sohyo maintained a predominant position in the labor movement in the public sector, the JSP lost leverage over many white-collar and blue-collar workers in the private sector through this realignment within the union movement just at a time when the private sector was growing rapidly because of the economic growth of the 1960s.

Meanwhile, the Japan Communist Party, which had suffered from suppression during the Occupation and from its own reckless policy of insurgency during the Korean War period, emerged in the 1960s under Kenji Miyamoto as a party with an effective leadership and a flexible party line. The JCP achieved notable electoral successes beginning in the 1967 general election, when its support increased to 2.2 million votes from .5 million votes in the previous general election of 1963. In the 1967 poll, the JCP gained five Diet seats. In that same general election of 1967, the newly formed Komeito, or Clean Government Party, which was affiliated with the Soka Gakkai, a Buddhist lay association, won 2.5 million votes and 25 seats. This successful performance was all the more notable since this was the CGP's first appearance as a contestant in an election for the House of Representatives.

Significantly, the combined votes and seats of the three minor parties in the 1967 general election—the JCP, CGP, and DSP—were sufficient to threaten the hitherto unchallenged positions of the LDP and JSP. In the subsequent 1969 general election, both the CGP and JCP did very well. The CGP doubled its strength to 5 million votes and 47 seats. The JCP increased its votes to 3 million, winning 14 seats. The JSP, in contrast, was the only party to lose seats in the 1969 general election, falling a full 50 seats short of their 1967 total of 140 seats.

The origins of these changes do not reflect changes in Japanese society in any simple way. Indeed, if we look into the social-structural variables associated with the CGP, JCP, and DSP vote, we are struck with the heterogeneity of those three parties. Moreover, analyses of voters in the 1967 and 1969 general elections showed that about half of CGP voters had been nonvoters in the elections before the CGP existed (Tanaka, 1977:89). In addition, the remaining half of the CGP's votes seemed to come equally from past voters for the LDP and JSP (Miyake, 1979:119). CGP votes also appear to have been recruited heavily from among women, especially those between their 30s and 50s. Among occupational categories the CGP recruited its support from nonunionized sales workers and blue-collar workers as well as from self-employed merchants and manufacturers (Komei Senkyo Renmei, 1970:277, 281).

The JCP votes came disproportionately from persons in their twenties. In terms of occupations, two major groupings, white- and blue-collar workers (both unionized and nonunionized) and self-employed merchants and manufacturers, contributed relatively more to JCP support than did other categories of employment. As a matter of fact, since its revitalization, the JCP has competed with the JSP for the votes of unionized white- and blue-collar workers and with the LDP and CGP for the votes of self-employed merchants and manufacturers in the cities. The DSP's special clientele are white-collar employees above the middle-management level, but DSP support also includes scattered votes from white- and blue-collar workers and self-employed merchants and manufacturers.

What we can see here is a kind of overlapping pattern where all three parties—the JCP, CGP, and DSP—are emphasizing their respective appeals and fiercely competing with each other and with the two major parties (the LDP and JSP) for the support of persons within the same social strata. The resulting social-structure base of the three minor parties could thus be seen as a mosaic of support. As shown in table 2.4, the mosaic pattern remained essentially the same in the 1976 elections, except for the presence of one more complication in the form of another new party—the New Liberal Club—which split off from the LDP in 1976. Thus, despite the oil crisis of 1973 and ongoing social change, the correlation between party vote and social structure seems to have remained largely an extension of those patterns that developed in the 1960s, at least up until 1976 when the JABISS study was conducted.

Thus, we can discern a progressive diversification of Japan's social struc-

Table 2.4   Occupational Composition of Minor Party Voters in 1969 and 1976

	1969			1976			
	JCP	DSP	CGP	JCP	DSP	CGP	NLC
Farmers and fishermen[a]	8	7	6	2	3	3	3
Merchants and manufacturers[a]	18	14	12	20	13	8	20
Managerial employees	0	8	1	3	7	1	1
White-collar workers	23	19	5	12	14	9	19
Sales and service workers	7	4	12	11	6	9	5
Blue-collar workers	17	10	16	15	13	14	6
Housewives	15	35	42	26	36	44	38
Others	12	3	6	11	8	13	8
Total	100%	100%	100%	100%	100%	100%	100%
N of Cases	(60)	(100)	(137)	(105)	(90)	(132)	(65)

	Percentage of above 1976 subtotal of white-collar, sales and service, and blue-collar workers supporting a minor party that are unionized			
	JCP	DSP	CGP	NLC
Union member	38	39	16	40
Nonunion	62	61	84	60
Total	100%	100%	100%	100%

Sources: 1969 Komei Senkyo Renmei survey; 1976 Akarui Senkyo Suishin Kyokai survey.
[a] Includes both self-employed persons and their family members who were working in the family business.

ture, increased complexities in the linkage between values and party support, and additional complexities in the development of multiparty support patterns, all of which weakened the direct and manifest correlations between social structure and party vote that had obtained earlier. The 1970s have also brought a number of other complicating factors to the party choices of the voters. One such factor was the decline of the salience of the Japan–United States Security Treaty as a partisan issue, because of changes in Japan–China–U.S. relationships that came about in the early 1970s. Another development was a series of corruption scandals culminating with the 1976 Lockheed scandal that brought the downfall of Kakuei Tanaka's cabinet in 1974, Tanaka's arrest in 1976, and his lower court conviction in 1983. These revelations increased political distrust among Japanese voters.

■ Social Structure and Partisan Choice in the 1976 General Election

I will turn now to a more detailed analysis of the patterns of association between social-structural variables and partisan choice at the time of the 1976 election. In this regard our JABISS study does not presume to present entirely new results. Indeed, many other surveys that have been conducted in Japan since the 1950s by scholars, the mass media, and others have already identified a number of well substantiated patterns. For instance, it has been repeatedly pointed out that neither the British-style causal chain from occupational prestige via class identification to partisan voting, nor the American-style differentiation of partisan voting by socioeconomic status (SES) exists in Japan (Yasuda, 1973; Flanagan and Richardson, 1977; Miyake, 1979). This finding is reconfirmed by our survey. We find that income and occupational status have no significant independent effects on vote choice when education is also entered into the multiple regression equation and that when class is added to these predictor variables, the combined model including education explains only little over 4 percent of the variance in the 1976 voting decision.

As indicated above, however, two social-structural variables, age and education, have occupied strategic positions in Japanese voting studies, beginning with those made in the 1950s. Indeed, the "cultural politics" theory, which has stressed the role of value differences in explaining electoral behavior, was developed to accommodate the association found between these two demographic variables and the vote. Age and education still proved to be at work as major predictors of political behavior in 1976. As shown in table 2.5, however, there has been a trend toward a decline in the explanatory power of age and

Table 2.5 Party Vote by Age, Education, and Occupational Category

	1963		1967		1972	
	Eta	Beta	Eta	Beta	Eta	Beta
Age	.27	.17	.23	.13	.24	.16
Education	.17	.05	.10	.01	.10	.01
Occupational Category	.38	.32	.37	.34	.30	.25
	$r^2 = .169$		$r^2 = .156$		$r^2 = .113$	

	1976		1976 Urban		1976 Rural	
	Eta	Beta	Eta	Beta	Eta	Beta
Age	.23	.12	.14	.11	.30	.14
Education	.11	.02	.02	.08	.20	.07
Occupational Category	.35	.30	.27	.25	.38	.31
	$r^2 = .132$		$r^2 = .084$		$r^2 = .171$	

Source: Calculated by Komei Senkyo Renmei survey data for 1963 to 1972 and Akarui Senkyo Suishin Kyokai survey data for 1976.

Notes: Based on multiple classification analysis in which the dependent variable is vote for Right (LDP), Center (DSP, CGP, NLC), and Left (JSP and JCP) parties. Four occupational categories (farmers, manufacturers and merchants, white-collar, and blue-collar workers) were used. Other categories are excluded from the calculation.

education in predicting leftist voting, especially in urban areas. Moreover, although the remarkable expansion of secondary and higher education after the war resulted in age and educational levels being strongly inversely correlated ($-.35$), age seems to have persisted more strongly than education as a factor influencing left-right voting. However, if we examine the party vote in 1976 in greater detail, we discover that education, even controlled by age, still exercises some independent influence in the 35–49 age group, with a fairly substantial correlation existing between higher education and leftist voting. In addition, when we look at the case for the minor parties—the JCP on the left, and the CGP, DSP, and NLC in the center—it becomes evident that these groups also rely on different age and education groups as the main sources for their vote.

Occupational categories such as white-collar, blue-collar, and self-employed have been used widely as powerful social-structural variables in predicting or explaining the voting behavior of people in various countries (Rose, 1974). In studies of voting behavior in Japan, four occupational categories—white-collar employees, blue-collar workers, self-employed/family workers in commerce and manufacturing, and farmers—have been used as social categories in most opinion polls and scholarly studies, from the first use of survey methods in the late 1940s up to the present, with only minor modifications by individual researchers.[8]

As exemplified in Richard Rose's (1974) compendium on the sociology of partisanship in Western Europe and North America, Japan also demonstrates some awkward spots in the categorization of occupations. Categories cannot be based only on a simple occupational classification, because they usually are combinations of employer, self-employed, and employee statuses, plus non-manual and manual occupational classifications, and industrial classifications, such as agriculture, commerce, and manufacturing. For instance, the fourfold Japanese classification of farmers, self-employed persons in commerce and manufacturing, white-collar, and blue-collar are based first on employment status—whether a person is self-employed or an employee. Sometimes we use this dichotomy of self-employed and employed with a further combination of other variables, such as unionization and/or size of enterprise, and find these composite indicators useful. A second criterion applied in defining the fourfold categorization is industrial sector, distinguishing between farmers and the self-employed in the nonagricultural sector. A third distinction is occupational, discriminating between white-collar and blue-collar jobs. Furthermore, if researchers' data provide a sufficient number of cases, more minute distinctions can be introduced, such as "sales and service workers" or "self-employed construction workers" using the industrial classification as a secondary principle, or "professional" employees versus self-employed professionals according to employment status, or "employees in managerial positions" versus white-collar employees based on subdivided employment status. We will develop a more complex scale using some of these distinctions where necessary and possible.

The validity for political behavior analyses of Japan's basic fourfold classification of occupational categories rests on the following points. First of all, despite the shrinkage in their numbers, farmers in Japan have long been the stronghold of conservative party support and they still form an important group in the electorate seen as a whole (12 percent by the 1975 Census).[9] The electoral

8. As mentioned earlier, it has become more common since the middle 1960s, in both opinion polls and scholarly studies, to insert a category of "sales and service workers" between the white-collar and blue-collar categories in occupational status scales or between the white-collar and blue-collar employee groups versus self-employed merchants in indices of political predispositions.

9. The ratio of those engaged in primary industries among the gainfully employed dropped to 12 percent in 1975 and 11 percent in 1980 (both are census figures). The number of households involved in agricultural work—some on a full-time basis and most on a part-time basis—is 4.66 million, however. The farm population, therefore, was 21.4 million, or 18.3 percent of the total population in 1980. All figures are from the Agricultural Census as reported in the *Asahi Nenkan*, 1982:334, 384.

impact of this group is further magnified by the overrepresentation of rural districts, especially in the House of Representatives.

Second, self-employed merchants and manufacturers have been a large group since before the war, and they have remained a sizable, tenacious set, recruiting new entrants even during the high economic growth period of the 1960s. Although this group basically remained a stronghold for the conservatives, in recent years support drawn from the group has also been essential to the electoral success of CGP, DSP, and JCP candidates in the cities (see table 2.4).

Third, the subclassification of employees into white-collar and blue-collar groups reflects a clear and valid distinction in terms of jobs—that is, whether manual or nonmanual—as well as differences in attributes such as education level. In Japan's case, however, though these differences are socially meaningful, white-collar and blue-collar workers are rather similarly distributed vis-à-vis class identification and partisan support. Since the 1950s, when the value-based "cultural politics" was most prominent, higher education has meant greater attachment to modern values and hence more support for the Socialists. In that case, the higher educational level of the white-collar group was a factor promoting support for the Socialists among white-collar workers. This factor, however, declined in relative importance in the 1960s through the effects of social change. Meanwhile, in both white-collar and blue-collar groups, widespread unionization has encouraged leftist preferences, a factor of no small significance given that the level of unionization is higher among white-collar employees than among blue-collar workers. As table 2.6 demonstrates, when we break down the two occupational groups by unionization, we find clear voting distinctions only between the unionized and nonunionized groups, with little or no differences between the respective white-collar and blue-collar categories.

Looking at industries by sector, we find that agriculture and fishing are predominantly LDP worlds, with more than 82 percent of the vote among persons working in those areas going to the LDP. People engaged in commerce are about equally divided between the self-employed and employed; sales employees, as mentioned above, incline toward support for the LDP. An interesting sector is that of construction, which has expanded through economic growth and concomitantly increasing government expenditure on public works. In the process, the construction industry has become known for its notorious connections with politicians of the ruling party, that is, the LDP. Interestingly, our data analysis tells us that the LDP garners 47 percent of the votes of people in the construction industry, including not only corporate and self-employed persons but also employees.

What is clear for this discussion is that while various kinds of occupational categories clearly distinguish voting tendencies in Japan, occupational status

Table 2.6　Party Voting among White-Collar and Blue-Collar Workers by Unionization in 1976 and 1986

	1976				
	Right	Center	Left	Total	N
Unionized white-collar	15	16	69	100%	(111)
Unionized blue-collar	27	7	66	100%	(71)
Nonunionized white-collar	42	22	35	99%	(161)
Nonunionized blue-collar	42	22	35	99%	(120)
	1986				
	Right	Center	Left	Total	N
Unionized white-collar	28	21	51	100%	(88)
Unionized blue-collar	36	26	38	100%	(69)
Nonunionized white-collar	66	14	20	100%	(229)
Nonunionized blue-collar	65	14	21	100%	(141)

Sources: Akarui Senkyo Suishin Kyokai surveys.

and income do not. Thus blue-collar workers in certain kinds of industries or contexts (that is, nonunionized, small enterprises) tend to vote conservative. Moreover, two of the most important occupational categories in Western voting studies, blue- versus white-collar workers, cannot be distinguished in their voting preferences in Japan. Here the meaningful distinction turns out to be not blue versus while collar, but union versus nonunion. Finally, the two categories most strongly associated with conservative voting—farmers, and merchants and manufacturers—both cover a wide range of status and income levels, from presidents of large companies to street peddlers.

Social Networks and Voting Choices

Both researchers on elections and the public at large in Japan recognize that LDP electoral strength is based on social networks of various kinds, such as those based on community, kinship, occupational, school, or other kinds of social ties. Candidates from other parties also cultivate such ties whenever possible in order to win in elections, although union ties, as mentioned above, are the main weapon of JSP candidates. In this connection, occupational categories carry with them different patterns of social network involvement.

One of the most political associational networks is the type of organization known as the *koenkai*. The koenkai is a personal sponsoring association set up by a particular candidate, based on personal networks built up around a variety of social ties. The koenkai is also a mechanism through which a number of benefits—tangible and intangible, material and spiritual—are distributed to members in exchange for support for the candidate at election time. Koenkai membership now makes up one-seventh of the total electorate, and koenkai are used by candidates of all parties, including the JCP, to seek support from persons in all occupational categories.

As shown in table 2.7, koenkai involvement flourishes most among self-employed merchants and manufacturers. Although the level of membership in koenkai even in this occupational group is only 22 percent, the koenkai organization exerts an influence beyond its direct membership through its links with various trade associations that are organized around common business concerns such as liquor sales, owning restaurants, and so forth.

Involvement in neighborhood contacts, a second kind of social network, also differs by occupational category. Similarly, the politicization of neighborhood contacts, as measured by involvement in neighborhood political discussions, varies by occupation. In both cases, farmers and merchants and manufacturers are more involved in neighborhood networks than people in other occupational categories.[10] Merchants and manufacturers are also the most involved group with regard to participation in trade associations.[11] As mentioned before, union ties that involve persons in different employee groups to different degrees—more in the cases of white-collar and blue-collar and less in the case of sales workers—are the "counter networks" that provide infrastructural support for JSP, JCP or DSP candidates. But neighborhood and trade association networks are overwhelmingly under the influence of LDP candidates, although all other parties try to utilize those networks, too, whenever possible.

Length and type of residence are also important factors associated with variations in involvement in neighborhood or community networks. The longer people reside in a community, the more they are apt to be involved in neighborhood networks. Also, persons who live in their own homes tend to have a greater stake in their communities and to reside in older, more integrated communities, and for these reasons they are also more likely to be involved in neighborhood networks than are renters. Finally, both length and type of re-

10. Often social networks in villages overlap with kinship ties. According to a sociological survey in a village in northern Japan, a stem family had twenty-nine families attached to its kinship organization out of a total of forty-eight households in the village. The researcher pointed out that each farm household usually had at least five or six relatives living in the same village (Takahashi, 1977).

11. In the case of trade association memberships, the figure of 34 percent for farmers seems too low considering the fact that Agricultural Cooperatives (*Nokyo*) include all farming households in Japan. We can argue that the coverage of Agricultural Cooperatives is so comprehensive and "natural," however, that many farmers fail to recognize their cooperative as a "trade association."

Table 2.7   Social Network Involvement of Persons in Different Occupational Categories
(In Percentages)

	Membership in Koenkai	Neighborhood Contacts	Neighborhood Political Discussions	Membership in Trade Associations	Membership in Union
White-collar employees	18	56	25	—	51
Sales and service workers	16	55	17	—	20
Blue-collar employees	17	71	32	—	43
Merchants and manufacturers	22	76	41	57	—
Farmers	18	98	43	34	—

sidence are related to occupation. Farmers, for example, are almost immobile and are only second in the tendency to own their own homes. Therefore, certain occupational categories are actually highly correlated with the variables that summarize residential status, and, in turn, reflect differences in social network involvement.

A Preliminary Summary Analysis of Voting Choice in the 1976 Election

We have conducted a multiple classification analysis (MCA), reported in table 2.8, to sum up the above discussion. The criterion variable was right, center, and left voting, and the explanatory variables included six social-structure variables. Here, social structure is defined broadly to include along with age, education, and occupation one organizational or social network variable (union ties) and two contextual residential variables (length of residence and home ownership). To simplify the analysis, these six variables were reduced to three by combining the two attribute variables, the two occupation-related variables, and the two residential variables into single scales. Finally, two other variables that are identified elsewhere in this volume as important predictors of the vote were used: a values variable (deference) and a partisanship variable (party images).[12] This analysis, then, is designed to test for the importance of social structure, particularly various kinds of occupational classifications, in predicting the vote relative to a number of other key variables. In so doing, it also serves as an introduction to several important variables or influences—values,

12. Multiple classification analysis is an analysis of variance procedure that produces standardized regression coefficients in the sense used in multiple regression but is particularly appropriate when analyzing intercorrelated independent variables that are measured at the nominal level. The age and education scale is a combination of age and education as follows: (1) under 34 years old, (2) 35 to 49 years old with low education, (3) 35 to 49 years old with medium and high education, (4) over 50 years old with low education, (5) 50 years old with medium and high education. The occupational categories and union affiliation scale has five categories: (1) unionized employees, (2) employees with some union member or members in their family, (3) self-employed but with some union member or members in their family, (4) employees without any union ties, (5) self-employed without any union ties. The length of residence and home ownership scale is constructed by dichotomizing and combining length of residence and home ownership. The deference scale was calculated by summing the responses to four questions measuring deferential values, the scalability of which was tested by the Guttman technique. Finally, the party image variable was obtained by adding mentions of the LDP in three questions that asked respondents to mention the name of a party which in their view had the best policy, was the best representative of the respondent's occupation, and was most capable of governing. In other words, the party image variable reflects the degree to which the respondents have a party image favoring the LDP. Party image was used here as the measure of partisanship because it greatly reduces the missing data problem associated with the standard affective partisanship question and because the party image variable is identified in chapter 10 as a measure of cognitive partisanship with strong predictive power. The operationalization of party image used in chapter 10, however, differs somewhat with that employed here.

Table 2.8   Multiple Classification Analysis of 1976 JABISS Data

	Nationwide		Urban Japan		Rural Japan	
	Eta	Beta	Eta	Beta	Eta	Beta
Age and education	.16	.03	.16	.07	.14	.10
Occupational cate- gories and union ties	.36	.24	.26	.17	.44	.36
Length of residence and home ownership	.25	.12	.25	.16	.18	.09
Deference	.23	.16	.23	.17	.23	.18
Party image	.45	.36	.43	.37	.46	.37
	$r^2 = .319$		$r^2 = .289$		$r^2 = .378$	
	$N = 999$		$N = 527$		$N = 471$	

Note: Criterion variable: partisan vote (Right, Center, and Left).

contextual effects, social networks, and partisanship—which will be considered in more detail in the following chapters.

The MCA revealed several interesting points. First of all, although the bivariate Eta coefficients for the relationship between the age and education scale and partisan vote as the dependent variable were moderately substantial, the Beta coefficients reflecting the strength of the relationship after the influences of other variables were excluded was insignificant, except in the case of rural Japan. These results coincide with our findings in table 2.5. Second, the composite variable of occupation and union ties is the most powerful explanatory variable among the three social-structural variables, especially in rural Japan. Furthermore, the contextual length of residence and house ownership scale, which can be regarded as an indirect indicator of involvement in neighborhood social networks, acts independently from occupational category, especially in urban Japan. In rural Japan, however, its Beta coefficient is markedly low, indicating that in rural areas social networks are so strong and comprehensive as to absorb even newcomers and tenants. In rural areas, therefore, it would appear that only being an employee or having union ties can weaken the effects of surrounding social networks and allow people the freedom to vote for opposition party candidates. Third, as shown in table 2.5 above, the amount of variance in voting choice that can be explained by such social structural variables as age, education and occupation have decreased in the 1970s in comparison with the 1960s, and is weaker in the cities than in rural areas.

In the face of the declining power of social-structural variables to predict vote choice in Japan, there have been attempts by a number of researchers to search for other variables that might explain electoral behavior. Thus, more and more attention has been paid to psychological and other intervening variables such as issue positions (Kohei, 1979: chap. 1), party images (Kohei, 1979: chap. 2), candidate evaluation (Shiratori, 1972: chap. 2), and life-style (Akuto, 1975). At the same time, value cleavage explanations have survived in the form of socio-psychological variables that effectively link social structure and voting behavior. In order to indicate the possible effectiveness of these variables in explaining partisan voting, we added values and party image to the MCA, as indicated above. The total variance explained by the five variables is fairly satisfactory, especially in rural areas. Moreover, the Beta coefficient for party images was the highest for the five variables included, thus suggesting the potency of psychological variables in the explanation of behavior in an increasingly complex society.

Religion and Partisanship in Japan

A remark on the implications of religion in explaining Japanese voting behavior is appropriate here. In many other societies, religious affiliations and frequency of church attendance still play a considerable role in differentiating the partisan orientations of voters (Rose, 1974). In Japan religious factors affect voting very little, however. Historically, Japan is a country of great religious diversity and frequent conflict. The fierce rebellion of a Buddhist sect in the sixteenth century and the rebellion of Catholics who suffered severe repression in the seventeenth century are examples. After the Meiji Restoration, Protestantism also exercised great influence among intellectuals, along with the spread of Western individualism. But despite the influence of Christianity on social thought, Christians—both Catholics and Protestants—remained a very small minority in prewar Japan and continue to constitute a small minority today. Even according to the evaluations made by Christian churches, which may be somewhat inflated, the Christian population in Japan is only 910,000 including 350,000 Roman Catholics, 10,000 Greek Orthodox, and 540,000 Protestants (Bunka Cho, 1981). Taken together, therefore, Christians make up less than 1 percent of the total population.

What are the remaining 99 percent who are not Christian? Are they Buddhists or Shintoists? The answer is both yes and no. Surveys show that those who believe in any religion—Buddhism, Shinto, or Christianity—make up only 25 percent of all adults (TSK-KCI, 1979). In addition to the limited number of believers, there is no sharp cleavage between those who believe in some religion and those who do not. Among those who do not believe in any religion, 69 percent indicate they are tolerant of religions, that is, they say that they respect religiosity. In addition, the doctrines of the dominant religions in

Japan—institutionalized Buddhism with 75,000 temples and 245,000 priests and Shrine Shinto organized under the Association of Shrines (Jinjahoncho) with 80,000 shrines and 10,000 priests (Bunka Cho, 1981)—are loosely organized and exhibit syncretic tendencies that tie them together and deeply connect both to community life. These qualities are not conducive to religious cleavage. Also, while Shinto was made the state religion from the Meiji Restoration until the end of World War II, under the postwar constitution Shinto lost its special status.

Notwithstanding these important trends toward the downgrading of religious belief and conflicts, Shinto practices and rituals have been a political issue in recent years.[13] Conservatives have insisted that certain aspects of Shinto are so closely associated with the Japanese way of life that they should be accorded special treatment despite the separation of religion and state stipulated by the 1947 constitution. Socialists and communists have fiercely opposed this, saying that the conservatives are attempting to revive prewar social values and practices. In this regard, the Shinto issue has been, and will remain, a focus of the value cleavage between modern and traditional ways of life.

The clergy and organizational arms of different religions themselves take different positions on the values issue and related conflicts. The minority Protestants are quite vocal, and sometimes alliances of socialists, communists, labor unions, and Christians emerge to oppose conservative policies, for example, concerning the Yasukuni Shrine and *Gengo* issues.[14] Indirectly, Buddhist monks and Shinto priests can be regarded as conservatively oriented, because as local notables they are involved in community life in parts of the country where conservative values are generally dominant. Yet they cannot be always

13. The following examples are instructive. To have a Shinto ceremony at a ground-breaking has been a widely held practice even for the construction of government buildings. In 1965, a JCP local assemblyman sued the City of Tsu for spending official money for a Shinto ground-breaking ceremony at the start of construction of a city building. The Supreme Court's final decision on this case in 1977, however, declared the city's action constitutional. Another example is the case of the Yasukuni shrine in Tokyo, which is dedicated to those who died in wars since the Meiji Restoration and which was heavily protected by the state until the end of World War II. Under the 1947 constitution, the Yasukuni shrine lost its privileged legal status and became an ordinary Shinto shrine. Moves to restore the Yasukuni shrine's special status have been persistent throughout the postwar period, however. From 1969 to 1974, the LDP repeatedly proposed a law to define the Yasukuni shrine as a "nonreligious institution" and to give it special governmental support; the LDP failed to get the measure passed because of fierce opposition and criticism both within and outside of the Diet, however. After 1974, the focus of the issue shifted to the problem of the official visits of the emperor and the prime minister to the shrine. Actually, each successive prime minister has visited the shrine, but they have refrained from calling their visits "official." So far, the emperor has made no visit to the shrine since World War II.

14. The *Gengo* issue concerns the debate over permitting official sanctioning of the traditional practice of designating the calendar year by the year of the sitting emperor's reign.

manifestly conservative because they must cater to heterogeneous parishes that include unionists as well as persons from conservatively inclined occupational categories.

There are two exceptions to the generally diminished significance of the religious factor in contemporary Japan. One is the well known case of the Soka Gakkai and its political arm, the Komeito (Clean Government Party). Another is the Shinshuren (Federation of New Religious Groups). It is well known that the CGP relies heavily on the Soka Gakkai membership for vote mobilization, despite the formal separation of the CGP from the Soka Gakkai since 1970. Our data show that about half of CGP votes in the 1976 general election came from Soka Gakkai members, which coincides with other estimates (Murakami, 1971; Asahi Shimbun, 1979). Meanwhile, the Shinshuren's leadership is in the hands of the Risshokoseikai, also a lay organization of a Buddhist sect and hence organizationally similar to the Soka Gakkai (although they are rivals both in proselytizing efforts and on political issues). The Shinshuren under the leadership of the Risshokoseikai avowedly supports LDP and DSP candidates, and as an indirect indicator of this religious organizational support, we find that 9–11 percent of LDP and JSP supporters indicate membership in a religious organization compared to only 2–4 percent for JCP, JSP, and NLC supporters.

These activities by religious organizations, however, do not mean that any significant religious cleavage as such exists. The CGP has refrained from manifest promotion of religious interests since 1970. And although the Shinshuren provides valuable support for the LDP and especially the DSP, where it often contributes the votes necessary to help candidates win, the majority of votes for the LDP and DSP come from nonreligious voters and for nonreligious reasons. Thus, Japan demonstrates not so much the presence of a religious cleavage as religious diversity with only a limited and partial manifestation of religious factors in voting.

■ Changes in the Social Structure and Voting Patterns since 1976

More than a decade has passed since the JABISS survey (1976) was conducted, and further changes in the industrial and occupational structure of Japanese society have occurred. As table 2.9 shows, between 1970 and 1985, the shift in the labor force from the primary industries to other industrial sectors has continued at a swift rate. In particular, the tertiary sector has been expanding rapidly, providing nearly ten million new jobs (see the bottom five categories in table 2.9).

Table 2.9 Change in Labor Force by Industry and Employment Status
between 1970 and 1985
(In Thousands)

Industry	Self-Employed and Family Workers	Employed	Total
Agriculture, fishing, and forestry	−4593	−63	−4656
Mining	−8	−121	−129
Construction	+220	+1151	+1371
Manufacturing	−567	+131	−436
Wholesale and retail sales	−27	+3393	+3366
Finance, insurance, and real estate	+56	+551	+907
Transport, communications, and other public utilities	+33	+363	+396
Service	+349	+4289	+4638
Public service	—	+295	+295

Source: 1970 and 1985 census.

Despite this continuing pattern of change, a comparison of the changes occurring over this fifteen-year period to those reported in table 2.3 for the decade of the 1960s reveals some interesting differences. The major shift is the onset of a decline in the self-employed in the manufacturing and sales industries. Over the 1960s the number of self-employed workers in these two industries grew by 1.5 million. From 1970 to 1985, the self-employed in manufacturing and sales decreased by nearly 600,000. This decline was nearly completely offset by increases in the number of self-employed in other industries outside of the primary sector, especially the construction and service industries. Given the gain of nearly ten million new employed workers, however, this change has meant that now, even outside the primary sector, the numbers of self-employed are in decline in relative terms. Since the two categories of farmers and self-employed manufactures and merchants in our four-type occupational scheme have traditionally been the foundation of LDP support, while the remaining two categories of blue- and white-collar workers have been the source of opposition strength, this change could spell trouble for the LDP (see table 2.2). At least in relative terms, both occupational categories that have strongly and consistently supported the ruling party are now in decline.

There have also been several notable changes in the distribution of employed workers by industry. The number of employees in manufacturing has leveled off. Although sales employees have continued to grow strongly in numbers, the biggest new surge in employed workers has occurred in the service industry. Since manufacturing has traditionally been one of the most heavily unionized industries and the left has not done as well among sales and service workers, this shift might be expected to impact negatively on the JSP, DSP, and JCP. Indeed, unionization has largely failed to penetrate the tertiary industrial sector in Japan. As a result, the number of unionized workers has stagnated around the level of twelve million from 1970 up to the present. Thus, the unionization rate has fallen from over 35 percent in 1970 to 33 percent in 1976, 31 percent in 1980, and finally to less than 28 percent in 1987. This decline hurts the JSP and DSP most directly, as they have relied heavily in the past on the Sohyo and Domei union federations respectively to mobilize the support of blue- and white-collar workers.

Further complicating matters is the fact that these two national labor federations decided to amalgamate into one national federation. As a result, the Rengo union federation (Japanese Private Sector Trade Union Confederation) was formed in 1987 as a first step in the amalgamation. The public sector unions joined this new federation in November 1989, and the organization's name was changed to the Japan Trade Union Confederation (Nihon Rodokumiai Sorengokai—still abbreviated as Rengo). Although several unions under the influence of the JCP opposed this unification and set up a separate, minority federation (Zenroren), the newly created Rengo federation covers 65 percent of organized labor. Rengo is expected to exercise more influence than either the previous Sohyo or Domei union federations in mobilizing support for the JSP and DSP. Moreover, this important unification of the labor movement should promote greater cooperation among the JSP, DSP, CGP, and other minor center parties while it sharpens the split between these parties and the JCP.

Survey data provided by the Akarui Senkyo Suishin Kyokai on four recent House of Representatives elections (1979 through 1986) help to clarify the relationship between social structure and voting in Japan since the JABISS study. The data demonstrate that in the urban sector, the minor parties have continued to recruit support from a broad variety of social groups. Here again the ability of personal and organizational networks to reach across different social strata is evident. While the minor parties have not been able to expand their vote significantly since 1976, their previously established support bases have clearly become firmly entrenched in the mosaic social structure of the Japanese urban world. Indeed, if any change can be detected in the structure of support of the JCP and DSP since the early 1970s, it is that both parties have become less dominated by white-collar supporters, making their support bases look even more similar to that of the CGP.

Despite the continuing shrinkage of the farming population and the emerging relative decline of the self-employed merchants and manufacturers, the LDP was not destined to continue losing support at the polls after 1976. While the numbers of farmers have declined, their level of support for the ruling party has been further strengthened in recent years. Also, though the minor parties have managed over the last two decades to penetrate the urban self-employed, the majority of the self-employed in the secondary and tertiary industrial sectors are still inclined to support the LDP. Most central to the LDP's continued success at the polls, however, has been its ability to increase its support among both blue- and white-collar employees. This shift in the occupational composition of the LDP's support base is clearly depicted in table 2.10. While the shift is a moderate rather than a dramatic one, it is in line with the changing composition of the Japanese work force and demonstrates the LDP's ability to adjust to changing societal conditions.

The LDP's growing inroads into the blue- and white-collar work force are even more apparent in table 2.6. The rather dramatic trends that appear in that table in nonunionized blue- and white-collar workers' levels of support for the LDP, rising from 42 percent in 1976 to 65–66 percent in 1986, should be interpreted with some caution. The 1976 election represented the low point in LDP fortunes, with the party receiving only 42 percent of the nationwide vote, a full seven percentage points lower than its 1986 vote totals. If we go back to the 1967 election when the LDP polled the same percentage of the nationwide vote as in 1986, we find that 55 and 59 percent of the nonunion blue- and white-collar workers were supporting the ruling party (Flanagan and Richardson,

Table 2.10   Occupational Composition of LDP and JSP Voters
              in 1976 and 1986

	1976		1986	
	LDP	JSP	LDP	JSP
Farmers	27	9	28	9
Manufacturers and merchants	35	13	24	11
White-collar workers	23	48	30	51
Blue-collar workers	15	30	18	28
Total	100%	100%	100%	100%
N of Cases	(490)	(258)	(664)	(156)

Source: Akarui Senkyo Suishin Kyokai surveys.
Note: Categories other than these four are omitted.

1977). These nonunionized employees tend to be the most volatile occupational category in Japan in their voting behavior, because they are neither as firmly tied into conservative community and occupational networks as the self-employed nor as involved in opposition party networks as unionized workers.

While the LDP has clearly been increasingly successful in gaining support among these nonunionized workers in recent years, perhaps its most impressive gains have been among the unionized workers. In 1967 only 15–22 percent of unionized blue- and white-collar workers were voting LDP, roughly in the same range as the 15–27 percent found for 1976. By 1986, however, LDP support among these unionized workers had jumped to the 28–36 percent range. Thus the growing erosion of opposition party support among unionized workers would appear to be a fairly recent phenomenon, one that has undoubtedly helped to sustain the ruling party in the face of the declining proportions of the self-employed in Japanese society.

As a result of these changes, the LDP has become increasingly balanced in its support structure, looking more and more like a true catch-all party on a national scale. In this regard, the minor parties could be viewed as mini-catch-all parties, primarily operative in the urban world only. On the other hand, as shown in table 2.10, the JSP has become increasingly a party of white-collar workers. This can be regarded as a legacy of the cultural politics of the 1950s and the JSP's growing reliance, as its support has declined, on its core supporters of white-collar unionists in public enterprises and more educated voters with more modern, libertarian values. This trend is not necessarily a bad one, since white-collar workers are the fastest-growing occupational category in Japan. Indeed, the future potential of the JSP would seem to lie in mobilizing and representing the urban, educated white-collar workers and cooperating more

Table 2.11 Party Vote by Age, Education, and Occupational Category

	1979		1980		1983		1986	
	Eta	Beta	Eta	Beta	Eta	Beta	Eta	Beta
Age	.21	.13	.19	.08	.21	.08	.21	.09
Education	.06	.04	.14	.04	.15	.05	.15	.05
Occupational category	.32	.28	.34	.31	.35	.32	.29	.24
	$r^2 = .116$		$r^2 = .126$		$r^2 = .132$		$r^2 = .092$	

Source: Akarui Senkyo Suishin Kyokui surveys.
Note: Categories and calculations are the same as those in table 2.5.

effectively with the new national union federation and the DSP and CGP center parties.

With the possible exception of the JSP, therefore, the trends I have identified depict an increasing blurring of the social-structural bases of party support. Indeed, table 2.11 reveals the continuing decline in the explanatory power of age, education, and occupation as predictors of the vote in the four elections between 1979 and 1986. Here we have repeated the same multiple classification analysis that was reported in table 2.5 for the 1963–76 elections. Minor fluctuations from election to election tend to disguise a trend that becomes more apparent if we average the percentages of the explained variance across successive pairs of elections. If we do that the explained variance drops continuously from 16.2 percent (1963–67) to 12.2 percent (1972–76) to 11.7 percent (1979–80) and finally to 11.2 percent (1983–86). While the major change clearly occurred in the early 1970s, a continuing erosion in the predictive power of these variables can be detected. From the perspective of social structure, Japanese voters appear to be becoming more volatile and more responsive to social network cues and psychological influences that are not based on nor exclusive to broad occupational and demographic categories. This conclusion regarding increased volatility, or at least the increased potential for volatility, is reinforced by the findings regarding the declines in the proportions of self-employed and the falling levels and party loyalty of unionists. The relative decline of these two groups, which have traditionally been firmly tied by organizational linkages to the LDP and JSP respectively, has meant that Japan's two major parties have had to rely increasingly on voters whose support was less firm and predictable. This change foreshadows a rise in electoral volatility, which to date has most notably been seen in the 1989 upper house contest.

The relationship between social structure and voting in Japan across the postwar era has not been a clear-cut one. The political alliance formed during the Meiji nation-building efforts in the nineteenth century, a coalition of the bureaucracy, local notables, and businesses, was maintained through the pre–World War II period to a remarkable degree. In postwar Japan, however, the late-developing socialist movement gained considerably, especially in the 1950s, by taking advantage of the salience of value issues. Modern values were linked to support for the Socialists, and traditional values were linked to support for the Conservatives.

Because of the high level of secularization in Japan, religion plays only a limited role in reinforcing these value cleavages. Moreover, economic growth and the low posture of the governing Conservative party in the 1960s and beyond have blurred the traditional/modern confrontation. Nevertheless, value differences continue to be correlated with voting behavior, as is shown above and in the following chapter, and that relationship accounts for the continuing associations found between age and education and voting choices.

Neither the British-style class voting nor the American-style socioeconomic status voting exists in Japan. Instead, different kinds of broad occupation categories—defined by self-employed versus employee status, type of industry, enterprise size, and the types of organizations tied in with a given occupation (that is, unions, trade associations, and so forth)—are the important social-structural predictors of the vote in Japan. Rather than a social cleavage model, therefore, Japanese voting behavior fits more of a mosaic or matrix pattern. Occupational type is important, but only when further specified by additional variables that more fully define the specifics of a given occupational context and the partisan influences with which it is associated. Moreover, there are signs of the declining power of social-structural variables in predicting the vote. This trend can be attributed to the emergence of various factors influencing vote choice that are independent of occupational context, including the rise of minor parties, the growing importance of psychological factors such as party and candidate images, and the increasingly complex patterns of partisan cues associated with the voter's immediate social networks.

Three ■ Value Cleavages, Contextual Influences, and the Vote

SCOTT C. FLANAGAN

This chapter begins with the proposition that two of the most compelling explanations of Japanese voting behavior are derived from the "cultural cleavage" and "social network" models. As was demonstrated in the last chapter, the kinds of religious, ethnic, and regional cleavages typically found in the European democracies were historically comparatively absent in Japan and hence not available to serve as social bases for political parties. Moreover, the principal social cleavage that is present—the division of class or socioeconomic status—does not have the strength or clarity of expression in Japan that it does in many other industrial countries (Flanagan and Richardson, 1977). These findings suggest the need to look beyond the European social cleavage model to achieve a satisfactory explanation of Japanese voting behavior.

Two decades ago, Joji Watanuki introduced the concept of "cultural politics" and suggested that this notion might better characterize the basis of political alternatives in postwar Japan. He defined cultural politics as a "politics in which the cleavages caused by differences in value systems have more effect on the nature of political conflict than the cleavages caused by economic or status differences" (1967b:456) Watanuki argued cogently that several societal conditions had combined to heighten the salience of value issues and value politics in the postwar Japanese political milieu: 1) the rapid socioeconomic changes in Japanese society that were inducing massive changes in values; 2) the prolonged period of high economic growth and prosperity that was deemphasizing the salience of economic conflicts and economic issues relative to more purely value-based issues; and 3) the persistence of a traditional, paternalistic form of hierarchic interpersonal relations and the relative absence of rigid status demarcations because of the openness of merit-based upward mobility, both of which diffused the potential for status discontent and class antagonisms. To these points we might add the fact that value conflict in Japan was greatly intensified by the Occupation's superimposition of Western political, educational, and social reforms upon an authoritarian tradition, epitomized by the emperor system and the family system. Given the Occupation's experiment in social engineering and the dramatic economic transformation of Japanese society in the post-Occupation period, it is not surprising that, as Watanuki notes, many of the major issues that have divided postwar Japanese politics have their basis in competing value systems.

A second voting model that is applicable to the postwar Japanese political context is the social network model. This model stresses the importance of both formal organizational networks and informal small group networks in the transmission of political opinions, voting cues, and other "influence communications." In elaborating this model, Richardson and I argued elsewhere that the organizational and small group communications networks in which the individual is enmeshed can potentially exercise an important short-term influence in mobilizing and channeling his or her voting choice. We also reasoned that these networks could potentially have a long-term impact on political attitudes and partisan attachments (Flanagan and Richardson, 1977). Although data on interpersonal influences were not available for that study, we were able to test for the contextual effects of certain kinds of occupational and residential environments using the 1967 Japanese Election Study.[1] We found, for example, that a respondent living in a conservative residential environment or a progressive occupational environment was apparently influenced by these social contexts and their associated informal communications networks in reaching his or her voting decision. Here this kind of contextual analysis will be revisited using the more recent JABISS data.

This chapter is designed to test the applicability of the cultural cleavage and social network models to the explanation of Japanese voting behavior and the interrelations between these two modes of explanation. The chapter begins with a theoretical discussion of what values have been changing in Japan over the postwar period and why. That is followed by an analysis of longitudinal data taken from the National Character Studies to demonstrate the patterns of change that have been associated with different value dimensions.[2] The remainder of the chapter is based primarily on the rich value and contextual items found in the 1976 JABISS Japanese Election Study. This analysis begins by defining three value scales and the various direct and indirect linkages between these

---

1. The 1967 Japanese Election Study was conducted by the Center for Japanese Studies of the University of Michigan with Robert Ward and Akira Kubota as the principal investigators in conjunction with the January 1967 House of Representatives election.

2. The findings of the National Character Studies are to be found in the numerous publications and research reports of the Institute of Statistical Mathematics and its research staff, which were led by Chikio Hayashi. Among these, the major publications are TSK-KCI, 1961, 1970, 1975, and 1982.

traditional-modern social value predispositions and voting preferences to explain why values are related to vote choice. Finally, we move toward an integration of the cultural cleavage and social network models by demonstrating that certain kinds of residential and occupational environments are related to voting behavior, at least in part, because they instill or perpetuate traditional or modern values. In other words, our two models are somewhat reinforcing; contextual factors affect values, which in turn guide voting choices.

■ Identifying the Politically Relevant Dimensions of Value Change in Postwar Japan

The basic social values that underpin Japanese society and culture have undergone very rapid and fundamental change in postwar Japan. So rapid has been the pace of change that Tadao Okamura (1968:567) has referred to the socialization process in Japan as the "political socialization of upheavals." As a result several authors have come to speak of two different cultures as existing side by side in Japan. (Nishihira, 1964; Richardson and Flanagan, 1984). At one end of the cultural continuum we find traditional attitudes and behaviors and at the other end we find a more modern set of attitudes. Several analyses have identified a number of different attitude clusters according to the rate and pattern of change associated with each cluster (Leghorn and Suzuki, 1985; TSK-KCI, 1985; Hayashi and Suzuki, 1984; Kojima, 1982). It appears that a number of discrete attitude dimensions have witnessed a marked parallel change throughout the postwar period, such that they may be assumed to be related to the same general process of change.

In each case, age and education emerge as the two demographic variables most highly associated with these changes. The older, less educated show a much greater tendency to hold to certain kinds of traditional Japanese values than do younger, more highly educated respondents. Elsewhere, it has been shown that on a number of important value dimensions these age differences reflect a strong pattern of intergenerational value change (Kojima and Akiyama, 1973; Ike, 1973; Flanagan, 1979). The rapid rate of socioeconomic change in postwar Japanese society has meant that each new generation has been socialized under a somewhat altered set of societal conditions. These differences in the social context in which the socialization process takes place have been producing substantial differences between the social values held by younger generations and those espoused by their parents and grandparents. At the same time, the rapid expansion of secondary and higher education across

the postwar period has had an independent effect on changes in value preferences, since education implies a process of enlightenment whereby traditional
folkways are gradually replaced by more modern concepts of human society.
Thus even within the same age cohort, we find that those with less education
cling to the more traditional societal value preferences.

There is a growing body of literature on Japan that has not only documented the presence of important intergenerational value cleavages but also
established the political relevance of these value differences. That evidence
demonstrates the existence of distinct value types that are associated with
contrasting political attitudes and behaviors (Kojima and Akiyama, 1973;
Kohei, 1974; NHK-HYC, 1975, 1979, 1985; Watanuki, 1977; Flanagan, 1979,
1980c, 1982, 1984).

Two factors, however, may potentially complicate an analysis of value
change in the Japanese case. The first is that the pattern of value change has
been somewhat uneven, at least from a Western, Parsonian perspective. A
number of value dimensions that can loosely be classified under the traditional-
modern rubric show marked movement in the modern direction. Several other
dimensions, however, that are equally associated with concepts of traditional-
ism and modernity in the Western mind show weaker signs of change. This
uneven pattern of change raises questions of convergence or divergence. Are
Japanese cultural values becoming more or less like those found in the advanced
industrial societies of the West? In the case of some kinds of attitudes, the
answer seems to be yes, but in other cases the answer is much more ambiguous.
We cannot, then, assume that all "traditional" Japanese values are undergoing a
uniform process of change in a modern or Western direction. That is an empirical question that needs to be answered, since values that are not changing
clearly cannot lie behind observed changes in political attitudes and behavior.
This first complicating factor, then, should be taken as a warning against the
pitfall of assuming that, because certain value dimensions are changing, all
other value dimensions associated with them in the Western mind are also
undergoing change and hence contributing to the explanation of political attitude change.

A second potentially complicating factor in a sense raises the opposite
problem—not that fewer than expected value dimensions may be experiencing
change but that too many different kinds of values may be changing at the same
time. This problem would make it difficult to isolate which set of values, among
those that are changing, are effecting shifts in political attitudes. Specifically,
the literature clearly distinguishes between two kinds of value change—those
changes in basic social values that are expected to be associated with the

transition from the agrarian to industrial phase of development and those changes believed to be associated with the industrial to postindustrial transition.

Modernization theories have typically focused on a more or less common set of value changes that are presumed to accompany early industrialization (Parsons, 1951; Almond and Powell, 1966; Pye, 1966; Inkeles and Smith, 1974). Often, at least in the early work on modernization, these changes were presented as a series of dichotomies. Traditional man living in agrarian societies was viewed as involved in diffuse relationships and holding particularistic, group-centered, and ascriptive norms while modern man living in industrial societies was seen as involved in specific relationships and holding universalistic, individualistic, and meritocratic norms. These theories in their most simplistic form suggested black and white differences in value orientations between traditional and modern man. While few would hold to that view today, the lingering implication of these theories is that with the advent of industrial society, the movement along these dimensions of change was complete. In other words, although one could never expect to find a contemporary society where 100 percent of the population espoused thoroughly "modern" attitudes, in these already highly industrialized societies, further economic development was not expected to be associated with further movement in the mass attitude distributions along these traditional-modern dimensions.

In contrast, most postindustrial theories of value change have identified other kinds of attitude dimensions that are expected to experience change during the stage of advanced industrialization (Roszak, 1969; Reich, 1970; Bell, 1976; Inglehart, 1977; Toffler, 1980). Perhaps the most developed theory regarding what kinds of values are expected to change with the advent of postindustrial society and why these changes occur is found in the work of Ronald Inglehart (1971, 1977, 1979, 1987). Inglehart identifies a set of materialist value priorities that are associated with the industrial stage of development and a distinct set of postmaterialist value priorities that are associated with the postindustrial stage of development.

In the Japanese case, this conceptualization of two distinct, discontinuous, and noncomplementary kinds of value change associated with two separate phases of socioeconomic development poses special problems. Because the modernization of Japan has been so recent and the pace of socioeconomic change so rapid over the past one hundred years, these two phases of value change are likely to overlap in Japan. If it is found that the same individuals who hold modern industrial values also tend to hold postindustrial values, then it will be more difficult to identify which kinds of value change are responsible for the emergence of newer kinds of political orientations.

I contend that this is an artificial problem created by a faulty conceptualization and identification of the politically relevant social values that are undergoing change in today's advanced industrial democracies (see Flanagan, 1987, and Flanagan and Lee, 1988). Certainly some kinds of values are more likely to change at the early stages of industrialization while other traditional values endure longer and begin to change at more advanced levels of industrialization. If we focus narrowly on the politically relevant dimensions of value change, however, those attitude dimensions that can be shown to be strongly related to key political attitudes and behaviors, it would appear that value change is more continuous than discontinuous. The politically salient value cleavage found in the advanced industrial societies of today is not a new one, but rather one that has been with us for some time, even if it has not always been strongly politicized. It is not so much that a different set of value dimensions is beginning to undergo change as a result of the advent of advanced industrialization but rather that further movement is taking place along the same value dimensions that began to experience change during the early stages of industrialization. This point becomes clearer when these politically relevant dimensions of value change and the associated environmental changes that are inducing movement along these dimensions are identified. It is the identifying of these latter causal factors, the changing conditions of life under which socialization is taking place, that is crucial to estimating the timing and duration of the value change phenomenon. If the changes in the relevant socializing life conditions are relatively new in origin, then so too must be the value cleavage. However, if the changes in these critical conditions of life can be traced back one hundred years or so, then the value cleavage must have much earlier origins.

A Theory of Value Change

In my view there are two politically potent dimensions of value change, one a shift from an emphasis on *authority* to *autonomy* and the second a related shift from *conformity* to *openness*. Agrarian societies are characterized by scarcity, inequality, rigid hierarchic social stratification, economic and physical insecurity, and personal dependencies on patrons. These conditions of life breed social norms that emphasize respect for authority, obedience, social order, resignation to one's station in life, and loyalty to and dependence on the symbols and offices of power. In addition to this emphasis on hierarchic authority we also find an emphasis on horizontal authority, namely conformity to collective group pressures. Conformity is nurtured by the static, slow-changing nature of agrarian societies, their isolated homogeneous communities, the economic interdependence of these communities on shared goods and services, and the widespread ignorance that gives rise to superstition and ignorance. These conditions promote norms of conformity that stress adherence to time-honored customs and traditional moral and religious beliefs, a distrust of new ideas, and an intolerance of what is different.

Innate in every person is a drive for self-actualization, to become the most that one can be. The conditions of agrarian life placed severe constraints on this drive and conditioned all but a very few privileged members of society to accept an existence ruled by one's superiors, one's group, and the unseen forces of nature. As the basic conditions of life began to change with industrialization and economic development, the emphasis placed on authority was tempered and replaced by a growing valuation on autonomy. Here *autonomy* means accentuating equality rather than hierarchy, a self-assertive individualism and independence rather than a passive compliance or submissive resignation. Similarly, the stress on conformity began to give way to demands for greater openness. A higher valuation on openness becomes vital for creating a freer environment to facilitate self-actualization through more openness to new ideas, more permissive attitudes toward new life styles, and more tolerance of and empathy with people or groups that are different from oneself. Openness presents the individual with more choices, and autonomy puts those choices in one's own hands rather than in the hands of one's superiors or one's society.

It is in identifying the causes of these shifts in values that the more continuous nature of these changes becomes apparent. Agrarian societies are characterized by conditions of scarcity and economic marginality. Scarcity breeds inequality and insecurity, conditions which inspire subjugation and social norms that emphasize and justify a highly asymmetric distribution of power and authority. Industrialization and economic development, however, require a much wider distribution of the traditionally scarce resources of education, knowledge, and technical skills than is necessary or possible in agrarian societies. This is a progressive relationship such that the higher the stage of industrialization the more broadly and equally these resources *must* be distributed. Industrialization, then, brings with it not only much higher levels of affluence, education, and knowledge but also a growing equality in education, life chances, incomes, and life styles. Social mobilization and social mobility increase freedom of choice and opportunities and blur rigid class lines. As the distribution of knowledge, skills, and other important resources broadens, it becomes increasingly difficult to justify an asymmetric distribution of power. This growing equalization of life conditions has successively diminished the scope and magnitude of authority that one individual can exercise over another and strengthened autonomy at the expense of hierarchic authority.

At the same time, other developments have been freeing the individual from personalistic dependencies and arbitrary power. With the development of the nation-state and the penetration of the means and instruments of state regulation have come a bureaucratization and rationalization of the exercise of power and a declining risk of physical attack. More recently, the rise of private and governmental insurance systems and the welfare state has further undermined the individual's traditional economic dependency on powerful families and local notables. Again, these are long-term progressive developments that have gradually reduced the need to identify strongly with external sources of power.

The process of economic development has also been associated with a progressive undermining of the norm of conformity. Traditional agrarian societies were based on stability, continuity, and custom. Industrial society, however, is based on innovation, the idea that new could be good. Again, it is apparent that those forces eating away at the norms of conformity and horizontal or group-centered authority are long-standing and progressive: the accelerating pace of change, which increasingly requires and rewards the creation and assimilation of new ideas; the successive emergence of new machines and technologies, which are progressively freeing us from a dependency on friends and neighbors for shared goods and services and thereby weakening the collective mechanisms of social control; the breakdown of the isolation and homogeneity of the community through increasing geographic mobility and media exposure to different groups, customs, and ideas, an exposure which is enhancing tolerance of different people and ideas; and the advance of scientific knowledge and education, which are undermining strict adherence to traditional moral codes and religious beliefs.

The Timing of the Political Emergence of the A-L Value Cleavage

Elsewhere I have identified these two major dimensions of value change, authority/autonomy and conformity/openness, as defining an overall process of value change in which the more traditional values and social norms are clustered under the label *authoritarian* and the more modern norms are identified by the label *libertarian*. As the above discussion suggests, this authoritarian to libertarian (A-L) value change process has been with us for some time, indeed at least since the advent of industrial society. There have also been earlier eras when the A-L value cleavage became politically important, although the disputes in those periods occurred at different points on this value continuum. For example, in earlier and more thoroughly authoritarian environments the issue may have been whether a lord's vassal had the right to kill a farmer on the spot for a lack of appropriate displays of deference, or whether scientific findings that disagreed with religious beliefs should be suppressed, or whether women should be allowed to own property or vote. The long-term trend of human history from agrarian society onward is moving us away from authoritarian values in a more liberal direction. There have been long periods of stagnation or even reversal in the direction of change, but from a long range perspective, the direction of change is clear. Thus we should not conceptualize the authoritarian-libertarian value cleavage as new. Rather, it is an old cleavage that has been running throughout human history but has recently been redefined around a new set of political issues at a more progressive point on this value continuum.

Because survey research is a rather recent phenomenon, we cannot demonstrate that an A-L value cleavage was present and latent in the society of, say, Elizabethan or Victorian England. We can look at contemporary societies at earlier stages of development, however. One of the most influential works in this regard is the study of Alex Inkeles and David Smith (1974) on the kinds of attitude changes associated with the early stages of industrialization in six developing nations. While the specific content of the items they employ differs from my own work, the same themes of a shift from authority to autonomy and conformity to openness are not only present but dominate the composition of their Overall Modernity (OM) Scale. The authority/autonomy dimension is clearly represented by items that tap one's obligation to parental authority, deference to the aged and to people from distinguished families, one's dignity valuation (whether in the punishment of subordinates, wives, children, defeated enemies, and others in general one selects a harsh authoritarian treatment or a more mild, empathetic treatment that recognizes the other's value), one's sense of personal efficacy, one's breadth of opinions and political assertiveness. The conformity/openness dimension is represented by items that assess the individual's openness to new experiences and to people who are different from oneself and that measure the extent of one's adherence to traditional morals, customs, and religious beliefs.

These same themes of authority/autonomy and conformity/openness have been found to divide, by education and generation, the advanced industrial societies of Japan, the United States, and Western Europe (Flanagan, 1987; Flanagan and Lee, 1988). Naturally, in these more highly developed nations, the specific content of the items used to tap these common themes reflects higher levels of autonomy and openness—that is, different points of division and debate along these attitude continuums. Also, at least in the cases of the advanced industrial nations, it has been shown that this A-L value cleavage is strongly correlated with key political attitudes and behaviors.

If the A-L value cleavage is of a long historical duration, what makes it politically salient and explosive at one period and latent and largely ignored at another? Clearly there are many factors at work here. Changes in the material/technological conditions of life, which have progressively accompanied the movement from agrarian to ever more highly industrialized and developed societies, occur in an uneven rather than continuous way in terms of both their timing and the groups and strata that they initially affect. As these changes begin to cumulate in significant ways and become diffused throughout society, new kinds of values also begin to emerge and spread. When there is a major change in the conditions of life in a society or a spurt in the rate of change in those conditions, when the old dominant values and views resist change and revision, when those holding new values reach a certain critical size and begin to openly challenge old beliefs and practices, then the A-L value cleavage is likely to be manifested in the emergence of salient political issues.

The literature on the Western advanced industrial democracies has argued that a new value cleavage emerged in these countries during the 1960s. This was associated with higher levels of political cynicism, more direct forms of political participation, and realigning changes in voting behavior (Inglehart, 1977; Barnes and Kaase, 1979; Dalton et al., 1984). If, as I contend, this was not a new value cleavage but rather a new expression of the old authoritarian-libertarian value cleavage, why did it not appear in Western Europe earlier in the postwar era? First, it did not emerge earlier in the nations of Western Europe because politics during the early postwar period in those societies was dominated by class and other economic issues that crowded value issues off the political agenda. Second, the wartime destruction temporarily slowed the pace of change, and it was only with the recovery in the 1950s that the pace of change quickened and once more began to drive the process of value change.

By the 1960s, however, the situation had reversed. First, the growing affluence in Europe and the success of the welfare state weakened class divisions, as rising wages and social guarantees lessened class differences in standards of living. At some point, when it began to be clear that adding still more redistributive measures and government benefits would require taxing wider and wider social strata more and more for the benefit of fewer and fewer, the appeal and salience of class and other related economic issues began to decline (Inglehart, 1987). Second, as the postwar technological explosion began and set off an era of change more rapid than had ever before been experienced in human history, many value-based issues started to accumulate on the political agenda. These issues first emerged as libertarians began pushing for change and registering a number of victories in the 1960s. In the wake of this unprecedented challenge, authoritarians began to dig in and countermobilize to halt or roll back the pace of social change, and value issues further multiplied. In time the political agenda became cluttered with a multitude of value-based issues, many new and seemingly unrelated, from immigration and minority rights, protest, social order, crime and punishment to defense, peace, nationalism, patriotism, and a host of religious and social issues from abortion and women's rights to divorce and family issues, pornography, and homosexuality. With the emergence of these issues we began to hear about a new politics in Western Europe with the rise of a New Left and a New Right.

At first the Japanese case appears to be somewhat of an anomaly or deviant case, because the A-L value cleavage emerged much earlier in Japan around a set of issues that peaked in salience during the 1950s and declined in importance since then. If the European value cleavage were a strictly postindustrial one, then its emergence in Japan as a predictor of the vote in the early postwar years, long before it was identified in Europe and long before Japan could be described as a postindustrial society, would be inexplicable. If we conceptualize the politically relevant dimension of value change in Japan and the West as the A-L value cleavage, however, the difference in timing in its emergence into politics can be readily understood. As we have already noted in reviewing Watanuki's arguments, class was not available during the early postwar years in Japan as a basis for political mobilization. At the same time, the discrediting of Japan's authoritarian past occasioned by the defeat and the radical nature of the Occupation's political and social reforms brought a set of issues to the top of the political agenda that were based on value divisions among the population.

Related Dimensions of Value Change

Before we turn to an analysis of the patterns of value change associated with the two major dimensions of the A-L value cleavage, identified above, mention should be made of several related value dimensions. First, a third and somewhat less central dimension of the A-L cleavage has been identified elsewhere (Flanagan, 1982; Flanagan and Lee, 1988). This dimension taps a shift from a survival to a self-fulfillment orientation. Survival values stress the importance of hard work, diligence, self-discipline, and a frugal, austere life style that is constantly preoccupied with laying up a surplus to provide for a rainy day. In contrast, a self-fulfillment orientation stresses the search for personal happiness and fulfillment through improving one's living environment and general quality of life, through a stronger emphasis on self-understanding, self-improvement, and the expansion of one's knowledge, skills, and capacities, and through a greater willingness to relax austere codes that inhibit the pursuit of personal pleasures and self-indulgences. Because many of the changes along this dimension require high levels of education, affluence, and government and private insurance guarantees against loss, it is to be expected that much of the change on this dimension is associated with the advanced industrial stage of development and hence is of fairly recent origins. Empirically, however, value preferences on this dimension have been found to cluster with the two major dimensions of the A-L cleavage. Therefore, it can be viewed as part of the same overall A-L value change phenomenon that seems to be occurring in all the advanced industrial democracies.

While all three of the A-L value dimensions are believed to be related to voting choices in all the advanced industrial democracies, there are other value dimensions whose political relevance may be of more special importance to the Japanese context. In particular, certain aspects of Japan's traditional culture have been under attack during the postwar period, because they have been viewed in some quarters as inherently "feudal" and undemocratic. One such value dimension is *personalism*.[3] Traditional Japanese culture stressed particularism and social relativism, which when translated into politics encourages an orientation toward one's personal and community ties with a candidate. Personalistic norms stimulate candidate support on the basis of the volume of favors and benefits candidates have brought or are expected to bring to one's family or local area. A second and related dimension is *parochialism*. The parochial orientation describes an attitude that highly values proximate objects that are familiar and close at hand and ignores or distrusts more distant objects. Parochial values also encourage the voter to form loyalties to politicians who are dispensing local benefits rather than to pursue public policies that would benefit a broader spectrum of similarly situated but geographically separated people with whom the voter is not personally acquainted. As a result, personalistic and parochial norms induce an inattention to considerations of party, ideology, or national issues, all of which simply reinforces a traditional authoritarian orientation to politics. Because the ruling conservative party is better situated to utilize these norms in its vote mobilization, personalistic and parochial values should also be related to vote choice.

■ Analyzing the Patterns of Value Change

I have discussed how I think values are changing and why, but is there any actual proof of change along any of the three subdimensions of the authoritarian-libertarian value cleavage or the personalistic or parochial dimensions? Virtually all the available data is cross-sectional or is panel data of too short a duration to test whether change is actually taking place. Instead, I have inferred that change must be occurring based on the sharp educational and age differences that are typically found associated with the attitude distributions along these value dimensions. In the case of education, there is a fairly sound logic to the argument of cross-temporal change in the distribution of mass

3. For a more detailed discussion of the personalism value dimension in Japan, see Richardson and Flanagan, 1984.

attitudes. Since it has repeatedly been shown that more libertarian attitudes are associated with higher levels of education, the fact that there has been a dramatic rise in educational attainment in all the advanced industrial democracies across the post–World War II period argues persuasively that some value change has accompanied this diffusion and rise of secondary and higher education.

How about age? Is age having an effect independent from education? Is there something else going on in the socializing environment other than the spread of education that is instilling more libertarian values in the younger generations compared with their parents? Naturally, I believe that the answer to that question is yes, but is there any proof? Here the evidence is much more difficult to come by because of the universal problem encountered in trying to demonstrate intergenerational attitude change with cross-sectional data. The problem here is that cross-sectional data do not permit us to distinguish between three distinct patterns of change: intergenerational change, life-cycle change, and period effects. In the first pattern, each successive age cohort emerges with somewhat more modern values, which are then maintained over the life cycle, thereby in time moving society in a more modern direction. The second pattern, life-cycle change, may also explain generational differences: age cohorts change over time so that their attitudes, though distinct when they were young, come to increasingly match those of the older generations as they age. Here generational differences may yield no net change over time in the marginal distribution of attitudes for a society as a whole. The third pattern, period effects, is typically reflected in shifts that affect all age cohorts equally, moving them uniformly in one direction or another. If age differences already exist on a particular attitude dimension, a period effect may resemble an intergenerational pattern of change. The problem here, however, is that the effect is not an enduring one, but only a short-term cyclical shift. So again what may appear as an enduring pattern of intergenerational change may be reversed down the road by a cyclical shift in the opposite direction.

Fortunately there exists in Japan an extensive set of time series data in the form of the National Character Studies that have been conducted every five years since 1953. While the data for most of the surveys in this series are not available for secondary analysis, the Institute of Statistical Mathematics (Tokei Suri Kenkyujo), which has conducted these studies, has published an exhaustive series of cross tabulations for each attitude item in their surveys with age, education, and a number of other demographics up through the 1988 survey.

Table 3.1 summarizes the patterns of change that have occurred between 1953 and 1988 for seven items taken from the National Character Surveys that

Table 3.1   Patterns of Change over Thirty-Five Years across Four
Value Dimensions

	Deference	Survival	Conformity			Personalism	
	I-1	I-2	I-3	I-4	I-5	I-6	I-7
Trad-Modern Scores							
1953	−6	−16	−20	—	8	−76	—
1958	12	18	—	—	8	−70	—
1963	24	28	0	−8	12	−72	4
1968	26	34	−8	−8	10	−76	16
1973	38(b-34)	54	8	−10	6	−72	16
1978	28(c)	50	0	−20	−16	−80	2
1983	30(c)	58	−10	−26	−14	−82	−2
1988	34(c)	62	8	−20	−14	−80	−4
Time change							
score	40	78	28	−12	−22	−4	−8
Age difference							
1953	112	66	30	58	56	4	6
1988	86	54	66	44	12	14	12
Educational difference							
1953	82	33	42	76	70	18	30
1988	62	16	74	42	22	14	10
Type of change (1953–83)							
Intergener.	1.59	.97	.73	.60	.70	(.22)	.30
Period eff.	.40	.68	(.28)	−.46	−.51	−.59	−.35
Life cycle	(.10)	(.37)	−.21	−.88	−.23	(.24)	−.06

Notes: *Item content* is as follows: I-1 Leader vs. people; I-2 Enjoy oneself vs. self-denial; I-3 Individual vs. nation; I-4 Social obligation vs. individual freedom; I-5 Personal choice vs. follow custom; I-6 Specific vs. diffuse relations with boss; I-7 Merit vs. connections in hiring. (See below for full content and coding of items.) There is a discontinuity in the time series on Item-1 owing to a shift in item format from a middle category to a forced dichotomy in the 1973 *b* version of the question, which appears to depress the relative proportions of modern responses compared to the traditional format that was also asked in that year. The dichotomized format was continued in the *c* version of the question beginning in 1978, but further word changes make it uncomparable with the *b* version. Thus, the analysis of the I-1 type of change was carried only through 1973. The time change and age and education difference scores reported in this table ignore these changes and use the 1988 rather than the 1973 data in their computations, however.

Traditional-modern scores were computed at each point by subtracting the percentages of responses classified as traditional from the percentages of those classified as modern, so that positive scores indicate predominantly modern responses.

(*continued*)

Table 3.1 *(Continued)*

Time change scores are the 1988 traditional-modern scores minus the 1953 (or first available) scores.

Age difference scores are the traditional-modern scores of the 20–24-year-olds minus those of respondents 70 years of age and older for the indicated years (where again 1963 is the first available time point for items 4 and 7).

Education difference scores are the traditional-modern scores of the college-educated minus those of respondents receiving only compulsory education or less for the indicated years.

Type of change: Our estimates of the relative magnitude of three different patterns of change—intergenerational, period effects, and life cycle change—are the means of the range of parameter variation statistic across each traditional and modern category and sex category for each item. These statistics are derived from a Bayesian logit cohort analysis conducted by the TSK-KCI covering the years 1953–83. The means of this statistic, reported in parentheses, indicate that the pattern of change was nonlinear, invalidating this measure as an estimate of the relative degree of change over time attributable to that type of change.

Item Content and Coding

The item response categories are designated with a *T* if they were classified as traditional responses, *M* if they were considered modern responses, and *U* for unclassifiable if they could not be classified as traditional or modern.

Item-1. Some people say that if we get good political leaders, the best way to improve the country is for the people to leave everything to them, rather than for the people to discuss things among themselves. Do you agree with this?

T — Agree
M = Disagree
U — Depends; other

Item-2. There are all sorts of attitudes toward life. Of those listed here, which one would you say comes closest to your feeling?

T — Study earnestly and make a name for yourself.
T — Resist all evils in the world and live a pure and just life.
T — Never think of yourself; give everything in service of society.
M — Don't think about money or fame; just live a life that suits your own tastes.
M — Live each day as it comes, cheerfully and without worrying.
U — Work hard and get rich.

Item-3. Which one of the following opinions do you agree with?

T — If Japan as a whole improves, then and only then can individuals be made happy.
M — If individuals are made happy, then and only then will Japan as a whole improve.
U — Improving Japan and making individuals happy are the same thing.

Item-4. If you were asked to choose two out of this list that are important, which two would you pick?

T — Being dutiful to one's parents
T — Repaying social obligations
M — Respecting individual rights
M — Respecting freedom

Item-5. If you think a thing is right, do you think you should go ahead and do it even if it is contrary to custom, or do you think you are less apt to make a mistake if you follow custom?

(continued)

Table 3.1 *(Continued)*

T — Follow custom
M — Go ahead
U — Depends

Item-6. Suppose you are working in a firm. There are two types of department chiefs. Which of these two would you prefer to work under?

T — A man who sometimes demands extra work in spite of rules against it but looks after you personally in matters not connected with the work.
M — A man who always sticks to the work rules and never demands any unreasonable work but never does anything for you personally in matters not connected with the work.

Item-7. Suppose you were the president of a company. The company decides to employ one person and then carries out an employment examination. The supervisor in charge reports to you, saying, "Mr. X (the son of parents who had been our benefactor) got the second highest grade. But I believe that either he or the candidate who got the highest grade would be satisfactory. What shall we do?"

T — Hire the son of your benefactor.
M — Hire the one with the highest grade.

fall into four conceptual categories. In order to condense the information from a multitude of tables, traditional-modern scores were computed at each time point by subtracting the percentage of responses classified as traditional from the percentage of those classified as modern. To avoid distortions resulting from changes in the proportions of missing data or the presence or absence of "middle" or other categories that could not be classified as either traditional or modern, the traditional and modern responses were in each case standardized so that they would total 100 prior to performing the subtraction to compute the traditional-modern scores. A score of −100, then, would mean that at any one time point all the classifiable responses were traditional and none was modern, while a +100 score would mean that all responses were modern. Of course, these extremes are never found, but by computing the score for each time point, we can track the degree and direction of change that is taking place.

The table also reports a time change score, which is simply the 1988 traditional-modern score minus the 1953 (or first available) score. Positive scores indicate a shift over time in a modern direction, and negative scores a shift in a traditional direction. The table also reports the age and educational difference scores, which represent the extent to which attitudes on a given item were polarized by age and education in 1953 (or the first available time point) as compared with 1988. In the case of age, the difference scores were computed by subtracting the traditional-modern score for those 70 and older from that of those 20–24. For education, the difference scores were derived by subtracting the traditional-modern score for those receiving only a compulsory level of education from that of those receiving higher education.

Finally, table 3.1 also indicates the pattern of change for each item by presenting the *means* of the *range of parameter variation* statistic across each traditional and modern category for each item. This statistic was derived by applying a sophisticated Bayesian Logit cohort model to each item. The analysis was conducted by the National Character Survey group at the Institute of Statistical Mathematics; these researchers were able to statistically measure and visually present the relative contribution of intergenerational, life-cycle, and period effects in explaining the pattern of change found on each item using seven data points up through the 1983 survey, covering a thirty-year period (TSK-KCI, 1985). As is typical for the Hayashi Quantification Scaling methods, preferred by most Japanese social scientists, the statistical treatments are performed for each category of a variable and permit cross-item regression and factor and dimensional analysis for nominal data. These procedures have certain advantages over the preferred Western techniques when variables have more than two categories that do not fit neatly into an ordinal scale.[4]

The reader is cautioned to understand that the numbers presented under "type of change" in table 3.1 are only estimates of the relative extent to which the change that is occurring conforms to an intergenerational, life-cycle, or period effect pattern. While these numbers are sensitive to the magnitude of each type of change taking place, they should not be viewed as absolute measures along a single standard interval scale. Moreover, since it is the means of this range of variation statistics across several distinct analyses that I am presenting here (one for each traditional and modern response category of an item), I clearly cannot assign any absolute, readily interpretable meaning to any particular number or range. Nevertheless, they provide us with a convenient though rough estimate of the relative impact of the three different patterns of change for each of our items. The reader should also bear in mind that our discussion of the patterns of change associated with each item represents a distillation of extensive graphic and statistical findings reported elsewhere (TSK-KCI, 1985), which enables us to determine the timing of the beginning of a pattern of change associated with a particular item that is attributable to, for example, a period effect and whether that change is linear or nonlinear over time. Our statistic, the range of parameter variation, is simply a range and therefore can only be employed as an estimate of the relative magnitude of change over time when the pattern of change is linear, monotonically increasing or decreasing. When the means of the range of parameter variation statistic are

4. For more on the Hayashi statistical treatments, see the more detailed discussion and appendix in chapter 6.

reported in parentheses, it indicates that the dominant pattern of variation associated with a given type of change was not linear but rather curvilinear, s-shaped, or nearly random. These nonlinear patterns render the statistic invalid as a indicator of the relative degree of change over time, and therefore in those cases the numbers should be ignored.

At first glance, two patterns stand out in table 3.1. First, there is clearly a period effect in the 1970s that slows, arrests, or, in a number of cases, reverses the direction of change taking place. Typically the pattern of change is in a modern direction up through 1968, but then it begins to halt or reverse in the 1970s. Several factors can explain this phenomenon. The 1973 Arab oil boycott sent shock waves through the Japanese economy; the oil crisis diverted attention from the environmental, quality-of-life, and participation issues that had come to the forefront in the 1960s and refocused national attention on economic issues, leading to a resurgence in conservatism. This period also coincided with a renewed interest in Nihonjinron (essays on what it means to be Japanese) as the Japanese began to reassess the enduring aspects of their culture in light of the previous three decades of massive importation of goods, ideas, and practices from the West. Toward the end of the 1970s this renewed interest in the enduring traditions of Japanese culture was reinforced by a growing nationalism and cultural self-satisfaction with Japan's new international standing and dramatic economic successes.

A second pattern apparent in the table is that across all seven items, the age and education difference scores demonstrate that the younger and more educated Japanese consistently hold more modern attitudes than those of their older and less educated counterparts. At the same time, however, we also see in most cases some narrowing in these differences across time. This suggests that after the dramatic pace of socioeconomic change in the first postwar decade, the rate of value change that these environmental changes precipitated slowed over the 1970s and 1980s.

Change along the A-L Dimensions

Having noted these two general patterns, however, we find that a closer inspection reveals substantial differences and complexities in the patterns of change across the different dimensions. The first three conceptual dimensions presented in the table were selected because they represent the three subdimensions of the authoritarian-libertarian scale identified above. The five items reported here under these three categories comprise essentially all the available items repeated across all or most of the surveys that could be considered conceptually related to each of these dimensions. There are, however, similar kinds of items that have appeared more recently and for shorter time periods, which can be found on this and other surveys and which appear to reflect the same patterns of change. Some of these other findings will also be mentioned.

The items representing the first two conceptual dimensions in table 3.1 reveal unambiguous patterns of intergenerational change. The representative item for the first dimension, authority/autonomy, asked if the country could best be improved by leaving everything to good political leaders rather than by discussing issues among the people themselves. Deference and unquestioning loyalty seem to be giving way to a demystification of authority and greater demands for responsiveness. Other surveys have found that younger age cohorts are much less likely to espouse strong loyalty for the company they work for or to believe that children need more discipline or should respect their parents more (Passin, 1975; Flanagan, 1979). Within the younger generation, then, and among those with higher education, we see a decline in the magnitude of authority that can legitimately be exercised over others within the family, the work place, and in politics.

The second dimension, survival/self-fulfillment, is here represented by an item that taps an austere, self-disciplined versus self-indulgent orientation. Here we find that the young and highly educated prefer to "live a life that suits your own tastes" or "live each day as it comes, cheerfully and without worrying" as opposed to "study earnestly and make a name for yourself," "resist all evils in the world and live a pure and just life," or "give everything in service to society." Other surveys have also found that the younger cohorts respond less to the traditional virtues of austerity and self-sacrifice but rather seek more personally fulfilling lives. Associated with this change in values among the younger generation has been found a decline in devotion to work, an increased concern for finding employment that allows the individual to develop his or her abilities to the full and to pursue leisure activities outside work, and a generally expanded desire for self-expression and personal freedom (Kojima and Akiyama, 1973; NHK-HYC, 1975; Flanagan, 1979).

On both of the first two dimensions intergenerational change has been the predominant pattern, although there have also been some significant period effects (moving strongly in a modern direction in the 1950s and 1960s and then reversing slightly in the 1970s). In each case, while the rate of change on these dimensions was substantially slowed in the 1970s, it appears to be continuing. This is more difficult to detect in the case of the authority question owing to the change in question format from a middle category to a forced dichotomy in the 1973b version of the question, which appears to depress the proportions of modern responses. That dichotomized format was continued in the c version of the question beginning in 1978, but further wording changes make it impossible to assess the trend between 1973 and 1978. Also, while both the age and educational differences have been narrowing across the time series, the age differences on these dimensions continue to be relatively somewhat greater than the educational differences.

On the third dimension, conformity/openness, we find a more complex pattern of change. This dimension contrasts collective, group-centered norms with independent, individualistic values. Individualism has a great appeal for Japanese youth, and we do note some real intergenerational change on all three of the conformity items presented in the table. In relative terms this pattern of intergenerational versus other kinds of change is most pronounced on the first of these conformity items (I-3), which juxtaposes individual rights with more abstract notions of public interest.

We also find significant life-cycle effects on all three conformity items, but especially on Item 4, which gauges the relative priority placed on filial piety and repaying obligations versus respecting freedom and individual rights. Interestingly, the life-cycle effect was much more pronounced on the repaying obligations than on the filial piety option. Thus it would appear that when individual interests are posed against those of the immediate, face-to-face group, the idealism of youth gradually gives way to the realities of Japanese society. This pattern of life-cycle change is quite understandable, as it is the young in Japanese society that feel most fettered by human relations with teachers, superiors, and senior colleagues and thus exhibit greater desire to be freed from the bonds of social relationships. As one ages, one's role in influencing the group and shaping the consensus-building process enlarges, and thus the norm of conformity becomes less burdensome and more personally beneficial. Certainly the growing social responsibilities and social obligations that come with maturity also play a role, but regardless of the motivating factors that induce attitude change on this dimension, it would appear that the collective, holistic norms of adult Japanese society are still sufficiently strong to ensure an increasing emphasis as one grows older on conformity, social obligations, and sacrificing individual desires for the sake of group harmony.

Finally, we also find a substantial period effect on all three conformity items. In the case of Item 3, the pattern of change is curvilinear, moving the population in a modern direction through 1963, then waffling and turning decidedly back in a traditional direction from 1978 through 1983. In the case of Items 4 and 5, however, there is no initial movement in a modern direction, and movement in a traditional direction sets in during the 1960s and proceeds in a continuous and decided fashion. On these items, then, the traditionalistic period effect is sufficient to obscure completely the intergenerational change that is actually moving successive cohorts in a more modern direction. Indeed, the time change scores for both of these items reveal a net change in the gross marginals over time in a traditional direction.

There is, then, some real intergenerational change taking place on this conformity versus individualism dimension, especially in terms of the individual versus the large group (nation or public interest). Moreover, on Item 3 we find that the age and education differences have actually increased substantially over time. We should also note that in nearly all cases the educational differences associated with these three items appear to be somewhat greater than the age differences. At the same time, when individual rights are posed against the interest of the small group, we see an important life-cycle effect that enhances the emphasis placed on group norms with age. This emphasis on conformity has been further reinforced by a period effect that is revitalizing certain kinds of traditional Japanese virtues, at least temporarily.

While this analysis suggests that the pattern of intergenerational change is weaker on the conformity/openness dimension than on the other two dimensions of the A-L cleavage, we should bear in mind that the National Character Studies items have not by any means enabled us to tap the full range of attitudes associated with this dimension. For example, there is nothing here on tolerance of out-groups, openness to new ideas, or permissiveness toward new life styles. At least in the case of the last of these, there is evidence from other studies that there has been a substantial generational shift in the adherence to the moral strictures of Confucian asceticism and a relaxation in attention to the moral standards of good conduct. This change is particularly noticeable in regard to social norms and individual values regarding sex. For example, dramatic generational differences have been demonstrated in the acceptability of women engaging in sexual relations before marriage (NHK-HYC, 1979, 1985).

We can conclude from this analysis of the patterns of change associated with the A-L value dimensions that although the pace of change may be slowing on some of its dimensions, Japan's postwar value cleavage is not disappearing. In part we have seen that a period effect reinforcing traditional values that set in during the 1970s has temporarily obscured a continuing pattern of intergenerational value change. In addition, other values that are not explicitly tapped by the National Character Study items may be experiencing an accelerating pattern of change. After all, the NCS questions were designed in the early 1950s to tap the social manifestations of value change that were perceived at that time. An effective indicator of a shift toward more open and autonomous values in one period may no longer serve as a useful indicator in a later period, as what once was viewed as an inappropriate, disrespectful, or even shocking practice becomes commonplace.

While the process of value change is more continuous, however, public awareness of important value cleavages tends to ebb and flow. From time to time, certain social problems and political issues bring the A-L value cleavage more sharply into focus in the public mind. In the 1950s it was the cultural politics issues and in the late 1960s it was the student campus closures, citizen's movements, and quality-of-life issues that focused attention on value differences and brought them into the political debate. In the last decade we have heard a great deal about the *shinjinrui,* the "new breed" of humankind that is emerging among Japanese youth. Public awareness of this generational cleavage has focused more on the survival/self-fulfillment dimension of the A-L value change—the declining devotion to work and growing pursuit of personal pleasures and self-indulgences—but the value change also includes a weakening commitment to traditional morals and customs (the conformity dimension) and a declining respect of and deference to one's elders (the authority dimension). To date, the issues surrounding the shinjinrui phenomenon have not been politicized, but this new values debate may ultimately bring new political issues to the fore. The fears that the shinjinrui are undermining the very values that have made Japan strong coupled with the fear of losing a distinct Japanese identity may fuel the rise of a new nationalism; such a movement would not sweep Japanese society but rather polarize it.

Value Change and Voting Trends

Even before we turn to testing for the relationship between the A-L value cleavage and political attitudes, a review of some additional items drawn from the NHK Values Studies, which have been conducted every five years from 1973 to 1983, suggests why change along this overall value dimension is so politically important in Japan. To the extent that deferential, conformist values, with their emphasis on respecting authority and avoiding conflict, remain primary norms of Japanese society, they encourage passivity and disassociativeness. Japanese respondents on the whole still exhibit a strong distaste for protest activity of any kind and a reluctance to become involved in movements or voluntary associations that engage in divisive or partisan activities.

To take one example, the 1973 NHK survey found that when respondents were asked, "What is the most desirable form of political behavior for the general public?" a full 63 percent chose, "We should select an excellent politician by election and entrust political affairs to him." By 1983 this percentage had fallen only slightly to 60, percent. Over the same period there is a gradual rise from 12 to 15 percent in those responding, "When a problem occurs we should see that the politician we support reflects our opinions," and an even smaller increase (from 17 to 18 percent) in those saying, "We should help the growth of the political party or body we usually support so that we can realize our views." Similarly, on questions related to working conditions and residential pollution problems, the survey found that respondents were much more likely to adopt a "wait and see" attitude or to ask a superior or local influential to handle the matter instead of seeking a solution through personal involvement in a labor union or citizens' movement. The prevalence of these passive, nonparticipatory attitudes may help to explain how a paternalistic, dominant party catering to local interests has been able to maintain a lock on political power for the past forty-five years without interruption. These attitudes also suggest how important the A-L value change is for Japan, if a fully competitive and accountable democracy is to be realized in that nation.

Looking ahead to the findings reported below of a substantial relationship between libertarian values and leftist voting, the patterns of change presented above can provide important clues for explaining postwar electoral trends. First, table 3.1 has demonstrated that all three of the A-L subdimensions have experienced significant intergenerational change across the postwar period. This intergenerational pattern of change helps to explain why, for much of the postwar period, younger age cohorts have been more likely to vote left than older cohorts. An intergenerational pattern of value change would also help to explain the gradual long-term rise in the support for the opposition parties in Japan. In each successive HR election after 1952, the conservative vote declined up through the 1976 election.

The patterns displayed in table 3.1 may also help to account for another aspect of Japanese voting trends. Beginning in 1979 the conservative decline was arrested, and LDP support levels entered a period of fluctuation within a narrow range of 45 to 49 percent of the vote in HR elections. The drop in the age differences over time reported in the table suggest that the rate of intergenerational value change in recent years has been slowing down. This phenomenon might in part explain the bottoming out of the LDP decline.

What may be a far more important contribution to the LDP recovery at the polls after 1976, however, is found in the period effects that have been shifting the entire population, at least temporarily, in a more traditional direction. As noted, significant period effects can be seen setting in during the 1970s and moving the marginal distributions back in a traditional direction, at about the time when the decline in the conservative vote began to level off. It should be kept in mind that period effects tend to exhibit stronger and more immediate influences than intergenerational patterns of change, because they effect the entire population and not just the newest cohort of voters. This stronger effect of short-term period influences on the distribution of the gross marginals is clear from table 3.1. In the case of Items 1 and 2, where the intergenerational and period effects are both working together in moving the population in a modern direction, the traditional-modern time change scores are in a strongly modern direction. In the case of Items 4 and 5, however, where the two are working against each other, the weaker range of variation in the period effects totally overwhelms the stronger range of variation in the intergenerational effects in determining the sign and direction of change in the marginal distributions across time. Thus the period effect that is observed in table 3.1 shifting values back somewhat in a conservative direction in the 1970s may be one contributory factor in the LDP resurgence at the polls.

Finally, the finding that some aspects of the A-L value cleavage are exhibiting a certain amount of life-cycle change should not be ignored. To the extent that the values one holds at any one time may influence his or her voting behavior, a life-cycle pattern of value change could also be related to voting trends. Here the predicted voting trend would be in the conservative direction, as voters become more conservative with age and as the proportions of older voters rise within Japan's aging society.

Change along the Personalism Dimension

Before leaving the National Character Studies' data, we may recall that value dimensions other than the A-L cleavage, such as personalism and parochialism, were also identified above as being potentially relevant to political attitudes and behavior. Table 3.1 reports the patterns for two items representative of what Chikio Hayashi and his associates refer to as the *giri-ninjo* items. Labeled *personalism* here, these items contrast the more diffuse, particularistic relationships found in Japan with the more specific, universalistic norms generally associated with socioeconomic relations in the West. These items appear to behave quite differently from the A-L items associated with the previous three dimensions. For example, these items exhibit very weak associations with age.

The first of these, Item 6, is related to Talcott Parson's diffuseness-specificity pattern variable, and yet we find highly traditionalistic response patterns in Japan that reflect no inclination toward movement in a "modern" direction over time. In 1988, 87 percent of the full sample would still prefer to work for a department chief who sometimes demands extra work in violation of the rules but looks after one personally in matters not connected with the job, compared to only 10 percent who would choose the boss who never demands any unreasonable work but never does anything for one personally outside the job. This strong cultural preference holds true for all age and educational levels, and the only interpretable, nonrandom pattern of change associated with this item is a slight period effect that has been moving the population in an even more conservative direction since the early 1960s. Other items show that Japanese highly prize social contacts with superiors outside the workplace and the kind of diffuse, hierarchic relationships that exchange loyalty and service for care and nurturing. Japanese respondents are also found to prefer overwhelmingly a firm with a family-like atmosphere to one with higher wages (TSK-KCI, 1982).

These findings suggest that items related to the diffuseness-specificity pattern variable are not appropriate for inclusion in an overall traditional-modern value change scale. Neither youth nor higher levels of education are substantially associated with the Western preference for more specific relationships with employers, work associates, and other friends and acquaintances outside the family. Still, before declaring this aspect of Japanese culture as unqualifiedly unique, we should consider the findings of the 1973–83 NHK Value Studies (NHK-HYC, 1985). These findings suggest that when a broader range of alternatives is presented a somewhat different pattern emerges. For example, in 1983 among those 70 years of age and older, 68 percent reported preferring unlimited relationships with work colleagues compared to only 35 percent of those 20–25. Moreover, judging from the proportions preferring this option by age cohort across the three data points and ten years for which these data are available, the pattern of change on this item appears to conform to an intergenerational one. The shift in the preferences of the younger generations, however, is not toward the Western type of limited relationship but toward a more intermediate level of interaction. Thus, while Japanese still overwhelmingly prefer social contacts with work colleagues after hours, among the young there seems to be some attenuation of the involvement and obligation of these relationships.

A second aspect of the personalism dimension is the strong emphasis on the affective side of human relations still found in Japan today. The representative National Character Studies' items here, for which thirty-five years of data are available, asked whether if cross-pressured it would be better to rush home to the bedside of a seriously ill childhood benefactor or attend a meeting that will decide whether the firm one is president of will survive or go bankrupt. While this item is not reported in the table, its analysis shows that a bare majority would rush home to the benefactor. More important for our purposes, there is no significant shift in the marginal distributions over time, and the only pattern of change observable is a moderate life-cycle shift toward the personalistic response. A similar, more recent NCS item reveals that most Japanese respondents feel that one should, as an airline company president, visit all the homes of crash victims to apologize rather than devote one's efforts to investigating the causes of the crash. Here the response distributions are completely unrelated to age and education and exhibit no signs of change over time.

These items reflect a strong cultural preference for a personalistic, affective orientation to interpersonal relationships rather than a more rationalistic, goal-oriented one. It may be that with several aspects of personalism, it is more appropriate to speak of Japanese versus Western rather than traditional versus modern differences. In other words, on some value dimensions Japan may not be moving in the Western direction, and in such cases we would have to conclude that modernization does not lead inevitably to Westernization. It is interesting to note that most Japanese who travel abroad view social relations in the West as excessively harsh, cold, and unfeeling.

There is still a third aspect of personalism, the particularism-universalism distinction that is represented by Item 7 in table 3.1. In spite of the coexistence of strong meritocratic norms in Japanese society, about two-fifths of the respondents continue to say that they would hire the son of a benefactor rather than the individual that scored highest on their company's entrance examination. While the rate of change here appears somewhat weaker than in the case of the A-L items, we find the same pattern as was associated with the conformity dimension. Thus Item 7 reveals evidence of an intergenerational change toward more universalistic preferences, a change which becomes obscured by a period effect that sets in during the 1970s and moves the gross marginals back in a more traditional direction.

It is this particularistic aspect of personalism that is likely to be most relevant to politics. The cultural emphasis in Japanese society on relying on personal connections and the exchange of special favors and gifts in the conduct of one's affairs has a tendency to spill over from the private to public spheres in economic and political dealings. In the political arena these cultural exchange practices become bribery and influence peddling, which traditionalists are more likely to excuse as inevitable while moderns are more likely to condemn. The conservative Liberal Democratic Party is more closely identified with this old style of politics, which stresses personalistic ties and the dispensing of favors and public works projects to individual constituents and local communities while the progressive parties place greater emphasis on mass organizations and movements and national issues. This conflict between a more traditional patron-client or pork-barrel mode of politics and a more modern, issue politics is rooted in conflicting cultural value orientations. In its more narrowly defined form, therefore, a personalism-universalism value dimension may also prove to be an important part of the value cleavage that divides Japanese society.

■ Value Preferences and Voting Behavior

Having now identified what kinds of politically relevant values are changing, why they are changing, and how they are changing, we will examine the relationship between these value cleavages and voting choices. The item content of our 1976 JABISS study permits the measurement of three separate value scales. The first of these is an *authoritarian-libertarian* scale, which is constructed from six items. Four of these are directly related to the authority/autonomy subdimension of the A-L construct—with authoritarians agreeing that leaders' opinions should be respected, politics should be entrusted to outstanding leaders, Dietmen and governors should command respect, and the traditional virtues of respecting parents and seniors should be honored—and two items tap the conformity/openness subdimension—with authoritarians preferring to donate without complaint to a community collection even if they did not agree with the purpose in order to preserve neighborhood harmony and, to avoid bad feelings, to cut short a group discussion if opinions are sharply divided.

A second scale tapping a *personalism-universalism* value dimension is composed of five items, with those at the personalistic end of the scale agreeing that it is important to save face, that one must take great care of personal relationships both in one's local community and place of work, that personal connections are very important in finding a job or doing business, that intermediaries are important if one is to be successfully received when making requests of local or national government officials, and that it is appropriate to give year-end gifts to officials that have taken care of you in the past. As the item content suggests, this scale taps not so much the diffuseness or affectivity aspects of personalism but rather the particularistic aspects of the concept, namely, the cultivation of personal relations for special advantage. This side of personalism conflicts with the more modern preference for being evaluated on the basis of merit and treated according to universalistic criteria rather than on the basis of personal connections and personal favoritism.

The third scale measures a *parochial-cosmopolitan* value orientation. Four items comprise this scale with parochials ranking local politics ahead of international, national, and prefectural politics as their focus of interest and believing that local events are more important than national incidents, that important community posts should be given to long-time residents rather than newcomers, and that voting choices should be based more on the candidates' positions on local rather than national issues. As discussed earlier, parochial orientations are believed to be related to other traditional values because they insulate the holders of these values from exposure to modern values. More important for our purposes, parochial values should be related to voting choices in much the same way that personalistic values are. Parochial orientations focus voters' interests on local personal and community issues, and this is an arena in which the LDP's candidate-centered, patron-client, pork-barrel style of politics holds the advantage.

Since all three of these value scales were found to be highly intercorrelated, a fourth overall *traditional-modern* scale was constructed by equally weighting and combining these three value scales.[5] Libertarian, universalistic, and cosmopolitan values can all be considered "modern" if by modern we mean those values associated with advanced industrial societies and recognize that neither the rates of change nor periods of greatest change associated with each of these dimensions over the last fifty to one hundred years have necessarily been uniform. Despite these presumed differences, we still find sharp value cleavages along each of these dimensions in contemporary Japanese society, and those that are found to be at the traditional end of one dimension are likely to also be found at the traditional end of the others.

Moreover, as shown in table 3.2, the age and education cleavages associated with change along these value dimensions appear to be holding up fairly well, at least in the case of the A-L dimension. The table first reports the correlations between four demographic variables and three authoritarian-libertarian scales drawn from surveys conducted across three decades. While these findings would suggest that the intensity of the value cleavage and pace of value change along the A-L dimension are still strong, some caution must be exercised in interpreting these findings. Each of the three A-L scales was measured by a different set of items, and an argument could be made that the three scales represent successive improvements in the richness and clarity with which the A-L subdimension is being operationalized.[6] Thus, a reduction in measurement error may be disguising some real reduction in the age and education differences along these dimensions. Also, while all three surveys were national ones, the 1984 Japan Successor Generation study was limited to the college-educated, thereby preventing any test of the impact of educational level on values for that data point. Regardless of these caveats, it is valid to conclude that the A-L value cleavage appears to be an enduring one in Japan and hence potentially still relevant to voting behavior.

The personalism and parochialism scales were only available for the 1976 JABISS study. In viewing this second part of the table, two points stand out. First, we note strong correlations between cosmopolitan values and education, suggesting that education plays a particularly central role in extinguishing paro-

5. The correlations between the A-L scale and the personalism and parochialism scales are .40 and .34, respectively, and .30 between the personalism and parochialism scales. For survey research, these correlations are quite high; thus, while these three value dimensions are not identical, they are strongly interrelated.

6. This point is particularly true when we contrast the 1984 scale with the two previous ones. The 1967 scale was composed of six items, with three items tapping the authority, two the conformity, and one the survival dimensions (for the full text of the items see Flanagan, 1982). The main differences between the 1967 and 1976 scales is that the latter scale omitted the survival/self-betterment dimension and the content of its items was more political. The 1984 scale, however, is much richer, being composed of seventeen items, with eight tapping the authority, six the conformity, and three the survival dimensions (see Flanagan, 1987).

Table 3.2 Association between Values and Demographic Attributes (Pearson's r)

Demographic Attributes	Authoritarian($-$)/Libertarian($+$) Values		
	1967	1976	1984
Age	$-.41$	$-.37$	$-.36$
Education	.25	.27	—
Income	$-.06$	.09	$-.17$
Sex (Male)	.10	.09	.10
	1976 JABISS Data		
	Personalism($-$)/ Universalism($+$)	Parochial($-$)/ Cosmopolitan($+$)	Traditional($-$)/ Modern($+$)
Age	$-.10$	$-.14$	$-.27$
Education	.16	.32	.33
Income	(.04)	.17	.14
Sex (Male)	(.03)	.16	.17

Note: All correlations are significant at the .01 level except those in parentheses, which are not significant even at the .05 level.

chial orientations. Second, we note that all the demographic correlations are substantially lower with personalism, particularly in the case of age. This pattern reflects our earlier finding of more modest rates of change along the personalism dimension. This could be either because the change induced along this dimension by the processes of industrialization, education, and other associated changes is nearly complete in Japan or because other cultural factors are delaying or slowing the pace of change. We are not in a position to decide among these alternative explanations with the available data, but it is interesting to note, at least in the case of this personalism scale, that the distributions are substantially skewed in a traditional direction.[7]

The other demographic relationships with all the value scales are on the whole much weaker than those with age and education. Women, as we might expect, are somewhat more likely to hold traditional deferential, conformist, and parochial orientations than men.[8] The relationships are rather weak, how-

7. For four of the five items in the personalism scale an average of 60 percent of the respondents picked the traditional responses (agree or agree somewhat) compared to only a mean of 13 percent who selected the "modern" responses (disagree or disagree somewhat). Only in the case of the item on giving gifts to public officials who have helped one do we find only 28 percent selecting the traditional and 43 percent the modern responses.

8. See Pharr, 1981.

ever, and there is no significant relationship between sex and personalism. The table also demonstrates that there are no strong positive relationships between income and modern values. Indeed, when these relationships are controlled by education, no significant positive relationships between family income and modern values are found, with the single exception of the parochialism scale.[9]

Our central question here, however, concerns the relationship between our three values scales and party preference. Table 3.3 demonstrates that regardless of whether party preference is defined as a conservative/progressive ideological preference, a party identification, or a party vote choice in the 1976 election, that partisanship clearly exhibits substantial correlations with all three of the value scales. Among the three, the highest associations are found with the A-L scale, but these relationships are further enhanced when all three are combined in an overall traditional-modern scale. This suggests that these values work together in shaping partisan preferences.

Table 3.4 provides a more concrete representation of what these levels of association mean. The combined traditional-modern (T-M) scale was first trichotomized so that one-third of the respondents were classified as traditional, one-third mixed, and one-third modern. For this trichotomized scale it was found that less than one-third of the moderns voted for the ruling LDP while over two-thirds of the traditionals did. To demonstrate how strongly values affect voting for those with more consistently traditional or modern values, these two categories were further divided in half between strong and "semi-" categories. As shown in the table, among that roughly 16 percent of the sample at the traditional end of the scale, a full 71 percent voted LDP, while for the same proportion at the modern end of the scale only 22 percent voted LDP. Value preferences, then, are very closely related to voting in Japan.

Table 3.5 strongly suggests that the relationship between values and partisan preferences has not declined in Japan over the last three decades, at least in the case of the A-L scale. Here we have pulled out the college-educated only from the 1967 and 1976 surveys to make the comparisons with the 1984 college-educated only survey more appropriate. If anything, these findings

9. Interestingly enough, a comparison of the 1967 and 1976 A-L scale relationships with both occupational status (not shown) and household income suggests that over the decade these associations shifted from weak negative to weak positive ones as the younger, better educated postwar generations, holding more libertarian values, began to move into positions of some importance. Indeed, when those 1976 relationships are controlled by education, both become insignificant. The finding of stronger negative relationships in the 1984 study between libertarian values and both occupation status (not shown) and income is due in part to the fact that this college-only sample already controls for education. In addition, those with high education but low income and status may tend to be drawn even more strongly toward antiestablishment and antiauthoritarian values than their more successful counterparts.

Table 3.3 Association between Values and Partisanship
(Pearson's r)

	Authoritarian(−)/ Libertarian(+)	Personalism(−)/ Universalism(+)	Parochial(−)/ Cosmopolitan(+)	Traditional(−)/ Modern(+)
Ideological camp	.26	.25	.22	.32
Party identification	.29	.23	.19	.31
Party vote	.28	.23	.22	.32

Note: All reported correlations are significant at the .01 level.

would suggest a strengthening of the values/partisanship association from the 1960s through the 1980s. We must be careful in forming this conclusion, however, because of the ambiguities introduced as a result of the differences between the three A-L scales in exact item content, as was noted in the discussion of table 3.2. In particular, the completely apolitical content of the 1967 scale contrasts with the other two scales, which mix purely private domain concerns with public domain issues. On the other hand, tests conducted elsewhere found only small differences in the ability to predict partisan preferences when comparing the performance of A-L scales based only on private domain items with those based on mixed public and private domain items (Flanagan and Lee, 1988). At the least, then, it would appear that the power of the A-L cleavage to predict voter preferences in Japan has not declined over the postwar period.

Table 3.4 Relationship between Traditional-Modern Values and the Vote, 1976

	Values				
	Modern	Semi-Modern	Mixed	Semi-Traditional	Traditional
Right	22	35	50	63	71
Center	15	20	19	11	13
Left	63	45	32	26	16
Total	100%	100%	101%	100%	100%
N of Cases	(184)	(184)	(486)	(202)	(204)

Table 3.5 Association between Values and the Vote, Party Identification, and Left-Right Ideology across Three Decades (Pearson's *r*)

| | Authoritarian(−) Libertarian(+) Values | | | | | |
| | Full Samples | | | College-educated Only | | |
	Vote	Party ID	Ideology	Vote	Party ID	Ideology
1967	.20	.18	—	.22	.14	—
1976	.28	.29	.26	.29	.35	.27
1984	—	—	—	—	.41	.42

Note: The data are derived from analyses of the 1967 Ward and Kubota Japanese Election Study, the 1976 JABISS Election Study, and the 1984 USIA Successor Generation Study. All reported correlations are significant at the .01 level.

Explaining the Values-Vote Linkage

Having demonstrated that a substantial relationship exists between traditional-modern value preferences and voting choices, we must ask, why do these associations exist? The most immediate answer to this question is that values are associated with partisan preferences because values have direct and obvious relationships to voter positioning on key issues. As shown in table 3.6, those with traditional values tend to report that the LDP is closer to their position across 12 issues, while those with modern values tend to name opposition parties as closer to their position across these same 12 issues. By far the highest correlations, however, are found between the value scales and the cultural

Table 3.6 Association between Values and Issues (Pearson's *r*)

	Authoritarian(−)/ Libertarian(+)	Personalism(−)/ Universalism(+)	Parochial(−)/ Cosmopolitan(+)	Traditional(−)/ Modern(+)
Issue closeness to LDP	−.19	−.15	−.07	−.19
Issue closeness to opposition	.20	.19	.24	.27
Cultural politics issues	.37	.27	.33	.43

Note: All reported correlations are significant at the .01 level.

politics issues. The cultural politics issues are those issues that emerged during the Occupation, polarized the electorate and political parties, and defined the emerging postwar party system in the 1950s (see chapter 7).

Again, among the three value scales, the highest correlation is found between the A-L scale and these cultural politics issues ($r = .37$). Table 3.7 demonstrates that there is almost a dimensional attitudinal identity between the A-L items and the four representatives of the cultural politics issues that were included in the JABISS study. We find that when both sets of items are combined in a single factor analysis, all the value and issues items load heavily on the first unrotated factor.

The first two cultural politics issues in the table, on strengthening the Japan–United States security system and strengthening defense forces, are strongly intertwined with authoritarian value preferences because authoritarians have a heightened anxiety about their own weaknesses and a strong sense of dependency, and thus they tend to seek security through power and identification with the symbols of authority. In contrast, libertarians are more suspicious of authority and concentrations of power, more likely to reject force as the preferred means of settling disputes and rather seek security through mutual self-determination and equality. The other two cultural politics issues tap the respondent's preference for strengthening the political role of the emperor, the source of all power in the prewar authoritarian system, and one's attitude toward the legitimacy of protest behavior, here represented by the right of public employees to strike. Again, the linkages are obvious. Authoritarians stress deference to the traditional symbols of authority and emphasize social

Table 3.7   Factor Loadings of Six Authoritarian-Libertarian Items and Four Cultural Politics Issues on the Same First Unrotated Factor

Authoritarian-libertarian value items	
Should respect leaders' opinions	.671
Should entrust politics to outstanding leaders	.634
Dietmen and governors should command respect	.605
Cut discussions short when divided to avoid bad feelings	.539
Honor traditional virtues of respecting parents and seniors	.504
Donate without complaint to preserve neighborhood harmony	.485
Cultural politics issues	
Should strengthen Japan-U.S. security system	.650
Should strengthen defense forces	.627
Strengthen emperor's political role	.563
Recognize public employee's right to strike	−.436

control, including strengthening police powers, restraining political demonstrations, and dispensing harsh penalties on all who threaten the public order. In contrast, libertarians value reforms that will enhance equality, freedom, self-determination, and more direct political participation.

The other two value dimensions are also related, though somewhat less strongly, to the cultural politics issues as shown in table 3.6. These associations would seem to be derived from a generalized preference among personalistic parochials for old rather than new political orientations and ways of relating to politics. When all three value scales are combined in the traditional-modern index, they yield a remarkably high correlation of .43 with the cultural politics issues.

While it is not surprising to find such high value/issue associations, what is surprising is to find that, despite their declining salience, these 1950s issues are still the issues that best predict the vote. Chapter 7 demonstrates that this low-salience set of cultural politics issues continues to yield high correlations with vote choice while other high-salience issues, like taxes, welfare spending, and corruption, yield insignificant to modest correlations with the vote. How do we explain this anomaly? This seems all the more puzzling when we realize, as Curtis (1988) correctly points out, that the party images engendered by the 1950s cultural politics issues—images of the LDP as a "feudal," traditionalist party bent on undoing the Occupation's reforms and reviving nationalist sentiment, images of the Socialists as defender of the new democratic order—no longer are the pervasive ones.

The explanations for this unexpected issue/vote relationship are detailed in chapter 7, but we may outline the explanation for this finding here by noting that it was the cultural politics issues that defined the postwar party system and left-right social alignments. No new polarizing issues have emerged as yet to displace this old set of issues by realigning the electorate around a new set of concerns. New issues did surface in Japan in the 1960s over such matters as citizen's movements, increasing citizen input in government decisions, environmental pollution, and other quality-of-life issues. These issues tended to reinforce the values/issue/vote alignments as the progressive parties emerged as the champions of the environment, local citizen rights, greater citizen participation in policy making, increased government spending on welfare, and green space and other quality-of-life concerns. The emergence of this second set of postwar value issues was associated with the rise of progressive support levels and prefectural and municipal progressive administrations in Japan's urban areas during the late 1960s and early 1970s. This trend was derailed in the 1970s, however, first as the ruling party began to respond effectively to these environmental and welfare concerns, thereby blurring public perceptions of the linkages between these issues and party stances, and second as the oil crises crowded these issues off center stage on the public agenda.

Since the early 1970s, the major issues that have commanded public attention have been "valence" rather than position issues, which neither divide the electorate nor clearly differentiate the parties and hence are not strongly correlated with vote choice (see chaps. 7 and 11). Almost by default, then, the cultural politics issues continue to predict vote choice. Their residual relevance for contemporary Japanese society would seem to lie in their identification of an establishment versus an antiestablishment orientation, which continues to be a politically meaningful distinction. This distinction has been reinforced and institutionalized by the patterns of alignment between social groups and political parties that became frozen in the 1950s. Those left versus right aligned social groups continue to reflect the value cleavage that runs throughout Japanese society.

While the association between value and issue preferences provides the strongest explanation for the values/vote linkage, there are two other interesting indirect connections. Table 3.8 demonstrates that those with modern values are more likely to be skeptical and cynical of politicians and government institutions and performance. The institutional support scale taps the extent to which respondents felt that political parties, elections, and the National Diet make it possible for the people's voices to be heard in politics. Those with modern values are somewhat more skeptical on this score. The government performance scale measures the degree of satisfaction with government performance across eight different areas, from the economy and area development to providing needed services to eliminating pollution and corruption. Again, modern values are associated with lower evaluations of government performance.

Our best measures of political cynicism are found in the two trust or support scales. The first, incumbent support, taps evaluations of politicians' responsiveness, capability, and honesty. Here those with modern values have somewhat lower evaluations of politicians, but in Japan even traditionals tend not to view politicians in an altogether positive light. Thus the largest correlations with values by far are associated with the system support scale. Here the moderns are found to exhibit less pride in their political system, to have less trust in politics at all levels of government, to feel that the problems that cause distrust are more difficult to eradicate, and to feel more cut off from political influentials and more convinced that politics are run for the benefit of big special interests rather than the common man. It is reasonable to expect that higher levels of political cynicism would be associated with lower levels of

Table 3.8   Association between Values and Political Trust (Pearson's r)

	Authoritarian(−)/ Libertarian(+)	Personalism(−)/ Universalism(+)	Parochial(−)/ Cosmopolitan(+)	Traditional(−)/ Modern(+)
Institutional support	−.14	−.07	—	−.11
Government performance	−.13	−.08	−.11	−.15
Incumbent support	−.12	−.09	−.08	−.13
System support	−.20	−.19	−.11	−.23

Note: All reported correlations are significant at the .01 level. A dash indicates that the correlation was not significant even at the .05 level.

support for the ruling LDP, which at the time of the survey had consistently been in power for over two decades. When we test for these relationships in the combined path analytic model below, it is this system support scale that will constitute our measure of cynicism.

A second indirect link between values and the vote is found in the associations between values and psychological involvement in politics. In table 3.9 we find five indicators of levels of psychological involvement in politics, with modern values most strongly related to political interest and efficacy. In addition, those with modern values are also more likely than traditionals to discuss politics more frequently, to follow politics in the media more attentively, and to exhibit greater political knowledge. Moreover, the relationships between these five indicators of psychological involvement and values are only slightly reduced when controlled by education. Libertarians tend to be more assertive and desirous of controlling their environment, which explains their higher levels of political interest and efficacy. The relationship between more interest and efficacy and support for the left may not be immediately obvious. One partial explanation may be that this latter association operates to some extent through the cultural politics issues. These issues embody the libertarian demands for less authoritarian and more responsive government and more popular self-determination and participation in politics, goals which those with higher levels of political interest and efficacy are likely to share.

The association that has been found between values and higher levels of efficacy and interest, however, raises a different question. Does this relationship mean that modern values are also associated with higher levels of conventional participation? Here the answer is no, because the effects that modern values have on increasing one's psychological involvement in politics are offset by the effect those values have on increasing one's political cynicism. Cynicism tends to dampen levels of participation in conventional political activities. As a result, we find in table 3.10 that modern values have only negative or insignificant associations with the three conventional participation scales of voting turnout, campaign participation, and other political activities.[10] The exception here is found in the case of unconventional participation. The dissent scale is not only related to modern values, as shown here, but also to both psychological

10. Indeed, if we control the relationships between the value and participation scales by efficacy and interest, we find that significant correlations emerge between traditional values and higher levels on each of the three conventional participation scales. In terms of scale item content, those scoring at the high end of the campaign participation scale attended political meetings during the campaign, were members of a candidate support organization, contributed money to a campaign, and did campaign work. Those scoring at the high end of the political activities scale contacted a local influential, a local politician, and a national politician, and they participated in political groups and local self-government associations.

Table 3.9 Association between Values and Psychological Involvement in Politics

	Authoritarian(−)/ Libertarian(+)	Personalism(−)/ Universalism(+)	Parochial(−)/ Cosmopolitan(+)	Traditional(−)/ Modern(+)	Partial Controlling for Education[a]
Political interest	.18	.11	.31	.26	.21
Political efficacy	.20	.18	.26	.28	.23
Discussion frequency	.12	(.05)	.18	.15	.13
Media exposure	.09	.08	.20	.16	.12
Political knowledge	.12	.09	.23	.17	.13

Note: All reported correlations are significant at the .01 level, except the one in parentheses, which is significant at the .05 level.

[a]These are the partial correlations of the combined traditional/modern values scale with the five indicators of psychological involvement controlling for education.

Table 3.10　Association between Values and Political Participation
(Pearson's *r*)

	Authoritarian(−)/ Libertarian(+)	Personalism(−)/ Universalism(+)	Parochial(−)/ Cosmopolitan(+)	Traditional(−)/ Modern(+)
Voting turnout	−.09	—	−.06	−.08
Campaign participation	—	−.08	—	(−.06)
Political activity	—	—	—	—
Dissent	.20	.13	.11	.19

Note: All reported correlations are significant at the .01 level, except the one in parentheses, which is significant at the .05 level. A dash indicates that the correlation is not significant even at the .05 level.

involvement ($r = .28$) and vote choice ($r = .26$).[11] This finding provides another explanation for the role that psychological involvement plays in stimulating leftist voting. Both modern values and higher levels of psychological involvement may enhance one's willingness to engage in protest behavior. In turn, those activities are likely to involve one with left partisans and may lead, as an expression of one's protest, to support for the opposition parties.

All of the above linkages between values and voting preferences are visually displayed in the multivariate path analysis presented in figure 3.1. Age and education are included in the analysis to demonstrate their strong independent effects on values and to control out of the associations between values and the other variables that portion of those relationships that is actually attributable to the effects of age and education. As expected, the strongest path is from values through positions on the cultural politics issues to voting choice. Modern values are also highly related to higher levels of interest and efficacy, which in turn are indirectly related to voting through dissent and issue preferences.[12] A third path goes from modern values through cynicism, which in turn induces opposition voting both directly and through those cultural politics issues which reflect a lessening trust in and greater challenge of the traditional authorities.

We may conclude that the traditional-modern value dimensions identified above are associated with voting choices in Japan for three reasons: 1) because

11. The dissent scale was composed of three items, which measured whether the respondent had participated in a demonstration over the previous five years and whether he or she would cooperate with or protest a salary freeze to fight inflation or a government rationing of basic necessities if there were no controls over hoarding.

12. The political efficacy and political interest scales were combined here to simplify the picture by using z-score transformations and additive procedures. These scales were strongly related ($r = .32$) and combining them did not disturb the relationships with any of the other variables in the figure in any significant way.

Figure 3.1 Path analysis of value cleavages and voting behavior

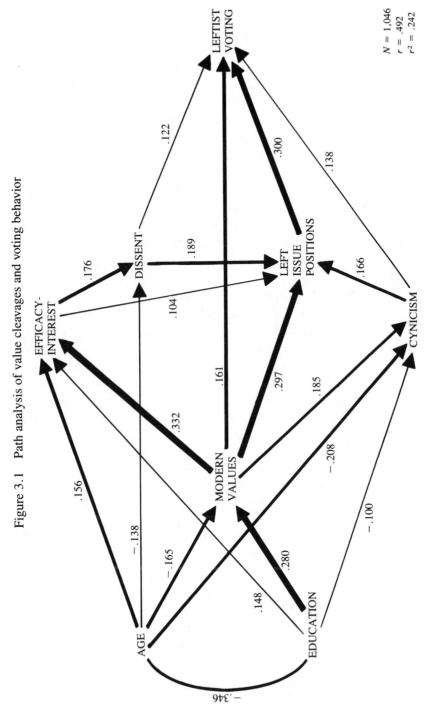

$N = 1,046$
$r = .492$
$r^2 = .242$

123

the cultural politics issues that defined the postwar partisan cleavage were originally based upon these values differences; 2) because modern values promote more distrust and cynicism vis-à-vis the ruling party and conservative political establishment; and 3) because modern values encourage a more critical, assertive, and conflictual approach to politics. In addition to these three indirect effects depicted in figure 3.1, values are also shown to have a direct effect on voting. I suspect that much of this residual direct effect is due to the contrasting style of appeals and modes of vote mobilization employed by the conservative and progressive camps. Traditionally oriented voters may be more responsive to the more traditional style of vote mobilization employed by some LDP candidates, with its emphasis on parochial loyalties, personalistic attachments, and so forth. Similarly, progressive campaign appeals, which tend to place more emphasis on national issues and party labels, may strike a more responsive chord among modern voters.

■ Contextual Influences and Vote Choice

Having demonstrated the role that values play in shaping electoral choices, I now turn to a discussion of the role that certain kinds of social environments play in Japanese voting behavior and the relationship between these contextual influences and value preferences. In our study based on the 1967 Japanese Election Survey, Richardson and I hypothesized that certain kinds of contextual settings, those that have a distinct conservative (rightist) or progressive (leftist) bias, should affect the voting behavior of those respondents located within them through the social network dynamic of attitude homogenization (Flanagan and Richardson, 1977). Specifically, we found that location in certain kinds of occupational and residential environments influenced voting behavior in the predicted manner. For instance, blue- or white-collar unionists were far more likely to vote progressive than those of the same occupational classification who were not organized into unions. Moreover, voting behavior was not only affected by the simple fact of membership but also by the quality of that membership. The longer the membership, the stronger the member's attachment to his or her union, and the more militant the union, the greater the member's proclivity to vote left. We also found that whether the employees were unionized or nonunionized, the size of the enterprise they worked in affected their votes. Workers employed in the smaller shops and business concerns, where a more traditional, paternalistic environment typically prevails, were more conservative in their voting behavior than those employed in large enterprises.

Residential environments may also affect voting behavior. The established residential areas in Japan's cities, towns, and villages are generally characterized by home owning residents with fairly long-standing ties to their area.

Indeed, 69 percent of the respondents in the 1976 JABISS study are home owners and, of those, 66 percent have lived in their present residency for sixteen years or more, 32 percent for their entire lives. These established residential communities stand in sharp contrast to the more transient communities of apartment dwellers found especially in the metropolitan areas. The established residential areas are characterized by high levels of community organization.[13] Local party politicians have found these community organizations useful in mobilizing support. Thus, politicians frequently are tied into such groups as official advisors, which means that they serve as a group's special political benefactor in return for campaign support.

While the more transient communities of apartment dwellers are likely to be serviced by progressive politicians, the progressive have had difficulty making inroads into the more established communities. This is because of the fact that in the older residential areas in both the cities and the countryside, the leadership of the neighborhood and hamlet associations and the numerous supplementary kinds of community organizations (young men's, women's, old people's, fire-fighters, crime prevention, temple and shrine associations, and so forth) almost invariably falls to members of the old middle class (upper and middle farmers, retailers, small manufacturers, and self-employed professionals). Such leaders generally establish ties with conservative politicians, because they are either economically conservative or culturally conservative. Thus the political coloration of community organizations in these areas tends to be strongly conservative (Flanagan, 1968).

Our findings for the 1967 election study demonstrated that integration into these established residential communities as measured by home ownership, length of residence, and deference to community influences was associated with higher levels of conservative voting. We also found that regardless of occupation, length of residence, or home ownership, urban-rural differences in community setting affected voting behavior. The reasons for this appear to relate back to the notion of integration into one's residential community. We know that in the rural areas community organization is much denser, in the sense that there are more community organizations and higher proportions of a community's inhabitants are organized into them. Moreover, the norms of community solidarity are stronger in the countryside. This is owing to the smaller scale of rural communities, their greater population stability, and par-

13. Of course, not all of the old, established residential communities are characterized by high levels of community organization and solidarity. For example, in the case of Tokyo, it has been noted that substantial differences that exist between the live-in, work-in shitamachi type of districts and the commuter type yama-no-te districts where we find large numbers of up-scale professionals who do not invest a great deal of emotional energy in neighborhood affairs. Nevertheless, when we contrast all home-owning communities with rental residential areas on a nationwide basis, the distinction regarding levels of community integration is valid.

ticularly their lower levels of competition from numerous external organizational attachments.[14]

In Sidney Verba and Norman Nie's (1972, 1975) terminology, rural communities are more bounded. Rural inhabitants not only reside but for the most part also work in their immediate communities. Their economic activities, social interactions, organizational associations, and recreational facilities are all focused within a relatively small, cohesive, geographically identifiable area. The process of urbanization tends to destroy this self-containment and with it community solidarity. Community boundaries become more permeable as residents move out of their residential areas to seek education, employment, social services, cultural experiences, and entertainment. As residential communities increasingly come under competition from outside attachments, and particularly those centering around one's place of work and occupational associations, the ability of areal-based associations organized within the community to influence the behavior of residents declines.

Specifically, in Japan we find that the solidarity of many established communities in urbanizing areas has been weakened by the arrival of large numbers of newcomers and the erection of high-rise apartments that cater to a highly mobile, transient clientele (Allinson, 1980). Other studies report more extreme examples where old neighborhoods are dissected by new highways or simply annihilated by development projects that dislocate many long-standing families (Falconeri, 1976). Moreover, the large suburban apartment complexes tend to isolate residents from their neighbors, with husbands commuting long distances to work and wives and children confined to physical spaces poorly designed for community interaction (Kiefer, 1976). Thus many local residents in urban neighborhoods in present-day Japan are simply not available for mobilization by traditional community networks, either because these networks cannot effectively integrate many new residents into the mainstream of community opinion or because the greater diversity of interests that have invaded the neighborhood render a holistic, areal mode of representation inoperative.

14. Despite the decline in the agricultural sector to slightly less than 10 percent of the work force by the 1980s, about 25 percent of the population continues to live in rural counties (*gumbu*). Moreover, there is evidence from the JABISS study that despite many of the occupational and residential mobility changes that have affected rural as well as metropolitan areas, levels of community integration are still much higher in rural areas. For example, we find correlations of .18, .24, and .26, respectively, between rural residence and living and working in the same neighborhood, having more close friends among one's neighbors, and being actively involved in community organizations. To put these associations in a more concrete perspective, if we compare the 25 percent of the sample living in the rural counties with the 20 percent living in the ten largest cities, 48 percent of the rural residents work at home compared to 29 percent of the metropolitan inhabitants, 67 percent of rurals had three or more close friends in their neighborhood compared to 38 percent of the big city dwellers, and 49 percent were highly involved in community organizations compared to only 16 percent of the urbanites. For more evidence on the higher levels of organizational density and community involvement in rural areas see Ikeuchi, 1974.

In Japan's rural areas, therefore, conservatively oriented residential networks experience less competition from external associational identifications that might have a progressive coloration, such as those emanating from a work place, particularly if it is a unionized, large enterprise. This is another way of saying that the associational networks in rural Japan are more uniformly conservative. Naturally, the less the partisan uniformity of an individual's associations, the less reliably we can predict voting behavior from contextual factors without knowing which associations are more central to his or her experience and more personally meaningful. Moreover, since we are here measuring the contextual environment rather than the partisan identifications of the groups within that environment or the specific partisan messages received, we must not only contend with a certain ambiguity in the relative salience of the different contextual influences that an individual is subject to but also an ambiguity in the partisan orientation of the associational networks in each contextual setting. For instance, neighborhood associations (*chonaikai*) and local retail dealers' shop associations (*shotenkai*) tend to be tied into conservative networks, but not in every case. Conversely, the self-government associations (*jichikai*) in high-rise apartment complexes and labor unions tend to have progressive ties, but this is not universally so.

Despite these ambiguities, Richardson and I (1977) found that our contextual variables had an additive effect. That is, two, three, or four contextual factors associated with progressive influences (for example, long-term union members, employed in large enterprises and renting their homes) substantially increased a respondent's proclivity to vote left compared to that probability when only one factor was known. Likewise, cumulative conservative contextual influences (for example, nonunionized, long-resident home owners working in small enterprises) heightened the probability of voting right. Conversely, the voting behavior of respondents associated with equally balanced conservative and progressive contextual influences did not differ significantly from the sample mean.

In table 3.11, the above-cited findings based on the 1967 election study are up-dated with data from the JABISS election study conducted a decade later. Here three occupational variables—occupation type, unionization, and enterprise size—were dichotomized. Again it is assumed that blue- and white-collar, unionized, large-scale contexts should be associated with progressive partisan influences and farming and old middle class, nonunion, small-scale contexts with conservative influences. In the table, the number of a respondent's occupational characteristics associated with conservative contexts have simply been counted to demonstrate the additive effect of these contextual variables. Respondents with no conservative occupational characteristics, therefore, have three progressive occupational characteristics, and we find that

Table 3.11 Percent Voting LDP by the Number of Occupational and Residential Characteristics Associated with Conservative Partisan Contexts

	Number of Respondent Characteristics Associated with Conservative Partisan Contexts[a]						
	0	1	2	3	4	5	6
Of three occupational characteristics:	20	40	54	64			
Occupation type (Farming and old middle class)	(211)	(200)	(223)	(377)			
Unionization (No union ties)							
Enterprise size (Small)							
Of three residential characteristics:	27	37	52	68			
Ownership of residence (Respondent's household)	(200)	(286)	(392)	(427)			
Length of residence (Long)							
Place of residence (Rural)							
Of six residential and occupational characteristics:	15	20	34	36	51	65	79
All of the above	(46)	(97)	(168)	(189)	(174)	(166)	(171)

Note: The figures in parentheses are the *N* of cases on which the percentage was computed.

[a] The categories of the dichotomized residential and occupational variables that are associated with conservative partisan contexts are indicated in parentheses.

only 20 percent of this category voted conservative. Conversely, 64 percent of those with three conservative and no progressive occupational characteristics voted LDP. The table shows that as we move from zero to three conservative occupational characteristics, the level of conservative voting monotonically increases.

The same pattern emerges when we turn to the three residential characteristics reported in the table—ownership of residence, length of residence, and place of residence. Rental, short-term, urban contexts are associated with progressive influences, and home owning, long-time rural contexts with conservative influences. Here we find that when these are all progressive, only 27 percent vote LDP and when they are all conservative, 68 percent vote LDP.

Finally, in the last row in table 3.11, all six occupational and residential variables are combined so that the count of conservative characteristics now runs from zero to six. Again we find a completely monotonic rise in the conservative vote as the number of conservative characteristics rises, but now the extreme differences are much greater. Only 15 percent of those with all six variables associated with progressive contexts voted LDP, while nearly 80 percent of those with all six describing conservative contexts voted LDP.

These social context variables have an additive effect on predicting vote choice, because the more contextual variables we consider, the more precisely we can identify a respondent's surroundings and the likely partisan proclivities of the social networks he is involved with on a day to day basis. If all six of the respondent's contextual indicators tend to be associated with conservative social networks, then there is a high probability that most of the influence communications he or she receives will reinforce a conservative partisan preference. At election time, the partisan cues received should be largely homogeneous and unambiguous, at least with respect to party choice, if not candidate choice as well. Conversely, those respondents located in mixed contextual settings will be subjected to mixed conservative and progressive partisan cues, making it impossible to predict their voting behavior without having additional information regarding which associational memberships are personally more salient and rewarding to the individual.

■ Social Context and Value Cleavages

Social context variables have an additive effect on predicting vote choice because adding variables enables us to paint in the partisan coloration of a respondent's social network context with greater precision. We might also expect to find that value preferences and contextual influences have an additive effect. Since modern values tend to induce support for the progressive parties, we might posit that the probability of voting left would be strengthened if a modern value orientation was also associated with union membership or working in a large enterprise. In the case of value preferences, however, perhaps more is involved than simply an accumulation of uniform influences. We might also argue that value compatibility may enhance the impact of contextual influences. In other words, a traditional is more likely to be receptive to the kinds of influence communications found within established residential community associations or small enterprises, whereas a modern value orientation might somewhat insulate an individual from such influences, because the transmission vehicle or the form of the message may appear inappropriate or uncongenial.

Whether these value and contextual effects are simply additive influences that reinforce each other or interactive influences whose combination further enhances the individual effects of each, table 3.12 shows that, for both the 1967 and 1976 data sets, value preferences have both cumulative and cross-cutting effects when combined with each of five of the principle occupational and residential variables introduced above in table 3.11. For instance, in the case of the moderns in 1976, only 19 percent of those with union ties, 22 percent of those employed in large enterprises, 22 percent of the renters, 29 percent of those living in their present residence for less than fifteen years, and 28 percent of the urban electorate voted conservative. In contrast, among the traditionals, 72 percent of the nonunion, 74 percent of those in small enterprises, 72 percent of the home owners, 75 percent of the long-term residents, and 76 percent of the rural electorate voted conservative. On the other hand, cross-cutting influences weaken the ability of either values or contextual factors to predict voting behavior, as demonstrated by the percentages along the other diagonals.[15]

I would also argue that the value cleavage and social network models are interrelated in another way. Over time, contextual influences may exert an impact on value preferences. That is, certain environmental settings will tend to instill or reinforce certain kinds of value orientations. Table 3.13 supports this contention. We find that all of the value scales are positively associated with engaging in modern occupations (blue- and white-collar wage earners versus farmers, proprietors, managers, and small retailers), employment in large enterprises, and union ties.

The residential environment variables in table 3.13 have been divided into two categories. The first differentiates the overall urban or rural character of the setting in which the respondent is located. Here we find that the more urban the environment, the more likely it is that the respondent will have modern values. The second category of residential variables is labeled community integration. In the 1976 study, we were able to tap the dimension of community integration much more convincingly than was possible with the 1967 study. Here, added to home ownership and length of residence, are the number of close friends the respondent has in his residential community, the number of community organizations he belongs to as well as his degree of involvement in them, and his commuting time to work. We find home ownership, long residence, many neighborhood friends, high involvement in community organizations, and short commuting time (working close to one's home) are all associated with

15. The sixth variable that appeared in table 3.11, occupation type, is deleted here for reasons of space. The same relationships hold, however, as can be seen from the findings of the 1976 study where only 22 percent of the blue- and white-collar workers with modern values voted LDP compared to 74 percent of the farming and old middle class traditionals.

Table 3.12 Percentage of Modern and Traditional Respondents Voting Conservative in 1967 and 1976, Controlling for Five Occupational and Residential Variables

	Union Ties		Enterprise Size		Home Ownership		Length of Residence		Place of Residence	
	Union	No Ties	Large	Small	Renter	Home Owner	Short	Long	Urban	Rural
1967 Study										
Modern	24 (135)	48 (262)	26 (120)	45 (215)	27 (144)	48 (262)	32 (156)	42 (136)	23 (124)	47 (291)
Traditional	39 (125)	72 (411)	43 (93)	66 (278)	50 (139)	69 (421)	54 (132)	68 (268)	62 (134)	64 (459)
1976 Study										
Modern	19 (134)	37 (232)	22 (223)	44 (135)	22 (141)	35 (265)	29 (222)	34 (191)	28 (247)	36 (165)
Traditional	45 (86)	72 (310)	51 (122)	74 (241)	37 (70)	72 (374)	49 (137)	75 (309)	53 (179)	76 (268)

Note: The figures in parentheses are the *N* of cases on which the percentage was computed. The values variable was trichotomized into roughly equal categories of Modern, Mixed, and Traditionals. Here the Mixed category was excluded to simplify the table. All of the residential and occupational contextual variables were dichotomized, with no excluded categories.

Table 3.13   Association between Values and Occupational and Residential Contextual Variables, 1976 (Pearson's r)

	Authoritarian (−) Libertarian (+)	Personalism (−) Universalism (+)	Parochial (−) Cosmopolitan (+)	Traditional (−) Modern (+)
Occupational environments				
Modern occupations				
(Blue- & white-collar workers)	.18	.10	.16	.19
Enterprise size	.18	.12	.24	.24
Union ties	.12	.07	.13	.14
Residential setting				
Urban	.12	.10	.23	.19
Community integration				
Home ownership	−.13	−.09	−.11	−.14
Length of residence	−.14	−.10	−.15	−.17
Close community friendships	−.16	−.12	−.18	−.20
Community organizational				
involvement	−.18	−.14	−.20	−.23
Commuting time to work	.19	.20	.23	.27

Note: All reported correlations were significant at the .01 level.

traditional values. If established residential communities in Japan are the preserve of a traditional ethos, then those individuals who are highly integrated into these environments are likely to reflect those same traditional values.

In figure 3.2, I have further tested the interassociations between value and contextual influences and voting behavior through the technique of path analysis. Here, for simplicity, I have combined age and education into a single *modern attributes* scale in which low age and high education are assigned high scores. I have also combined modern occupations, large enterprises, and union ties into a *modern occupational environments* scale and the five community integration variables into a single index. Note that age and education have the strongest impact on values but that the occupational environment and community integration still have an independent effect. Regardless of one's age or education, then, the character of one's occupational and residential environments affects one's values. High integration into an established residential community will tend to reinforce traditional values, while joining the wage-earning force as a blue- or white-collar worker and union member in a large enterprise will tend to instill modern values.

Figure 3.2 also demonstrates that occupational environment, community integration, and values all have a direct, independent effect on voting behavior even when the effects of issue preferences are controlled. In the case of values, I argued above that value orientations affect the ability of the more modern, progressive and the more traditional, conservative styles of voter mobilization to effectively reach and attract voter support. I have also shown that modern values are associated with a more cynical and dissident approach to politics, a perspective that is not likely to induce support for the conservative establishment and its "money power" politics. The impact of occupational environments is not surprising in that the organizations and informal groups within the various occupational contexts undoubtedly collectively perceive certain economic advantages in supporting one party or another and convey these messages to their constituent members.

The role of community integration is somewhat distinct in that I argue that integration within an established residential community is likely to bring one into contact with community organizations and small group networks that have a conservative partisan orientation. High community integration, then, leads to integration into conservative social networks. Low integration, on the other hand, simply removes the individual from such influences but does not have any direct partisan effect. It may be assumed, however, that such residentially unintegrated individuals are more susceptible to influences from other social networks, such as those revolving around their place of work, recreational activities, and friendship associations.

To sum up, the findings in this section have brought us closer to an integra-

Figure 3.2 Path Analysis of Value Cleavages, Social Contexts, and Voting Behavior

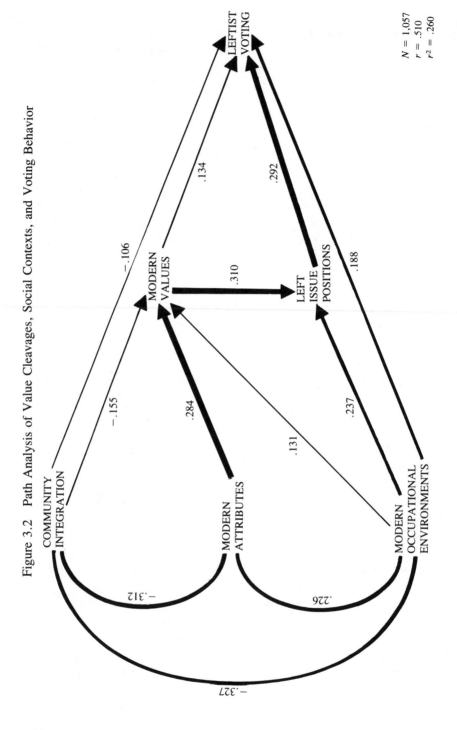

N = 1,057
r = .510
r² = .260

134

tion of the value cleavage and social network models of voting behavior. There appears to be a mutually reinforcing interaction between social values and contextual influences. In the short run, values play an important role in sorting out the various influence communications that are directed at an individual. Where many diverse communications are received, an individual will place a higher valuation on those that are most compatible with his values in terms of their rhetoric, mode of presentation, and source. In the long run, high integration into a particular set of social networks with a pronounced and uniform value orientation will tend to preserve such value preferences among the constituent members and socialize new members into the same set of values.

Urban and Rural Differences

From what we know about Japan, there are good reasons to believe that the relative influence of the cultural cleavage and social network models and their component variables may vary somewhat between urban and rural settings. A final series of tests, therefore, will examine the differences between the influences that the value and contextual variables exert in the cities and the countryside. Here the residential setting variable has been dichotomized into urban areas defined as cities of 100,000 and above and rural areas that include all small cities, towns, and villages with populations of less than 100,000.

Table 3.14 repeats the analysis presented in table 3.12 for the urban and rural subsamples respectively. Comparing the distribution of cases across the various cells, we can see how different the two environments are. The number of cases tends to be greatest in the upper-left-hand cells in the urban areas and the lower-right-hand cells in the rural areas. We not only find more modern value orientations in the urban areas but also more union members, large enterprises, renters, and short-term residents. One simple way to gauge the relative impact of each variable is to average the summed differences down each table column for the *values effect* and across each table row for the *contextual variables effect*.[16] We note that overall, the values effects are higher in the rural than in the urban areas. In addition, the occupational environment variables also appear to exert a greater influence in the rural as compared to the urban areas. The community integration variables are more ambiguous, but length of residence seems to be more important in the urban areas.

While these results are suggestive, they do not permit us to make conclusive statements about the relative impact of the different variables. For that purpose

16. As noted in table 3.12, the values scale was trichotomized with roughly one-third of the sample falling into a central mixed category that has been deleted from these tables. Since the contextual variables were dichotomized with no categories deleted, our simple measure of value and contextual effects in table 3.14 will exaggerate the impact of values relative to that of context on voting behavior. This measure, therefore, should not be used for comparisons across types of effects but rather to roughly gauge the relative impact of each type of effect across urban and rural settings.

a return to the more sophisticated technique of path analysis is required. In figures 3.3 and 3.4, the figure 3.2 model path coefficients have been recomputed for the urban and rural subpopulations. In this case both the standardized betas and (in parentheses) the unstandardized B's have been reported for each path. To aid in the interpretation of the unstandardized B's, I have standardized all the variables in the model so that their scale scores range from zero to one. The standardized betas enable us to make comparative statements regarding the relative strength of any path within a given model, while the unstandardized B's permit us to compare the strengths of identical paths across our two models.

In the rural model, the occupational environment clearly has a stronger effect on the vote than it does in the urban model. In the former case there is a strong direct path from occupational environment to vote, while in the latter case there is no direct path at all. In addition, the unstandardized B's reveal that values have a stronger direct impact on both the vote and issue positions in rural areas than in urban. Conversely, when we turn our attention to the urban model, we find a stronger emphasis on issues in determining the vote than in the case of the rural inhabitants. We also find that community integration has a direct impact on voting, whereas in the rural model it had a strong influence on one's values but no direct effect on voting.

These findings suggest that in rural environments community integration perpetuates a strong traditional ethos and that values in general play a pronounced role not only in determining one's vote but also in the way one perceives the issues. In other words, issues have a stronger value coloration in rural areas than in urban. In such an environment, where traditional influences are so pervasive in the residential communities, the work place plays a highly significant role in breaking the hold of conservatism on the Japanese voter. We note, for instance, that the inverse correlation between modern occupational environments and community integration is much higher in the small cities and villages than in the large urban areas.

Movement into modern occupation environments in the rural areas, then, constitutes a greater break with the typical pattern of life found in the countryside than that found in the city. Evidently, for rural inhabitants, it is through being pulled out of the communal solidarity of the residential environments and pushed into a modern occupational status as blue- and white-collar wage earners and union members in large enterprises that both values and voting behavior change. In table 3.15 for instance, we see that without the stimulus of modern occupational environments, the pervasiveness of conservative influence communications and associational networks greatly attenuates the impact of values on voting behavior. For those living in rural areas who are not union members or who are employed in small enterprises, even the semi-

Table 3.14 Percentage of Urban and Rural Respondents Voting Conservative by Values, Controlling for Occupational and Residential Variables

Values	Union Ties		Enterprise Size		Home Ownership		Length of Residence	
	Union	No Ties	Large	Small	Renter	Home Owner	Short	Long
Urban areas								
Modern	20	21	25	30	20	35	26	31
	(80)	(140)	(138)	(80)	(122)	(133)	(147)	(100)
Traditional	38	57	45	62	36	60	40	67
	(45)	(116)	(60)	(90)	(52)	(127)	(90)	(88)
Values effect	22		26		20.5		25	
Contextual effects	15		11		19.5		16	
Rural areas								
Modern	17	46	18	64	31	36	35	36
	(54)	(92)	(85)	(55)	(29)	(132)	(74)	(91)
Traditional	54	81	56	82	39	78	66	78
	(41)	(194)	(62)	(151)	(18)	(247)	(47)	(221)
Values effect	36		28		25		36.5	
Contextual effects	28		36		22		6.5	

Note: The figures in parentheses are the *N* of cases on which the percentage was computed.

137

Figure 3.3 Path Analysis of Value Cleavages, Social Contexts, and Voting Behavior in Rural Japan

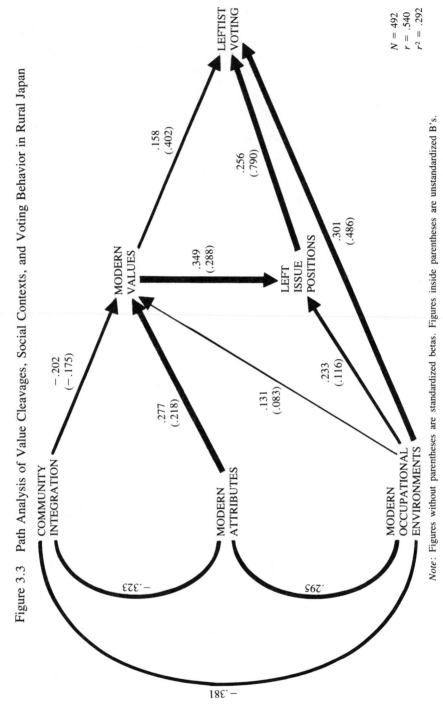

Note: Figures without parentheses are standardized betas. Figures inside parentheses are unstandardized B's.

138

Figure 3.4   Path Analysis of Value Cleavages, Social Contexts, and Voting Behavior in Urban Japan

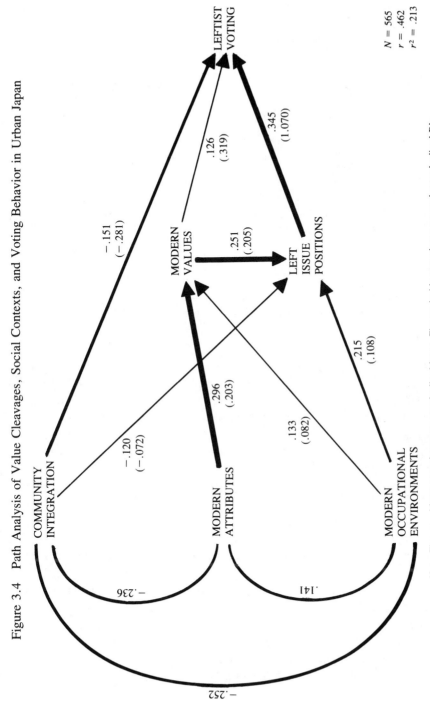

Note: Figures without parentheses are standardized betas. Figures inside parentheses are understandardized B's.

139

Table 3.15 Percentage of Respondents in Traditional Occupational Environments Voting Conservative by Residential Setting and Values

	Modern	Semi-Modern	Mixed	Semi-Traditional	Traditional
Respondents with no union ties					
Rural	29	61	67	78	83
	(45)	(47)	(125)	(83)	(111)
Urban	25	35	43	60	54
	(63)	(77)	(141)	(62)	(54)
Respondents employed in small enterprises					
(less than 30 workers)					
Rural	46	76	69	79	83
	(22)	(33)	(106)	(68)	(83)
Urban	22	37	41	66	59
	(37)	(43)	(93)	(44)	(46)

Note: The figures in parentheses are the *N* of cases on which the percentage was computed.

moderns vote heavily conservative. In the rural areas, in the absence of the influences that emanate from modern occupational environments, it requires a much stronger or more consistently modern value orientation for those values to link up successfully with progressive partisan preferences. Thus, the role of occupational environments is central to partisan change in the rural areas.

In contrast, urban voters seem to be more issue-oriented, and values play a somewhat smaller role in determining either issue positions or the vote. The interesting finding in the urban model concerns the role of community integration. Table 3.16 helps to clarify what that role is. We note in both urban and rural areas that respondents who are highly integrated into their residential communities are strongly influenced in their voting behavior by their value orientations. For all value types, rural voters more strongly support the conservatives than do urban voters, vouching for the higher proportions of rural communities that have ties to conservative as opposed to progressive politicians and the greater competition in urban areas from progressive oriented associational attachments outside the community. In both urban and rural areas, respondents with high community integration *and* modern values are more likely to vote progressive than conservative, either because they ignore the conservative political influences emanating from their communities or because they live in communities with progressive party attachments.

In the case of those with low integration into their communities, however, we find striking urban-rural differences. In the rural areas in the absence of

Table 3.16   Percentage of Respondents with High and Low Levels of
Community Integration Voting Conservative by Urbanization
and Values

	VALUES		
	Modern	Mixed	Traditional
High community integration			
Rural	44	69	83
	(55)	(86)	(180)
Urban	32	51	67
	(37)	(47)	(51)
Low community integration			
Rural	27	54	55
	(68)	(54)	(40)
Urban	24	27	31
	(129)	(98)	(51)

Note: The figures in parentheses are the *N* of cases on which the percentage was computed.

community influences, traditionals are still able to make the linkage between
traditional values and conservative partisan preferences. There are, then, in
rural environments other sources of conservative influence than those associated with the residential community setting. In the urban areas, however, low
integration into one's residential community greatly attenuates the impact of
values on voting behavior. Evidently, in the large cities, in the absence of strong
residential ties, there are few other environmental cues that will enable traditionals to make a meaningful connection between their value preferences and
voting choices.

The analysis above has presented evidence that strongly supports the applicability of both the value cleavage and social network models of voting
behavior in Japan. I first identified what values are changing in Japan and
presented a theory to explain why they are changing. Next I demonstrated that
these identified dimensions have been characterized by a significant pattern of
intergenerational change and substantial age and educational cleavages across
the postwar period. Finally, I showed that respondents with modern values are
far more likely to vote for opposition or leftist candidates than are those holding
traditional values. This was found to be primarily because these value differences lay at the base of the cultural politics issues that defined the postwar party
system, but secondarily because modern values are associated with cynical and
protest orientations toward politics that further induce leftist voting.

I then turned to a preliminary investigation of the social network model. While the next chapter will analyze that model more directly, here I presented indirect evidence of its applicability to Japan by examining contextual effects. There have been many studies in other electoral settings of the impact of context on voting decisions. Typically these studies have found that the more homogeneous the partisan coloration of one's living or working environments the more consistently one is likely to vote for the predominant party preference associated with those settings (Butler and Stokes, 1976; Huckfeldt, 1986). While the relevant contextual variables may be somewhat differently defined in Japan, the same finding was demonstrated—the more partisanly homogeneous one's context, the more predictable one's voting choice.

This analysis has moved us closer to an integration of the value cleavage and social network models by showing that values and contextual factors exert mutually reinforcing influences. A respondent's value orientations affect his receptivity to the various kinds of influence communications that emanate from the several principal social networks with which he is associated. Particularly when the respondent receives mixed cues from different sources, he is likely to place greater weight on those that are most compatible with his value orientations. Conversely, a respondent's long-standing integration into a stable set of social networks with a strong, coherent value orientation will tend to instill and reinforce those shared values.

Finally, the analysis has shown that while values and occupational and residential environments play significant roles throughout Japan, there are important urban-rural differences in their influences. In the cities, issues play a somewhat larger role in voting behavior, and high integration into a residential community is necessary to offset the strong progressive influences that prevail in urban settings. In contrast, in the rural areas, values play a heightened role, and movement into a modern occupational environment is necessary to counteract the influences on voting behavior of the pervasive conservative associational networks found in village, town, and small city settings.

Four ■ Mechanisms of Social Network Influence in Japanese Voting Behavior

SCOTT C. FLANAGAN

In the last chapter it was found that cultural cleavages and certain kinds of occupational and residential contexts were strong predictors of vote choice in Japan. The finding of contextual effects on voting behavior assumes that social networks are the mechanisms that explain the associations between these geographic or associational environments and the vote. This chapter looks inside these contextual settings to gain further insight into the various means by which social networks shape voting behavior.

The chapter begins with a discussion of the social network model that reviews the cross-national evidence on contextual effects and introduces a typology of the various mechanisms through which social networks influence voting choices. This theoretical discussion is followed by a description of Japanese campaign practices and cultural norms from the perspective of that typology to demonstrate the special relevance of a social network approach to the study of Japanese electoral behavior. Turning to the data, I move beyond a contextual effects analysis to uncover the internal dynamics of the social network model. I argue that social networks exert several kinds of long-term influences on vote choice through the development of group loyalties, which can guide vote choice, and through group socialization processes, which promote attitude conformity. Evidence is presented that demonstrates the ability of social networks to induce these kinds of reference group and partisan socialization effects.

■ The Social Network Model and the Study of Contextual Effects

The social network model posits that an individual's social characteristics and early socialization experiences alone cannot explain political behavior. Class, religious, partisan, and other identifications may well represent early childhood and adolescent social learning that has been internalized. While these identities and the perceptions surrounding them play a continuing role in helping the individual to interpret political phenomenon, an individual's political attitudes and actions are also conditioned by current influences from his daily environment. The individual is repeatedly subjected to influences stemming from those primary social contexts in which his most valued social interactions take place—the family, the neighborhood, the work place, and other habitual formal and informal associational settings. The patterns of social relationships within these valued contextual settings provide the individual with trusted communication networks, which supply information and interpretations that can shape the individual's political perceptions and behavior.

The study of the role of social networks in voting behavior both in the United States and Europe has curiously been neglected (Sheingold, 1973). This seems ironic in light of the fact that the early Columbia voting studies pointed to the conclusion that the receipt of information and influences through interpersonal communications was a decisive element in the decision of many voters. The Columbia findings—regarding the "two-step flow of influence," the role of opinion leaders, the role of organizations in mobilizing their members, the homogeneity of primary groups and their rising uniformity in voting choice throughout the campaign—all point to the importance of social networks as a research agenda (Lazarsfeld et al., 1944; Berelson et al., 1954).

There are several reasons why a social network approach to voting behavior has been neglected. The first of these is methodological. With the shift from the Columbia community studies to the Michigan large-scale nationwide survey samples, the individual's social context became randomized, thereby obscuring its effect (Huckfeldt, 1986:5–6). Also, though sociologists have been developing sociometric techniques that permit a mapping of structural patterns of interpersonal relations and roles, the detailed information on all interpersonal contacts required for such studies severely limits their utility for the study of voting behavior (Holland and Leinhardt, 1970; White et al., 1976). Although these approaches have discouraged political scientists from investigating social networks, such limitations can be overcome by a focus on personal networks, that is, egocentric networks which take the individual respondent as the center and trace the pattern of contacts outward from him (Weatherford, 1982). Although such an approach is not without problems, it can, in the context of local surveys or specially designed national surveys, permit an investigation of information flows and interpersonal influences.

A second reason for the neglect of social networks may reflect the influence of traditional democratic theory. Democratic theory places heavy importance on the individual and his ability to make personally meaningful, self-interested choices. Indeed, external influences have typically been viewed as corrupting or exploiting forces. Vote buying, machine politics, and the use of patron-client relations to mobilize bloc voting all suggest distortions of the democratic process, the manipulation of the voting public, and the failure of the individual to make a politically aware, self-conscious choice. This kind of politics is generally viewed as being characteristic of developing Third World countries or earlier political eras in the advanced industrial democracies. The conclusion would be that external influences are largely negative and/or largely irrelevant to the study of contemporary American and European electoral behavior. Yet external influences need not be manipulating or irrational or limited to voters with low education and political awareness. Given the complexity of party platforms and campaign issues and the high cost of gaining sufficient information on all of the candidates to make an informed choice, turning to trusted others among one's family, friends, neighbors, and co-workers who share similar interests and viewpoints can be a cost-effective approach to making a self-interested electoral decision. Beyond that, individuals do not exist in isolation but rather are enmeshed in social interactions that not only provide much of their information about politics but also shape their political perceptions and behavior.

Probably the most important reason, however, for the inattention to social networks is that voting research in the United States and Europe has historically been dominated by voting models that minimize the role of interpersonal influences. The Michigan studies have been based on a psychological approach that lays stress on the individual's attitudes and partisan loyalties. While these may very well have been originally imparted in an interpersonal context, such as the family, they have typically been viewed as being acquired rather early in life and, once acquired, as being very stable. This perspective tends to discount the continuing socializing influences found in the individual's adult living and working environments.

The emphasis in the psychological approach on the isolated individual and his attitudes and perceptions implicitly assumes that individuals are members of groups only by choice and that if they happen to adhere to a group voting recommendation it is only as a result of an independent assessment of political self-interest. While the individual does ultimately settle on a voting choice and physically cast his ballot, the information, perceptions and evaluations on which the decision is made are drawn from, or at least filtered through, his environment. A focus on the respondent's party preferences, candidate evaluations, and issue positions may predict vote choice with great success, but it simply begs the question of where these attitudes and perceptions are coming from.

On the other side of the Atlantic, European voting studies have been dominated by a social cleavage model, which stresses the importance of large categorical social group memberships. Here, long-standing cleavages and antagonisms based on class, religion, region, or ethnicity have been seen as defining political competition. Hence, certain social group memberships are viewed as implying a particular party choice. Little attention, however, has been placed on determining which of an individual's demographically defined social group memberships are meaningful to him or on identifying the mechanisms through which such meaning is imparted. Also, the linkages between social group memberships and voting choice have been largely left to the imagination.

In contrast to these two approaches, the social network model highlights the role of both formal organizational networks and informal small group networks in the transmission of political opinions, voting cues, and other influence communications. Organizations often have definite ties with a particular party, and many organizations, such as labor unions, frequently engage in self-conscious efforts aimed at both the long-term socialization of their members into an explicit partisan orientation and their short-term mobilization to support specific candidates in election campaigns. For many voters these organizational networks are a major source of the ideas, opinions, and images through which they view parties and politics. Thus, beyond their explicit efforts to influence electoral choice during campaigns, such organizational networks may also serve as vehicles for socializing and politicizing voters by molding political attitudes, alerting members and followers to group-related issues and interest, promoting loyalties to a particular party, and mobilizing other forms of political participation in addition to simply voting.

Informal small group networks operate both inside and outside of large organizations. Small group networks are embedded in large organizations, and frequently informal, face-to-face, leader-follower or peer group relations are the vehicles through which organizational communications are transmitted. In addition, informal small group networks are found in all of the social settings in which the individual is involved, including the home, neighborhood, and work place. Since any social contact may be the source of a voting cue or some other political message, the more homogeneous the messages being received from different network sources, the greater their influence is likely to be in shaping an individual's political attitudes and behavior. Also, among the different networks, the more trusted and valued the source and the closer the individual's identification with it, the greater its influence is likely to be.

Over the past decade, a growing number of studies in the advanced industrial democracies have pointed to the declining power of class to predict voting behavior (Lipset, 1981; Stephens, 1981; Rose, 1982; Kelley et al., 1985). Indeed, many of these analyses have shown that virtually all demographically derived categorical social group memberships are playing a weakening role in explaining electoral choice. There have been many explanations offered to account for this change, from embourgeoisement theories that stress the role of growing worker affluence in decreasing the relevance and strength of class identifications to realignment theories that suggest that the old cleavage alignments are in the process of being replaced by new lines of division cutting across social groups (Dalton et al., 1984).

A social network explanation, however, may also account for the change. A close inspection of even the earlier sociological studies of European voting behavior reveals that it was not so much the categorical social group membership as the tangible organizational expression of that membership that was influencing electoral decisions. For example, numerous multivariate analyses demonstrated that it was frequency of church attendance rather than denominational preference or union membership rather than class that were the stronger predictors of vote choice (see Liepelt, 1971, and the national studies in Rose, 1974). Moreover, other evidence suggests that while the relationship between individual class characteristics (occupation, education, and so forth) and voting has declined over the last few decades, the relationship between contextual indicators of class (union membership, type of housing, and so forth) and vote choice has been increasing (Miller, 1978; Rose, 1982).

Social group categories may have been good predictors of European voting behavior in past decades because of the segmenting or pillarization of those societies, which, for example, isolated manual laborers in working-class ghettos and mobilized different religious groups and social strata into exclusive social and organizational networks. It is argued, in fact, that in a number of countries there were conscious attempts to insulate the various socially defined constituencies from the heretical ideologies emanating from other self-contained communities (Lorwin, 1966; Daalder, 1966; Lijphart, 1968). What may be happening is not so much a detachment of voters from previously held group identifications or a rejection of their principal social networks as sources of voting cues, but rather a change in the patterns of social network involvement.

With the destructuration of society and the growing homogeneity of life styles, voters are coming into contact with more diverse kinds of social networks (Murakami, 1982). For example, Stephens (1981) argues that the decline in class voting in Sweden is closely tied to the change in contextual influences that accompanied the declining residential segregation of society by class. Heterogeneous residential environments have become common in recent years in Sweden because of rising working-class incomes, an urban housing short-age, and a conscious policy of class mixing on the part of city planners. As workers come increasingly into contact with middle-class neighbors, they receive fewer network communications that reinforce a socialist party preference.

It may be, then, that both the effectiveness of social group categories in predicting voting behavior and the deviations from those predictions are, in large part, attributable to the operation of social networks. For example, the growing literature on contextual effects has demonstrated a substantial relationship between the probability that a member of a given social class will vote for his class party and the class composition of the individual's neighborhood. Thus, heavily working-class neighborhoods substantially increase the probability over the sample mean that working-class respondents will vote for a party of the left, while predominantly middle-class neighborhoods substantially decrease the probability that workers will vote left (Tingsten, 1963; Przeworski and Soares, 1971; Segal and Meyer, 1974; Langton and Rapoport, 1975; Butler and Stokes, 1976; Huckfeldt, 1986).

Studies of contextual effects are closely linked to the social network model. Indeed, the contextual effects literature assumes that social networks are the mechanisms through which environmental influences are transmitted. Moreover, there is evidence supporting the contention that the location of a respondent's living and working environments largely defines the demographic characteristics of the main participants in his primary social networks. For example, it has been found that the more middle-class the neighborhood a blue-collar worker lives in the more likely he is to have middle-class friends (Fuchs, 1955; Putnam, 1966). As Huckfeldt (1986:40) puts it, "the social class content of friendship groups is influenced by associational opportunities and constraints imposed by the neighborhood social context." And the same could be said for the social context in the work place. While the contextual effects literature in the United States has tended to focus on the neighborhood and ignore the work place, one cannot successfully study contextual effects in Japan without recognizing that the environment of the work place is the principal alternate "community" setting that provides the individual with primary social relationships.

To begin to move from the concept of social networks to a model of social network effects, we need to specify in clearer detail the various mechanisms through which social networks may exert an influence on voting behavior. I will outline four different kinds of influences, two with long-term and two with short-term effects.

The first of these can be labeled *assimilation effects*. Individuals tend to assimilate the attitudes of those around them. This is true for political as well as nonpolitical attitudes. If an individual is surrounded by a particular set of political opinions, he is likely to develop attitudes congruent with them, even if these attitudes deviate from his early political learning and partisanship.[1] To a large extent, then, political beliefs are a product of informal group living. One explanation for this phenomenon is found in the study of small groups, which has shown that small group contexts exert subtle pressures on members for attitude conformity to preserve an atmosphere of harmony and rapport (Janis, 1982). Members derive psychological support from their small groups, and the more important group acceptance is to the individual the more likely that he will be sensitive to the sanctions and rewards associated with approval or rejection of group norms. Newcomb (1957), for example, found that students from conservative homes living in a liberal college environment were likely in time to adopt more liberal views, especially if they were desirous of cordial relations with those around them. In an important recent study of interpersonal neighborhood networks, Weatherford (1982) found that network partisanship had a significant impact on a whole range of political attitudes, covering economic and social liberalism and evaluations of presidential performance, even when the effects of the individual's party affiliation were controlled.

The more stable and homogeneous an individual's social networks and the more closely he is tied into them, the greater the likelihood that he will conform to the views of those around him. Interestingly, Weatherford found that while the frequency of contact had little effect, the duration of the friendships and their intimacy had important effects. Thus, it is not so much the repetition of the message as trust in the sender that stimulates receptivity and conformity. Over time, these assimilation effects can induce change not only in issue opinions and other political attitudes but in partisanship as well. One indicator of that is Huckfeldt's finding (1986) that the neighborhood social environment is at least as important as individual characteristics in predicting partisanship.

A second type of social network influence can be labeled a *reference group effect*. In identifying this effect, Huckfeldt (1986:20–24) notes that social networks may influence individual voting decisions even if politics are not discussed. The idea here is that people surrounded by a group are more likely to identify with the group and view politics, as well as other social phenomena, from the group's perspective. For example, the social context may structure

1. As Huckfeldt (1986) notes, assimilation to the attitudes held by the dominant social group surrounding one is not the only possible response. If one perceives the dominant social group in one's environment as threatening and fundamentally different, perhaps owing to racial or ethnic differences, higher concentrations of the dissimilar social group may actually lead the individual to develop more hostile attitudes toward it.

interpersonal interactions such that repetitive, informal contacts in an individual's neighborhood, work place, and other settings of more casual encounters (like a neighborhood store or local park), predominantly involve interactions with one particular social group. In such cases, the individual is likely to see his interests as somehow bound up with that group.

Different economic groups, such as manual workers, farmers or small businessmen, different churches, and even different social settings, such as inner-city versus suburban residence, are associated with different social beliefs. Thus, even apolitical interactions within a given social context can influence political behavior by structuring the perceptions and social beliefs through which political events are interpreted. The primary mechanism here, then, is the reference group. Interpersonal contacts within a particular social context shape social loyalties, which in turn influence political perceptions. Voting behavior may then be structured not by the communication of ideological political attitudes but by essentially issueless messages that provide the individual with the set of social perceptions from which he interprets politics and seeks to identify that party which is closest or most favorable to his group.

A third type of influence that social networks may have can be labeled *opinion leader effects*. These are short-term effects that typically occur during the course of election campaigns. In most social networks, politics are typically not a common topic of conversation. During election campaigns, however, discussions about politics are much more likely to come up, and particularly discussions that make reference to the candidates and campaign issues. In these exchanges, the political influence communications are likely to be asymmetric, since some people have much more interest in and knowledge about politics than others. Politics are rather remote from the daily concerns of most citizens, and hence large sections of the electorate fail to invest sufficiently in gaining an adequate understanding of the issues and candidates that surround any electoral contest. Faced with the task of making a voting decision, these voters, consciously or unconsciously, turn to trusted others within their social networks for voting cues, frequently found in unsolicited comments about the candidates.

If the voter becomes convinced of the personal correctness of a particular candidate choice, he is likely to pass the communication on to others with whom he frequently interacts. Because such influence communications typically reflect a partisan bias, once these social networks become activated by the election campaign to carry political communications, they exert a homogenizing effect within small groups on electoral choices. Lazarsfeld and his associates refer to this kind of two-step flow of communications in explaining the rising levels of homogeneity within small groups that they observed during the course of the campaign. More recently, in a 1976 American panel study,

Huckfeldt and Sprague (1990) found that, whereas the social composition and partisan context of the locality failed to structure vote preferences early in the campaign, they had a substantial effect on postelection reported votes. They conclude that the campaign mobilized social influences that brought the voters in line with the social groups surrounding them.

The first three of our four mechanisms of interpersonal influence all suggest some kind of balance between internal and external influences. In the case of the two long-term effects, political attitudes, partisan preferences, or social group loyalties are acquired through interpersonal contacts and then become internal bases of electoral choice. Even in the case of the opinion leader, though the voter may somewhat uncritically accept biased information from a trusted source, that information is still processed through his own system of political beliefs in reaching a decision. In the case of our fourth type, *mobilization effects,* external influences totally dominate, due to the virtual absence of internal political reasoning processes.

The absence of internal political reasoning processes in deciding whether to act on a particular interpersonal message may reflect a low level of knowledge or understanding about politics that leads the individual to defer to the opinions of others. Or the individual's political beliefs may be discounted in the face of other more salient concerns, stemming from an emotional loyalty to the sender of the message or a sense of personal obligation to comply with the recommendation based on some past favor. Some voters, then, lack the internal resources to make an independent voting decision and simply jump on the candidate bandwagon that his friends and neighbors favor. Others have the internal resources, but those concerns are overwhelmed by personal considerations stemming from strong emotional ties to others or patron-client relationships.

As shown in figure 4.1, these four types of mechanisms by which interpersonal communications can influence voting choice fit neatly into a two-by-two table defined by the duration of the effect and the level of political content of the

Figure 4.1   Mechanisms through which Interpersonal Communications within Small Group Networks Influence Voting

	Message Characterized by	
	High Political Content	Low Political Content
Long-term	Assimilation effects	Reference group effects
Short-term	Opinion leader effects	Mobilization effects

message. In the case of both the assimilation and opinion leader effects, the political content of the information being communicated is high and the messages are designed to persuade others to accept certain political attitudes and evaluations. In the case of reference group effects, however, the communications have no political content. In the case of mobilization effects, also, the most that is being communicated is a candidate's name, without the embellishment of any political arguments, or, at least in terms of the message received, any attached political content is irrelevant. It should also be noted that these four kinds of effects are not mutually exclusive, but rather may interact with each other. In particular, both of the long-term effects may set the stage for opinion leader effects by favoring certain messages and message sources. Reference group effects may also enhance mobilization effects by defining who the trusted message senders are. And finally, the accumulation of opinion leader effects over time can have an assimilation effect.

■ Japanese Political Culture and Campaign Practices

Different methodologies frequently yield different results. While survey research tends to obscure the role of social networks, the participant observer approach to the study of election campaigns tends to emphasize personalistic influences. Despite these built-in biases, it is remarkable how dominant a role social networks play in the descriptions of Japanese campaigns. From the early postwar studies (Beardsley et al., 1959; Dore, 1959) through Gerald Curtis' influential study (1971) to an important new study by Kyoji Wakata (1986), both the investigators and the candidates themselves appear to share the view that social network communications and transactions are the most important factors in shaping voting behavior in Japan.[2]

One reason for this emphasis on social network explanations is the relatively minor role that many other kinds of campaign practices widely employed in the United States play in the Japanese setting. For example, the media play a very limited role in influencing Japanese voting decisions owing to strict election laws that forbid all candidates from buying any advertising in newspapers or on television or radio. Only national candidates are allowed any access to the media, and that is strictly regulated. In the case of television, national candidates are now permitted three five-minute spots in which all the district's

2. Wakata's study is based on interviews with ninety-one municipal and prefectural assemblymen in Japan's Kansai area and includes a comparative American study based on forty-two California city councillors and county supervisors. See also Richardson, 1967b; Flanagan, 1968; Iga and Auerbach, 1977; and Allinson, 1979. Nobutaka Ike (1978) has gone so far as to argue that the social network model is the central paradigm that explains Japanese politics.

candidates are presented, one after another, in seated head-shots reading their statements without any visual aids. In addition, the slick campaign brochures, mailings, and door-to-door canvassing that play a large role in American campaigns are strictly prohibited (Curtis, 1983; Wakata, 1986).

Thus, appeals to the anonymous public are limited to a prescribed number of sound trucks, posters, and postcards, which are used primarily to gain name recognition. Indeed, the public is typically kept at arm's length from the formal campaign by regulations and practices that discourage volunteer participation. Most campaign workers are young students who are hired for pay on a part-time basis. While there are other means to contact the public—through side walk speeches, joint candidate meetings, and other gatherings—a candidate's efforts are not primarily directed at unattached floating voters, which even in some national election districts have been viewed as constituting no more than 20 percent of those who actually turn out to vote.[3] Rather, his major effort is directed at mobilizing social networks to appeal to voters through personally mediated ties.

The prominent role of social networks in Japanese election campaigns is attributed not only to the limited role that the media and other impersonal forms of communication are permitted to play but also to various cultural norms that govern social behavior. This has resulted in relatively weak party loyalties among the electorate and candidate-centered campaigns that stress personal ties and emotional appeals rather than ideology or major national issues. It would be useful, then, to review the linkages between cultural norms and campaign practices from the perspective of the four mechanisms of network influence introduced in the previous section. This review will demonstrate that social networks should be expected to play an even more pronounced role in Japanese than in European or American voting behavior.

First of all, there are several reasons why we might expect to find a stronger *assimilation effect* within the Japanese small group context. Japanese small groups tend to make heavier demands on their members and enforce higher levels of conformity than are typically found in Western countries. Doi's discussion (1973) of the high level of psychological and emotional dependency on the group and Lebra's emphasis (1976) on social preoccupation and interactional relativism as two of the primary distinguishing characteristics of the Japanese ethos all suggest a greater sensitivity to the views and feelings of other

3. Significantly, the term *floating voter* in Japan refers not to the absence of a party attachment but rather to the lack of a personally mediated tie to one of the candidates. Floating voters are those who cannot be reached through the established networks of interpersonal relationships that flow down and outward from the candidates, their core supporters, and supporting organizations (Curtis, 1971:105).

group members and a greater desire for group acceptance. Other analyses of Japanese culture focus on its *holistic* dimension and the great importance placed on maintaining group solidarity, avoiding conflict, and presenting a single unified voice to the outside world (Richardson and Flanagan, 1984).

In addition to these cultural inducements for greater group attitudinal conformity, other characteristics of Japanese social networks also promote homogeneity. For example, while Japanese are more likely that Americans to be members of at least one organization, they tend to be involved in a narrower range of associational memberships (Verba and Nie, 1972:176; Ikeuchi, 1974:439–65). Moreover, as Nakane (1970:21) argues, no matter how many group affiliations a Japanese citizen has, he is likely to view one of those as primary, and hence "a single loyalty stands uppermost and firm." Other memberships, then, tend to be viewed as secondary or they involve similar types of groups that are likely to share a common political outlook.

Added to this picture is the fact that social networks in Japan are more stable and enduring because personal ties, once established, tend to be cultivated and maintained over one's lifetime. These network ties are further stabilized by the Japanese lifetime employment system, which reduces occupational mobility. In addition, residential mobility, although rising substantially in urban centers over the postwar period, is still remarkably low. Our 1976 survey found that 25 percent of the respondents had lived in their present residences for their entire lives, and 53 percent had done so for sixteen years or more. All of the above suggests a higher level of consistency or crystallization in network influence communications and a greater homogeneity of attitudes within Japanese small groups. Assimilation effects, therefore, should be stronger in the Japanese case.

Given the emphasis on loyalty to one's group in Japanese culture, we might expect to find a strong *reference group effect* as well. That is, even in groups in which politics are not typically discussed, group membership may serve as the basis of voting choice. In Japan, all kinds of groups that are organized for nonpolitical purposes—religious groups, sports and recreational groups, PTA or retailers associations, and so forth—are frequently mobilized to deliver their vote for a particular candidate.

In rural areas, the most important of these groups is still the hamlet association (*burakukai*). The thirty to one hundred households that live in these close-knit, tightly bounded communities display a strong sense of belonging. In the local assembly elections, a candidate is typically recruited from among the community's leadership; if the hamlet is too small to elect its own representative, a joint candidate is put up with another nearby hamlet. These election campaigns often take on the character of a village festival, in which the campaign headquarters becomes the site for social gatherings, with food and drink served (Dore, 1978). Wakata (1986) reports that even today, with the hamlet's prestige on the line, the community leadership is typically able to deliver 60 to 80 percent of the vote for their candidate. Moreover, Wakata finds that the major cause of defections to other candidates is the presence of more pressing personalistic ties based on kinship or other bonds.

This pattern of community-based, bloc voting has been empirically demonstrated using aggregate voting returns in a number of studies (Curtis, 1971:88–90; Flanagan, 1980b:153–68). What these studies have found is that the more rural and more local the election, the greater the tendency for each candidate's vote to be highly concentrated within a very small geographical section of his election district. As one moves up to the prefectural and national assembly elections in these rural districts, the levels of concentration weaken slightly, but it is still clear that community is the primary reference group in voting decisions.

In more urban areas, residential communities are often more heterogeneous and transient, and hence community solidarity is not as high. Nevertheless, Allinson (1979:201) reports that even in these large metropolitan settings the neighborhood associations often play an important role in voting decisions, but not so much through official endorsements of candidates as by creating "a climate of social harmony characterized by informality, reciprocity, and a sense of common purpose." In this way, the residential community continues to serve as an important reference group in urban settings.

On the other hand, the more urbanized the residential environment, the less bounded it is likely to be and the greater the competition the neighborhood association faces from other sources of group loyalty. For this reason, the geographical concentration of the vote, while still high in many urban and suburban local elections, begins to dissipate in higher-level elections. Takeshi Ishida (1961) has argued that all kinds of organizations and institutions in Japanese society are based on the village community model, which therefore stress diffuse, enduring, face-to-face relationships and group solidarity and loyalty. Given the Japanese lifetime employment system, the work-place community can become an individual's primary reference group and the company and its union an important vehicle of vote mobilization. Particularly in the private sector, the company's management and union are often extremely close. For example, all blue- and white-collar employees in a factory, including lower management levels, typically belong to the same union; these unions have diffuse functions that include social and recreational activities; many company executives begin their careers in union staff positions; and unions have on occasion been reported to behave more like company enforcers than representatives of worker grievances.

A number of studies have shown that the work place or the union can deliver blocs of votes in much the same way as the rural hamlet. What is particularly interesting about Wakata's report (1986) is his finding that it is the work-place community, not a broader union identification, that is the effective mobilizer. For example, in the local at-large elections, the union's district federation will often divide its support among a number of candidates by allotting certain locals to certain candidates. If a candidate is a union official in a particular local or a present or former employee of a particular company he can expect those workers' full support. Among the other union locals allocated to the candidate, however, where he is not known and has no personal ties, the workers are likely to be indifferent to the union's call for support. In contrast, the union candidate's "home company" support often extends beyond his company to its *shitauke* companies. In these smaller companies that have subcontracts with the main company, both management and workers will frequently support whole heartedly the candidate even though these smaller companies are typically not unionized. Wakata (1986:59) concludes, "even mobilization of union votes is contingent on the availability of chains of personal connections for the candidate."

In Japan, then, an individual is likely to have at least one reference group identification that has special meaning for him. Regardless of whether this is a community, company, union, religious group, or some other identification, and despite the fact that politics may rarely if ever come up as a topic of discussion within the group, loyalty to the group may be harnessed to deliver the vote to a particular candidate.

There are also good reasons to expect that *opinion leader effects* would be more strongly felt in Japan than in the West. One reason for this expectation stems from Nakane's argument (1970) that Japan has a vertical society that lays stress on hierarchic relations between people in different status positions. Yet I doubt that hierarchy and deference explain this effect today, except perhaps in certain rural areas. Rather, what enhances the opinion leader effect in Japan has more to do with the fact that Japan is still pervasively a personalistic society. This means that there is a heavy emphasis on doing things through known people, and thus chains of face-to-face personal connections play an extremely important role in the average citizen's daily life. For this reason, Japanese are taught from an early age the importance of using every opportunity to cultivate personal ties and, once established, to maintain them across their lifetime— beginning with their first kindergarten class reunion six months after graduation. As a result, we find in Japan extensive and complex hierarchic and lateral communication networks that broaden the reach of interpersonal messages.

In the towns and villages in the more rural areas, local influentials play the opinion leader role in initiating candidate support messages aimed at mobilizing the neighborhood vote. These influentials typically include present and former officers of the neighborhood or hamlet associations and of other community groups such as the agricultural cooperatives, young men's associations, and fire-fighters' associations. Like their rural counterparts, the neighborhood associations in suburban areas, representing three hundred to three thousand "new town" residents, serve as the primary basis of vote mobilization. In the suburban case, however, where the male breadwinners usually commute long hours to their jobs and often return home late at night, it is mostly middle-age housewives and a few retired elderly men who perform the opinion leader role. These energetic housewives, who are concerned about community welfare and development issues, utilize their webs of personal ties to circulate the word about what their candidate has done or will do for their community (Wakata, 1986).

What enhances the power of the opinion leader effect in the Japanese case is that personal ties are consciously, not casually, activated to spread the message about a particular candidate. Moreover, in these chains of personal connections, the individual often plays a dual role, first as opinion receiver and then as opinion leader, transmitting the message on to others. Organizations often provide a framework for this endeavor. But the target of this activity is not simply the organization's membership but, through the members, the community itself. For example, a small factory and its union with two hundred employees may be expected to deliver six hundred votes through the employees' families and other personal ties. If the organization is large, more formalized procedures may be employed to line up the vote. These might include personally contacting each member to assess how secure his vote is and how many additional votes outside the organization he can deliver, or asking the member to sign a document pledging his support to the candidate in an effort to heighten his sense of obligation to vote for the organization's choice. If the organization is small and represents a special interest, such as small businessmen, a formal organizational endorsement may not be even sought or desired by the candidate (Wakata, 1986:52–53; Allinson, 1979:195). What is desired is the active participation of the organization's influential leaders and other members in soliciting support for the candidate through their individual networks of personal connections.

Curtis (1971:189–93) provides us with a classic illustration of just how effective these efforts can be in some cases. The dental association in a candidate's hometown, a medium-sized city, decided to throw its whole-hearted support behind the candidate's bid to gain a seat in the National Diet, because he was a "local boy" and had served as their official "advisor" and worked for their interests while he was in the prefectural assembly. Of the sixty-three dentists in the association, only five were permitted to abstain from actively campaigning for the candidate because they were either sick or had relatives that were running against him. Because dentists are geographically dispersed throughout the city and hold positions of respect in their local communities, they were in a good position to play the opinion leader role. In each of the city's eleven school districts, one of the dentists was designated as campaign manager and given a quota of votes to collect, which he was to divide among the other dentists in his district. During the campaign, each district manager had to meet regularly with the dental association's election committee to report on the progress of his team members and provide detailed explanations if any dentist in his district was failing to keep pace. Through enlisting laboratory workers and dental supply dealers and contacting their many clients and other personal connections in their districts, these fifty-eight dentists were able to collect nearly sixteen thousand promised votes for their candidate.

Finally, there are at least two reasons to expect that the *mobilization effect* of social networks would be stronger in Japan than in the United States. The first concerns the apolitical type of voter who has so little interest and knowledge about politics that he lacks the internal resources to make a considered voting choice. These voters typically cannot be influenced by information regarding a candidate's issue positions, ideological leanings, or even party label. Rather, these voters are likely to make their voting decisions based on a favorable image they have of the candidate.

Some may acquire this favorable image as a result of their personal exposure to the candidate through television and other media. As we have noted, however, such opportunities are rather limited in Japan. Thus, it is more likely that the apolitical Japanese voter develops a personally mediated image of the candidate through messages received from trusted acquaintances who assure him that candidate *A* is a good man and the right person for "people like us" to support.

In the United States, most apolitical voters are unlikely to vote, even if they do receive such personally mediated images of one or more candidates. In Japan, however, integration into community or other group networks can transform the voting act into a social obligation. Thus, Japanese social networks will in many cases supply an apolitical voter not only with name recognition and a favorable image for a particular candidate but also with a strong motivation to vote. Given the high levels of educational attainment and media saturation in Japan, we should not expect to find that apolitical voters constitute a larger share of the Japanese than the American electorate, except perhaps among women who did not receive the right to vote until 1947 and have been traditionally discouraged from taking an active interest in politics (Pharr, 1981). It can be argued, however, that more of these apolitical voters actually turn out to vote in Japan.

The second reason that social networks can be expected to exert a stronger mobilization effect in Japan is associated with the cultural meaning of voting in Japan. Instead of being an individual expression of political preference, the voting act in many cases may represent the repayment of a debt. Japan is still largely a personalistic society that draws the individual into interdependent webs of personal obligation. There is a strong cultural emphasis on reciprocity and the repayment of all debts incurred through the receipt of some gift or favor, no matter how small. This provides the politician with the opportunity to instill a sense of obligation among his constituents by performing a host of small favors.

Many voters, for their part, still seek a personalistic relationship with the candidate. There is a great deal of discussion in the literature revolving around such concepts as *amae,* dependency, and the psychological motivations found in Japanese culture for seeking out benefactors to attach oneself to in a kind of senior-junior or patron-client relationship.[4] We can explain this phenomenon on purely instrumental grounds, however. Japan continues to be a highly particularistic society that operates on the basis of personalistic exchanges. As a result, Japanese continue to feel that, whether one is seeking a business deal or assistance from a government office, the meeting will go much better if it is preceded by a letter of introduction or call from a mutual acquaintance. For example, in our JABISS study, 58 percent of the respondents agreed and only 13 percent disagreed with the statement, "When one lacks personal connections, one is greatly handicapped, either in finding a job or doing business." Also, 51 percent agreed and 17 percent disagreed with the statement, "When one goes to request something from a national or local government office, things go well if a Dietman or prefectural or municipal assemblyman serves as an intermediary." Apparently many of those in the middle, "depends on the circumstances," category on these two items also believe in the efficacy of personal ties.[5]

4. *Amae* refers to childhood socialization patterns thought to instill a preference for passive, dependent relationships with benevolent superiors, as discussed in Doi, 1973, and Nakane, 1970. In fact, Ike (1972) has labeled Japan a "patron-client democracy" but, as noted below, the term *patron-client relationships* should only be applied to these kinds of hierarchical ties in Japan if the term is broadened beyond that meaning typically assigned to it in Third World contexts.

5. This conclusion is suggested by findings from an earlier study where it was shown that the largest proportion of those feeling that they could contact an official directly without an intermediary were rural inhabitants living in small communities where direct personal ties to local officials were well developed (Ikeuchi, 1974:320–32; Richardson and Flanagan, 1984:179–81). In other words, in some situations where direct personal connections are already well established, intermediaries are not necessary.

In postwar Japan the politician has displaced the traditional local notables and leading families and become the principal intermediary in citizen dealings with the bureaucracy. While Americans, especially middle-class Americans, typically bring their requests directly to government agencies through well-established channels, such a direct approach in Japan is often ineffective. For example, Wakata (1986:82–83) reports an example of a president of a neighborhood association who met with repeated frustration in getting the city administrators to respond to his community's requests. Once he was elected to the city assembly, however, his requests on behalf of his community to these same city bureaucrats suddenly received a great deal of respect and attention.

Japan's political culture, then, has institutionalized and protected the politician's role of go-between. On major national and local issues, the policy making process in Japan is typically depicted as being dominated by the executive and bureaucracy, allowing the legislator only a weak role. Instead, it is in the area of constituency service requests, many of which are handled by purely bureaucratic or other channels in the United States, that the legislator's principal activities lie. Indeed, it often appears that the major role of the Diet and Assembly representatives is one of bestowing benefits on their constituents (*jimoto rieki*) in the form of personal favors and improved government services within their districts. According to some accounts, Japanese politicians typically devote 80 percent of their time to such activities.[6]

While constituent service and pork-barreling activities are also basic to the success of American politicians, Wakata's comparative study of Kansai and California politicians reveals a number of important ways in which these activities differ between the two settings.[7] First, casework activities in Japan are more personal and diffuse in nature and are not limited to simply running interference with government administrators. Instead, casework activities extend well beyond the realm of government to include playing the role of mediator in settling conflicts among neighbors in the politician's community (conflicts over noise, drainage, accident compensation, and the like) and assisting constituents with purely personal matters (finding jobs, arranging marriages, securing loans, settling marital disputes, attending funerals, and so forth).

Second, Japanese politicians are much more active than their American counterparts in soliciting personal and community requests, but typically do so within a more limited segment of their districts. Rather than try to blanket the entire electoral district with networks of personal ties, the politician will carve

6. Wakata, 1986:69. One LDP prefectural assemblyman has been quoted as saying, "The most important work of the politician is to bring governmental funds back to his *jimoto* (home area). This is all the politician is elected for" (Naganuma, 1983:18).

7. The following two pages draw extensively on Wakata's findings (1986:69–94).

out a territory, usually centering on his residential area and other group ties, such as a particular union or enterprise association. Within that territory, he will actively solicit constituent service requests. These services are perhaps most aggressively sought by municipal assemblymen in urban areas, who advertise their "consultation services" on neighborhood billboards, make themselves available twenty-four hours a day, and even visit their constituents door-to-door to "take orders" (Wakata, 1986:70–71). The Japanese politician can afford to limit these activities to a more or less contained portion of his constituency, because most municipal, prefectural, and national assembly elections are conducted in multimember or at-large districts. Within this territory, the representative will attempt to monopolize constituency service work, while at the same time he adheres to a gentlemen's agreement not to raid the territory of other politicians with such activities, thereby reducing conflict within as well as among the parties. Naturally the purpose of all these energetic service activities is to instill a sense of obligation on the part of the beneficiaries to vote for the politician. Indeed, this obligation is often formalized by enrolling into the politician's *koenkai* (supporters' association) all those who have received some benefit through his good offices.

Third, the Japanese politician is able to extend these personalistic networks that tie the voter to him well beyond his own reach. Even in the United States, there are always some voters who support a candidate purely because he is a friend or has done some favor for them in the past. Typically, however, there are not enough of these voters to make a difference. In Japan, the bonds of emotion and obligation reach much further than the politician's own ability to cultivate face-to-face relationships, through the use of middlemen. On the local level, the leaders of the neighborhood associations often serve as middlemen, soliciting and forwarding requests to the politician. Here the neighborhood association official is playing the opinion leader role by propagandizing the successes of the assemblyman on behalf of one or another family in the community. These activities take place on a daily basis throughout the year, but it is at election time that the middlemen will call in these obligations by reminding the residents of past favors received.

On the national level, the middlemen are typically local officials who already possess their own personal followings—mayors, municipal and prefectural assemblymen, heads of agricultural cooperatives or chambers of commerce, and so forth (Curtis, 1971:43). In these cases, support may be mobilized for the Dietman not because of any favor he has done for the voter but because of a favor the middleman has done. It is a well-established cultural norm in Japanese society that one can meet one's obligation to A by doing a favor for B at A's request. There is also a more direct instrumental benefit that underlies these indirect ties to the Diet representative. The voter recognizes that his municipal and prefectural representatives are able to assist him effectively with his community and personal problems because of their ties to the sources of power from above. Thus, the Dietman played a role, albeit an indirect one, in the services his local assemblyman performed, and it is in the interests of the voter to keep these vertical power relationships functioning by supporting the Diet candidate that his local assemblyman endorses. In this way, the national candidate is able to gather the "hard vote" of local politicians and thereby extend the bonds of obligation beyond what he can directly cultivate through his own constituency service activities.[8]

The fourth and final way in which constituency service activities differ between Japan and the United States is in the interpretation of the transaction that is taking place. In both countries these activities have an instrumental basis—the representative's services are exchanged for voter support. In the Japanese case, however, the instrumental aspects of the transaction are hidden behind a thick emotional veneer. In any dyadic relationship, the Japanese is not seeking fairness or justice in any universalistic sense, but rather assurances that the other understands the special circumstances of his situation. A relationship on a personal level is always preferred because it is in the context of a warm, family-type relationship that both parties are induced to bend the rules in the other's favor. In the granting of these special exceptions and indulgences, the emotional bond tying the parties together is strengthened. In turn, a stronger emotional bond increases the expectation that larger favors will be performed in the future. In Japan, then, constituency service is viewed not as a responsibility of office but as a personal favor. By granting these personal favors, the politician creates an emotional tie with the voter and instills a sense of obligation.[9]

These four characteristics of constituency service work in Japan—the diffuse, personalistic nature of the services done; the tendency toward exclusive monopolies on these activities within defined territories; the role of middlemen; and the emotional interpretation placed on these transactions—make them sound a lot like the kinds of patron-client relationships typically found in Third

8. The concept of the "hard vote" (*koteihyo*) is in common parlance among both politicians and academics alike; it is defined by Curtis (1971:38) as the "vote that goes consistently and repeatedly to a particular person as a consequence of personal ties." Curtis (48–49) also cites estimates that one-half to one-fifth of the vote received in local elections by municipal or prefectural assemblymen is sufficiently securely tied to them to be successfully transferred to a Diet candidate at these local politicians' request.

9. Austin, 1975:18–75; Richardson and Flanagan, 1984:117–92, Wakata, 1986: 69–94. Wakata identifies a telling contrast in the conduct of casework in Kansai and California that results from this difference in meaning attached to the activity. In California, casework is actually handled by the representative's staff, while the Japanese representative does the work himself and attempts to maximize face-to-face contact in the process.

World countries. While the latter are also based on personalistic cultural norms, the Japanese transactions lack the intimidating and exploitative dimensions found in the Third World cases. Furthermore, in the Japanese case the patron and client are separated more by differences in role definitions conferred by elective office rather than by great hierarchical distinctions in social status. Moreover, the Japanese voter is free to seek a new patron if disappointed with the performance of the incumbent, and indeed many communities play an important role in selecting who they want to run for office to represent their locality. Finally, in the Japanese case, as we have noted, the initiative for performing a specific service activity often comes from the patron seeking to create a bond of obligation rather than from the client who benefits from the service.

The important point to note about these personalistic ties between candidate and voter is that they can overwhelm the political predispositions of the voter. Allinson (1979) offers many examples of voting that is based more on affective bonds than partisan preferences. For example, an LDP identifier may vote for a progressive governor because the governor's family used to live in his area and shop at his father's store. Or a Socialist identifier may support the incumbent conservative mayor because of the cultural and recreational center he built in her neighborhood for her children to use. Or a conservative supporter may vote for a Democratic Socialist municipal assemblyman because his wife shops in the corner store where they offer discounts to anyone who joins that assemblyman's koenkai.

Naturally, it is in local elections that these obligation-induced mobilization effects have their greatest impact. This is because 1) voters are more likely to have some sort of personal tie to a local rather than a national candidate; 2) most local candidates, while having clear partisan ties, choose to run as independents; and 3) even those running under a party label tend to see their role as one of representing a particular geographical territory within their districts rather than a particular class or interest.

Nevertheless, evidence of a substantial mobilization effect can be seen in national elections as well. The ability of the fifty-eight dentists mentioned above to line up sixteen thousand promised votes for a Diet candidate undoubtedly had something to do with the political content of their message, which reportedly stressed the dual themes of hometown boy and the need for new blood in the LDP in the wake of a corruption scandal (Curtis, 1971:191). But undoubtedly many of these votes were promised out of a sense of personal obligation to the dentist who was making the request. We also find socialist and communist candidates tapping the same kinds of emotional bonds to line up support in unlikely quarters. For example, socialist Diet candidates are typically able to utilize hometown neighborhood and classmate ties to build personal support organizations around small retailers and other businessmen who would otherwise support the conservatives. Even the Communist Party has been able to build strong support among small businessmen in urban areas because of the services its Democratic Merchants and Manufacturers Associations provide these businessmen in tax, licensing, and other matters and the sense of obligation those services create.

To sum up, this review of Japanese political culture and campaign practices argues strongly for the importance of social network explanations of voting behavior in that cultural setting. As noted, there are good reasons for believing that all four of the social network mechanisms for influencing voting behavior—assimilation, reference group, opinion leader, and mobilization effects—will be more strongly felt in the Japanese electoral context.

■ An Analysis of the Mechanisms of Social Network Influence

The remainder of this chapter will turn to an analysis of survey data to determine what evidence can be found through a survey research methodology to demonstrate the effects of one or another of the social network mechanisms of influence that have been identified. It should be noted, however, that if the survey method tends to obscure the effects of social networks, participant observation of election campaigns tends to exaggerate their influence. Observing the campaign from the candidate's perspective overemphasizes the behavior of those firmly enmeshed in a web of mutual obligation and ignores those voters that lie beyond the reach of its snares. Also, such analyses are flawed by a short-term perspective that deemphasizes the role that assimilation and reference group effects play in developing the partisan preferences, political attitudes, or group loyalties that condition the voter's receptivity to opinion leader and mobilization effects.

In chapter 9 below, Bradley Richardson analyzes in vivid detail the extent of individual and group communications in election campaigns designed to mobilize and persuade voters on behalf of a particular candidate. He introduces the term "influence communications" to include both informal face-to-face communications as well as the more formal organizational communications that take the form of candidate recommendations and endorsements. As Richardson demonstrates, social networks exercise a significant short-term influence on vote choice by communicating these candidate specific messages. Since chapter 9 reports the evidence on the short-term effects of social networks on influencing vote choice, our analyses of opinion leader and mobilization effects here will be limited to demonstrating the existence of the opinion leader and mobilized voter roles and profiling the characteristics of the respondents that fall into each of these two categories. This will be accomplished by analyzing the face-to-face interpersonal communications that took place during the 1976 election campaign and identifying some of the attributes of the participants on both sides of those exchanges. In the case of the long-term assimilation and reference group effects, direct and indirect evidence will be presented to demonstrate the role these influences play in conditioning vote choice.

The Opinion Leaders

While Japanese society is very densely organized, Japanese groups are not highly politicized. Indeed, politics are not frequently discussed in many Japanese groups, and many Japanese do not exhibit a high degree of psychological involvement in politics (Ikeuchi, 1974; Flanagan, 1978). If Japanese social networks are to perform a role in influencing political attitudes and behaviors, much of the responsibility for originating influence communications is likely to fall to a relatively small number of "opinion leaders" within associational settings.

It is quite apparent that interpersonal influence communications are extremely widespread in Japanese election campaigns. In all, 47 percent of the people surveyed in the JABISS study report receiving at least one request to vote for a particular candidate, while 14 percent say they made at least one vote request to someone else. As we would expect, there are far fewer askers than asked. Moreover, the askers are on the whole very active, with 44 percent of them asking four or more voters for their support. Few respondents report receiving that many requests, but still 34 percent of the entire sample reported receiving two or more requests.

The findings of a concentration of vote requesting activity among a relatively small segment of the sample suggests that we may to some extent be identifying the political opinion leaders within Japanese associational contexts. Particularly in the case of that 6 percent of the sample who were active canvassers, we might expect to find the attributes that we associate with the opinion leader role. In order to test this hypothesis, the sample was divided into four categories—active canvassers (making four or more requests), occasional canvassers (one to three requests), those who received but did not make any requests, and those who were not personally contacted. Tables 4.1 and 4.2 provide an analysis of the differences among these four groups on a number of demographic and attitudinal variables. The reported numbers are the mean z-scores for each of the four categories of respondents on each attribute variable. Standardizing the attribute or criterion variables provides an easy way to interpret the direction and magnitude of the deviations of each group from the sample mean of zero on any particular variable.[10]

My discussion of table 4.1 focuses on the demographic differences between the canvassers and the contacted to determine whether or not these exchanges continue to flow today primarily through vertical channels. In the prewar period local notables and high-status families reportedly engineered much of the vote mobilization activity. Table 4.1, however, shows little evidence of marked status differences between the askers and the asked. We note that the canvassers are somewhat older than those being contacted, have somewhat higher incomes, and are substantially more likely to be male. On the other hand, there are no significant differences in the social status between those requesting and those being requested, and the education of the canvassers is, if anything, slightly lower than that of those receiving their requests. On balance, then, canvassers are somewhat older and more well-to-do than those they are contacting, but one would have to conclude that horizontal communications are more prevalent than vertical ones, except perhaps in some of the more traditional community settings.[11]

What distinguishes the opinion leader in Japanese society today, therefore, is not his status in society but the role he performs for his community. Opinion leaders would be those in one's neighborhood, social or work-related organization, or informal circle of friends who are more knowledgeable about politics and more interested and active in it. They are more likely to bring political topics into their conversations with friends and neighbors and, because of their

10. In both tables 4.1 and 4.2, and also in tables 4.4 and 4.5 below, all the dependent or criterion variables were standardized across all their nonmissing cases with means equal to zero and standard deviations of one. Thus, if we find that on a particular variable one category of respondents is .50 and another −.50, that would indicate a very high level of polar differences between the two groups, standing a full standard deviation apart from each other on that variable.

11. As noted in our previous discussion of campaign practices, it appears that in the rural areas older, higher-status males in community leadership positions continue to play an important role in activating social networks to request votes. Many of the actual requesters differ little from their neighbors, however, except in their levels of network involvement and perhaps also in their interest in politics. Also, since the community leaders are no longer drawn from the families of the traditional feudal lords, great status differences no longer separate community leaders from nonleaders. Thus, among the rural counties (*gumbu*) in our sample, the frequency of requesting others' votes was only weakly correlated with occupational status ($r = .09$) and education ($r = .06$). There is only a slight tendency, then, for requests to still flow down vertical channels of influence, even in the rural areas. In the urban areas, because much of the requesting activity often falls to housewives and long-term residents (whose status may be considerably lower than the newcomers—e.g., farmers and small retailers versus white collar professionals), any hint of vertical channels of influence disappears. Thus, in cities of 100,000 or larger the correlations between requesting votes and both status and education are weakly negative ($-.03$ and $-.09$, respectively).

Table 4.1 Demographic Profiles of Canvassers, the Contacted, and Noncontacted

	Actively Canvassed	Occasionally Canvassed	Received Requests	Received No Requests	Eta
Age	.18	.19	−.11	.10	.11
Income	.11	.22	−.03	−.06	.08
Sex (male)	.36	.10	−.07	−.07	.11
Occupational status	−.01	−.06	.04	−.02	[.03]
Education	−.06	−.20	.04	−.07	.07
Urbanization	−.14	−.04	.09	−.17	.12
N of cases	(93)	(119)	(601)	(723)	
Percent	6	8	39	47	

Note: All reported eta are significant at the .05 level, except the one in brackets. Each variable was standardized on all of its nonmissing cases. In some cases the reported group mean scores across a variable do not quite average to zero because of missing cases associated with the made and received requests variables used to construct the group types.

greater knowledge and more firmly held views, to play a larger role in forming political opinions and preferences within small, informal groups.

Table 4.2 demonstrates that the active canvassers possess many of the attributes associated with the opinion leader role. Across all four of the reported network involvement scales,[12] those receiving requests do not deviate significantly from the sample mean. In contrast, the active canvassers score highly on all four and, in particular, on the organization involvement and candidate

12. The four social network involvement scales are all additive scales. The composition of the first of these, community integration, has been introduced above. The informal associations involvement scale is composed of three items, measuring the number of intimate friends the respondent has in his neighborhood, the number in his work place, and his frequency of chatting with family, friends, neighbors, relatives, and colleagues. The formal organizations involvement scale measures the respondent's number of memberships and level of activity in the following six types of nonareal organizations (i.e., those not limited to one's immediate neighborhood): business or professional organizations, unions, religious associations, PTA, sports or hobby groups, and classmates or study groups. These first three scales were also merged into the combined social network involvement scale introduced at several points in the text. The fourth scale reported in table 4.2 is the candidate networks involvement scale, which taps whether there was a candidate running 1) whose supporters' association (*koenkai*) the respondent belonged to; 2) who had done some special favor for the respondent or some member of his family, such as helping someone get a job or gain admission to a school; 3) who had sent a postcard to the respondent or a member of his family; 4) who had done something for the people of the respondent's local area such as getting roads paved or acquiring government grants; or 5) who had an especially deep relationship with the respondent's local area.

Table 4.2 Levels of Network and Psychological Involvement, System Support, and Partisanship of Canvassers, the Contacted, and Noncontacted

	Actively Canvassed	Occasionally Canvassed	Received Requests	Received No Requests	Eta
Network involvement					
Community integration	.37	.20	−.03	.04	.10
Informal associations	.66	.31	.08	−.13	.22
Formal organizations	.74	.27	.05	−.18	.23
Candidate networks	1.08	.43	.02	−.24	.34
Psychological involvement in politics					
Political interest	1.03	.57	.05	−.27	.35
Knowledge	.85	.59	.08	−.26	.32
Discussion	.94	.51	.10	−.24	.32
Media exposure	.77	.28	.04	−.17	.24
Efficacy	.63	.25	−.10	−.08	.20
System support					
System trust	.41	.18	−.06	.02	.12
Institutional support	.40	.21	.00	−.06	.12
Strength of partisanship	.86	.56	−.04	−.13	.27
N of Cases	(93)	(119)	(601)	(723)	
Percent	6	8	39	47	

Note: All reported eta are significant at the .05 level. Each variable was standardized on all of its nonmissing cases. In some cases the reported group mean scores across a variable do not quite average to zero because of missing cases associated with the made and received requests variables used to construct the group types.

networks scales lie three-quarters to a full standard deviation above the sample mean. Of course, we would expect active canvassers to be closely tied into candidate networks, and in fact 60 percent of them reported being members of a candidate's support association and 63 percent said they attended a candidate report meeting or public address, figures that are three to four times the sample mean.[13] The active canvassers are also three-quarters to a full standard deviation above the mean in terms of their interest in politics, their level of political

13. In addition, 7 percent reported that one of the candidates had done some special favor for themselves or their families, a small number but five to six times as high as the sample mean.

knowledge, and their frequency of discussing politics and following politics in the media. They also score vastly higher on a political efficacy scale than those receiving their requests. Finally, they exhibit substantially higher levels of system trust and institutional support[14] and are much stronger partisans. Indeed, 48 percent of the active canvassers were strong partisans compared to only 9 percent of those contacted.

There is a second way in which we might try to isolate the opinion leaders. The JABISS respondents who reported discussing politics with family, friends, neighbors, or work colleagues were also asked if they mainly talked, listened, or did both during these discussions in each of the different contexts. From these questions a scale of passive, mixed, and active discussants was constructed. Without repeating the same kind of analysis presented in tables 4.1 and 4.2, I can report that the same general pattern of relationships was found to hold, although in some cases the differences were not quite as dramatic. Thus, the active discussants tend to be significantly older, more often male, more strongly integrated into all four kinds of social networks, and higher in psychological involvement in politics, system support, and strength of partisanship than the mixed or passive discussants. Here we find, for example, that 38 percent of the active discussants are strong partisans, compared to 18 percent of the mixed discussants and 13 percent of the passive discussants.

In table 4.3, a fourth category of those who rarely or never discuss politics is added and the percentage distributions reported across several variables not included in the previous tables. Again, the active discussant category is a rather elite one, comprising only 6 percent of the sample. Significantly, 61 percent of those who participate in political discussions categorize themselves as playing only a passive, listening role in these conversations. The table shows that the active discussants are much more likely to follow politics regularly between elections and to be most concerned about the larger national and international issues rather than purely local, parochial matters. They also exhibit more fixed or stable political attitudes and somewhat higher levels of civic responsibility.[15]

There are several further points that can be made about the opinion leader role by referring back to these last two tables. Table 4.2 presents some evidence

14. The system trust scale was composed of five items measuring the respondent's pride in the Japanese political system, trust in national politics, confidence that problems that cause distrust can be improved, belief that politics work on behalf of all the people, not just a few big interests, and the ease with which one could find a necessary intermediary in contacting a government official. The institutional support scale was comprised of three items stating respectively that parties, elections, and the National Diet "make it possible for people's voices to be heard in politics."

15. Those scoring high on the civic responsibility scale disagreed with each of two items, the first stating that it was useless to vote if your party or candidate doesn't have a chance to win, and the second that so many people vote that it doesn't matter if you vote or not.

Table 4.3 Political Interest, Attitude Stability, Civic Responsibility, and
Canvassing Activity by Discussion Role
(In Percentages)

	Discussion Role			
	Active Discussant	Mixed	Passive Discussant	Rarely or Never Discuss
Follow politics between elections "all the time"	42	26	18	8
More interested in national & international than local or prefectural politics	69	53	48	30
Changed political way of thinking due to Lockheed scandal	35	55	52	42
Stable party ID across survey panels	92	76	78	76
High scores on civic responsibility scale	58	52	47	36
Made one or more vote requests	31	24	16	4
N of Cases	(116)	(260)	(576)	(855)
Percent	6	14	32	47

of the chain effect discussed earlier, where the individual is first persuaded by an opinion leader and then assumes the role of opinion leader in contacting others. The active canvassers may be viewed as the candidate's core supporters, while the occasional canvassers lie further from the centers of candidate networks and play an auxiliary role in passing on messages that have been relayed to them by the core supporters. Indeed, a full 58 percent of the occasional canvassers report also receiving a request for their vote.[16]

Of course, not all the active canvassers are core supporters, and undoubtedly there are several echelons of support and activity even within the active canvasser classification. Nevertheless, the finding that levels of activity are related to levels of proximity to a candidate and integration into other social networks suggests a kind of ripple pattern in canvassing activity, emanating outward in all directions from core supporters to community opinion leaders to

16. This is only slightly higher than the 52 percent reported by active canvassers, but it may be more of a significant difference, in that more requests were received despite their substantially lower levels of network involvement and, hence, lower probability of coming in contact with an opinion leader soliciting their vote.

other friends and neighbors through chains of interpersonal relationships. The further down the chain, the lower the message receiver's levels of psychological and network involvement are likely to be and the lower the probability that the message will activate him to assume the opinion leader role in passing the recommendation on to others.

Second, we can also detect evidence in table 4.2 of an important opinion leader effect. Those not receiving any requests are substantially lower in psychological involvement than the contacted. It may well be that the opinion leader plays an important role in his conversations with others in stimulating their interest in the campaign and their attention to politics in the media and in increasing their political knowledge. To test for that possibility, the canvassers were excluded and a partial correlation, controlling for contaminating influences, was computed between the frequency of being contacted and a combined psychological involvement scale. Reviewing the differences between the contacted and uncontacted reported in the tables, the only variables that appear capable of accounting for a spurious relationship with psychological involvement are education, network involvement, and possibly urbanization. Whether we control singly or simultaneously for these three variables, however, the bivariate relationship is hardly attenuated, yielding a substantial third-order partial of .18 between frequency of being contacted and level of psychological involvement. Opinion leaders, then, not only persuade others to accept their preferences but also may stimulate political involvement.

Finally, we may view the active discussants in table 4.3 as potential opinion leaders who may or may not become activated to play that role in the context of a given election campaign. Whether they become activated may depend in part on their own level of psychological involvement. For example, if we further subdivide the table categories into high and low frequencies of discussion, we find that the frequent-active discussants come closer to our image of the opinion leader, with 47 percent strong partisans, 42 percent members of candidate support associations, and 40 percent requesting others' votes. Another way to look at this is to divide the active discussant category into the roughly one-third who canvassed for votes and the two-thirds who did not. If we average these two groups' mean z-scores across four of the five psychological involvement scales (excluding discussing politics), we find that the noncanvassing active discussants' average score was .20 while that for the canvassing active discussants was .96.

Some of these potential opinion leaders, therefore, may be much more highly motivated to get involved than others. Another factor that may affect participation is how well the individual's attributes suit him for that role. For example, if we look at the age, sex, occupational status, and education variables reported in the first table, the average group score across those four variables for the noncanvassing active discussants was .06, while it was .32 for their canvassing counterparts. Potential opinion leaders, then, are more likely to assume that role if their personal attributes equip them to be more comfortable and effective in its performance—that is, if they are older, male, and higher in education and occupational status.

There is also evidence to suggest that involvement in social networks draws the individual into the opinion leader role. For example, there is a very high correlation ($r = .35$) between the combined social network involvement index and frequency of discussing politics. In addition, canvassing active discussants score substantially higher on all four of the network involvement indexes than their noncanvassing equivalents. In particular, the group mean scores on the organizational involvement scale were .54 for the canvassers and $-.03$ for the noncanvassers. Particularly in the context of national elections, these formal organizations play an important role in structuring vote mobilization activities. Indeed, looking across the entire sample, only 7 percent of those falling in the bottom fifth in levels of organizational involvement asked anyone to vote for a particular candidate, compared to 27 percent in the top fifth.

There is evidence, then, to support the notion that opinion leaders can be found within most Japanese small groups and associational networks and that they play a role not only in transmitting partisan messages but also in increasing the political knowledge and interest of those with whom they come in contact. We can detect distinctions between potential and mobilized opinion leaders and different levels of activity among those assuming the opinion leader role. The greater their psychological involvement in politics, the more their personal attributes equip them to perform the opinion leader role effectively. On the other hand, the more closely they are tied into candidate and other associational networks, the more likely they are to become mobilized by the election campaign to assume the opinion leader role and the more active their efforts in that role are likely to be. Once activated, the influence of these opinion leaders can be felt through at least three of the four social network mechanisms discussed above. That is, the individual performing the opinion leader role may 1) persuade his listener of the superior policies or qualities of his candidate (opinion leader effects); 2) over an extended period of time, condition those with whom he regularly interacts to accept his political attitudes and partisan biases (assimilation effects); or 3) otherwise mobilize the support of those who cannot be reached through political arguments (mobilization effects).

The Mobilized Voter

The opinion leader is not the only type of voter that we can identify. Our discussion of mobilization effects suggested that there were two distinct types of voters who assumed the passive role in these kinds of influence communications. The first was the apolitical voter who lacked the internal resources to reach a voting decision on his own. The second was the personally obligated voter, who has a political predisposition but finds his own proclivities overwhelmed by bonds of affection or obligation to a candidate or one of the candidate's supporters. Actually, both types of mobilized voter are often motivated by the same kind of incentive—the vote is offered up as just one more exchange in the web of interpersonal obligations. What distinguishes these two types is that without the opinion leader's stimulation the personally obligated voter would have settled on another candidate, whereas the apolitical voter would simply have abstained.

One indirect indication that mobilization effects exert a substantial influence in Japanese elections is the sheer magnitude of vote requesting activity. Since requests from strangers are considered totally ineffective, a large proportion of the population is mobilized to make a relatively small number of requests from among their friends, neighbors, and other acquaintances. As reported above, 14 percent of the population was mobilized to canvass votes in the 1976 lower house election, and these personalistic influence communications are believed to be even more pervasive in local elections. Much of this vote requesting is done without the benefit of supporting arguments to show why a particular candidate is superior. Indeed, much of it would hardly qualify as a political discussion, except that the name of a candidate was mentioned. Rather, we find the core supporters of a candidate making endless rounds of visits during a campaign, not to argue their candidate's case but simply to show their faces to reinforce a sense of obligation to them personally and to use that sense of obligation to mobilize those contacted to support their candidate.

Once again, this chapter will not attempt to demonstrate the impact of these short-term mobilization effects on vote choice. Moreover, this analysis will not identify the personally obligated voters, although their numbers are thought to be quite large. Instead, my effort here will be to profile the apolitical voter and to demonstrate the effectiveness of social networks in getting apathetic voters to the polls.

Verba, Nie, and Kim (1978) begin their seven-nation study with a puzzle that asks why the correlation between an individual's socioeconomic resource level (an index of income and education) and overall level of political participation is so high in some countries (for example, in the United States, $r = .35$) and so low in others (in Japan, $r = .12$). They respond to this puzzle by developing a model that posits two paths to political involvement, one an individually based process and the other a group-based process. Individuals with high levels of education and income possess the internal resources and motivations to become involved in politics. Lacking those internal resources, however, an individual may still become active as a by-product of his membership in a group or organization, which provides the individual with the channels and motivations to participate.

What we are looking for here is evidence that network involvement can mobilize otherwise apolitical voters to turn out to the polls. This is most clear in the case of our index of community integration, because it is the only one of our three principal network involvement scales that has no significant relationship with the individual's socioeconomic resource level ($r = -.02$) and at the same time it has the highest correlation with voter turnout ($r = .25$). In table 4.4, the respondents' socioeconomic resource levels (SERL) and community integration were trichotomized into low, medium, and high categories, but the middle categories have been deleted to simplify the table. The reported numbers are the mean z-scores for each category of respondents on a scale of their frequency of turnout across four recent national and prefectural elections. We see very starkly that the individual's SERL by itself does not have any independent effect on voter turnout, whereas regardless of the voter's individual resources, community integration has the same strong effect in raising turnout levels above the sample mean of zero. We also note that the highest frequency of cases falls in the low SERL/high community integration classification.

Table 4.4   Standardized Group Mean Scores on Turnout Levels for Voter Categories Defined by Levels of Community Integration, Socioeconomic Resource Level, and Psychological Involvement

	Level of Community Integration		
	Low	High	Eta
Socioeconomic Resource Level:			
Low	−.34	.22	
	(127)	(167)	
			.28
High	−.39	.23	
	(104)	(116)	
Psychological involvement:			
Low	−.44	.26	
	(139)	(115)	
			.34
High	−.22	.34	
	(108)	(152)	

Note: The figures in parentheses are the N of cases on which the group mean was computed.

This finding suggests that SERL has no effect on turnout levels unless, perhaps, these personal resources stimulate higher levels of psychological involvement. That leads us to the second part of the table, where the same analysis is performed with the combined psychological involvement scale substituted for SERL. Surprisingly, we still find that the individual motivations for participation are overwhelmed by group processes. True, psychological involvement does exert some detectable, albeit small, influence. Nevertheless, those falling into the top third on psychological involvement but the bottom third on community integration are strongly inhibited from participating (−.22). In contrast, those scoring in the bottom third in psychological involvement but the top third in community integration are strongly mobilized to vote (.26).[17]

This evidence suggests that social networks play an enormous role in motivating people to vote and hence may even be capable of mobilizing completely apolitical voters. To further test this hypothesis, two indexes of voting turnout were constructed. The first is an index of *aware voters*. Aware voters are those who could name the party affiliation of the candidate they voted for across each of four recent elections. The index is a measure of the proportion of times the respondent said he voted and named a party as opposed to the proportion of times he reported abstaining from voting in the four elections. This index was significantly correlated both with an overall index of psychological involvement in politics (.19) and the combined index of social network involvement (.25).[18] So we find here a mix of reinforcing internal and external influences. Effective integration into social networks stimulates the individual's psychological involvement in politics, and both factors have independent effects on motivating the individual to vote.

A second type of voter, however, was excluded from the index of aware voters. These were the respondents who said that they had voted but had forgotten either which candidate they had voted for or which party the candidate was affiliated with in one or more of the four elections. There seems to be quite a substantial portion of *forgetful voters* in Japan. In fact, 30 percent of the sample reported forgetting their vote at least once across the four elections. In

17. Naturally, if we had looked at the other types of more active participation that Verba, Nie, and Kim investigate, we would have found that SERL and psychological involvement do play substantial roles in raising participation levels on these kinds of activities. See also Flanagan and Renten, 1981.

18. The combined index of social network involvement reported throughout the text includes the community integration, organizational involvement, and informal associations scales, the first three of the four network involvement scales described in note 12. The candidate network involvement scale was excluded to test for the political influences of networks that were not explicitly political.

addition, 17 percent reported abstaining in one or more elections. In all, 40 percent of the sample reported either forgetting or abstaining in one or more elections and hence were included in the index of forgetful voters. The index was constructed by subtracting the number of times a respondent reported abstaining from the number of times he reported forgetting his vote across the four elections.[19] This second index demonstrates that the forgetful voters are significantly lower in their levels of psychological involvement than even the nonvoters ($-.13$). Most forgetful voters admit to no party identification and are very low in political interest and other measures of psychological involvement. If they have less interest in politics than the nonvoters who in turn have much less interest than the aware voters, why do these forgetful voters bother to vote? The answer would seem to lie in their higher levels of social integration. The correlation between the forgetful voters index and the overall social network involvement index is .12, and that with the single community integration sub-dimension of that index is .23. This demonstrates that forgetful voters are substantially more likely to be involved in various kinds of community, informal, and formal group networks than the nonvoters.

Since these indexes included a number of mixed types, three more or less pure types were extracted from the sample to permit a comparison not only among all three classifications but also between these three types and the sample as a whole. For this purpose the aware voters were defined as those who named a party for which they had voted across all four elections. The forgetful voters are those who said they forgot who they voted for three or four times across the four elections, while the abstainers reported that they had not voted two to four times.

Table 4.5 reports the number of respondents who fell into each of the three categories and the mean levels for each category type across a number of indicators of psychological involvement and social integration. In order to facilitate the interpretation of these means, z-scores were again computed for all reported variables. As expected, the aware voters in table 4.5 are substantially above the sample mean on all five indicators of psychological involvement, while the abstainers fall significantly below the mean in all cases. The forgetful voters are not only below the mean in all cases but are roughly twice or more as far below the mean as the abstainers, especially on the dimensions of political interest, frequency of discussing politics, and political knowledge.

19. A small portion of the responses classified as "voted but forgot who for" were actually "Don't Know" (DK) responses. Overall 18.9 percent of these responses were DK responses while the remaining 81.1 percent were of the "forgot" type. For technical reasons it was difficult to remove these DK responses and so they were left in. Since the typical profile of the DK respondent—old, rural, female, low in education, and apolitical—is precisely the same as that of the forgetful voter, however, it is unlikely that these few DK responses had a distorting effect on the findings.

Table 4.5   Group Means for Three Categories of Voters Based on
Indicators of Psychological Involvement and Social Network
Involvement

	Aware Voters	Abstainers	Forgetful Voters	Eta
Psychological involvement				
Political interest	.25	−.40	−.78	.39
Frequency of discussing politics	.20	−.12	−.51	.26
Frequency of following politics in media	.20	−.33	−.47	.27
Political knowledge	.31	−.29	−.85	.42
Strength of partisanship	.32	−.35	−.64	.38
Social network involvement				
Community integration	.26	−.74	.00	.30
Frequency of interaction in informal association	.21	−.40	−.21	.23
Active participation in formal organizations	.17	−.39	−.32	.22
Involvement in Candidate networks	.24	−.58	−.52	.33
N of Cases	(766)	(95)	(160)	

Note: All reported eta are significant at the .01 level. See note 12 on the composition of the
Social Network Involvement Scales.

The picture changes when we turn to the social integration measures. Once
again the aware voters are significantly above the mean on all four indicators of
network involvement, and the abstainers are well below the mean. Now, however, the forgetful voters fall above the abstainers on all four of these network
measures. In the case of the measures of involvement in candidate networks and
active participation in formal organizations, the forgetful voters are only very
slightly and not significantly better integrated than the abstainers. This should
not surprise us. It has been shown elsewhere that high levels of involvement in
formal and informal group networks not only stimulate higher levels of political
participation but also exert a strong influence on enhancing one's level of
psychological involvement in politics (Flanagan and Renten, 1981). If the
forgetful voters exhibited high levels of network involvement, they would not
have such low levels of psychological involvement.

The forgetful voters, therefore, are not active members of their communities. They are not likely to be involved in formal organizations and certainly not in candidate networks. On the other hand, neither are they isolated

from more casual, less formal forms of social interaction. Thus, on the index of interaction in informal groups, we find that the forgetful voters are likely to have substantially more close friends and chat with them more frequently than the abstainers. And the differences are most striking on the community integration index. Despite their proclivity to inaction, the forgetful voters exhibit average levels on integration into their communities, while the abstainers lie three-quarters of a standard deviation below the mean. It would appear, then, that integration into informal community social networks provides the motivation that stimulates and the voting cues that enable these disinterested, apolitical respondents to vote.

In table 4.6, the distinctions between the aware and forgetful voters are further clarified by comparing them across an index based on the respondent's levels of political interest and knowledge and active versus passive role in political discussions.[20] The table reveals that nearly a quarter of the aware voters exhibit the characteristics of opinion leaders. That is, they have medium to high levels of political interest and knowledge and play mixed to active roles in political discussions. Slightly over half of the aware voters fall in the same medium to high levels of interest and knowledge but play only a passive role in political discussions or typically do not engage in such conversations at all. When we turn to the forgetful voters, however, the picture of disengagement from politics is almost complete. Nearly three-quarters of them not only are low in interest and knowledge but also play a passive to nonparticipatory role in political discussions.

By using the same breakdown procedure with demographic variables, we begin to get a clearer picture of who these forgetful voters are and how they differ from the abstainers. Abstainers tend to be younger than the sample mean ($-.58$), urban (.42), and highly educated (.33). In contrast, forgetful voters tend to live in more rural areas ($-.21$), to work in small enterprises ($-.23$), to be female ($-.30$), and to have low educations ($-.26$). Moreover, if we break the sample into occupational and family role groups, we find that 44 percent of the forgetful voters, compared to only 24 percent of the aware voters, are classified as housewives or family workers in blue-collar, white-collar, or professional households. Another 12 percent of the forgetful voters were unemployed.

20. The psychological involvement and discussion role variable was constructed by first dichotomizing interest and knowledge levels and combining those two variables into a single additive scale yielding three low, medium, and high categories with roughly equivalent numbers of respondents. This new variable was then dichotomized by combining the medium and high categories. The discussion role variable appearing in table 4.3 was also dichotomized by grouping the rare and passive discussants and the mixed role and active ones. These two-by-two categories were then combined into four discrete types, as shown in table 4.6.

Table 4.6 Association between Voting Types and the Respondent's Level of Psychological Involvement and Role Played in Political Discussions (In Percentages)

	Aware Voters	Forgetful Voters
Medium-high political interest & knowledge & mixed-active role in political discussions	23	5
Medium-high political interest & knowledge & passive-nonparticipant role in discussions	54	21
Low political interest and knowledge and mixed-active role in political discussions	4	3
Low political interest and knowledge and passive-nonparticipant role in discussions	19	71
Total	100%	100%
N of Cases	(697)	(150)

Note: The measure of association for the two variables in the table is Eta $= .44$; $p < .001$. See note 20 on the construction of the psychological involvement and discussion role variable.

The forgetful voter category suggests that there are a substantial number of voters in Japan that lack the internal motivations to induce them to go out to the polls and vote. Moreover, forgetful voters typically lack the partisan identifications that could guide their voting decisions in the absence of any substantial interest and knowledge about politics. Only 28 percent of the forgetful voters admit to any party identification, and almost all of those were weak identifications. In contrast, 74 percent of the aware voters were party identifiers and nearly a third of those were strong identifiers. Given the forgetful voters' low levels of psychological involvement in politics, their absence of partisan ties, and their need for cues and guidance in reaching a voting decision, it seems likely that not only the motivation to vote but also the choice of candidate is derived from external influences.

While the forgetful voter classification is not a perfect indicator, its identification does suggest the existence of a sizable group of voters whose participation in elections is mobilized by the more involved and knowledgeable opinion leaders within their own circles of associates. The lack of a perfect fit between the apolitical voter concept and the forgetful voter category is demonstrated by two groups of respondents that were only very slightly more represented among the forgetful voters than they were within the sample as a whole. These were the farm wives and family workers, and the retail sales wives and family workers ($N = 132$ and 90, respectively). When the full sample was broken down into fifteen groups by household head's occupation, union membership, and family role, the above two groups emerged as most closely fitting the model of the apolitical voter. Applying the same procedures as above, only now breaking the standardized variables down on these fifteen occupational types, these two farm and retail sales categories were substantially lower than the sample mean in psychological involvement ($-.61$ and $-.12$, respectively), much higher in community integration (.82 and .59), and higher in voter turnout (.24 and .32).[21]

We do, then, find an asymmetry in roles in the vote mobilization process in Japan. Many of the more active and psychologically involved community members apparently play an important role in mobilizing the more disinterested and apolitical members to go to the polls and vote. Moreover, the mobilized voters' choice of candidate does not seem to be attributable to either a partisan loyalty or media exposure, since these sources of voting cues have been found to be quite low to nonexistent for these kinds of voters (see table 4.5). Thus, it is plausible to argue that these mobilized voters are deriving voting cues from interpersonal sources.

Evidence of Reference Group Effects

The evidence presented above suggests that opinion leaders may take an important part in mobilizing the vote for particular parties and candidates, especially among the least politicized portions of the electorate. As I have argued, however, there are other kinds of long-term effects that social networks can exert that also do not involve sophisticated political communications. The reference group effect is not limited in its impact to the apolitical voter, nor does it depend for its effectiveness on a sense of personal debt or obligation to someone actively canvassing for votes. Rather, this long-term aspect of social network influence operates through a very simple mechanism. The individual closely identifies his interests with those of a particular social group, organization, or informal network of family and friends. In that context, the individual does not need to be told the policies, past performance, character strengths, or even the party affiliation of the candidate. The only message that needs to be communicated is that candidate A is "our candidate." The greater the individ-

21. It is instructive to compare these two occupational classifications of respondents with the white-collar nonunionist category. These white-collar workers are above the mean on SERL and psychological involvement (.50 and .15, respectively), but because of their low levels of involvement in either their community social networks or nonareal organizations ($-.35$ and $-.27$, respectively) are inhibited from participating and fall below the mean in turnout levels ($-.13$).

ual's loyalty to a group, the greater the likelihood that that message alone will suffice to gain the individual's compliance with the group's choice.

One test of a reference group effect would be to see if those who identify more strongly with a group conform more to its partisan preference when casting their ballots. While the JABISS study did not ask respondents how strongly they identify with each of their group associations, we can infer differences in levels of identification from the respondent's level of activity within a group and the length of his association with the group. The more active the group member and the longer his membership, the greater the likelihood that he will view his own interests as closely bound up with those of the group and turn to the group for voting cues.

We find strong evidence of this kind of reference group effect in table 4.7. In order to identify groups that had clear and unambiguous partisan preferences, this analysis had to be limited to three kinds of formal organizations. Neighborhood associations are known to have strong ties to the Liberal Democratic Party, especially in the old, established neighborhoods. To try to identify those established neighborhoods, that analysis was limited to home-owning, lifetime residents. The analysis of the second organization in the table, enterprise associations, was limited by occupation to farmers and the old middle class (mostly small retailers). Here the enterprise associations in question are largely agricultural cooperatives and merchants associations, which again are known in most cases to have close ties to the LDP. Finally, the largest of the national labor federations, Sohyo, is a long-standing, staunch backer of the Japan Socialist Party. Across all three cases, we find that 71 to 75 percent of the organization members who say that they participate frequently or always in their organization's activities report a group-conforming vote compared to levels of 53 to 58 percent for those who say that they participate occasionally or never. Respondents in both the high and low activity-level categories identified themselves as members of the respective group. The organizations clearly meant a lot more to the more active members, however, and that stronger attachment enabled the organization to perform more of a reference group role for these members in reaching their voting decision.

We find similar confirmation of the reference group effect when we turn to length of membership. Here we only have data for residential communities and unions. In both cases, however, the longer the member has been associated with the group, the greater his voting conformity to established group preferences, rising from levels of 44 to 47 percent for short-term members to levels of 66 to 78 percent for long-term members. We may hypothesize that the longer the duration of the tie, the greater the likelihood that the individual will perceive his own identity as somehow bound up with the group. Clearly a longer association

Table 4.7 Percentage of Group Members Casting Votes That Conform to Their Organization's Preference by Level and Duration of Group Involvement

Category of Respondents	Organization	Level of Activity in Organization	
		Low	High
Home-owning lifetime residents voting LDP	Neighborhood association	58 (60)	73 (128)
Farmers and small businessmen households voting LDP	Enterprise association	53 (59)	71 (143)
Union members and their families voting JSP	Sohyo-affiliated union	56 (16)	75 (59)

	Length of Residence		
	1–16 years	Over 16	Entire Life
Home-owners voting LDP	44 (310)	59 (333)	66 (297)

	Length of Union Membership		
	0–5 years	6–15 Years	Over 16
Sohyo households voting JSP	47 (15)	69 (32)	78 (32)

Note: The figures in parentheses are the *N* of cases on which the percentage was computed.

would provide more opportunities for the individual to assimilate the group's values and preferences, which of course would reinforce a reference group effect. For whatever reason, long-term members are apparently more likely to rely on their organization for voting cues.

We can also find additional indirect evidence of a reference group effect. If formal and informal associations were acting as reference groups in guiding vote choices, we might expect to find that some individuals who identified very closely with a particular groups would not perceive that their vote was being solicited, when that group was the source of a candidate-specific influence communication. In processing that voting request, the individual would interpret the communication as an identification of "our candidate" rather than "your candidate." If this were true, when the respondent was asked to report how many people had asked him to vote for a particular candidate, he would be more likely to underreport requests that came from the most intimate circles of family and friends or from an acquaintance in an organization with which he strongly identified.

If this kind of reference group effect were not operating, we would expect to find that the more tightly the individual was tied into formal and informal groups and their communication networks, the more influence communications he would receive seeking to mobilize his support for a particular candidate. Yet the evidence does not support this expectation; this leads me to conclude that considerable underreporting of requests takes place in associational contexts with which the individual closely identifies. For example, we find higher levels of interpersonal voting requests in urban rather than rural areas ($r = .10$). Yet we know that both formal and informal social networks are much more pervasive in rural areas.[22] We also find no relationship between the community integration index and receiving requests ($r = .01$). This conflicts with reams of descriptive evidence that have demonstrated over the years that interpersonal influences are extremely prevalent and effective in highly integrated communities and certainly among those most closely tied into such community networks.

Other anomalies can also be found in the data between the expected frequency of influence communications and the frequency of reporting requests. For example, less than 5 percent of the respondents reported receiving requests from someone in their family, a figure that is certainly not reflective of the degree of political communication that takes place at election time within families. We also find no associations between receiving vote requests and membership in highly cohesive and mobilized organizations, such as religious groups like the Soka Gakkai, reform organizations such as local residents' movements, or enterprise associations such as the neighborhood retailers' associations. Conversely, membership in these associations is substantially correlated with asking others for votes ($r = .20, .15$, and $.07$, respectively). It appears, then, that the members of these organizations do not perceive as "requests" for their votes many kinds of influence communications within their

22. Thus, the JABISS data demonstrate negative correlations among all four of our network involvement scales and level of urbanization. These correlations are extremely high in the case of community integration ($-.2$) and moderate in the case of informal associations and candidate networks ($-.15$ and $-.18$, respectively). We even find a small but significant correlation of $-.05$ with level of involvement in formal organizations, which is somewhat surprising since most of those kinds of organizations are not directly community-based as are the organizations included in the community integration scale.

group, which nonetheless result in high levels of group conformity in voting choices.

On the other hand, the evidence suggests that the larger the organization and the weaker its emphasis on traditional bonds of communal solidarity, the more likely the respondent will perceive that a personal request is being made for his vote. Thus, we do find significant associations between receiving voting requests and membership in larger and less cohesive organizations, such as labor unions, PTA, and recreational groups. Another sign of underreporting is the fact that the correlations associated with membership in these broad, nonareal kinds of formal organizations are much higher with reporting having asked others for votes (.20) than having received requests (.14). The same pattern is found in the case of the candidate network scale, where the correlation with asking others for votes is .22, compared to .12 with being asked.

Another interesting finding is that reporting voting requests turns out to be associated with location in an environment in which the formal and informal groups one is associated with exhibit less homogeneous partisan cues. Respondents were asked to identify the partisan preferences of four informal group associations (family, friends, neighbors, and co-workers) and of the formal organizations to which they belonged (among the ten different types identified on the survey). Looking across all of these formal and informal associations, the group partisan preferences for each respondent were coded into a dichotomous variable distinguishing those with all consistent partisan cues from those with inconsistent cues. While all respondents have essentially the same opportunities to report vote requests from their family, friends, neighbors, co-workers, neighborhood association, and the other organizations to which they belong, a significant monotonic relationship emerges between the number of vote requests perceived and the proportion of respondents reporting conflicting cues ($r = .15$). This finding implies that awareness of specific requests for one's vote is associated with conflicted, cross-pressured voters. These voters may identify closely with one network communication source and more or less reject the others, or they may feel simply confused by the conflicting requests. In either case, these voters receive a greater number of requests that they are likely to view as "external requests" and hence are more likely to report.

Finally, the number of voting requests received was found to be associated with leftist voting (.06). This is perhaps the most surprising finding of all, since we know that personalistic influences are most characteristic of conservative campaign organizations. Thus, paradoxically, 55 percent of those who voted LDP reported receiving no requests for their vote, while only 44 percent of those voting for the center parties (DSP, CGP, and NLC) and 49 percent of those voting left (JSP and JCP) reported no requests. On closer inspection it appears that the reason those voting for the small center parties report receiving the most requests for their votes is that, here again, they are subjected to the highest numbers of conflicting cues. Looking across the same fourteen kinds of formal and informal associations reported above, among those who report receiving any requests, only 29 percent of the center party voters reported receiving two or more exclusively consistent cues, compared to 34 percent for the leftist voters and 47 percent for the LDP voters.

As we would expect, the number of conflicting cues received seems to be a function of party size and ideological location, with the supporters of the smaller parties and of parties in the center of the ideological spectrum being subjected to the greatest number of conflicting cues. The most important point for us, however, is that this finding and the others reported in this section support the conclusion that, all other things being equal, an individual is more likely to interpret an interpersonal communication as a request for his vote to the extent that the "request" is viewed as coming from outside a group he strongly identifies with and as conflicting with other requests. Thus, we find a significant degree of underreporting of voting requests in rural areas, within the family and other intimate circles, among those living in highly integrated communities or belonging to highly solidaristic organizations, and among conservative voters. I argue that this finding is indirect evidence of a reference group effect. Integration into a particular social network has over time created such a close identification that the interpersonal influence communications emanating from that source may not even be perceived as external influences attempting to manipulate one's voting decision. The reference group communicates its choice and the loyal member accepts it as his own.[23]

Evidence of Assimilation Effects

The assimilation effect focuses on the tendency of an individual to acquire attitudes that are compatible with those espoused by the valued people and groups that populate his daily life. This results in an attitude homogenization process within social networks that is stimulated by both positive and negative inducements—the desire to emulate trusted role models in one's immediate environment and the desire to gain acceptance and avoid group sanctions by blending in with those around one. We might view assimilation as a two-step

23. This phenomenon of underreporting those vote requests that emanate from one's most important and valued group associations may explain in part Richardson's findings in chapter 9 that the rates of compliance with reported vote requests and group recommendations are in many cases lower than the descriptive literature would lead us to expect.

process in which the individual first becomes aware of the attitudes of those around him and then gradually adopts new attitudes or adjusts old attitudes to accommodate his belief system to his interpersonal milieu.

Evidence of contextual effects reported in chapter 3 has already demonstrated the impact that certain types of residential and occupation environments exert on shaping the individual's basic social values. This assimilation of shared community or work-place values has important political effects, as the previous chapter has shown. Chapter 3 demonstrated that those who assimilate traditional values are then predisposed to adopt conservative positions on the important set of cultural politics issues, to exhibit higher levels of system trust and support and lower levels of efficacy and protest behavior, and to be more receptive to traditionalistic campaigning styles (for example, obligation-induced voting). In turn, all of these consequences of traditionalistic value systems were shown to be associated with voting LDP.

In this section we will look at the assimilation of political rather than social attitudes and analyze the impact of an awareness of group partisan preferences on the respondent's vote choice. An awareness of the partisan preferences of the valued people with whom one is involved will tend to induce the individual to adopt the same partisan identification or, if not a stable identification, at least political attitudes that guide the individual to a similar vote choice. We will also expect to find that the more consistent the partisan preferences of one's family, friends, neighbors, co-workers, and fellow members in the various organizations one belongs to, the greater the likelihood that one's vote will conform to those preferences.

To demonstrate this kind of assimilation effect, we turn again to the questions asking what party was supported by the members as a whole of each organization to which a respondent belonged, and to the four additional questions on what party the respondent's family, friends, neighbors, and co-workers generally supported. As there were ten types of organizations, respondents could have identified the partisan orientation of a maximum of fourteen formal and informal groups with which they were associated, although membership in more than four kinds of formal organizations was extremely rare.

In coding the partisan preferences of these reference groups, one simplifying assumption was employed. To reduce the task of differentiating the number of cues received across fourteen groups for six parties to a manageable exercise, the parties were grouped into right, center, and left. This simplification, however, should not adversely influence the validity of our findings. The LDP is the only party on the right and the Socialist Party (JSP) is the dominant party on the left. The only other leftist party, the Communist Party (JCP), is relatively small, capturing only 20 percent of those identifying with these two leftist parties. The

JCP is also very close to the JSP in terms of policy and the kinds of organizations to which its supporters belong. Finally, the center parties are very small and, in fact, the left and right together captured over 85 percent of the perceived group partisan preferences.

Fifty-one percent of the total sample and 56 percent of the voters were able to identify the partisan preference of the members of at least one formal or informal group with which they were associated. There are two reasons why this total is not higher. First, there were filter questions in each case. Naturally, a respondent had to be a member of an organization in order to be asked about its members' partisan preferences. A full 86 percent of the sample were members of at least one of the ten kinds of formal organizations, but only 58 percent were members of at least two; 30 percent, members of at least three; 13 percent, at least four; 5 percent, in at least five. So 14 percent had no memberships, and another 56 percent were asked to identify the partisan preferences of only the one or two organizations to which they belonged. We might have expected higher frequencies in the case of the more intimate groups, since everyone presumably has family, friends, and neighbors. In these cases there were two filter questions. Respondents who either reported they had no social contacts with neighbors, work colleagues, friends, or family *or,* on a second question, said politics did not come up as a topic of discussion with them, were not asked about those groups' partisan preferences. Across these four kinds of intimate groups, that meant that only 67 percent of the sample were asked about the partisan ties of at least one of the four intimate groups and only 21 percent were asked about three or more of these groups.

A second factor that limited the reported numbers of group partisan preferences was that substantial proportions of the people who were asked these questions said that they could not say or did not know the partisan preferences of the other group members. For instance, in the case of the four intimate groups, 34–46 percent reported that they could not say and another 15–21 percent said that they did not know. This meant that only 51 percent of those questioned about the partisan ties of their family and relatives reported a party preference, as did 47 and 45 percent for co-workers and neighbors, respectively, and 34 percent for friends. Moreover, 39 percent of those who were members of at least one formal organization were aware of the partisan preferences of at least one organization to which they belonged.

These findings suggest that three types of respondents are being eliminated from this analysis of assimilation effects. The first are those who are largely isolated from social networks and thus could not be influenced by those effects anyway. The second are the apolitical voters and those with low levels of political interest and sophistication, who are being eliminated because they either do not discuss politics with others or do not know the partisan preferences of those around them (perhaps because they do not perceive politics in partisan terms). For example, only 10 percent of the forgetful voters identified the partisan preference of a single formal or informal group with which they were associated. Again, we would not expect to find any assimilation effect in their case. The third type of respondent would be one who does not report any group partisan preferences because he is not receiving any clear, unambiguous partisan cues from any of the groups with which he is associated. This may be either because the people and groups he interacts with are essentially apolitical or because they have mixed and conflicting partisan preferences. Once again, no assimilation effect would be expected.

We are left then with 56 percent of the voters who may have experienced some kind of long-term assimilation effect that could exert an impact on their vote choice. The possibility of a strong assimilation effect is enhanced by the fact that among those respondents identifying more than one associated group's partisan preference, 73 percent reported only consistent preferences. Indeed, only 15 percent of those respondents perceiving one or more group partisan preferences reported any inconsistent or conflicting cues. This extremely high level of consistent and reinforcing group partisan cues should increase the assimilation effect.

In table 4.8 we find that the greater the number of group partisan cues and the more consistent they are, the greater the likelihood that the respondent will develop a strong partisan identification of his own. The respondents in table 4.8 represent the subsample of those who are aware of at least one group partisan preference among their informal and formal group associations. The first category includes both those who received balanced cues (for example, an equal number of left and center cues) and those who received confused cues (those receiving all three kinds of partisan cues—left, center, and right). The unbalanced cues category includes those who received, for example, one center cue and two to four right cues. Since the subsample of respondents in table 4.8 excludes many of the least sophisticated voters, it is not surprising to find that there are fewer leaners and nonidentifiers in it than in the full sample (26 versus 40 percent). But within this subsample we find that as we move from those with balanced, confused, or only one cue, to those with three or more unbalanced cues, or to those with two, three, or more consistent cues, the proportion of strong identifiers increases while the frequencies of leaners and nonidentifiers drops.

The table also demonstrates significant relationships between the number and consistency of cues received and the respondent's reported partisan and voting stability. Since Japanese associational networks tend to be quite stable

Table 4.8 Association between the Number and Consistency of Group Partisan Preferences and Strength of Partisanship and Stability (In Percentages)

	Distribution by Partisan Type					N of Cases	Partisan Stability	
	Strong	Weak	Leaners	Non-ID	Total		Always Supporting Same Party	Voting Same Party over Last 10 Years
Balanced or confused group partisan preferences	8	58	10	24	100%	(59)	48	72
1 consistent group partisan preference	13	54	10	23	100%	(365)	79	78
3 or more unbalanced group partisan preferences	18	56	5	21	100%	(61)	57	79
2 consistent group partisan preferences	18	61	3	18	100%	(127)	75	89
3 or more consistent group partisan preferences	31	55	4	10	100%	(178)	84	87
Comparison of above subsample and total sample								
Respondents aware of at least one group partisan preference	18	56	7	19	100%	(790)		
Total Sample	13	46	8	32	99%	(1,563)		

over the individual's lifetime, the more politicized these networks are and the more consistent their partisan message, the more stable the individual's partisan leanings and voting behavior are likely to become.

An inconsistency in the percentage rank orders for the partisan stability variable, however, suggests that while the number and consistency of the cues are important in all three of the relationships reported, the number of cues may be somewhat more related to strength of partisanship, while their consistency has more to do with their stability over time. Katz (1979) has argued that strength and direction of partisanship are two different dimensions, with strength of partisanship being more related to the individual's level of politicization rather than the duration of the tie. Thus, the more politicized one's social networks, the more politicized the individual becomes, the greater the likelihood that he or she will identify a partisan tie, and the stronger that designation is likely to be. We find, then, that three or more unbalanced cues are associated with 18 percent strong identifiers and only 26 percent leaners and nonidentifiers, while the corresponding figures are 13 and 33 percent for one consistent cue. More cues indicate more politicized groups and stronger politicizing influences, even if some conflicting cues are present in the environment.

On the other hand, the consistency of the cues perceived is by far the most important factor in influencing partisan stability over the long term. Thus, 79 percent of those perceiving one consistent group partisan preference report having always supported the same party, compared to only 57 percent of those perceiving three or more unbalanced group preferences. A tie to a group with dissonant partisan preferences presents the possibility that earlier in a respondent's life, perhaps before some of his other network ties were established, that currently dissonant tie, to perhaps his family or neighborhood, may have loomed much larger in shaping his partisan loyalties. Since the table shows that its effect is not apparent on his voting stability over the past ten years, its dominant influence is likely to have occurred more in his distant past. As his network ties developed and changed after leaving his parents' home, entering the work force, and settling into a career, so did the balance of partisan preferences among his associated networks, in time leading to a network-induced partisan conversion.

To estimate the effectiveness of these group partisan preferences in influencing the respondent's vote choice, a variable was constructed that measures the direction and well as the numbers and consistency of the cues received. In table 4.9 this is cross-tabulated with vote choice and yields an extremely high Tau C of .60. So we find that among those receiving three or more right partisan cues, 91 percent voted LDP in the 1976 election. Conversely, among those receiving three or more left partisan cues, 92 percent voted Socialist or Communist. The fewer the cues and the more mixed the cues, the lower the conformity to group preferences.

One recognized problem with this mode of analysis is that self-reporting of others' partisan preferences tends to overestimate consistency with the respondent's preferences. Apparently some respondents project their own partisan preferences upon those around them without really knowing where the other people stand. This is more likely to be the case among those who never discuss politics or those who do all the talking when they discuss politics and hence may not know where their listener stands. In an effort to minimize this problem, table 4.9 also reports the relationship between the respondent's party vote and the direction and consistency of his groups' partisan preferences for that subset of the sample who reported that they were mainly passive listeners when they discussed politics with others. As the statistics show, the group preference–respondent vote relationship is even slightly higher among the passive discussants, with a remarkably impressive Tau C of .64.

Table 4.9 Relationship between the Number, Direction, and Consistency of Partisan Cues and Vote Choice

Number and Consistency of Partisan Cues	Whole Sample Percent Voting:				Passive Discussants Only Percent Voting:			
	Right	Center	Left	N	Right	Center	Left	N
Three or more, all Right	91	6	3	(112)	91	7	2	(45)
Two, Right	89	7	4	(55)	85	8	8	(26)
One, Right	77	10	13	(144)	80	6	14	(55)
Mixed, more Right	53	10	37	(30)	—	—	—	(14)
Balanced	30	21	49	(43)	43	14	43	(21)
All or more Center	13	66	21	(77)	3	88	9	(32)
Mixed, more Left	25	0	75	(16)	—	—	—	(8)
One, Left	26	9	64	(118)	21	9	70	(56)
Two, Left	10	5	85	(40)	9	9	83	(23)
Three or more, all Left	3	5	92	(37)	0	10	90	(19)

Tau C = .60   Tau C = .64

Note: The figures in parentheses are the N of cases on which the respective percentages were based. The percentage distributions for Ns with fewer than 15 cases were considered too unstable to report. In a few cases the percentages do not add to 100 owing to rounding error.

These findings may exaggerate somewhat the degree of group partisan homogeneity by focusing only on that 56 percent of the voters who perceive the members of at least one of their associated groups as having a discernible partisan preference. Nevertheless, the degree of consensus both between the group and the respondent and across the respondent's different groups is strikingly high. Perhaps this should not surprise us in a group-centered society such as Japan.[24] Indeed, it seems quite reasonable to expect that the perception that those around one all tend to support the same party in election after election would induce a long-term process of partisan crystallization. In this process, favorable images and political evaluations will form regarding the group's supported party. Election campaigns will then stimulate additional communications within the individual's important circles of family, friends, neighbors, and work colleagues, which will tend to reinforce those favorable partisan images. The greater the partisan consistency of these communications, the greater will be the individual's tendency to internalize them and perceive them as his own.

We also should expect to find that the further along this process of partisan crystallization is in terms of developing a leaning toward a party into weak and then strong partisan attachment, the greater would be the individual's conformity to his group's partisan preferences in his vote choice. Thus, as we move from leaners to weak to strong identifiers, we find the Tau C's measuring the strength of the relationship between one's groups' partisan preferences and one's own vote choice rise from .50 to .61 to .72, respectively. Even among the nonpartisans, however, who do not admit to even leaning toward any party, we still find a strong correlation of .39 between their groups' partisanship and their vote choice. Thus, 67 percent of those nonpartisans who perceived all consistent group partisan preferences conformed to that preference in their vote choice. The proportion conforming rises to 78 percent when we look only at those nonpartisans perceiving two or more consistent group partisan preferences. Many of these nonpartisans may simply be conforming to their group's preference out of a sense of obligation or loyalty (reference group or mobilization effects). But it is also likely that some of them have not only gained an awareness of their groups' partisan preferences but have also assimilated some favorable attitudes and images of their associates' preferred party. While they may be in the early stages of this assimilation process, its effects on voting behavior are nevertheless clearly evident.

This chapter has examined the social network approach to the study of

24. There are many works that stress the importance of the group in Japanese culture, from Nakamura (1964) to Doi (1973) to Lebra (1976). For one synthesis of this literature see chapter 4 in Richardson and Flanagan, 1984.

voting behavior as it applies to the Japanese case. This approach argues that a focus on intragroup long-term socialization processes and short-term influence communications is a fruitful one, because long-standing formal and informal groups based on close interpersonal ties tend to develop fairly homogeneous and stable political attitudes over time and tend to induce high levels of uniformity in their members' voting choices. To gain further insight into the processes through which groups and interpersonal networks affect the individual's voting decision, a typology of four different mechanisms of influence was introduced. Evidence was then presented to argue that the impact of each of these four mechanisms of influence should be greater in the Japanese case as compared to the advanced industrial democracies of the West. That discussion of Japanese political culture and campaign practices established the greater relevance of the social network approach to the study of voting behavior in Japan.

In turning to the data, evidence was presented to demonstrate that opinion leaders and mobilized voters are very much in evidence in the context of Japanese election campaigns. The asymmetry between these two types of voters in discussion roles and in levels of political knowledge, interest, and media exposure suggests a strong asymmetry in influences in the interactions between them. In addition, the discussion identified factors that motivate potential opinion leaders to assume an active canvassing role in a campaign, which in turn was shown to enhance the psychological involvement of some of those who were contacted and to mobilize other apolitical voters to go out to the polls.

Also analyzed were the long-term reference group and assimilation effects of social networks. It was shown that the stronger the individual's identification with his group, the greater his conformity to the group's voting preference. Also noted was a tendency for individuals closely associated with a reference group to identify the group's candidate choice as their own choice; consequently, an influence communication that solicits the member's vote is not always perceived as an external request. It was also shown that individuals assimilate not only the values of their groups and networks but, more directly, political attitudes as well, including party preferences. The more politicized the groups the individual interacts with, the greater the likelihood he will develop a party identification; the more consistent their party preferences, the more stable his own partisanship will be. Finally, the greater the number and consistency of the group partisan cues the individual receives and the further he has progressed in assimilating group partisan preferences, the higher his voting conformity to his group's chosen party will be. While these relationships are likely to hold in all settings, their impact may be somewhat greater in Japan, because of the high level of partisan homogeneity found across the respondents' different formal and informal groups.

There is strong evidence, therefore, to conclude that social networks play an important role in guiding vote choices, at least in the Japanese setting. Over time, within the context of stable and long-standing interpersonal ties, group identifications develop and homogeneous attitudes are formed. In the context of an election campaign, these political attitudes and group loyalties become mobilized and condition receptivity to the voting cues that are being diffused throughout the group. Often through spontaneous, informal discussions, group attitudes begin to crystallize concerning candidate preferences. Since the levels of political interest and partisanship vary within the group, those with stronger and more firmly held views take a greater part in this homogenization process. For those who have already acquired firmly held partisan preferences, interpersonal influences may only serve to mobilize the individual to go out to the polls and vote. But even in these cases, given the relative unfamiliarity of voters with many of the candidates in a district, interpersonal influence communications may guide the voter trying to decide which of a party's candidates to support. Other voters who do not have a great deal of interest or knowledge about politics will search for voting cues to enable them to make a personally meaningful choice. Especially if they feel some obligation to vote but lack the confidence to sort out the candidates, they may tune in more consciously to the political messages coming from their family members, other intimate associates, and acquaintances. In screening the myriad influence communications with which they are bombarded, their group identifications and the group attitudes that they have assimilated help them to assign relative values and validities to each communication, enabling them to decide which to act upon and which to reject.

From the opposite perspective, social groups and interpersonal networks influence their members not only because some members seek direction but also because many groups seek to direct. While many voters may be confused about what they hear the candidates saying and how to relate their vote choice to their interests, some of the groups they belong to are likely to have clearly defined interests and preferences, which they actively try to communicate to their members. While a group cannot enforce uniformity in the context of an open democratic society, it can condition its members' choice of candidate by providing them with certain reference points and political outlooks. These may be concrete references, such as a party preference or a preferred candidate position on a key group issue. Or the reference point may be a formal tie between the candidate and the group, established by designating the candidate as the group's "official advisor" and even as a group officer. Or the group may diffuse a set of attitudes that condition choice more indirectly—a preference for a certain style of leadership or an ideological perspective that narrows the range of acceptable choices.

A group member may enter a conversation with no firm ideas as to who the candidates are and how he is going to vote yet come away with a firm decision based on the information that a trusted opinion leader has given him. The message may have been that candidate X is more progressive, is more sympathetic to the group's concerns, or is simply the best man. While the actual balance between internal and external influences is a subtle and complex one in these exchanges, the more a voter has been conditioned by assimilation and reference group effects to validate a particular communication, the more likely he is to view his decision as internally derived.

By treating each of the four mechanisms of network influence separately, I may appear to be suggesting that any one of them is potentially determining. These influences, however, do not operate in isolation either from each other or from other influences stemming from the media or the voter's own early political learning and partisan socialization. In the Japanese case, however, the influences of the media and early partisan socialization appear to be comparatively weak. Hence, although a reference group effect, by itself, may not be sufficient to determine one's vote, when that effect is reinforced by assimilated group attitudes and values, by the arguments of trusted opinion leaders, and by a sense of obligation to a particular vote canvasser, all crystallizing around one candidate choice, that decision may be highly determined. One reason why context predicts vote choice as well as it does in Japan is that in some social settings, such as the farming village or the large urban factory, all four mechanisms tend to reinforce a single voting decision.

The test of any voting model can be found in its ability to explain stability and change. In this regard, social network explanations shed important light on some of the patterns and paradoxes in Japanese electoral behavior over the postwar period. First, Richardson (1977) has found comparatively very high levels of stability across the postwar period from one election to the next in the percentage of the vote received by each party in Japan. This pattern of high voting stability exists side by side with unusually low and weak levels of party identification (Miyake, 1967 and 1970; Richardson, 1975; Flanagan and McDonald, 1979). Recently, Richardson (1986) has identified a sizable category of *habitual voters* in Japan, who lack stable party identifications and yet vote consistently for the same party. Compared to the stable identifiers, the habitual voter's choice of party is much more likely to be devoid of issue content, based on candidate rather than party considerations, and lacking in either favorable party images or positive party affect. Only 25 percent of the habitual voters had positive feelings toward the party they consistently voted for, and only 22 percent reported any significant differences that favored their own party over the other parties.

It would appear that what explains the consistent behavior of these habitual voters is being rooted in stable social contexts and interpersonal networks that, in election after election, prompt voting choices for the same kinds of candidates. Richardson reports that 18 percent of the JABISS sample qualify as habitual voters and 53 percent as stable identifiers. However, the habitual voting phenomenon may be somewhat more widespread than his analysis indicates, because the stable identifiers only had to report stable identifications across two panel survey waves spaced about one month apart. In contrast, habitual voting required a combination of inconsistent or absent identifications and stable voting over four different kinds and levels of election across a four-year period. A longer panel interval, therefore, certainly would have yielded fewer stable identifiers, many of whom would likely have been reclassified as habitual voters. Also there are the "forgetful voters" who cannot tell you what party they voted for and yet, because they are being cued by their social networks, may in fact consistently be supporting the same party.

A second phenomenon illuminated by social network explanations is the substantially higher level of individual compared to aggregate volatility. With the exception of the 1989 upper house election, a given party's electoral fortunes have typically varied by no more than one to three percentage points from election to election. Yet there is considerably more individual change taking place. Voting choices based on interpersonal ties to candidate networks limit aggregate volatility. The reach of any one candidate's personal networks is circumscribed. The Japanese voter will typically forgo a distant, marginal tie to a more powerful politician for a closer tie to a less influential candidate. As a result, the ruling party can field two to four candidates in the lower house two-to-six-member election districts without a great deal of concern that one of their stronger and more popular candidates will attract all the conservative votes and cause the defeat of the party's other district candidates. The powerful attraction of proximity in the voter-candidate tie also means that even socialist or communist candidates can stand for election in rural districts and expect support from many of the small businessmen in their hometowns who otherwise would typically vote conservative. The fact that we still find considerable community and organizational bloc voting, means that these groups can shift their votes from one candidate or party to another, if a new candidate should emerge who has a closer personal tie to the group. The limited reach of candidate networks ensures that these bloc shifts will not result in major aggregate swings in party fortunes. At the same time, community bloc voting, which is often based on the exchange of community votes for government funding of local projects and the rounding up of personally obligated votes, favors the ruling party and helps to explain its uninterrupted majority control of the Diet for over thirty years.

A third and final aspect of Japanese voting behavior clarified by a social network perspective is the pattern of electoral and partisan change. While short-term influences—the rise and fall of political issues, corruption scandals, the appeal of party leaders, and so forth—have had only minor effects in changing party fortunes from election to election over most of the entire postwar period, the ruling party and the conservative forces in general have experienced a long-term decline in voting support. This decline began in the early 1950s and was not arrested until the end of the 1970s. As discussed elsewhere, this long-term decline is best described as an ecological realignment (Flanagan, 1984). Rather than stemming from changes in the social bases of party support, this Japanese realignment in party vote shares was the result of socioeconomic forces that were shrinking the LDP's traditional constituencies. The dramatic decline in the relative size of the farming population, inroads in some old middle-class occupations, the rise of the new middle class, the increasing number of large enterprises, the unionization of blue- and white-collar workers, and greater mobility undermining the solidarity of some residential communities—all changed the social environments in which Japanese lived and worked. Rather than an issue realignment or a social group realignment, electoral change over those three decades was largely explained by socioeconomic forces that were moving the Japanese population out of traditional settings and social networks where conservative influences prevailed and into new kinds of settings where more modern values and progressive influences dominated.

Why a change in their social networks has had such a pronounced effect on Japanese voters in the space of only a few decades is explained in the next chapter. There, Ichiro Miyake demonstrates the weak durability of early partisan learning in the face of adult changes in occupation, living environment or the partisanship of one's formal and informal groups. While a number of Western studies have shown that a change in occupational class or peer groups can induce defections from parental partisanship (Butler and Stokes, 1976; McClosky and Dahlgren, 1959), the homogenizing influences that encourage attitude conformity within Japanese small groups and social networks appear to be substantially stronger and more effective than they are in the West. All of these findings along with the evidence cited throughout this chapter seem to confirm the importance of social network explanations in accounting for the patterns of stability and change we find in Japanese electoral behavior.

Five ■ Agents of Partisan Socialization in Japan

ICHIRO MIYAKE

Early studies on the American electorate concluded that citizens were likely to inherit the partisan affiliation of their parents and to retain it during their lifetime. This stability of party affiliation across generations contributed to the stability and durability of the party system and, in turn, of the political system in general.[1] In the case of Japan, there are reasons to believe that the family may not be the most important agency of political socialization. For one thing, the Japanese party system has undergone several changes over the last fifty years. The biggest change is the one that took place after the defeat in World War II. At the time of the JABISS survey, less than half the electorate had experienced their early political socialization under the postwar party system. Moreover, the major postwar parties did not consolidate and adopt stable party labels until 1955, and so as of 1976 only about a quarter of the electorate had been socialized under the current party system. These discontinuities have greatly weakened the familial transmission of partisanship.

A second reason to expect lower levels of successful parental transmission of partisanship in Japan compared to the United States or Britain is related to the rate and magnitude of socioeconomic change in postwar Japan. Postwar development has brought about high levels of occupational and geographic mobility. The proportion of the work force engaged in farming and fishery was reduced from 40 percent in 1955 to 15 percent in 1975, while the proportion of new middle-class occupations, such as clerks, professionals, and managers, jumped from 15 percent in 1955 to 25 percent in 1975. Most of these changes occurred through intergenerational mobility, with sons forsaking the traditional family enterprise for new opportunities in burgeoning urban centers. Thus, occupational changes have been related to a pronounced pattern of geographical mobility from rural villages and towns to metropolitan cities and then to suburban cities. During the years 1965–70, more than 50 percent of those who were younger than 35 years old reported that they had experienced at least one such

1. Representative works here are Campbell et al., 1960, and Easton and Dennis, 1969.

move. Clearly the young have been most affected by this occupational and geographical mobility, moving in great numbers into occupational and residential contexts markedly different from those of their parents.

A third reason to expect that the family may not be the most important agent of socialization stems from the pronounced degree of intergenerational value change in Japan, discussed above in chapter 3. The resultant value conflict between the old and the young is believed to be an obstacle to the transmission of parental partisanship to children. In fact, age ranks along with type of occupation as one of the two most important demographic factors that account for one's partisan preference. The older one is, the more likely one is to be conservative, while younger age cohorts are more progressive. At the time of the JABISS survey, in 1976, forty years of age roughly marked the cutting point between earlier generations and a postwar generation, which received its early socialization in a postwar environment and came of age politically after the consolidation of the party system in 1955. Across this generational divide, we find many parents with traditional values and conservative partisan preferences facing children with modern values and progressive partisanship.

Despite the situational evidence unfavorable to the hypothesis of a dominant parental role in partisan socialization, the studies by Kubota and Ward (1970), Massey (1976), and Iwase (1977) on early socialization in Japan uniformly have confirmed that the extent to which parents succeeded in transmitting their partisanship to their children was not much less than that in Western nations. They show that the family does indeed play the leading role in the child's early political socialization despite the large and rapid political, social, and cultural changes that have been taking place in Japan. Their common conclusions, however, are largely constrained by the characteristics of their data, which are based on paired parents and children who were independently interviewed or asked to fill out questionnaires. As their child-respondents are mostly high school students or younger who live in the same households with their parents, they are more likely to follow their parents' political views than older offspring who, as adults, live independently of their parents. For these teenagers living with their parents, the social milieu in which the whole family lives naturally reinforces the familial transmission of partisanship.

The question we have to answer is not to what extent parents and children are correlated in their partisanship, but rather to what extent Japanese youth are moving away from their parents as they are drawn into new social contexts and become surrounded by independent and frequently quite different kinds of social networks. The durability in some countries of early partisan preferences learned in the home may have more to do with the stability of class lines and types of occupational and residential contexts across generations than to the indelibility of early childhood learning. For example, Butler and Stokes (1976) found that, in Britain, respondents were far more likely to defect from their parents' partisanship and their own early party preferences if they, as adults, moved into a different occupational class than their parents'. Still, even with marked intergenerational differences in class, occupation, and education, most British respondents remained consistent with their parents' party identifications. For reasons already discussed in chapter 4, long-term partisan commitments are likely to be even more strongly affected by changes in social context in Japan than in many Western nations. The question to be addressed here, therefore, is how well does early parental partisan learning in Japan withstand contrasting influences in the adult environment?

It should be noted at the outset that this analysis is based on recall data and hence is subject to some bias. Our respondents were asked the party support of their parents during the years when the respondents were growing up. The recall data allow us to include in our sample children who live under a different set of social pressures from their parents and to collect a large number of parent-child pairs over a broad range of age groups. A number of researchers, however, have found that recall data contain a substantial degree of inaccuracy. For example, Joseph Massey (1976:83) found that only about two-thirds of his respondents claiming knowledge of their parents' partisanship correctly identified their parents' party affiliation. It has also been shown, however, that the bias associated with recall data is consistently in the direction of exaggerating the consistency between parents and child (Niemi, 1974). Respondents are likely to err in the direction of assuming that their parents' party matches their own. This bias will not invalidate the findings presented here, because the bias works against the major thesis of this chapter. Since we are looking for change rather than continuity, the bias inherent in recall data will provide us with conservative estimates of the amount of change that has really occurred.

This chapter begins with an analysis of the role of parental socialization, looking at both the awareness of parental partisanship and the level of transfer. The investigation then turns to a study of the impact of other socializing groups and contexts on both the strength and direction of partisanship and goes on to test the relative importance of the parental transmission of partisanship compared to adult socialization. Finally, the effects of other agents of socialization that are more indirect and difficult to assess, such as the media, are discussed.

■ Intergenerational Partisan Consistency

Awareness of the father's party appears to be correlated to a child's own partisanship. As shown in table 5.1, in 1967, if the father's party was recalled, 89 percent of the respondents reported that they also supported a party. In

Table 5.1   Recall of Father's Partisanship and Respondent's Party Support

Survey Year	Respondents Recalling Father's Party	Respondents Recalling Father's Party Who Support a Party	Respondents Not Recalling Father's Party Who Support a Party
1967	37%	89%	64%
1976	42%	79%	60%

Note: The 1967 survey was conducted by the Center for Japanese Studies, the University of Michigan; the 1976 survey is the JABISS survey.

contrast, among those who could not recall their father's party, only 64 percent reported a partisan preference. In 1976, the levels of party supporters were lower in both cases, but the effect of an awareness of the father's party is still quite apparent.

The effect of the father's partisanship, however, is limited in many ways. First, in light of the discontinuities in the Japanese party system discussed above, we could assume that a smaller portion of the electorate can recall their father's partisan position in Japan than is reported in the United States and Britain, where the party systems have remained largely unchanged across several generations. In fact, the proportions of those who can recall their father's party are only 37 percent in 1967 and 42 percent in 1976. While a slight rise can be noted over time, these figures contrast strikingly with the much higher figures reported for the United State and Britain.[2]

Second, a high proportion of the electorate remains unaware and presumably uninfluenced by their father's partisanship in their formative years, but they have nevertheless developed their own partisanship at a rather high rate of 64 percent in 1967 and 60 percent in 1976. This fact suggests that, besides familial learning, there are other important pathways of political socialization through which one comes to hold a partisan attachment.

Last, among those who are aware of the father's party, the intergenerational transfer of partisanship has begun to weaken recently. Table 5.2 suggests that across the survey years there has been a trend in the direction of more children abandoning the preferences of their fathers to become independents. Interestingly enough, the table reveals two contradictory trends. On the one hand, there appears to be a marked trend among those in the younger age cohorts increasingly to be able to recall their father's party. The break between relatively high and low levels of recall falls between those in their twenties and

2. The comparable American (1976) and British (1979) recall rates are 75 percent and 79 percent, respectively.

Table 5.2 Father-Respondent Relationship on Party Support
by Age Group
(In Percentages)

		Age Group				
	Survey Year	20s	30s	40s	50s	60s or above
1967	**Those who can recall father's party**					
	Consistent with respondent's party	25	12	15	10	6
	Inconsistent with respondent's party	14	13	10	2	3
	Respondent has no party	4	3	4	1	2
	Total	43%	28%	29%	13%	11%
	Those who can't recall father's party					
	Respondent has party to support	33	54	51	54	46
	Respondent has no party	24	18	19	33	43
	Total	57%	72%	71%	87%	89%
	Total sample	100%	100%	100%	100%	100%
	N of cases	(346)	(391)	(278)	(205)	(211)
1976	**Those who can recall father's party**					
	Consistent with respondent's party	18	17	15	15	9
	Inconsistent with respondent's party	13	13	8	4	4
	Respondent has no party	13	10	4	3	4
	Total	44%	40%	27%	22%	17%
	Those who can't recall father's party					
	Respondent has party to support	25	34	47	51	51
	Respondent has no party	31	26	26	27	32
	Total	56%	60%	73%	78%	83%
	Total sample	100%	100%	100%	100%	100%
	N of cases	(336)	(360)	(320)	(214)	(211)

thirties in 1967 but between those in their thirties and forties in 1976. This is consistent with the greater stabilization of the Japanese party system after 1955. Thus, the potential range of parental influence has been expanding. While respondents are remembering their father's partisanship more, however, they are apparently following it less. For example, in 1967, 58 percent of those in their twenties who recalled their father's party supported the same party, while in 1976 the corresponding figure for the new twenties cohort was 41 percent.[3] The trend that appears here, however, is not one of defection to another party but of higher proportions of independents.[4] In the Japanese case, therefore, the greater continuity in the Japanese party system after 1955 and the greater awareness of parental party that has accompanied that change has not (at least as of 1976) been translated into rising rates of parental transmission of partisanship.

Owing to discontinuities in party labels, the recent development of new small parties, and the large imbalance in power and size between the LDP and the other parties, it would be better not to engage in a party by party analysis as we explore partisan consistency between parent and child. Instead, we will focus on two broad ideological camps: conservative (LDP, NLC, and old conservative parties) and progressive (the rest of the parties and old socialist parties). Those who are fifty years old or above will hereafter be excluded from the sample, because they spent their adolescence before the World War II and hence their early partisan learning could not be easily transferred to the postwar party system.

The literature on early socialization in Japan suggests that the mother is as important as the father as an agent for the generational transmission of partisanship (Kubota and Ward, 1970; Massey, 1976; Iwase, 1977). Therefore, not only the father's but also the mother's partisan location should be examined. We will deal with the following questions: 1) which camp is more successful in transmitting the parent's party; and 2) does parental partisan homogeneity or heterogeneity affect the rate of partisan transmission?

Table 5.3 provides the basic data on the relationship between early parental partisan influences and the respondent's subsequent partisanship. The data show that the category with the largest number of cases is the one in which the

3. For the relationship by age cohort between the strength of the child's partisanship and awareness of the father's partisanship, see Miyake, 1983a.

4. The actual trend toward higher levels of independents from 1967 to 1976 may be somewhat larger than reported here, because the wording used for the party support question in 1967 seemed to depress the levels of identifiers and hence inflate the numbers of independents obtained. This can be seen from comparing the 1967 Japanese Election Study conducted by Ward and Kubota with other surveys fielded at the same time but using the more standard Japanese wording that was also applied in our JABISS study.

Table 5.3   Agreement of Parental Partisanship and Its Impact
            on Respondents

| Parents' Party Affiliation | Respondent's Partisanship | | | | |
	Conservative	Progressive	None, DK	Total	Nᵃ
Both conservative	54	27	19	100%	(293)
Conservative-Noneᵇ	48	31	21	100%	(258)
Both unaffiliated	31	28	41	100%	(933)
Conservative-Progressive	30	50	20	100%	(20)
Progressive-Noneᵇ	15	58	27	100%	(71)
Both progressive	13	58	29	100%	(69)

ᵃRespondents older than 50 are excluded from the sample.
ᵇ"None" includes DK's.

child cannot recall the partisanship of his parents or recalls that both of them were nonpartisan. A child's inability to recall his parental partisanship negatively affects the probability that the child himself will support any party. Forty-one percent of these cases report that they are independent or apolitical. The second biggest group is a homogeneous one in which parents are in agreement on conservative partisanship, while the "both progressive" category has less than one-fourth as many cases. On the whole the progressive families show a slightly higher success rate of transmission than conservative families, particularly if only one parent's partisanship is recalled. This is not an unexpected finding, since extrafamilial influences across the postwar period have favored an intergenerational progressive trend.

Politically heterogeneous families appear to be extremely rare in Japan. Only 1 percent of our sample were aware of conflicting parental party preferences. Interestingly enough, these conflicting cues do not appear to lead to higher levels of nonidentifiers (if we can rely on the small number of cases here). The sex of the parent in these cases also appears to have no effect on the outcome. The higher proportion of progressive party supporters found among those socialized in these heterogeneous families again suggests the effects of extrafamilial influences.

Our data clearly confirm earlier findings, based on paired parent-child interviews, that the family is an effective agent of political socialization in Japan and that mothers as well as fathers play a role. According to our findings, however, the parents' influences appear to be more homogeneous and reinforcing than was supposed, at least as perceived by the child.

■ Group Influence on the Strength of Partisanship

It has been shown that an awareness of parental partisan preferences affects the development of a child's partisanship. The proportion of those who are aware of at least one parent's partisanship is still less than half of the electorate, however, and the success rate of the transmission of partisanship appears to be decreasing. Alternative agencies of political socialization are undoubtedly also at work. Such agencies may be informal groups and formal organizations with which respondents are affiliated as well as the mass media, schools, and the like. Since we do not have data on the roles these groups play in the early socialization process and the data are cross-sectional, our analysis here will be centered around the adult socialization process at the time of our survey.

We have information on whether respondents know persons in their immediate neighborhood intimately and whether they have intimate contacts at their work place. We also have information concerning whether political matters come up as a topic of discussion with neighbors, co-workers, other friends, and family or relatives. Finally, we have information on whether they know what party these persons support. We find that those who know these persons' partisanship and talk about politics with them are relatively small in number, from 9 percent of the sample in the case of "other friends" to 24 percent in the case of "family or relatives." As for formal organizations, we have similar data. First, respondents were asked whether or not they were members of such formal organizations as enterprise associations, labor unions, community associations, religious organizations, and the like. Then, they were asked what political party the other members of those groups support as a whole. Of the sample, 86 percent reported that they are members of at least one such organization, and 29 percent identified their organization's partisan orientation.

Table 5.4 shows the impact of informal and formal group memberships on the partisan strength of respondents. The entries in the table are the mean scores on the strength of party support index, which is constructed by counting "strong partisan" as 4, "weak" as 3, "leaning" as 2, and "independent" and "don't know" as 1. In each category of informal and formal groups, those who can identify the group's party support are likely to be stronger partisans themselves. In contrast, those who have no friends or relatives with whom they discuss politics, and those who do not belong to a formal organization with a political orientation tend to be weaker partisans. The magnitude of the effect shown in the table does not appear to vary much by the type of group. But, since the greatest number of cases fall into the "family or relatives" and "formal organizations" categories, the effect of these two types of groups is more extensive.[5]

5. For a multivariate analysis with strength of partisanship as a dependent variable and parents

Table 5.4 Impact of Informal and Formal Groups on Strength of Party Support

| | Informal Groups | | | | |
Category of Respondents	Friends in Neighborhood	Colleagues in Work Place	Other Friends	Family or Relatives	Formal Organizations
Those who know group's party support	2.97	2.97	2.98	2.88	2.81
Those who don't know group's party support	2.47	2.36	2.45	2.27	2.26
No friends who talk politics or no membership	2.27	2.29	2.30	2.23	2.07

Note: Entry is mean score on Strength of Party Support Index.

These findings demonstrate that the family plays a continuing role after the completion of the preadult socialization process. The individual who discusses politics with family members and other relatives and is aware of their partisanship is likely to be a stronger identifier. Hence the family is also an important agent in the adult socialization process.

■ Early Socialization versus Adult Socialization into Partisanship

We have focused on the direct role of the family in transmitting party support. As table 5.3 has shown, the probability that a conservative family will successfully transfer its partisan tradition to its children is about 50 percent. In the case of a progressive family this figure becomes almost 60 percent, which is somewhat larger but still not big enough to say it is decisive. Moreover, these figures may be deceptive in that they may depend on extrafamilial reinforcing influences. Throughout their adult lives individuals are subject to extrafamilial agents of socialization, which may either reinforce or conflict with their early partisan learning. In the case of conflict, resocialization may move the younger generation away from the political view of their parents.

and informal and formal organizations as independent, see Miyake, 1983a. Some of the results (partial correlation coefficients) are as follows: father (when young) .13, mother (when young) .04, neighbors .10, co-workers .07, other friends .02, family/relatives .16, and organizations .16; Multiple $r = .39$.

We have found above that informal and formal organizations play a large role in determining the strength of partisanship. We would also expect them to function as a reinforcing factor for parental partisanship when they are in agreement or as a deviating force from the early familial impact when they are in conflict. Figure 5.1 represents the two way pressures of early parental and of groups' current partisanship on the child's party position. The partisanship of informal groups is defined by the combined direction of partisanship of the four categories of informal groups.[6] Following the conservative-progressive party designation defined above, the partisan positions of the respondent and two socializing agents (parents during child's adolescence and current informal groups) are divided into three categories: conservative camp, progressive camp and nonpartisan. Accordingly, the figure is divided into nine subfigures— vertically by the three partisan categories of the informal groups and horizontally by the three categories of perceived parental partisanship during the child's adolescence. Each subfigure presents the percentages of respondents identifying themselves as conservative or progressive party supporters. The percentage of respondents falling into the nonpartisan category is omitted from each of the subfigures for the sake of simplicity. If 75 percent of the respondents in a particular category are identified as conservatives and 10 percent progressives, however, the remaining 15 percent are the nonpartisans.

The percentages of conservative and progressive respondents in each category are plotted with a line connecting the two points so that in situations of conflicting influences we can readily see, from the slope of the line, which influence is dominant. For example, if the parent's party is conservative and the group's party is progressive, a positive slope with the line inclined upward from a low conservative to a high progressive proportion suggests that the respondents' informal groups, rather than their parents, have played the dominant role in partisan socialization. Conversely, a negative slope with the line declined downward under the same set of conditions would indicate that early parental socialization played the greater role. On the other hand, if the conditions are reversed, with the parents progressive and the groups conservative, a positive slope suggests a stronger parental influence and a negative one a stronger group influence. We can then compare these situations of conflicting influences with those of reinforcing influences. When the two socializing agents are reinforcing each other (both conservative or both progressive), the slopes of the lines should be at their steepest and hence those slopes can serve as benchmarks in determining the relative weight of the two influences when they are in conflict. In the limiting case, if, for example, the slope for reinforcing progressive

6. The informal group partisan index is constructed so that it represents the majority of the partisan directions of groups of which the respondents are members. When they are even (two conservative and two progressive, for example), they are considered as nonpartisan.

Figure 5.1 Effects of Parental Party and Informal Groups on Respondent's Partisanship

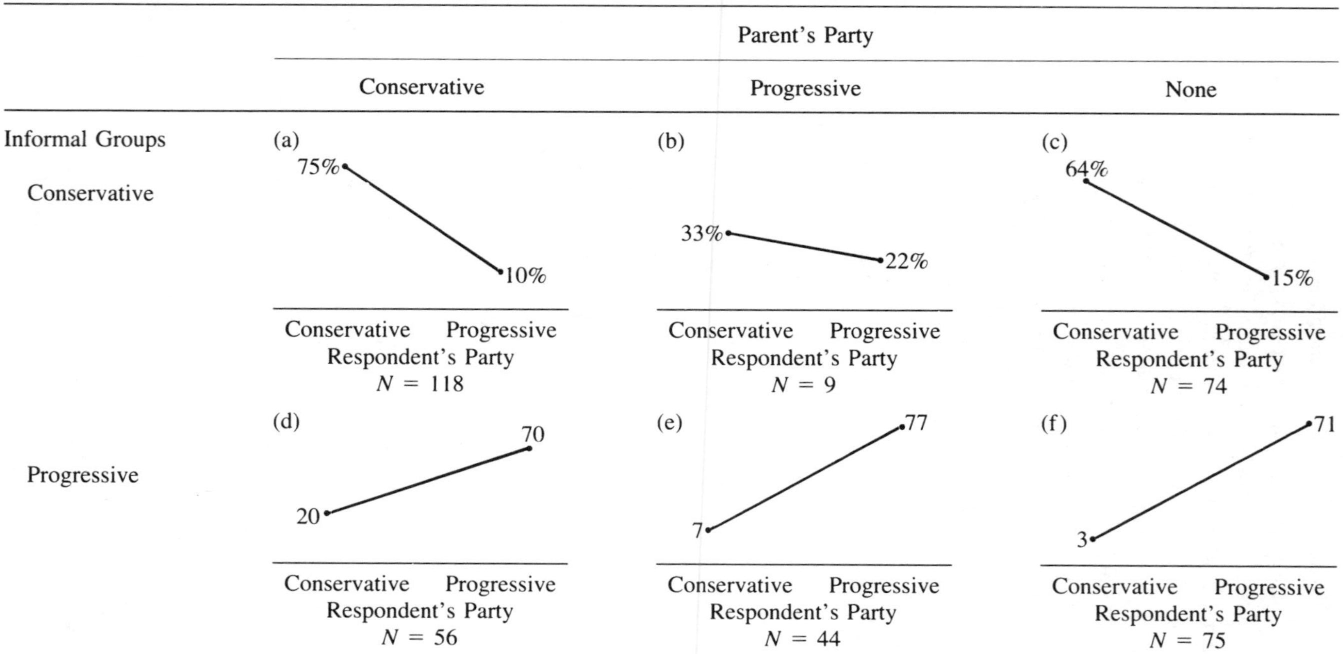

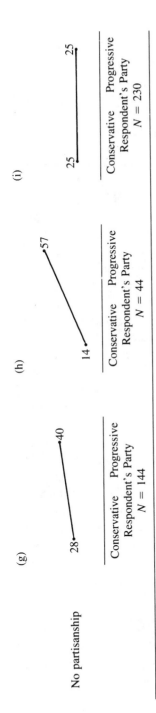

(g)

No partisanship

28• •40

Conservative	Progressive
Respondent's Party	
N = 144	

(h)

14• •57

Conservative	Progressive
Respondent's Party	
N = 44	

(i)

25• •25

Conservative	Progressive
Respondent's Party	
N = 230	

Note: Percentages shown do not total 100% because nonpartisans are excluded.

209

influences remains unchanged when one of the two agents moves to the conservative side, then that agent that has moved from reinforcing a progressive influence to counteracting it has essentially had no effect on the distribution of respondent partisan preferences. In such cases we can say that the influence of the dominant agent has overwhelmed and virtually washed out the influences of the other agent. When neither of the two socializing agents is at work, because the respondent cannot assign any partisan coloration to either, the slope of the line cannot be predicted and will depend on some third factor that we have not identified.

The subfigure (a) positioned at the upper-left corner of figure 5.1 represents the distribution of partisanship of the respondents whose parents and informal groups are both conservative. Among the 118 cases of respondents who fall into this group, 75 percent are conservative while 10 percent are progressive. This is clearly a case of the reinforcing influence of parents and groups on the respondent's partisan attachment. The subfigure (b) is an example of the conflicting influence of progressive parents and conservative groups. The appearance of the line in this subfigure is so much less inclined as to be almost flat. But the proportion of conservative respondents is 11 percent more than that of progressive respondents. This suggests that the informal groups have played a more dominant role in imparting partisan preferences. The same pattern recurs in subfigure (d), where progressive informal groups are posed against conservative parents. In this case the slope is almost as steep as in subfigure (e), where the influences of both agents are reinforcing in the progressive direction. This suggests that progressive informal groups exert a strongly dominating influence over early family learning, to the point of virtually nullifying the effects of a conservative parental upbringing. All in all, the figure suggests that when parents' partisanship conflicts with one's group partisanship, the latter tends to prevail. While the number of cases upon which some of the subfigures are based is quite small, the consistency of the findings across figure 5.1 and the other three figures presented in this section reinforces our conviction that the patterns depicted in the figures are not the product of random sampling error.

It should be remembered that one of the informal groups, "family or relatives," has been combined with the other kinds of informal groups. In this case, however, the category "family or relatives" is most likely to refer to one's spouse and only secondarily to relatives outside the household such as siblings, parents, and other relatives. Of course, there are still many households in Japan where the parents continue to live with the eldest son, but whatever the familial referent, it is clear that latest family influence dominates early family learning. When the "family or relatives" category is singled out and examined, it works as the other informal groups do.

The effect of formal organizations on a member's partisanship is almost the same as that of informal groups. The pattern of data shown in figure 5.2, which represents the two-way pressures of early parental and formal organizations' partisanship on the respondent's partisan preference, is quite similar to and a little clearer than that seen in figure 5.1. Again the key comparisons to be made are between the reinforcing patterns of influence in subfigures (a) and (e) and the conflicting patterns in subfigures (b) and (d). These patterns show that when members perceive their organizations as party-affiliated in one way or another, the organizations become far more effective in guiding their members' partisanship than family tradition. Thus, the more politically relevant the formal organizations are, the stronger their effect.[7]

Soka Gakkai may be the best example of a formal organization whose political orientation is completely unambiguous. Two-thirds of the Clean Government Party supporters are Soka Gakkai members. Soka Gakkai has so recently and rapidly expanded that most of its members appear to be first-generation believers. The JABISS data reveal that the Gakkai plays the dominant role in determining its members' partisanship (though this finding is qualified by the fact that the number of cases in which a father's partisanship is known among Gakkai members is very small). Labor unions provide another good example. The data show that a member of a union that reportedly supports progressive parties is far more likely to be progressive, whatever his father's partisanship may be. There is apparently little room for the retention of a parent's party preference that is not in harmony with the union's affiliation. Because of the limited number of cases, however, all formal organizations were lumped together to be analyzed.

The social network of which one is a part is found to be an important socializing agency, often more effective than family in the early socialization process.[8] In many cases these early networks reinforce family partisan learning. When people as adults move into a new social network, however, they often encounter new partisan influences that are in conflict with their early socialization. Japanese scholars of electoral politics have argued that this change in social context is likely to be associated with a shift away from early parental influences (Miyake, 1979).

In order to provide empirical tests for this argument in the absence of direct

7. The partisan index of formal organizations is constructed in the same way as is the informal group partisan index (see note 6).

8. Aside from the Soka Gakkai and unions that are linked closely with political parties, many professional organizations and some neighborhood organizations play the same role as those party-affiliated organizations. When these organizations are perceived to be politically neutral, they do not work as agents of socialization. However, when members perceive them as having a party attachment—that is, when their partisan activities come to the fore—these organizations become far more effective in guiding their members' partisanship than family, regardless of whether these groups are progressive or conservative.

Figure 5.2 Effects of Parental Party and Formal Organizations on Respondent's Partisanship

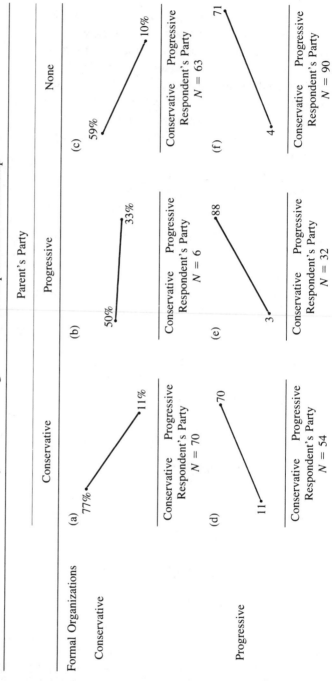

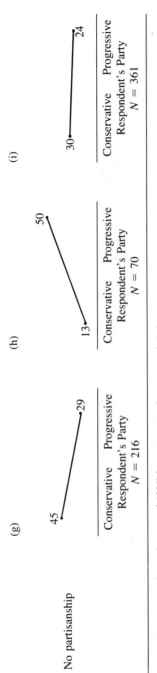

No partisanship

(g)

	Conservative	Progressive Respondent's Party $N = 216$

45
29

(h)

	Conservative	Progressive Respondent's Party $N = 70$

50
13

(i)

	Conservative	Progressive Respondent's Party $N = 361$

30
24

Note: Percentages shown do not total 100% because nonpartisans are excluded.

evidence, a broader perspective may be needed. People are born into a family and that family is, in turn, placed within a community where various social networks interact. In a static society, parents and children are engaged in the same occupation and live out their lives within a single community. The political homogeneity of a community helps facilitate the parental transfer of partisanship. A rapidly changing society may be quite different. Intergenerational occupational mobility from the farm sector to the secondary and tertiary sectors takes place on a large scale. Most occupational mobility takes people from their birthplace to urban areas where they are exposed to quite new social environments. They are placed in new settings and new interpersonal relationships. They may change their familial or their own initial partisan affiliation to conform to their new political environment. To what extent, then, does occupational and geographical mobility affect the parental transmission of partisanship?

First, we will turn to the effect of intergenerational occupational mobility, which is often considered a cue to intergenerational partisan change. Occupations are lumped into two broad groups. Occupational group I includes business owners and managers, those who are engaged in sales and services, and farmers; they are likely to support conservative parties (the LDP and the NLC). Occupational group II contains those who are engaged in technical and professional work, other white-collar workers, and blue-collar workers; they are more likely to support the progressive parties. This classification is made for the purpose of the present analysis on the basis of the general partisan orientation found among those falling into these occupational categories, rather than on any neat sociological grouping of the categories.[9] We will call group I "conservative-oriented occupational groups" and group II "progressive-oriented occupational groups." A combination of the father's and respondent's occupational groups constructs four types of father-respondent pairs in terms of intergenerational occupational mobility. Type A is the pairing in which both are in conservative-oriented occupational groups; in type B, both are in progressive-oriented occupational groups; in type C, the father is in a conservative occupational group and the respondent in a progressive group; and in type D, the father is in a progressive occupational group and the respondent in a conservative group. Type D, however, has so few cases that we can omit it from the following analysis.

We assume that the partisan orientation of the occupational group to which the son or daughter belongs would have some impact on his or her partisanship.

---

9. For the partisan orientation of each of the occupational categories, see chapter 2.

If so, this impact should be particularly clear in the case of type C, the inter-generational movers from a conservative-oriented occupational group to a progressive-oriented group. As they go into a new occupational environment, leaving their father's, they acquire a new partisanship more suitable for their own occupation. This is not the case with types A and B, in which father and respondent share a common occupational environment in terms of the partisan influences that predominate therein. In these cases of "occupational stayers," the partisan socialization that the respondent receives in his or her adult occupational environment is likely simply to reinforce the political training he or she received as a child.

The data shown in figure 5.3 seem to confirm this assumption. Among type A and B respondents, who experience no intergenerational mobility, when the parent's party matches that of the father's and respondent's occupational context (subfigures a and e), they reinforce each other. When the parent's partisanship is not known (subfigures c and f), the respondent's occupational context dominates. When the partisan orientation of father's and respondent's occupational category is in conflict with the parent's party (subfigures b and d), however, the early parental socialization appears to be as or more important than the occupational influences, though the differences in percentages between the proportions of conservative and progressive respondents are rather slight. For type C, the intergenerational movers from a conservative-oriented occupational setting to a progressive one, the new occupational partisanship overwhelms both the early familial transmission of partisanship and the early socialization within the network associated with the old occupational context. The lines in the subfigures (g, h, and i) for type C are all inclined upward to the right, which means that progressive respondents outnumber conservatives in each of these subfigures.

The data in figure 5.4 show the relative effect of a geographical mobility versus parental transmission of partisanship on the child's party position. Even if people change their occupation, as long as they remain in the community where they were brought up, they are still exposed to the same kinds of influence, and this may keep them from changing their partisanship to conform to their new occupational interests. If this hypothesis is plausible, a clear pattern may appear among movers from rural small towns or villages, where residents often share a conservative orientation, to a big metropolitan area, where they have far more chance of being involved in a new political environment that is progressively oriented. Based on the size of the community where respondents currently reside and the community where they were brought up, we can set up the following typology of geographical mobility: type A is "small town or

Figure 5.3   Effects of Parental Party and Occupational Mobility on Respondent's Partisanship

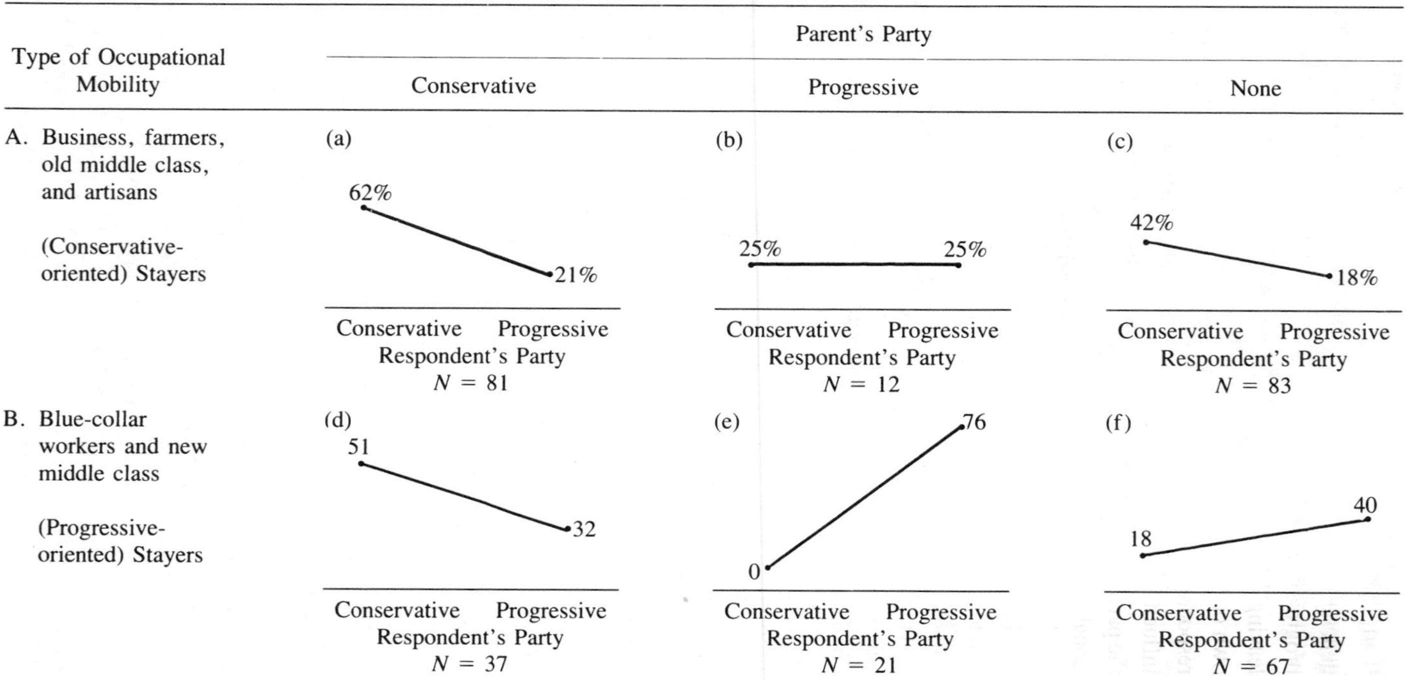

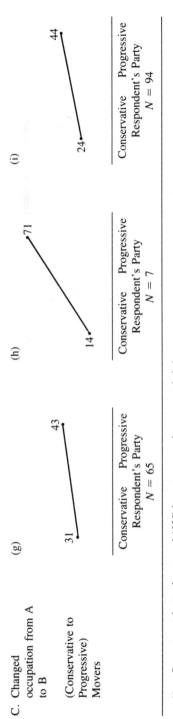

C. Changed
occupation from A
to B

(Conservative to
Progressive)
Movers

(g)

31
43

Conservative Progressive
Respondent's Party
N = 65

(h)

14
•71

Conservative Progressive
Respondent's Party
N = 7

(i)

24
44

Conservative Progressive
Respondent's Party
N = 94

Note: Percentages shown do not total 100% because nonpartisans are excluded.

Figure 5.4 Effects of Parental Party and Migration on Respondent's Partisanship

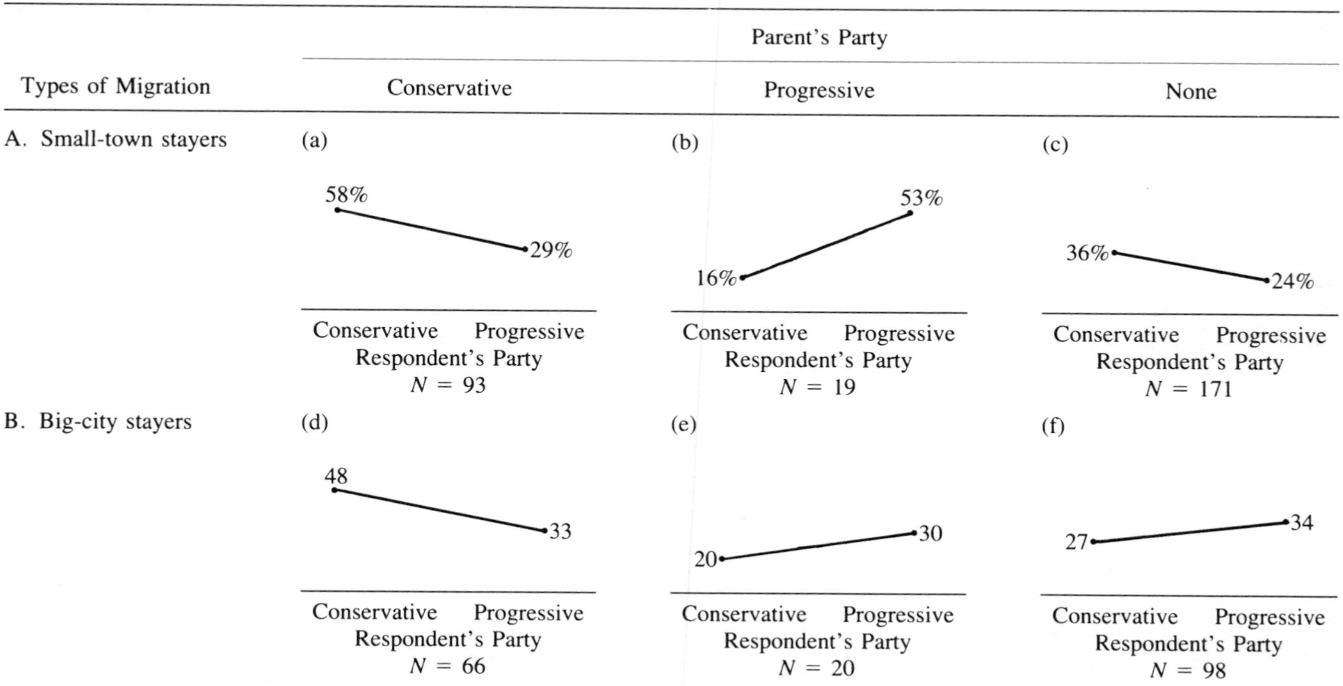

C. Small-town to
bigger-city movers

(g)

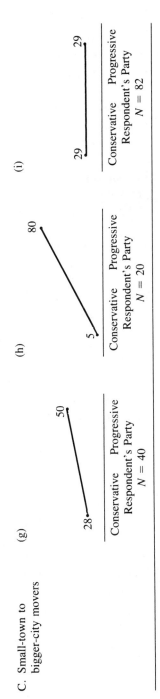

28

50

Conservative Progressive
Respondent's Party
N = 40

(h)

80

5

Conservative Progressive
Respondent's Party
N = 20

(i)

29

29

Conservative Progressive
Respondent's Party
N = 82

Note: Percentages shown do not total 100% because nonpartisans are excluded.

219

village stayers"; type B, "big city stayers"; type C, "movers from a small town or village to a metropolitan area"; and type D, "other kinds of movers."[10] Here again, type D is omitted from the analysis because it contains a variety of movers, within and across community size categories.

The effects of migration should be the same as those of occupational mobility. Those who have stayed in a community since their childhood are likely to conform to the partisan orientation of the community. In cases where such partisanship is not clear enough or where the parents' partisan position is in conflict with the community's, however, it is plausible that stayers would be less subject to the influence of their community's partisan orientation. The parents may have been in the minority, but they were likely to be surrounded by a comfortable social network that their children may continue to enjoy. Thus, for types A and B, if the child is aware of his or her parent's partisan position, the parents' impact should exceed that of the general political orientation of the community. In contrast, movers from a small town or village to a big metropolitan city are likely to be exposed to the political culture of the urban center, which is generally more progressive than the political culture they left behind. Thus, so far as these movers are concerned, the effect of the partisan orientation of the new community might prevail.

The data in figure 5.4 provide evidence favorable to the expectations stated above. If our assumption is correct that the political orientation of rural communities is conservative while that of a big city is progressive, subfigures (a), (e), and (h) are cases of reinforcing community and parental influences. Subfigures (b), (d), and (g) are the examples of the competing pressures of the two. As predicted, both in subfigures (b) and (d), the parental impact surpasses the community's influence, whereas in subfigure (g) the reverse is true. Among "stayers," regardless of their community size, the parental transmission of partisanship is dominant. In contrast, among movers from a small town or village to a metropolitan area, community influences have a greater effect than the parental partisanship.

In sum, politically relevant formal organizations and informal groups are in many cases more effective than the family in instilling partisanship. This is particularly likely to be true if one has changed his or her occupation from, for instance, farmer to business clerk or moved from a rural village to a metropolitan city.[11]

10. A "big" city or "metropolitan" area is here defined as cities with more than 100,000 population.

11. For a multivariate analysis (Hayashi Quantification Scaling, type II) with party support (conservative-progressive) as the criterion variable and with the partisan locations of socializing agencies as independent variables, see Miyake, 1983a. Some of the results (partial correlation

■ Other Agents in the Adult Socialization Process

As we have seen in the preceding section, the family and social networks of various kinds are important agencies in political socialization. When the directions of partisanship of these agencies are in agreement, their influences reinforce each other. When the directions are in conflict, either one of them may prevail. In the 1976 JABISS study, however, the proportion of those who report being aware of their father's partisan position during the years when they grew up is only 42 percent. Those who talk politics with friends or relatives and can identify these persons' partisanship are about a third of the respondents. The proportion of those who belong to formal organizations and can identify the partisanship of the general membership is 29 percent.

A fairly sizable proportion of the electorate, therefore, would appear to be free from any of the above socializing influences. Undoubtedly some unconscious socialization is actually taking place in the home, work place, union or trade association, and other formal and informal associational contexts that some respondents are not able to verbalize. Those who do not think of themselves as discussing politics or do not think of their formal or informal group as a politicized one that endorses a particular party may nevertheless be receiving consistent partisan messages that more or less unconsciously shape their own partisan preferences. Unfortunately, we have no way of estimating these effects. Even if we could, we would still be left with a substantial number of respondents who are not socialized into a partisan identification in any clear way by any of the agents of socialization discussed above. It is very likely that a large portion of these respondents will be nonpartisans. We are also likely to find, however, that even some of these respondents have developed partisan attachments.

The question that arises, then, is how do we account for the partisan socialization of these respondents? The answer, of course, is that there are other socializing agents that we have not considered. Partisan learning must come from somewhere, but where? One plausible candidate is the schools. In Japan the textbooks themselves are an unlikely agent of partisan socialization because they are scrupulously nonpartisan, to such an extent that one finds very few mentions of any specific parties or postwar political leaders. One might suspect, however, that the clear leftist ideological coloration of the strong Japan Teachers Union (Nikkyoso) would be reflected in classroom lectures and hence exert a partisan socializing influence. The JABISS study does not contain any

---

coefficients) are as follows: parents, .09; neighbors, .08; co-workers, .08; other friends, .05; family/relatives, .24; organizations, .28; eta, .54.

items relevant to such a question, and indeed few studies have been made of the role of schools in the Japanese socialization process. The available evidence, however, suggests that despite the teacher union's proclaimed partisan preferences, the direct effect of classroom socialization on political attitudes is small and contributes more to producing political cynicism than partisan attachments.

A second plausible candidate is the media. Here again there are reasons to expect small direct effects. Studies in the United States have shown that the media have little effect on children's partisan political orientation (Chaffee et al., 1970). In Britain, where the press has clear partisan biases, one finds high correlations between the political orientation of the newspaper a respondent reads and the respondent's own partisanship. In this case, however, it appears that the selection of a newspaper depends on prior partisan preferences shaped by other socializing agents and that the role of the British press is primarily to reinforce rather than to instill partisanship (Butler and Stokes, 1976:80–83).

As reported in chapter 8, in the Japanese case perceptions of media partisan bias are very low. While there is some perception that the weekly magazines favor the leftist parties, few perceive any bias on the part of the press or television, and those who report a bias are nearly balanced between those who perceive a bias in favor of the ruling party versus those who see these media as favoring the opposition. While there is a slight tendency for more respondents to perceive the press as favoring the opposition and television the ruling party, the differences are so small that it is unlikely that these media have any significant direct effect in imparting a partisan orientation. On the other hand, it is also reported in chapter 8 that the print media play some role in instilling modern, cosmopolitan values, especially among the young. Since these values are associated with progressive partisan preferences, the media may play an indirect role in propagating values that favor the progressive parties. We might expect higher levels of exposure to the press, then, to be associated with a shift in partisanship toward the progressives.

To test this hypothesis we will focus on the young, those in their twenties, who are likely to be less tied into established politicized social networks, to have less well developed partisan preferences, and hence to be more susceptible to the influences of the press. Table 5.5 reports the partisanship of those aged 20–29 who do not perceive clear partisan preferences within their primary social networks. The table looks first at those who report no partisanship for their parents and *formal* groups, and then at those who perceive no preferences for their parents and *informal* groups. As expected, the effect is small, but we do find a slight increase in the proportion supporting the progressive, relative to the conservative, parties as exposure to political articles increases.[12]

12. The suggestion here, then, is that media exposure may play some kind of indirect role by shaping other attitudes, such as basic social values, which themselves are associated with partisan-

Table 5.5 Frequency of Reading Print Media and Partisanship among the Young (Age 20–29)

Partisan Direction of Respondents	Number of Articles Read about Election in Newspapers		
	None	1–2	3 or more
(A) Who report no partisan preferences for parents or *formal* groups			
Conservative	21	21	8
Progressive	19	21	19
Neither	60	57	73
Total	100%	99%	100%
N of cases	(67)	(42)	(37)
(B) Who report no partisan preferences for parents or *informal* groups			
Conservative	20	12	12
Progressive	20	22	25
Neither	60	65	63
Total	100%	99%	100%
N of cases	(71)	(40)	(40)

Note: While the above patterns are suggestive, given the small magnitudes of the differences and the small numbers of cases involved, neither the A nor B distribution pattern is significant at the .05 level.

Somewhat surprisingly, however, higher exposure levels have no apparent effect on increasing levels of partisanship. We would expect greater exposure to be associated with a growing interest in politics, higher levels of political knowledge and sophistication, and the development of partisan attitudes, especially among the young. The lack of media impact may have something to do with the nature of political reporting in Japan. While the media are strongly supportive of Japan's democratic institutions, political reporting often portrays party politics in a critical, negative light by reporting on factional in-fighting or corrupt practices associated with the parties. In this way the media might

_____

ship. The evidence presented in table 5.5 is only suggestive of such a possible set of relationships, since we cannot be sure what it is about newspaper reading that favors the acquisition of progressive party attachments, or even the direction of causality, since it may be that those with modern values read newspapers more. Other evidence, however, demonstrates that many Japanese journalists have attempted to play a self-conscious socializing role in the diffusion of more modern and democratic values across the postwar period (Kim, 1981).

actually exert a slight dampening effect on the initial acquisition of a partisan preference.

In the final analysis, we can never hope to measure the effects of all the various sources and agents of socialization. In the context of large-scale, urbanized, advanced industrial societies, individuals contact and interact with so many potential sources of political learning that even the individual himself is unlikely to be able to identify where his partisan images and preferences have come from. What is so interesting in the Japanese case is the extent to which Japanese, who are aware of the partisan preferences around them, take on the partisan coloration of their environment and, even more strikingly, change that partisanship when they move from one context to another.

The Japanese family plays an important role in early political socialization and some continuing role in adult socialization. Its influence is felt both on the development and strength of partisanship and on its direction. Though many Japanese voters cannot recall their parents' partisanship or, if they can, many perceive it as "independent" or "apolitical," an awareness of parents' partisanship is the most broadly perceived among the competing socializing agents. As time goes on, the proportion of those who have been socialized under the current party system will increase; thus, barring a major realignment, the role of the family could potentially increase in the future.

Although awareness of a parent's party preference is the most widespread socializing factor, it accounted for less than a half of the respondents' partisanship in 1976. Even among those who failed to recall their fathers' partisan position, roughly three-fifths have developed their own partisanship. Thus, there are other important sources of childhood and adult socialization in operation within Japanese society. Two important socializing agencies for adults are informal groups and formal organizations. When the partisan directions of these groups or organizations agree with that of the parental one, both reinforce each other in transferring partisanship to the respondent. When they conflict, they do not appear to suppress each other by causing confusion and nonpartisanship. Rather, in most cases the partisanship of the more recent influences, the formal and informal groups, seems to be the dominant force. Therefore, adult socialization appears to exhibit a strong potential to undo and reverse early partisan learning in the home. This is particularly the case when respondents have changed occupations from farming or small business to a new middle-class occupation and/or have moved from a rural area to a metropolitan area. Those who experience these changes leave their old social networks and family influences behind and enter into new social and political environments in which very different kinds of partisan influences may be at work.

The effect of these organizations and groups is important, but many respondents do not perceive any clear partisan preference within the various formal and informal groups they are associated with. When the partisanship of their group is ambiguous to them, family influences have a more enduring effect. When partisan information is missing or is nonpartisan, then other agents of socialization such as the schools or the media may exert some indirect influences on partisan affiliation.

Which camp, the conservative or the progressive, gains more from these processes of political socialization? Conservative parents by far outnumber progressive ones. Informal groups are more or less inclined to be conservative. But the partisan orientation of most formal organizations tends to be progressive. In terms of the range of possible influence, the conservative camp has the advantage. In terms of real impact, however, the progressive camp has a higher rate of transmission of its partisanship. In addition, newspapers instill modern values and critical images that may indirectly favor the progressive despite the fact that the press is perceived as being neutral. While it is impossible to add up these diverse influences in any reliable manner, my impression is that they slightly favor the progressive camp. This is even more apparent when we consider, as shown in chapter 3, that the socioeconomic changes that have been taking place in Japan over the postwar decades have been moving the younger generations out of conservatively oriented social contexts and into progressive contexts. In these new environments, the younger age cohorts have come into contact with very different kinds of socializing partisan influences than their parents experienced.

One final caveat that warrants mentioning is that while the range of people who can potentially be influenced by their parents is expanding and the number of organizations is increasing, the direct influence of parents and formal groups is apparently decreasing. The young are found to deviate increasingly from the norms of their families, work groups, and other affiliated organizations. In partisan terms these declining group loyalties are associated with a rise in independents. What about the effects of informal small groups? Are small groups becoming more and more important political socializing agencies? If not, will the mass media begin to play a growing role? Or will dealignment set in? These are questions that our JABISS data cannot address, but they should be noted as issues for future research.

Six ■ Types of Partisanship, Partisan Attitudes, and Voting Choices

ICHIRO MIYAKE

It has often been noted that one of the important features of party support in Japan is its low intensity. Among voters, there seem to be far more independents and apathetics in Japan than in other advanced industrial countries. Even when there is an attachment to one of the parties, it is likely to be weak (Richardson, 1975). Another important feature of party support in Japan is the poor or negative image of political parties. The number of responses to questions of what respondents like or dislike about each of the parties is much smaller in Japan. Even when substantive responses are given, they are often negative comments, even about one's own party (Kubota, 1974; Flanagan and McDonald, 1979; White, 1976). Even though simple cross-national comparisons of frequencies in survey data may be sometimes unreliable, we would still have to conclude that these are the important features of party support in Japan.

Both the weakness of party support in Japan and the negative tendencies in party imagery have historical roots that I cannot discuss in the present chapter. Furthermore, they have not appeared at the same time nor do they come from the same sources. They have emerged in complex ways, and they are related to other attitudes and attributes in a complicated fashion. Until the middle of the 1960s, education, political involvement, and certain values were linked to levels of party support: the higher the educational background and the more modern the value orientation, the more likely a person was to be interested in politics and to report strong party support. Persons who had less education and more traditional values were less interested in politics and more likely to be independent (Watanuki, 1967b; Richardson, 1975). Among political attitudes, political interest or involvement was the key variable. "Political involvement could be a more genuinely prior variable" to party support in places like Japan according to one interpretation (Richardson, 1975:18–19). In contrast with the clear link between party support and political involvement, some fragmented survey evidence indicates that political cynicism, which was already widespread among Japanese voters, was not closely related to any of the relevant political variables.[1]

In the 1970s the relationship among education, political involvement, other variables, and party support changed. An increase in educated independents and in negative partisans was conspicuous in this period. The young and the educated became more cynical and less involved in politics, partly because they had benefited from economic growth and were content with their everyday lives and partly because they were dissatisfied with the governing party—itself the scene of several major scandals as well as appearing far less efficient and more traditional than other institutions. At the same time, they were disappointed with the fragmented, weak, and overly ideologically oriented opposition parties.

The new groups of educated independents and negative partisans contributed to shifting patterns in voting behavior and different perspectives on the political scene. The major portion of abstentions in Japanese elections used to come from the less-educated independents and apathetics; some persons in this category also consistently voted for the Liberal Democratic Party and thus contributed to the stability of conservative support. In the 1970s the educated independents contributed more to abstention; this group and the negative partisans helped to increase the ratio of opposition support as they became floating voters and sources of fluidity in party support.

■ Party Support in the Contemporary Literature

The discussion thus far has focused on relatively simple trends and relationships. Scholarship both inside and outside of Japan, however, indicates that partisanship is more complicated than we have assumed so far. Several Japanese studies have noted that the American conceptualization and measurement of party identifications must be modified in the Japanese context to accommodate Japan's multiparty system (Ikeuchi, 1960; Miyake et al., 1967; Akuto, 1970). Recent scholarship outside Japan has further complicated party identification theory by pointing to the multidimensionality of partisanship. To understand party support in Japan, therefore, we should begin with results of recent relevant studies.

As earlier studies pointed out (Converse, 1976), party identification consists of two components: the direction of partisanship and the strength of partisanship. Initially these two components were represented on a one-dimensional scale with strong support for the Democrats constituting one pole and strong support for the Republicans the other. But recently, many scholars

---

1. For the relationship between cynicism and other political variables, see Miyake (1983b). See also Miyake (1982) for a discussion of the content of politics in the 1960s.

have suggested that attitudes toward the two major parties should be conceptualized as separate dimensions (see, for example, Maggiotto and Piereson, 1977; Weisberg, 1982). Each dimension can then be dealt with separately, and attention can be paid to whatever properties are deemed inherent to that dimension. Thus, conceptualization of the directionality of party support should include voters' attitudes not only toward their own party but toward each of the parties in the system, since these attitudes affect other partisan attitudes and electoral behavior. (For this reason I have developed an index of "support range," introduced later in this chapter.)

Scholarly concern with the dimensionality of partisanship also focuses on the strength component. For example, Katz (1979), among others, has suggested that the currently used scales of party identification—strong support for one party at one end and for the other party at the opposite end, with independence in the middle—are not suitable for multiparty situations. Moreover, the argument on dimensionality does not remain this simple. Weisberg (1980) argues that each aspect of the strength component constitutes an independent dimension—that is, strength of identification, strength of independence, and attitudes toward the political party system are separate dimensions. Elsewhere, Dennis (1981) suggests that the separate categories of partisanship differ with respect to three underlying factors: partisan direction, party system support, and political involvement.

Building on these arguments, I will assume in this chapter that partisanship has multiple underlying dimensions. I further assume that there are several types of partisanship based on various combinations of the multiple dimensions of partisanship drawn from a dimensional analysis. I will argue that this development of a complex typology can better explain the recent trends in political attitudes and electoral behavior in Japan than earlier analyses that examined primarily the links between political involvement and party support.

This chapter begins with the introduction of indexes that are designed to represent the major aspects of partisanship. These indexes are then entered into a dimensional analysis from which two major dimensions are derived. On the basis of these results, four types of partisanship are constructed. The characteristics of these types are then examined in terms of their relationship with some background variables and basic attitudinal scales. Last, their effects on the stability of partisanship, issue attitudes, and electoral behavior will be analyzed.

■ Measures for Different Aspects of Partisanship

The party support question employed in the JABISS survey is one of the most commonly used measures of partisanship in Japan. The respondents were asked, "What party do you support?" To those who did not mention any party name, we then asked, "Is there any political party that you ordinarily like?"; if so, "What is it?" Those who named a party they supported were asked, "How strongly do you support that party: enthusiastically or not so enthusiastically?" This is a close replication of the party support questions employed in the Japan Participation Survey in 1966 (Ikeuchi, 1974; Verba, Nie, and Kim, 1978) and similar to the new party support questions in the American CPS election studies of 1980 and 1982.[2]

From the answers to these questions, I constructed one index of strength of partisanship from each set of these items that were repeated on both the first (W1) and second (W2) waves of the survey. Besides these two partisan strength indexes, the JABISS survey included four measures of positive-negative feeling toward parties: (1) a measure of party anti-support that is commonly used in Japanese surveys; (2) feeling-thermometer questions tapping the degree of positive or negative feeling toward each of the parties; (3) open-ended party affect questions about the respondent's likes and dislikes regarding three parties—the LDP, JSP, and JCP; and (4) party evaluation questions—a series of questions that ask the respondents to name the party they think is most capable of resolving different problems or performing different functions (such as representation of occupational interests).

The first of these four party affect measures is an index of the number of opposed parties. The respondents were asked if there were any parties they would never support. People who answered affirmatively were then asked to name these parties. This is the measure of what we call "party anti-support." About half of the respondents mentioned at least one party that they would never support. From the replies to this question we developed two indexes. One is the "support range" index that will be introduced later in this chapter. The other is the "number of opposed parties" index, which is computed by simply counting the number of parties respondents mentioned as ones they would never support. The resulting index turned out to be highly correlated with the strength of partisanship index. The stronger respondents are in terms of partisan attachment, the more parties they tend to oppose.

The second index we developed is based on responses to a feeling-thermometer question like that used in various CPS American election studies.[3]

---

2. Question A9 of the CPS 1982 election survey questionnaire reads as follows: *A9:* "In your mind, do you think of yourself as a supporter of one of the political parties, or not?"; *A9a:* (If yes) "Which political party do you support?"; *A9b:* (If no) "Do you ever think of yourself as closer to one of the two major parties, or not?"; *A9c:* (If yes) "Which party do you feel closer to?"

3. Our wording for this question is somewhat different and goes as follows: "People have all kinds of feelings toward the people and groups that are influential in politics. In answering the following questions, if you neiither like nor dislike a person or group, would you indicate this by giving them a rating of fifty degrees? If you like the person or group would you give them a rating

Since respondents were asked how they felt about each one of the six parties contesting the 1976 election, we have feeling scales for each of these parties. A summary index for positive-negative feelings across the six parties was then constructed; each of the scales was collapsed so that thermometer values 51 degrees and higher are considered as positive feelings, a reply of 50 degrees is coded as neutral, and an answer of 49 degrees or below is treated as negative.

The categories of the index (see the left side of table 6.1) are those employed by Crewe (1976) and Weisberg (1982). The positive, neutral, or negative designation to the left of the hyphen refers to the respondent's feelings toward the party he or she supports, while the label to the right of the hyphen refers to feelings toward other parties. For multiparty systems, categorization becomes a bit more complex. Thus, by "Positive-Pos/Neg" I mean that a respondent is positive toward his or her own party and has mixed positive and negative feelings toward other parties, identifying at least one disliked party. Twenty-eight percent of the sample who manifested other than neutral feelings displayed this kind of response pattern. The "Positive-Negative" category signifies that one likes only one's own preferred party and dislikes others. Thirty-three percent of the sample (excluding persons who gave neutral responses) replied in this fashion. "Other Types" combines the other possible categories that are not specified in table 6.1; some of the patterns are fairly illogical, such as the case of a respondent who dislikes the party he supports and likes one of the other parties. Four percent fell within this category. "Negative-Negative" was also a small category, accounting for only 4 percent of the respondents who manifested other than neutral feelings.

The third index is constructed from positive-negative party affect items. The CPS American election survey normally asks respondents what they like and what they dislike about each of the parties. My colleagues and I sought similar information from the 1976 Japanese respondents, using a slightly different but almost equivalent question to that employed in the CPS surveys.[4]

In their answers to our questions, most party supporters said more positive than negative things about their own party and were either negative or neutral about other parties. A series of scandals involving high officials of the govern-

---

between fifty and one hundred degrees, and if you dislike them a rating between zero and fifty degrees? Then how do you feel about . . . "

4. Our wording for the party affect question was as follows: "How do you feel about the LDP—you may mention whatever you have in mind—for instance, what you like about the LDP or dislike about it?" This question was repeated for the JSP and JCP. The responses were then coded into "positive," "negative," and "neutral" references to construct a positive-negative party affect index.

Table 6.1   Positive-Negative Pattern and Strength of Partisanship

Positive-Negative Partisanship	Feeling Thermometers and Strength of Partisanship			Party Affect and Strength of Partisanship		
	Strong	Weak	Leaning	Strong	Weak	Leaning
Positive-pos/neg	30	29	23	8	5	6
Positive-negative	49	30	25	51	39	20
Positive-neutral	4	5	2	7	7	11
Neutral-negative	10	13	14	15	12	14
Negative-negative	1	5	8	5	9	14
Neutral-neutral	3	5	14	3	6	9
Apathetic	2	8	6	7	18	17
Other types	1	5	8	4	3	9
Total	100%	100%	100%	100%	99%	100%
N	(169)	(618)	(111)	(130)	(542)	(81)

ment and spiraling inflation probably made the LDP unusually unpopular at the time of the survey, however, as was reflected in the fact that views regarding the LDP were much worse than those of other parties.[5] Indeed, only 5 percent of the supporters of the five opposition parties expressed positive views about the LDP, whereas 64 percent of them held negative views. Even more dramatic evidence of the unpopularity of the LDP is found in the fact that among LDP supporters, those who held positive images were in the minority (45 percent), while the majority of the LDP supporters were either negative (10 percent), neutral to their own party (11 percent), or remained silent (32 percent). Actually, the figures for the JSP, while better than those for the LDP, are not as positive as might be expected. The ratio of positive versus negative views among JSP supporters is 57 to 13 percent. Thus, the unpopularity of the governing party is not accompanied by the high popularity of the opposition, even among opposition party supporters.

A party affect index was constructed from the replies to the likes-dislikes items in the same way as the partisan feeling index explained above. Table 6.1 shows the relationships between strength of party support and both this index and the party feeling-thermometer index. One would expect that the stronger

5. The responses given by more than 10 percent of the sample are as follows: LDP—"Lockheed scandals, corruption, money power politics," "Favors big business and industries"; JSP—"Always opposes the government; their ideas and policies are impractical and unrealistic," "In favor of working class, salaried people"; JCP—"Emotional repulsion toward JCP." Most of these responses represent negative views of parties.

one was in partisanship, the more likely one would be to be a polarized partisan ("Positive-Negative"), and the weaker one was, the more likely one would be a negative partisan ("Negative-Negative"), a neutral partisan ("Neutral-Neutral"), or apathetic (no affect). The data in table 6.1 confirm this expectation. About half of the strong partisans expressed a polarized pattern in regard to feelings and party images, whereas less than a quarter of the leaners did so. Correspondingly, negative partisans are rare among the strong partisans, whereas they occupy a small but not negligible portion among the party leaners.

Our fourth measure of positive-negative feelings toward the parties was constructed from a set of questions asking respondents about their evaluations of the parties. Party evaluations were derived from eight closed-ended questions in the postelection survey, asking respondents to name the party they thought best, most suitable, or most capable of resolving a particular problem or performing a particular function, depending on the specific wording of each question. Most party supporters saw their own party in a favorable light. Since we had found quite a few "negative partisans" on the basis of the replies to open-ended questions on party images, however, there should have been some party supporters who did not name their own party but one of the opposing parties in their replies to these evaluation questions. In fact, such a pattern emerged in certain instances. In response to the question of which party best represents the area the respondent lives in, the supporters of the NLC, a splinter party from the LDP, referred more often to the LDP than to their own party. Even among JCP supporters, who were the most loyal to their own party, 34 percent and 27 percent named the JSP and the LDP, respectively, as the parties most competent to represent their place of residence.

We tried to compose a positive-negative party evaluation index, using the eight-party competence items, that would be similar to the indexes of partisan feeling and party affect introduced above. Because it was not possible to register negative replies to this question, we coded references to one's own party as "positive" and references to other parties as "negative." The categories in this index may be summarized as follows:

Positive-None   named only one's own party;
Positive-Positive   named both one's own party and another party or parties, but named one's own party more often than others;
Negative   named one's own party less often than another party or parties *or* did not mention any party name;

All the Same   mentioned "all parties are the same" in place of naming a
                      specific party label.[6]

In addition to the two strength of partisanship and four partisan affect indexes just described, two indexes of cognitive partisanship level were also constructed using the information on partisanship collected in the JABISS survey. Values on the first index are the total number of responses to the six thermometer questions and the party like-dislike open-ended questions used in the pre-election interview. The second index is based on the total number of parties named in response to the eight party competence questions from the postelection interview.

■ Types of Partisanship

The eight indexes introduced above were entered into a factor analytic type of quantitative analysis developed by Chikio Hayashi and known as Type III Quantification Scaling. (See the appendix to this chapter for an explanation of this statistical procedure; see also Hayashi, 1985, 1988a, 1988b, and 1989, and Torgerson, 1958:338–43). One major advantage of the Hayashi techniques, which are widely used in Japan, is that they present scores for each value of a variable, not just one score for the entire variable. These statistical techniques assume that all variables, whether independent or dependent, are measured at the nominal level and hence they are most useful for categorical variables and for ordinal variables that do not conform to linear relationships. This statistical

6. The table below shows the relationship between the party evaluation index and the party affect index.

Party Evaluation (Wave II Interview)

Party Affect (Wave I)	Positive-Positive	Positive-None	Negative	All the Same
Positive-Pos/Neg	32	19	25	9
Positive-Negative	32	41	24	31
Positive-Neutral	3	4	5	3
Neutral-Negative	13	10	12	13
Negative-Negative	4	2	9	6
Neutral-Neutral	2	4	5	13
Apathetic	4	7	9	13
Other types	10	13	11	12
Total	100%	100%	100%	100%
N	(197)	(375)	(224)	(32)

method was used to analyze the underlying structure of the relationships between the different scales.

Table 6.2 contains a listing of the weights (roughly comparable to loadings in factor analysis) that are assigned to each category of the indexes entered into the analysis.[7] The weights are adjusted so that the grand mean of each scale is zero and the variance from it is one hundred times the correlation coefficient of each solution. Only the results of the first two solutions or dimensions appear in table 6.2.[8] This statistical treatment differs markedly from factor analysis treatments that are standard in Western nations. In those analyses that generate only one number per variable, the exercise is to identify which variables load heavily on each dimension. One looks then for high and low loadings and expects to find that one set of variables will load highly on one dimension and a different set of variables will have low loadings on that dimension but high loadings on another dimension. In the Hayashi Type III Quantification Scaling it is not unusual to find that nearly all variables have high positive and negative weights on all dimensions. The key to interpreting the meaning of each dimension is to identify not simply the magnitude of the positive and negative scores but how they are polarized across each variable. The pattern through which a dimension differentiates each variable's categories provides the clue to grasping its meaning.

With this in mind, a variable-by-variable examination of table 6.2 reveals that arrayed at the opposite ends of the first dimension are strong identifiers versus "Don't Know" (DK); cognitions of opposed parties versus no such cognitions; positive, negative, or other partisan feelings or party affect versus no partisan feelings or affect; positive or negative party evaluations versus all the same or none; and high cognitive levels versus low cognitive levels. This dimension, then, is tapping an affectively neutral, cognitive level of party and partisan awareness. The second dimension, on the other hand, does not distinguish cognitive level but rather affective orientations toward the parties. Here we find arrayed strong identifiers versus independents; opposition to no parties versus DK or opposition to many; positive or none versus negative or neutral

7. The criteria for the construction of the positive-negative partisan indexes were originally twofold: whether a reference was positive, neutral, or negative and whether the party referred to was one's own party or not. The latter criterion is sometimes disregarded for the sake of simplicity and generalizability. To be more concrete, the positive-negative partisan patterns that appeared in table 6.1 were collapsed so that, in each of the pattern labels reported in table 6.2, the right side of the hyphen (attitudes toward parties other than one's own) is disregarded. The party evaluation index was not collapsed, however.

8. The other dimensions were considered irrelevant on the grounds that the correlation coefficients of the solutions were less than .50 and their substance and interpretations were not easily identifiable.

Table 6.2 Dimensionality of Partisanship Based on Hayashi
Quantification Scaling

	Dimension 1	Dimension 2	N of Cases
Strength of partisanship (W1)			
Strong	−126	149	227
Weak	−49	35	824
Leaning	−9	−110	148
Independent	106	−163	425
DK	190	131	150
Strength of partisanship (W2)			
Strong	−131	157	178
Weak	−41	14	906
Leaning	70	−152	17
Independent	150	−209	173
DK	185	88	77
N of opposed parties (W1)			
More than two	−102	67	129
One	−73	15	774
None	70	−72	664
DK	129	114	229
Partisan feeling (W1)			
Positive	−75	41	947
Neutral	97	−173	136
Negative	11	−193	415
None	264	262	241
Other	−72	14	57
Party affect (W1)			
Positive	−95	63	648
Neutral	77	−126	58
Negative	−34	−102	559
None	168	46	502
Other	−82	−50	29
Party evaluation (W2)			
Positive-positive	−69	28	292
Positive-none	−43	50	580
Negative	−64	−79	240
All the same	164	−214	96
None, DK	87	1	558
Cognitive level of party image (W1)			
Lowest	302	308	184
	99	48	135
	39	−99	139
Middle	65	−121	298
	−64	−59	450
	−104	45	385
Highest	−91	−29	205

(continued)

Table 6.2 (*Continued*)

	Dimension 1	Dimension 2	N of Cases
Cognitive level of party evaluation (W2)			
Lowest	29	−34	216
	−29	−34	281
Middle	−60	−20	151
	−92	68	258
Highest	−117	94	215
Correlation coefficient	.68	.50	

Note: W1 (first wave) refers to the preelection survey; W2 (second wave) refers to the postelection survey.

partisan feelings and party affect; positive versus nègative or all the same evaluations and less clear linear alignments on cognitive levels.

As shown in table 6.3, four types of partisanship were established by using these two dimensions to construct a two-by-two table classification. The zero value was used as the cutting point for each of the two dimensions. *Loyal partisans* are high on both dimensions, combining a high level of cognitive awareness of parties with a strong positive affective attachment to their supported party. These respondents tend to be "strong" partisans who indicate "more than two" opposed parties, "positive" feelings toward parties, "positive" party affect, and "higher" or "middle" cognitive levels. Moving counterclockwise around the diagram, we find a second type labeled *negative partisans*. Negative partisans share high levels of political awareness with loyal partisans but lack a strong positive affective tie with the party they regularly vote for. We may view these respondents as shallow partisans, and, indeed, because of the lack of an affective tie, the attachment may not be deep or necessarily durable. On the individual indexes, these respondents are more likely to be leaning partisans and holders of "negative" partisan images or feelings; they also report "middle" or "higher" levels of political cognition.[9]

Our third type are low on both dimensions of partisanship and hence logically should be labeled *nonpartisans*. Indeed, as will be shown in table 6.4, nearly 70 percent of nonpartisans emerge as independent or DK on the standard party support question. While some do claim to support a party, these are likely to be either very nominal or volatile attachments or attributable to measurement error. Our fourth type, the *uninformed partisans*, are analogous to the mobilized voters discussed elsewhere in this volume. They have positive, trusting

9. The labels *loyal partisan* and *negative partisan* are adapted from Crewe (1976:52–53). Though the substantive meanings of our categorization are similar to Crewe's, the methods of deriving our categories were quite different.

Table 6.3   Four Types of Partisanship

Dimension 1

Cognitive Partisanship

High ——————————— Low

		Loyal partisans	Uninformed partisans
	High		
Dimension 2		(38%)	(15%)
Affective Partisanship		Negative partisans	Nonpartisans
	Low		
		(25%)	(22%)

feelings toward the party they regularly vote for but have very little knowledge or awareness about politics. On our individual indexes, this uninformed group falls mainly into the "don't know" groups.

The figures in parentheses in table 6.3 are the percentage distributions for each type in the total sample. These percentages represent a relative measure because the scores on our two dimensions were standardized. Thus, we cannot tell the absolute size of each type of partisanship through the method we are using. This is somewhat of a drawback since the purpose of the analysis is to examine the utility of this new classification of partisanship. Nevertheless, in relative terms the reported distribution pattern is meaningful.

Tables 6.2 and 6.3 suggest the nature and meaning of each type of partisanship. This chapter will also demonstrate how the different types are correlated with people's general political attitudes and their social backgrounds, an analysis which provides additional confirming evidence of the meaning of the different partisan types. To conduct this analysis, three general political attitude scales—a psychological involvement in politics scale, political cynicism scale, and cognitive level scale—were created as factor score scales from a single factor analysis of individual political attitude items and scales that included such attitudes as political interest, efficacy, cynicism, trust, mass media exposure, issue and candidate familiarity, and the like.[10] Figure 6.1 shows the mean scores on these three general scales for each of the four types of partisanship.

10. In an attempt to identify the underlying dimensions of an attitude structure broadly called "psychological involvement in politics," a factor analysis was conducted on ten indicators of political involvement and trust. The items used are identified below along with the results of the

The results in figure 6.1 further confirm the distinctions that define each of our partisan types. Loyal partisans are shown to be the most psychologically involved and the most informed regarding politics; they also are very low on the cynicism scale. In sharp contrast, the uninformed partisans are the least involved in politics and have the lowest levels of political information, but they are just as trusting of politics as the loyal partisans. Negative partisans have the same levels of political information as loyal partisans, and while their level of psychological involvement is slightly lower than that of the loyal partisans, it is far higher than the levels found for either the uninformed partisans or nonpartisans. Negative partisans, however, have one salient characteristic that distinguishes them from the loyal partisans, and that is their high level of cynicism. Finally, the nonpartisans are as cynical as the negative partisans and almost as low in psychological involvement as the uninformed partisans. On the cognitive level scale, they fall about halfway in-between the loyal and negative partisans at the high end and the uninformed partisans at the low end of the scale, making them low in political awareness in relative if not absolute terms. In figure 6.1 and in subsequent figures and tables the partisan types are ordered *loyal, negative, nonpartisan,* and *uninformed.* It may seem counter-intuitive to list nonpartisans third rather than fourth, but note that in figure 6.1 this listing conforms to the four types' rank order on the psychological involvement and cognitive level scales. These distinctions will have important impact on other characteristics of the types discussed below.

_____

factor analysis. The first dimension represents political interest or involvement, with high loadings on political interest, mass-media exposure, political discussion, political efficacy, citizen duty, and issue familiarity. The second dimension is clearly political cynicism. The third dimension can be interpreted as signifying the cognition level, since the two familiarity or awareness indexes have relatively high loadings on this dimension.

Dimensions

	Involvement	Cynicism	Level of Cognition
Political interest	.73	.02	.14
Mass media exposure	.58	−.03	.30
Political discussion	.34	−.02	.33
Political efficacy	.29	.01	.01
Citizen duty	.28	−.01	.10
Issue familiarity	.44	.08	.48
Awareness of governmental performance	.10	.05	.52
Political cynicism	.02	.64	.06
Political trust	.00	.63	−.01
Institutional support	−.02	.39	.03

Figure 6.1 Psychological involvement, cynicism, cognitive level, and type of partisanship

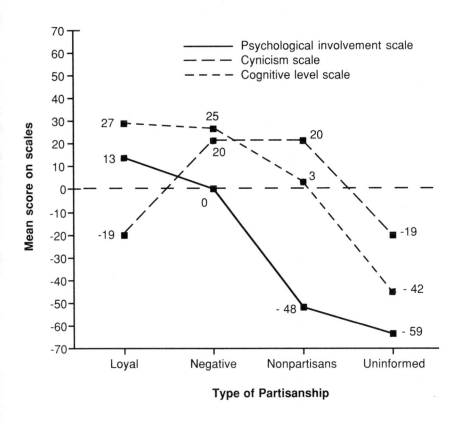

We can anticipate, from our analysis of the four types of partisanship above, that persons in each partisan category will be distinct in regard to social background. The cross tabulation of the types of partisanship with several key social background variables in table 6.4 confirms our expectations. Loyal partisans tend to be middle-aged and older men, with somewhat above-average educations; they are least likely to be found in the big cities. Negative partisans tend to be young, urban, and highly educated. As expected, nonpartisans are far more likely to be young and somewhat more likely to be women; they tend to be found in big cities and rural areas. Finally, the uninformed partisans are heavily older, female, rural, and low in education. All four partisan types are dispersed fairly evenly across all occupational categories, except that loyal partisans are somewhat overrepresented among white-collar workers and self-employed merchants and manufacturers, while farmers are less likely to show up as negative partisans and more likely to uninformed or nonpartisan.

Table 6.4 also includes an analysis of the partisan preferences of each of our four types of partisans. The vast majority of the nonpartisans naturally appear in the categories of "independent" and "don't know," while only 5 percent of the loyal partisans fell into those two categories. The uninformed partisans were much less likely to be independents than the nonpartisans, but more likely to fall into the "don't know" category, yielding only slightly higher levels of party preferences than those found among the nonpartisans.[11] Not surprisingly, given our image of the traditionalistic, mobilized bases of LDP support, the ruling party did disproportionately well among the uninformed partisans, attracting nearly two-thirds of those offering a party preference. When the row percentages, rather than the reported column percentages, are computed, we find that among all the parties, the JCP followed by the DSP supporters contain the highest proportions of loyal partisans, while the CGP has the highest proportion of negative partisans and the NLC the most nonpartisans.

■ Stability and Change in Partisanship

The Japanese party system has undergone remarkable changes over time. The biggest discontinuity occurred between the prewar and the postwar periods, when the shape of partisan alternatives was dramatically altered. The establishment of the "two-party system" in 1955 also began a new era in the history of Japan's party system. Finally, the recent rise of several new parties seems to represent a gradual shift to a multiparty system from the two-party system of 1955. Whether a new party system has replaced the old one is yet to be seen, even today, over a decade after the 1976 election. But there was a systematic shift away from support for the two establishment parties—the LDP and the JSP—toward support for the smaller opposition parties, especially during the 1960s and 1970s. While the Liberal Democratic Party, until the end of the 1960s, held an absolute majority of party support among those supporting any party, the LDP lost its majority status around 1976 (the time of our JABISS survey). The rate of decline in support for the Japan Socialist Party was even

11. These distinctions are almost true by definition, since the variables on which the dimensional generation of the types of partisanship was based included indexes of partisan strength, which, in turn, contain "independent" and "Don't Know" categories. See table 6.2 above. This analysis and figure 6.1 are presented primarily to demonstrate that our statistically sophisticated dimensional identification of the four types of partisans produced the expected differences in tendencies and characteristics among the types.

Table 6.4 Demographic Attributes, Type of Partisanship, and Direction of Partisanship (In Percentages)

Partisan Type by Demographic Category	Loyal	Negative	Nonpartisan	Uninformed	N
Sex					
Male	45	25	22	8	(777)
Female	31	22	26	21	(1,019)
Age					
20–29	29	26	33	12	(371)
30–44	34	27	26	13	(659)
45–59	43	20	20	17	(484)
60 and over	44	17	16	23	(282)
Education					
Primary	34	21	24	21	(811)
Secondary	39	24	25	12	(726)
Higher	40	31	25	4	(259)
Urban-rural residence					
Big city	31	28	31	10	(325)
Middle-sized city	42	28	21	9	(607)
Small city	38	19	20	23	(370)
Town/village	35	17	28	20	(494)
Occupation					
White-collar	50	24	21	5	(237)
Sales/service	37	26	25	12	(225)
Blue-collar	40	26	25	9	(185)
Farmers	33	18	30	19	(170)
Merchants/manufacturers	44	26	22	8	(218)

Direction of Partisanship (W1) by Partisan Type

LDP	46	32	17	28
JSP	27	22	8	9
JCP	8	5	2	0
CGP	6	2	1	3
DSP	5	6	2	1
NLC	3	5	1	1
Other	0	2	0	1
Independent	2	25	57	25
DK	3	1	12	32
N	(683)	(449)	(395)	(269)

greater than that for the LDP. By the mid-1970s, the proportion of support for the JSP among all party supporters fell from 42 percent to 23 percent, which was half of its original level in 1955. Meanwhile, during the 1955–59 period only 2 percent of party supporters were followers of the minor parties, but in the 1977–78 period 32 percent of all party supporters were inclined toward the small parties (including the new splinter parties).

In 1976, many voters would not have been surprised to see the LDP or the JSP split further and some new parties established. Also, party officials of the CGP and the DSP, the two most enthusiastic promoters of coalition government at that time, were apparently ready to dissolve their parties to establish a more broadly based party. Many voters also appeared to be ready to support such movements, according to their responses to appropriate questions in the JABISS survey.

The trends in the aggregate vote in Japan in recent decades, which include a gradual but steady shift of party support and a seemingly ongoing process of realignment and dealignment among voters, suggest that party support at the individual level in Japan would be less stable than that in countries with a more stable party system. We might assume further that the degree of stability or instability differs from one type of partisanship to another. Loyal partisans should be more attached to their own party and should not change their support during a short period of time. The uninformed partisans might tend to be stable for a different reason—their lack of information concerning political events and the stands that the parties take. Negative partisans, in contrast, are well-informed and usually appear to have relatively strong reservations toward their own part; thus they should be able to switch their party more easily than loyal partisans or the uninformed. The behavior of the nonpartisans is difficult to predict. They fall in the middle on information levels, they have little or no experience with party affiliation and exhibit high levels of political distrust, and hence they are more detached from party politics than any other group. As a result, nonpartisans may be the most frequent switchers. Because they often have no party to support, they may move back and forth between partisanship and independence rather than between support for alternative parties.

This section will compare the four types of partisanship in terms of their degree of stability. I will deal with two kinds of data: recall of past party support and the observed patterns of party support during the electoral campaign based on data from the pre- and postelection interviews. The analysis will pay attention to the hypothesis that there is a phenomenon that might be called "support range." I shall argue that persons who switch their party are likely to switch to a party within their "support range" and that party changes beyond the "support range" seldom occur. Finally, if movements beyond the "support range" take place, they occur more often among negative partisans and nonpartisans.

Partisan changes may take place during the period of an electoral campaign. The electorate is subject to fairly intense partisan as well as nonpartisan forces during the campaign period. As a result, some independents may come to support a party, and some partisans may change their party preferences. According to our 1976 findings, 20 percent of the partisans of the six major parties changed the party they supported during the relatively short two- to three-week interval between the pre- and postelection surveys. Furthermore, the rate of change actually goes up to 33 percent when those who changed from independents to partisans or the reverse are included in the calculation. One reason for this low stability was the high propensity to change found among the NLC supporters. Most of the NLC supporters from the preelection interview defected by the time of the second interview, but new NLC supporters emerged in the postelection interview. The group of NLC supporters seems to have been in a process of reorganization—something that all splinter parties undergo sooner or later. We cannot attribute all changes in partisanship to the emergence of that small splinter party, however.

Table 6.5 shows the frequencies of party changes among the supporters of the six major parties and the frequencies of changes between partisans and independents according to type of partisanship. As can readily be seen, negative partisans and nonpartisans are twice as volatile with regard to party support as are loyal and uninformed partisans. Meanwhile, the nonpartisans and uninformed partisans are substantially more disposed to change from the uncommitted category to support a party, and vice versa, than are the negative partisans, and they are dramatically more prone to such behavior than are loyal partisans. It is likely that the recent increase in the number of negative partisans and nonpartisans within the electorate brought about the current trend toward the instability of party support.

These findings demonstrate that Japanese party support is quite volatile, especially that of negative partisans and nonpartisans. We can hypothesize,

Table 6.5   Change of Party Support between Pre- and Post-Surveys

	Loyal	Negative	Nonpartisan	Uninformed
Change of party support				
Among six-party supporters	10%	22%	26%	11%
N	(463)	(223)	(57)	(73)
Between supporters & independents	6	28	41	40
N	(496)	(327)	(162)	(149)

however, that change will be limited to the relevant "range" of party support. There are probably very few partisan changes that involve a move from one extreme to the other of the party spectrum. Rather, we can expect most of the changes to take place within a "support range." A conservative voter may switch from the LDP to the NLC or DSP because of the Lockheed scandal, but he will only rarely go beyond the DSP to the JSP, if the Socialists lie beyond his support range, and he is even less likely to leap over the Socialists to support the more extreme JCP. The breadth of one's support range, however, is likely to vary from voter to voter. Some will be so inclusive as to not exclude any party, whereas others will be very narrow and only permit movement between one center party and another or between the JSP and JCP.

The "support range" is a concept my colleagues and I have developed to represent voters' own conceptualization of their partisan choices (Miyake et al., 1967; Miyake, 1971, 1985). In effect, a voter selects one party as his preferred party at any point in time but may switch his voting choices and even his partisanship in different elections. These shifts in voting and partisanship, however, rarely go beyond the boundary defined by his reply to our question about parties that he would never support. Thus, we composed the "support range" index on the basis of the usual preelection party support questions and the party anti-support data.[12]

To facilitate ease of construction and simplify the resultant support range index, we made five assumptions. (1) The LDP and its splinter party, the NLC, are within the same sector of the support range and thus can be merged (that is, NLC partisans are considered LDP partisans and NLC nonsupport is considered LDP nonsupport for the purposes of the index). (2) The CGP is excluded from the construction of the index because it is closely connected with a new religion (Soka-Gakkai) that has been associated with some unpopular proselytizing tactics. Therefore, rejection of the CGP has little to do with the placement of the other parties on the left-right ideological continuum. Since it would require a second dimension to accommodate these anti-CGP voters, I decided, for the sake of simplicity, to ignore CGP rejections and construct a one-dimensional support range index. (3) In defining the support range, I assumed that the respondent

12. The drawback of these data is their asymmetry. We asked the respondents whether or not they were opposed to each of the parties, but we did not ask them whether they supported parties in the same way. Therefore, we only know the party that they support most and those parties, if any, that they clearly oppose.

An index of support range could also be constructed using thermometer feelings toward the six parties. At first glance, the party feeling thermometers seem a better choice than the party nonsupport question. They can classify the six parties in either "supportive" or "nonsupportive" categories so that a "support range" index is easily composed. "Feeling" toward a party, however, is conceptually different from support, and for this reason the thermometer approach was not adopted here.

would not select parties that are *not* located side-by-side on the ideological continuum but might select a range of two or more contiguous parties. (4) Explicitly opposed parties define the limits of the range of supported parties, a range which begins from the respondent's explicitly supported party and moves outward to the left and right until encountering an explicitly opposed party. (5) All parties falling within that range, thus defined, are considered within the respondent's support range.

Based on these assumptions, a series of ranges of support were defined based on a unidimensional ideological continuum in which the four remaining parties are arranged from right to left in the order of LDP, DSP, JSP, and JCP. This set of ranges can be seen in the left-hand column of table 6.6. The first thing to note is that our support range classification procedures were able to accommodate all but 2 percent of the cases. While this finding would seem to support the utility of the support range concept for describing the Japanese electorate, two caveats need to be mentioned. First, a support range that violates our classification criterion and permits only movement between the two major parties, the LDP and JSP, was permitted on the grounds that in the 1955 party system these two parties were contiguous and respondents who developed their partisan orientations at that time may have developed a support range based on the

Table 6.6   Distribution of Respondents
by Range of Partisan Support

Range of Party Support	Percentages
LDP	2
LDP-DSP	4
LDP———JSP	27
DSP-JSP	3
DSP———JCP	6
JSP	2
JSP- JCP	3
LDP & JSP	9
Other types	2
All parties	42
Total	100%
N	(1332)

Note: The CGP has been excluded from this unidimensional construction of the range of party support.

partisan options that existed then. As shown in table 6.6, 9 percent of our sample fall into an LDP and JSP only support range category.

A second caveat is that table 6.6 demonstrates that our procedures yield extremely broad and undiscriminating support ranges for the large majority of our cases. Forty-two percent fail to exclude any party while another 27 percent exclude only the JCP. Only 7 percent have support ranges limited to within the right, center, or left ranges of the ideological spectrum,, and only another 13 percent have moderately limited ranges including only center-right or center-left parties. While it should be noted that another 12 percent of the sample had more constricted support ranges than identified in table 6.6 in that they excluded the CGP, that excluded information, if retrieved, would not help in locating the left or right boundaries of a respondent's support range. Our conclusion is that the support range concept is a valid one for the Japanese electorate, but that its utility is limited by our operationalization to date. These measurement problems in turn plausibly stem from two limiting factors. First, uninformed partisans and nonpartisans are probably incapable of conceptualizing Japanese parties and politics in terms of an ideological continuum and hence are unlikely to limit consciously their voting behavior within any support range. Second, many Japanese are likely to be reluctant to name opposed parties in a face-to-face interview situation, even if they conform to a narrowly defined support range in their behavior. As a result, our procedures do not permit us to determine whether those who mentioned no parties should be treated as missing data or as potentially willing to support any of the five or six competing parties.

Despite these limitations, it is still interesting to find in table 6.7 that nearly all party switchers confined their defections to within their range of support. Among those who switched parties between pre- and postelection interviews, only twenty-four persons changed their partisanship to a party outside their range of party support as defined above. The entries are the real numbers of deviant cases accruing to each type of partisanship. The percentages shown at the bottom of table 6.7 are the ratios of inconsistent cases to total partisans at the time of the postelection interviews.[13] While the numbers involved here are too small to permit statistical significance, it is nevertheless suggestive to find that once again the negative partisans are the most volatile.

Negative partisans also reported the most frequent changes in response to a question about past partisan consistency. Respondents to the JABISS survey were asked if they had ever supported some party other than their present one. Logic

13. Even when "other types" and "all parties," which by definition never result in inconsistent cases, are excluded from the bases for percentage calculations, the percentages do not go up much. The differences are 3 percent for loyal partisans, 6 percent for negative partisans, and 7 percent for the nonpartisans.

Table 6.7 Partisan Changes beyond the Party Support Range by Type of Partisanship

Range of Party Support	Type of Partisanship			
	Loyal	Negative	Nonpartisan	Uninformed
LDP		2	1	
LDP-DSP				
LDP——JSP	1			
DSP-JSP	2	1		
DSP——JCP	1	2		
JSP	1	2		
JSP-JCP	2	2	1	
LDP & JSP	1	4	1	
Other types				
All parties				
Total *N* of deviant cases	(8)	(13)	(3)	(0)
Percent of total cases	2	4	1	0

dictates that all supporters of new parties should be composed of party-switchers from older parties, former independents, or persons who came of voting age after these parties were formed. About half of the 1976 supporters of the DSP and the CGP and two-thirds of those who supported the NLC were in fact found to be former supporters of other parties. Moreover, half the supporters of the JCP, which had recently increased its number of supporters, reportedly came from other parties. Even within the two established parties, the LDP and the JSP, from 10 to 20 percent of their supporters were actually switchers.

The recall data on party change are actually fairly difficult to interpret. Table 6.8 shows the extent of changes during different year periods among different party types on the basis of the recalled data. In general, we found that the stronger a voter's partisanship, the more likely he was to report he had changed his party in the past, whereas the weaker the voter's partisanship the less likely he was to report changing his party. Since stronger partisans should rather be more stable, this finding suggests that the high rates of persons who "never changed" among the uninformed and nonpartisans can most likely be attributed to higher rates of forgetting. Indeed, compared to the loyal and negative partisans, these categories seem particularly unlikely to have recalled any change that occurred more than four years earlier. In contrast, in the case of more recent changes, within one to four years, where recall is likely to be better even for those with low political involvement, the two alienated or distrustful

Table 6.8 Change of Party Support in the Past (In Percentages)

	Type of Partisanship			
	Loyal	Negative	Nonpartisan	Uninformed
Never changed	74	72	81	87
Changed				
1–4 years ago	9	13	11	4
More than 5 years ago	16	14	6	6
DK	1	1	2	3
Total	100%	100%	100%	100%
N	(503)	(337)	(286)	(206)

categories, the negative and nonpartisans, exhibit the highest levels of switching.

To summarize, tables 6.5 through 6.8 demonstrate that in the very short-term, loyal partisans have switched their party least, though many loyal party supporters recalled changing parties several years back. Among the uninformed who were also party supporters, we found the lowest levels of recall regarding party switching in the past, and few of these persons changed parties between the two interviews. They did often alternate between partisanship and "DK" or "independent" responses, however. In contrast, negative partisans tended most commonly to be party switchers. They often admitted that they had changed parties in the recent past, and just about half of the negative partisans either changed parties or switched from partisanship to nonpartisanship between the two interviews. Moreover, when changing parties, negative partisans were the most likely category to move to parties beyond their party support range. The nonpartisan group had difficulty recalling partisan changes in the distant past, but they changed parties or moved between partisanship and nonpartisanship between the pre- and postelection interviews more often than the voters in any other category.

■ Issue Attitudes and Types of Partisanship

Past surveys in Japan have accumulated evidence that party support or partisanship, as we have broadly defined it here, functions much like the narrower American concept of party identification. That is, we can view partisanship in Japan largely as a "perceptual screen" for political information that structures political attitudes and guides political behavior. Most Japanese parties are not ideological and most Japanese voters are not ideological either. Voters do tend to have vague ideas about the ideological differences between parties, however, and to place themselves, when asked, in either the conservative or the progressive camp. And it is not uncommon for Japanese voters to develop their own political attitudes toward issues and to make partisan choices on this basis.

I shall demonstrate in this section that the types of partisanship discussed throughout this chapter are in fact related to people's degree of familiarity with political issues and to the consistency of their issue attitudes. The respondents were asked about their opinions on twelve issues that were salient in 1976 (see chapter 7 for a more extensive discussion of the issue items). Immediately following their response to each of the twelve issue questions, those respondents who expressed an opinion were asked, "Which party is closest to your opinion on this issue?"

Frequencies of responses to the issue questions should be related to the respondents' level of political knowledge; frequencies of responses to the party issue proximity question should in turn be more closely related to people's degree of psychological involvement. If this is indeed the case, the curve for the response frequency to the issue opinion items and curve for the frequency of replies to the party issue proximity questions should be similar to the curves for level of cognition and political involvement, respectively, shown above in figure 6.1. The data reported in figure 6.2 clearly demonstrate that this is the case. Negative partisans have a degree of familiarity with current political issues similar to that of loyal partisans, while the nonpartisans and the uninformed are far behind those two groups of well-informed partisans with regard to issue knowledge. In contrast, the curve for responses regarding party issue proximity falls more quickly and steadily than the issue familiarity curve and closely resembles the pattern found for psychological involvement in figure 6.1.

Among those who named a party closest to their own views, on the average only half named their own party as closest to their opinions. There were many "don't knows" and "no such party exists." The "defection" rate for replies to this question was higher, for example, than in the case of the party evaluations mentioned earlier. Partisanship does have some effect, however. On whatever issue they are asked about, party supporters tend to believe that their own party is closer to their opinion than any other party. We also found a tendency among supporters to evade the issue and refuse to answer, or to answer "no such party exists," when, as was the case with the LDP supporters being asked about the Lockheed scandal issue, their party's perceived position was unpopular. There are exceptions, however. Among supporters of the DSP and the NLC there were relatively few who named their party as the closest to their own opinions; such

Figure 6.2   Issue familiarity and type of partisanship

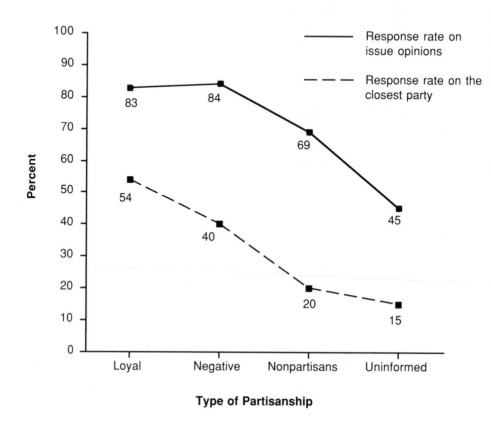

persons were, in fact, in the minority. NLC supporters were the most extreme case. Only 13 percent of the NLC supporters named the NLC as the party closest to their views, whereas 51 percent named the LDP and 45 percent named the JSP as closest on at least one issue across the twelve-issue battery.

The frequencies of mention of one's own party as opposed to some other party as close to one's position on the issues may be related to one of two factors. One of these would be the voter's cognitive level. Higher levels of political awareness should give voters more knowledge of other party's positions relative to one's own party and hence increase the chances of realizing that some other party may actually better represent one's own opinion on a particular issue. Another factor would be the voter's affective attachment to their party.

The stronger the affective attachment, the greater the likelihood that one would select one's own party whatever the logic of the situation. If the former factor were the more influential, the same proportions of own versus other party mentions should be found among loyal partisans as among negative partisans. The data shown in table 6.9 demonstrate that, on the contrary, the ratios of reference to own party over other party are lowest among the negative and nonpartisans and highest among the loyal and uninformed partisans. Affective detachment from party politics therefore appears to be the more important factor. The fact that the highest ratios are found among the uninformed partisans, however, suggests that the cognitive argument may also exercise some influence.

Partisan attachment is said to have the effect of structuring individual attitudes on issues along party lines. Thus, party supporters should manifest consistent issue attitudes reflecting the presence of a unified general ideology toward politics. Attitude consistency in this sense should be highest among persons who are loyal partisans according to our typology of party support. In contrast, negative partisan and nonpartisans should be less dependent on parties when they form issue opinions, with the result that their attitudes should be less consistent. This expectation seems intuitively obvious in the case of nonpartisans but may need more justification in the case of negative partisans who, after all, exhibit high levels of issue familiarity. Despite this cognitive awareness, however, we would expect that the negative partisans' lack of positively evaluated ties with a party would inhibit their exposure to their party's ideologically structured positions on the issues.

The findings shown in figure 6.3 seem to confirm our expectations. The curve shown in figure 6.3 represents the coefficient of correlation between an

Table 6.9 Issue Competence and Type of Partisanship

Issue Competence	Type of Partisanship			
	Loyal	Negative	Nonpartisan	Uninformed
Ratio of references to				
(a) One's party	49%	25%	21%	31%
(b) Other party	18	18	16	8
(a)/(b)	2.7	1.4	1.3	3.8

Note: The ratio of references is the result of division of the number of references to one's party (other party) by the total possible references to any party. Nonpartisans are excluded from the sample on the basis of which the percentage is calculated.

Figure 6.3   Ideology and type of partisanship: strength of the association
              between an issue position scale and ideological self-placement

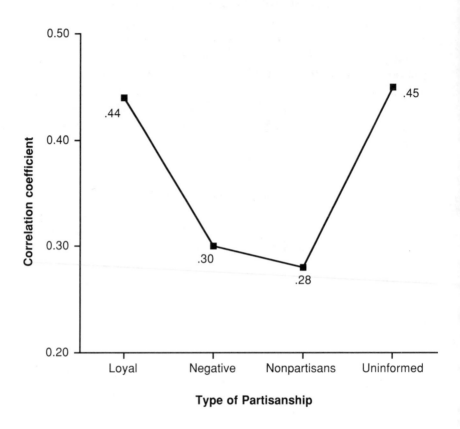

issue position scale and an ideology measure for different types of partisans.
The issue position scale is a factor score scale based on the respondent's
position on the three "cultural politics" issues, the tightly intercorrelated set of
issues that was found to be most strongly associated with partisanship (see
chapter 7). These issues covered the respondent's feelings about the emperor's
power, Japanese defense power, and the Japan–United States Security Treaty.
The ideology measure represents the respondent's self-placement with regard
to the conservative, center, and progressive camps. Interestingly, the curve in
figure 6.3 is the reverse shape of the curve for the cynicism scale shown in
figure 6.1. This suggests that cynicism or affective detachment from party
either directly or indirectly affects the level of partisan attitude consistency.

One may be surprised to find that the uninformed partisans, along with the loyal partisans, are the most able to make the appropriate linkages between their ideological self-placement and their positioning on partisan issues. The relationship here could reasonably have been assumed to be the lowest from among those for the different partisan types, since the uninformed should lack the information to make the appropriate linkages. The same results were shown, however, when we reanalyzed the Ward-Kubota 1967 Japan election survey data. First we should note that the levels of missing data among these uninformed partisans were very high, as only a small proportion of this category had both an ideological self-placement and issue positions. Beyond that, recalling that these uninformed partisans are conservative, older, female, and rural residents, we could argue that for them the cultural politics issues represent "easy issues" in the sense that their traditional value orientations lead them naturally to associate themselves with the conservative side of these value issues and with the conservative camp without referring cognitively to their party's stands (Carmines and Stimson, 1980).

■ Types of Partisanship and Voting Choices

Now I turn to the last problem for analysis: the effect of type of partisanship on voting decisions. Most studies of voting behavior in Japan agree that partisanship is the key to the vote. Persons who support a party tend to vote in elections, and the stronger their partisanship, the more likely they are to turn out. Most persons also vote consistently for their supported party's candidates in elections, and the stronger their partisanship, the more likely they are to do so. Correspondingly, we would expect that people manifesting different types of partisanship would vary with regard to their turnout rates and propensity to vote for their supported party in the 1976 general election. Loyal partisans would be expected to turn out most often, while the nonpartisans, who tend to have little stake in elections, should turn out the least. The voting rates of negative partisans and the uninformed would fall in between those of the other two types mentioned just above. This is because negative partisans, who exhibit low interest in which party will win in the election, are still higher in interest than the persons who are uncommitted to a party. Meanwhile, the uninformed are also the least interested in politics, but their susceptibility to being mobilized to vote may cause them to turn out fairly often.[14]

14. The JABISS survey contains questions to tap the effect of influence communications operating through social networks. The respondents who said they were asked by someone to vote for a particular candidate were then asked, "In regard to deciding whom to vote for in this election, what kind of effect did this recommendation that you received have on you?" The table below is formed from the responses to this question among persons in different categories of partisanship. "Conver-

Voters' propensity to defect from their supported party in voting choices, which is calculated by dividing the number of defecting votes by a party's total number of supporters who voted in the election for each of the six main parties, is easy for us to predict except in the case of the uninformed partisans. The frequency of defection among the uninformed category would actually depend on the way in which they are being mobilized; when such persons are mobilized by campaign activists whose partisanship is the same as their own, their rate of defection would be lower than it would be if the persons seeking their vote represented a different party.

Three kinds of findings are shown in table 6.10 for different types of partisans: abstention rates, frequencies of defection from one's own party, and rates of defection from one's support range. The results are quite consistent with our expectations. The rate of defection from their supported party among persons in the uninformed category is as high as the rates for the negative partisans and nonpartisans, but they are much less likely to defect outside their support range. Probably the uninformed partisans are mobilized by the group networks they are involved in to vote for candidates who are not always from their own party.

In addition to data on behavior in the 1976 election, the JABISS survey results include information on voting participation and choices in three other recent elections: the 1972 general election, the 1974 House of Councillors election, and the 1975 prefectural assembly election. From this information, two kinds of

sion or activation" signifies the combination of the following two responses: (1)"I was thinking of voting for another candidate, but I decided to vote for the recommended candidate," and (2)"I had not decided whom to vote for, but ultimately voted for the recommended candidate." "Reinforcement" means "since I had been intending to vote that way from the beginning, I voted for the recommended candidate." "No effect" includes both "I ignored the request and voted for another candidate" and "I did not vote." The table demonstrates that received vote recommendations were most effective in mobilizing the vote of the uninformed.

Effect of Influence Communications in Relation to Type of Partisanship

	Loyal	Negative	Nonpartisans	Uninformed
Successful Recommendation				
Conversion & Activation	14	13	21	25
Reinforcement	45	32	27	43
Unsuccessful Recommendation				
No Effect	41	55	52	32
Total	100%	100%	100%	100%
N	(503)	(337)	(286)	(206)

Table 6.10 The 1976 Vote and Type of Partisanship (In Percentages)

1976 Vote	Type of Partisanship			
	Loyal	Negative	Nonpartisan	Uninformed
Rate of nonvoting	3	10	20	11
	(429)	(324)	(245)	(177)
Rate of defection from own party	9	19	15	18
	(420)	(250)	(111)	(104)
Rate of defection from support range	3	12	21	0
	(250)	(189)	(67)	(30)

Note: The figures in parentheses are the *N* of cases on which the percentages were based.

scales representing behavior over the four elections were constructed. The voting and campaign participation scales, the mean scores of which are shown in figure 6.4, are factor score scales derived from a factor analysis of participation items including voting behavior in the four elections. The scales are based on two of the four modes we obtained from the analysis.[15] Following the results of Verba, Nie, and Kim (1978), who demonstrated that campaign participation is related to psychological involvement in politics, the level of campaign participation is the highest among loyal partisans in our analysis, while being monotonically less in descending order for negative, uninformed, and nonpartisans. In comparison, voting was less related to psychological involvement, as Verba, Nie, and Kim argued and our findings in figure 6.4 show. The frequency of voting among persons in the uninformed category was higher than that among both the nonpartisans and negative partisans.

The second kind of index developed from the multiple election data represents inconsistent patterns or deviant choices relative to party support over the four elections. The impact of partisanship clearly appears in the proportion of the electorate who voted repeatedly for the same party over time. The JABISS data show that 60 percent of those who provided sufficient information to construct the index voted consistently with their party support over the three elections. The rate of consistent voting should be much higher among loyal partisans and lower among negative partisans and nonpartisans. The consistency rate for the uninformed is hard to predict. Table 6.11 reports cross tabulations between the types of partisanship and the index of consistent party voting. The category "consistent party vote" is self-explanatory. The category "consistent within an ideological stance" means that some of the votes cast by a

15. The remaining two modes are communal activity and protest.

Figure 6.4   Participation and type of partisanship

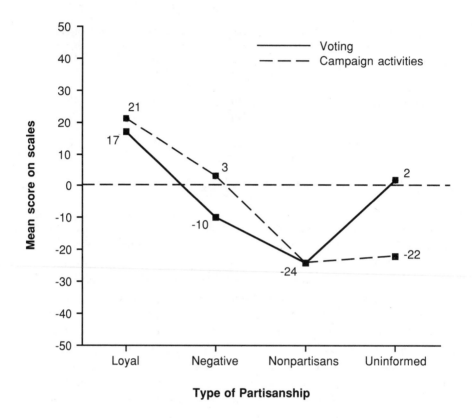

respondent are not consistent with his own party support but these inconsistent votes are for parties within the ideological stance (conservative, middle-of-the-road, or progressive) of his party. The category "cross-ideological tendency" represents a voting pattern that excludes the first two categories; that is, these are persons who deviate from their preferred party to vote for a different party from their own and one that is not ideologically similar. When missing cases are excluded, three-quarters of the loyal partisans are consistent party voters, compared to only about half of the negative partisans and nonpartisans. The rate of "consistent party vote" among the uninformed partisans falls in between that for loyal partisans and the other two categories.

Our typology of partisanship better explains recent trends in political attitudes and electoral behavior in Japan than does the ordinary index of partisan

Table 6.11 Consistent Party Voting by Type of Partisanship
(In Percentages)

Partisan Voting Choices	Type of Partisanship			
	Loyal	Negative	Nonpartisan	Uninformed
Consistent party vote	69	36	25	33
Consistent within an ideological stance	8	21	15	16
Cross-ideological tendency	13	19	11	8
Missing cases	10	24	49	43
Total	100%	100%	100%	100%
N	(503)	(337)	(286)	(206)

strength (strong-weak-leaning-independent). Two dimensions—representing the cognitive and affective aspects of party attachments—were extracted by a multiple dimensional scaling analysis performed on eight scales tapping a broad set of orientations relevant to partisanship. Four *types* of partisanship were constructed by combining these two dimensions: loyal partisans, negative partisans, nonpartisans, and uninformed partisans. These types were found to vary significantly with respect to their general political attitudes.

Loyal partisans are the most involved, the most informed regarding politics, and low in cynicism. They are also the most stable where past support is concerned. Though many reported having changed parties several years back, they still switched their party least compared with other types of partisans. They are also the most familiar with partisan issues, the most likely to form issue attitudes that reflect a consistent position with regard to conservative-progressive ideology, and the most likely to name their own party as the party closest to their position on the issues. Loyalists also vote and participate in campaign activities more often than other kinds of voters. When loyalists vote, they tend to vote for a candidate from their own party. Thus, their "defection" rate was the smallest in the 1976 general election, while they were also most likely to have been consistent party voters in the prior national elections and the 1975 prefectural assembly election. In short, loyalists fit very well the model of party identifiers that the Michigan school describes. Our best estimate, how-ever, is that only 38 percent of the Japanese electorate falls into this category (see table 6.3). While we cannot be completely confident in the proportions we have reported for each partisan type, for reasons already discussed, this figure is probably not far off.

It is important, therefore, to note that our other three types of partisans all deviate in one way or another from the attributes commonly associated with the Michigan concept of party identification—attributes such as the presumed stability of the tie, its independence from a short-term voting intention, and a positive affective attachment that bolsters one's loyalty and commitment to the chosen party. While we cannot be highly specific about the degree of deviation from the assumptions of the Michigan party ID concept here, the purpose in creating a typology of partisans is to suggest that we find large numbers of partisans in Japan that have somewhat different attributes than those typically associated with the concept of party identification.

It is, of course, no surprise to find that the respondents in our nonpartisan category do not behave like party identifiers, nor does this finding challenge the applicability of the party ID model to the Japanese case. As we would expect, nonpartisans display a mirror image of the loyal partisans. Thus, they are high in cynicism and low in psychological involvement in politics. The only exception to this pattern occurs where the nonpartisans are found to be moderately familiar with the issues and near the mean of the sample on several other cognitive indicators rather than being the least informed type. The great majority of the nonpartisans, naturally, consistently fail to offer any choice in response to the party support question. A substantial number of them do, however, and when they do, as was shown in table 6.5, these partisan choices emerge as the most unstable of those offered by any of our four types, in terms of shifting from one party to another and from party support to independence.

The major contribution of our typology, therefore, is found in the identification of the off-diagonal types found in table 6.3, those respondents that are high on one dimension of partisanship but low on the other. These two types, the negative and uninformed partisans, differ from the Michigan party ID model in important ways. As newly identified types, they manifest a partisan anchoring in ways not suggested by the party ID model, while at the same time pointing to two distinct patterns of voting behavior in Japan. The negative partisans lack a positive affective tie with the party they regularly support. Negative partisans support the best alternative from among what they perceive as a relatively unattractive set of options. This provides Japanese electoral behavior with a conditional stability, voting patterns remain stable so long as the contending parties and the relative attractiveness of their perceive images remains unchanged. But as suggested in chapters 10 and 11, this conditional stability masks a high potential for volatility should certain things change. In table 6.4, we find that the majority of negative partisans claim to be supporters of the LDP or JSP. If many of these attachments represent nominal or conditional loyalties, the anchoring effects of partisanship may be weaker in Japan than the party ID model would lead us to believe.

Indeed, we have found that negative partisans together with the nonpartisans demonstrate the highest levels of volatility in party support, defecting from their party in their partisan attitudes and voting choices far more than those in the other two categories. Unlike the nonpartisans, however, negative partisans have high levels of political awareness and are moderately psychologically involved in politics. As a result, negative partisans participate more often in voting and campaign activities than do the nonpartisans. The higher levels of political awareness and participation on the part of the negative partisans lead them to play a much more important role in elections than do the nonpartisans.

Our second new type of partisan, the uninformed partisan, points to a markedly contrasting pattern of voting behavior frequently found in Japan. The uninformed partisan fits our model of the mobilized voter, and in many ways seems to parallel the characteristics associated with the "forgetful voter" identified in chapter 4. Uninformed partisans are found in greater numbers among rural older women with low levels of education. The majority of these voters typically fail to identify a party they support when asked, with more falling into the "don't know" than the independent category. Those that do mention a supported party manifest a high level of instability in their party attachments, not in switching from party to party but rather in vacillating between partisanship and nonpartisanship. This instability is clearly associated with their low level of political awareness. They are the least familiar with partisan issues, the lowest on political awareness, and at the bottom on levels of psychological involvement in politics. Their levels of political trust, however, match those of the loyal partisans, and they exhibit positive feelings toward the party or candidates they usually support.

Here an apparent instability in partisan attitudes masks fairly high levels of stability in voting behavior. While many of the uninformed partisans fail to identify the party they support in public opinion surveys, they are likely to be habitual voters for the same party in election after election (Richardson, 1986). In this regard, their narrow political frame of reference, as noted in their very high rate of mentions of their own party relative to any other party on the closest party questions, contributes to this stability. Indeed, their lack of information on current political events and policy stands often insulates them from short-term electoral influences and permits them to vote consistently for the same party. The most important source of their stability, however, is believed to be their nesting in stable social networks that routinely mobilize them in election after election to turn out and vote for candidates of the same party. Indeed, they are second highest in voting levels after the loyal partisans, despite their very low levels of psychological involvement in politics. It is this mobilized consistency that undoubtedly enables some of them to develop images and attach-

ments to the party they regularly vote for. Ironically, however, it is their susceptibility to mobilization that explains not only their frequent voting stability but
also their higher rates of defection than the loyal partisans, as noted in table
6.10. When their mobilizing networks swing their support to another party,
these uninformed partisans are unlikely to exhibit much resistance to that
change. In different ways, then, both the negative and uninformed partisans
represent sources of potential instability in voting patterns because their partisan attachments are not anchored in the same way as are the attachments of the
loyal partisans.

The findings in this chapter suggest that, at least in the Japanese case, we
need to broaden our conceptualization of partisanship to include a number of
additional types that differ in important ways from the set of attributes associated with the Michigan concept of party identification. By introducing four
types of partisans, we are moving the standard indicator of party support back
on more solid theoretical ground and safeguarding ourselves from easily falling
into the assumption that all partisans in Japan will behave as the Michigan
model suggests. While our method of classification of partisan types does not
permit us to identify the exact figures for the distribution of the four types of
partisanship, we believe that all four are presently found within the Japanese
electorate in substantial numbers.

In light of the increase of political cynicism among the Japanese electorate
in the early 1970s, there is little doubt that the negative partisans and the
nonpartisans have increased within the electorate. The uninformed, in contrast,
must be decreasing in numbers through generational replacement. Many
among the nonpartisans who are young may become either loyal partisans or
negative partisans as they become older and accumulate political experience.
Some of the negative partisans, in turn, may evolve into loyal partisans, if a new
political situation enhances the attractiveness of a particular party. As long as
the present situation, characterized by a competent but corrupt governing party
and a divided and unreliable opposition, continues, however, the proportion of
persons who are negative partisans is not likely to decline.

APPENDIX The Hayashi Quantification Scaling

This is a method of classification of individuals based on the similarity of their
responses to questions having several categories. This method is especially
important here as no other method exists for classification.

The response pattern of individuals is shown in the following table or
chart. We assume that individuals are interviewed with L questions and give
only one response to each question.

In order that individuals with similar response patterns may be listed in a certain order in the chart, so that they are located in roughly the same area of the chart as well as in categories having similar characteristics, we want to classify individuals and categories simultaneously.

From this, we can find the configuration of both the individuals and response categories in multi-dimensional Euclidean space, in order to be able to make inferences from them.

Inferences can be made easily if we have these configurations in one-dimensional space. This means that we can summarize the information on similarity among individuals and among response categories on one axis. If the configurations cannot be summarized on one axis, we shall have to interpret configurations in multi-dimensional space. So, first, we will start our interpretation in one-dimensional space and then continue to multi-dimensional space.

We define $\delta_i(j)$ as

$$\delta_i(j) = \begin{cases} 1, \text{ if the } i\text{th individual (or type) selects the } j\text{th response} \\ \quad \text{category} \\ 0, \text{ otherwise,} \end{cases}$$

where $i = 1, 2, \ldots, Q$, and $j = 1, 2, \ldots, R$, and

$$R = \sum_{j=1}^{L} K_j; K_j \text{ is the number of response categories in the } j\text{th item}$$

$$l_i = \sum_{j=1}^{R} \delta_i(j);$$

$$n = \sum_{j=1}^{Q} s_i; n = \sum s_i; \bar{l}n = \sum_{i=1}^{Q} l_i s_i$$

where L is the number of items, s_i is the number of respondents that fall into the ith type, and n is sample size.

We want to quantify types (individuals) and categories by assigning numerical values to them which will maximize the correlation coefficient between individuals and categories. This is the idea of simultaneous grouping of individuals and categories and also is considered to be one method of taxonomy of individuals and categories based on response pattern.

So let the types be $1, 2, \ldots, Q$ and response categories be $l(C_{11}), \ldots,$ $K_1(C_{1K_2}), K_1 + l(C_{21}), \ldots, R(C_{LK_2})$. Then we require $y_1, y_2, \ldots, y_Q$

given to types and x_1, x_2, . . . , x_R given to categories to maximize the correlation coefficient $^1\rho$ between x and y, where

$$^1\rho = C_{xy}/\sigma_x\sigma_y$$

$$\sigma_z^2 = \sum_{i=1}^{Q} \sum_{j=1}^{R} \delta_i(j)s_ix_j^2/(\bar{l}n) - \left\{ \sum_{i=1}^{Q} \sum_{j=1}^{R} \delta_i(j)s_ix_j/(\bar{l}n)^2 \right\}^2$$

$$\sigma_y^2 = \sum_{i=1}^{Q} s_il_iy_i^2/(\bar{l}n) - \left\{ \sum_{i=1}^{Q} s_il_iy_i/(\bar{l}n)^2 \right\}^2$$

$$C_{xy} = \sum_{i=1}^{Q} \sum_{j=1}^{R} \delta_i(j)s_ix_iy_i/(\bar{l}n)$$

$$- \left\{ \sum_{i=1}^{Q} \sum_{j=1}^{R} \delta_is_ix_i/(\bar{l}n) \right\} \left\{ \sum_{i=1}^{Q} s_il_iy_i/(\bar{l}n) \right\}.$$

And in order to maximize $^1\rho$, it is to solve

$$\frac{\partial^1\rho}{\partial x_k} = 0, \frac{\partial^1\rho}{\partial y_e} = 0, (k = 1, 2, \ldots, R; e = 1, 2, \ldots, Q)$$

which implies

$$\sum_{j=1}^{R} h_{jk}x_j = {}^1\rho^2 \sum_{j=1}^{R} f_{jk}x_j, \quad (k = 1, 2, \ldots, R)$$

where

$$f_{jk} = \begin{cases} -b_{jk}; & (j \neq k) \\ d_k - b_{jk}; & (j = k) \end{cases}$$

$$h_{jk} = a_{jk} - b_{jk}$$

$$a_{jk} = \sum_{i=1}^{Q} \frac{\delta_l(j)\delta_i(k)}{l_i} s_i$$

$$b_{jk} = \frac{1}{\bar{l}n} \sum_{i=1}^{Q} \delta i(j)s_i \cdot \sum_{i=1}^{Q} \delta_i(k)s_i$$

$$d_k = \sum_{i=1}^{Q} s_i\delta_i(k).$$

For further convenience, the matrix representation

$$HX = {}^1\rho^2 FX$$

will be used in the following discussion, where the elements of the matrix H are h_{jk}, those of the matrix F are f_{jk}, and X is a column vector. Then calculate the latent vector corresponding to the maximum latent root of ${}^1\rho^2$, where we can set $\bar{x} = \dfrac{1}{ln} \sum_j \sum_i \delta_i(j) s_i x_i = 0$ and $\sigma_x^2 = 1$ without loss of generality. And we obtain

$$y_e = \frac{1}{{}^1\rho} \frac{\sigma_x}{\sigma_y} \left(\frac{1}{l_e} \sum_{j=1}^{R} x_j \delta_e(j) \right), \quad (e = 1, 2, \ldots, Q)$$

which implies

$$y_e = \frac{1}{l_e} \sum_{j=1}^{R} x_j \delta_e(j) \text{ in case } \frac{1}{{}^1\rho} \frac{\sigma_x}{\sigma_y} = 1.$$

This method is equivalent to that of maximizing $\eta^2 = \sigma_b^2/\sigma^2$, where σ_b^2 is between type variance of σ^2 is total variance (σ_w^2 is variance within type and is equal to $\sigma^2 - \sigma_b^2$).

We generalize this idea to multi-dimensional quantification. We want to quantify types (individuals) or categories by assigning numerical vectors to them to minimize the within generalized variance, $|W|$, with the total variance being constant. In other words, it is to minimize $|W|/|VT|$, where $|VT|$ is generalized total variance with respect to vector ${}'X_i$ (or ${}'Y_j$) for $s = 1$, $2, \ldots, S$ and for all i (or j), and S is the number of dimension of the space.

The process mentioned above is described in detail below. We want to maximize $1 - |W|/|VT|$ under the reasonable condition that the nondiagonal elements in matrix W vanish, and this means to maximize $1 - |\bar{W}|/|VT|$ where $\bar{W}$ is the diagonal matrix of W. As $|\bar{W}|/|\overline{VT}| \geq |\bar{W}|/|VT|$ and $|\overline{VT}| \leq |VT|$ hold, $1 - |\bar{W}|/|\overline{VT}| \geq 1 - |\bar{W}|/|VT|$. Thus, it is desirable to quantify the individuals and the categories (in other words, to require vector x_i (or y_j) for all i (or j)), so as to minimize $|\bar{W}|/|\overline{VT}|$, or to maximize $1 - |\bar{W}|/|\overline{VT}|$. This reduces to the maximizing of $\prod_i^s {}'\eta^2$ for ${}'\eta^2$ is the correlation ratio with respect to ${}'X_i$ for all i, and it is equivalent to maximizing $\prod_i^s {}'\rho^2$ where ${}'\rho$ is the correlation coefficient between ${}'X_i$ and ${}'X_j$ for all i and j.

Thus, it leads us to solve the latent equation $HX - \rho^2 FX$, and ${}'X_i$ is the latent vector corresponding to the sth largest root of H.

Table 6.12 Spatial Representation of Individuals (Types) and Response Categories in Question Items Based on the Information of Response Pattern

A			1	......	2	......	L
B			$1, 2, \ldots, K_I$	......	$K_I + 1, \ldots$	......	$\ldots\ldots, R$
C			$C_{11}, C_{12}, \ldots, C_{1k_1}$	......	$C_{21}, \ldots\ldots, C_2 k_2$	......	$C_{L_1}, \ldots\ldots, C_{LK_I}$
D	E	F					
l_1	s_1	1	V				V
l_2	s_2	2	V		V		V
l_3	s_3	3	V		V	V	
⋮	⋮	⋮					
l_Q	s_Q	Q	V		V		V

"V" sign shows the response category of an individual.

The categories contain neither "DK" nor "other" responses.

No sign is shown when one selects "DK" or "other." Thus, the number of responses (l) may vary from one type to another.

A: item (question)   B: consecutive number
C: category   D: total of signs
E: frequency   F: response type (individuals)

Part III ■ Short-term Influences on Voting Behavior

Seven ■ Issues and Voting Behavior

SHINSAKU KOHEI, ICHIRO MIYAKE,
AND JOJI WATANUKI

The role of issues as determinants of voting choice has been a central topic in voting studies in every democracy. In spite of a considerable accumulation of voting research in the advanced democracies, however, that role has not been made entirely clear. As an article reviewing voting studies in the United States noted, issues as determinants in voting can be identified as having a certain limited importance—neither overwhelming nor completely insignificant (Niemi and Weisberg, 1976:162–71). Thus, the impact of issues on voters' decisions may differ from country to country, election to election, or even from study to study.

In the Japanese case, it has been argued that several factors associated with the political context are likely to further limit the role of issues, as compared with their role in other advanced democracies. First of all, the electoral system for the Japanese House of Representatives is a unique system characterized by three- to five-member districts, the plurality principle, and a single nontransferable ballot. As a result, the two largest parties, the LDP and JSP, frequently run two or more candidates in a given district who then find themselves competing for the same voter's single ballot. In this context, national partisan issues tend to be downplayed in favor of local issues connected with regional or group interests.

Second, the LDP, the largest and governing party for roughly thirty years, has been a catchall party, accommodating many interests and juxtaposing a number of policies with little attention to the systematic integration of those policies. This was not always the case. In the 1950s, the LDP (and both major conservative parties before they merged in 1955) was explicit on the revision of the 1947 constitution. This created a confrontation with the opposition parties—especially the Japan Socialist Party—concerning the basic values of polity and society. These value differences reflected a set of cultural cleavages that underlay the left-right issue polarization of the party system. As discussed elsewhere and in chapter 3 of this volume, this phenomenon has been labeled

Japan's "cultural politics" (Watanuki, 1967b). After 1960, however, under the late Premier Hayato Ikeda, the leading issues shifted from the constitution to an emphasis on economic growth, and this brought about a lower posture of confrontation on the part of the LDP.

In the 1960s, the opposition parties—the JSP, JCP, and newly formed CGP—clung consistently to the Japan-U.S. Security Treaty as the basic issue in the confrontation with the LDP. Moreover, the decade of the 1960s brought with it new issues, such as increased pollution and environmental destruction. These quality-of-life issues versus economic growth seemed to provide a new basis for confrontation. After some initial foot-dragging, however, the LDP administration moved to respond effectively to those problems by legislating various pollution control laws and allocating monies for abating pollution in the late 1960s and especially in the early 1970s. As a result, by the mid-1970s the environmental issue had lost much of its momentum (Pempel, 1982:218–54).

Thus, Shinsaku Kohei (1979), comparing the general elections of the 1960s with those of the 1970s, comments that earlier elections appear to be issue-vote based, centering on the Japan-U.S. Security Treaty issue and on the problems of the negative consequences of high economic growth. In contrast, the elections of the 1970s have become "issue-less," in the sense that both the security treaty and economic growth have ceased to be the main political concerns, and other issues, such as corruption and political scandals, cannot be clearly identified as to partisan direction.

Although limited, the role of issues in Japanese general elections is not nil.[1] Our JABISS survey was an attempt to determine the extent of that role, using twelve issues. The full text of these issues is presented in table 7.1, where they have been grouped into four categories according to type and content.

■ The Twelve Issue Questions

The selection and characterization of the twelve issues requires some comment. First of all, the 1976 general election is known as the "Lockheed election." In February 1976, at the U.S. Senate Foreign Relations Subcommittee on Multinational Corporations, former Lockheed Aircraft Corporation President Carl Kotchian testified that his company had paid a huge sum of money to certain Japanese businessmen and officials to promote its business prospects in Japan. Shocked by this news, the Japanese Diet decided to inquire into the matter

---

1. Although based on local data, Miyake and others tried to measure the weight of issues in six elections at different levels. The partial correlation between issue opinions and voting was highest in mayoral elections (.354) and lowest in general elections for the House of Representatives (.087) (Miyake et al., 1967:486–87).

Table 7.1   Text of Twelve Surveyed Issues by Issue Area

Money Politics Issues
1. The "money power" politics and political corruption that came to light in the Lockheed scandal should be swept away.
2. Political donations by corporations should be prohibited.
3. The people's interests should be protected against the growing power of big corporations.

Economic Issues
4. Social welfare programs such as pensions and medical care for the elderly should be improved even if taxes go up.
5. Stronger measures should be taken to stimulate business even at the risk of inflation.

Cultural Politics Issues
6. The Emperor should have more political power.
7. Japan's defense forces should be strengthened.
8. The Japan–United States security set-up should be strengthened.
9. Civil servants and public employees should have the right to strike.

Foreign Relations with Communist Neighbors
10. A treaty of peace and friendship should be concluded with China as soon as possible.
11. More efforts should be made to improve relations with North Korea.
12. Japan should make stronger demands on the Soviet Union to return the Northern Territories.

and summoned witnesses during February and March. The mass media—especially television—gave detailed coverage, including scenes of the hearings. The climax came in July when former Prime Minister Tanaka was arrested and in August indicted for taking bribes from the Lockheed Corporation. Three other LDP Diet members were also indicted for bribery, and a dozen other LDP politicians were rumored to be involved in the case as well. Four of the politicians prosecuted, including Kakuei Tanaka, withdrew voluntarily from the LDP when they were arrested but subsequently ran in the general elections as independents. Three of them, including Tanaka, succeeded in maintaining their seats. Moreover, Tanaka continued to lead the largest LDP faction and to play a highly influential role in internal LDP politics up through and even after his conviction on the Lockheed bribery charges in the fall of 1983.

All the opposition parties demanded a more rigorous and thorough inquiry into the matter, especially of borderline cases concerning LDP politicians who had not been prosecuted. The LDP position became somewhat blurred. The LDP called for a "purification of politics," and Prime Minister Miki and Minister of Justice Inaba took a positive stand promoting further inquiry. The majority of

LDP politicians, however, were critical of the Miki-Inaba position, denouncing them as lacking sympathy for their colleagues and insisting that the whole case be left to the courts (that is, exempting the borderline cases from any further inquiry). Given the fact that the LDP was divided on the issue and that socialist and other party politicians have not escaped involvement in corruption scandals in the past, the Lockheed affair did not constitute a clearly partisan issue.[2]

When Miki succeeded Tanaka as prime minister in late 1974, he tried to reform the law regulating political funds, as a concrete measure to "purify" politics. Miki's position on this issue differed from that of the LDP mainstream. He sought to introduce legislation prohibiting political donations by business corporations. Because of opposition by the LDP majority, however, the result was a more moderate reform of the law approved in 1975, which merely set ceilings for political donations by private corporations based on the size of their capital. The JSP, JCP and CGP continued to insist on total prohibition of political donations by private corporations, and they made this part of their party platforms in the 1976 general election. This appears as our second issue in table 7.1. The other opposition parties, however, the Democratic Socialist Party (DSP) and New Liberal Club (NLC), did not favor such a complete prohibition, and even the JSP was less than enthusiastic in supporting it because the party feared the possibility of a similar prohibition against political donations by unions.

Partly related to the issue of political donations and partly caused by the reported price-rigging and withholding of goods in expectation of higher prices by major trading and oil companies during the 1973 oil crisis, the big corporations became targets of antipathy and criticism in 1974–76. As a result, the opposition parties made regulation of the actions of the big corporations an issue (#3 in table 7.1). Reform of the antimonopoly law in the direction of more strict regulation was attempted by the Miki cabinet. In the spring of 1975, a reform bill was presented to the Diet and, after negotiations, all opposition parties including the JCP agreed to it. In the end, however, the bill was shelved as a result of persistent opposition by certain LDP politicians as well as pressures from big business behind-the-scenes. The bill was not discussed in the Diet at all in 1976, in spite of Miki's repeated efforts to promote it. Finally, in February 1977, under the Fukuda cabinet formed after the 1976 general election, the bill was passed by both houses. At the time of the 1976 general election, the opposition parties, especially the JSP, JCP, and CGP, called for reform of the antimonopoly law, and the JSP and JCP emphasized further measures to regulate

2. Despite this ambiguity, however, there is evidence that the opposition parties benefited somewhat from the Lockheed issue, as seen later in this chapter and in chapter 8. For a more detailed analysis of the Lockheed incident and the LDP, see Baerwald, 1976; Passin, 1979:14–17.

the big corporations (the so-called democratization of the economy). On the other side, the LDP remained silent on reform of the antimonopoly law because of disunity on this issue within its ranks.

The first three issue items reported in table 7.1, then, are all related to the themes of corruption and morality in politics and efforts to curtail the undue influence of big money and big business. These were not new issues to Japanese politics in the 1970s. Indeed, it seems that Japan has witnessed at least one major corruption scandal in every decade across the postwar era. Beginning with the 1967 "Black Mist" scandal, the media have played a major role in keeping public attention focused on corruption-related problems for extended periods of time, perhaps in a somewhat self-conscious effort to counteract the more forgiving attitudes toward corrupt practices often associated with traditional values. The 1988–89 Recruit Scandal (discussed in chapter 11) is only the most recent manifestation of this continuing problem.

While the corruption-related issues tend to command public attention periodically when scandals arise and then disappear again from public debate, the second set of economically related issues in table 7.1 are constant fixtures in all political campaigns. Indeed, welfare measures and the economy have been consistent foci of electoral interest in every recent election in Japan, as in other advanced industrial democracies. According to other election survey data, the issues that attracted most attention in elections throughout the 1970s were "commodity prices," "social welfare," and "business conditions."[3]

Our survey included two such economic items presenting problems of trade-off relationships, that is, social welfare versus increased tax burden, and stimulating business versus inflation. Compared to the 1980s when the trade-offs on these issues became really serious, however, 1976 was a rather fortunate year where favorable economic conditions prevented these trade-offs from being sharply drawn in the voters' minds. It is true that the Japanese economy had suffered seriously in the 1973 oil crisis and had recorded a minus 1 percent real growth rate in 1974. From 1975 on, however the economy again began to grow (2.3 percent in 1975 and 5.3 percent in 1976 in real terms), and rampant inflation (24.5 percent for consumer prices in 1974) was quickly brought under control (11.3 percent in 1975 and 9.3 percent in 1976). This new growth was stimulated by rationalization efforts by private corporations aimed at reducing production costs and increasing efficiency and by massive increases in govern-

3. According to nationwide sample surveys conducted by the Akarui Senkyo Suishin Kyokai (formerly the Komei Senkyo Renmei), in the 1972, 1976, 1979, and 1980 general elections, the top issue mentioned in the sample was "prices" (53, 57, 51, and 61 percent, respectively), and the second "welfare" (51, 35, 30, and 36 percent, respectively); Komei Senkyo Renmei, 1973; Akarui Senkyo Suishin Kyokai, 1977, and 1980.

ment spending for public works (a 21.2 percent increase over the previous year in fiscal 1976). Moreover, in spite of the 1973 oil crisis, recession, and rationalization in business, unemployment increased only moderately (reaching levels of 1.3 percent in 1972 and 1973, 1.5 percent in 1974, 1.9 percent in 1975, and 2 percent in 1976). Thus, both recovery from recession and control of inflation were achieved without much appreciable increase in unemployment. As for social welfare, increased expenditures began from 1974 and continued throughout the 1970s, with increases over the previous year of 36.7 percent in 1974, 35.8 percent in 1975 and 22.4 percent in 1976, without introducing any new tax.

The secret to all this was reliance on the national debt, through the issue of huge quantities of governmental bonds. The percentage of reliance on bonds for governmental revenue jumped from 5.4 percent in 1970 to 9.4 percent in 1975, 29.9 percent in 1976, and eventually to 39.6 percent in 1979. From the viewpoint of the 1980s, the overissuing of government bonds and overreliance on expanding the national debt in the 1970s, especially after 1975, has proved to be a serious financial handicap. Legal procedures for the issuance of so-called deficit bonds, as distinguished from construction bonds, were proposed under the Tanaka cabinet in late 1974, and approved for amendment to the 1975 budget under the Miki cabinet.[4] Thus, in terms of economic and fiscal policy, Miki adopted Tanaka's expansionist line and increased governmental spending, postponing all the trade-off relationships between spending and tax burden. Although opposition parties spoke against this proposal, their opposition amounted to little more than ritualistic posturing and was not systematic or sincere except in the case of the JCP. Because the opposition parties were in favor of expanding governmental spending, especially on welfare (CGP and JSP) and on wage increases for public employees (JSP), they were ready to bargain with the LDP and lend their tacit approval by not obstructing the closure of discussion and voting on the bill.

In the years following the 1976 election, as deficit spending climbed, the spending/taxation trade-off finally had to be confronted and debated in the public forum. Even then, however, the classical confrontation between those desiring to increase welfare spending and those trying to hold down taxes and government spending did not emerge in Japan and divide the parties along the liberal/conservative lines found in the West. Ironically, in Japan it has been the

4. Under the postwar Japanese Government Finance Law, bond-issuing has been allowed only for public works since 1964. This had been the practice before 1975, and bonds issued for that purpose were called "construction bonds." Since 1975, a special law permitting the issuance of bonds to compensate for a general deficit in revenues for that particular year has been legislated each year, and bonds issued under the special law are called "special bonds" or "deficit bonds," as distinguished from "construction bonds."

fiscally conservative LDP that has been calling for tax increases. These LDP efforts to increase taxes have been extremely unpopular with the public and have negatively affected the ruling party's fortunes at the polls both in 1979 and 1989.[5] While the opposition parties have jumped on this issue to gain popular support, however, their opposition to LDP tax increase proposals has not been completely credible, given the fact that their own spending proposals would probably require even larger budgets than those of the ruling party. The other side of the taxation/welfare spending issue has also been blurred by the fact that the LDP has been able to raise the ratio of welfare spending to national income steadily since the early 1970s while still lagging well behind European or even American levels. As a result, steady improvements in government benefits at still comparatively modest cost levels, which have not as yet created a demand to retract previously provided benefits, have further veiled a potential partisan cleavage on this issue. Finally, not only has the LDP consciously rejected the model of the Scandinavian type of "institutionalized welfare state" in favor of a "Japanese-type welfare society," but by and large the opposition parties seem to have done so too (Watanuki, 1990; Esping-Anderson and Korpi, 1987). In 1976 and beyond, therefore, the trade-offs either between higher taxes and increased welfare spending or between higher inflation and increased spending to stimulate business did not sharply divide the parties. Thus, as in the case of the "money politics" issues, we would not expect to find strong correlations between preferences on these issues and the partisan direction of vote choice.

In contrast to these two sets of issues, the third cluster of issues included in the survey has sharply divided the parties since the early 1950s (see table 7.1). These are the "cultural politics" issues that arose following the conclusion of the Occupation in 1952 when the conservatives ushered in the "reverse course" period and moved to roll back many of the Occupation reforms. These issues dominated the political stage, at least through 1960, and fueled an intense, sometimes violent, confrontation between the right and the left. Our study included three representative thematic foci of this class of issues—issues concerning the structure of government and the distribution of power, those regarding the values of peace versus military defense and security, and those dealing with the rights of citizens to press forward legitimate demands versus the need

5. In 1979, Prime Minister Masayoshi Ohira announced his intention to introduce a new "general consumption tax," similar to the value-added tax in European countries, just before the general election of October 1979. The public uproar that followed his announcement forced him to disavow his proposal in short order. Despite this retraction, the tax issue was believed to be responsible for the ruling party's poor showing in the election. The number of seats the LDP won was even less than in the previous "Lockheed election" of 1976 (248 in 1979, compared to 249 in 1976), and far below the expectations of the LDP or the predictions of specialists. On the impact of the tax issue in the 1989 upper house election, see chapter 11.

for public order. While the salience of most of these issues has declined greatly since 1960, much of the public still perceives the parties on the left and right as holding clearly divergent preferences on this set of cultural politics issues.

There were many issues in the 1950s revolving around the Occupation's reforms to the Japanese political structure, but perhaps the most central of these concerned the role of the emperor. In the late 1940s, many Japanese of conservative sentiments were incensed by the Occupation's dismantling of the emperor system and relegation of his august station to an inconsequential symbolic role. While virtually none advocated a total return to the prewar system, voices were heard, at least throughout the 1950s, calling for an expansion of the emperor's power. It was widely reported, however, that the imperial family itself was content with its new position as "symbol of the Japanese nation," and with time this issue has been virtually removed from the political agenda. Indeed, no clear revision on this point has been discussed in any recent election, including the 1976 general election.

Nevertheless, from time to time, an event or ritual that involves the emperor becomes a matter of controversy among the parties. The LDP has taken the side of defending such events or rituals, while the JSP and JCP are ranged on the other side against them. Usually the DSP is close to the LDP and the CGP vacillates between the two poles. Just prior to the 1976 general election, on November 10, 1976, the government held a major official ceremony in Tokyo, attended by 7,500 representatives from various parts of Japan and guarded by 2,700 riot police, to commemorate fifty years of the reign of Emperor Hirohito. The JSP and JCP had opposed this ceremony, and members of the Diet from both parties boycotted the ceremony in protest. The CGP left the issue of attendance of invited Diet members to individual judgment, while the DSP took a positive stand on participating in the ceremony. Issues such as these and events such as the passing of Emperor Hirohito in January 1989 undoubtedly rekindle old feelings regarding the role of the emperor.[6]

6. On the issue of enhancing the emperor's role, there was some speculation at the time of Hirohito's death that the right wing might use that occasion to resurrect the issue. While the assassination attempt on the life of Nagasaki Mayor Hitoshi Motoshima in January 1990 (for saying that the emperor had to bear some responsibility for World War II) may be a sign of increased activity on the extreme right, the ascension to the throne of the more traveled and cosmopolitan Emperor Akihito will make it even more unlikely that the issue of expanding the emperor's powers will ever again be seriously engaged in public debate. Other emperor-related issues, however, may surface from time to time as they have in the past. Besides the commemoration of fifty years under the reign of Emperor Hirohito, there have been other examples. It has been a practice for the emperor to make an appearance at the opening of the regular session of the Diet in January and give a short statement. The JCP Dietmembers have protested this practice by boycotting the ceremony. In 1973, the JCP went even further, denouncing the emperor's statement as being too political and favoring the party in power. Despite the fact that the other opposition parties, including JSP, did not

The security issues have revolved around article 9 (the "peace clause") of the constitution, the role of the military in Japan and the advisability of maintaining a close military alliance with the United States. The JSP and JCP have consistently argued that the very existence of the Self-Defense Forces (SDFS) is unconstitutional and therefore they should be dissolved. Public opinion polls, on the other hand, show that the SDFS have met with growing acceptance among the general population, reaching levels of 80 percent approval consistently throughout the latter 1960s and 1970s (Nishihira, 1980:95, 101). On this point, the JSP and JCP positions have come to reflect a definite minority of the Japanese electorate. On the other hand, a majority of about 60 percent of the populace favored maintenance of the present scale of the SDFS throughout the 1960s and 1970s; in other words, those who support the expansion of the SDFS also have been in a minority (roughly 20 percent). Thus, the LDP position in favor of strengthening the SDFS has not been in harmony with the majority of the Japanese populace either. In the 1976 general election, the LDP as a whole did not enthusiastically support the strengthening of the SDFS, and the actual increase in the government budget for defense was slightly below the average increase of the budget. But the LDP has been definitely committed to the Japan-U.S. Security Treaty and has emphasized the importance of its bilateral relationship with America. It tends, therefore, to be sensitive to American pressures on Japan to augment its defense strength, even beyond the limits of incrementalism, as became clear in the drawing up of the 1982 budget onward. Among the opposition parties, both the JSP and JCP toned down their insistence on "dissolution" of the SDFS, and the CGP drew closer to the position of the DSP in approving both the Japan-U.S. Security Treaty and the SDFS. This change in the CGP position on defense was announced more explicitly following the 1976 general election (Yoshihara and Nishi, 1979).

In 1960, the security treaty between Japan and the United States had been the issue over which public opinion and partisan politics were most sharply divided. In 1970, when the treaty again came up for renewal or revision, the JSP

---

support the JCP attack on the emperor, the upshot of the incident has been that the emperor's statements to the Diet have become shorter and more abstract since then. Another example was the *gengo* (emperor's reign year) issue. Traditionally in Japan the calendar year was officially designated according to the emperor's reigning name and the year of his reign; e.g., 1975 was Showa 50, the 50th year of the reign of the Showa emperor, Hirohito. Since the war this has been a mere optional, customary practice without any legal basis. Triggered by the fiftieth anniversary ceremony of the emperor's reign in 1976, the LDP started a move to provide a legal basis for the use of the emperor's reign year. The law approving the use of the *Showa* reign year during Hirohito's remaining years on the throne and providing for a shift to a new reigning name and year count each time a new emperor ascends to the throne was legislated in 1979. The JSP and JCP were fiercely opposed to this, while the CGP, after oscillation between opposition and support, eventually voted for the bill. In contrast, the LDP, DSP, and NLC consistently supported the bill.

and JCP sought to mobilize opposition once more around this issue. Late in 1973, the CGP tried to polish up its party image by presenting itself as "progressive" and changing its stand on the treaty from "early abolition" to "immediate abolition." The tide of public opinion has been rapidly changing in favor of the treaty, however, since around 1974 (Nishihira, 1981:26). In the 1976 general election, even the JCP removed the abolition of the treaty from the policy goals of its proposed "provisional coalition government."[7] The CGP, as mentioned above, moderated its position as well. Positions on the treaty remained fairly clear, however, with the LDP on one side and the JSP on the other. The LDP called for strengthening cooperation with the United States based on the treaty, while the JSP remained committed to its abolition.

The last of the "cultural politics" themes covered by our study was the issue of the rights of citizens and groups to protest and demonstrate versus a preference for order and stability. There were a host of salient issues in the 1950s revolving around the issues of union rights, police powers, treatment of demonstrators, disruption, and political violence. One of the most enduring of these was the right of public employees to strike, which remained an unrealized goal of the socialists and the largest union federation in Japan, Sohyo. By the mid-1970s, the unions of government employees and workers in public corporations, and especially the two unions of the National Railways Corporation, had been demanding the legalization of the right to strike for close to three decades, insisting that it was guaranteed under the 1947 constitution but retracted during the Occupation period. These two unions, in spite of the legal prohibitions against strikes, had participated in the so-called Spring Offensive almost every year, incurring a number of penalties. In November 1975, they decided to launch a prolonged strike demanding legalization of their right to strike, and they sought a promise from Prime Minister Miki, a "liberal" among LDP politicians, at least to give the matter favorable consideration. The strike lasted for eight days, halting most National Railways trains, but in vain. The unions gained nothing. In the 1976 general elections, the JSP, which has close organizational ties with these unions, made this issue—legalization of the right to strike for public employees—part of its party platform.

The last set of issues that appears in table 7.1 deals with diplomatic relations with Japan's communist neighbors in Northeast Asia—China, North Korea, and the Soviet Union. Despite the fact that the conservatives are perceived as

7. The idea of a "provisional coalition government" was suggested by JCP chairman Kenji Miyamoto in December 1976, just before 1976 general election. This concept differs from the JCP's usual proposal of a "unified front government," where the abolition of the Japan-U.S. Security Treaty has always been included as a policy goal. The idea of a "provisional coalition government" was that of a coalition government just to handle the domestic issues of political corruption and coping with the emergence of fascism (Yoshihara and Nishi, 1979:17).

aligning themselves with the Western camp and the JSP and JCP with the socialist camp, these issues have not been particularly divisive in recent years. For example, on the issue of diplomatic relations with China, many conservative politicians and business leaders pushed for recognition of the Peking regime for years. Indeed, it was a conservative party leader, Prime Minister Tanaka, who set the stage for the normalization of relations with China in 1972 by his visit to Peking earlier that year. Negotiations for a peace treaty with China were launched in 1975, and all Japanese political parties were in favor of its early conclusion. China, however, insisted on inclusion of the so-called hegemony clause (a clause supporting a common stand against "hegemony" which implicitly meant hegemony by the Soviet Union in the region). The Japanese government sought to moderate the expression in order not to provoke retaliation from the Soviet Union. From September 1975, when negotiations were temporarily suspended, to January 1977 following the general election, when the CGP chairman brought a message to Peking from the new prime minister, Fukuda, no negotiations were made. The treaty was finally concluded in August 1978, and mutual concessions were made on the expressions concerning hegemony, although the clause itself was kept in the treaty. During the 1976 general election, no negotiations were going on, and all political parties supported the early conclusion of the treaty. It was known that the JCP was particularly critical of the hegemony clause, and the DSP was cautious with regard to maintaining the balance between China and the Soviet Union (Masuda, 1979:106).

Japan's relationship with Korea is complicated by thirty-five years of colonial rule, that nation's division by occupation which was further intensified by the Korean War, and Korea's geopolitical location between Japan and the Soviet Union. Not until 1965 was the Japan-Korea Basic Treaty concluded and diplomatic relations established with the Republic of Korea (South Korea), after prolonged negotiations. This treaty had faced stiff opposition both in Japan and South Korea. In Japan, the LDP and DSP had supported the treaty while the JSP, JCP, and CGP were opposed.

From 1965 through 1976, when our survey was conducted, and up until today (1990), diplomatic relations between Japan and the Korean Democratic People's Republic (North Korea) have yet to be established, although trade and various kinds of exchange have begun and been maintained between the two countries. Basically, North Korea has insisted that relations with Japan can only be normalized after abrogation of the Japan-Korea Basic Treaty. The JCP has echoed that position and at the time of our survey was explicitly calling for the abrogation of the treaty. The JSP's position has not been so clear-cut, although it has sent missions to North Korea and once (1974) issued a joint statement emphasizing the need to establish diplomatic ties between the two countries. The CGP has been even more vague in its Korea policy, and in 1976 took an equidistant position vis-à-vis North and South Korea and went no further than support for the autonomous and peaceful unification of the peninsula (the CGP position changed in 1981 to support of South Korea). The DSP supports South Korea most clearly among all Japanese political parties, but even it does not oppose increased contact with North Korea.

The LDP position has been somewhat more complicated than those of the other parties. On the one hand, it has attempted to preserve close relations with South Korea in spite of incidents such as the KCIA kidnapping of Kim Dae-Jung from Japan. On the other hand, thirteen LDP politicians visited North Korea for the first time in July 1975, and the LDP interpretation of the Japan-Korea Basic Treaty, which includes article 3 stipulating that the Government of the Republic of Korea is the sole legitimate government in Korea, has been different from that of the South Korean government (Yamamoto, 1978:97–99). The South Korean government's interpretation is that "Korea" in this article means the entire Korean peninsula, while the Japanese government's interpretation is that it means the area south of the armistice line, leaving room for intergovernmental contact with North Korea. Thus, while the treaty with South Korea was sharply contested, the issue of improving relations with North Korea should not be expected to reflect strong partisan divisions.

The last of the three diplomatic issues concerns relations with the Soviet Union, a giant and aggressive neighbor. These relations have been important in the past and will remain so in the future. A variety of problems have intervened between Japan and the Soviet Union, such as implementing economic cooperation for the development of Siberia, arrangements for mutual fishing rights in adjacent waters, and the Soviet military build-up in Northeast Asia. The core problem, however, has been the absence of a peace treaty after more than forty years following the end of the Second World War. Although relations between Japan and the Soviet Union were normalized in 1956 by joint declaration, a peace treaty has yet to be signed and the major obstacle to its conclusion has been the "Northern Territories" issue. Japan regards this region as its own territory, but the Soviet Union continues to occupy the area, refusing to return it to Japan.

The Northern Territories consist of three parts. First, there are two islands (Habomai and Shikotan, although to be precise, Shikotan is a group of tiny islands) off Hokkaido, which have been considered part of Hokkaido. Even the Soviet Union agreed in the 1956 joint declaration to return these two islands when a peace treaty was concluded. Second are two other islands, Kunashiri and Etorofu, lying south of the Kurile Islands, which were never Russian territory in any sense until the Soviet occupation just after the end of the Second World War. (These four—Habomai, Shikotan, Kunashiri and Etorofu—are known as the Four Northern Islands.) Third are the Kurile Islands, stretching from Urup to Shumshu, which belonged to Japan not by annexation through war but by a treaty concluded in 1875 between Russia and Japan, in exchange for South Sakhalin.

Although all political parties in Japan unanimously take the position that the Soviet Union should return the Northern Territories to Japan, there are two different positions concerning the scope of the territory to be returned and the conditions for return. The position taken by the Japanese government, the LDP, DSP, CGP, and NLC has been that Habomai, Shikotan, Kunashiri, and Etorofu should be returned upon conclusion of the Japan-Soviet peace treaty. In other words, return of those four islands in a package is the condition for conclusion of a peace treaty. The JSP and JCP take the position that, at the time of conclusion of the peace treaty, only Habomai and Shikotan must be immediately returned. After conclusion of that treaty, however, and after dissolution of the Japan-U.S. Security Treaty, which would eliminate the Soviet fear and suspicion of military use of the Kurile Islands by the United States, Japan should and could negotiate return of all the Kurile Islands from the Soviet Union. The JSP and JCP positions on the return of Northern Territories have been perceived as being more con-ciliatory toward the Soviet Union. Despite minor party differences on the three issues dealing with Japan's relations with her communist neighbors, the ab-sence of sharp partisan divisions, and in some cases even clear party positions, coupled with the low salience of these issues to the Japanese voter, should greatly weaken any potential association between them and vote choice.

■ Issues Types and Issue Salience

Table 7.1 above organized twelve issues into four clusters on the basis of their common thematic content or issue area. Table 7.2 suggests a somewhat differ-ent ordering of these issues. Here the issues are ordered from high to low values based on the difference between the percentages agreeing with the issue state-ment minus the percentage disagreeing.

The issues that cluster at the top of the table are *valence* issues, issues on which there is overwhelming support with essentially no disagreement. These are generally moral issues or other kinds of issues that are impossible to oppose because they are stated in good/bad or positive/negative terms. Everyone is for honesty in politics, prosperity, better schools, better care for the elderly, and motherhood; and everyone is against crime, corruption, pollution, inflation,

Table 7.2   Issue Opinion Distribution and Issue Salience of Twelve Issues Ordered by the Level of Agreement Minus Disagreement on Each (In Percentages)

Issue	Agreement	Disagreement	Salience
Reform money power politics	77	3	62
Increase welfare at cost of tax hike	73	4	73
Protect public interests against big corporations	67	2	62
Demand Soviet return of Northern Territories	65	1	47
Conclude Sino-Japanese peace treaty	56	2	40
Prohibit political donations by corporations	56	4	52
Improve Japan–North Korea relations	32	7	24
Stimulate business at risk of inflation	34	19	58
Legalize public employees' right to strike	30	31	42
Strengthen defense forces	22	28	36
Strengthen Japan-U.S. security ties	18	24	34
Increase the emperor's power	14	39	19

Note: Salience percentages are the sum of the "very important" and "important" responses. Agreement percentages are the sum of the "agree" and "agree somewhat" responses, and disagreement percentages the sum of the "disagree" and "disagree somewhat" responses, with the remaining unreported percentages falling into the "can't say," DK, and NA categories. Both salience and issue position percentages are based on 1,564 cases.

unemployment, and a host of other social ills. Not surprisingly, the "money politics" issues cluster at or near the top, with strong support and essentially no opposition. One of the two economic issues, the welfare issue, also emerges as a valence issue. This may seem surprising to Western readers whose own liberal and conservative parties often espouse markedly different positions on this issue. As we have noted, however, in 1976 the voters were not forced to face the welfare/tax burden trade-off, thanks to deficit spending. Instead there was, at the time, a broad consensus on the need for both holding down taxes and increasing welfare spending, and indeed the government was doing just that.

At the bottom of the table we find the *position* issues, those issues that have two sides and divide the electorate between conflicting preferences. Here the four "cultural politics" issues neatly cluster at the bottom of the table. Not surprisingly, they are joined by the second of the two economic issues, the "stimulate business versus inflation" issue. In an era of stagflation in which societies have had to learn to cope with the simultaneous ill effects of both recession and inflation, some elements of the public will inevitably be more negatively affected by the former while others will suffer more from the latter.

The "foreign relations with communist neighbors" issues fall somewhere in between these two polar types of issues. They are valence issues in the sense that there is little or no dissent on the issues, but they are also issues which, on the whole, attract lower levels of support than those that we have identified as valence issues. In other words, these are *low-salience valence issues* and hence are issues that are not likely to influence voting behavior.

This analysis suggests a three-cluster grouping of the issues into valence issues, position issues, and a residual, low-salience foreign relations cluster. When we look at the salience rankings of the issues reported in table 7.2, however, we find that the average salience of the foreign relations issues is almost the same as that for the five position issues. This finding points to a contaminating bias between issue type and issue salience. It can be clearly seen from the table that there is a fairly strong rank order correlation between the percentage agreeing with an issue and the salience of the issue (Spearman's *rho* = .86). It appears that people who disagree with an issue statement are not strongly disposed to say that it is an important issue. This means that our salience measure somewhat underestimates the importance of position issues to the voter in relation to valence issues. Thus, for example, the economy position issue ranked fourth in salience despite the fact that it has consistently emerged as the number one priority of voters on open-ended questions, well ahead of the corruption issue. Again, the strike position issue ranked in the lower half of the issues on salience, despite the fact that it was a clearly articulated election issue and one that had caused a great deal of public inconvenience during the 1975 railway strike. Clearly the cultural politics issues in 1976 were not as salient as they had been in the 1950s or even 1960s and certainly were not as much on the minds of the voters as the money politics issues. Undoubtedly, however, they were more salient than the foreign relations issues, which, as other studies have shown, consistently rank very low in the Japanese voter's preference schedules.

More evidence of the contaminating effects of issue position on issue salience can be found in table 7.3, which examines the breakdowns on issue salience by party support. A positive sign means that support for the indicated party is significantly associated with attaching high salience to a given issue while a negative sign indicates an expression of the issue's low importance. Turning to the cultural politics position issues, we find that the signs completely conform to the party's position on the issue. The communist and/or JSP supporters on the left attach high importance to the strike issue, which they support, and low importance to the defense, U.S. ties, and emperor issues, which they oppose. Conversely, the LDP supporters attach importance to the emperor issue but unimportance to the strike issue.

The reader may detect two deviant cases that do not appear to fit the pattern. These cases also can be shown to confirm the position-salience relationship,

Table 7.3 Relationship between Issue Salience and Party Support

Issue	LDP	NLC	DSP	CGP	JSP	JCP	Chi Sq.
Valence Issues							
Reform money power politics		−*			+*		p .001
Prohibit corporate political donations		−*			+*		p .05
Protect public against corporations				+	+		p .25
Increase welfare							p .75
Foreign Relations							
Sino-Japanese treaty						−*	p .73
North Korean relations							p .42
Return Northern Territories	+						p .36
Position Issues							
Stimulate business vs. inflation			+			−	p .001
Public employees' right to strike	−		−		+*	+	p .001
Strengthen defense forces						−*	p .01
Japan-U.S. security ties						−	p .09
Increase emperor's power	+*	−*				−*	p .001

Note: A (+) means that support for the party indicated is associated with attaching high importance to the issue in question, while a (−) means that support for the party is associated with attaching low importance to the issue. All reported correlations were significant at the .05 level and those that are starred (*) are significant at the .01 level, indicating stronger correlations.

however. The "New Right" NLC supporters attached low importance to the emperor issue because on the issue position item they were strongly opposed to expanding the emperor's power, more opposed than the Socialist supporters. While the NLC supporters were found to be conservative on economic and communist relations issues, it has also been shown that they were far more likely to have libertarian and cosmopolitan values than LDP supporters. As a result of these more modern value orientations, NLC supporters tended to hold more progressive positions on many of the cultural politics issues, especially those related to the political structure, the emperor, and associated traditional practices (Flanagan, 1984). In the second seemingly deviant case, the supporters of the moderate but labor-oriented DSP were found attaching low salience to the strike issue. The DSP, however, was affiliated with Domei, a federation composed almost entirely of private employees' unions, which assigned low importance to the strike issue because it concerned the interests of their archrival Sohyo, the union federation that heavily represented public employees. To legalize the right of public employees to strike would have only enhanced the power and prestige of Sohyo at the expense of Domei.

Clearly, then, a respondent's position on an issue influences the importance he is willing to attach to it. If an issue is stated in such a way as to oppose his interests or if it simply takes no position, the respondent is not likely to attach as high importance to it as to one that unambiguously endorses his preferences.

■ Issue Cognition and Partisanship

As shown in table 7.2, many of the twelve issues are perceived as being important by large proportions of the Japanese electorate. Nevertheless, issue cognition, both in terms of the individual's own position on the issues and an awareness of the parties' stands, seems to be extremely low. As shown in table 7.4, on the average, 27 percent of the respondents failed to take any position on these issues and 57 percent were unable to name any party that represented their

Table 7.4   Levels of Issue Cognition (In Percentages)

	"Don't Know" on Issue Position	No Close Party Identified on Issue	Named Voted Party as Closest Party
Valence Issues			
Reform money power politics	18	50	26 (28)
Prohibit corporate political donations	23	51	21 (25)
Protect public against corporations	23	51	25 (29)
Increase welfare	15	49	28 (33)
Foreign Relations			
Sino-Japanese treaty	30	59	24 (28)
North Korean relations	39	70	16 (18)
Return Northern Territories	27	56	26 (31)
Position Issues			
Stimulate business vs. inflation	29	61	23 (27)
Public employees' right to strike	28	55	24 (28)
Strengthen defense forces	31	57	24 (29)
Japan-U.S. security ties	35	57	25 (30)
Increase Emperor's power	30	60	22 (26)

Note: The figures in parentheses are the perentages computed on the basis of 1976 election voters only.

own opinion on the issues. Only if a voter is able to make a linkage between his own position on an issue and the various stands of the parties and make an assessment, either correctly or incorrectly, as to which party best represents his views can it be said that the issue played some role in influencing that person's vote.

Another, and somewhat surprising, finding reported in table 7.4 is that on any given issue only slightly more than half of the respondents identifying a party that best reflects their views named the party they voted for. On average, 43 percent were able to name a party that they felt was closest to their position on a given issue, but only 24 percent mentioned the party for which they voted. These findings might lead us to question the potential for issue voting in Japan. If over a quarter of the voters have no positions on the issues, over half are unable to identify any party that represents their views, and over three-quarters fail to link their issue preferences with the party they voted for, then it seems unlikely that a study of issues will contribute greatly to an explanation of voting outcomes.

It could be, however, that different voters are concerned with different issues and that although they are unable to identify which party represents their views on most issues, on that *one* issue that is most important to them, the parties' stands are well known to them. Thus, if a respondent could name the party that was closest to his views on only one issue, an issue voting model might still be applicable. When we take this approach, we find that only 33 percent of the respondents are unable to name any party that represents their views on any of the issues. Similarly, while a respondent might not name his party as closest to his preferences on all the issues, it may be perceived as being closest to him on most of the issues. Table 7.5 reports the extent to which the respondents named the party they voted for or named some other party as closest to their position a majority of the time. In this case we find that those supporting the LDP, CGP, JSP, or JCP named their own party a majority of the time in 72–85 percent of the cases in which some party was named. These findings might lead us to reassess our initial pessimism regarding the potential for issue voting in Japan, for we have found that two-thirds of the respondents are able to identify a party that is closest to their views on at least one issue, and of these three-quarters or more identify the party they voted for a majority of the time.

For a substantial proportion of the Japanese electorate, therefore, we do find a perceived linkage between the respondent's position on the issues and the party he voted for. What we do not know is the origins of that linkage. An issue voting model suggests that voters confront the problem of electoral choice with a prior set of firm issue commitments and select the party they perceive as being

Table 7.5 Perceived Issue Position Congruence between Respondents and Chosen Party

Party Voted For	LDP	NLC	DSP	CGP	JSP	JCP
Own party named[a]	52	17	21	62	57	57
Other party(ies) named[b]	13	50	55	11	20	22
No satisfactory party exists and DK	35	33	24	27	23	21
Total	100%	100%	100%	100%	100%	100%
N of Cases	(626)	(60)	(75)	(73)	(355)	(91)

[a] Percentage of respondents who named the party they voted for a majority of the times they named any closest party across the twelve issue questions.

[b] Percentage of respondents who named other parties more often than the party they voted for.

closest to them on the issues. It is more likely in many cases, however, that the direction of causation is reversed. That is, voters may develop a party loyalty for other reasons and then are either socialized by partisan communication networks to adopt certain issue positions or have little hard factual information regarding party stands and simply assume that their party best represents their views. Thus, the voter's issue positions may play more of a reinforcing than a determining role, in that they provide the voter with the ideological and pragmatic rationale for supporting a party that he or she has already chosen for other reasons.

Some differences across issues and parties that emerge from tables 7.4 and 7.5 are worthy of mention. In the former table, we find that significantly fewer of the respondents are able to identify a party that represents their views on the four cultural politics position issues than on the four valence issues. This seems unusual since the parties' positions are so much clearer on the cultural politics issues than on the valence issues. When we control for the proportion of the sample identifying their own position on the issues, however, this difference between issue types drops out. Moreover, a significantly higher proportion of the respondents who identified a close party named their own party on the cultural politics issues than on the three money politics valence issues. This may be in part a reflection of the clearer party differences on the cultural politics issues, but it also is related to the fact that the supporters of the largest party, the LDP, were significantly less likely to name their own party as best representing their views on these valence issues. For example, in the case of the "reform money power politics" issue, which focuses on the Lockheed scandal associated with the LDP, only 16 percent of LDP supporters identified the LDP as the party closest to them on the issue. The fact that most of these LDP supporters went ahead and voted LDP despite their recognition of their party's shortcomings on the corruption-related issues suggests either that other issues were more important to them or that issues played no role in their voting choice. This is not the first time that the LDP has demonstrated its relative immunity from attacks based on corruption-related issues.

Table 7.5 reveals one significant difference among the parties. The DSP and NLC have substantially lower proportions of supporters naming their own party. As center parties, these parties have less clearly articulated positions and, particularly in the case of the NLC, as newer parties their supporters have had less opportunity to learn their positions. Thus, we find that only 21 percent of the DSP voters and 17 percent of the NLC voters named their own party a majority of the time.

■ Issue Cognition and Communication Networks

As many studies have shown, there is a strong relationship between level of issue cognition and political interest or psychological involvement in politics. It has also been found that an awareness of the parties' issue stands is related to strength of partisanship. Stronger partisans simply have more information regarding their party's stands on the issues. These relationships are well known and are confirmed by our JABISS data as well.

Rather than reviewing these established findings, this section will explore the relationships between issue cognition and communication networks in both formal and informal groups. For this purpose, we have computed an issue cognition scale by counting the number of times a respondent identified his position on an issue across the twelve issue questions (responses other than "don't know" [DK]). These scale scores were then transformed into standardized scores, with a mean of zero and a standard deviation of 100. Positive scale values indicate high levels of issue cognition and negative scores below average levels. A second "closest party cognition" scale was also created using the same procedures on the twelve "closest party" items.

In table 7.6 these scale scores are broken down by the respondent's involvement or lack of involvement in informal groups in which the election was discussed. Respondents were asked whether they had discussed the 1976 House of Representatives election prior to election day with family, friends, neighbors, relatives, or work colleagues and if so whether they actively expressed their opinions in those discussions or mainly listened to the views of others. In the case of issue cognition, the table shows that even passive listeners seem to have a considerably higher level of cognition than those who are not involved in such politicized communication networks. In the case of closest party cogni-

Table 7.6   Issue and Closest Party Cognition by Involvement in Informal
Communication Network

	Involved			
	Active	Depends	Passive Listeners	Not Involved
Issue cognition	52	29	24	−46
Closest party cognition	64	28	3	−36
N of Cases	(163)	(408)	(386)	(964)

Notes: Involvement in informal communication networks is measured by the response to a question concerning the role played by the respondent in discussions about the general election that occurred among family members, neighbors, relatives, work colleagues, and other friends prior to the election.

The issue and closest party cognition scores reported for each category are the means of the respondents' standardized scores (mean = 0, SD = 100) based on the number of nonmissing responses (position identified or party named) given on the twelve issue questions.

tion, the gap between active discussants and passive listeners widens. These findings suggest that issue cognition can be easily improved by simply being exposed to informal communication networks, whereas improvement of closest party cognition requires more than mere exposure.

Naturally, how much one discussed the election and how active a role was taken in those discussions could simply be a reflection of one's prior level of interest in politics. Thus, we need to control the relationships reported in table 7.6 by interest level in order to determine the independent effect of involvement in communication networks. In table 7.7 this control is applied, dividing the sample into low and high interest groups. As can clearly be seen, in all cases those with high interest score higher on both cognition scales than those with low interest. We also find, however, clear evidence of the independent effect of communication networks. In the case of high interest respondents, even those who are uninvolved in such informal networks stand well above the mean in cognition levels. Involvement in politicized informal communications networks, however, is associated with a substantial additional boost in cognition scores. For those with low interest in politics, network involvement plays a larger role and the quality of that participation has a quite dramatic effect. As learning theory research has found, active discussion requires a greater command of the facts than passive listening. Therefore, those who are drawn into active discussion or for whatever personality or attribute reasons typically assume a leading role in conversations are more likely, when those discussions turn to politics, to develop issue positions and perceptions of the parties' stands.

In table 7.8 we turn to the effects of membership in formal groups on

Table 7.7   Issue and Closest Party Cognition by Involvement in Informal
Communication Networks and Political Interest

	Involved			
	Active	Depends	Passive Listeners	Not Involved
Issue cognition				
Low interest	45	18	14	−39
High interest	55	62	64	33
Closest party cognition				
Low interest	41	14	−10	−38
High interest	77	62	52	29

Note: Political interest is measured by a scale constructed from the following items: (1) extent that respondents pay attention to political events, (2) extent that respondents have interest in campaigns, (3) extent that respondents care about which party will win, and (4) extent that respondents expressed interest in the Lockheed scandal.

cognition scores. We selected union membership because among the large formal groups for which we have membership data, unions are believed to be the most politicized. Here, membership is broken down by frequency of participation in group activities. Also, the nonmember category is a residual category that does not control for membership in other formal or informal

Table 7.8   Issue and Closest Party Cognition by Union Involvement and
Political Interest

	Union Member Participation in Union Activities			
	Often	Occasionally	Never	Nonmember
Issue cognition				
Low interest	63	45	36	−14
High interest	66	54	52	55
Closest party cognition				
Low interest	57	43	20	−21
High interest	74	62	106	54
N of Cases[a]	(77)	(118)	(25)	(1694)

Note: Calculation of scores follows the same procedures as in tables 7.6 and 7.7.

[a]The N of cases is reported for the closest party cognition portion of the table, because the much lower numbers here bring into question the stability and significance of the reported mean scores. In particular, the "never" category had only 25 cases and the highly aberrant score for the "high interest" portion of that category is clearly a reflection of the fact that only 7 cases fell into their cell.

groups in which political discussions may or may not be taking place. While there is some instability in the "never participate" category of union members due to the small number of cases, what the table shows is that union membership has essentially no effect on cognition levels among those respondents with high levels of political interest. For those with low interest in politics, however, union membership and frequency of involvement in union activities has a marked effect on both levels of issue cognition and closest party cognition. This analysis suggests that informal and formal social networks play an important role in communicating and instilling pertinent information on issue positions and party stands relevant to voting decisions, especially among those constituents that are not greatly interested in politics and not motivated to acquire such information on their own.

■ Issue Areas, Issue Types and the Vote

If issue voting is occurring, we would expect to find some associations between issue positions and party vote. In table 7.9, these correlations are reported for

Table 7.9 Association of Issue Positions and Party Vote (Tau B)

Money politics issues	
Reform money power politics	.15
Prohibit corporate political donations	.22
Protect public against corporations	.15
Economic issues	
Increase welfare despite tax burden	.08
Stimulate business despite inflation	−.06
Foreign relations with communist neighbors	
Conclude Sino-Japanese treaty	.08
Improve North Korean relations	.13
Demand return of Northern Territories	.00
Cultural politics issues	
Legalize public employees' strikes	.31
Strengthen defense forces	−.32
Strengthen Japan-U.S. security ties	−.34
Increase Emperor's power	−.21

Note: A positive correlation indicates that agreement with the issue statement is associated with leftist voting, while a negative correlation indicates that agreement is associated with a vote for the conservatives. All reported correlations are significant, except for the Northern Territories issue, but the weak correlation with the "stimulate business" issue is significant only at the .05 level.

the twelve issues grouped into the same four issue areas presented in table 7.1. Note that there is a rough but not perfect fit between these four issue areas and the issue-type classification presented in table 7.3 that divides the issues into high-salience valence issues, low-salience valence issues, and position issues. We find the highest correlations with vote among the cultural politics issues. These are all position issues, and since they played a central role in shaping the party system and defining partisan cleavages in the early postwar period, these relatively high correlations are not surprising. The next strongest group of correlations are found among the money politics issues. These are all high-salience valence issues. It may seem surprising to find any correlations at all between these issues and the vote, since we reported virtually no disagreement at all on these issues in table 7.2. Issue positions were measured on a five-point agree-disagree scale, however, with a neutral midpoint. Since these issues were pointedly directed against certain politicians, practices, and interests closely associated with the LDP, it is not surprising to find that the more intensely one supported these issues the lower one's likelihood of voting conservative.

The other two issue areas demonstrate only weak to nil correlations with the vote. The low correlations with the "foreign relations with communist neighbors" issues are expected from our previous discussion. The only association meriting mention among these three issues is the one with the North Korean relations issue. The somewhat higher correlation here undoubtedly stems from the fact that it is associated in some respondents' minds with the South Korean treaty issue, which had a history of sharp partisan division.

In the case of the economic issues, our previous discussion of the virtual consensus on the welfare issue would lead us to anticipate the low correlation that we find here. On the other hand, the low correlation with the "stimulate business" issue might seem unexpected, since that was shown to be a position issue. The issue was not posed as a trade-off between inflation and unemployment as is often the case in the West, however, since unemployment was not and has not been a serious issue in Japan. Since the issue was framed as a trade-off between overcoming a business recession versus inflation at a time when both had fairly successfully been brought under control, the absence of strong partisan divisions is quite understandable. While the electorate reported divided responses to this issue, by and large the divisions were not along partisan lines. Thus, all we find is a very slight tendency for leftist voters to be more concerned with inflation.

We have seen that in our issue-type classification, the economic issues category disappears, with the welfare issue classified as a valence issue and the "stimulate business" issue as a position issue. The lower correlations reported in table 7.9 for both the economic issues raise the question of whether these economic issues can properly be grouped with the other two issue clusters as suggested by the issue-type classification. To answer this question, we have conducted a factor analysis, presented in table 7.10. We find that all four high-salience valence issues load heavily on the first factor, although the welfare issue has the lowest loading of the four. Three of the cultural politics position issues load heavily on the second factor, and the three communist relations issues (the low-salience valence issues) cluster neatly on the third factor. Significantly, the "stimulate business" issue does not load on any of these three factors.

We will label the first factor a "salient valence issues" factor, the second a "cultural politics" factor, and the third a "communist relations" factor. The only anomaly in this neat labeling is caused by the ambiguities between issue content and issue type associated with the strike issue. The strike issue is a position issue like the other three cultural politics issues, but in content it is clearly associated with a business versus labor issue cleavage. Two of the four high-salience valence issues have a clear antibusiness connotation. So in terms of content, the strike issue has more in common with those valence issues. As a result the strike issue straddles the first two factors, loading equally on both.

By applying the same type of transformation procedure used in the last section, we can standardize factor scores and report the mean factor scores

Table 7.10 Factor Loadings of Twelve Issues in a Three-Factor Solution

	Factor 1	Factor 2	Factor 3
	Salient Valence Issues	Cultural Politics	Communist Relations
Reform money power politics	.626	−.072	−.047
Prohibit corporate political donations	.568	−.011	−.045
Protect public against corporations	.520	.022	−.161
Increase welfare	.494	.079	−.079
Legalize public employees' strikes	.304	−.309	.021
Increase Emperor's power	−.002	.545	.098
Strengthen defense forces	−.091	.674	−.026
Japan-U.S. security ties	−.864	.793	−.025
Sino-Japanese treaty	−.040	.011	−.965
North Korean relations	.068	−.093	−.463
Return Northern Territories	.181	.113	−.487
Stimulate business vs. inflation	.078	.208	−.017

broken down by party vote. This will enable us to observe party-by-party differences across the three issue dimensions. In table 7.11 we find as expected the sharpest differences among the parties on the cultural politics dimension. The valence issue dimension also demonstrates a clear progression from positive to negative scores across our right to left array of the parties. In contrast, the communist neighbors factor reveals no consistent left-right pattern. On the cultural politics position issues, the nonvoters appropriately fall squarely at the mean; they fall at one of the extremes on the other two issue dimensions, however. This occurs because the other two dimensions represent valence issues, where most of the variation takes place between a strongly agree and a noncommittal, neutral center point on the issue position items. Thus on the salient valence issues factor, which is mostly defined by the money politics issues, the nonvoters and the LDP voters cluster at the noncommittal end of the dimension, while on the communist neighbors factor, the nonvoters and NLC voters cluster at the noncommittal end.

It is interesting to observe that the two major center parties, the DSP and CGP, stand much closer to the right on the cultural politics dimension and much closer to the left on the valence issues factor. Thus, while these center parties are very critical of various corrupt practices associated with the LDP, they have on a number of position issues, especially the security issues, been moving closer to the right over the last two decades. What these standardized factor scores on the cultural politics dimension suggest is that the emergence of the center parties has greatly reduced the ideological distance between parties in the party system and enhanced the potential for workable coalition governments should the LDP lose its parliamentary majority in the future.

Table 7.11   Standardized Factor Scores on Three Issue Dimensions by Party Vote

	Factor 1	Factor 2	Factor 3
	Salient Valence Issues	Cultural Politics	Communist Relations
Party Vote			
LDP	22	36	3
NLC	10	0	−31
DSP	−13	15	12
CGP	−24	13	−10
JSP	−26	−37	16
JCP	−49	−73	31
Nonvoter	27	1	−21

■ The Lockheed Scandal and Issue Voting

Since the 1976 election has been called the "Lockheed election," we should look more closely at the "reform money power politics" issue, which specifically mentions the Lockheed scandal. The question raised here is to what extent this one issue caused longtime LDP supporters to defect from their party and vote for some other party. In table 7.12 we have selected out the subset of respondents that reported LDP party identifications during the first wave of our panel survey, two weeks prior to the election. The table reports the cross tabulation between party vote and closest party on the Lockheed-related issue as reported in the postelection survey wave, for these LDP identifiers.

First, we note that only a little over 40 percent of those LDP identifiers who voted named any party as being closest to their own views on the "reform money power politics" issue. Second, of those who named a party, slightly over 50 percent named their own party, the LDP. Thus, at best this issue could potentially only induce about 20 percent of the LDP supporters to defect. Of those 111 cases who mentioned one of the five largest opposition parties as closest to them on the issue, 86 percent stood firm and supported the LDP, and only 9 percent voted for the party they designated as closest to them on this issue. From this analysis, therefore, it appears that only slightly over 2 percent of the LDP identifiers were induced to defect from their party as a result of the Lockheed issue. This may explain why the so-called Lockheed election did not produce a landslide victory for the opposition parties.

On the other hand, a 2 percent shift is not inconsequential and could be crucial in a tight election. Hence it would be wrong to conclude that the

Table 7.12 Party Vote of LDP Identifiers by Perceived Closest Party on the Reform-Money-Power-Politics Issue

Closest Party on Money-Power-Politics Issue	Party Vote							Total	N of Cases
	LDP	NLC	DSP	CGP	JSP	JCP	Independent		
LDP	95		1	1	1		2	100%	(115)
NLC	82	18						100%	(17)
DSP	100							100%	(5)
CGP	90			10				100%	(10)
JSP	86	2			7		5	100%	(59)
JCP	85			5		10		100%	(20)
Missing	93	2	1	1	2	1	1	101%	(312)

Note: The "missing" category includes those that responded DK, NA, No Party, or Other on the closest party question.

Lockheed incident had no effect. Furthermore, the effect we find, though small, does not seem to be the product of random noise, since in most of the cases of defection, the party vote is predicted by the closest party response on the Lockheed issue. In addition, as shown in chapter 8, the Lockheed issue appears to have had a much more pronounced effect on floating voters who had no previous partisan loyalties. Finally, it is probable that a number of long-standing LDP supporters switched their partisanship as a result of the Lockheed issue well before the first wave of our December 1976 survey. After all, the Lockheed scandal had broken in February 1976 and dominated the front page of the Japanese press for nearly a year. If the effect of the issue was strong enough to shift partisanship as well as vote, that effect would have been missed by our table 7.12 analysis. In fact, 6 percent of our survey respondents reported that they had changed party support because of the Lockheed scandal. Aggregate voting data reveal that the LDP received nearly 11 percent fewer votes in 1976 compared with the number of votes it amassed in the previous HR election. It is likely that a sizable proportion of this loss was either directly or indirectly (through the emergence of the NLC) related to the Lockheed incident. In the next chapter, the role of media attention to the Lockheed scandal in influencing this vote swing against the LDP is analyzed.

■ Effects of Economic Conditions

As mentioned earlier, 1976 was a year of recovery from the shock of the 1973 oil crisis for the Japanese economy; inflation was brought down to one-digit percentages, unemployment remained around 2 percent, and the economy began to grow at a 6-percent annual rate in real terms. People were very much concerned about prices, however, and among many there was a sense of relative deprivation. Asked whether they felt their living conditions had become better or worse off in comparison with the previous year (that is, 1975, when Japan experienced double-digit inflation and only 1.4 percent economic growth), 29 percent of the respondents said that their living conditions had worsened, more than double the number who answered that they were better off (13 percent).

We do find a fairly modest relationship ($r = .12$) between this item and direction of vote. In other words, those who felt that their economic situation had worsened recently were somewhat less likely to vote for the ruling LDP than those whose economic condition had improved. In fact, declining economic fortunes appear to be associated with a protest vote phenomenon. Table 7.13 reports the percentage of the voters, for each of the six parties, who reported that they were worse off than in the previous year. These categories were further subdivided between those whose vote was consistent with their partisanship and those whose vote was inconsistent, including both defectors and nonpartisans.

Table 7.13   Percentages of Those "Worse Off" than the Previous Year,
Controlled by Party Identification and Party Vote

Consistency between Party Identification and Party Vote	Party Vote					
	LDP	NLC	DSP	CGP	JSP	JCP
Consistent	24	52	29	32	33	45
Inconsistent[a]	25	69	22	30	30	44

[a] The "inconsistent" category includes defectors from other parties and nonpartisans.

We note that those who voted LDP were less likely to have suffered economically, while those who voted communist and the NLC were far more likely to have experienced a decline in fortunes. Thus, we find in Japan evidence of a phenomenon that has long been reported in many countries. The incumbent party is rewarded for good times and punished for bad times. Moreover, the preferred instrument for registering a protest against the LDP regime appears to be a vote for the communists and the NLC. The fact that the percentages of those "worse off" for "consistent" and "inconsistent" voters for each party are almost parallel suggests that in Japan short-term economic declines can result in not only voting defections but also changes in partisanship.

In this chapter, we have looked closely at twelve issue items that were grouped around four issue area classifications—the corruption-related money politics issues, economic issues, cultural politics issues, and issues concerning relations with Japan's communist neighbors. We found that these same twelve issues fell into three types—high-salience valence issues, low-salience valence issues, and position issues—and that our measure of the salience of the position issues was likely to be somewhat depressed by a reluctance of respondents to attach great importance to issue statements with which they disagree.

Among these issue clusters, we found that only the cultural politics position issues yielded fairly strong correlations with vote, while the money politics valence issues exhibited moderate associations. Only these two issue clusters could be expected to exert any influence on voting behavior, and that influence is weakened by the fact that many voters have no positions on the issues and a majority are unable to identify the party that is closest to their view on virtually any given issue. Even more threatening to an issue voting model is our finding that nearly half of the respondents naming a close party named some other party than the one they voted for. Moreover, it could be that much of the association we find between issue positions and party vote is a function of the long-term socialization of party loyalists and others who are tied into partisan networks.

Those integrated in such networks are likely to gradually internalize partisan views and issue positions. Thus, in some cases, exposure to certain politicized communication networks may be causally antecedent to both a respondent's issue positions and vote choice.

On the other hand, issues are not without some influence on the voting behavior of the Japanese electorate. Issues undoubtedly play an important role in reinforcing party preferences and mobilizing the electorate to turn out to vote. We found, for instance, that those who were involved in politicized formal and informal social networks exhibited higher levels of issue attitude formation and information regarding party stands, even when the level of political interest was controlled. Pronouncements of party platforms and issue positions, therefore, may serve to strengthen partisanship, and, as this information becomes diffused through the media and works its way through formal and informal social networks, it may galvanize partisans to participate in voting and other election-related activities. In this same process, partisan issue appeals are brought to the attention of weak partisans and nonpartisans and may serve as the rationale for short-term voting decisions.

When we think of issues as determinants of voting choice, we normally expect to find a short-term influence that shifts an electorate temporarily in one direction or the other. Mitigating against our ability to detect short-term issue effects in this case is the fact that the issues most related to voting are the cultural politics issues, which are long-standing issues and indeed are the very ones that to a great extent defined the cleavages around which the party system and partisan alignments took shape. Moreover, the House of Representatives multi-member constituency system, which pits candidates of the same party against each other, somewhat insulates district races from the influences of national issues and focuses attention on personality and performance assessments— candidate ties, candidate images, and perceptions of which candidate is likely to bring more benefits to one's area or group. Nevertheless, we did detect some short-term issue effects. For example, it was shown that the Lockheed issue increased defections somewhat among LDP partisans. Also, the state of the economy issue was shown to exert some influence over the fortunes of the incumbent regime. Despite the fact that the election was held under relatively good economic conditions, those respondents who felt their economic situation had worsened exhibited some tendency to register a protest vote against the LDP. This suggests that a serious economic recession in the future might increase this tendency to the benefit of the opposition parties. That is only likely to happen, however, if the voters also begin to feel that some party or coalition of parties could run the economy better.

Eight ■ Media Influences and Voting Behavior

SCOTT C. FLANAGAN

One of the most profound changes that has accompanied the advent of the advanced industrial society has been the unprecedented expansion of the mass media. Recent studies have shown that Americans are exposed to one or another type of media an average of seven hours a day. Whether in the form of political information or entertainment, the mass media have become a pervasive and important part of our lives. In particular, television has been singled out as having the most profound effect on our images and evaluations of the world around us. Studies have shown that the average recent high school graduate in the United States has spent a greater share of his eighteen years watching television than he has attending classes in school (Graber, 1980). Television presents us with role models and portrays a set of cultural values that tend to become accepted as national norms. Many commentators have concluded from this kind of evidence that the media must also be playing an important role in shaping political attitudes and behavior.

As we will see, media diffusion and media consumption levels are as high or higher in Japan as they are in the United States. Thus, the media should play as important a role in Japan as they do in the United States. Does this role extend into politics? More specifically, do the media in Japan play an important role in influencing voting behavior either directly or indirectly? While the evidence presented in this chapter will demonstrate that the media can play some role in voting outcomes, both indirectly through shaping long-term attitudes and directly through portraying candidate images and setting the issue agenda, we will find that these influences are rather muted. This modest role for the Japanese media seems to be attributable to two major factors— one associated with theories of political learning found in media effects literature and one associated with the specifics of media use in the Japanese context.

297

■ The Media Effects Literature

If we were to characterize the American literature, we would have to say that despite expectations and a multitude of research undertakings, it has been difficult to demonstrate substantial media effects on attitude change in any context, especially in electoral campaigns. From the turn of the century into the 1940s, with the growth in media-delivery technologies and the rise of total-itarian regimes and state-controlled propaganda campaigns, there were predic-tions from many quarters that the media, and especially the state-controlled media, would increasingly be used to mold mass attitudes. With the advent of public opinion surveys in the 1940s, however, this view quickly began to change. Perhaps the most influential early works in this literature were the studies of the presidential elections of 1940 and 1948 by the Columbia school (Lazarsfeld et al., 1944; Berelson et al., 1954). These studies gave rise to the widely accepted view that the media exert minimal effects on changing citizen attitudes. So pervasive did this view become among the academic community that the comprehensive *American Voter* analysis of voting behavior that ap-peared in 1960 virtually ignored the role of the media in American elections. The image of the American voter presented by the Columbia and early Michi-gan studies was one of apathy and inattention to political information in the media, with the result that many voters, and particularly the independent swing voters, were basing their election decisions on little accurate information about the major issues and the candidates' respective stands on them.[1]

Beyond these election studies, numerous other studies found little evidence of a direct media effect on changing attitudes (Hovland et al, 1950; Klapper, 1960; Trenaman and McQuail, 1961). This nonfinding was explained by such concepts as perceptual screening, selective perception, and cognitive disso-nance, among others. Thus, it has been shown that individuals tend to gravitate to media that reflect their previously formed political dispositions and prefer-ences. It has also been found that core beliefs and attitudes are highly resistant to discrepant information. Instead of changing their beliefs, individuals are likely to emphasize selectively and retain incoming information that conforms

---

1. For example, a 1961 American survey, conducted just after the construction of the Berlin wall, found that a large proportion of those supporting military retaliation did not realize that Berlin was encircled by East Germany. In another case, it was found that the bulk of pro-peace candidate McCarthy's strong showing in the 1969 New Hampshire primary came from hawks who wanted a more forceful prosecution of the war (Converse, 1975). A more recent example of voters selecting candidates without any apparent awareness of the candidates' stands on the issues can be seen in the March 1986 Illinois Democratic primary. In that election two radical fringe Larouche candidates, Mark Fairchild and Janice Hart, won the lieutenant governor and secretary of state races over party stalwarts George Sangemeister and Aurelia Pucinski, presumably because of the voters' preference for all-American, Anglo-Saxon over ethnic-sounding names (*Newsweek,* 3/31/86; 4/7/86).

to their preexistent perceptions and to discount and discredit information that challenges the validity of their beliefs (Sears and Freedman, 1967; McClure and Patterson, 1974; Lang and Lang, 1959; Larson, 1973; George, 1980).

In addition to these cognitive consistency theories, other cognitive processing theories, such as attribution theory and schema theory, have reinforced the general finding that preexistent beliefs can condition our evaluation of new information (West, Gunn, and Chernicky, 1975; Heradstveit, 1979; Fiske and Kinder, 1981; Conover and Feldman, 1984). These theories view human beings as problem solvers or cognitive misers that apply certain rules to the processing and evaluation of information to cope with the problems of either too little or too much information. For example, schema theory argues that individuals develop pyramidal cognitive structures consisting of organized knowledge about events and people drawn from past experience to create simplified mental models of the world. These schema or mental constructs are then used selectively to identify what parts of any new incoming information are important, how that new information should be interpreted and evaluated so that it fits with established perceptions, and how the information is to be stored, which in turn effects its retention (Graber, 1984).

Because of these and similar processes, studies have not simply found that there is no relation between level of media exposure and attitude change, but rather the seemingly perplexing finding that the greater the individual's level of exposure to political information in the media, the more stable his political attitudes, issue positions, partisanship, and voting behavior. One line of argument based on cognitive elaboration theories has been offered to account for this phenomenon: high levels of media exposure over time produce a more sophisticated understanding of politics, which better equips voters to handle large amounts of new information without changing their issue positions and, at the same time, creates denser perceptual screens that explain away information that might challenge their current partisan choice.[2]

The minimal effects hypothesis, therefore, has argued that if the media have any effect on attitude change, it is only on those citizens that have little or no prior information or opinions. In the context of election campaigns this means that only those voters with shallow to nonexistent images and attitudes regarding the parties and candidates are likely to be influenced by the media in their voting decisions. This effect is further mitigated by the fact that these politically unsophisticated citizens who could potentially be influenced are also the least interested in politics and hence least likely either to expose themselves to

2. For an alternate view, which argues that the media exposure/voting stability relationship is spurious, caused by the association of both of these variables with an antecedent variable, strength of partisanship, see Norpoth and Baker (1980).

political information in the media or to vote. The conclusion is that the media have little power to change attitudes and at best exercise a secondary role of reinforcing preexistent partisan attitudes and mobilizing interest in the campaign and voting turnout.

The minimal effects hypothesis, of course, has not gone unchallenged. The growing role of the American media over the last two decades in communicating political information, articulating the issues, projecting candidate images, and in some cases even creating the news has made it hard to believe that the media are not having some effect. As a result, beginning in the late 1960s and early 1970s a revisionist school has grown up to contest the minimal effects conclusion. One tack in this revisionist literature is to argue that the media do influence attitude change, but that our methods are at fault. The effects of media exposure may simply be smaller than originally expected and hence require more precise forms of measurement. Or else the effects may be limited to more localized impacts or to special subgroups of media users (Wagner, 1983). Given the great variety of conflicting messages emanating from different media and other sources, it is understandably quite difficult to isolate and measure media influences with a one-shot national survey design. Media effects on attitude change, therefore, may be significant and important, but simply missed owing to the inappropriate research designs and data analysis methods typically employed in nationwide surveys.

A second tack in the revisionist challenge to the minimal effects view is to concede that the media do not play an important role in attitude change, but nevertheless exert a number of other kinds of important effects such as agenda setting and political mobilization (McCombs and Shaw, 1972; Erbring et al, 1980; Iyengar et al, 1982). Perhaps one of the most intriguing kinds of effects demonstrated here come out of the work of several American election campaign media specialists who have claimed that one powerful TV ad has in some instances raised the support for their candidate by 25 percentage points or more in the space of a couple of weeks. It is interesting to note that these TV ads appear to be most influential in primary campaigns, where the candidates are less well known and where partisanship cannot guide voting decisions. Most important, the ads appear to be successful not because they persuade the voter to adopt a certain issue position or even because they persuade the voter of the importance of a particular issue, but because they powerfully influence the voters' positive or negative images of one or more of the candidates along the dimensions of competency, trustworthiness, service and attentiveness to local concerns. As has been repeatedly shown, television is not a very effective medium for conveying hard information. But it is a very effective medium for conveying feelings and images, and the rise of negative campaign ads in American elections demonstrate the power of television in manipulating images.

The ballot is still out on the media effects debate, but what this review of the American literature suggests is that we should begin our analysis of the role of the media in Japanese elections with rather modest expectations. Even in the best of cases—that is, in the American electoral setting where we know that the media are heavily used in politics and election campaigns—it is difficult to document significant media effects.

■ The Role of the Media in Japanese Election Campaigns

When we turn to the Japanese context, we will find that our job of detecting media influences becomes all the more difficult owing to factors associated with the Japanese political setting and the manner in which the media are utilized in election campaigns. First, there are several factors limiting the voter's need to rely on the media for the basic information and guidance needed to make voting decisions. Japanese electoral districts are typically smaller than those found in the United States, and Japanese voters are generally faced with only one race to decide on rather than the multiple campaigns associated with the American long ballots.[3] These fewer Japanese candidates, then, are closer to the voters and better known by them. There are also no primary elections, in the American sense, and hence Japanese voters are not forced to make their voting decisions in the absence of any partisan or ideological cues.[4] Moreover, organizational ties and informal social networks within the neighborhood,

3. Japanese normally participate in four types of elections: 1) House of Representatives elections, in which they cast one vote for a district representative; 2) House of Councillors elections, in which they cast one vote for a candidate in a local constituency race and one for a party in a nationwide proportional representation race; 3) prefectural elections, where they vote for a governor and a representative to sit in their prefectural assembly; and 4) municipal elections, where they elect a mayor and a representative for their city, town, or village assembly. The last two types of elections are typically held one week apart in what is called the unified local elections. In many municipalities and prefectures, however, the chief executive elections no longer coincide with the unified local elections, because once a municipality or prefecture experiences a vacancy in the office of chief executive in mid-term, owing to death or resignation, the term of the new executive elected in a special election to fill the office is four years from the time of that elections. On the other hand, in recent years the elections for the two houses of the National Diet have occasionally been held on the same day. In any case, Japanese voters have far fewer choices to make than Americans when they go to the polls.

4. Recently, primary elections have been established by the LDP and JSP to play some role in the selection of these two parties' presidents. These are party offices, however, not public ones, and they involve only the relatively small formal memberships of each party. Selection of official party candidates for public office is controlled by the leadership of each party. Candidates for the offices of mayor or governor often run as independents, but the party coalitions endorsing each candidate are explicit and well publicized. The closest thing to nonpartisan elections in Japan occurs in village assembly elections, where often most candidates are conservatives running as independents. Media coverage of these elections is minimal and hardly necessary for the voters to reach their decision.

work place, and other contexts provide many Japanese with an extensive and often compelling set of cues upon which to base their evaluations of the candidates. All these factors reduce the Japanese voters' need to seek information about the candidates in the media in order to make their voting selection.

The role of the media in Japanese elections is also lessened by the manner in which Japanese media have chosen to cover politics. Traditionally, the leading national dailies and television networks in Japan have adopted a position of strict partisan neutrality. In countries like Norway and Britain, many of the leading newspapers are strongly committed to one party or a group of ideologically compatible parties that they continuously defend (Campbell and Valen, 1966; Butler and Stokes, 1976). Thus, the press plays a major role both in articulating the differences between the parties and in advocating a particular ideological position or partisan preference. In the United States, the press tends to be more politically neutral between election campaigns, but many papers nevertheless come out and endorse specific slates of candidates during campaigns. Either party advocacy or candidate endorsement may be expected to exert some influence on the electorate's voting decisions.[5]

In contrast, both the Japanese press and the electronic media scrupulously avoid partisan advocacy or the endorsement of any candidates. Indeed, perhaps because of a cultural distaste for conflict, the newspapers often seem so eager to avoid controversy that they go beyond neutrality to actually censoring newsworthy items that might be seen as differentially favoring or disfavoring one party or another. Instances have been reported when the major dailies refused to print advertisements of one party that were directly critical of another party, omitted or downplayed stories or incidents that were critical of or cast one of the political parties in a bad light, and suppressed their own preelection polls because they feared that one-sided findings might influence voter behavior.[6] Moreover, as Kim (1981:107) has observed, Japanese newspaper editorials "are unusually ambiguous, making it difficult to ascertain the position of a newspaper on a given issue." This strict partisan neutrality, therefore, should reduce the capacity of the media to influence election outcomes.

Finally, as noted in chapter 4, the use of the media by the parties or candidates to reach the electorate is severely restricted by law. All candidates are forbidden to buy any advertising in any of the media. Only party leaders and

5. For example, some American studies have demonstrated that these newspaper candidate endorsements prior to an election have a small but significant effect on voting behavior (Robinson, 1974; Adams, 1984).

6. Shinohara, 1970; Yanai, 1972b; Kim, 1981. It should also be noted that these omissions in news reporting do not tend to favor any one party or to bear any relationship with the ideological leanings of a paper's editorial staff. Indeed, the beneficiaries have often been the smaller fringe parties such as the Communist Party and the Buddhist CGP.

Diet candidates are permitted access to the media, and that is strictly regulated. For example, Diet candidates are limited to five-minute speeches that are aired on television one after the other in large time blocs of one hour or more. The format of presentation is exceptionally dull, allowing only seated head shots of the candidates reading their statements without the benefit of any visual aids. Moreover, the viewer typically will not know when in the order of the twelve to fifteen or more candidates being presented the candidates standing in his district will appear. As one can readily envision, few voters are hearty enough to sit through these long time blocs of candidate speeches. It is hard to imagine a media format for candidates to present themselves to the public that would be more poorly designed for influencing voting decisions.

While all these factors suggest a very limited role for the media in Japan, it should also be noted that several key ingredients are present that should permit the media to play some role in shaping mass attitudes. First, Japanese society is highly saturated with both the print and electronic media. Japan ranks highest in the world in terms of per capita circulation figures, and the average citizen watches three to four hours of television a day (Donovan, 1981). In our JABISS study, only 1 percent of the respondents reported that they either did not have a television or did not watch TV, while 89 percent reported watching for one hour or more every day. In addition, 95 percent of the respondents reported that they read one or more newspapers regularly. These high levels of exposure to the media translate into high levels of exposure to political information that is being transmitted through the media. For example, 62 percent of the JABISS respondents report that they watch television news programs daily, while 92 percent report watching at least once a week. Moreover, 50 percent say they watched three or more special election-related TV programs, while 86 percent watched at least one such program during the 1976 House of Representatives election campaign. Finally, of the 95 percent who say they read some newspaper regularly, 85 percent read at least one election-related newspaper article.

In some form, then, media information directly related to the election campaign was reaching nearly all Japanese voters. This information may well have been highly regarded because it was coming from a highly trusted source. The Japanese media enjoy the special status of being viewed as one of the most trustworthy institutions in Japanese society. Indeed, Ellis Krauss (1986) cites a 1978 poll which found that NHK, Japan's public television and radio networks, is the most trusted institution in Japanese society, surpassing government institutions, the police, courts, business, and labor. In a more recent 1984 survey, 81 and 75 percent of the public expressed confidence in television news and the press, respectively. Out of a list of fifteen institutions, these media ranked third and fourth in confidence levels, following the constitution and the courts.

Conversely, the parties, Diet, and Self-Defense Forces brought up the rear, with only 21–39 percent expressing confidence in those institutions (Flanagan and Marshall, 1987).

In a comparative perspective, these high levels of trust in the Japanese media seem rather remarkable. For example, in similar kinds of questions asked of American respondents over the last three decades, the American media have consistently ranked near the bottom in levels of confidence, with few Americans reporting great trust in television news or the press.[7]

One explanation for the comparatively high levels of trust in the media in Japan may be found in the media's strict adherence to the principal of partisan neutrality noted above. This practice is not lost on the public. Indeed, the JABISS findings show that only 19 to 22 percent of those exposed to television, magazines, or the popular press reported an awareness of any partisan bias. Among those perceiving a bias, many more saw the weekly magazines as favoring the opposition parties, while the numbers perceiving a left or right bias in the press and television were nearly balanced, with slightly more seeing the press as favoring the opposition and television as favoring the ruling party. This pattern of direction of bias parallels the partisan preferences of the heavy consumers of these respective media. We also find that there are virtually no significant correlations between direction of perceived bias and any of the demographic, attitudinal, or behavioral variables. There are only slight significant correlations between the perception of a conservative bias and both high community integration and high levels of activity in community neighborhood associations. Again this conforms to the partisan preferences of these respondents. Thus, there may be a slight tendency for those who perceive a bias to view the media as being friendly to their views and preferred party rather than hostile. This is a weak association at best, however, as there is only a slight positive correlation ($r = .05$) between direction of perceived bias and partisan preference. But it does suggest that the perception of a bias is not likely to be associated with cynicism.

Indeed, if we test instead for the attributes of those who perceive a media bias regardless of partisan direction, we find that the perception of a bias is slightly related to higher levels of trust in and support of the political system ($r = .07$). We also find stronger relationships between perception of a bias and the strength of partisanship (.16), interest in politics (.14), and active participation in political discussions (.14). Thus, the perception of a bias is not a function of

7. Abramowitz, 1980; Graber, 1980. In a recent 1987 American poll, the top three institutions in public confidence levels were churches, the military, and the Supreme Court, with 61–51 percent expressing high levels of confidence, while the press, television, and unions brought up the rear with 31–26 percent expressing confidence (*The Star*, 9/8/87).

distrust in Japan but rather one of strong partisan involvement and perhaps the tendency of strong partisans to expose themselves more selectively to media that reinforce their partisan preferences.

On the question of the most trusted media, frequent television viewers choose television, while those who rely more on newspapers tend to choose the newspapers. On the question of the media least trusted, many respondents seemed unable to identify any media as untrustworthy, with 40 percent declaring that they cannot say. Only 3 percent said they distrusted all media and only 5 percent named television, the press, radio, or monthly magazines. A full 52 percent of the respondents named weekly magazines as the least trusted media. This response, however, was not associated with higher levels of political distrust or cynicism; it seems rather to reflect the more sensational approach to journalism of a number of the weekly magazines. In other words, these magazines are viewed as being unreliable but not untrustworthy in the sense of disseminating biased and distorted information to promote a partisan cause.

In conclusion, the lower dependency on the media in Japan for providing the basic candidate information and cues needed to reach a voting decision, the legal restrictions on media use in campaigns, and the partisan neutrality of the media should all greatly limit the effect of the media on partisan choice. On the other hand, the high levels of media exposure and trust might increase the media's potential for effecting other kinds of attitude change.

■ Media Exposure to Political Information

While most Japanese have at least some exposure to the media, *levels* of exposure to the media in general and to political information carried by the media in particular differ markedly throughout the Japanese population. Who are the high consumers of the mass media in Japan, and what are the implications of the frequency of exposure and the type of media one is exposed to?

Table 8.1 reveals that there are important differences between the high consumers of print and visual media. A greater frequency of watching television is related to lower socioeconomic status.[8] Those who exhibit high levels of TV viewing also tend to be women and to have low levels of social integration; that is, they have few close friends and are neither well integrated into their residential communities nor are members of nonareal organizations outside their residential communities. In contrast, newspaper readership, frequency of reading weekly magazines, and reliance on newspapers as opposed to television

8. The index of socioeconomic status was constructed by equally weighing and combining respondent's education level, household income, and the head of household's occupational status.

Table 8.1 Associations between Media Exposure and Demographic, Social
Network, and Attitudinal Variables

	Frequency of TV Viewing	Number of Papers Read	Frequency of Magazine Reading	Reliance on Print Media	Exposure to Election Information
Demographics					
Age	(.02)	(−.02)	−.29	−.07	.04
Sex (Male)	−.14	.13	.13	.22	.27
Urbanization	(.03)	.05	.13	.08	.05
Socioeconomic status	−.11	.22	.22	.17	.18
Social Integration					
Social ties to friends	−.06	.09	.10	.07	.23
Community integration	−.06	(.01)	−.12	−.06	.12
Members of nonareal organizations	−.09	.20	.13	.13	.22
Values					
Traditional (−) Modern (+)	(−.04)	.11	.18	.15	.15

Note: All reported correlation coefficients are significant at the .05 level, except for those in parentheses.

for political information all demonstrate similar patterns of association.[9] High consumers of print media tend to be young, male, urban, high in socioeconomic status, and socially integrated in friendship networks and nonareal organizations, but not in their immediate residential communities. High consumption of print media is also associated with more modern values.[10]

These differences are not surprising in view of the fact that exposure to the print media is not as easily accessible and requires more effort than viewing

9. The survey question on reliance on the print media versus television for political information actually asked the respondent specifically what media source he chiefly relied on for information regarding the Lockheed scandal. Since this was a prolonged issue that dominated the media for virtually the entire year prior to the survey, we can assume that the item is a fairly good indicator of the respondent's general tendencies in seeking political information. Over 98 percent of the respondents selected either television (65 percent) or the press (33 percent), leaving less than 2 percent for all other media.

10. Here the traditional-modern value scale is composed of the same three value subscales introduced in chapter 3. All three of these component scales are significantly related to frequency of exposure to the print media and exposure to election information in the media. The strongest relationship, however, was found between the parochial-cosmopolitan value scale and exposure to campaign information ($r = .20$).

television. Women and the elderly spend much of their time at home and thus have fewer opportunities to purchase print media. In rural areas, the fewer newsstands and the greater distances between them in comparison with the cities may also limit the accessibility of the print media and induce more respondents to turn to television, which is in virtually every home. Low education may also make newspaper reading a much more difficult task than television viewing, particularly if a respondent is not familiar with all the terms and Chinese character compounds used in newspaper articles.

Of course, our interest here is exposure to political information in the media, not media exposure in general. These two types of exposure are necessarily related in that citizens that are not exposed at all to television or the press cannot be exposed to political information through these media. Television and newspapers are so full of political information that it is difficult for the consumers of these media to avoid any contact with such information. As noted in the last section, extremely high proportions of the Japanese population had at least some exposure to the 1976 election campaign through the media, and not surprisingly we find that simply frequency of watching television and numbers of newspapers read are positively related to our political information index ($r =$ .10 and .27, respectively).

In constructing this index of exposure to political information through the media, I tried to eliminate these inherent biases in exposure to television versus print by selecting one item for each of these two types of media. The items also refer not simply to a broad perusal of political information but rather a seeking out of information directly relevant to a highly salient political event—the election campaign. Respondents were asked how many newspaper articles they read about the election and how many election-related television programs they watched prior to election day. These two items were combined into the index of exposure to election information reported in table 8.1. Since neither the print nor electronic media are more heavily weighted in the index, we should get a fairly accurate assessment of overall exposure levels to information about the campaign through the media.

We could argue, therefore, that the differences found on the election information exposure index are not attributable to problems of access but rather to the respondents' motivations for seeking political information. Thus, we find some interesting changes between the patterns described above for overall media exposure and the patterns associated with the exposure to political information. The youth bias in access to the print media now disappears, and if anything it is the older respondents who have marginally higher levels of exposure to political information. The urban-rural differences also decline to the point of near insignificance. In contrast, the sex bias increases. Although women spend more hours every day watching television than do men, their exposure to political information is much less. Undoubtedly this is a reflection of traditional cultural norms in Japan, which have viewed politics as an inappropriate activity for women. Where these cultural norms remain widespread—especially among older women, in rural areas, and among those low in education—women are evidently inhibited from even following politics in the media.

The one area where we find little change is on socioeconomic status. Those with higher levels of education, income, and occupational status—perhaps because of more knowledge and interest in politics, a greater perceived stake in political outcomes, and a greater sense of personal political efficacy—are motivated to seek higher levels of exposure to political information through the media. One important conclusion that we can draw from this pattern of findings is that when we turn to testing the relationships between media exposure to election information and other variables, we will need to introduce controls for sex and socioeconomic status to ensure that the associations found are attributable to media exposure levels and not these demographic characteristics.

Table 8.1 also demonstrates that political information exposure is positively related to all three of our measures of involvement in social networks. The more friends an individual has and the more frequently he interacts with them, the more organizations he belongs to, and the more deeply he is integrated into community networks, the more he is likely to follow politics in the media. Not only are these relationships uniformly positive, but they exhibit greater magnitudes than in the case of general media exposure levels. Evidently integration into various social networks stimulates interest in and discussion of election campaigns, which in turn encourages higher levels of information seeking in the media. Finally, traditional values appear to inhibit political information seeking in the media, as demonstrated by the association with the overall traditional-modern value index reported in the table (see note 10).

Table 8.2 suggests that the type of media one relies on can also effect levels of exposure to political information. Here we find that those who rely on the print media for political information and subscribe to national dailies exhibit the highest levels of exposure to election information and psychological involvement in politics. The table also shows that both reliance on television and reading local newspapers tend to be associated with lower levels of exposure to election information. There is some question about the direction of causation here. Subscription to local dailies and reliance on television may reflect a prior disinterest in politics. On the other hand, it is also true that local newspapers tend to assign less space to political news, and it is easier to avoid political information on television by just changing the channel. For those subscribing to national dailies, in contrast, the largest headlines and first few pages of their

Table 8.2   Media Exposure to Election Information and Psychological Involvement
by Type of Media (In Percentages)

	TV or Nothing	Rely TV & Local Press	Rely TV & Nat. Press	Rely Print (Local Press)	Rely Print (Nat. Press)	Tau B
Respondents medium-high to very high on						
Exposure to election information	0	36	40	47	54	.19
Psychological involvement	13	34	41	40	58	.18

Note: Both reported Tau's are significant at the .01 level.

newspapers are typically devoted to political news. Thus, the individual's selection of media may also have some effect on his or her levels of exposure to election and other political information.

■ Long-term Indirect Effects of Media Exposure

The remainder of this chapter will be devoted to an assessment of a number of different ways in which the media in Japan can be shown to have some effect on voting behavior. First, we will look at long-term indirect effects. Here we are addressing a number of different ways in which long-term media exposure can induce changes in individuals that in turn shape their electoral choices. The argument here, then, is that media exposure over time stimulates changes in third variables and that those variables can be shown to be related to voting. Specifically, we will be looking at the impact of media exposure on levels of political knowledge and psychological involvement in politics, on instilling system support and modern values, and on eroding partisanship and increasing volatility.

Political Information and Psychological Involvement

A number of studies in the United States and Britain have shown that higher levels of political exposure are related to higher levels of information. By controlling for education and other variables and using a panel design, it has been shown that media use results in gains in knowledge during election campaigns. In addition, individuals with high levels of exposure exhibit more accurate information and a broader and deeper understanding of political matters even when the effects of education are controlled (Becker et al., 1975; Robinson, 1972; Trenaman and McQuail, 1961).

While we cannot reconfirm the direction of causation, the available data demonstrate the same patterns of association in Japan. For instance, the Uji study by Ichiro Miyake and his associates found that media exposure was related to both greater familiarity with the candidates and political efficacy (Miyake et al., 1967). A secondary analysis of James White's 1972 Tokyo survey, as shown in table 8.3, demonstrates similar findings.[11] Exposure to political information in the media is related to higher levels of political knowledge and political efficacy, even when the effects of education are controlled. The pattern of associations presented in table 8.3 suggests that following politics in the media leads to higher levels of political efficacy through increases in political knowledge. In fact, when the media exposure-efficacy association is controlled by political knowledge, the partial drops to a very weak and nearly insignificant one. Media exposure, then, raises the citizen level of political competence, through direct gains in political knowledge that in turn are associated with gains in efficacy.

Other evidence suggests that media exposure can also increase levels of psychological involvement in politics. For example, the early Columbia studies by Lazarsfeld and his associates found a complex interactive relationship between media exposure and psychological involvement (Lazarsfeld et al., 1944; Berelson et al., 1954). They found that the media stimulated interest in election campaigns and subsequently this heightened interest was associated with increased information seeking and attentiveness to the media. Since then numerous studies in the United States and elsewhere have reported associations between media exposure and political interest as well as various modes of political participation such as voting turnout and campaign participation. Most of these latter studies have not had the sophisticated panel designs to permit a determination of the direction of causation, but it seems reasonable to assume that Lazarsfeld's finding can be generalized. That is, we should expect that exposure to politics in the media does play some role in stimulating interest and participation. Obviously, the reverse causal flow also has important effects; that is, higher levels of interest and participation lead to more information seeking in the media.

As shown in table 8.4, when we turn to the JABISS study, we find a very strong association between frequency of exposure to politics in the media and

11. James White's 1972 survey was conducted in three Tokyo wards, representative of downtown, uptown (yamanote), and suburban settings and realized 839 completed surveys. For a complete report on the findings of his study, see White, 1982.

Table 8.3 Association between Media Exposure, Political Knowledge, and Political Efficacy, Controlling for Education and Political Knowledge

	Knowledge	Efficacy	Efficacy
	(Controlling for Education)		(Controlling for Knowledge)
Media Exposure	.29	.12	.06
Political knowledge	—	.21	—

Source: Secondary analysis of James White's 1982 Tokyo Survey.
Note: All reported partial correlations are significant at the .05 level.

an index of psychological involvement in politics ($r = .46$).[12] Media exposure to politics is also related to higher levels of turnout at the polls (.17) and greater participation in campaign activities (.30).

To probe the effects of the media in stimulating political involvement and participation further, respondents who had discussed the election prior to voting day were asked if they ever had a political discussion started by something they saw on television or by something they read in the newspapers; 62 percent responded in the affirmative to both questions. Moreover, respondents who were stimulated by the media in this way evinced higher levels of political interest and were more likely to have engaged in campaign-related political activities than those who did not report having a discussion started by the media.[13] The Japanese media, therefore, do appear to play a significant role in stimulating political interest, political discussions, and participation.

The finding that media exposure increases political competence and mobilizes participation finds substantial support in the comparative literature and hence is not unexpected. Thus, we find in table 8.4 that strong relationships remain between media exposure and both psychological involvement and political knowledge even after the effects of socioeconomic status and sex have been controlled. What may appear surprising and unexpected are the relationships between involvement, knowledge, and the vote. Those with higher levels of information and interest are more likely to vote for the progressive parties. Again these relationships remain essentially unchanged after appropriate controls are applied. Why?

In trying to unravel the causes and meaning of these associations, it will be

12. The psychological involvement index was constructed by combining and equally weighing a "political interest" scale and a "frequency of discussing politics with others" scale, which were based on four and eight items, respectively.

13. The index of reported media-stimulated discussions exhibited correlations of .22 and .12, respectively, with the political interest and campaign participation scales.

Table 8.4 Association between Media Exposure and the Vote and Levels of Psychological Involvement and Political Knowledge

	Psychological Involvement	Political Knowledge	Vote (Left)
Media exposure	.46	.38	.07
Vote (Left)	.13	.21	—
Controlling for SES *and Sex*			
Media exposure	.40	.30	.05
Vote (Left)	.11	.21	—

Note: All reported simple correlations and partials are significant at the .05 level.

useful to refer to other studies where similar associations have been tested. A number of studies based on other Japanese surveys have reported even stronger associations between political interest and voting left (White, 1982: Flanagan, 1980b). In one of these, a multivariate path analysis helps to illuminate the causes of this association (Flanagan, 1980b). Apparently higher levels of psychological involvement in politics in Japan are associated with more ideological frames of reference for interpreting politics and more modern voting criteria— that is, voting on the basis of parties and issues rather than on the basis of the candidate's personality or his relationship to the voter or his district. So what we really may be measuring here is the respondent's orientation toward politics.

A similar conclusion can be reached by looking more closely at the knowledge/vote relationship. For example, while White (1982) reports a fairly high association between political interest and leftist voting ($r = .21$), he finds no significant association between his political information index and the vote. The explanation for the difference between his finding of no association and the fairly substantial correlation of .21 reported in table 8.4 would seem to reside in the differences in the item content of our respective information scales. White's scale is based on more standard kinds of informational items, such as "name the Foreign Minister of Japan" and "name the Lower House Representatives from this district." Possession of this kind of factual information does not distinguish progressive from conservative voters, particularly since much of the information being asked for concerns local political figures. In contrast, the political knowledge index derived from the JABISS survey was based on the number of times respondents were willing to take positions on twelve preselected national issues, the number of times they could identify a party that they felt was closest to their position on each issue, and the number of specific comments or characteristics they offered about each of three of the largest parties in Japan. A high score on this knowledge index, therefore, would require a strong orientation toward national issues and parties.

The associations we find between psychological involvement or political knowledge and the vote, then, may be attributed to differences found between progressives and conservatives in their orientations toward politics. These differences in turn can be explained in part by traditional-modern value differences, in part by conservative-progressive differences in political style, and in part by differences in party campaign strategies.[14] Given this pattern of associations we could argue that those who relate to politics in terms of candidates, local issues, personalities, and the like tend to be drawn to the LDP, while those who relate to politics in terms of national issues, party issue positions, and other party characteristics may be drawn to the progressive parties.

Based on these findings, a case could be made for a long-term indirect media effect on electoral behavior. If the media play a socializing role in altering the way citizens orient themselves to politics—from more traditional personalistic to more modern issue and party orientations—then that impact on changing perceptions of politics over time might indirectly affect voting behavior.

Value Diffusion and System Support

Media exposure can also be shown to be related to other kinds of variables that have more obvious associations with voting behavior. For example, I have argued elsewhere that the media played a significant role across the first three postwar decades in changing the Japanese political culture (Flanagan, 1986). Especially during the early postwar years, many in the media were convinced that traditional Japanese values were incompatible with the role the citizen was meant to play under the new constitution, and they set about self-consciously to resocialize the Japanese population into more democratic social and political values. Indeed, during this period, many were drawn to media careers out of a sense of mission to root out "feudalistic" ways of thinking and build support for Japan's new democratic institutions. From the Occupation days onward, the media consistently have exhorted the Japanese population to take seriously the responsibilities of citizens in a democracy, have searched for and pointed out shortcomings in mass attitudes and behavior, and have encouraged higher levels of political participation.

As shown in chapter 3, social and political values have been undergoing

14. This last distinction stems from the differences encountered by candidates of large versus small parties in Japan's multimember districts. Because of the ruling party's large size, several LDP candidates typically run against each other in each district and hence emphasize candidate personality over party. In contrast, most of the smaller opposition parties only nominate one candidate per district and therefore need to stress the importance of party differences to achieve election.

rapid change across the postwar period, at least up until the late 1970s. It is not unreasonable to suggest that the media may well have played an important role during this period in diffusing more modern, cosmopolitan values among postwar generations. Other studies have shown that the media's message in Japan is a state-legitimizing one (Krauss, 1986), and so it could also be argued that the media over time have played a role in building system support. With the JABISS data we do find consistent correlations between media exposure levels and modern values (.15), system support (.13), and citizen duty (.19).

We should not make too much of these associations here, because our research design is ill-suited to test for the posited pattern of causal interaction. First of all, there is the problem of reciprocal relationships. Media exposure may diffuse modern values and build system support, but it is also true that modern values and support for the political system may stimulate greater interest in politics and increased information-seeking activities. Thus, part of the correlations reported above must be attributed to the reverse pattern of causation.

On the other hand, our cross-sectional approach inevitably fails to capture much of the change that has taken place. The change we are trying to test is one that occurs over time and across generations as a function of prolonged media exposure. Our only estimate of that effect possible with the JABISS data is by means of the assumption that habits of media exposure endure, such that high consumers of the media at one point in time tend to be consistently so, while low consumers hardly vary their indifference to following politics in the media. Thus, heavy users of the media should internalize more of the media's message. That may be true, but such a cross-sectional perspective greatly underestimates the potential media effect over time. All Japanese are exposed to the media to some extent and thus the effect we should expect is a more generalized one that is moving all of society in a given direction, despite and granted the fact that there are differences in exposure and receptivity levels.

Our findings here, then, are only meant to be suggestive of one pattern of causation that may be taking place. As summarized in the path analysis diagram reported in figure 8.1, we do find significant positive relationships between increased levels of exposure to political information in the media and both modern values and system support.[15] These relationships hold despite the

15. In the path analysis reported in figure 8.1, path coefficients of less than .10 were considered too marginal an effect to merit reporting and thus such paths of influence were dropped from the equations and model. Pairwise deletion was selected to avoid the distortions that occur from losing too large a portion of the sample to missing data, a problem associated with listwise deletion in the Japanese case where the proportions of missing cases are comparatively rather high. Nevertheless, the listwise model was also constructed and yielded an identical structure with the reported figure with two small exceptions, namely that sex (male) was found to predict to both modern values ($B = .11$) and system support ($B = .10$).

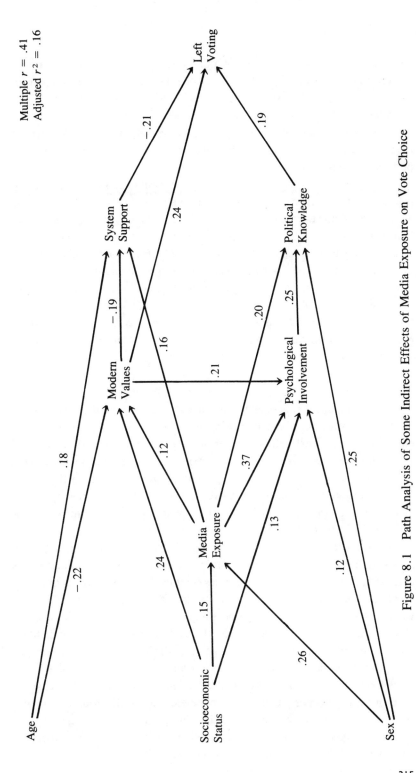

Multiple r = .41
Adjusted r^2 = .16

Figure 8.1 Path Analysis of Some Indirect Effects of Media Exposure on Vote Choice

multivariate controls for the effects of other variables. We also find, as already demonstrated in chapter 3, that modern values are associated with support for the leftist parties while system support is associated with support for the right. Therefore, to the extent that the media diffuse modern values, they may increase support for the opposition parties. Conversely, to the extent that the media project positive images of the political system, they may increase support for the conservative party.

The figure also demonstrates the effects of media exposure on increasing psychological involvement in politics and political knowledge. As we have already noted, however, our political knowledge variable appears to be a stand-in measure for an orientation toward national issues and parties versus a more local, personalistic orientation. Thus, we could argue that media exposure increases psychological involvement and that both media exposure and involvement are directly related to voting decisions that are based more on modern criteria (knowledge about national issues and parties), which in turn are related to progressive voting. In sum, then, the media may indirectly affect voting behavior by propagating certain attitudes and values that favor some parties over others.

Eroding Partisanship and Increased Voter Volatility

One final indirect effect that the media may be having on voting behavior is in eroding partisanship and increasing volatility in voting. This possibility emerges from the fact that with the growing diffusion of television more and more individuals are reporting that they are relying on television rather than the print media as their primary source of hard political information (Flanagan, 1986). For example, in our JABISS survey, 65 percent said that they had relied mainly on television for their information about the Lockheed incident compared to 33 percent who relied on newspapers.

Several scholars have argued that this shift from the print media to television is having a number of important political consequences. According to this argument, television communicates images rather than facts, turns politics into stories and personalities, and captures its audience through the entertainment value of visual action shots. Because it requires so little effort on the viewer's part to receive television's messages, little real learning takes place and little is remembered of what has been seen. The viewer is left with images and vague impressions that decrease his ability to discriminate among the candidates on the issues and reduce his cognitive understanding of his own political behavior. Thus, it has been charged that the advent of television as the medium of choice for receiving political information is eroding partisanship, increasing voter volatility, encouraging shallow political thinking, and decreasing interest in politics (Manheim, 1976; Smith, 1981; Wagner, 1983).

To test for the possibility of these effects, two measures were employed. The first divides the two questions on the number of election-related newspaper articles read and TV programs watched into high and low levels. This measure selects out and compares only the 163 respondents that were high on TV exposure and low on newspaper exposure with the 210 respondents that were high on newspaper exposure and low on TV exposure. The advantage of this measure is that it is based on reported *behavior* and isolates the two categories that should exhibit the greatest differences if the above hypotheses are correct— namely, those whose exposure to the campaign was predominantly through what was seen on television from those whose exposure was predominantly through the press. The problem with the measure is that it has a very short-term perspective with which to attempt to identify a set of effects, at least some of which should take some years to show up.

The second measure is the item asking respondents what media source they mainly relied on for information about the Lockheed scandal. Since the Lockheed scandal filled the media for nearly one entire year prior to the survey, this item may capture more enduring media exposure tendencies than the campaign items can and may also better identify the media source that the respondent pays more attention to regardless of exposure levels. On the other hand, this item cannot control for the fact that those who rely on television may nevertheless also be heavily exposed to the print media and vice versa.

Given the imperfect nature of our measures, we cannot draw any definitive conclusions about the long-term effects of reliance on television rather than the print media for one's political information. As shown in table 8.5, however, at least in the short term, heavy exposure to television to the relative neglect of newspapers has no significant effect on weakening partisanship or increasing voter volatility. Indeed, when the appropriate controls are applied it has no significant relationships with any of the seven dependent variables in the table except for turnout, and that relationship is the opposite of the one hypothesized. As the negative sign indicates, it is the high TV/low press exposure respondents that were more likely to turn out to vote than the high press/low TV exposure respondents.

The only confirming evidence that emerges from the table is found in the fairly modest partial correlations, ranging from .07 to .14, between reliance on newspapers as one's information source concerning the Lockheed incident and higher levels of political knowledge, psychological involvement in politics, and campaign participation. Even here the direction of causation is in doubt, since it may well be that those who are more psychologically involved in politics have a stronger motivation to seek out the print media where more detailed political information can be found. We must conclude that while the potential may be there, perhaps because of the rather modest utilization of the

Table 8.5   Association between Media Relied on for Political Information and Strength of Partisanship, Voting Stability, Political Involvement, and Knowledge

| | Reliance on TV (−) versus Print (+) Media for Information about | | | |
| | | | Controlling for SES and Sex | |
	Election Campaign	Lockheed Incident	Election Campaign	Lockheed Incident
Strength of partisanship	(.01)	(.03)	(−.03)	(.00)
Perceived stable vote	(−.07)	(−.03)	(−.08)	(−.02)
Reported stable vote	(−.01)	(−.01)	(.01)	(−.01)
Voting turnout	−.11	(.02)	−.13	(.02)
Campaign participation	.09	.11	(.02)	.07
Psychological involvement	.13	.21	(−.03)	.13
Political knowledge	.15	.23	(−.03)	.14

Note: All reported correlations are significant at the .05 level, except those in parentheses.

media in election campaigns, there is little evidence to suggest that the increasing reliance on television for political information in Japan is having the hypothesized negative effects of eroding partisanship, increasing voter volatility and decreasing interest in politics.

■ Short-term, Election-specific Effects of Media Exposure

This section will identify two short-term kinds of media effects that can be shown to influence election outcomes directly. These kinds of effects are limited to one election, however; they do not alter long-term political attitudes and frames of reference, such as partisanship, party evaluations, issue positions, or ideology. Since these basic political attitudes remain essentially unchanged, the impact of these media effects are confined to a single election campaign. Because of their direct effect on election outcomes, however, these are probably the two most important media effects that can be identified in Japan.

Image Campaigns

Studies have shown that people process information through preexisting attitudes and belief systems. The information and images an individual derives from the media regarding objects with which he is already quite familiar and for which he holds stereotyped beliefs are largely "perceiver-determined." On the other hand, an individual is most likely to accept the views and evaluations projected by the media without reinterpretation in those areas for which he lacks familiarity, personal experience, or guidance from social contacts. In these cases the images the individual derives from media exposure will be largely "stimulus-determined" (Graber, 1980:117–51).

It could be argued that television is shifting the criteria upon which voting decisions are being made in a direction that enhances the media's influence. As noted in the last section, television conveys images better than hard factual information. While television may stimulate little political learning, it does provide the voter with vivid candidate images and first-hand exposure to personality attributes. As a result, these criteria have become increasingly important vis-à-vis party loyalties and issue preferences in the voter's choice (Graber, 1980; Tannenbaum et al., 1962). While media images and messages concerning party platforms and positions tend to be perceiver-determined, because parties are familiar objects, assessments of candidate personalities and capabilities tend to be stimulus-determined.

Thus, television is augmenting the importance in the voter's decision of those very criteria—candidate images and perceived personality attributes— that are largely shaped by the media. Many times in American politics the media have caught a candidate at an awkward moment or in a slip of the tongue—for example, George Romney's brainwashing statement, Edmund Muskie's crying episode, or Gerald Ford's misstatement on Eastern Europe. In each case, the media played up the incident and projected a negative candidate image that rebounded to the detriment of the candidate at the polls. Conversely, the media became fascinated by the Carter story in the 1976 primaries and accorded him far more coverage than his Democratic rivals, rescuing him from obscurity and greatly increasing his voter recognition and acceptance (Graber, 1980). Perhaps the most dramatic examples of the life and death power of media images over American candidate fortunes occurred in 1987, when the media effectively destroyed the presidential candidacies of Gary Hart and Joseph Biden by playing up personal character issues that some have argued were either trivial or irrelevant to the leadership capacities of these two highly qualified and respected men.

Candidate image also appears to be an important factor in voting choice in Japan, particularly in the gubernatorial elections where media attention is frequently focused on the contrasting styles and personalities of the candidates. The role of candidate image is well revealed in Michio Yanai's study of the 1971 Tokyo gubernatorial election (Yanai, 1972a, 1972b). In that election the incumbent governor, Ryokichi Minobe, was endorsed by the leftist JSP and JCP while his opponent, Akira Hatano, was supported by the LDP. The center parties took a neutral stand, neither running a candidate of their own nor endorsing Minobe or Hatano. Judging from the results of previous Tokyo elections, these left versus right party coalitions were fairly evenly balanced. Yet Minobe won a landslide victory, gaining 65 percent of the vote to Hatano's 35 percent, even though Hatano had an impressive record in public service and had promised a virtual cornucopia of new national developmental funds to improve the quality of life in Tokyo.

Yanai's work demonstrates that the deciding factor in this election was the contrasting media images of these two men. In his preelection Tokyo survey, 52 percent of the respondents reported that they attached more importance to candidate personality than parties in their voting decision, while only 28 percent stressed party over personality. Minobe had been a familiar TV personality in Tokyo, with a popular series of lectures on economics prior to his election. Both in his TV programs and as governor, he projected a warm, friendly personality. In several semantic differential studies conducted with the candidates as object, Minobe continually emerged with a friendly, accessible, conciliatory, honest image while Hatano was perceived as having a harder, less reassuring personality. Among those respondents in the Yanai study who said they based their decision on candidate personality, 59 percent supported Minobe to only 8 percent for Hatano (Yanai, 1972a; Flanagan, 1980).

In the absence of television, it is unlikely that the public would either hold such vivid images of the candidates' personalities or place such weight on this criterion in their voting decisions. In the national Diet elections with many more candidates running, each candidate naturally receives much less media coverage, and candidate images are less compelling in the voters' decisions.[16] Nevertheless, some studies have reported a "party image" effect in the lower house elections that is similar to the above kind of short-term candidate image effect. For example, Fukashi Horie and Yoko Kidokoro (1978) found that there was a strong media effect on boosting the fortunes of the fledgling New Liberal Club (NLC) in the 1976 lower house election. The NLC was born shortly before

16. One familiar item that frequently appears on Japanese surveys asks voters whether they made their voting choice based on the man or his party. Large proportions typically select "the man," particularly in local level elections. The fact that even in national elections one-third to one-half of the respondents continue to select "the man" option, however, is not evidence of a media image effect. Instead, this response has referred to something quite different than the media-projected personality characteristics we are discussing here. Traditionally, the criteria that many respondents have in mind when they select "the man" option are the candidate's personal ties to their family and their locality; his reputation, power, and connections; and his ability to bring benefits to the district. For others, this response simply reflects the fact that the two largest Japanese parties often run more than one candidate per district and hence supporters of those parties are often forced to choose between two or more of their party's candidates.

the election, when six LDP Dietmen, five of whom were members of the lower house, defected from the LDP in reaction to the Lockheed scandal and launched the new party. Typically, new parties do poorly in Japan unless the defectors are able to bring large numbers of sitting Dietmen with them. The content analysis conducted by Horie and Kidokoro, however, discovered that Japan's three leading dailies allocated much more space to the NLC than was warranted by the party's size and number of candidates, with coverage of the NLC increasing up to election day. At the same time, the papers' evaluations of the new party were largely favorable. Indeed, in computing each newspaper's average sympathy scores for the five largest parties competing in the election, Horie and Kidokoro found that the NLC had the most favorable scores of any party in the Yomiuri, while ranking a close second behind the Japan Socialist Party in the Asahi and Mainichi newspapers.

In a context in which little was known about the NLC, it appears that this media coverage had a lot to do with the party's surprising success, electing seventeen of twenty-five candidates despite that fact that 80 percent of their candidates were inexperienced newcomers. This media effect seems all the more plausible in light of the party's poor showing in subsequent elections after the party had developed a record that could be evaluated by the public. Indeed, in the last three lower house elections in 1980, 1983, and 1986, the party's seats consistently fell from twelve to eight to six, and shortly following the 1986 election the party was dissolved and its members reabsorbed into the LDP.

It appears, then, that the media can have a significant short-term effect in helping or hurting the fortunes of candidates and parties when voter decisions are based more on considerations of image rather than either the modern criteria of issues and ideologies or the traditional criteria of proximity and personal connectedness. These conditions are most likely to hold in Japan either in the case of new parties, which as unfamiliar objects are likely to be perceived as initially portrayed by the media, or in the case of a small number of candidates running for important offices in contests that have national significance. Since there are no presidential elections in Japan, candidate image is most likely to be a force in gubernatorial elections in key urban prefectures.

Naturally, the more local the election, the less media coverage it attracts and the less the dependency of the voters on the media to form their images of the candidates. Thus, given Japan's parliamentary system and restrictions on campaign advertising in the media, the ability of media-induced images to affect election outcomes is much more limited in Japan than in the United States. Nevertheless, as discussed above, under some conditions these media effects can be documented in Japan, and it is to be expected that the role of media images in influencing voting decisions will increase in the future.

Former Prime Minister Nakasone (1982–87) was the first Japanese leader to recognize the full potential of the media for building popular support. His ability to utilize the media adroitly to increase his popularity is in part responsible for the rise in his party's support in the opinion polls to its highest levels ever by the mid-1980s and the LDP's landslide victory in the 1986 lower house election. In the past, many Japanese candidates have been anything but photogenic and spellbinding. If, as expected, however, the media come to play a larger role in Japanese election campaigns, one media effect we are likely to see is an increasing recognition of the need to field candidates that project positive, attractive media images that will help their parties draw support from the expanding pools of urban floating voters. Thus, we should expect an increase in image campaigning in the future, which will further enhance the ability of the media to affect electoral outcomes.

Agenda-Setting

There is a second way in which the media may exert a short-term influence on voting decisions. Studies have found that the media play an important role in agenda setting. That is, the coverage devoted to an issue in the media is directly related to the awareness and salience of the issue among the public. For instance, panel studies have shown that respondents tend to give quite similar rankings to the importance of current issues and that their rankings reflect the cues they are receiving from news stories (Shaw and McCombs, 1977). Cohen (1963) has argued that while the media may not be very successful in telling people what to think, they are extremely successful in telling people what to think about.

If some of the issues are viewed by the voters as being better handled by one or another party, a change in the relative salience of the issues can affect the outcome of the election. In the British case, for example, it has been argued that certain parties "own" certain issues. Thus, an increase in the salience of welfare, health, education, and other social-justice and social-service issues is seen as favoring the Labour Party. Conversely, an increase in public concern over such issues as defense, law and order, public morality, and foreign immigration will favor the Conservatives (Budge, 1982; Butler and Stokes, 1976). In the United States, the Republican Party was stereotyped for many years as the party of economic depression and the Democratic Party as the party of war. Thus, it has been argued that a rise in the salience of economic issues (unemployment, welfare, and consumer issues) has tended to benefit the Democratic Party, and a rise in the salience of foreign-policy issues has favored the Republicans. If the media, then, can play a role in setting the issue agenda, they can indirectly influence election outcomes.

A number of studies have demonstrated an agenda-setting function for the

Japanese media (Maeda, 1978; Kaga, 1975). The 1976 Japanese election also provides evidence for the potential of the above kind of party-preferential, agenda-setting effect. First, certain parties are clearly favored by a rise in the salience of certain issues. At least since the mid-1960s the opposition parties have owned the welfare, pollution, quality-of-life, and reform issues. Conversely, the ruling party has owned the economic stability and growth issues. If it can be shown, then, that the Japanese media gave disproportionately extensive coverage to a single issue that clearly favored either the ruling party or the opposition, the necessary conditions for a party-preferential, agenda-setting effect will have been met.

In the Lockheed incident story we find such an issue. This story gradually unfolded and dominated the front page of Japanese newspapers for virtually the entire year of 1976. The Lockheed scandal, which implicated a number of senior government officials in a pattern of undercover political payoffs over seventeen years, highlighted the long-standing system of corruption and bribery associated with the ruling party and its money-power politics. Given the media's intense, extended coverage of this bribery scandal, we would expect that if the media did influence perceptions of issue salience, it would be to increase the perceived salience of corruption-related issues. In turn, a rise in the importance of these issues in the voter's mind would be expected to favor the opposition parties at the expense of the LDP.

As reported in chapter 7, the corruption-related issues were in the forefront of the voters' minds. In fact, among the twelve issue items addressed in the JABISS survey, the three related to the excessive and unethical practices of politicians and big business ranked second, third, and fifth in salience. Moreover, only these three issues exhibited the following pattern of associations: in each case a higher salience ranking on these issues was associated with (1) higher levels of exposure to politics in the media and (2) higher levels of support for the opposition parties.

These findings are reported in table 8.6. The "reform corrupt practices" question specifically referred to the Lockheed scandal and the money-power politics and political corruption that incident brought to light. The "prohibit corporate donations" question raised the issues of the corrupting effects of the massive amounts of money infused into Japanese politics in general and into election campaigns in particular by large corporate donations. The "control the power of big business" question tapped the same issue in the voters' minds—namely, that big business and big money had too much influence in Japanese politics and as a result the interests of the people were suffering. These three issues were then combined into a single index of the salience of corruption-related issues.

Table 8.6 Associations between the Salience of the Corruption Issues to Respondents and Their Media Exposure, Partisanship, and Vote

	Reform Corrupt Practices	Prohibit Corporate Donations	Control Power of Big Business	Combined Index
Media exposure	.15	.17	.13	.18
Partisanship (Left)	.08	(.06)	(.06)	.07
Vote choice (Left)	.10	.10	.08	.11

Note: All the reported statistics are partial correlation coefficients controlling for SES and sex and are significant at the .05 level, except for those in parentheses.

As the table shows, high media exposure was associated with a higher salience ranking for each of these three issues and the combined index. In each case, a higher salience ranking was also associated with both lower levels of identification with the LDP and a reduced tendency to vote LDP. The party ID–issue salience relationship simply suggests that supporters of the leftist parties, following cues from their party leaders, were likely to view the corruption issues as being very important, while the supporters of the LDP were more likely to downplay somewhat the importance of those issues. Given the relatively high volatility of party identifications in Japan, as reported in chapter 6 and elsewhere (Flanagan and McDonald, 1979), it is also possible that some former conservative supporters changed their party support to one of the opposition parties because of the great importance they attached to the corruption issues. When we control the relationship between issue salience and party vote by strength of partisanship, however, we find that the relationship is much stronger for strong partisans than for weak partisans; this finding suggests that the former explanation of partisanship affecting the perceived salience of the corruption issues is the more appropriate one.

More important, then, for our purposes, is the finding in table 8.6 that in each case the vote–issue salience relationship is stronger than the partisanship–issue salience relationship. Some LDP partisans evidently were defecting from the LDP if they attached high salience to the corruption issues. An even more likely cause of this finding is that nonidentifiers were strongly inclined to vote against the LDP, if they viewed the corruption issues as being very important.

These relationships can be more effectively explained if we simultaneously control the correlation between vote and the salience of the corruption issues index by strength of partisanship and education. As reported in table 8.7, when we break the sample down into partisan and nonpartisan and high and low

Table 8.7 Percentage of the Vote Cast for the LDP by the Salience of the Corruption Issues, Controlling for Education and Partisanship

	Unimportant	Mixed	Important	Very Important	Tau
Full sample	59	47	43	42	.09
	(127)	(233)	(530)	(172)	
Subsamples					
Low education	54	50	51	53	[.02]
(primary or less)	(56)	(76)	(226)	(68)	
Partisans with high	64	42	42	38	.10
education	(33)	(90)	(153)	(61)	
Nonpartisans with	50	48	29	26	.21
high education	(26)	(40)	(70)	(19)	

Note: The figures in parentheses are the *N* on which the percentage was computed. All reported Tau's are significant at the .05 level except the one in brackets.

education categories, we find that for those with low education (primary schooling or less), there is no relationship between vote and issue salience regardless of whether the respondent reported a party identification or not. Since partisanship had no effect on the relationship for those with low education, the partisan and nonpartisan low-education categories were combined in table 8.7. Evidently, if a respondent's educational level is quite low, he is likely to lack the political information and sophistication to make the appropriate linkage between concern over certain issues and vote choice. We must conclude that these voters made their choices not on the basis of issue concerns or issue preferences but rather on the basis of some other criteria such as group recommendations, personal ties to a candidate, or candidate image.

For partisans with high education (secondary or more), a strong issue salience–vote relationship emerges. Not only were high issue salience partisans likely to vote more strongly for the left, however, but low issue salience partisans were more likely to vote for the LDP than the sample mean on party vote. We would not expect a lack of concern over the corruption issues to affect the vote, unless a low salience ranking of these issues was a function of the respondent's prior partisan ties to the LDP. In other words, here is further evidence that for partisans, party preference determined one's salience ranking of the corruption issues rather than the reverse.

For nonpartisans with high education, however, we also find a strong issue salience–vote relationship. Moreover, for those who view the corruption issues as unimportant or of mixed importance, the percentages supporting the LDP do not differ significantly from the reported LDP share of the party vote for the entire sample (50 and 48 percent compared to the sample mean of 49 percent). But among those who viewed the corruption issues as important or very important, only 29 and 26 percent, respectively, voted LDP. In other words, we find a strong tendency to vote against the LDP among those respondents who lacked party loyalties, if they viewed the corruption issues as highly salient and if they had sufficient education to make the appropriate linkages between issue salience and vote choice. For these nonpartisans with a secondary education or more, increased exposure to the media heightened the importance they attached to the Lockheed-related issues, and this heightened salience was directly related to an unusually high level of voting support for the opposition parties.

The Lockheed incident, then, is a good example of the role the media can potentially play in agenda setting and how that can influence electoral outcomes. By headlining the Lockheed issues day after day, the media increased the salience of those issues in many voters' minds. If those voters had the necessary education and sophistication to link the Lockheed and other corruption issues to a condemnation of the LDP and if they lacked strong prior partisan ties, their media-induced concern for these issues was very likely to be translated into a vote against the LDP.

The media stress on the Lockheed incident, then, helps to explain why the LDP vote dropped sharply from 47 percent in the 1972 lower house election to an all-time low of less than 42 percent in the 1976 election, when all other signs had been pointing to a leveling off in the decline of conservative popularity at the polls. Indeed, following that election, the LDP rebounded to 45 percent of the vote in the 1979 lower house elections and averaged 47.3 percent in the last four lower house elections between 1980 and 1990.

Our findings also explain why the Lockheed incident did not have a greater influence on the electoral outcome in 1976. In order for the scandal to have affected a voter's decision, he had to (1) be highly exposed to the media; (2) be convinced that the corruption issues were very important; (3) lack prior partisan loyalties; and (4) have sufficient education and political sophistication to recognize that the corruption issues were directly related to the long-term rule of the LDP and that the way to register his concern for those issues was to vote against the ruling party. Clearly, the proportion of the electorate that met all these criteria was not all that large.

In the Lockheed incident, then, we find both the potential and the limits of the media's party-preferential, agenda-setting effect. We can conclude that it would be inappropriate to label the 1976 lower house election as a "referendum on Lockheed," as some have done. Nevertheless, for that subset of the electorate that was susceptible to being influenced in their vote choice by the corruption issues, the magnitude of the shift against the LDP was striking.

■ Direct Media Effects on Political Attitudes

Do the media influence any lasting change in political attitudes? If so, their influence would extend beyond any specific election campaign and affect voting behavior for years to come. We should begin this analysis without great expectations. Given the time span of only a few weeks between the pre- and postelection surveys and the virtual absence of attitude items that were repeated on both waves, the JABISS survey is poorly designed to test attitude change. Here we will have to rely on self-reported changes, which raise some issues of reliability. Our literature review has also cautioned us to expect few detectable effects.

Under what conditions is the media most likely to shape opinions? It can be argued that the impact of the media depends on (1) exposure levels, (2) the absence of preconceived or stereotyped opinions (as, for example, among the young or uninformed), and (3) the motivation for receiving something from the media (that is, the perceived need for guidance). Clearly, those who are not exposed to the media cannot be influenced by the media. In addition, those with firmly held opinions are highly resistant to media influences and rather tend to block, screen, or reinterpret media messages that are at odds with their views. Finally, the user-gratification model and similar functional approaches to media influence suggest that the impact of the media is a function not only of one's motivation to expose oneself to its messages but also of one's need for guidance and evaluations (Graber, 1980). Thus, the media are most likely to influence those attitudes of attentive media consumers that are not well formed and that concern matters about which the user has a strong motivation to gain information. Voting is certainly one context in which individuals may feel some need to acquire views and information on which to base their decisions. In the context of election campaigns we might also expect to find fresh personalities or events or new issues that have not been widely discussed and about which the individual has little personal experience. So the expectation of a media effect on attitude change in some areas related to voting should not be completely ruled out a priori.

On the other hand, the attitudes that are most susceptible to change are by our definitions those which are most likely to be campaign-specific and hence will have little enduring effects on subsequent elections. In addition, those with the highest levels of media exposure also tend to be those with the most firmly held opinions. For example, it is typically found that media exposure is directly related to strength of partisanship (Norpoth and Baker, 1980). Thus, studies have tended to find little direct media influence on changing partisan preferences, basic political attitudes, or even candidate choice as a result of media coverage during election campaigns.

We also find little evidence of such direct media effects in the JABISS election study. When asked if anything they had seen on television or read in the newspapers had changed their opinions about any of the candidates or political issues, 92 and 93 percent, respectively, replied in the negative. Nevertheless, one could argue that 7–8 percent of the respondents report media-induced opinion changes, and in a close election such shifts could decide the outcome. With so few reporting any effect, however, the impact on the election outcome would be negligible, unless it could be shown that the influence was a uniform one. In this case, there is no significant correlation between a reported media impact and party vote choice.

Clearly the media do send mixed messages. Not everyone is exposed to the same media and the same messages, so conflicting effects can occur. We need to ensure that the reported media effects are stimulus-determined and not perceiver-determined, however; that is, that the message received is the one that is being sent. Here we will return to the Lockheed scandal, because in that case the content of the message being sent and its implications for partisan and other political attitudes are clear.

The Lockheed scandal was clearly a media phenomenon. It had long been widely believed that the kinds of practices uncovered in the Lockheed case were a deeply entrenched aspect of the covert side of politics, conducted on a daily basis beyond public scrutiny. By playing up the Lockheed revelations day after day, the media made these practices a political issue. Because the Lockheed incident reflected very negatively on the ruling party and because it was taken up as a campaign issue by the opposition parties, we might expect, in this unusual environment, to find stronger direct media effects than have generally been reported in other studies of media influences.

Some studies have argued that media skimmers, that is, those with moderate to low exposure, are more likely to be influenced because they tend to have less firmly held views and are weaker partisans than high consumers of the media (Becker et al., 1975). Indeed, as the JABISS data reveal, high Japanese consumers of the media do tend to be the stronger partisans ($r = .17$). Moreover, despite their higher media exposure, the stronger partisans were somewhat less likely to have reported that they changed the party or candidate they supported ($r = -.11$) or their ideology ($r = -.07$) as a direct result of the Lockheed incident. This suggests that more firmly held views are in fact more resistant to change from media influences. Nevertheless, table 8.8 shows that the percentage of respondents reporting that they changed their opinions about any of the candidates or issues as a result of something they saw on television or read in the newspaper or that they changed their ideology or vote because of the Lockheed incident increases consistently with the level of media exposure. Thus, despite the fact that many heavy media consumers have strongly held views, the greater the media exposure, the stronger the media influence.

Judging from table 8.8, the impact of the media on political attitudes and vote choice was not at all inconsequential. It should be noted that the chronic know-nothings and apathetics were excluded from the table by filter questions or DK responses. The size of that group averaged over 20 percent of the interviewed respondents, and we would expect that the media had little or no impact on them. Moreover, as already noted, the Lockheed media blitz created an atypical context in which media influences could be expected to be greater than in more normal election years. Nevertheless, the levels of influence reported in Table 8.8 are rather substantial, especially among those with high levels of exposure. Among that category, 54 percent felt that their political thinking (ideology) had been affected in some way by the Lockheed incident, 17 percent reported that their opinion of some candidate or issue had changed as a direct result of their exposure to the media, 13 percent said they changed the party they supported because of the scandal, and an additional 9 percent reported changing their candidate but not their party choice.

It is only common sense to conclude that the media cannot influence those who do not receive the message. Table 8.9, however, unfolds the exposure–attitude change relationship in greater detail. Studies in the United States have

Table 8.8   Respondents Reporting a Change in Attitudes or Vote Choice by Level of Media Exposure (In Percentages)

| | Level of Media Exposure | | | |
	Low	Medium	High	Tau
Changed opinions about candidates or issues owing to media	3 (211)	8 (578)	17 (580)	.12
Changed political way of thinking owing to Lockheed	33 (148)	47 (410)	54 (451)	.14
Changed candidate or party choice owing to Lockheed	12 (115)	17 (321)	22 (386)	.06

Note: The figures in parentheses are the *N* on which the percentage is based. All reported Tau's are significant at the .05 level.

Table 8.9 Respondents Reporting Changing Their Way of Thinking about Politics Owing to the Lockheed Incident, Controlling for Education (In Percentages)

| Education | Level of Media Exposure | | | Tau |
	Low	Medium	High	
College	56	37	49	(.04)
	(18)	(60)	(80)	
Secondary	44	54	57	(.08)
	(59)	(174)	(198)	
Primary	18	44	53	.23
	(71)	(176)	(173)	

Note: The figures in parentheses are the N on which the percentage was computed. The Tau's in parentheses were not significant at the .05 level.

shown that well-informed, politically sophisticated individuals pick up a great deal more information than poorly informed individuals from the same level of media exposure (Tichenor et al., 1970). It is easier to learn and remember new information when the individual can relate it to things he already knows. Also, the individual with greater conceptual skills is more likely to make the appropriate linkages among bits of newly acquired information, so that they may effectively influence his political attitudes and behavior. In contrast, the less sophisticated fail to see the pattern or significance of events or to relate them to more overarching ideological frameworks (Converse, 1975). Thus, those with high levels of prior political knowledge and sophistication may require substantially less exposure for a media message to influence attitudes and behavior. In table 8.9, we have used education as a rough measure of prior political knowledge and conceptual sophistication. We find no consistent relationship between level of media exposure and attitude change as a result of the Lockheed incident for the college educated. Conversely, we find the strongest relationship for the lowest educational category. Evidently, for those with low levels of education, a more intensive exposure is necessary to affect attitudes, while for those with high education and political sophistication, even relatively modest levels of exposure are sufficient for them to get the message.

We have found that the media play a rather limited role in influencing election outcomes in Japan. In part this finding mirrors the conclusions of much of the comparative media effects literature, and in part it reflects the more restrained and restricted use of the media in Japanese election campaigns.

Nevertheless, we have found that the media virtually saturate Japan and that few Japanese are completely isolated from political information transmitted through the media. The pervasiveness of the Japanese media, coupled with the remarkably high levels of public trust in its messages, enhances its potential for influence.

While the media do not exert dramatic, decisive influences on Japanese voting behavior, they do play an important role in raising the level of citizen competence, psychological involvement, and political participation. Beyond that we found that the media may indirectly affect voting behavior by propagating certain kinds of attitudes and values that are themselves related to partisan preferences. Perhaps the strongest evidence of media influence was found in certain kinds of campaign-specific effects related to (1) shaping the content and heightening the importance of candidate images vis-à-vis party and issue preferences in the voter's decision and (2) reordering the salience of political issues that may favor one party over another. Finally, some evidence suggested that the media may also play a role in shaping more enduring political attitudes and frames of reference among some respondents under certain conditions, where high exposure, high education, and nonpartisanship all enhance the potential for a media effect.

While undoubtedly the Japanese media perceive their task as one of informing rather than persuading, the media nevertheless do play a significant role in shaping the context and occasionally even the outcome of electoral contests. Moreover, in the case of the Lockheed incident, the media may have contributed in another way to political change in Japan. Those reporting that they changed either their ideology or vote choice as a result of the Lockheed incident scored substantially lower on the strength of partisanship and system support scales than those reporting no change. The media's emphasis on the Lockheed incident, therefore, may have contributed to the growing cynicism and detachment from the party system that has been reported in Japan.

Nine ■ Social Networks, Influence
Communications, and the Vote

BRADLEY M. RICHARDSON

This chapter addresses the impact on individual voting behavior of electoral
mobilization in Japanese elections. Emphasis is placed on the effects of informal solicitations of one's vote by means of communications that depend on
existing social networks and structures. These are often seen as especially
influential owing to special characteristics of Japanese society and culture. The
focus of the analysis is on the candidate component of voting choices. Normally, solicitations of people's votes and other mobilizing activities are initiated
on behalf of candidates, not parties.

Extensive efforts by candidates, communities, and groups to influence
people's voting choices via face-to-face contacts and appeals have been frequently described in political science research on Japan (Ward, 1951, 1960;
Steiner, 1956, 1965; Richardson, 1967a, 1967b; Flanagan, 1968; Curtis,
1971). Some scholars have seen these activities as the major component of
Japanese election campaigns. Japanese community studies have also paid considerable attention to local electoral mobilization. Enduring ties between community leaders and their rank and file, and the general intimacy and redundancy
of local social relationships, have often been cited as critical elements in electoral mobilization in rural communities and the older, small merchant- or
entrepreneur-dominated *shitamachi* districts of cities (Beardsley, Hall, and
Ward, 1965; Dore, 1958, 1959). Informal efforts to mobilize the vote in national elections have generally appeared to be concentrated more in local elections and in rural and small city constituencies than in other kinds of settings.
But they are to a lesser degree found everywhere in Japanese elections, regardless of place or level of election.

■ **Japanese Electoral Mobilization and Voting
Behavior Theory**

A mobilization theory of Japanese electoral behavior is present in the Japanese
election and community studies literatures. According to this research tradi-

tion, the vote is gathered via informal pressure exerted through external social relationships. Instead of the vote being motivated by individuals' internalized political attitudes—as most political behavior research would expect—what counts in electoral choices, according to this approach, is the opinions and appeals of one's neighbors, co-workers, work-place superiors, and community leaders. Where motivation comes into play, individuals are believed to be moved by personal loyalties or group or community ties and interests rather than by attitudes toward general political objects such as political parties or national issues.

A mobilization perspective on Japanese voting is congenial with interpretations of Japanese society that stress the importance of social conformity, group consensus, and social hierarchy (Nakane, 1970; Dore, 1959; Richardson and Flanagan, 1984). There is also some parallel between the mobilization paradigm and aspects of comparative political behavior theory. The Japanese mobilization literature shares with European political sociology the belief that people's social affiliations largely determine their vote. Japanese mobilization studies have more in common with European micropolitical sociology (for example, Goldthorpe, 1968; Sani, 1974a; Liepelt, 1971), however, than with broad social cleavage interpretations of European party support (for example, Lipset, 1960; Lipset and Rokkan, 1967). Micropolitical sociology looks to the effects on voting of specific small group relationships within the family, work group, peer group, or neighborhood, and sometimes includes the relationships and communications within formal organizations like trade unions or churches. The social cleavage perspective common to much political sociology looks more to the electoral effects of vast, society-wide social divisions, something not really relevant to Japan today (see chapter 2 and Flanagan and Richardson, 1977). Also, somewhat differently from most political sociology elsewhere, Japanese electoral mobilization research looks mainly at short-term mobilization in single elections. Most European political sociology has, in contrast, stressed the "freezing" effects on the vote of repeated mobilization and other longer-term processes.

Filling a Gap in Political Behavior Analysis

While the external aspects of activation of social ties in election campaigns have been described in considerable detail in the Japanese electoral mobilization literature, their effects on behavior are mainly imputed. The ordinary voter is simply assumed to be influenced in many cases by external pressures, even though we do not know precisely how often and why this might happen. The result is a gap in our understandings of these important processes. Addressing this gap by showing how individuals respond to external electoral mobilization is the goal of this chapter.

A second gap somewhat like that in Japanese research exists in voting behavior research in general. Mass behavior theories universally recognize that people's social relationships and organizational ties affect their political loyalties and voting. Yet these theories are not uniform in their treatment of social milieus as potential sources of political attitudes and actions. Nor is their coverage of the processes linking social structure with individual choice complete. Sociological research, as we have seen, is mainly concerned about the effects of external social structures on political behavior. The attitudes that presumably link structure with behavior at the individual level are not specified. In contrast, social psychological explanations treat social networks and contexts largely as externalities, a given in regard to which individual exposure, identifications, and involvement vary (Campbell et al., 1960; Converse, 1977).[1] There is an obvious gap in these two traditions, in the sense that neither approach completely identifies the intervening links that make social processes relevant to individual actions. This chapter will address the gap in models of voting by identifying and linking external and internal factors that affect behavior in Japanese elections within the limits imposed by our survey information.

An Integrated Picture of Electoral Mobilization's Impact

Two paradigms from American research are useful as beginning points to trace the link between external electoral mobilization and internal individual attitudes and behavior. One is Herbert Kelman's (1961) conceptualization of attitude change, which relates the effects of the characteristics of different external social agents to internal psychological responses. Kelman thinks attitude change is a result of alternatively (a) people's deference to powerful persons, (b) their identifications with liked persons and groups (including those with whom intimate personal relationships exist), or, (c) their responses to credible messages. Kelman's interest was with fundamental processes of compliance leading to attitude change. My concern is with conforming or nonconforming behavior in the face of specific external solicitation of the vote or similarly biased cues from individuals or groups with whom persons have social relationships. Even though we deal with shorter-term and less fundamental processes, the relationships and motivations leading to opinion change that Kelman identified are still an attractive heuristic for the processes of electoral mobilization and their effects in Japan. Thinking in terms of Kel-

1. An exception would be socialization studies that have looked at different combinations of mothers' and fathers' party loyalties and political interest in order to see how these differences in external influences affected child adoption of parental political identifications (Jennings and Niemi, 1968). McClosky and Dahlgren's (1959) study of peer group effects on party identification is also an exception.

man's trichotomy of sources of attitude change enables us to distinguish between different aspects of people's external ties—specifically dependency versus identification—and to treat these as variables affecting conformity or compliance.[2]

The model of voter reactions to election campaigns from *The People's Choice* (Lazarsfeld, Berelson, and Gaudet, 1944) provides a useful supplement to Kelman's attitude change model in conceptualizing the effects of electoral mobilization. Following Lazarsfeld and his associates, this chapter views the effects of influence in Japanese elections as alternatively *reinforcing* existing predispositions, *activating* latent inclinations, or *converting* persons to behave in ways they normally would not. Using candidate images and party identification as evidence of an existing predisposition, we will see if external requests for people's vote and other cues of a biased nature stemming from election campaigns merely reinforce existing feelings or move people to depart from established loyalties in their vote choices.[3]

■ Electoral Mobilization in Japan: Definitions and Perspectives

Besides determining the effects of electoral mobilization on people's voting decisions, this chapter employs survey evidence to systematically describe patterns of electoral mobilization in Japan. Many writers have described efforts to organize people's votes in Japan that depend on activation of microsocietal relationships and structures. Some of their characterizations of election campaigns have been superficial and unsystematic in use of terminology. Diverse phenomena have been portrayed either via oversimplified models or terms that have not distinguished accurately the different kinds of campaign activities and influence structures found in Japanese elections.

One of the most common oversimplifications of Japanese election processes has been that which describes influence as revolving around patron-client ties. Patron-client ties certainly exist in Japanese politics, for example, as

---

2. Many people could obviously defer to some person and also perceive that person as being credible. Belief in a source's credibility could also result from identification with that source. We have omitted source credibility from consideration for that reason.

3. We did not attempt to test the Lazarsfeld et al. hypothesis that election campaigns also may activate latent predispositions. The Lazarsfeld group made the assumption that people having certain social characteristics should vote a particular way, even if there was no overtly observable partisan commitment such as a party identification. In Japan such an assumption is difficult to make because of the "social matrix" patterns described by Joji Watanuki in chapter 2. The exception would be rural districts, which normally support the Liberal Democrats, but their homogeneity is assumed to be so great that there is no point to pursuing the relevant analysis.

the "cement" that links faction members to their leaders and local politicians to national counterparts (Scalapino and Masumi, 1962; Thayer, 1969). But specific patron-client relationships are rare in Japanese mass society today. They have nearly disappeared in the rural areas, according to Japanese village studies (for example, Norbeck, 1961), and can only be found in some residual form among such diverse groups as day laborers, gangsters, and graduate students. To speak of patron-client ties as the basis of influence at the mass level in Japanese elections would consequently be highly inaccurate today.

A second approach to mobilization in Japanese elections avoids the terminology of clientelism but stresses the importance of community influentials. This "influentials" model is undoubtedly a more accurate picture of important relationships in Japanese electoral mobilization than the clientelistic approach. The concept of the local influential is universally recognized in Japanese life. Persons such as well-to-do farmers or leading merchants in Japan's ubiquitous urban shopping street associations exist in most settings and are readily identified by the term *yuryokusha* (literally, persons who have influence). Clearly this sort of person has the potential to influence or try to influence political behavior.[4] Scholars of the "social influence" persuasion commonly assume that ordinary voters, many of whom lack high social status or may be economically dependent on a particular influential, are led or pressured to vote in particular ways by such persons of superior social position in local community settings or at the work place.

Toward a Social Network View of Japanese Elections

Our own evidence demonstrates that the social influence model of Japanese voting is still only part of the story. Even granting the pervasiveness of local economic and social hierarchies in Japan, it would be inaccurate to see the majority of Japanese election campaigning as dominated in any simple sense by a class of local influentials. Probably the most suitable comprehensive picture of Japanese society would be one that stresses the universality and centrality of social networks. The sources of efforts to manipulate the vote mentioned by respondents to our 1976 survey indicated clearly that electoral mobilization works through networks of many complexions and types rather than visibly

4. I will not address the question of *whether* influentials choose to use their power at election time or *how* influentials actually use their influence, in part because these are very complicated matters requiring different methodologies from survey research. But my dissertation field experience (Richardson, 1966, 1967b) made it clear that not all influential persons in a particular locale get involved in electoral mobilization. Nor are the sources of influence uniform—some persons inherit high status, some gain it, some dominate others in economic relationships, some are respected for their ability and expertise, some are liked. In no sense are we dealing with a broadly identified social class of exploitative persons whose sources of power are solely economic relationships, although certainly some local elites would demonstrate these characteristics.

flowing downward through social hierarchies. Efforts to win people's support came from such diverse sources as politicians' lieutenants, friends and acquaintances, relatives, storekeepers, delivery persons, work colleagues, community influentials, supervisors at the place of work, and many others. Within this broadly defined framework of social relationships, some ties clearly were based on hierarchical relationships between inferiors and superiors. But the widespread use of relationships that lacked specific and identifiable elements of hierarchy for mobilizing the vote was also clear. Consequently, it is best to see influence in Japanese elections as a "horizontal" as well as a "vertical" process.[5] Whether we call these *kankei* (Flanagan, 1968) or use some other term, widespread and complex patterns of social ties are the major vehicles by which "influence" is exercised in Japanese elections. This qualified view of electoral mobilization influence is further examined below.

Electoral Mobilization and Social Change

An implicit modernization model has been present in many studies of electoral mobilization in Japan and should inform our search for patterns in efforts to influence people's votes. Solicitation of the vote via social hierarchies and community networks is seen as the domain of Liberal Democratic candidates in rural areas, provincial cities, and older *shitamachi* neighborhoods in large cities. According to this picture of Japanese society and politics, influence thrives primarily in settings where two conditions are present—intimate interpersonal relationships influence and mobilize the vote, and parochially defined community and neighborhood loyalties and interests are used as a rationale for appeals for political support.

It is widely believed that electoral mobilization via local social structures will diminish in importance or vanish as Japanese politics and society modernize (Scalapino and Masumi, 1962). Efforts to mobilize the vote using interpersonal networks and community ties should die out as people become more mobile and therefore less involved in local community activities and less dependent on economic and social ties with local community leaders (Flanagan, 1980). The growth of cities—and particularly the modern parts of cities, where people are less active in community affairs, commute out to work, and may even live in the large anonymous *danchi* apartment blocks—is logically viewed

5. For the best statement by a political scientist of the social networks theory, see Scott Flanagan (1968). It is also important to realize that the justifications for vote solicitations vary significantly and depart from the simple influence or social obligations model of behavior. Some evidence (Richardson, 1966) indicates that solicitations of the vote are often laden with instrumental content, ranging from arguments that a particular candidate for election has good character and would therefore be a good representative to contentions that a specific nominee would advance specific community or group interests.

as a manifestation of such processes (Flanagan, 1980). According to some versions of the modernization approach, formal organizations like political parties will take the place of informal influence communications networks in mobilizing electoral support as the older ways become less viable (Scalapino and Masumi, 1962; Ward, 1960).

Actually much can be said for these perspectives on electoral mobilization and influence in Japan and the projections they subsume. In many ways they are accurate representations of reality. Yet like many theories of politics originated before detailed empirical research, their pictures of reality can be qualified through close empirical examination. Like many other areas of political behavior, influence in Japanese elections is more complex than has been typically viewed thus far. In addition, some of the existing hypotheses about Japanese style electoral mobilization can be refuted, and with the insight derived from qualification, a more satisfactory picture of the role of these activities in Japanese political life can be gained.

■ Influence Communications Processes

There are two kinds of election campaigns in Japan, a *formal* one where candidates and party leaders give speeches before crowds of citizens or make statements that are transmitted or printed via the mass media, and an *informal* effort wherein a variety of appeals for support are made via word of mouth through people's social network contacts. Use of existing social structure for political mobilization is a common phenomenon in Japan, perhaps a more visible or a more frequent activity there than in any other industrialized country.

Organized groups also play a well-known role along with interpersonal networks in efforts to mobilize voting support in Japan. Many kinds of groups are used as channels for mobilizing the vote. Communities play an especially prominent role in local election campaigns, given frequently intense local loyalties and interests, and the special suitability of parochial social relationships for small-scale electoral mobilization. Some communities are active even in the relatively more remote and larger-scale national contests. Labor unions, shopping street associations, agricultural cooperatives and production unions, voluntary fire fighter groups, parent-teacher associations, and many other organizations are included in the inventory of groups that actively support candidates and may even campaign on their behalf at election time.[6]

6. Perhaps company "group" members should be added to the roster. In some House of Councillors elections there have been instances of an individual company's support for individual candidates. In a few lower house constituencies, such as the district including Toyota City (Allinson, 1975), close cooperation between companies and unions to support particular candidates have been reported. But Japanese surveys have not asked questions on this pattern of mobilization.

One of the most conspicuous examples of group electoral mobilization is the *koenkai* or support association, an organization set up explicitly for mobilizing a body of voters and community leaders in support of a particular candidate (Richardson, 1967b; Curtis, 1971). The koenkai is a curious organization sociologically; it represents a kind of borderline between the formal and informal sides of Japanese elections. It is part of the open, public campaign, in the sense that this is an explicit instrument set up for winning votes. At the same time, many of its internal relationships revolve around social ties found in any Japanese community, and we include koenkai as part of our treatment of influence communications for that reason. As we will see, koenkai membership is widespread at all election levels in Japan.

A generic term is needed for the kinds of activities that go on in Japanese elections where people's voting support is sought via mobilization of social networks and group affiliations. These electoral mobilization efforts are labeled *influence communications* in the remainder of this chapter. Influence communications are interpersonal and organizational communications designed to directly mobilize and manipulate voting support through activation of personal obligations, feelings of deference, or other kinds of sentiment pertaining to specific ongoing social relationships that extend well beyond any given election campaign. I include in this category a substantial variety of behavior, such as interpersonal requests (*irai* or *tanomare*), informal arrangements in some community or social group (*moshiawase*), and endorsements by organizations including communities and labor unions (*suisen*). I also include koenkai, since these are generally set up with some kind of relationship to local community social structures and rely on those networks in many ways. Even candidates' use of postcard greetings in Japanese election campaigns (and between elections at New Year's and *chugen*) can be seen as a peripheral form of influence communication. Sending postcards is a traditional social activity for political purposes, as would be the case were American congressmen to send Christmas cards to their constituents. But we cannot tell exactly what kinds of influence they exert, since the relationships they invoke are impossible for us to identify. Excluded from the influence communications category are the absolutely formal aspects of campaigns—the speeches and public efforts that do not involve interpersonal contacts and group activities as the primary mode of contact— and general political discussions that are not specifically designed to influence people's votes even if they have this effect.

The Nature and Patterns of Influence Communications

Many people feel that influence communications are a major part of Japanese election processes. Despite excellent anecdotal descriptions of these phenomena, however, there has been little systematic information provided to assess the precise role of influence communications in Japanese campaigns. Nor has the stability or change of these activities been examined over time, despite considerable speculation about how these might change as Japanese society continues to modernize.

Table 9.1 shows information from a long-term series of survey research reports to answer the overall "extensiveness" question and some related questions about the importance of influence communications in Japanese elections. Four *kinds* of influence communications activities are identified in table 9.1— interpersonal requests, endorsements by groups, membership in candidate support associations, and receipt of a postcard from a candidate. People's discussions of their voting choice are also included for purposes of reference. We have no way to judge which discussions involve an effort to influence the vote and which do not. For this reason, discussions will not be claimed as a form of influence communication. Nevertheless, talking about one's vote choice constitutes a useful comparative datum with which to judge the importance of other kinds of specifically influence oriented-communications. The data are presented by *type* of *election* and *time* as well as by type of influence communication.[7]

The figures in table 9.1 indicate a general picture of the frequencies of different kinds of influence communications in different kinds of elections in Japan between 1960 and 1987. There are interesting variations in frequencies in regard to all three main dimensions—type of communication, election level, and year of survey—shown by table 9.1. First, there is a crude hierarchy of frequencies of influence communications activity independent of differences reflecting the effects of time or election level.[8] Interpersonal requests for the vote are the most common form of influence communication in Japanese elections. This tendency is most clear at the national level. But even in local elections, requests are beginning to pass organizational environments in importance. Requests are followed in order of importance by receipt of postcards, koenkai membership, and group endorsements. Requests are probably more prominent than many people would anticipate, especially in recent House of Representatives elections where they actually exceeded discussions of voting

7. The questions about influence communications exposure upon which table 9.1 data depend solicited respondents' *perceptions* of particular kinds of activities. This means that some underestimation could occur where people are less politically aware.

8. The estimates of total frequencies of particular kinds of activities (for example, requests) were made by adding together different subtypes of these activities without regard to possible overlap, that is, cases where a single person engaged in more than one kind of activity. This was done because the data are taken from research reports over which we have no control; they are not from our own data manipulations.

choices. In contrast, group and community endorsements are much less frequent than anecdotal evidence from scholarly and journalistic sources would suggest. In part, the "low" levels of group endorsements or support reflect rather lower levels of some kinds of group memberships than are normally anticipated for Japan. According to our JABISS survey findings from 1976, outside of union memberships (13 percent of those interviewed), businessmen's organizations (18 percent), and hamlet and neighborhood associations, which are semicompulsory groups, only a small fraction of the respondents belonged to a formal group. For PTAS, reform groups, political groups, fire fighters and similar organizations, recreational groups, and religious organizations, an average of 13 percent of the respondents were members. Membership in one formal group was a special case. Seventy percent of our respondents cited their *households* as belonging to hamlet and neighborhood associations. Figures such as these often lead scholars to expect high levels of group mobilization in Japanese communities. But membership in these groups is largely compulsory, and many family members did not participate in this group's activities; thus, reported memberships are not a meaningful gauge of the importance of the organization.

Setting aside the low levels of membership in some groups, relatively few members actually saw their groups as supporting candidates. Labor unions had the highest levels (26 percent of their members) of reported group support or endorsements. Religious groups were next in importance with 18 percent of their members reporting that their group supported a candidate (but few people were members of religious groups). Small businessmen's groups were third in frequency of perceived group support for a candidate (13 percent of their members). Members of other organizations perceived their group as supporting a candidate even less frequently—young people's and old people's groups (5 percent), communities (4 percent), and PTAS (2 percent). Mobilization in Japanese parliamentary elections relies on interpersonal requests and other voter contacts initiated by candidates much more than on the visible mobilization of interest groups or local communities.[9]

In addition to an observable hierarchy in the frequencies of different kinds of influence communications, some remarkable changes took place in influ-

9. Percentages in each case are those persons who said they were members of a group (or that their household was an affiliate in the case of community associations) who also identified the name of a candidate supported by their group. This is a indicator of "hard" information about group political climates. We actually had replies to an easier "yes, a candidate was supported" or "no, nobody was supported" series of filter questions about group support for candidates. In most of this chapter I use "harder" measures of different kinds of influence communications rather than "softer" ones, in part because it is necessary to know which candidate was supported when the actual effects on voting are examined. Where both types of data are used, as in general descriptions of population frequencies or tendencies among persons of different education or persons living in cities versus the countryside, this will be clearly indicated.

Table 9.1 Influence Communications, 1960–87

	House of Councillors[a]			House of Representatives[b]							Local Assembly[c]			
	1974	1977	1983	1960	1963	1972	1976	1979	1983	1986	1964	1975	1983	1987
Interpersonal requests														
By telephone	7	6	10	—	—	12	21	26	40	41	—	—	—	—
From friends	13	14	12	10	—	17	16	18	25	26	—	—	—	—
From friends/ influentials	—	—	—	—	—	—	—	—	—	—	—	19	26	28
From influentials/ work superiors	3	3	2	3	—	2	3	3	6	8	—	—	—	—
Candidate endorsed by														
Unions	7	7	6	6	8	6	8	8	10	9	—	—	—	—
Unions/business	—	—	—	—	—	—	—	—	—	—	—	10	10	13
Business groups	7	6	7	—	—	5	5	7	11	11	—	—	—	—
Community groups	2	2	1	1	1	4	3	6	4	6	16	15	13	11

342

Respondent a koenkai member	17	—	14	9	11	10	14	20	16	18	—	—	—	—
Talked over voting choice														
In family	23	20	17	—	37	33	32	31	30	30	—	22	21	26
At work	8	7	6	—	—	12	13	12	14	16	—	—	—	—
In neighborhood	7	5	3	—	—	13	11	10	11	9	—	—	—	—
Perceived postcard from candidate	—	—	—	—	—	25	23	34	33	35	—	—	—	—

[a] Figures are not cumulative, i.e., do not sum to 100 percent, as multiple answers were permitted. Figures pertain to national constituency phenomena; prefectural constituency patterns are somewhat more like those of lower house contests. Data are from the *Sangiin Tsujo Senkyo no Jittai* series of reports from the Komei Senkyo Renmei (KSR), and lately, from the Akarui Senkyo Suishin Kyokai (ASSK).

[b] Sources are *Shugiin Giin Sosenkyo no Jittai* report series from the KSR and the ASSK.

[c] Sources are *Toitsu Chiho Senkyo no Jittai* report series from the KSR and, after 1979, the ASSK. The relevant question asks respondents to name source of information "useful" in voting decisions. Surveys from which data on national elections are cited simply asked respondents to name activities to which they were "exposed during this election campaign," a less qualified question.

ence communications over the relatively short span of time between 1960 and the 1980s. In the 1960s and early 1970s, that is, prior to our JABISS study, requests to vote for a particular candidate were seldom received by more than one-third of the electorate, according to national election surveys run by the Komei Senkyo Renmei (Clean Election League) or its successor, the Akarui Senkyo Suishin Kyokai (Association for the Promotion of Clean Elections). Likewise, in this same period, less than 10 percent of the electorate were aware that some group *endorsed* a particular candidate, and about 10 percent of the electorate on the average were members of a koenkai. Influence communications overall probably reached a maximum of 40 percent of the electorate.[10]

But as table 9.1 clearly demonstrates, people's reports of influence communications increased quite dramatically in Japan beginning in the early 1970s. In House of Representatives elections, reports of requests by telephone increased twofold, while other kinds of requests and koenkai memberships also increased substantially according to survey respondents' self-reports, as did the reported frequencies of receipt of postcards sent by candidates. Even frequencies of perceived group endorsements increased, although at a much slower rate than requests and other activities. Some of the same trends could be seen in local elections and, in a limited way, in House of Councillors elections. Evidence of increasing influence communications activity would seem to explicitly reject the hypothesis that influence communications will decline as Japan's society modernizes. There was ample social change in Japan in the form of massive population movement to the cities and suburbs in the 1960s and early 1970s (Richardson, 1977; Flanagan, 1980). But this movement to the cities was not paralleled by a general decline in influence communications frequencies. Only modest declines of community endorsements of candidates in local elections seem to fit modernization theory's expectations of a decline in community life and related kinds of electoral mobilization as the result of urbanization and greater social mobility. The increased frequencies of requests is striking evidence of the continuing importance of informal interpersonal relationships in Japanese elections.[11]

The information in table 9.1 on activities in different kinds of elections suggests some further qualifications on the role of influence communications in Japan. In the earlier years of the postwar era, higher levels of influence com-

---

10. This figure is an estimate based on our understanding of overlapping patterns from analyses of the JABISS 1976 data, since the data series used in table 9.1 lacked an explicit figure for persons engaged in more than one kind of influence communications behavior.

11. An alternative explanation to the patterns in table 9.1 is that they could reflect greater openness in people's replies to survey questions as time goes on. This possibility is hard to evaluate. The influence communications items were multiple answer-questions, and patterns in "Don't Know" answers, which might be one indication of a change in people's openness about influence communications, are hard to interpret within the contour of the multiple-answer format.

munications were found in local elections than in national contests, and more influence communications activities by and large could be seen in HR than in HC elections. Influence communications seemed to increase in frequency as the size of electoral districts diminished, reflecting the parochial nature of many of the groups and social networks activated in efforts to informally shape the vote. More recently, though, both interpersonal requests and organizational endorsements in national elections have paralleled or even perhaps surpassed the levels of local election mobilization. (A slight noncomparability in question categories makes absolutely precise comparison impossible.) Change has meant use of different informal channels of intermediation rather than an overall, simple decline in the volume of influence communications processes. Once again, we are reminded of the changing nature of electoral mobilization in Japanese elections and of patterns that on the surface do not conform to simple social modernization theories.

Some other interesting patterns emerge from the cross-level data in table 9.1. Clearly, communities and neighborhoods are of only minor importance in the endorsement of candidates in national elections. This pattern, which has not changed over time, challenges the folkloric assumption of high levels of visible community involvement in electoral mobilization regardless of election level. Labor unions and economic groups (mainly shopkeepers associations, agricultural cooperatives, and groups of manufacturers who make the same kind of product) are more important than community groups in national elections. Unions and business groups are also becoming more important in electoral mobilization in local elections as time goes on. In this one sense—the ascendancy of economic groups over community social structure—the expectations of modernization writings are borne out, although in rather a weak way insomuch as neither are of marked importance with regard to interpersonal requests.

Taken altogether, two principles appear as major factors influencing the use of various kinds of social networks and organizational ties for electoral mobilization in Japan over the past three decades. One is the principle of *parochialism,* by which smaller-scale election districts were earlier characterized by more intensive use of community and neighborhood channels of communications. This principle became qualified over time as social change reduced the relevance of community-based social ties, while *political expediency* led politicians and their lieutenants to seek to exploit more fully the essential network nature of Japanese society in their search for votes. It is totally plausible that these two "principles" are in fact causally linked, since as natural communities declined, the need for votes gathered via other kinds of social ties increased.

Question Wording Effects on the Reporting of Influence Communications
The figures in table 9.1 are people's answers to straightforward questions

about their *perceptions* of particular kinds of communications activities. Survey respondents were simply asked whether or not they had been contacted and asked to vote a particular way, or if they were aware of community or group endorsements. Direct questions of this variety run the risk of underestimating levels of influence communications for two reasons. Some election practices, such as visits to people's homes and the presentation of token presents in exchange for supportive votes, have been outlawed in Japan. Election authorities have also conducted campaigns to eliminate traditional campaign practices, which have conveyed the image that some of the activities we described earlier are somehow undemocratic.[12] Some people may be reluctant to answer questions about activities they consider to be undemocratic or verging on illegality, which naturally would depress frequencies of reported exposure to these activities.

In contrast to the simple, straightforward method of soliciting information on people's influence communications, one local prefecture survey (Shimane, 1960) added to questions about influence communications a long disclaimer that respondents should not confuse their reports of exposure to influence communications with illegal activities. The effect of this disclaimer was dramatic. Frequencies of reported exposure to influence communications actually reached an overwhelming 85 percent of the persons interviewed in this predominantly rural prefecture. On the assumption that question wording was extremely important, our 1976 JABISS survey followed a similar approach to that used in the Shimane local survey. A lengthy disclaimer as to the intent of the questions was included to introduce the items in this potentially sensitive area.

As shown in table 9.2, the JABISS results showed somewhat higher levels of influence communications activity in some categories than those indicated in table 9.1 based on national surveys from the same time period (the 1970s), which lacked an introductory disclaimer as to question intent. Reports of interpersonal *requests* to vote a particular way "rose" to 51 percent, awareness that some group *endorsed* a candidate stood at 14 percent, while 18 percent of the respondents reported membership in a candidate's support association. One form of specific campaign or between-campaign activity—constituents' receipt of postcards from Diet members—was a little more common (55 percent) than most of the influence communications processes considered in this chapter. Altogether, 77 percent of the electorate sampled were exposed to some kind of influence communications activity when multiple contacts were accounted

12. The Komei Senkyo Renmei and the Akarui Senkyo Suishin Kyokai, mentioned earlier in connection with data sources, have both been part of the Home Ministry's efforts to publicize "fair" election practices, which could have heightened respondent sensitivity to legal and normative nuances in the relevant questions.

Table 9.2   Communications Behavior in the 1976
General Election (In Percentages)

Watched election programs on television	82
Read about the election in newspapers	76
Discussed some aspect of the election	61
Exposed to some form of influence communication[a]:	77
Received a postcard from a candidate	55
Received a request to vote for a candidate	51
Member of group(s) that supported candidate(s)	14
Members of a candidate's koenkai	18

Source: 1976 JABISS survey. The percentages are based on the panel portion of the total sample.

[a] The percentage is based on the number of persons exposed to any kind of influence communication, whether exposure was to only one form or to several. The percentages for different combinations were as follows: one of multiple combinations of postcards, requests, group endorsements, or support association membership, 34%; requests only, 15%; postcard only, 13%; koenkai only, 1%; group endorsement only, 1%.

for. In effect, use of different question wording considerably increased the frequencies with which the various kinds of influence communications were reported.

The table 9.2 data also permit comparison of influence communications with other forms of political communications at election time. It is clear that exposure to influence communications is not as common a form of electoral behavior as watching television or reading the newspaper. Influence communications were an important component of people's overall exposure to sources of information about politics at the time of the 1976 election, but they were not the exclusive nor the dominant source of information by any means.

At this point, we should note an important qualification to the "levels" data presented in table 9.2. Our JABISS questions provide the most comprehensive survey of influence communications activities ever attempted in Japan, and my associates and I feel very comfortable with the estimates of the frequencies of these activities that they permit. Altogether, forty-three questions were asked about organized group environments, seventeen questions were asked about political climates within social networks, and a shorter battery of queries focused on koenkai membership and other contacts with the candidates, including receipt of postcards. In addition to asking people whether they experienced some kind of influence-seeking contact or were members of a group that supported a candidate, these questions also sought precise identifications of what parties and/or which candidates were favored within groups or in social networks. The resulting information is an indicator of levels of explicitly remembered influence communications activity, which I assume may be the most meaningful information for many people for the simple reason that it is stored in memory. Still, given the redundancy of human relations in rural hamlets and small towns, it is possible that less clearly remembered cues about the election may have influenced some people.

There is a considerable drop-off between levels of simply stating that a particular kind of activity occurred and knowledge that a specific candidate was mentioned. Numbers in the category showing receipt of a request declined from 42 to 18 percent using the more qualified information, that showing receipt of a postcard dropped from 55 to 45 percent, and that identifying koenkai membership declined from 18 to 16 percent. This information about "meaningful" influence communications is used in later analyses of the effect of the different kinds of influence communications on people's electoral decisions, since effect can only be measured with these more concrete data. As we shall see shortly, these data also provide interesting insights in regard to urban-rural and social status patterns of influence-seeking activities.

Urban-Rural Patterns in Influence Communications

Journalistic and scholarly discussions of elections in Japan have long recognized that efforts to mobilize the vote via group endorsements and interpersonal requests are found in both the countryside and the cities. Still, since requests and endorsements would seem to depend for their existence and effectiveness on the presence of dense social networks or strong loyalties to communities or other social groups, one might expect that overall levels of influence communications would be higher in the rural areas than in the cities. According to the evidence presented in table 9.3, this does not appear to be the case. Not only were influence communications frequencies relatively similar between the city and the countryside, but interpersonal requests—the main form of informal influence communications activity in both sectors—actually displayed the highest levels in middle-sized cities.

To explain these urban and rural patterns of influence communications it is necessary to examine both the respective social milieu and the types of political organization found in both sectors. In other words, frequencies of influence communications that rely on social networks or groups depend both on the presence of a congenial social setting and the actual choice to use the social setting for purposes of political mobilization. Initially, Japan's rural districts appear on the surface to be a more fertile setting for influence communications than the cities. Table 9.4 demonstrates that rural residents more commonly have intimate ties with their neighbors than their urban counterparts, and they are

Table 9.3   Urban-Rural Patterns in Influence Communications
(In Percentages)

	Major Cities	Cities over 100,000	Other Cities	Rural
Interpersonal requests				
Asked to support a candidate (1976)	53 (25)	51 (29)	42 (14)	42 (23)
Asked by telephone (1972)	27	27	19	10
Asked by friends (1976)	23 (14)	26 (19)	28 (6)	15 (10)
Asked by neighbors (1976)	16 (12)	14 (12)	9 (4)	12 (9)
Asked by co-workers (1976)	14 (7)	18 (13)	16 (8)	11 (8)
Group endorsements				
Hamlets and neighborhoods (1972)	2	2	5	6
Hamlets and neighborhoods (1976)	4 (2)	2 (2)	4 (2)	11 (7)
Koenkai membership				
(1972)	10	13	18	15
(1976)	15 (9)	15 (13)	17 (11)	19 (16)

Sources: 1976 JABISS study and Komei Senkyo Renmei, *Shugiin Giin Sosenkyo no Jittai* (1973). Major cities are those so designated in Japanese statistical practice, i.e., Tokyo, Osaka, Yokohama, Nagoya, Kobe, Kitakyushu, Fukuoka, Kawasaki, and Sapporo.

Note: Figures in parentheses indicate proportions of cases where respondents indicated a candidate's name.

members of groups about twice as often, even omitting community groups from the calculations.[13] Only in levels of reported ties with persons at one's place of work are the urban and rural populations fairly similar. If frequencies of influence communications activity at election time depended solely and directly on urban-rural differences in extrafamilial social contacts, one would indeed expect greater activity in the rural sector, particularly in those forms of influence communications that focus on community and neighborhoods.

Probably the differences in the rural and urban social settings are linked in a less visible way to the trends in influence communications than our data indicate. The rural social milieu is, presumably, relatively more supportive of *long-term* political organization than the city environment because of the intimacy of interpersonal ties and overall density and redundancy of social contact there. Consequently, the relatively greater influence communications activity at election times in the cities could simply be a corrective in the absence of more permanent political organization of the kinds possible in the rural areas. This

13. Neighborhood and hamlet associations figured very little in endorsements. Furthermore, these groups are much less active and therefore less meaningful as group environments in urban settings. We left them out of urban-rural comparisons of group memberships for this reason.

Table 9.4   Urban-Rural Social Patterns in 1976 (In Percentages)

	Major Cities	Cities over 100,000	Other Cities	Rural
Knew persons in the neighborhood intimately	58	67	77	85
Had intimate contacts at work place	47	49	50	52
Member of one or more groups	13	19	19	24

Source: 1976 JABISS survey.

interpretation seems highly plausible when we note that rural voters indicated in surveys that they make their election decisions before the campaign in substantially greater frequencies than do urbanites.[14] It is not news that electoral organization is more permanent in the rural areas, but it is intriguing that this is apparently associated with greater influence communications activity at election time in the cities. These urban and rural patterns are also obviously linked to trends over time in the incidence of influence communications, since recent social change has resulted in far larger proportions of the population living in urban areas. As we observed earlier, when natural communities decline through social mobility, politicians and their lieutenants apparently turn to other kinds of social networks that at least on the surface are not so parochially defined. Concretely, this means more influence-seeking activity through economic groups, in requests from colleagues at the work place, and via telephone solicitations—the patterns which characterize urban residents more than their country counterparts.

The relative dependence of the different political parties on influence communications for mobilized voting support is also probably a factor in the urban-rural patterns. As was noted earlier, there is a tendency among observers of Japanese politics to identify "traditional" vote-seeking activities, such as requests for the vote and the use of the koenkai form of support organization, with the Liberal Democratic Party style of mobilization. But in reality *all* the Japanese parties depend upon requests, group endorsements, and koenkai to some extent in their efforts to gain support, as shown in table 9.5.[15] This fact certainly contributes to the relative extent to which influence communications processes resemble each other between the cities and the countryside. Indeed, the higher frequencies of interpersonal requests from some opposition parties (especially

14. Akarui Senkyo Suishin Kyokai (1977:173). Twenty-three percent of major city residents said they made their choices before the campaign while the figure for rural areas was 36 percent.
15. The national data series cited in table 9.1 confirms the JABISS evidence on this point.

Table 9.5 Influence Communications by Political Party of Candidate
(In Percentages)

	LDP	JSP	JCP	CGP	DSP	NLC
Vote request	35	16	9	33	7	1
Group support	46	29	4	17	5	—
Koenkai	56	18	8	9	7	2
1976 party vote	48	27	7	6	6	3

Source: 1976 JABISS survey.

Note: The percentages are proportions among all requests, all group support/endorsements, and all koenkai memberships of requests originated by each party (according to respondents' perceptions). Comparison with the party vote makes it possible to see where party efforts were unusually concentrated relative to a party's "electoral support."

the JSP and CGP) in relation to their voting strengths undoubtedly contribute to the slightly higher use of interpersonal requests in the cities.

An alternate explanation for these urban-rural and party differences in reporting receipt of influence communications is presented in chapter 4. There Scott Flanagan argues that the reported frequencies for rural areas are depressed by a tendency for individuals who identify very closely with a particular group to fail to perceive the influence communications directed at them from that source as an external request. Conversely, those who are cross-pressured and receive a number of conflicting influence communications—for example, people living in the cities—may more likely be aware of and report requests and endorsements. This phenomenon would obviously help to explain the patterns we find in tables 9.3 through 9.5.

The percentages in the different residential settings for persons who reported exposure to some kind of influence seeking activity *and* who also knew which candidate was being supported are shown in parentheses in table 9.3. Viewed this way, levels of influence communications tend to be much more balanced between urban and rural settings than the reports of exposure to influence communications noted above implied. The urban-rural differences actually are smoothed out in some instances, especially with regard to electoral mobilization that involves general requests to support a particular candidate. There is also a kind of bounded cities effect in the case of cities of over 100,000 inhabitants with regard to some kinds of requests and membership in support associations.

Influence Communications and Social Status

As was noted earlier, one of the most popular versions of influence communications theory in Japan describes request activity as flowing downward from persons of higher social status to persons of lower station. In the most simplified version of the model, Japanese society and politics, particularly rural society, is believed to be dominated by "feudal" relationships wherein community and economic elites defend their interests through manipulations of the vote.

It is impossible to test a social hierarchy theory of influence communications thoroughly with data collected from a randomly drawn sample survey. Snowball sampling that captures both sides of an influence communications exchange would be more appropriate. Still, it is interesting to see whether the data gathered from a normal mass survey meets the expectations of a social hierarchy model even if only in a simplistic way.

If a social influence or social hierarchy model were to operate in some pure sense, persons in upper-status positions in society would typically originate efforts to manipulate the vote while persons in lower-status situations would be the targets of these manipulative activities. If the social hierarchy model were to reflect reality, findings from a sample survey should at least show fairly high exposure to influence communications among persons in lower social strata relative to that of their social superiors. Analysis of our JABISS data (see table 9.6), however, actually shows a pattern that severely qualifies these expectations. Using educational attainment as an indicator for social status, it was found that people at higher status levels usually reported exposure to influence communications processes at higher frequencies than people in lower social positions.[16] Rather than flowing downward through social hierarchies, receipt of a request is in most instances concentrated among persons of middle and higher relative status.

The higher frequencies reported among better-educated persons may be a function of some underreporting among persons with lower educations, since it is this category that comprises a large part of the population in highly integrated rural communities. In this instance, social elites (typically the better educated) would receive requests for support, which are then translated into community endorsements or "arrangements" (moshiawase). These arrangements then

16. Education is obviously not the only criterion for social status. Nevertheless, I felt comfortable in its employment in Japan, in part because it is such a central criterion in ordinary people's evaluations of success in Japan. Also, the influentials in the districts I studied in Japan in 1962–63 were almost always better educated than other people. Income might be considered, but measurements of income are often inaccurate. Occupation is also typically employed in social status measures, even though controversy about appropriate classification of specific occupational groups is very common (see, for example, Heath, Jowell, and Curtice, 1985). I felt unsure about using our own occupational status data because of precisely the kinds of problems in its applications that reflect disagreements elsewhere. But an even bigger problem is the need to separate local status system criteria, which are those most important in Japan, from more general occupational status data; consequently, I stayed with education.

Table 9.6   Influence Communications and Educational Strata, 1972–76

| | Level of Education | | | | | |
| | KSR 1972 | | | ASSK/JABISS 1976 | | |
	Low	Middle	High	Low	Middle	High
Koenkai membership				16 (12)	18 (14)	14 (10)
Received request				43 (22)	50 (26)	49 (23)
Received telephone request	8	14	22	16	24	31
Neighborhood vote discussion	14	13	8	11	11	6
Work place discussion	9	13	10	10	16	16
Friends' suggestion	14	19	22	14	17	21
Friends' request				17 (11)	21 (13)	21 (19)
Colleagues' request				14 (9)	15 (9)	19 (14)
Neighbors' request				13 (9)	13 (11)	7 (6)

Sources: 1972 Komei Senkyo Renmei and 1976 Akarui Senkyo Suishin Kyokai studies (see table 9.1) and the 1976 JABISS survey.

Notes: Persons having "low" education graduated from elementary or middle school; "middle" education designates high school graduates; and "high" education means college and university completion. Figures in parentheses are persons who remembered the name(s) of candidates recomended by others or supported by support associations.

would become known to other community residents by word of mouth, although in a less conspicuous form than a request. Our finding that people of low education do report disproportionately higher exposure to requests to vote from *neighbors* and *discussions* of voting choices in the *neighborhood* context fits such an interpretation, although the actual percentages of persons exposed to such activities at all education levels are still fairly low. In addition, persons with low levels of education may also be less politically aware and hence less likely to recognize or remember influence communications.

At this point, the best sense that can be made from these data is to assume that there are actually different kinds of influence communications processes and that these processes involve social hierarchies more in some cases than others. Thus, influence communications may flow from persons of superior status to people in lower social positions where the focus is on communications within the community and neighborhood, given the higher proportions of lower-status people reporting exposure to activities having a local focus. Since these kinds of communications processes tend to be found more in the rural areas, it seems that vertical influence networks are a little more prevalent in the rural sector. (But, to repeat a point emphasized earlier, the evidence also points to very small frequencies of persons being involved in some of these activities.)

Ultimately, customary sample survey data cannot settle the issue of whether influence communications flow mainly from higher- to lower-status persons in Japan. For example, the finding of high frequencies among those persons with low education could simply mean that a particular kind of activity is more prevalent in some areas, such as rural districts, having concentrations of less well educated persons. Both senders and receivers might share the same relatively low status levels in such an instance. Moreover, the opposite finding of higher frequencies among those with high education or no variation across education levels could mask the fact that more subtle status differences with little relation to educational levels still structure the flow of influence communications. Overall, within the limitations of normal sample-based survey data, we find little direct support for a hierarchical model of influence communications. Where hierarchical patterns do still exist I suspect that they are on the decline, since urbanization tends to narrow the social differentials between those with whom one commonly interacts, specifically with regard to education level. And as one tends to associate more with social equals, influence communications should flow increasingly within those less hierarchical relationships, just as our data suggest.[17] But complete confirmation of this view must await better evidence.

■ The Impact of Influence Communications

People's reactions to outside efforts to influence their voting choices can be studied in several different ways. Respondents can be asked to evaluate subjectively the role these communications played in their voting choices. Or patterns in congruence between the cues received in influence communications interactions and actual voting choices can be examined. The Komei Senkyo Renmei and Akarui Senkyo Suishin Kyokai have studied influence communications using the first of these two approaches. The 1976 JABISS study also employed this technique. But we also asked an extensive battery of direct questions about the substance of influence communications—what candidate was recommended or supported—and cross-tabulated these data with information about

17. The real test is, of course, whether there is a differential impact of influence communications within different categories of educational status. I made the appropriate tests using methods reported in the next section of the main text. According to the results, university graduates tended to conform more than their educational inferiors where requests were concerned. The reverse was the case in regard to both group support and candidate contacts, including both koenkai membership and postcard receipt. But the latter activities also produced conforming votes in the rural areas more than in the cities, and it is in the rural areas that there are more people of low levels of educational accomplishment. So it is hard to tell if the effects are related to social status or to the circumstances of rural life. I favor the latter.

specific candidate voting choices. The results from both kinds of analysis methods are reported here to demonstrate the general impact of influence communications in Japan and the effects of particular forms of influence communications.

Simple Estimates of Impact

The best estimate I can make from the various data sources is that the choices of roughly one-quarter to one-third of the Japanese electorate are directly affected in some way by influence communications processes in House of Representatives elections. According to the 1986 Akarui Senkyo Suishin Kyokai study cited earlier, 37 percent of the persons interviewed found some kind of influence communications—that is, requests, discussion of the vote, koenkai membership, and group endorsements—"useful when they made their voting decision." This is a 7 percent increase over comparable figures for 1976, and parallels the overall increase in influence communications activity noted earlier, albeit with a much lower gradient.[18] Among those interviewed in the JABISS study a somewhat lower proportion (compared with the national figures for the 1980s) of 19 percent attributed their vote decision to the effects of requests from other people to vote a particular way.[19] Within this overall group 13 percent said that outside requests had reinforced their preexisting decisions, while only 6 percent reported that the outside requests actually "influenced" their voting intentions. These findings make sense from a common perspective of voting research, where communications about elections are generally shown to exist more between persons with congenial political views and loyalties than between persons with different ties and opinions (Berelson, Lazarsfeld, and McPhee, 1954; Huckfeldt and Sprague, 1987). Still, given the amount of attention reportedly paid to influence communications by Japanese politicians and by scholars who study them, the actual fairly modest impact of influence communications, according to different kinds of self-evaluated evidence, is perhaps anticlimactic.

One possible qualification on the findings just cited would acknowledge that self-assessments of external influence could underestimate its effects sim-

18. Once again the figures for the total of all influence communications exposure are somewhat inflated for the simple reason that multiple answers were allowed to this question. The measure itself also appears to be rather "soft," in the sense that taken on its face, only very weak kinds of influence—having simply thought a little about a request or endorsement rather than actually having conformed to it—might be present in many instances. This could of course result in some overstatement of influence impact.

19. One factor depressing our figure relative to those from the Akarui Senkyo Suishin Kyokai is that multiple answers were more readily handled in the JABISS analysis. In our analysis multiple answers were analyzed so as to total 100 percent regardless of individuals' experiences of more than one kind of communication exposure.

ply because many people lack adequate insight into their own thought processes to answer questions about external influences on their vote. Pride in having made one's own independent decision might also be involved, as witness the high proportion of replies that the vote choice was made "independently" in answers to Komei Senkyo Renmei/Akarui Senkyo Suishin Kyokai questions on these matters. Both conditions could lead to an underestimation of the effects of external efforts to influence the vote. One corrective to these defects is to cross-tabulate people's answers to questions about which candidate was recommended in requests for support with individuals' self-reports of which candidate was chosen at the polls. This was made possible with the JABISS data, where these identifications were made through direct questions (for example, "Which candidate was that?") if a person said he or she had received a voting request. We also identified people's perceptions of the specific candidates supported by youth, women's and elders' groups, enterprise groups, community associations, labor unions, religious organizations, parent-teacher associations, sports clubs, reformist groups (*jumin undo, shimin undo* and women's rights groups), voluntary firemen's and security associations, political associations, and koenkai. Finally, questions were also asked about the identity of respondents' candidate choices in the December 1976 election. If we add together all persons affected by at least one kind of influence communications using this more concrete evidence, just 14 percent were "influenced" by group processes and social network requests. If we add the effects of koenkai membership and receipt of postcards to the other named activities, we get a total figure of 22 percent of the electorate whose votes in some way were measurably affected by exposure to some kind of influence communications. The use of this approach produced roughly the same impressions as to general levels of influence communications' impact in 1976 as did the previously cited attribution method. Roughly one out of every five or six Japanese voters is thus "influenced" by external social relationships and group memberships, according to both kinds of data. Perhaps influence communication is an overrated component of the Japanese electoral process relative to Japanese election folklore. Still, these processes are important to the votes of quite a few people, even if significant sectors of the electorate are unaffected.

In addition to measuring general influence communications effects within the total population, the JABISS data also make possible precise identification of the voting impact of *different kinds* of influence communications (within the limits imposed by use of perceptual information). By looking at the percentages of persons who voted in accordance with the perceived preferences of a particular group or the suggestions of individuals who requested their support within different categories, we can estimate the relative influence of different kinds of influence communications sources. The results are shown in table 9.7.

Table 9.7 Impact of Influence Communications on the Vote by Type of Communication

	N	Conforming Vote[a]	Total[b]
Requests within the family	(39)	80	4
Requests from neighbors	(101)	36	10
Requests from co-workers	(111)	48	11
Requests from friends	(142)	35	14
Small business group endorsement/support	(33)	70	3
Union endorsement/support	(40)	70	3
Community group endorsement/support	(34)	70	3
Support association members	(158)	80	15

[a]Percentage of persons who conformed to outside requests or endorsements among knowledgeable individuals, i.e., those who could identify names of candidates supported/recommended by others and who knew concretely for whom they had voted. "Conforming Vote" refers to people who experienced the designated form of influence communications and conformed thereto.

[b]Percentage of conforming persons of *all* voters who knew the name of the candidate they supported ($N = 823$). (The total voting population was 1,026.)

In the discussion of tables 9.1 and 9.2, a hierarchy of frequencies of influence communications activity was noted. Requests were the most prominent kind of contact. According to the 1976 data in table 9.7, however, the most effective form of influence communications was clearly support associations, and not most kinds of requests. This is not surprising since koenkai membership is in itself an affirmation of support, with the exception of people who join because they are forced to do so by social pressure. Within the multiple categories of request experience, only family requests were equal in importance to koenkai, followed by group endorsements (aggregated across various groups). Seventy percent of community and small businessmen's organization members (which groups are often territorially based in some shopping or manufacturing district) voted for the candidate supported by their group. Unions were equally influential. Requests coming from social networks *outside* the family were not too effective, and influenced only 35 to 48 percent of those whom they reached. If we apply Kelman's (1961) approach to influence, *identification* with *persons and groups* (including where this reflects intrafamilial intimacy) is the mechanism invoking the greatest effect on people's voting choices in Japanese elections. If we keep in mind our earlier findings that indicated minimal social status effects, Kelman's assertion that deference would be a common motivation is not supported.

In thinking about the findings in table 9.7, we should keep in mind also that levels of group member awareness of support for a candidate were extremely low, even though conformity was fairly high among those persons who were actually exposed to groups that supported a candidate. This means that the percent of persons who actually conformed to group political climates was very small as a percentage of the total voting population (see last column in table 9.7). Relatedly, requests still proved to be of greater overall importance within the total population because of their substantial frequencies.

Patterns of External Reinforcement

Some individuals interviewed in 1976 received communications designed to influence their vote from more than one outside source. In fact, we were able to identify a number of persons who received more than one cue to vote for a particular candidate, either in the form of personal requests from several sources and/or perceptions of support for a candidate in more than one group. Of those for whom we had information on both requests and group candidate cues (that is, specific candidate *names*), as well as actual voting choices, 9 percent received cues from more than one external source in the case of requests while 36 percent were exposed to multiple cues via group processes. The remainder in each category received information from just one source.

The effects of multiple versus single external cues on the vote are both theoretically and substantively interesting. Theories of persuasion (McGuire, 1985) and information processing (Fiske and Taylor, 1984) postulate that multiple, reinforcing messages enhance the potential for attitude change (although repetition beyond a certain number of times may be counterproductive). If we once again assume that attitude theories can be used as a heuristic for short-term effects of influence communications in Japanese elections, we would anticipate greater conformity among persons who receive multiple reinforcing cues than among persons who receive only a single request. Multiple, conflictual cues should be even less potent. Table 9.8 presents findings on the effects of single and multiple communications from groups and requests to vote a particular way. The data are arranged by origin of cues, that is, whether they came from groups or face-to-face relationships, and patterns of cues, that is, multiple and reinforcing, single, or multiple but conflicting. From the voting conformity figures within these different combinations, it is clear that in the case of both groups and face-to-face relationships, reinforcing cues exert greater influence than a single stimulus, just as theory would dictate (see also Nisbett and Ross, 1980). As would also be anticipated, conflictual patterns of external voting cues resulted in even lower levels of conformity (with at least one of the cues) than single requests or group endorsements. (This conclusion is limited to face-to-face requests because of the small number of cases of conflictual cues from groups, an interesting point in its own right.)

Table 9.8   Voter Conformity to Single and Multiple Cue Patterns from
Groups and Other Persons (In Percentages)

Cue Structure	Groups	Face-to-Face Relationships	Both
Two or more: reinforcing	85	84	96
Single	76	51	—
Two or more: conflictual	—	22	—

Source: 1976 JABISS study.

Notes: Percentages are of persons who were exposed to a particular cue pattern—e.g., a single cue from a group—who voted in a conforming way. Dashes indicate no information or small numbers. Once again, the relevant population is persons who named the candidate for whom they voted in 1976 and who also knew which candidate was supported in an organized group or endorsed in requests from persons in social networks.

Within the general tendency for multiple reinforcing cues to produce higher levels of conformity, face-to-face relationships are still less influential as a general category than group influences. This finding might be counterintuitive in industrialized societies other than Japan, where more intimate interpersonal relationships might be expected to foster conformity more readily than impersonal groups. The greater impact of groups is also curious from the point of view of Kelman's proposition that identifications are a potent source of conformity (if we repeat the assumption made earlier that interpersonal relationships should be more intimate than other social contacts). But it is also true that group consensus is a potent force in Japanese society where this is invoked. Great effort is spent on developing a group consensus through multiple consultations, with the result that persons would likely identify strongly with those groups that do reach a consensus on candidate support. It is also true that not all interpersonal relationships are intimate in Japan, and this fact undoubtedly lies behind the lower potency of interpersonal requests in electoral mobilization in Japan when these are taken as an aggregate. Japanese rely on social networks as intermediaries in a wider variety of circumstances than do people in most Western societies. Reflecting in part this pattern of broader usage, such relationships can be at times fairly impersonal relative to the greater intimacy of familial relationships or friendships. The use of external sales people and delivery persons in efforts to woo the vote was cited above and is an example of dependence on relatively impersonal networks for electoral mobilization. Where network ties are less intimate, identifications with cue-givers are less likely, which means that conforming behavior is less likely to occur. Such a wide variety of interpersonal ties are activated by requests, including many that are not very intimate, that some weakness in their effects might be anticipated.

These very differences are reflected in the big gap between the higher level of conformity with intrafamilial and co-workers' requests that with those stemming from other kinds of relationships (table 9.7). Ultimately, intimate interpersonal ties within the family and work place are as influential as group processes, just as Kelman's prediction that people identify with persons with whom they are intimate anticipates, even though requests as an aggregate are less potent because of the many less intimate channels they exploit.

Influence Communications, Candidate Perceptions, and Voting Choices

We have seen that 14 percent of the voting public in Japan made choices in the 1976 general election that were congenial with communications received from groups and individuals who sought to manipulate or influence their votes directly, or through their awareness of the climate of support for a particular candidate in some group. An additional 8 percent were influenced by koenkai memberships and receipt of postcards. Many of these persons were probably influenced in their vote by considerations other than requests and/or group endorsements alone, even though we have treated influence communications in isolation so far. To evaluate the role of influence communications properly, it is necessary to look at their effects in a broader context that includes internalized voting motivations in addition to external voting cues.

A variety of evidence, both folkloric and empirical, suggests that loyalties to candidates or attitudes toward candidates exist in Japan that may be relatively impervious to short-term efforts to influence the vote. People's candidate images and loyalties might be one of the more powerful influences on voting in Japan's multimember districts, where competition between nominees of the same party occurs with some frequency (Richardson, 1974; Rochon, 1981). To evaluate this possibility, the JABISS survey included a specially designed battery of questions on people's feelings about candidates. Multiple-answer questions that solicited different images of candidates for whom respondents voted have long been the stock and trade of the Komei Senkyo Renmei/Akarui Senkyo Suishin Kyokai surveys mentioned earlier. Several of the characteristics that were cited most often in people's reasons for their candidate vote choice in the KSR/ASSK surveys were used in the JABISS questionnaire to develop a candidate image battery.[20] The resulting series included items that solicited perceptions of which candidate was "a pride of the local area," which person seemed to have

20. A similar procedure, discussed in chapter 10, was used to measure party images. The same procedure was also used to develop summary indexes for group climates and request patterns. First, in each instance of exposure to some kind of influence communications, or feeling that a particular candidate had attractive characteristics, the respondent was asked for the name of that person. Then candidates were given a code in each election district that corresponded to a national code, such as "1st LDP candidate," "2nd LDP candidate," and so forth. From this information, we developed aggregate codes for specific item answers across all election districts and aggregate indexes for

such laudable qualities as seriousness and sincerity, or which nominee would appear to represent a specific local area, occupation, or type of business. To explore the effects of candidate images and influence communications simultaneously I examined the patterns of requests received from external sources along with answers to the questions asked about images/perceptions of the candidates. Table 9.9 summarizes the findings of this analysis and presents fascinating evidence of both the independence and interplay of candidate imagery and external vote requests.[21]

I analyzed the preferences of the entire group of respondents who reported receipt of interpersonal requests or favorable images of some candidate(s), or both, and who also indicated which candidate they had chosen. Among those persons who did not receive a request to vote for some candidate but did have one or more favorable images of some candidate, 82 percent were influenced in their vote by their images. A smaller 47 percent of those who received a request to vote a particular way, and who possessed no favorable image of a candidate, conformed to that request. Among people who had *both* a favorable image of a candidate and who had received a request to support that candidate, the conformity ratio was a very high 88 percent. Finally, in cases of conflict between these two stimuli, one external and one internal, which occurred in under 10 percent of all cases where one or another type of stimulus was present, candidate images prevailed over requests three times as often as requests overwhelmed candidate images. While it will be noted in chapter 10 that these candidate images are not as deeply rooted temporally as partisan loyalties, it is clear from our analysis here that internal motivations are a stronger force in the vote than external face-to-face requests to vote in some particular way.[22] Since many more people had favorable images of some candidate than received a request, a higher proportion of the electorate was affected by images than by requests. Candidate images were both causally and compositionally important.

---

dominant preferences for "1st LDP candidate" or whatever within categories of group climates, requests, candidate images, and so on.

21. We considered the image-request patterns of all persons who remembered whom they were asked to vote for or who indicated a specific candidate as the object of one or more candidate images. Only those persons who also reported a specific candidate choice and provided this person's name were included in this analysis. This group does not constitute, therefore, a representative sample of the Japanese electorate; the figures reported pertain only to a candidate-oriented subset thereof. The failure of many people to name their chosen candidate was part of a general tendency in the 1976 electorate to be more aware of parties than candidates. The reader is referred to chapter 10, where various combinations of candidate images, group support climates, and interpersonal requests are considered as variables in a path analysis of candidate voting choices. A related analysis also appeared in Richardson (1988).

22. I omitted the effects of group support patterns from this portion of the analysis because of their extremely small numbers.

Table 9.9 Candidate Attitudes, Influence Communications, and Voting
Choices, 1976 (In Percentages)

	Face-to-Face Requests	Candidate Images	Both
Conforming by category[a]	47	82	88
Conforming by composition[b]	13	44	8
N	(114)	(370)	(64)
			(Total N = 845)

Source: 1976 JABISS survey.

Note: The effects of group endorsements were ignored in the analysis because of small numbers.

[a] Those persons for whom candidate names were known and who conformed to particular cue patterns. The relevant percentages demonstrate the effects of particular patterns of influence considered separately.

[b] Voters who either received requests or perceived a candidate favorably or both and who conformed to these influences. This category demonstrates the relative frequencies of a particular kind of conformity among persons who both voted and indicated the name of the person for whom they voted.

Party Loyalties and Influence Communications

Party loyalties are an important factor in people's voting choices in addition to candidate images, as discussed elsewhere in this book. Indeed, candidate images were dealt with here first simply because of their assumed importance in Japan's multimember district electoral setting, and despite the fact that an overwhelming body of electoral research in industrial societies shows that psychological party loyalties are the most important factor in people's voting choices in national elections.[23] Several patterns of interaction between party loyalties and influence communications processes are possible in Japan. Influence communications may flow primarily between supporters of the same party and have a reinforcing effect on the partisan component of the vote. Or they may involve unsuccessful attempts by supporters of other parties to persuade loyal partisans to vote for a different party. Finally, requests from persons who support parties other than the respondent's own preference may produce a deviation from party loyalties in voting choices.

23. The classic statement on the importance of party identifications in the United States is Angus Campbell et al. (1960) while that on Britain is David Butler and Donald Stokes (1969). Many studies show a high consistency between responses to party identification questions and voting choices both in the United States and abroad. The dominant role of party identification in voting has, however, been challenged by some studies, as was noted in chapter 1. For persuasive arguments from this opposition, see Budge, Crewe, and Farlie (1976), Borre and Katz (1973), Kaase (1970), Thomassen (1976) and Crewe (1976). For counterevidence supporting the importance of some kind of psychological partisanship outside the United States, see Norpoth (1978), Heath and McDonald (1988), and Richardson (1991).

In order to determine which of these patterns of the effects of partisanship and influence communications best fit Japanese reality in 1976, the influence communications exposure of specific party supporters and their voting choices were examined simultaneously for adherents of the Liberal Democratic and Japan Socialist parties, the two partisan groups whose representation in the sample provided numbers sufficient for meaningful analysis in most cases. The results presented in table 9.10 indicate different patterns of influence communications among supporters of Japan's two major parties, as well as strong residual influence on the vote from party identification.

Comparison of the combined effects of party identification and efforts to

Table 9.10 Party Identification, Influence Communications and the Vote (In Percentages)

| | LDP Identifiers | | | | | |
| | Asked LDP | | | Asked Other Party | | |
	Voted LDP	Voted Other	N	Voted LDP	Voted Other	N
Family request	85	15	(11)	—	100	(4)
Relatives' request	100	—	(14)	50	50	(13)
Co-workers' request	74	26	(16)	38	62	(13)
Neighbors' request	81	19	(20)	64	36	(15)
Friends' request	100	—	(18)	60	40	(19)
Koenkai members	100	—	(57)	—	100	(9)
Group support	89	11	(35)	50	50	(4)

| | JSP Identifiers | | | | | |
| | Asked JSP | | | Asked Other Party | | |
	Voted JSP	Voted Other	N	Voted JSP	Voted Other	N
Family request	100	—	(3)	40	60	(5)
Relatives' request	100	—	(2)	33	67	(9)
Co-workers' request	85	15	(20)	53	47	(15)
Neighbors' request	50	50	(4)	55	45	(22)
Friends' request	75	25	(4)	62	38	(26)
Koenkai members	100	—	(16)	42	58	(28)
Group support	85	15	(27)	80	20	(5)

Note: All figures are percentages of the combined categories falling under the "identifier" and "asked" headings. Rows total to 100 percent within categories of being "Asked LDP/JSP" or "Asked Other Party."

influence the vote shows that influence communications flowed within partisan networks in many cases. This pattern was particularly clear in the case of the LDP supporters, whose group, work-place, and neighborhood environments tended to support Liberal Democratic nominees. A tendency for influence communications to flow outside of partisan networks was more pronounced among JSP partisans. Interestingly, here the patterns are somewhat different from those observed for LDP supporters. Reinforcing requests came most frequently from co-workers, reflecting the importance of efforts to mobilize the vote centering on the work place and labor union memberships. Deviating requests overwhelmingly predominated in the cases of relatives, neighbors, and friends, who tended to make requests mainly on behalf of other opposition party candidates, that is, nominees of the Democratic Socialist, Clean Government, and Communist parties. These patterns were much more common in urban than in rural settings, as could be expected from the greater prominence of both small party candidacies and heterogeneous social contacts in the cities. In contrast, rural districts were more homogeneous with regard to the partisan characteristics of influence communications.

Among persons who received requests congenial with their partisanship, conforming votes were very common, occurring in slightly fewer cases among Liberal Democrats than among Socialists. In addition, despite the substantial extent to which efforts to influence voting choices in some contexts contradicted party loyalties, partisanship actually "overcame" requests from other persons in many instances. This can be ascertained by looking at the data in the right side of table 9.10. If we select only those who were asked to support some party other than their own, around half of the LDP supporters defected and voted for the other party in response to specific cues in that direction. In the case of JSP supporters, defections in response to external cues were slightly lower. While party identifications appear to be less emotionally intense among Japanese than among citizens of some other industrialized nations, where those loyalties exist they seem to be reasonably resistant to efforts to mobilize the vote using networks and group relationships believed central in Japanese society. At least this was the clear pattern in the 1976 election. Following the Lazarsfeld et al. (1944) paradigm, *reinforcement* of existing predispositions appears to be the dominant pattern of effects. On the other hand, the rate of defection to vote for a nonsupported party as the result of external influence is not insignificant. There were some *conversions*.

Many students of Japanese elections have stressed the role of interpersonal influence and group consensus in people's voting choices. Influence and group pressures are believed to be especially important to the vote in rural areas. Relatedly, the impact of external influences on voting decisions has been believed to be on the decline over time in the face of the modernization of Japanese society via urbanization and other connected social processes.

Findings from surveys conducted at the time of the 1976 general election and results of a longer time-series of Japanese behavioral studies indicate that influence communications are still present at substantial levels. Slightly over three-quarters of the Japanese electorate we interviewed in 1976 were exposed to some kind of outside interpersonal vote request or group endorsement, or received a candidate's, postcard or belonged to a support association. Although a somewhat greater number of persons reported having followed the campaign on television or in the newspapers, still the figure for influence communications was very substantial. And, even if we eliminate persons who couldn't remember the actual name of the candidate who was recommended to them or the nominee supported in a group of which they were a member, a sizable 14 percent of the electorate were influenced in their voting choice by external pressures within face-to-face relationships or groups. If koenkai membership and receipt of a candidate's postcard—both of which involve adaptations of traditional social relationships to political ends—are added to requests and group support/endorsement, altogether 22 percent of the Japanese voters who named the candidate they supported actually conformed to some kind of external influence.

Further exploration of hypotheses about the patterns and effects of influence communications in Japan indicated the following:

1. Modernization theories concerning influence communications in Japan were not supported either by declining trends in manipulative activities in the face of marked urbanization and social change or by higher frequencies of influence attempts in the rural districts. Instead, there were different patterns in the urban and rural settings, with visible influence communications activities being at least as frequent in the cities (especially in "bounded" cities) as in the countryside, while cross-time trends of sharp increase in some kinds of influence communications could be seen.

2. Pictures of communications processes that stress the downward flow of influence from high to low status persons do not seem to be generally warranted in today's Japan. In reality, persons of higher education levels, and therefore typically of higher status, were more often aware of requests and group cues than were persons of lesser educational accomplishment. Only in the case of influence communications that focused on community and neighborhood did persons of lower status appear to be the targets of manipulation efforts more often than people of higher status, and even this finding was qualifiable.

3. Analysis of the impact of influence communications "cues" indicated that

roughly one in six persons in the candidate oriented portion of the electorate voted according to external suggestions, or one in five if postcards and koenkai membership are considered along with these interpersonal requests and group endorsements. Where influence communications effects were compared with the contribution to choices by candidate images, the latter were more important to voting choices. Influence communications were also observed to produce deviations from party loyalties in 1976 voting choices in only about half of the cases where contradictory cues were received.

Evidence on the nature and impact of influence communications presented in this chapter suggests that Japan is still very much a network or group society, in the sense that interpersonal and group attempts to affect the vote are a highly visible feature of electoral mobilization, even though they are not the exclusive nor in many cases the dominant component of people's voting decisions. It should also be clear that these activities are a self-conscious kind of behavior in Japan, and not simply a casual component of the more general informal communications processes found in all industrial societies at election times. In other words, Japanese social networks and group ties are used for specific political functions at election times in a highly visible and deliberate way. Social networks are indeed important in Japanese-style electoral mobilization. There is little support, however, for believing that political life in Japan is dominated by social elites through hierarchies of influence to the degree asserted by Marxian sociology or theories that stress the vertical dimensions of Japanese social organization.

Part IV ■ Conclusions

Ten ■ The Japanese Voter: Comparing the Explanatory Variables in Electoral Decisions

BRADLEY M. RICHARDSON, WITH
SCOTT C. FLANAGAN, JOJI WATANUKI,
ICHIRO MIYAKE, AND SHINSAKU KOHEI

This book has addressed the question of how people vote in Japan, why they choose particular political parties, and when and why they support specific candidates. In considering these issues, we have dissected the voting behavior of the Japanese people from a number of perspectives: traditional sociopolitical cleavage theory, value cleavage hypotheses, and propositions about contextual effects and social network influences, partisanship, issue opinions, media effects, and candidate-focused constituency mobilization and influence communications processes. Some of the analytical orientations were inspired by comparative research traditions; some reflect ideas about voting indigenous to Japanese scholarship. This chapter will summarize and integrate these hypotheses and the related findings.

All electoral behavior contains four common processes: mobilization, nurture and reinforcement, information processing, and response. *Mobilization* usually involves direct action in some specific time span, such as an election campaign. Appeals to residents of a rural hamlet to vote for a native son are an example. Mobilization can also be a repeated, intermittent activity—for example, labor unions asking members to vote for a particular party in many elections over time. Mobilization can and does use existing social structures as channels of communication and activation. Mobilization can also be unmediated by social structures, as in television and radio appeals made directly to viewer and listener audiences. Japanese voting studies have often stressed mobilization (see chapter 1). By doing so, they are standing outside the individual voter, observing what parties, candidates, elites, and groups do, and, at times, inferring how individuals respond.

Electoral behavior is also shaped by *nurture and reinforcement*. By nurture and reinforcement we mean three distinct things: 1) the initial fostering or socialization of attitudes; 2) ongoing support of attitudes and cognitive rationales through sustained, repetitive exposure to social groups' "biased" messages; and 3) the psychological support that groups provide for their members' compliance with those attitudes, a process contributing to further internal attitude strengthening. People respond to sustained information exposure through social groups by developing attitudes and cognitive rationales. Sometimes these attitudes and rationales are inherited through an early total immersion and socialization in one specific social group, the nuclear family. These attitudes and rationales are reinforced by subsequent and continuous exposure to the partisan climate in the family and other similarly situated groups.

Nurture and reinforcement occurs when people learn through normal interactions how other important persons feel about some socially relevant topic. Social interactions, including those with people upon whom the individual is dependent, provide information that complements intermittent mobilizing appeals and/or provides cues as to how persons in significant reference groups think and behave. The relevant social processes are often latent and informal (for example, unintended consequences of ongoing conversations), unlike the more direct, intentional efforts that characterize electoral mobilization. At times, the line between these two external processes is actually very fine, and a great deal of social experience relating to politics, particularly that at election time, probably mixes the two.

Various aspects of group processes also encourage conformity to group norms in actual behavior. People are economically dependent on some groups, they seek approval from others, or they are affected by ongoing group processes that contain a variety of sanctions or rewards favoring conformity. These attributes of groups enhance groups' socializing and attitude reinforcement roles. They also encourage conforming behavior among group members. Conforming behavior is itself conducive to further attitude strengthening.

Much of political sociology deals with the externalities of reinforcement processes, by analyzing the effects of social groups and other aspects of social structure on people's preferences. Political psychology also considers reinforcement processes to be important but looks more to their effects on internal attitudes and motivations. Obviously both outlooks provide insight into the external and internal dimensions of social group nurturing and reinforcement. Both of our first two electoral behavior processes, explicit campaign mobilization efforts and group nurture and reinforcement, clearly send specific kinds of messages to ordinary voters. The information gained from efforts to mobilize support is naturally biased information, favoring a particular person or party. Group nurture and reinforcement processes also send messages, and while these messages tend to be more continuous and more politically indirect, they nevertheless are likely to favor one or another party or political viewpoint. In addition to these biased messages, electorates receive a great deal of neutral *information,* either in the form of political coverage within the electronic and written mass media or discussions with other people about likely implications of particular political events. In modern electorates, this third behavior-molding process is also quite important, owing to the abundance of readily available neutral information. Although it is true that mass media sources are politically biased in some cases, in free societies there is still a great deal of open neutral information. As we shall see later, this abundance of open, neutral information is highly significant to how people process information and form cognitive rationales in support of specific political attitudes.

Finally, people's *responses* to mobilizing appeals can be quite varied. They may consist of simply acceding to an outside request through complying behavior. Responses to mobilizing appeals may accumulate over time to form an attitudinal disposition to support a particular party or candidate. These predispositions to behave in particular ways are supported in many instances by other responses that consist mainly of cognitive rationales. Such rationales can be formed as the result of either experiencing efforts to mobilize one's vote or receiving messages from groups or more neutral sources. The important feature of cognitive rationales is their support via internal argumentation of affective attitudes and behavioral predispositions. Responses can also include simply affective feelings of likes and dislikes that exist independently of cognitive support. Political psychology has emphasized the responsive aspects of electoral behavior and has essentially looked from the inside of people's mental processes outward toward the mobilizing actions and other informational cues that stimulate internal affective and cognitive processes. In charting these internal response patterns, political psychology has called attention to the strong possibility that affective motivations, and perhaps even cognitive rationales, can be inherited from earlier generations, as well as acquired more directly from specific experiences.

In this chapter we will organize our observations on Japanese voting behavior around the processes shaping electoral behavior that we have just described. Our picture of the Japanese voter contains three central components: *psychological partisanship* (our main example of voters' *response* to external forces), *constituency mobilization* (and related attitudes toward candidates), and *environmental nurture and reinforcement*. In this treatment, we will draw on ideas from political psychology, political psychology, and Japanese mobilization theory. (The media and "neutral" information, the fourth type of theoretically relevant influence, are of secondary importance in Japanese behavior, as far as can be determined directly with analysis focused on the time span of a single election. Nevertheless, the neutral news media undoubtedly have a strong effect on some attitudes over the long term, as will be suggested below in an analysis of the sources of party images.) Findings within the first three component sectors of this integrated model of Japanese voting behavior will be addressed sequentially starting with psychological partisanship. Our review, then, will move more or less outward from chapter 6 through the different chapters of the book. The interactions between comparative theory, Japanese hypotheses, and our findings are discussed for each sector of the model. As we proceed, we will consider the origins of each hypothesis briefly, note the major findings relevant to this hypothesis, and observe how Japanese conditions affect the findings. We will also speculate on how the Japanese findings instruct comparative theory.

As we move through the different concerns, we will present a path analysis of the different components of the vote in Japan. The resulting causal model of the vote will supplement our summary of the findings from different chapters to provide a comprehensive picture of the forces behind the vote in Japan. Since our findings stem from a survey conducted in the context of one particular election, we will also briefly consider how the general structural characteristics of Japanese electoral politics in the 1970s and 1980s, and the more transient aspects of elections at different times, affect the applicability of our evidence from 1976.

■ Psychological Partisanship and the Vote in Japan

Political psychology deals with people's internal political attitudes and motivations, their mental pictures of politics, and related processing of information about politics. Much of the psychological approach to electoral behavior has focused on people's attitudes toward parties and partisan issues. Psychological partisanship is widely felt to be a dominant factor in people's voting behavior, an assumption supported by our findings in Japan.

Party Identification and Japanese Behavior

Party identification has long been the core concept of political psychology, and it retains this status in current research despite various criticisms and revisionist suggestions on how to better characterize its basic nature. Seen from the start as a long-term emotional tie to a particular party, party identification was initially believed to be the major factor directly influencing vote choice. As the most durable attitude in the cluster of people's responses to elections, party identification was also usually assumed to have some kind of indirect influence on voting through its structuring effects on attitudes toward the issues and candidates in particular elections.[1]

1. Recent research in the United States has in some cases qualified party identification's role and demonstrated that short-term evaluations of candidates or appraisals of parties' performance

Following the practice of some contemporary American and Japanese scholarship, Ichiro Miyake delves into the various dimensions of partisanship in Japan in chapter 6. Using multiple measures of attitudes toward parties and a factor analytic technique developed by Chikio Hayashi, Miyake uncovers two central partisanship dimensions among Japanese voters, *affective partisanship* and *cognitive partisanship*. These dimensions in turn serve as building blocks in a partisan attitudes scale of which the four types of response groups are "loyal partisans," "negative partisans," "nonpartisans," and "uninformed partisans." People falling in the different categories in turn display distinct patterns of political involvement, cognition, and cynicism. Particularly interesting are the negative partisans, whose cynicism toward all aspects of politics is profound, and who, as a result, are potentially motivated more by these negative feelings than by positive commitments. Often what anchors the vote of these partisans is the more negative images of other rejected parties rather than any positive affinity to the "supported" party.

Miyake's uncovering of the negative partisanship dimension helps high-light the varieties of motivations that affect the vote in Japan and complements similar findings on negative partisanship and attitudes toward alternative parties conducted in the United States and elsewhere (Goot, 1972; Maggiotto and Piereson, 1977). In applying these categories to actual voting, Miyake shows that loyalists tend to vote on the basis of their party attachments more than persons in the other three categories do. Negative partisans are especially interesting, as they are more prone to defect from their party "ties" in particular elections than persons in the other categories. The vulnerability of these negative partisans could, in turn, help explain the considerable volatility noted in urban voting in the 1960s and 1970s (Richardson, 1977; Flanagan, 1980; Campbell, 1987) and in the nation as a whole in the 1989 upper house election (see chapter 11).

Miyake's discovery of multiple dimensions of psychological partisanship in Japan, and subsequent tracing of the behavior of different kinds of partisans, enriches political psychology in general. Party identification research initially saw identifications as a single dimensional affective tie to parties. By looking at negative out-group feelings, the concept of psychological partisanship is expanded. By including the depth and richness of information, imagery, and evaluations of the parties as a component of psychological partisanship that, like affective ties, shapes voting propensities in an enduring way, elements of cognitive structure are added to what was previously seen mainly as an affective

---

can play a central role in attitude formation and/or behavior (Page and Jones, 1979). Outside the United States, the party identification concept has been both challenged and defended in recent studies, as was noted in chapter 1 and elsewhere in this book.

attitude. Adding cognitive information is an important step in partisanship research.

Partisan Components of Choice

In conceptualizing partisanship in Japan for the purposes of this analysis, we will begin with Miyake's view of partisanship as a multidimensional notion. Here, however, to avail ourselves of a simpler measurement strategy, we will directly operationalize his two conceptual dimensions using easily computed indicators, thereby yielding only two types of partisans—*affective partisans* and *cognitive partisans*. In this scheme, the affective partisans are the party identifiers who essentially conform to the expectations of the Michigan concept and have a long-standing affective tie to a particular party. The cognitive partisans are those who, whether they have any durable, emotional bond with a party or not, still have images and perceptions of one or more parties that provide an evaluative basis that guides their voting choices. Our measure of affective partisanship will be a standard party ID indicator; we will use images and evaluations of the parties as our measure of cognitive partisanship.

In this conceptualization, affective partisanship is expected to set the higher standard of inclusion. Thus we expect our measures to yield many more cognitive partisans than affective partisans. Many of our cognitive partisans, then, do not meet the qualifications of the party ID concept because their party perceptions lack the dimension of positive affect always emphasized in prior political psychology. In addition, these cognitive perceptions may lack the degree of long-term stability associated with the identification concept. Nevertheless, even without internalizing an identification with a party, citizens can hardly escape holding some kinds of images of one or more political parties, and these images are likely to figure prominently in shaping short-term voting decisions.

These two dimensions of partisanship—the affective (that is, party identification) and the cognitive (that is, party images)—are graphically displayed in the simple causal model of the vote shown in figure 10.1a. It should be noted that the gains in ease of measurement that the procedures employed here yield over Miyake's approach are somewhat offset by sacrifices in precision and reliability. Our two types are not mutually exclusive. Indeed, it is expected that many of our affective partisans will also be cognitive partisans. In distinguishing between our two types, we will be particularly interested in the cognitive partisans who lack any affective attachment to their party, since these partisans include what Miyake labels the "negative partisans." We rely on our multivariate techniques to separate out to some degree the effects of affective and cognitive party attachments.

Our strategy for operationalizing these two dimensions is also simple and

Figure 10.1 Psychological Partisanship and the Vote

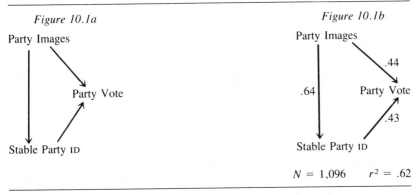

Figure 10.1a

Party Images

Party Vote

Stable Party ID

Figure 10.1b

Party Images

.64   .44

Party Vote

.43

Stable Party ID

$N = 1,096$ $r^2 = .62$

straightforward. As noted in chapter 1, the question wording we employed to tap party identifications is a form frequently used in Japan, where there are no common vernacular terms for party identifications such as exist in the United States. Respondents were asked which party they "supported" out of a list of the six significant parties running candidates in the 1976 election. We recognized that "supporting" a party was not the same as thinking of oneself as a Liberal Democrat or Japan Socialist, the essence of the identification concept. In other words, our threshold for inclusion for identifying those that have an affective party tie was too low. Therefore, a second criterion was applied that required "consistent" support across our short two-to-four-week panel to qualify as identifiers. Application of this criterion also made sense given the central assumption of party identification theory that most people's loyalties are long-term in nature. So whereas 59 percent of the full sample and 64 percent of the voting JABISS respondents indicated a party identification on the first wave, with higher numbers reported on the second wave, just 47 percent of the full sample and 59 percent of the voters consistently supported the same party at both time points.[2] The remaining 41 percent of the voting public either wavered between an identification and an apolitical stance of "no party" or "don't know," which was the dominant alternative pattern, or actually switched parties between interviews or were consistently apolitical (see also Miyake, 1985; Richardson, 1986).

In defining our measure of affective partisanship we should note that one important group of partisans identified by Miyake is overlooked by our procedures, namely, the uninformed partisans. We would expect these low cogni-

---

2. Throughout this chapter, we deal principally with the characteristics of persons who actually voted, since they are the population of interest to our analysis.

tive partisans to fall out of our cognitive measure, but they also tend to be missed by our affective party support measure, and particularly by the consistent support measure used here, as can be seen from tables 6.4 and 6.5 in chapter 6. This limitation imposed by our procedures means that the uninformed partisans, who are frequently mobilized by their social networks to vote in consistent ways, will be largely excluded from our partisanship measures as missing data. This problem is not unique to our approach, since the high level of "don't know" responses characteristic of the uninformed partisans makes them a difficult group to estimate and analyze through any survey research method.

Our measure of cognitive partisanship is an indicator of party images and evaluations that was operationalized through closed questions that solicited voters' opinions across eight items concerning which parties were seen as having the best candidates, leaders, or policies, which parties were most capable of representing local or occupational interests, and which parties could best stop inflation, end corruption, or rule Japan. Seventy-seven percent of the full sample and 89 percent of the voters had at least one favorable image of a political party, a figure substantially higher than that for our "consistent" identifiers.[3] Among the various image themes submitted to the electorate's scrutiny, the most commonly held image was that of a party "having the best candidates." Sixty-three percent of the voting electorate were able to select one of the parties on that dimension. Nominations of parties "best suited to govern" and "best representing my occupation" were close runner-ups.

The levels we have found for stable self-conscious identifiers are rather low relative to patterns in other countries, where, as reported in one comparative study, average long-term partisanship was over 60 percent (LeDuc, 1981).[4] The Japanese patterns were all the more remarkable given the fact that the period between the two panel waves was less than one month, whereas higher cross-time stability figures are shown for other countries for much longer periods of time. As various studies of party identification in Japan have noted, comparatively low levels of stability are normal for self-designated party loyalties

3. Although the party image questions were relatively easy to answer, which could have facilitated high response levels, there is no indication that they were essentially easier than the direct question about party support employed to identify affective party loyalties. Rather, as we point out in the text, we strongly suspect that the affective element of party loyalties is considerably less developed in Japan than in the United States, where the party identification concept was developed. Party images have been the subject of earlier writing by members of the Japanese team, and their work is reflected in the discussion in this chapter. See Shinsaku Kohei (1979:75–85) and Ichiro Miyake "Seito Shiji to Seijiteki Shinishizumu," in Watanuki et al. (1986).

4. The three countries for which long-term stability levels are cited were the United States, Canada, and Britain. Lower levels of partisanship more like those in Japan (given the shorter time period in the Japanese case) were shown by LeDuc for the Netherlands. But the Netherlands was going through a period of realignment at the time of the survey on which these data are based.

in Japan. Findings reported elsewhere, however, suggest that even these levels may be too high if we are trying to tap party identifiers in the Michigan sense of the term as a positive, substantive identification (Flanagan and McDonald, 1979). For example, the predominant pattern of "unstable" partisanship noted in our own and other analyses is one of moving back and forth from the "no party–don't know" category to support for a party. Moreover, these latent partisans constitute a larger proportion of the Japanese public than these types of partisans do in other countries. These latent and volatile identifiers would also obviously increase in number were our panel to have covered a longer time span (as would have persons who actually changed parties, who form a some-what smaller group). From a purely conceptual perspective, latent or volatile "identifiers" are better classified as cognitive partisans, because their party perceptions are neither sufficiently positive nor enduring to qualify as affective identifications.

This finding of rather low levels of "true" party identifiers in Japan has always led to a discounting of the importance of partisanship for the Japanese voter. Our point, however, it that party still may play an important guiding and anchoring role in the Japanese electorate, even in the absence of long-standing affective ties. This is accomplished through the cognitive and evaluative im-ages voters hold of the various parties. As shown above, party imagery is reasonably well developed in the Japanese case. Party images are understood to be people's broad, general mental pictures of the individual political parties, and they have been seen by some scholars as major, independent forces in voting behavior in addition to party identifications (Matthews and Prothro, 1966; Butler and Stokes, 1969; Baker et al., 1981). Party images are usually viewed as intermediate term attitudes that capture qualities of parties that transcend the events and issues of particular elections. For many voters those images may be quite durable and long-standing.[5] In the causal analysis depicted in figure 10.1a, party images affect voting directly; they also are seen as influencing the vote indirectly though party identification, since we strongly believe that imagery constitutes the cognitive rationale for affective identifica-tions in many instances.

5. The durability of party images has never satisfactorily been determined by empirical analysis. In research reported elsewhere, Richardson (1991) has demonstrated that party images measured by closed questions—the practice we employed in the JABISS survey—are more durable than issue opinions and nearly as stable as party identifications over the term of a three-year panel. (The locale is Britain in the 1980s.) In our own case, since party images were solicited only in the postelection wave, their stability over time is actually unknown. But their face content is quite broad and implies evaluation of party performance and qualities over time. Moreover, a summary index of respondent dispositions on all eight image dimensions showed a correlation of .647 with stable party identification. Thus, images were linked closely with an attitude likely having signifi-cant durability.

Before turning to our empirical analysis, we must acknowledge some nagging problems associated with a gap between our two conceptual types—affective and cognitive partisans—and their respective indicators, "consistent identifiers" and "party images." Our "consistent partisans" indicator may be somewhat overestimating the numbers of affective partisans in Japan because the stimulus word was "support," but that need not greatly concern us here, because we expect that most of these misspecified affective partisans would qualify as cognitive partisans anyway. For our purposes, both dimensions of partisanship should serve equally well, as both are expected to be excellent predictors of the vote, at least in the short term.

The more serious problem arises in terms of who does and does not qualify as a cognitive partisan. If we are really identifying partisans, then their partisanship should carry with it certain behavioral implications stemming from its characteristic as a "reasonably" stable and constrained array of rationales. The presence of varying degrees of stability in the kinds of party images we encounter was already noted. But variations in stability also likely reflect untapped dimensions of internal structure. Some voters surely have highly complex, differentiated, and enduring party images that function much like party identifications. Others are likely to have much less articulated, even ephemeral images. What is the threshold of inclusion for this concept, and what kinds of behavior fall below its definitional limits? This point may be argued, but we feel that to qualify as a cognitive partisan one's party images must have been essentially developed before the campaign and endure well after the election is over. In other words, we would exclude from the concept those whose party images are so new that they were products of the campaign or so transitory that they represent no more than an individual's rationalization after the fact of his or her short-term voting choice. While we can conceptualize this boundary of inclusion, we cannot at this point measure it. Thus some indeterminate proportion of our "image partisans" and perhaps even our "consistent partisans" should not be classified as any type of partisan. As noted below, this concept/indicator gap problem can potentially overestimate the predictive power of partisanship in Japan. Having said this, however, we hasten to add that we do not expect this problem to be of an order of magnitude that would fundamentally invalidate our results. Thus, while these indicator problems should be borne in mind, they should not in any way alter the basic structure of our path analysis models below.

Testing a Model of the Vote in Japan

For purposes of testing a model of the partisan forces affecting the vote, party identifications and images were represented by summary indices. The party image index was designed to reflect plurality preferences for one of the six main parties active in the election—the Liberal Democrats, New Liberal Club, Democratic Socialists, Clean Government Party, Japan Socialists and Japan Communists—as determined by the patterns of responses to the eight individual party image questions. The stable party identification index summarized the direction of consistent preferences for these same six parties and treated all deviations from consistency as missing data.

When the effects on the vote of stable party identifications and party images were examined through a multiple regression analysis as shown in figure 10.1b, party images, with a beta coefficient of .44, proved to be the strongest factor directly influencing voter decisions. Party images further outweighed party identifications in impact when their indirect effects were added to their direct influence. Stable party identifications were a close runner up as a direct factor in the vote, having a beta coefficient of .43.

Party imagery is clearly important to voting in Japan. Party images have been suggested as an important form of electorate response to parties in earlier writings on the United States and Europe. But the status of party images has never been completely clear. To some scholars, they are mainly correlates of party identifications. To others, they are independently important. To us, party identifications and party images are two distinct but somewhat overlapping dimensions of partisanship. Most identifiers have complementary images of their favored parties. In addition, however, 30 percent of the voting public also maintain favorable images of parties without being firm identifiers. It is this group within the electorate, which we have noted may be somewhat larger than estimated here, that gives imagery a special importance in Japan. When the effects of imagery are combined with those of stable identifications, these two dimensions of partisanship explain a remarkable 62 percent of the variance in the 1976 House of Representatives election vote!

Political psychology has long emphasized the affective content of party identification. Party images can best be seen as constituting a cognitive rationale for support of a political party, which for many people simply complements and augments the affective content of party identification. Prior research has shown that the affective content of Japanese identifications is fairly weak and that some persons even vote "habitually" for the same party without maintaining any self-conscious affective partisan tie (Richardson, 1986). For many Japanese, then, identifications are accompanied by cognitive evaluations of the parties that buttress otherwise weak, but not entirely missing, affective attitudes. The path from images to stable identifications in our model highlights this role played by party images. For many other Japanese, however, party imagery stands alone as the main indicator of a party tie, as is already indicated by the direct path between imagery and the vote. Clearly cognitive partisans and party images are important concepts for understanding voting behavior in Japan.

The Negative Partisanship Hypothesis

It was impossible to represent the complex patterns of positive and negative affect and cognitive awareness addressed by Miyake in chapter 6 in single dimensional indices of party identifications or imagery suitable for inclusion in regression analysis along with other more straightforward indices.[6] In order to show the link between our simpler measures of party identification and imagery and Miyake's more complex analyses, we have summarized the different patterns of liking and disliking regarding one's own favored party and alternative parties among persons with stable identifications and favorable images toward the Liberal Democratic and Japan Socialist parties, respectively. This illustration of the patterns of affectivity among an important subset of Japanese voters demonstrates well that sizable numbers of people are either affectively neutral, negative, or nondiscriminating toward their own supported party. It also illustrates other patterns indicative of the complicated ways in which people relate affectively to parties, patterns which complement the concept of dimensionality introduced by Miyake.

In table 10.1, the proportions of the various combinations of persons who like (+), dislike (−), or are neutral (0) toward their own party and its major opposition are shown for groups of stable identifiers and persons with favorable images. In each case, the opposition party is the other major party in the system, the Japan Socialists in the case of Liberal Democratic supporters and the Liberal Democratic Party among Japan Socialist followers. Here the image partisans are defined broadly as those persons who held one or more image favoring one of the two major parties, regardless of whether this measure overlapped empirically with that for the stable identifiers.

Patterns of in-party and out-party likes and dislikes were complex among both conservative and progressive partisans. The ideal type of "loyal" partisanship, liking one's own party and clearly disliking its major opponent, constituted a modest plurality (ranging from 29 to 38 percent) only among the identifiers of the LDP or JSP. Many other identifiers were warm toward their own party but just neutral or less warm toward the opposing party. For image partisans of both parties, the dominant or tying pattern was neutrality. Negative partisans, if defined narrowly as people who were neutral toward their preferred

6. As will be clear to anyone who has toiled with analysis of attitudes in multiparty systems, multiple parties make it impossible to collapse a second additional dimension into one partisanship scale as is done frequently in American political behavior research.

Table 10.1   In- and Out-Party Affect among Major-Party Supporters
(In Percentages)

Own/Other	Liberal Democrats		Japan Socialists	
	Stable ID	Images	Stable ID	Images
+/−	29	20	38	33
+/0	28	19	19	18
+ > +	10	8	9	3
0/−	12	13	10	8
Equal[a]	21	33	15	33
Other	1	7	9	6
Total	101%	100%	100%	101%
N	(305)	(411)	(196)	(199)

Notes: + = 51 or more degrees; 0 = 50 degrees; − = 49 degrees or less; + > + refers to persons who liked their own party while also liking its major opposition, but at a lower positive affect.

[a]Persons who evaluated their own party with the same valence (either position, neutral or negative) as the main alternative party. (Respondents were divided into five groups with regard to their thermometer scores toward both their own and alternate parties: these were negative, neutral, 51–65 degrees, 66–80 degrees, and 81 and above degrees. The patterns summarized here are collapsed and + patterns are simplified where possible, but both the "+ > +" and "equal" groups reflect the full range of distinctions among different degrees of warmness.)

party while negative toward the alternative party, accounted for just 8 to 13 percent of each group of partisans. Altogether 34 percent of the LDP and JSP identifiers and 47 to 53 percent of these two parties' image partisans were either neutral or negative in affect toward their own party or had the same levels of positive affect toward their party and its principal opposition.

Taken as a whole, the findings in table 10.1 indicate that party identification in the Michigan sense of the term is a meaningful concept that applies to a substantial proportion of Japan's electorate. At the same time, we must also realize that our measure of "stable identifiers" is still somewhat contaminated with partisans who lack any meaningful affective ties with their preferred party. Indeed, Miyake's tables 6.4 and 6.5 demonstrate that substantial proportions of his negative partisans emerge as stable identifiers.

Issue Opinions and Voting

Issue opinions are treated as a major factor in voting choice in most approaches to voting behavior. In chapter 7 of this book, Shinsaku Kohei, Ichiro Miyake, and Joji Watanuki examine the issue attitudes of the 1976 Japanese electorate. They employ ideas from American and European research (for example, Butler and Stokes, 1969) to document linkages between issue opinions and voting. That analysis deals sequentially with the extent of voter assessments of the *importance* of specific issues, people's actual awareness or *knowledge* of these issues, and the *perceptual links* made by the electorate between issues and party positions.

In 1976 two kinds of issues were "important" to more than half of the electorate; these were corruption and money politics and the felt need for expanded social welfare programs. The remaining eight issue topics were evaluated as being important by less than half of the public, with the emperor's political role and two other "1950s" issues—defense forces' strength and U.S.–Japanese mutual security ties—being seen as important by only about a third of the electorate.[7] Somewhat relatedly, levels of issue awareness, measured in terms of the respondent's ability to express an opinion about issues or designation of a party "close" to his or her own position, also seem fairly low, even in the case of issues emphasized by the parties and the media.

Issue opinions were also relatively weakly linked to party choices, in the sense that fewer than two out of three party voters saw their own parties as being close to their own positions. According to the analysis by Kohei and his colleagues, the failure to relate issues to preferred parties was slightly more conspicuous among conservative party followers than among adherents of most other parties. The inability of many conservatives to find a party close to their own opinions on particular issues may reflect the unpopularity of perceived conservative issue positions on the corruption and other valence issues. But it also may be a product of the lower education of many conservative supporters.

There were also differences regarding particular issues. The main issue cleavage related to voting preferences in 1976 was the "1950s cultural politics" cluster, which included attitudes toward defense and security issues, labor strikes, and the position of the emperor. This was a little surprising since these issues were not seen as very important in people's replies to the issue saliency questions. Other issue domains had less of an effect on the vote, as in the case of the corruption issues, or virtually no effect at all. In the Japanese example, the less salient long-term issues are most closely associated with the vote, because it was these "cultural politics" issues that played an important formative role in defining the Japanese party system and partisan cleavages in the early postwar period.[8] One striking feature of Japanese politics from the 1950s through the 1970s was the more or less stable differentiation of the parties along lines of

7. The "emperor's role" issue was actually seen as important by fewer than one elector in five.

8. It should also be noted that these issue stands have been repeated many times over the years, so one can assume that the socializing role of partisan alternatives enforces this conformity in many instances. It is also worth noting that the 1950s issues are those where partisan alternatives have been most clear and consistent across all five parties. In the case of many domestic issues, party stands are simply too close together or too complexly arrayed across parties to be clearly

cleavage drawn early in the postwar era, and under conditions of this kind transitory issues were of less electoral importance.

Chapter 7 concludes that while issues do affect voting choices in certain instances, partisanship emerges as the stronger of the attitudinal forces influencing Japanese voting behavior. This point is also demonstrated in the summary regression analysis presented in figure 10.2. Partisan issue domains were tapped by an index that summarized the partisan direction of people's opinions on three of the cultural politics issues mentioned above.[9] When this index was entered into a regression analysis in a modified version of our model of the 1976 vote, feelings of party proximity on the cultural politics issue dimensions had much lower effects on voting than stable party identifications and party imagery. Significantly, addition of the issue variable to the regression equation added only 1 percent in explained variance to the results produced by party imagery and stable party identifications.[10] Chapter 7 shows that issue partisanship is of only qualified importance in Japan. Issue partisanship mainly confirms and buttresses party imagery and party identifications, rather than constituting a strong independent force affecting the vote. In addition, rather than being a short-term influence on voting, as is expected in most voting theory, the issue opinions in Japan that counted most in actual voting were related to issue dimensions over two decades old.

Some analyses of issue dimensions of Japanese voting in past electoral studies have found that issues exercised greater weight in voting than the research in this book indicates. Journalistic accounts of Japanese elections likewise place heavy emphasis on the role of issues, sometimes speculating that particular issues motivate detached voters—those who participate infrequently—to come to the polls. There are several reasons for the discrepancies between our findings and those of these earlier studies. The analysis of this book has been much more complete than most earlier research. By showing the inadequacy of people's knowledge and weak sense of linkage between salient issues and party positions, we reach a relatively pessimistic view of the importance of issues as significant factors in voting in Japan. In addition, many of the

---

cognized by the electorate. An example from recent election manifestos is pension policy, where all parties support the concept of national pension, and differences are confined to actual amounts of benefits. As discussed in chapters 2, 3, 7, and elsewhere, cultural politics refers to the issue cleavages of the early 1950s, a time when some prominent conservatives felt that Japan should return to prewar constitutional and political arrangements while the opposition parties struggled to preserve the more open postwar system.

9. Following the procedures employed in chapter 7, the "strike" issue was excluded here from the cultural politics issue position scale because that issue did not load cleanly and exclusively on the cultural politics dimension in a factor analysis.

10. A validating analysis using issue questions on all twelve issues covered by the JABISS interview questions produced virtually identical results.

Figure 10.2   Issue Opinions and the Vote

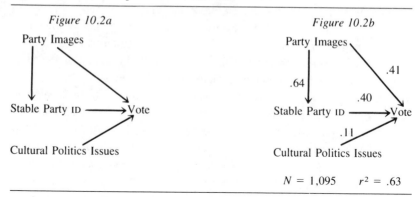

earlier analyses of issue voting in Japan did not include the effects of party identifications or party images in their voting research designs. Our inclusion of these variables weakens the direct impact of issues because of shared variance effects. Issues clearly have played a role across the postwar period in developing progressive-conservative kinds of images and evaluations of the parties within the electorate, and these undoubtedly have helped to form partisan loyalties. It is in this shaping and defining of party images and partisan loyalties that political issues appear to have had the greatest impact on electoral behavior in Japan.

We would conclude that issue opinions exert a visible but subdued influence on voting in Japan under normal circumstances. In a sense, the cultural politics set of issues constitutes a cleavage divide not unlike that seen in European electoral competition over the past century, even though the cleavage is not one drawn on lines reflective of deep and enduring social divisions. Moreover, beyond that cluster of 1950s issues, the Japanese electorate from the 1960s, through the 1980s was generally somewhat passive regarding most specific issues. From time to time salient short-term issues have emerged, like the corruption issue in the 1976 election, yet such issues have typically produced important but relatively small effects on voting patterns, as noted in chapters 7 and 8. As will be discussed in chapter 11, the 1989 upper house election represented an exception to this pattern in that a host of highly salient short-term issues combined to create a rather sizable impact on party fortunes.

■ Other Explanations of the Vote

Some readers might at this point question why we should proceed any further in trying to explain the causes of voting choices in Japan. We have already accounted for an extremely high proportion of the variance in voting decisions—indeed, unusually high levels for survey analysis—and we are unlikely to improve statistically on our result by adding other variables. In fact, a quick scan of the alternative models presented in the succeeding section demonstrates that alternate sets of variables explain far lower proportions of the variance than does psychological partisanship, and they add little statistically to the explanation in the final combined model.

There are two important reasons, however, for looking at other sets of variables. The first concerns those issues, raised in the general comparative voting behavior literature and reviewed in chapter 1, of the duration, stability, and independence of conventional measures of partisanship. In any kind of a causal model of voting, partisanship, whether measured as party ID or party image, should explain a large amount of the variance in the voting decision simply because the concepts of party support and party vote inevitably will be closely linked in the voter's mind. Partisanship represents the respondents' reactions to the most general of the objects of politics, the political parties themselves. For some people, this general attitude is a long-term loyalty, that is largely independent of or insulated from short-term influences. (This loyalty is what we are trying to tap with our measure of stable identifications at two points in time.) For others, it may be more of a running decision on which party to support, a decision that can be strongly affected by recent events. This second kind of partisan is likely more prominent among those cognitive partisans whose main indication of a party tie was their reported image that a particular party was "best." These partisans lack an emotional commitment that can serve as a barrier to shifts in evaluations.

A problem arises when measures of partisanship and vote choice become so close as to lack meaningful independence. This occurs when the party perceptions tapped by our indicators are so weak, temporal, and fluid that they cannot play any independent role in anchoring the vote, but rather shift in tandem with changes in vote choice. Theoretically this should not be a problem with our measure of party identification, because by definition party identifications are long-standing, affective attachments. But, as we have noted, we suspect that to some degree the measure of party identifications we employed may fail to screen out not only all the cognitive partisans who lack any emotional commitments to their supported party but also those whose partisan instability could not be identified by the very short interval between the two waves in our panel study. In the case of the cognitive partisans, their images and perceptions of the parties are expected to be somewhat more unstable those of the identifiers, if for no other reason than the fact that these images are not backed by any intense emotional commitments. Undoubtedly for many that we have classified as cognitive partisans party images are quite stable and function much like party identifications in anchoring and guiding voting decisions over time. For others, however, especially the less informed and cognitively sophisticated, their party images may be too weak, fluid, and transitory to qualify them as any type of partisan. Some indeterminate proportion of our respondents, therefore, have been misspecified as partisans (see Flanagan and McDonald, 1979).[11]

These caveats raise some notes of caution concerning our findings in figures 10.1 and 10.2. As in surveys anywhere that employ essentially a cross-sectional design, for some number of voters, there is likely to be a reverse direction of causation from vote choice to party image, and even to party identification. For this subset of voters who reported partisan sentiments based

11. Measurement of partisanship in Japan faces a number of difficulties. Latency of partisanship, for example, is one special problem. The major alternative pattern to stable identifications, according to replies in our two-wave panel, was alternation between "no party" and "don't know" in one wave and party support in another. In this group of "latent partisans," the most prominent pattern was "no party" or "don't know" in the first wave and support of a party in the second, postelection interview wave. This could imply that the election campaign activated party ties that were so latent as to be unknown to the respondent during the first wave interview. Such a pattern is possible in view of the frequencies of report of a consistent vote in the past even in the absence of a stable party tie in 1976 (Richardson, 1986). But these second-wave partisans could also simply be short-term supporters who reflect their most recent vote on their replies, and therefore persons who should not be counted under the party identification concept.

In addition, imagery solicited by closed-ended questions, which were the basis for our findings thus far, might inflate evidence of a stable party tie by tapping mainly current but essentially fluid mental pictures of the parties. For one thing, parties are only weakly salient to Japanese voters. Comparisons of the Japanese and American frequencies of response to open-ended questions regarding what people like and dislike about party *A,* party *B,* etc., were carried out by both Richardson (1975) and Flanagan and McDonald (1979) based on the 1967 Japanese Election Study and the 1960 and 1968 University of Michigan American presidential election studies. Both studies found that, compared to over 80 percent of the Americans, only one out of two Japanese respondents mentioned anything that he or she either liked *or* disliked about any of the parties. Moreover, when Japanese respondents did offer a response, it was more likely to be negative than positive, while Americans were more likely to offer positive than negative responses.

Still more problems lurk behind these findings. The emotional level of Japanese political culture is clearly lower than that in most other industrialized countries, according to comparisons of thermometer evaluations of parties, leaders, groups, and political institutions in different countries. This was noted briefly in chapter 1 and is also reported elsewhere (Richardson, 1986). The effects of the more emotionally neutral Japanese environment may actually depress levels of "liking" and "disliking" parties, the information sought by the traditional open-ended party image question in American research. This could mean that parties are more salient than they appear to be from the traditional party image questions, because people feel so emotionally neutral about them that they don't answer "like" and "don't like" questions. Our own open-ended question about images of the Liberal Democrats, Japan Socialists and Japan Communists—"What kind of party do you think (*blank*) is . . . are there things you like or don't like about that party?"—was specifically designed to capture the cognitive dimensions of imagery more directly than the simpler American "likes" or "dislikes" format. This change in question format resulted in higher levels of imagery (which were also close to those reported in replies to our closed-ended questions) than had been noted in 1967 using the American question. This discovery obviously enhances the credibility of our closed-ended question responses.

solely on their short-term voting intentions, the correlation between party vote and partisanship will always be a perfect 1.0. Adding them into the analysis, therefore, necessarily inflates the statistically demonstrated explanatory power of partisanship.

The first point then is that our conceptualization that affective and cognitive party attitudes determine vote choice may be an inaccurate representation of reality for some people, because their party attitudes are not stable nor long-standing nor independent of short-term voting intentions. The second point is equally important and also refers us back to a major criticism of the concept of partisan identification in the literature that was cited in chapter 1. This is the criticism that while psychological partisanship can be shown to have great predictive power, it is of little theoretical interest. Critics observe that partisanship in and of itself tells us very little about voting behavior and simply begs the question of where these partisan perceptions come from. The question is just as important in Japan as in other countries. We turn to an analysis of other variables, then, to elaborate our explanation of voting behavior in Japan.

We may view partisanship as a summary, aggregated evaluation of which party best represents the respondent's interests, which has the most attractive or trusted candidates, which is closest to the respondent's major reference groups, and which is supported (or even endorsed) in the primary and secondary groups of which the respondent is a member. Because partisanship summarizes and aggregates a variety of responses to politics and elections, it is bound to have a stronger correlation with the vote than the separate components themselves. At the same time, the component elements are themselves still theoretically important, and examining their contribution is essential to understanding political behavior.

The following two sections present further sets of variables and in doing so help us to elaborate our explanation of the vote. We turn first to the candidate and constituency dimensions of the voting decision in Japan's 1976 general election. The candidate dimension of the voting decision has always been viewed as important in studies of Japanese elections, given the *candidate*-rather than party-centered basis of Japanese campaign organizations and the apparent importance of mobilization based on personal ties to the candidates (or to other persons linked in some way to the candidates) in getting out the vote. The candidate and constituency mobilization variables may influence the vote in three ways. For some voters, a candidate tie of some kind, or a short-term attraction to a candidate set in the context of efforts to mobilize the vote through local social networks or secondary group endorsements, may actually "drive" the partisan element of the vote. For other voters, constituency and campaign influences may lead to deviations from partisanship, although candidate-oriented voting decisions that deviate from partisan preferences are much rarer in Japanese parliamentary elections than in presidential contests in the United States. In addition, constituency influences and attraction to candidates may play an important role in guiding voting decisions for nonidentifiers, somewhat analogous to that played by party images for less emotionally committed voters.[12]

The second alternate set of variables that we will consider are the long-term environmental influences. These variables contribute to our voting model by explaining the sources of partisanship. Here we will examine the socializing environment in which party images and loyalties develop. These variables help us to understand who becomes an LDP or JSP supporter and why. As we turn to these alternate sets of variables, we are moving away from political psychology, with its heavy emphasis on the responsive side of electoral behavior, that is, attitudes and cognitions. Instead, we will be dealing more with the direct actions of individuals in social groups. Social groups and social networks typically are more prominently featured in sociological, as opposed to psychological, theories of political behavior. For example, in political sociology, secondary groups, geographical regions, and community settings are seen at various points as playing critical roles in the *mobilization* of electorates and the *reinforcement* of political attachments. In political psychology, secondary groups are generally relegated to the status of background variables, even though in reality they are probably important agents of socialization. In Japan, we look to social groups as direct forces on the vote, whose cumulative effects are also to reinforce political allegiances. For this reason we side more with political sociology in our consideration of the role of social structure, even though we also look more to the effects of microaspects of social relationships than to macrosocial cleavages. We turn first to the short-term, direct effects on voting of different group contexts and subsequently their long-term role in attitude reinforcement.

■ Constituency Mobilization and the Vote in Japan

In our analysis of constituency mobilization and related communications processes, we will employ the construct of candidate images. Actually an attitudinal response, imagery is intimately connected with direct efforts to mobilize people's support in Japan's candidate-oriented electoral system. Candidate images are people's broad mental images of the candidates, and therefore, like

12. Indeed, our measure of party images may already in part account for some of these constituency influences, since one of the items included in the party image index asked respondents to identify the party that had the "best candidates."

party imagery, they can be an intermediate or long-term attitude, if the candidates themselves are durable political objects, that is, long-time incumbents or frequent contestants in parliamentary contests in a particular district's elections. While our concept of candidate images is similar to that typically employed in American electoral research, as operationalized in our JABISS analysis it differs by focusing more on the generic and lasting attributes of the candidates.

A Profile of Constituency Mobilization and Influence Communications

In chapter 9 of this book, Bradley Richardson focuses on direct manifestations and consequences of social group and network influence, specifically the frequencies and effects of direct efforts to mobilize the vote through requests for people's support and other efforts at *influence communications*. Japanese political scientists and journalists have long reported that direct solicitation of the vote is a common feature of Japanese election campaigns at both the national and local levels. Anthropological and sociological studies of local community life have described these and other forms of explicit electoral mobilization, including such actions as community endorsements of particular candidates.

Group mobilization and other kinds of group influences are normally seen in political sociology and political psychology research conducted in Western settings as having long-term effects somewhat removed from the events and processes of specific elections. Even when their role in specific electoral contexts is more clearly recognized, the processes involved in group mobilization are not specified. The social group in Japan also serves as a long-term setting for the reinforcement of political loyalties. But in addition to that important role, these groups are prominent and visible in direct efforts to bring family, friends, and acquaintances to the polls and to influence their vote choice. For this reason, the social group's short-term influences within the context of the campaign cannot be ignored.

Requests from one person to another are the most common form of explicit influence communications, according to the evidence presented in chapter 9 from a series of Japanese studies on electoral mobilization and the vote extending over time. Significant variations exist, however, between the practices emphasized in different kinds of elections. Community endorsements of candidates, for example, exceed social-network-based requests for the vote in local elections, whereas personal requests are more prominent in national elections. In addition to group endorsements and personal requests, in some cases more casual and routine interpersonal political communications may act as influence communications even though they are typically less explicitly designed to gain support for a particular candidate. Discussions of voting choices within the family, at work, and in residential neighborhoods, which took place at levels considerably exceeding those of solicitations of the vote, are thus a kind of borderline type of influence communications. Many of these network-based political communications do involve an effort to solicit the vote. Others, such as those within families, may rather involve consideration as to how to respond to various outside solicitation efforts. And, in another sense, we may view these more frequent and intimate small-group political communication processes as the dense network at the base of the political communications flow, which permits a broader coverage of the vote solicitation messages that originally emanate from organizations and candidate campaigns.

Chapter 9 provides a profile of constituency mobilization set within the context of the total communications process concerning politics. When we examine the role of constituency mobilization and influence communications in the overall communications behavior of the 1976 electorate, we can see a kind of hierarchy of information exposure. The written and electronic media are, not surprisingly, the dominant mode of political communications. Still, talking about politics and receiving a request to vote for a particular candidate are behaviors reported by over half of the electorate. Exposure to candidates in the form of receipt of a postcard was also quite common. Informal communications are important.

Some surprising and counterintuitive patterns in constituency mobilization processes can also be seen. Despite folkloric assumptions to the contrary, some kinds of influence communications, namely social-network-based requests, were more common in the cities than in the countryside. As suggested in chapter 4, this finding may be the result of selective underreporting owing to the respondent's failure to recognize the more proximate and intimate vote solicitation as an external request. But it is also highly plausible that specific requests are more necessary in urban environments, simply because constituency communications processes are generally less redundant there. In effect, mobilization may go further in rural areas, and perhaps has greater cumulative effects over time as well, because of the overlapping nature of all social processes. In both instances, the need for requests may be lower than in the less dense social context of urban life. Relatedly, both support organization membership and community endorsements still occurred at higher levels in the rural areas than in towns and cities, and direct requests to supplement these activities may have been unnecessary for reasons already stated.

In another area, however, the belief that influence communications are mainly a province of the Liberal Democratic Party's candidate machines does appear to be contradicted by the evidence from the 1976 interviews. All parties attempted political proselytization. Significantly, the Clean Government Party sponsored more kinds of influence-seeking communications relative to its voting strength than any other party. Indeed, these Clean Government Party actions partly account for the higher urban frequencies of influence communications observed in our research.

Assessments of the impact of efforts to influence people's votes are made difficult by reluctance to admit that one's vote was influenced by outside manipulation. For this reason, direct questions about the effects of external influence in most earlier Japanese surveys have not produced very conclusive evidence in favor of a constituency mobilization/influence communications model of voting. In the JABISS study, a special effort was made to allay people's concerns by clearly indicating the scholarly intent of the interviews. In addition, information was collected regarding a comprehensive array of activities and attitudes related to influence communications processes and constituency mobilization. Exposure to the various modes of influence communications, images of the candidates, and respondents' candidate choices were each measured separately by a series of question batteries. These included queries about (a) group support for specific candidates, (b) vote solicitation on behalf of specific candidates via face-to-face social contacts, including those within the nuclear family, (c) exposure to specific candidates' constituency campaigns, and (d) images of the candidates on five separate dimensions.

As reported in chapter 9, in the 1976 election, group endorsements and support were the most effective kind of influence communications, even though very few people were members of groups actually perceived to support a particular candidate. Face-to-face requests were also an important factor in people's votes for particular candidates. Within the spectrum of people's contacts within social networks, requests for the vote originating in the immediate family circle were the most successful mode of influence. This finding demonstrates how far influence communications processes originating within candidate's campaigns penetrate into people's most intimate social contacts. The importance of requests from within the nuclear family may also signal an increase in the mediating role of the nuclear family as other social groups become less important in people's lives through the effects of urbanization and industrialization of the rural periphery.

Probably the most striking finding of the analysis reported in chapter 9 is that *most* vote solicitation activity flows between campaigners and partisans of the same party. In Japan's comparatively homogeneous rural areas, such a pattern is to be expected. But in the cities the political climate is much more heterogeneous, which could produce a great many cross-party attempts at mobilization. Some occur, but even in the cities candidate campaigns focus more on the party faithful than on others. This means that from the point of view of the decision-making processes of the individual voter, influence communications play a dual role. They direct voters' attention toward a particular candidate, sometimes activating favorable candidate images developed as the result of earlier campaigns or activities and events between elections. They also play an activating and reinforcing role relative to people's partisan attachments. The role of constituency mobilization relative to the initiation and sustenance of partisanship over time is very important and will be the subject of later comment.

Some deviations from party identifications in people's vote choices could also be attributed to candidate-centered influence communications processes, especially those in urban and metropolitan districts where a more heterogeneous flow of influence communications was encountered. But in most instances "influenced" decisions about candidates were made within the boundaries of declared partisan loyalties, and the effects of external mobilization on partisan voting was more reinforcing than otherwise. In this manner, candidate machine politics in Japan performs the role attributed to social cleavage organizations in European political sociology.

A second significant finding of the analysis reported in chapter 9 was the evidence that candidate imagery and perceptions played a greater role in actual voting than direct influence communications and mobilization. Visible, direct efforts to mobilize the vote in one election are less essential to people's decisions than the evaluations they form of candidates in the context of the total campaign or their feelings toward particular candidates that have developed over time. In one sense this finding is intuitively obvious, since questions about campaign activities, such as vote requests, are measuring external attempts to manipulate perceptions, while respondent attitudes, such as candidate images, are measuring the net result of combined external and internal influences on shaping perceptions. Candidate images, then, by definition stand closer to the voting act than vote requests. The only exception here might be the totally apolitical voter who is simply following "instructions" when he casts his ballot, but the numbers of these voters in Japan today are likely to be relatively small. Still, candidate images must come from somewhere, especially since the media play such a minor role in disseminating candidate specific information or imagery in Japan. Thus, candidate images are likely to be the product of campaign activities and other external campaign influences, even though respondents do not always consciously remember the activities in question. One of the problems in assessing the relative influences of perceptions and various kinds of environmental influences is that we still do much better at measuring the former than the latter.

Modelling Constituency Mobilization

In view of the strong support for an influence communications/constituency politics model of the vote in Japan, it is interesting to see how far influence communications and people's images of the candidates go to explain people's voting choices. A model of the effects of the campaign and images of the candidate is proposed in figure 10.3a. Four aspects of the voting public's exposure to local campaigns were identified: candidate images or perceptions, direct contacts with candidates' campaigns, exposure to group climates favorable to particular candidates, and receipt of requests for a supportive vote. All but the first of these are what we have called influence communications. Each of these dimensions of voter exposure to constituency candidates and campaigns is postulated as directly affecting voting choices. In addition to their direct effects on voting, exposure to campaign activities, awareness of group support for candidates, and requests themselves probably help people form candidate images, as was suggested already. Social network requests and other aspects of candidate campaigns are especially important as possible information sources, since so little media attention is paid to constituency candidates. The causal diagram shown in figure 10.3a depicts these highly plausible indirect effects of our constituency mobilization variables through candidate images. Looking at things this way should help round out our understanding of how people learn about constituency candidates.[13]

In figure 10.3b, the results of a multiple regression of the vote for candidate on the three core components of voter reactions to local constituency campaigns are shown.[14] Two things stand out in this analysis of constituency influences on

13. Obviously, incumbents and candidates who ran in earlier elections also potentially benefit from the effects of prior campaigns and from efforts to maintain stable followings between elections. Some of these processes are tapped by our questions about receipt of postcards and membership in support associations, but some important informal communications processes in the past lie beyond the scope of our survey.

14. To facilitate testing of the influence communications and candidate image models of voting choice, summary indexes were created for the attitudes and experiences in each of the dimensions of voters' exposure to candidates and constituency campaigns. Each candidate index summarizes the candidate direction of a plurality or more of each individual's experiences. Both the indices for influence communications (i.e., requests to vote a particular way) and "campaign contact" (a measure tapping attendance of speeches in addition to the influence dimensions [see chapter 9] of being a member of a koenkai or receiving a postcard from the candidate) and the candidate vote choice variable were coded in each constituency as "first LDP candidate," "second LDP candidate," and so on. Using this procedure, the responses could be analyzed among voters throughout Japan without reference to district. The codes for candidates were also themselves keyed to the codes for parties. The LDP was represented by a 1 in all analyses; LDP candidates were coded 11 for the first candidate, 12 for the second candidate, 13 for the third candidate, and 14 for the fourth candidate. Where party voting was the dependent variable, as in this chapter, candidate codes were collapsed to their first digit.

Figure 10.3   Candidates, Constituency Mobilization, and the Vote

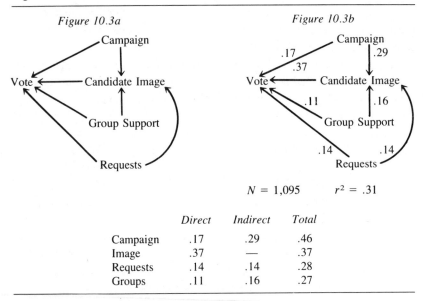

	Direct	Indirect	Total
Campaign	.17	.29	.46
Image	.37	—	.37
Requests	.14	.14	.28
Groups	.11	.16	.27

Note: Campaign experiences include receipt of postcard, joining a support association, and attending a speech. Group support is perceived candidate support in ten secondary group contexts, including unions and community associations.

the vote. First, our four measures of voter experience with constituency candidates and their campaigns do a pretty good job in explaining candidate choice. Altogether they account for 31 percent of the variance in the candidate vote. Clearly constituency candidates and their campaigns are important in Japan!

The second notable feature of the regression findings in figure 10.3b concerns the effects of the different aspects of voters' constituency campaign experiences and attitudes. Not surprisingly, given our discussion of the findings in chapter 9, candidate perceptions and imagery have a stronger direct effect on voting than any of the three influence communications variables. At the same time, the direct consequences of efforts to mobilize the electorate via requests, group support, and campaign contacts are still found to be significant. Moreover, having received a request, being a member of an organization that supports a candidate, and being exposed to the campaign (through receiving a postcard, attending a candidate speech, or joining a candidate support association) each had substantial indirect effects on candidate images, as predicted in our elaborated model of the vote. In terms of total effects, campaign experience ranks first in importance, followed by candidate images, requests, and group support.[15] Later, when we evaluate the full model with all three sets of variables, we will discuss the relative impact of and interaction between the constituency mobilization and partisanship variables. At this point, however, suffice it to say that the constituency mobilization variables play an important role in voting decisions in Japan.

■ Environmental Nurture and Reinforcement

This section deals with what we have called "environmental nurture and reinforcement." Borrowing from political sociology and psychology, we turn first to the specific social group contacts people have which are assumed to play some kind of role in the initiation of political loyalties and formation of favorable imagery of particular political parties and which also function as legitimizers of people's ongoing partisan predilections. This formative and reinforcing role is, we believe, extremely important in Japan. Social groups— secondary organizations, communities, peer groups, and social networks—are the mechanisms employed by politicians to mobilize support in particular elections. Over time, through long-term affiliations with particular candidates or parties and/or through repeated mobilization on behalf of specific candidates or parties, groups take on a partisan cast. This is true for secondary organizations as well as for the smaller groups and networks that are activated through the campaigning efforts of particular candidates or that themselves are embedded in social milieu reached by particular secondary organizations' activities. It is to the consequences of the partisan traditions of social groups that we turn in this section.

Political sociology and political psychology both look to the effects of social context on political behavior, as has been pointed out. Social groups mobilize the vote in particular elections, a process which in Japan is linked with local constituency campaigning. This is the short-term role of social groups dealt with above and in chapter 9. Groups also play a role in a longer time perspective, in the sense that they provide a flow of cues about parties that shape party images, the spark that ignites a party identification, or the continuing supportive information that reinforces people's already-established partisan images and preferences. Within this broader temporal context, the nuclear

15. The dependent variable in the analysis reported in figure 10.3 was the party vote in the 1976 general election. Use of party vote made it possible to maintain consistency throughout the analysis reported in this chapter, even though it would have been a little more precise to use candidate vote— e.g., first LDP candidate, second LDP candidate, and so on—as the dependent variable. An analysis that followed this second procedure, reported elsewhere (Richardson, 1988), however, yielded nearly identical results to those reported here.

family—one kind of social group—functions like other small groups. In some instances, the nuclear family provides the initial spark of partisanship, but parents also likely perform a reinforcing function as well.[16]

Our findings up until now have shown that party identification and party images are the broadest and conceptually most proximate, and hence most important, variables in the voting decision in Japan. The origins and reinforcement of these party loyalties and images within primary and secondary groups are addressed by Scott Flanagan and Ichiro Miyake in chapters 4 and 5. The links between group memberships and activities and informal social networks were given special emphasis in the JABISS survey. People's contacts with both formal secondary groups, like labor unions and agricultural cooperatives, and smaller, informal groups or networks, such as co-workers, neighbors, family, and friends, were ascertained in a series of JABISS question batteries. The JABISS respondents were also asked to indicate their perceptions of the partisan climates within different groups and social contacts. Flanagan used this information in his analysis of the long-term contribution of congenial social environments to the development of partisanship. According to Flanagan, virtually all persons who were members of multiple social groups and who received reinforcing partisan cues from those groups supported the parties favored within their social environment. In contrast, persons who had fewer than three contacts with homogeneous partisan reference groups or who were members of groups with different, cross-cutting partisan preferences tended to reflect the dominant partisan patterns in their social environment to a lesser degree. Exposure to multiple, overlapping, and reinforcing group cues thus enhanced the likelihood of people's conformity to their social context. The same forces were associated with greater cross-time stability in party identifications.

In analysis closely related to that conducted by Flanagan, Miyake examined the effects on party loyalties of parental party preferences—what "traditional" political psychologists have seen as the main source of party identifications. Miyake's analysis also looks at the effects on respondents' partisanship of climates within adult reference groups. As might be anticipated from Japan's recent history of party system discontinuity, and perhaps even more significantly, its experience of very rapid social and economic change—which involved moves to the large cities from parental homes in rural areas and small cities and towns for literally millions of young Japanese—respondents could identify their parents' party ties less often than people surveyed in other indus-

---

16. Parental influence early in life is captured through questions about the father's and mother's partisanship at the time respondents were growing up. Ongoing influence from the nuclear family was also tapped in questions about the contemporary party preferences of family and relatives.

trialized countries. Many contemporary Japanese are simply not conscious of the partisan loyalties of their parents. Relatedly, many people who themselves are partisans appear to have developed party ties in the complete absence of the kinds of familial traditions that seem to be relevant to the development of party identifications in the United States and to a lesser degree in Western Europe.[17]

There were also striking examples of people's deviation from their parents' party traditions in the Japanese case, as reported by Miyake. Those who did break with their parents' party did so in response to the partisan climate of their immediate face-to-face groups or secondary organizations. People in these circumstances actually tended to follow partisan cues from co-workers or to imitate the partisan tendencies of people in other informal groups to a remarkable degree. In some cases these more recent socializing contexts are so dominant that, if the individual is aware of the partisan preferences of his organizations and small informal groups, parental partisanship appears to be virtually irrelevant in shaping his adult partisan preferences.

On the one hand, this finding agrees with the well-articulated notions in the literature regarding the higher emphasis placed on conformity and consensus within the group in Japanese culture (Richardson and Flanagan, 1984). On the other hand, Miyake's findings are extremely important insomuch as they indicate the fragility of parental cues in the face of rapid social change. Clearly, disruptions in individuals' adherence to parental influences were coupled with the presence of potent *adult socialization* experiences. In his analysis of adult learning, Miyake joins the ranks of those scholars from other countries who are beginning to recognize the importance of adult socialization and resocialization experiences as alternatives to overly simple acceptance of the enduring influence of youthful socialization. In many senses, Miyake's work on the effects of massive *social mobility* parallels in importance earlier research by Converse (1969), which showed how much *institutional change* can severely disrupt what were earlier seen as "normal" patterns of intergenerational partisanship transmission and adult attitude maturation.

The processes by which people respond to partisan cues from their immediate social environment, and the separate contribution of parental partisan loyalties, can be readily included in our causal paradigm of the forces affecting voting in Japan. In this case, we are dealing with forces at least some of which were causally prior to conforming party identifications and images. While we expect these socializing influences to affect the vote indirectly through partisan-

17. Although recall of parental partisanship and self-reported conformity with parental ties are both much higher in the United States than in European countries, as is shown by analysis of surveys from nine political systems by Richardson (not reported here), Japan ranks with Italy in indicating the lowest levels of parental effects.

ship, in some cases they may also directly affect voting. This might occur where people lack clear party identifications or images of their own but are highly integrated into family, small group, and organizational environments with clear partisan preferences. It is also possible in some instances that a strong short-term obligation to persons in some social network could temporarily override the respondent's own partisan preference. To encompass all these possibilities, paths that represented the direct and indirect effects on the vote of partisan climates within secondary organizations, primary groups, and the nuclear family were included in the model of group reinforcement processes shown in figure 10.4a.

Two conclusions emerged from the estimates of this model presented in figure 10.4b. First, the direct effects on voting of all group traditions were negligible and statistically insignificant. One important reason for this finding is that virtually all those who could identify the partisan leanings of their families, small groups, or organizations also had partisan preferences and images of their own. These tended to be conforming partisan preferences. In contrast, the effects of group partisan climates, both within and outside the family, on party images and identifications were moderately strong and signifi-

Figure 10.4   Environmental Reinforcement: Parents, Small Groups, and Secondary Organizations

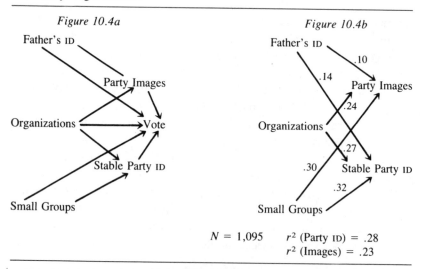

Note: Organizations are secondary groups, such as unions and community associations. Actual indicators are summary indexes of plurality group party support patterns for each respondent. Groups are friends, neighbors, co-workers, and nuclear family/relatives. Father's ID is father's party identification as respondent was growing up.

cant. Group partisan traditions, therefore, appear to be much more important in the formation and reinforcement of long-term partisan attitudes than they are as direct influences on the vote itself.

Our second conclusion, as demonstrated by the relative magnitude of the path coefficients in figure 10.4b, is that small group and organizational attachments and related partisan traditions were more important to both images and identifications than was parental socialization. This finding was of course anticipated in light of the evidence reported in chapters 4 and 5. A respondent's awareness of the political traditions within his affiliated organizations and informal small groups is developed over time as a result of the accumulated effects of individual short-term campaigns and other between-campaign political influences. As such, these group partisan cues provide both stimulus and reinforcement for the development and sustenance of favorable party images and stable party identifications.

Social Structure, Social Context, and Partisanship in Japan

Our analysis has shown that people's immediate social group memberships and face-to-face interactions play a significant role in developing and sustaining psychological attitudes. In addition to looking at microgroup influences such as those we have just reviewed, political sociology has also placed enormous emphasis on the part played by broader, macrosocietal cleavages in structuring political behavior. Political sociology developed intellectually in response to Marx and others who saw class cleavages as the core structural determinant of political life. Contemporary political sociology's concern for the role of sociopolitical cleavages also reflects the importance over the past century of multiple, highly conspicuous social cleavage/party linkages in European politics.

Japan is an interesting case for a test of political sociology's cleavage hypotheses. As Watanuki has chronicled in chapter 2, Japan lacks some of the basic sociopolitical cleavages that have been important in European electoral politics. Neither religion nor region has been important to political party support in the modern period in Japan to the degree found in Europe. In addition, other potentially significant political cleavages have been either wholly or partially attenuated in their development in Japan. A potential division between urban middle class business elites and rural landowning interests, a cleavage pattern prominent in the histories of some European systems, did not result in the formation of opposition parties in the Japanese case. Rather, prewar conservative parties were always coalitions of urban and rural interests.

Paralleling these events, mobilization of the emerging working class was largely suppressed until after World War II, while even after the war the union movement was fragmented and characterized by a national-local dualism with regard to its political and economic influence. More than anything else, the Japanese experience demonstrates the importance of the nature and effects of specific elite coalitions at critical junctures in the development of party systems, along with the enormous importance of organizational activities in electoral mobilization. Japan has an organizationally mobilized electorate, but not an electorate significantly divided by social cleavages of the European variety.

Specific prewar patterns of political mobilization continued into the postwar era, albeit with some important modifications. There is no religious cleavage in contemporary Japan, in the usual sense of competing church-supported or church-versus-secular parties. There is a significant religious party that promotes clean government and probably its own social visibility, but this is not the same as the reflection in party politics of a societal rift between opposing religions or between religious and secular forces. Regionalism also is of very little importance. Regional concentrations of support for particular parties, like those of the Clean Government and Democratic Socialist parties in some Kansai and Chubu constituencies, have nothing to do with regional sentiments as such.

Of the remaining traditional social cleavage bases, social class has itself gained dramatically more expression in postwar Japan than in the prewar era. This is manifested in the emergence of viable leftist and center-left parties supported at least in part by the appropriate labor unions. Unionized workers in Japan typically support the Japan Socialists and the Democratic Socialists, just as political sociology would predict. The Japan Communists likewise gain some union member support. On the other end of the political spectrum, persons in the upper ranges of middle-class occupations—for example, professionals and managers—tend more to support the conservative Liberal Democrats. Up to a point, the symmetries of political sociology can be observed.

The tidiness of the fit, however, between traditional political sociology's cleavage theory and Japanese electoral behavior stops with these symmetries. The white-collar sector of Japanese society, which traditional political sociology would place in the conservative camp, is actually divided between conservative and opposition party support. Among white-collar workers who are also union members, a fairly common pattern in Japan's larger companies, support for working-class parties is three times that of adherence to the conservative movement. Among nonunionized white-collar employees the split between progressive and conservative party support is more even. Meanwhile, nonunionized blue collar workers, who might be mobilized into leftist party support in some political systems, are themselves split relatively equally between supporters of the conservative and opposition parties! In a curious way, the asymmetry between occupations and partisanship in Japan parallels emerging patterns in "postindustrial" Europe, where new social class alignments have eroded traditional class cleavage alignments (Baker, Dalton, and Hildebrandt, 1981; Dalton, Flanagan, and Beck, 1984). The patterns in Japan, however, are much more reflective of secondary group alignments than has been shown to be the case elsewhere.

The most cohesive pattern of broad social sector support for a political party in Japan has been that of farmers for the Liberal Democrats. The underlying axis of this attachment has been, however, parochial and paternalistic, in the sense that the Liberal Democrats have favored farmers in general, and specific subgroups of farmers in particular, while also providing residents of specific rural communities with a broad system of financial supports and subsidies. Farmers are not a middle class united behind a middle-class party in conventional terms.[18]

The significance of the patterns of social structure support for parties in Japan lies, therefore, in the deviant patterns as much as it does in the areas of conformity with social cleavage hypotheses. Japan does not have sharply defined cleavages wherein entire social classes or other large and opposed population groupings support particular class- or group-oriented parties. Compared to nineteenth- and twentieth-century Europe, Japan simply has a more homogeneous society with less regional diversity, less pervasively felt religious differences, and a somewhat weak and fragmented labor union movement. Enterprise-based labor unions, which are organized around individual companies and include both blue- and white-collar workers in the same union, cut across class lines while the union movement as a whole has failed to penetrate large sectors of the traditional working class.[19] Watanuki calls the resulting fairly complex patterns of political mobilization in Japan a *matrix* rather than a cleavage array of social sector and party links. The complicated social coalitions represented in particular party camps are fairly stable, although certainly not fixed. So a kind of symmetry prevails in Japan, but it is not a cleavage-based symmetry. Each party attracts followers from several different social groups, and most social groups split their support between parties.

While the patterns of alignment between the social structure and political

18. Although many farmers have achieved middle-class affluence over time as clients of the Liberal Democratic Party's largess, the rural sector was formerly economically depressed relative to urban living standards.

19. The union movement's failure to penetrate a large part of the working class has a great deal to do with the dualistic nature of the Japanese economy. The survival of a very large sector of small-scale enterprises is a dominant feature of Japanese economic organization. Within these small firms, familial and paternalistic norms are believed to prevail, which adds to the effects of other characteristics inhibiting unionization, such as their small size.

parties in Japan do not conform to a traditional social cleavage model, microsocial contexts are quite important predictors of electoral behavior. For example, even though occupational status is not correlated with the vote in Japan, Watanuki clearly demonstrates in chapter 2 that there are consistent and substantial variations in party vote by occupational categories. Moreover, in chapter 3, Flanagan reports strong patterns of association between location in certain kinds of occupational and residential environments and voting for left versus right parties. Those respondents who were engaged in small-scale, nonunionized enterprises, and especially those in the farming, small retail, and other "old" middle-class occupations, tended to vote conservative. Conversely, those employed in large-scale, unionized enterprises as either blue- or white-collar workers, tended to vote left.[20] In a similar vein, it was found that those living in established home-owning communities or neighborhoods, which in provincial cities and rural areas are dominated by conservative mobilization networks, will tend to vote conservative to the extent that they are integrated into their community. Conversely, those living in the transient, rental apartment complexes, which tend to be drawn into the networks of progressive politicians, are more likely to vote for the progressive parties.

What is clear from that analysis is that these contrasting voting patterns cannot be explained by any social group identifications based on social cleavages. Rather, it is the tangible associational linkages between specific partisan networks and the formal organizations and informal small groups found within these different contexts that account for the observed behavior. For example, in the case of occupational environments, we are contrasting those dominated by progressively linked union networks with those where conservatively linked agricultural cooperative and trade association networks prevail. More than anything else, Japan demonstrates the validity of Sartori's (1969) dictum that links between social groups and parties depend more on the development of channels of communications and the mobilizing efforts of political elites than they do on the automatic eruption into political life of social cleavages.

Japan's Cultural Cleavage

In addition to social context, and partly conditioned by it, another factor that contributes to the prevailing broad patterns of party support in Japan has been the division of Japan's electorate along cultural lines. A cleavage between

20. Here union membership can be viewed as a contextual variable rather than as a voluntary association, since a person employed by a company that has a union in Japan virtually automatically becomes a member of that union and, conversely, if the company has no union, there is no opportunity to join a union.

persons on one side who adhered to traditional values and supported the conservative party movement and those who prefer modern norms and who supported the opposition parties, especially the Japan Socialists, was very prominent in the 1950s. Differences between camps then reached a hysterical pitch at times, as evidenced by the intensity of street demonstration activity and Diet conflict between proponents of both sides. At stake was the very legitimacy of Japan's postwar political institutions and acceptance of the participation in politics of the leftist parties and union movement.

The cultural politics cleavage emerged in the early postwar years around a series of issues related to very basic debates concerning the appropriate role of the emperor and the military, the form of the political structure, the legitimacy of political protest, and the nature of foreign alliance patterns. The pattern of social alignments around these issues had very little to do with economic interests and a great deal to do with basic value orientations. These cultural politics issues, to a great extent, defined electoral alignments and the postwar party system. While the salience of the cultural politics issues, which gave rise to the progressive-conservative political polarization in the 1950s, has declined greatly in recent years, the relevance of value differences to voting behavior has not, as demonstrated by Flanagan in chapter 3. There is some complexity to the pattern of value change in Japan, and some evidence suggests that the rates of change associated with several of the dimensions of the value cleavage may well have peaked, at least by the mid-1970s. Thus the degree of differentiation on such traditional/modern dimensions as parochialism and personalism may now be declining as Japanese society approaches a new cultural equilibrium on these values. In contrast, the authoritarian-libertarian value cleavage, which is associated with the postindustrial transformation, still seems to sharply differentiate voting patterns.

The cultural cleavage in Japanese politics, which was first identified by Watanuki, anticipates later concern for value change and value cleavages in other countries. The combined traditional-modern value cleavage introduced in chapter 3, and especially its authoritarian-libertarian subdimension, is closely linked with differences in age and education, just as that same A-L value cleavage reflects identical patterns of division in the European case (Flanagan and Lee, 1988). Important urban-rural differences in the values-vote linkages can also be seen, as well as clear differences in the relative effects of occupational and residential environments between these contrasting urban and rural settings (see chapter 3).

The value cleavage hypothesis provides one explanation for the tendencies of younger, well-educated, and more urban persons to vote for the opposition parties, while older, less educated, and more rural people support the conservative parties. These value differences also reinforce the patterns of political mobilization discussed earlier that are found within certain kinds of occupational and residential contexts. Elsewhere, it is shown that these value cleavages help explain why many persons in the middle and working class deviate from the "normal" patterns of class partisanship predicted on the basis of European experience (Flanagan, 1980). There, as well, the cultural values explanation and the effects of organizational mobilization converge, as in the case of the frequency of opposition party support among well-educated and unionized white-collar workers and conservative party allegiance among poorly educated and nonunionized workers in Japan's medium and small enterprises. The matrix patterns of social group–party links, therefore, reflect the reinforcing and sometimes interactive effects of value cleavages and social context. This pattern finds its clearest expression in support for the Liberal Democratic Party on the right and the socialist and communist parties on the left.

Modeling the Effects of Social Structure, Social Context, and Values

In the model displayed in figure 10.5a, both a traditional explanation of voting based on political sociology's cleavage theory and ideas about the role of social context in socializing partisan attitudes and mobilizing political support in Japanese elections are explored. The model contains causal paths for occupational status, education, and income, all of which could indicate aspects of social structure connected with class cleavage interpretations of voting. Three additional variables are included as plausible antecedents of voting, which should capture important aspects of electoral mobilization in Japan. These are urban-rural residence, community integration, and size of one's work place (the indicator employed here for the occupation environment).[21] Following the social context interpretation of demographic-voting linkages, people living in rural areas, working in small firms, and highly involved in local community life are expected to be immersed in a social milieu that is dominated by conservative political attitudes and conservative candidates' campaign mobilization networks. In contrast, those who live in the cities, who work in large firms, and who are weakly integrated into established home-owning residential communities are assumed to be exposed to progressive influences most of the time and hence expected to support opposition parties more often.[22]

21. Community integration is represented in this analysis by a summary indicator based on people's length of residence in their present home, distance from place of work, home ownership, and levels of interaction with neighbors.

22. In figure 10.5a, the dependent variable is the 1976 partisan vote. Use of the vote as the dependent variable makes it possible to look at links between social structure and political behavior in their most direct and simplest form (even though it is very likely that social structure works on the

Figure 10.5 Environmental Reinforcement: Social Structure and
Traditional-Modern Values

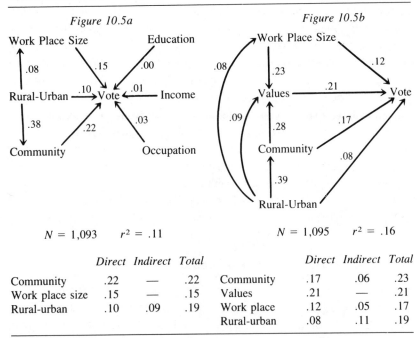

Figure 10.5a
Figure 10.5b

$N = 1,093$ $r^2 = .11$ $N = 1,095$ $r^2 = .16$

	Direct	Indirect	Total		Direct	Indirect	Total
Community	.22	—	.22	Community	.17	.06	.23
Work place size	.15	—	.15	Values	.21	—	.21
Rural-urban	.10	.09	.19	Work place	.12	.05	.17
				Rural-urban	.08	.11	.19

Note: Community is community integration (see text for composition). Occupation is an occupation status variable that reflects respondent occupation if employed and household head occupation if not gainfully employed.

Analysis of the effects of social structure on 1976 electoral choices indicated that social status variables—education, income, and occupational status—had no significant effects on voting. This result agreed with Watanuki's findings that Japan's party system is characterized by a *matrix* pattern of support, wherein links between social status and partisan support are so complex as to have no single, consistent, and discernible effect on the vote. Of the plausible demographic factors linked to voting in Japan, only the contextual variables— community integration, occupational environment, and urban-rural residence— made significant contributions to the vote. Clearly these contextual variables are significant because they identify social settings in which distinctive patterns of conservative or progressive electoral mobilization and partisan-affiliated organizations are found.

vote mainly indirectly through its effects on political attitudes like party identifications and party images, as was found to be the case earlier for social groups). More verisimilitudinous indirect linkages between social structure, psychological partisanship, and the vote will be examined below.

The effects of context or social setting on electoral behavior in Japan also interact with, and are reinforced by, traditional-modern values. Persons living in more traditional, integrated rural communities are exposed more to conservative party candidates' mobilization than they are to the organizing efforts of opposition party candidates. Likewise, as Flanagan has shown in chapter 3, they tend to subscribe more to traditional social norms, which enhance their receptivity to conservative issues and campaign styles. Similarly, urban residence and other characteristically "urban" experiences, such as being employed in large firms, are associated with both exposure to opposition party electoral mobilization and subscription to modern values. Figure 10.5b adds traditional and modern values to the contextual variables, to show how value cleavages and different social settings combine as factors contributing to political behavior. We integrate these variables into a general model of the vote below and show at that point how these forces work though partisanship variables to influence the vote.

■ Summing Up the Sources of the 1976 Vote

Figure 10.6 contains a representation of the entire array of factors believed to influence the 1976 partisan vote in Japan. Preliminary explorations of this model led to retention of certain variables as direct influences on the vote. These were the now familiar party images, stable party identifications, the cultural politics issues, constituency candidate images, and requests for one's vote. To be included at this stage a variable had to have a beta coefficient of over .05 and be significant at the .05 level. All other variables in the equation were determined to have mainly indirect effects and were included in the model only after multiple tests were conducted to show where their impact was greatest and/or where they met the same two criteria of significance and importance as were just mentioned. Paths representing the effects on stable party identifications and party imagery of partisan traditions in organizations and face-to-face groups, along with those of parental partisanship (all shown earlier in figure 10.4b), are included in our general model of the 1976 vote. The structure of the model follows rationales already stated in earlier sections of this chapter. Following this principle, requests for voting support and respondents' campaign experiences are also represented by indirect paths linking them to candidate imagery, as well as by direct paths to the vote in the case of requests, since it is likely that these contacts are one way in which images develop. The two contextual variables—community integration and plant size—proved to be related to organizational and face-to-face network partisanship and to requests and campaign experiences, and they were included in the relevant equations for

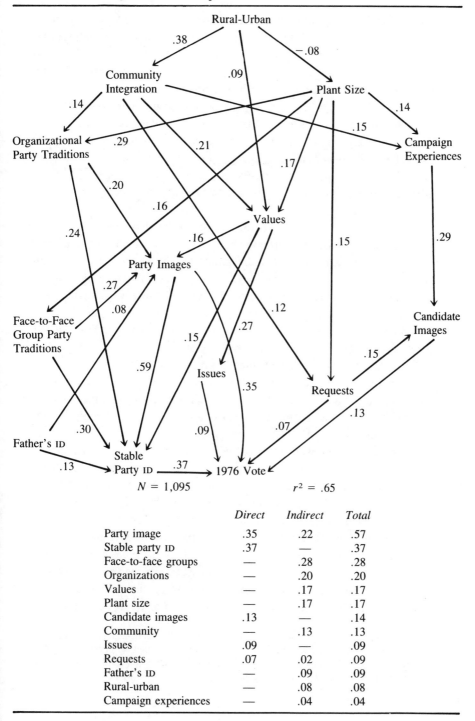

Figure 10.6   Comprehensive Model of the Vote

	Direct	Indirect	Total
Party image	.35	.22	.57
Stable party ID	.37	—	.37
Face-to-face groups	—	.28	.28
Organizations	—	.20	.20
Values	—	.17	.17
Plant size	—	.17	.17
Candidate images	.13	—	.14
Community	—	.13	.13
Issues	.09	—	.09
Requests	.07	.02	.09
Father's ID	—	.09	.09
Rural-urban	—	.08	.08
Campaign experiences	—	.04	.04

this reason. Finally, rural-urban residence proved to be a contributing factor to variations in community integration and size of plant, and they are linked via these variables to later variables in the model for this reason.

General cultural values were also represented in the general model of the forces affecting the vote in Japan. Values clearly permeate society and could be responsible for many mutations in party support in different contexts and at different junctures. At this point, consistent with Flanagan's analysis in chapter 3, we chose only to trace the effects of traditional versus modern values on the cultural politics issues, as well as to examine their impact on stable party identifications and party imagery. Paths from community integration, rural-urban residence, and size of work place to cultural values were introduced to complete the model.[23]

The results of our tests of the total model of the 1976 vote are shown in figure 10.6. The findings of prior analyses are confirmed with regard to most variables in the equation, as could be anticipated. Naturally, with the various individual and group partisanship variables entered into the equations, it is not surprising to find that the contextual and value cleavage variables are now related to the vote indirectly through partisanship. Indeed, a substantial linkage is found between values and party images and identifications as indicated by the standardized beta coefficients for the relevant paths in the model. We also find that occupational and residential contexts influenced to which parties' constituency campaigns people tend to be exposed and the partisan coloration of the formal and informal group networks found within these social settings. Finally, consistent with our earlier findings, residential and occupational settings made healthy contributions to value preferences.

Persons who were well integrated into their neighborhoods or hamlets of residence or who worked in small firms, where group traditions generally tended in the conservative direction, and whose values were also traditional, tended to have conservative party ties and/or imagery favorable to the conservative party, which ultimately led them to support the Liberal Democrats at the polls in 1976. Persons also favored conservative candidates as the result of a similar chain of relationships linking congenial social environment, specific campaign appeals and requests, candidate imagery, and the vote. The genesis and reinforcement of centrist and leftist party and candidate attitudes is similarly embedded in the chain of relationships shown in the figure 10.6 model.

23. A path representing the effects of group support for particular candidates was omitted from the final model, even though it was included in an earlier analysis of solely constituency forces. The omission of this variable was designed to avoid a statistical redundancy between the effects of group party traditions and group support for candidates.

■ A Theory of the Vote in Japan

Figure 10.6 presents a kind of funnel of causality representation of Japanese voting behavior. Those influences most proximate to the voting decision, such as party identifications and party images, and the more short-term influences, such as issues, voting requests, and candidate images, all exert direct effects on the vote. In contrast, the various environmental reinforcement variables, such as group partisan traditions, contextual settings, and values, all exert only indirect effects. In a statistical sense, then, these environmental variables are of secondary importance. In a theoretical sense, however, they are of crucial importance because they enable us to elaborate our model of voting and explain how party images and loyalties develop.

Our analysis of Japanese electoral behavior, as summarized in the figure 10.6 model, presents us with a number of interesting findings, some of which conform to and reinforce the traditional picture of Japanese voting found in both Japanese and American scholarship and some of which challenge or amend this traditional view. These points will become clear as we discuss the contribution of and interaction between our three sets of variables.

The Role of Partisanship Versus Constituency Mobilization

Perhaps one of the most important findings of our work is in reassessing the importance of partisanship in Japanese elections. The view has long been prevalent that partisanship played a rather muted role in voting decisions in Japan because of the findings that large portions of the electorate had weak, unstable, or missing party identifications (Richardson, 1975; Flanagan and McDonald, 1979). One important refinement to this view is that even where party identifications are missing, party images play a very important role in guiding voting decisions.

A focus on party images suggests that we need to broaden our conceptualization of partisanship in Japan and elsewhere. While party identifications require affective ties, party images are based more on cognitive rationales that can exist in the absence of strongly positive affective feelings. Traditional political psychology mainly stressed the role of affect, but it is becoming increasingly clear that affective attitudes are generally *buttressed* by cognitively derived rationales (Nisbet and Ross, 1980). People use information they receive from various sources to develop and test hypotheses about persons and institutions, in our case candidates and parties. As information accumulates, evidence and inference-based rationales supportive of particular attitudes develop. We might argue that cognitive images of political parties and other political objects develop first and therefore precede and contribute to formation of identifications, or in some cases produce changes in existing identifications in a similar causal sequence. For example, accumulated information may gradually convince a voter that a particular party has had several attractive candidates, an impressive leader, a favored policy, or a good service record in one's local constituency. In time, these party images may lead to the development of a positive affective tie to that party, but, in the meantime, these images alone, in conjunction with relative images of other parties, may be enough to guide voting decisions.

While it is logical to assume that cognitive partisanship may in time lead to affective partisanship, what is perhaps most interesting in the Japanese case is the extent to which this progression has apparently not as yet taken place for many voters. Miyake's identification of the negative partisans as an important type in Japan demonstrates that many cognitive partisans hold largely neutral images of the party they regularly support (while disliking other parties). The more critical perceptions that many Japanese have of parties and politics in general and the greater distance at which they hold the political world than, say, Americans necessarily influences the nature of partisanship as we find it in Japan.

While the concept of affective partisans—identifiers in the Michigan terminology—is clearly defined, our notion of cognitive partisans is as yet less precise, because it covers a greater possible range of behavior. As we have noted, the depth and complexity of party images is likely to vary greatly among voters, with those with the least political interest, sophistication, and education tending to have the most fluid, weak, and transitory images. For some cognitive partisans, then, their party images may be little more than running evaluations based on their current pool of perceptions as ever new increments of information are acquired and old information is forgotten.[24] To qualify at a minimal level as cognitive partisans, however, the perceptions and evaluations that dominate the shaping of their party images would have to at least predate the campaign. At the other end of these continua of interest, education, and sophistication, we would expect to find cognitive partisans with very rich and complex party images that act much like affective identifications in anchoring the vote over long periods of time. In those cases the main difference would be that the stable behavior of these cognitive partisans would be more dependent on the stability of the party system than in the case of the identifiers. That is, their voting stability is more dependent on the relative stability of the present parties' policy stances and the absence of any new parties that might appear more attractive. Despite these interesting caveats we conclude with an important

24. This view of party images has much in common with Fiorina's (1981) concept of retrospective partisanship.

modification to the traditional view of Japanese voting behavior. Our finding of the major role party images play suggests that even nonidentifiers in Japan tend to orient themselves to the voting act in terms of parties and party evaluations. Despite the vicissitudes of partisanship in Japan, as chronicled by Miyake in chapter 6, figure 10.6 demonstrates that party loyalties or party images are the most important predictors of vote choice.

A second and related important modification to the traditional view of Japanese electoral behavior emerges from figure 10.6. Previous studies held that electoral campaigns in Japan are almost uniquely candidate-centered. Japan's traditional culture and small, multimember electoral districts have tended to engender parochial, personalistic campaigns dominated by candidate support associations and candidate records and promises concerning local interests rather than party organizations or national issues. Perhaps nowhere in the industrialized world can so plausible a case be made for the importance of local constituency mobilization factors relative to partisanship in influencing voting outcomes. Our findings, however, challenge this view. Despite the great emphasis in the extant Japanese election literature on the importance of local candidate-oriented campaigns, party identification and party image emerge as much more dominating factors in the figure 10.6 model. While the constituency mobilization variables were important, they clearly played a secondary role to psychological partisanship.[25] In this area, then, in place of the traditional view, we find a Japanese voting model that looks a good deal more like the familiar American political psychological paradigm than has been imagined. One source of the domination of partisanship over our constituency mobilization variables is the fact that constituency mobilization apparently occurs mainly within party lines, in the sense that respondents reported exposure mainly to influence communications that favored a candidate from their preferred party. Candidate choices could themselves thus be seen as made under the "umbrella" of a partisan identification or some kind of partisan image. Thus candidate influences, in most cases, tend to reinforce rather than conflict with people's partisan attachments. In the statistical manipulations conducted to produce figure 10.6, the controls entered into the equations for the partisanship vari-

25. A problem of multiple regression analysis is a tendency for inclusive variables to dominate other variables to a degree out of proportion to their real contribution. To ensure that our results were valid, stepwise regressions were run in different ways so as to compensate for the effects of the stronger psychological partisanship variables, and the sequential explanations of variance in the different combinations were compared. In one run, the candidate and campaign variables were introduced first; subsequent addition of the partisanship indicators added 36 percent to explained variance. But when stable identifications, image partisanship, and issue partisanship were entered first, inclusion of candidate and campaign variables added only a further 4 percent in explained variance. Clearly, partisanship is more important than the short-term constituency mobilization variables in explaining parliamentary voting in Japan.

ables obviously reduced some of the impact that might otherwise have been attributed to candidate imagery and constituency mobilization experiences.[26]

A second and more important factor contributing to the dominance of psychological partisanship is the simple fact that substantially more people are oriented toward parties than candidates. For example, table 10.2 demonstrates that party imagery is much more developed than candidate imagery in Japan. Eighty-nine percent of the Japanese voting electorate reported one or more favorable images of some party compared to only 45 percent who reported one or more favorable candidate images. The table also shows that even issue positions, despite being of relatively low self-assessed importance to most voters, are considerably more developed than candidate imagery. Similarly, the overall frequencies of constituency-focused influence communications, while reaching substantial portions of the electorate, are still much thinner than the combined frequencies of party identifications and party imagery. Just over 50 percent of our entire sample had some kind of exposure to candidate campaigns or related group endorsements or social network–based requests.

The reasons behind the richer development of party versus candidate imagery in Japan lie to a marked degree in the nature of communications about politics and related aspects of people's processing of political information. Parties are a frequent topic of the electronic and written communications media, which are widely diffused in Japan and deal with politics on a *regular* and *repetitive* basis. Information about parties is also conveyed across multiple election levels by party and candidate campaign appeals. In contrast, constituency candidates are mainly the subject of informal, verbal communications, which for most people are *intermittent* and for some may occur only at election time. These differences in the regularity with which people are exposed to political information are extremely important. Repetitious information enhances cognitive processing, since it encourages repeated confirmation of rationales and provides even stronger buttressing of attitudes (Fiske and Taylor, 1984). More vivid information, the result of repetition, is more readily remembered and, hence, is more likely to be used.

To a considerable degree, the mass media are highly centralized in Japan and their news coverage deals mainly with national and cosmopolitan information. Many Japanese read only national newspapers (Richardson, 1966, 1988),

26. Treating candidate- and party-related influences and attitudes as competitive variables, as is done here, lacks verisimilitude. The problem has conceptual, measurement, and statistical dimensions. In Japan the vote choice really has two components for many people, and the candidate and party can be essentially separate entities in people's decision making processes where there is intraparty competition. But it is hard using the information normally gathered through survey interviews to determine where people's decisions proceed with two separate elements in mind, where they are fused, or where one dominates the other.

Table 10.2   Multiple Images of
Candidates, Parties, and Multiple Issue
Positions (In Percentages)

Candidate images:	
Two or more images	20
One image	25
No image	56
Party images:	
Two or more images	85
One image	4
No images	11
Issue positions:	
Three or more positions	60
One or two positions	10
No positions	30

Note: Figures are simple response frequencies for all voters. $N = 1,096$. Categories are adjusted to maximally standardize for different numbers of questions in different areas.

whose coverage of local affairs is especially scanty relative to their treatment of national and international news. Television coverage of politics and elections is also centrally administered and focused on national and international politicians and events. Some of the public, slightly over one-third of all newspaper readers (not counting overlapping readerships), do read regional, prefectural, or local newspapers where the news fare is more local in orientation (Asahi Shimbunsha, 1987). (Local newspapers are defined as those whose coverage focuses on a particular small city and surrounding areas. Regional newspapers include such well-known journals as the *Hokkaido Shimbun* and *Chubu Nippon Shimbun*.) Local pages that carry news for each prefecture (and which are different for each prefecture) are also found in all the centralized dailies. But, as far as can be discerned, neither prefectural and local newspapers nor local pages in the national dailies provide extensive coverage of individual candidate's campaigns.[27] The diminished media coverage of individual campaigns is aug-

27. Japanese election constituencies are themselves small. Candidate's campaigns are also often geographically focused within each election district, most typically in rural constituencies. A given prefecture has normally between three or four constituencies, and within each constituency several individual candidate support "territories" may exist. Although the national dailies and regional papers do carry long series of articles on local campaigns, these rarely go beyond brief references to each candidate and his organizational activities. The neglect of candidates in the news media reflects this small size of the relevant areas of candidate activity (and therefore their restricted

mented by the fact that little or no attention is paid by the media to the activities of rank-and-file members of the Diet. The activities of party leaders, cabinet members, and the parties' policy spokesmen in the Diet are reported. But, for a variety of reinforcing reasons, the inner workings of Diet committees and the role of ordinary members of the Diet in initiation of legislation or other legislative functions go largely unnoticed.[28]

In contrast with the abundance and regularity of messages about parties, information about candidates is only received on an intermittent basis by many people. Even though many candidates maintain permanent organizations that have regular meetings, our data show that these efforts involve at best only about one out of every eight voters, namely those who are koenkai members.[29] For the remainder of the electorate, candidates are normally salient mainly at election time or occasionally between elections at public events. Under these conditions of irregular and intermittent exposure, it is unlikely that many people develop sufficient information to support robust attitudes even where they actually favor particular candidates.

Flanagan's analysis in chapter 8 of the nature and impact of media involvement suggests a further way to test the linkage between media exposure and voters' cognitive processing of information. Flanagan demonstrated that media involvement was the key to a variety of differences in overt political participation and other behaviors. People who are more exposed to the media also participate covertly in politics more frequently than other people, in the sense that they actively process more information about politics and have more developed cognitive rationales for their attitudinal dispositions toward politics. Further evidence of this is presented in table 10.3, which shows levels of party image development among persons having different frequencies of media involvement. While we cannot test our general information processing hypothesis across time with currently available data sources, it is clear that cross-sectional data support

---

newsworthiness to broader audiences) and/or the fact that local candidacies are not seen as interesting or legitimate topics for other reasons.

28. Japan's parties almost invariably exercise tight internal discipline within the Diet, with the result that individual member's parliamentary initiatives are virtually unknown outside of the parties themselves. In addition, only meetings of the Lower House Budget Committee, where the most important parliamentary interpellations take place, receive much media attention. As a result, only a handful of prominent party spokesmen actually get a "mention" in the normal news.

29. The figures for actual participation in political groups were even more revealing. Only 3 percent of the population said they "regularly" participated in the activities of political groups, a figure which probably accurately indicates interelection levels of koenkai mobilization. Its plausibility as a true indicator of reality is enhanced by information on participation in political party organizations in other countries, where similar levels of participation are observed (e.g., Shell, 1969).

Table 10.3   Effects of Media Exposure on Party Imagery

Party Imagery	Media Exposure			
	High	Moderate	Low	Very Low
7–8 images	63	50	38	26
1–6 images	32	43	50	49
No images	5	7	12	25
Total	100%	100%	100%	100%
N	(122)	(370)	(439)	(156)

Note: High media exposure—viewed 10 or more TV programs and read 10 or more articles related to 1976 election; moderate media exposure—viewed 3–10 programs and read 3–10 articles; low media exposure—saw fewer than 3 programs and read fewer than 3 articles; very low media exposure—neither saw TV election programs nor read newspaper articles on election.

our interpretation of the communications exposure/attitude development linkage.

We have argued that differences in the regularity and abundance of information about parties as opposed to candidates is an important factor leading to the strength and salience of psychological partisanship in our combined model. In the short-term, constituency factors were not nearly as important, partly because fewer people were exposed to constituency campaigns or had favorable images of candidates than held images of the parties. In addition, constituency campaigns tended to focus on followers of the same party as that of the candidate, which produced some drop-off in the effects of constituency variables when controls for partisanship were introduced. Buttressing these more proximate causes, however, is the simple fact that partisan attitudes were much more developed across the board, which reflects not only the differences in media focus discussed above but also the fact that parties are generally more durable objects than candidates, permitting the development and reinforcement of cognitive images and affective ties over a much longer period of time than is possible in the case of candidates.

Even though most of us have long believed that constituency machines and campaigns are very important in Japan, constituency mobilization variables in the short-term are of fairly modest importance when their effects are compared with those of party identification and party images. Perhaps one problem we have in assessing the significance of constituency mobilization is our time perspective. The real implication of constituency campaigns may not be found in their short-term mobilizing effects but rather in their long-term implications for attitude formation and reinforcement. In this altered frame of reference, it is interesting to observe that party images and loyalties and favorable images of local candidates are intertwined in people's thinking in many ways. Japanese parties historically began as coalitions of politicians and interests having strong local ties, and they remain intimately linked to their local bases today through candidate organizations and informal associational networks. Constituency considerations actually enter people's normal frame of reference when thinking about parties at several points. Answers to different items in our closed question battery on party images showed that feelings that specific parties "have good candidates" or "represented local interests" were highly correlated with other components of imagery that had an exclusively partisan focus. Thus, the national and local dimensions of party imagery are tightly integrated, such that the local dimensions are a constituent part of the voter's mental pictures of parties. Constituency mobilization variables, then, clearly play an important role in the development and nurturing of party images.[30]

The Role of Environmental Reinforcement

Up to this point, it appears that the most important paths to vote choice lead through partisanship. Even constituency mobilization factors seem to play a larger role through developing and reinforcing partisan orientations than in effecting deviations from partisan preferences. The same of course is true for our environmental variables—group partisan traditions, occupational and residential contextual influences and cultural values. The usefulness of adding these variables into our model is that they enable us to better understand the processes through which party ties and images are nurtured.

Social settings, social groups, and group process provide the context in which political information is transmitted and political attitudes are acquired.

30. Clearly, if direct paths between the constituency mobilization and partisanship variables had been entered into the equation for the figure 10.6 model, highly significant path coefficients would have been found. For example, correlations of .45 were found between candidate images and party images and .40 between candidate images and stable party identifications. There are, however, unanswerable questions about the directions of causal interactions here. Constituency mobilization and influence communications may accumulate over several elections to stimulate the development of national party psychological ties and imagery for many voters and in single elections surely play a role for many in reinforcing partisanship. But a reverse process in which party loyalties influence candidate attitudes is also likely, just as classic American electoral behavior theory would postulate. The relationship, therefore, plausibly moves in both directions at different points in time, and depends on combinations of individual experiences and attitudes such as the saliency of different levels of politics, intensity of partisan attachment, and the character of candidates in different elections. A cross-time analysis of these relationships is needed to fully determine directionality in the interactions between psychological partisanship and constituency mobilization. For this reason, there are no arrows designating directional relationship between candidate and partisan attitudes in the causal model presented here.

The mobilization of the electorate through candidates' campaigns and social network requests is a repeated activity, even though it is an activity that is fairly intermittent relative to the constancy of the media's treatment of party politics. The fact that intimate social settings are involved implies unusually high levels of credibility relative to more remote sources of information, while the repetitive nature of group support adds some dimension of vividness to information from these sources. As information sources, people's group environments have a lot to offer in the way of salient and credible information, which can buttress information received from unmediated sources or even dominate the messages received from unmediated sources.

Group processes have additional implications above and beyond simply providing credible, vivid information. A variety of group processes encourage conformity, and these processes add special significance to information received from groups. Since we have shown that efforts to mobilize the vote through groups take place more often than not between partisans of the same party, it is logical that mobilization effects build up over time in the form of group climates favoring particular parties. The *group processes* that encourage conformity—representation of interests, economic dependence, reference group orientations, community norms, and face-to-face small group pressures—in turn give these traditions a special appeal. There are payoffs for conforming to group decisions or climates of opinion. This is precisely the chain of events reflected in our information on the effects on partisanship of partisan traditions within both primary and secondary groups in Japan, as was demonstrated both in Flanagan's chapter 4 and earlier in this chapter.

These socially anchored partisan climates in turn are nurtured by, but extend beyond, the effects of intermittent constituency mobilization in Japan (see again figures 10.4b and 10.5b). From the short-term perspective of a single election campaign, we found that no more than a third of the Japanese electorate perceived their organizations or informal small groups as supporting a particular candidate. This suggests that the campaign mobilization effects of group processes are important but limited in their reach, although there may be more unreported or unconscious group mobilization occurring than our data were able to uncover. In a broader sense, however, the family, community, work place, and other principal group involvements constitute the primary contexts of political socialization. Given the more neutral and restricted role of the media in Japan, the high levels of involvement in and dependency on formal and informal groups, and the high levels of conformity to group partisan preferences as documented in chapters 4 and 5, we would conclude that group processes are inextricably bound up with the development of party images and partisan support. Still, the actual number of Japanese consciously affected by political cues from social groups was much lower than we had expected. Traditional views of Japanese electoral processes appear to have been somewhat erroneous, or else overtaken by social change.

Groups, then, play important roles in attitude formation and voting behavior in Japan. Their informational inputs mix with those from other sources. As we have seen, familiar and important groups provide credible information that is used in the development of the cognitive rationales which support different attitudes (Fiske and Taylor, 1984). In some cases, groups may provide the initial stimulus by which a partisan tie is formed, and information from the mass media is subsequently used to develop a cognitive rationale to support that affiliation. However, information processing does not depend on the unmediated information sources provided by the modern media alone. Rather, group mediated information is mixed with media and other information sources to form lasting images of particular parties. Party images in turn form the rationale that supports affective loyalties.

The implications for electoral behavior and related attitude development of the enormous social change that occurred in Japan during the 1960s and 1970s must be considered again briefly. A variety of constituency influence communications processes still existed in Japan in the mid-1970s according to our findings, as they also do today (Akarui Senkyo Suishin Kyokai, 1986). Likewise, organized groups endorsed parties or provided a setting for informal political communications about candidates and political parties, which were tapped in people's replies to questions about group partisan tendencies in the JABISS research effort and shown to be significant in our analysis. Social context remains important in Japan.

Nevertheless, both short-term and long-term parochial influences have probably been becoming less relevant to many Japanese throughout the 1970s, 1980s, and beyond than they had been in earlier years. Increasingly the effects of local constituency mobilization and group reinforcement have become intermingled with the effects of mass media information and other cosmopolitanizing influences. Greater media penetration of the entire nation has been accompanied in critical degrees by regional industrialization, a process which has pulled farmers from their fields and lured housewives from their homes. This social mobility has had the effect of removing many people from direct contact with traditional political mobilization channels or altering the role played by these information sources in their overall outlooks toward politics. It is becoming increasingly unlikely that Japanese voters will be located within sets of social networks that not only have a uniform partisan preference but also completely shield and isolate them from all conflicting partisan cues. The growing exposure of the Japanese voter to a variety of conflicting partisan messages is undoubtedly increasing his or her autonomy in picking and choosing which to credit. Although Japan probably remains a more parochially organized society than many (see again chapter 9), the forces of change are taking their toll.

■ The 1976 Election in the Context of Time

This study of Japanese voting behavior has focused primarily on one point in time, the 1976 election of the House of Representatives. In some circumstances, electoral behavior in one election could be so idiosyncratic that a study of its genesis and component attitudes and processes would not be representative of broader patterns in electoral motivation. This is not the case in Japan for a substantial number of reasons, some of which were outlined in chapter 1 and others of which will be reviewed here.

In a summary of the elements of political continuity or change that could affect voting behavior, it is useful to distinguish between structural parameters and more transient aspects of politics. Most of our focus will be on structural parameters of politics. The implications of more transient election issues and context will also be considered, although they are seen as less important by and large in the period under consideration. We will also consider both factors that affect continuities in the *direction* of the vote as well as those influencing underlying voting *motivations*. Overall, influences affecting the direction of the vote could also have something to do with motivations. But these two are also separable in many instances. We will see that by and large the factors affecting the direction of people's preferences and the causal elements reflected in behavioral motivations are both very stable.

The structural parameters that affected Japanese voting behavior in 1976 have in several ways remained remarkably stable since then and essentially across the entire post–World War II period. First, the electoral arrangements for selection of members of the House of Representatives have themselves been unchanged, with only minor exceptions in the form of the creation of new districts in large cities. These election rules are believed to be of profound importance to Japanese voting behavior, particularly for the role of constituency mobilization in voting behavior. This institutional parameter, consisting of multimember districts without a proportional rule for selection of winners, has remained unchanged throughout the postwar era, despite many discussions and proposals in the Diet and party circles for reform.

Second, the party system itself has remained essentially the same since 1976, although the small New Liberal Club, which split off from the LDP in that year, recently disbanded, with its members returning to the LDP fold. Otherwise, the main party alternatives were much the same as they had been from the late 1960s forward. Parallel to this stability in the parties themselves, there was no drastic change in the long-term partisan alignments of major organizations. This stability in party alternatives and organizational alignments is very important, because ongoing channels of political mobilization were generally not challenged by new party formations nor use of new supplementary organizations to assist in "gathering" the vote after 1976. Unlike the case in the 1960s and early 1970s, when several new channels of political mobilization were developed, the organizational infrastructure of voting remained highly stable in later years.

What changes have occurred are changes of degree more than of kind. Some shifts occurred in the importance of particular groups that normally mobilize support, as both the agricultural cooperatives and labor unions experienced declines in strength by the mid-1980s. But even if these declines meant lower levels of organizational support for parties affiliated with these groups in some districts, the group-party ties themselves remained constant (except in the 1989 House of Councillors election as will be noted in chapter 11).[31] Stability in the party system and interest group infrastructure is probably more important for understanding the directionality of people's voting preferences. But the nature of party alternatives and group support patterns, particularly whether or not they are constant, is also important to the formation and stability of party loyalties.

A third factor enhancing the stability of electoral patterns since 1976 are demographic trends. Rapid shifts in urbanization and occupation were associated with a destabilization of electoral politics from the 1960s to mid-1970s. These changes slowed as the population and occupation distributions became more stable in the late 1970s and 1980s. Demographic change has been seen by many as a cause of declining conservative support in the 1950s and 1960s. A high rate of population mobility from agricultural to industrial employment and from rural to urban areas was accompanied by massive shifts in support away from the "establishment" parties in favor of smaller center and left parties in both urban constituencies and in "suburban" constituencies on the periphery of the major urban centers. In this overall process, extreme social mobility also is believed to have produced "social isolates," persons who lacked social contacts in their new urban environment. Many of these people were probably absorbed politically by the Clean Government and Communist parties.

31. A major realignment in the union movement was underway at the time of writing, as noted in chapter 2, but the long-term significance and impact of the movement's unification under Rengo are still unclear.

The first oil crisis in 1973 and subsequent slowing down of economic growth, combined with the introduction of the rigorous regulation of industrial pollution, began to dampen urban growth in the 1970s and early 1980s. Other factors, such as conscious local government luring of industry and private enterprise's search for cheaper labor in small towns and rural communities, also contributed to these changes in the pace of large city growth. According to census and election register statistics, further population increases slowed down dramatically in the big cities in the late 1970s and 1980s. Constituencies in the older parts of Tokyo, Osaka, Kyoto, and Nagoya actually lost voters, while the suburban fringe continued to expand, albeit much more slowly than in the previous decades. Simultaneously, quite a few medium-sized local cities that are also prefectural seats of government have begun to grow at a rapid pace, even though their growth in no instances has been as dramatic as that experienced in some metropolitan areas in the 1960s. Occupational mobility also began to slow down somewhat after 1980, as can be seen by comparing tables 2.3 and 2.9 in chapter 2. In most cases, it took a fifteen-year period from 1970 to 1985 to match the magnitude of occupational shifts that took place in the 1960s.

The slowdown of population movement and related changes had several kinds of consequences. Partisan tendencies in organized groups and related details pertaining to the "matrix" patterns of social structure support for parties can be expected to have remained largely constant since the JABISS survey. As shown by Watanuki, the decline in geographical and occupational mobility was also a factor contributing to a halt in the decline of support for the Liberal Democrats, as there were fewer social isolates to be attracted to the Clean Government and Communist parties or to the newer splinter parties, the New Liberal Club and Social Democratic Federation. These latter very small parties have depended more on a popular image to attract floating voters and, unlike all the other parties, have lacked any significant organized interest group support to provide bases for electoral mobilization. The slower pace of change since the mid-1970s has proven to be an uncongenial environment for these splinter parties, leading to the disbanding of the NLC after the 1986 election and the failure of the SDF as of yet to attract even 1 percent of the total national vote.

A final factor bolstering stability since 1976 of the electoral patterns presented here has been the Japanese economy, which has fared fairly well over the past decade. Even though there have been ups and downs, the economic record in Japan has been remarkably better than that in other industrialized countries. Annual real growth since the mid-1970s has averaged between 3 and 5 percent annually, inflation has been restrained to single digits, and unemployment has been only a modest 2 percent. Even *yendaka*, the rise in the value of the

Japanese yen relative to the U.S. dollar, has not slowed the economy down significantly, according to the very latest statistics, although the long-term effects of an expensive currency remain to be seen. We have not seen economic conditions as a major variable in our research in this book. It is important to realize that the conditions under which our attention was *not* drawn to economic issues, or other effects of the economy on voting, were themselves plausibly the product of stable times.

The stability of the environmental parameters that affect the vote is paralleled by the continuity observable in various indicators of political motivations. One of the most prominent of these is the long-standing Komei Senkyo Renmei–Akarui Senkyo Suishin Kyokai series on the role of "candidate" versus "party" in House of Representatives' voting choices. Table 1.4 in the introductory chapter, it will be remembered, demonstrated a weak, long-term trend up to the early 1970s by which "party" had slowly come to surpass "candidate" as the rationale for choice among a plurality of Japanese voters. That table also shows, however, a reversal of that trend in the 1970s, followed by a more gradual resumption of a growing emphasis on party in the 1980s. As a result, we find little long-term change since the early 1970s. Thirty-eight percent of the voters in 1972 said they preferred "candidate" compared to 39 and 37 percent in 1986 and 1990,respectively. Conversely, 48 percent relied more on party in 1972 compared to 49 and 51 percent in the 1986 and 1990 elections. Similar patterns of continuity could be seen in other indicators within the KSR-ASSK series, specifically with regard to the relative frequencies of different kinds of influence communications and constituency mobilization activities discussed in chapter 9. Relatedly, an analysis of the 1983 House of Representatives election (Watanuki, et al., 1986) showed no significant variations from the findings reported here with regard to the basic political motivations and influences that lie behind voting decisions in Japan.

Although more than a decade has passed since the JABISS study was fielded, major aspects of the Japanese electoral landscape and major voting motivations have, up through the 1990 HR election, remained generally stable and constant. Stability has not been, however, the complete story. Some aspects of voting in Japan have changed. But, on the average, what changes have occurred have been fairly modest and more relevant for the directions of preferences than for their underlying motivational structure. The year 1976 was the nadir of Liberal Democratic Party success in lower house elections in Japan. Since that time the Liberal Democratic Party has recouped support somewhat, as is shown in both the results of newspaper polling efforts and election outcomes. According to party support data from the monthly opinion polls conducted by the Jiji Press averaged on an annual basis, support for the Liberal Democrats declined from

40 percent in 1964 to just 25 percent in 1974 and 1976. After that low point, however, the Liberal Democrats climbed to nearly 50 percent by 1986.[32]

As is well known, the Liberal Democratic Party generally did better at the ballot box in the lower house elections between 1976 and 1990, after gaining only 42 percent of the vote in 1976. Chapter 1 notes that the long-term decline in conservative strength across the 1950s and 1960s was checked by forces that were already set in motion by 1976. Thus the unusually low LDP vote in that year was mainly attributable to a short-term media effect occasioned by the Lockheed scandal, as discussed in chapter 8. Since then, the LDP vote in HR elections has fluctuated within a narrow range of three to four percentage points, as can be seen in table 10.4. Thus some change occurred and must be acknowledged. Nevertheless, these voting trends in Japan still look remarkably stable viewed from the perspective of either the recent volatility of the vote in some European countries or the electoral fluidity in Japan in some constituencies during the years of high population mobility and related party fragmentation (Richardson, 1977; Flanagan, 1980). Clearly, if we exclude for the moment consideration of the 1989 upper house election (see chapter 11), the long-term downward trend in conservative support appears to have been firmly arrested. Indeed, if we look only at the HR elections reported in table 10.4, Japanese voting behavior seems to have entered a period of minor fluctuations around a basic pattern of remarkable stability.

Despite considerable evidence indicative of stable voting motivations and electoral results, all elections were not alike between 1976 and 1986. Votes and seats both fluctuated somewhat, with seats in the House of Representatives being the more volatile of the two as the result of Japan's electoral system's vulnerability to small movements around the margin between winning and losing. A movement of 1 percent or less in the vote for a particular candidate can determine a win or a loss, which means that slight movements in the popular vote are magnified in seat distributions. Issues also varied in the different elections, and they are usually seen as underlying the relatively modest variations that can be observed in the vote. Corruption within the ruling party was the dominant issue in 1983 as it was in 1976. In 1979, one of the main issues was a proposed consumption tax increase, which worked against the ruling party. In 1980 this issue was absent and voting may have been influenced by a nonissue event, the death of Prime Minister Ohira, which reputedly produced a "sympathy vote" for the conservatives. In 1980 the prospect of a coalition government between the different opposition parties, a possibility introduced by the opposition parties themselves, may also have affected voting, since this raised the

32. For similar figures see Flanagan, 1984. Post-1986 fluctuations in LDP support are noted in chapter 11.

Table 10.4   Number and Percentage of Party Votes in General Elections,
1976–90

Party	1976	1979	1980	1983	1986	1990
LDP	23,653	24,084	28,262	25,982	29,875	30,315
	(42)	(45)	(48)	(46)	(49)	(46)
JSP	11,713	10,643	11,400	11,065	10,413	16,025
	(21)	(20)	(19)	(19)	(17)	(24)
CGP	6,177	5,282	5,329	5,745	5,701	5,243
	(10)	(10)	(9)	(10)	(9)	(8)
JCP	5,878	5,625	5,803	5,302	5,313	5,227
	(10)	(10)	(10)	(9)	(9)	(8)
DSP	3,554	3,663	3,896	4,129	3,896	3,179
	(6)	(7)	(7)	(7)	(6)	(5)
NLC	2,363	1,631	1,766	1,341	1,115	—
	(4)	(3)	(3)	(2)	(2)	
Others/independent	3,272	3,078	2,567	3,221	4,136	5,715
	(6)	(6)	(4)	(6)	(7)	(9)
Total	56,612	54,010	59,028	56,779	60,449	65,704
	(100)	(100)	(100)	(100)	(100)	(100)

Source: Jijisho Senkyobu (1987).

Note: Raw figures are in 1,000 persons; figures in parentheses are percentages.

issue of the opposition camp's ability to govern. Finally, the personal popularity of Prime Minister Nakasone may have been an issue in the 1986 election, slightly increasing the LDP's vote total.

Aside from these short-term issue considerations, most of the major issues in elections up until 1989 have not been altogether different from those present in 1976 or even preceding years. Although the significance of specific election issues has always been dramatized by the media, in most cases these issues probably failed to capture the attention of most voters in a way that altered their voting behavior. For this reason, the issue environment, like other aspects of Japanese elections between 1976 and 1986, exhibited a pattern of minor variations amidst a pattern of great stability.

Nevertheless, one aspect of the saliency of different issues in different elections highlights a shortcoming of cross-sectional analysis, including that reported in this book. According to some views of voting in Japan, the prominence of specific issues in some campaigns contributes to a waxing and waning of electoral participation by a pool of "floating" voters, whose participation tends to favor the LDP. According to this hypothesis, issues that worked against the Liberal Democrats, like corruption and proposed tax increases, led to abstentions in 1976, 1979, and 1983 by some marginal voters who in more favorable circumstances could have been mobilized to vote LDP. In contrast, Ohira's death in 1980 and Nakasone's popularity in 1986 are believed to have motivated people who are weakly supportive of the ruling party or marginally connected to conservative organizational networks to turn out to the polls and vote. An organizational mobilization hypothesis is favored by some to explain this phenomenon, because these two highly successful elections for the LDP in 1980 and 1986 are Japan's only postwar *double elections,* where the lower house election is timed to coincide with the regularly scheduled upper house election. It is believed that these double elections favored the LDP because more interest groups and LDP candidates' machines were activated to mobilize the vote. A marginal voter who was brought to the polls by one LDP candidate's machine was likely to vote for LDP candidates in other races as well.

The floating Liberal Democratic voter hypothesis cannot be tested definitively with the JABISS data, since they pertain only to one election. Recent aggregate data findings (Campbell, 1987), which demonstrate greater stability in party vote as a share of the total electorate than as a share of the actual voters who turned out in specific elections, offer better insight than a cross-sectional analysis into the floating voter idea. Miyake's category of uninformed partisans constitutes a likely source of behavior fitting the floating voter model. But we are limited in the extent to which past behavior can be credibly analyzed using cross-sectional data, and we have refrained from pursuing this point further for this reason.

One of the major conclusions of this book has been that partisanship is the strongest predictor of the vote in Japan. This may seem like a rather startling finding given the fact that only 47 percent of our sample were found to support the same party across a two-to-four week period. Moreover, we have found from chapter 6 and table 10.1 above that not all of these "stable partisans" have positive affective attachments to their supported party. Rather, than discounting the role of partisanship in anchoring the Japanese vote, however, these findings led us to broaden the conceptualization of partisanship. Both in chapter 6 and herein we have viewed partisanship in Japan as a multidimensional concept. The question we have asked ourselves is, Can party images anchor the vote without a positive affective component? We believe the answer to that question is yes, and for that reason we have introduced the concept of negative partisans and the more inclusive concept of cognitive partisans to conceptualize what we believe to be taking place. While affective partisans, in the traditional sense ascribed to the term *party identifiers,* may only be a minority of the Japanese electorate, we have found that almost 90 percent of the voting public have some images of the parties. Moreover, we believe that most of the nonidentifiers holding party images can be classified as cognitive partisans, many of whom are likely to have rather stable images of one or more parties that function much like identifications in anchoring their voting behavior.

In one sense we have not made a very radical statement, because partisanship may simply be viewed as the psychological *response* to all the other forces and influences we have studied—social structure, social contexts, value orientations, the socializing and mobilizing influences of organizations and networks, the processing of media information, issue preferences and issue salience, and so forth. Ultimately the decision must come down to which candidate of which party. It is nearly impossible to make this kind of decision without developing some images of one or more parties. Given the relative stability of the party system and electoral context in Japan, it is logical to expect that over time these party images have become more informed, differentiated, and durable. While there may be special reasons why more cognitive partisans have not as yet developed into affective partisans in the Japanese context, we believe that for most of those that we have labeled as cognitive partisans, their evaluative images and perceptions of the party they regularly vote for are not just ephemeral but rather become an important rationale in justifying their voting decisions. So while a respondent's party images might change if the party system were restructured or if their principal social environments were to change dramatically in partisan orientation, at least from a mid-term perspective, these factors tend to be relatively stable for most Japanese. What is new, then, is our finding that partisanship, in some form, is relevant to the great majority of Japanese voters.

Turning to an assessment of short-term influences, we have also found that issues move a few voters, but not as commonly as they do in the United States. For example, in Japan we typically do not find deviations from identifications in response to short-term issues, a pattern which commonly occurs in America. Our evidence, then supports the long-held view by a number of Japanese scholars that issue voting is not particularly pronounced in Japan. The first of two exceptions here, of course, is the set of 1950s cultural politics issues that continued to predict electoral decisions (despite their declining salience) due to their important early role in shaping the postwar party system and voter alignments. The second is the overwhelming constellation of short-term forces that upset nearly a half-century of stable voting patterns in the 1989 upper house election, as will be discussed in chapter 11.

In a similar vein, media effects were shown to be fairly subdued in the Japanese context, which accords with our understanding of the limited role they are permitted to play in Japan's election campaigns. Still, significant effects could be identified and it appears that the LDP's roughly 5 percent dip in the

1976 election below "normal" levels of support typically achieved across the 1967 to 1986 period can be largely attributed to the media's agenda-setting function in the context of the Lockheed scandal. On an even larger scale, the media were the source of much of the information that produced deviating votes in 1989.

Our evidence also demonstrates that voting in response to a candidate image, or as a result of communications associated with candidates' efforts to mobilize the constituency vote, is an important pattern in Japan. Again this conforms with the traditional folklore regarding Japanese elections, but our conclusions were based on the most thorough documentation of constituency mobilization and environmental reinforcement ever attempted in Japan. In contrast to the traditional view, however, we have found that while constituency influences during the campaign certainly play an important mobilization role that may well determine the ruling party's margin of victory, they do not play a very important "decision" or "conversion" role, at least in the short-term. Rather than inducing deviations from partisanship, constituency mobilization influences tend to act over both the short and the long term as a confirming and reinforcing element in developing and buttressing party images and loyalties.

Long-term forces in Japanese society and culture, in the form of the partisan tendencies embedded in occupational, residential, organizational and small-group settings, and a traditional-modern value cleavage, are the Japanese equivalents of the social cleavages so prominent in European political sociology and have served to shape and sustain partisan ties to a degree that overshadows parental influences. But in the final analysis, partisanship drives the vote in Japan exactly as it has often been asserted to do in other industrialized societies. Indeed, we might conclude that so long as the voting decision requires a choice between different parties, partisanship—however conceptualized and measured—will always yield the strongest predictions of vote choice. What is different about Japanese behavior is how fragile and unstable these partisan attitudes appear to be when the individual moves from a reinforcing to a conflicting social environment. This increases the importance of understanding the contexts in which individuals shape their partisan attitudes and make their voting decisions in Japan.

The role played by partisan versus candidate attitudes is also different in Japan. Both party loyalties and imagery are more important in Japan than they are in American presidential elections, where responses to highly salient presidential candidates dominate voting according to recent analyses. Japan is more like Europe, where party rather than candidate image constitutes the major element in voting. In the European case, however, the social group forces that buttress and structure party loyalties have in the past been defined by social cleavages that divide the population into almost hereditary social contexts that remain rather stable throughout the individual's life. In Japan social group forces are not defined by ethnic, religious, or even class divisions, but within the matrices formed by the intersections of multiple demographic and contextual variables. Therefore, a movement from one city, neighborhood, or company to another can change the partisan coloration of one's social networks, and hence one's partisanship, even without a significant change in class or income. Nevertheless, these social contexts tend to be rather stable and hence these social matrices in Japan can play a similar anchoring role to that traditionally performed by social group cleavages in Europe.

This book has reported findings on Japanese electoral behavior during a period of relative social, economic, and political calm. The fact that our research deals with electoral behavior at the end of two decades of massive change and at the beginning of a more quiescent period in Japanese social development is significant in that we have been looking at the end products of change rather than a continuously fluid phenomenon. Whether the future promises the same degree of tranquility for Japanese electoral politics is unclear. Thinking of the 1990s, there are several factors that were absent in the 1970s but now must be taken into consideration. First of all, we must pay more attention to the effects of international factors that could influence voting, the foremost of which are the implications of trade conflicts between Japan and other industrialized economies. Domestically, but also linked with international events and trends, the performance of the Japanese economy will be a key factor for future electoral stability. Some danger signs are already present as a result of dislocations in some industrial sectors. Short-term responses to these problems in the form of pump-priming public works expenditures bear the promise of continued and possibly expanded fiscal deficits, themselves a constraint to expansion of government welfare support or other kinds of responses to population needs in a crowded, environmentally fragile, rapidly aging "post-industrial" society.

As noted above, issue attitudes have played a fairly restrained role in the vote in the relatively quiescent 1970s and 1980s. Future elections could witness a much greater impact from issue opinions and a greater volatility in electoral outcomes as a result. However, the absence of a credible alternative party or party coalition to take charge of the government in an economic crisis has so far mitigated against the possibility that a major economic downturn would significantly penalize the ruling party at the polls. Even the socialist success in the 1989 Councillors election was followed by intraparty disagreements and opposition camp disagreements that did not bode well for the long-term credibility of these parties to perform a governing role. A more likely possibility is that under conditions of declining resources or constraints on resources, what Richard Rose and Guy Peters (1978) have called "political bankruptcy" (that is, heightened political apathy and the lowering of political legitimacy) could occur. Such an event could obviously affect the mix of psychological forces described in this volume by weakening party identifications and intensifying the already appreciable negative component in party imagery.

How long the present electoral system of multiple seats and limited, nontransferable candidate voting will be continued remains to be seen. Voices favoring reform are numerous, in part because of the extreme unrepresentativeness of the present system. Overrepresentativeness has reached a proportion of 4.4:1 between the rural and urban vote in the most extreme examples.[33] This distortion will likely not last indefinitely. Two radical possibilities under discussion are the introduction of a single-member constituency system with increased seats for urban areas or proportional representation similar to the system used in the House of Councillors national constituency races since 1983. Any politically feasible alternative to the present system is likely to combine these two systems to fill different proportions of the lower house seats, and the way that balance is set will likely affect the balance of party power and perhaps also influence the political psychology of the vote in ways different from the profile presented in this book. The possibility of such changes makes the future uncertain.

From a comparative perspective, our multidimensional conceptualization of partisanship and our discovery that party images are central to psychological partisanship have important implications for political behavior research beyond Japan. Party identification has long been a suspect variable in comparative political behavior studies. Our broadening of the concept of partisanship by introducing the notions of cognitive, "image," and negative partisans as "deviant" but meaningful psychological responses that anchor vote choice enhances the relevance of psychological approaches to voting research in non-American settings and fits well with new developments in social cognition scholarship. Thus, for instance, our finding that party images operate as an independent influence on how people vote is a significant finding in its own right, given the dominant American research tradition that has viewed party identification as the main partisan component of political behavior.

For political sociology, we offer a somewhat different perspective from the traditionally favored cleavage hypotheses on the linkage between social structure and the vote. Persuaded that social cleavages are the main link between

33. In the fifth Hyogo district, the most "rural" or least populous of the contemporary cases, the mean number of voters per seat is 81,000. In Chiba's fourth district the equivalent figure is 360,000.

society and politics, political sociology has often overlooked the fact that elite coalitions and resultant patterns of mobilization are the key that determines which group loyalties are activated in politics and which group interests are ascendant on the political stage. Our view that the relevant socializing environments in Japan are defined by matrices of demographic and contextual variables rather than social cleavages focuses one's attention on the voter's immediate environment and patterns of social interaction rather than on latent social group identifications. Our focus on constituency mobilization, which depends on organizational and small group networks, also shifts political sociology's concerns away from macrostructure to consider how microsociety is "used" in the midst of election campaigns. The importance demonstrated herein of these factors in Japanese electoral behavior should help clarify sociological theory, especially insomuch as the latter is itself in the midst of extensive adjustments to the effects of social change on traditional patterns of group support.

Finally, our understanding of the importance of value cleavages and new theoretical insights into the origins and timing of the emergence of these cleavages in Japan also contribute to comparative theory. What is of interest in the Japanese case is the extent to which, since the early postwar years, basic social value orientations have transcended class and other potential social group cleavages in shaping the voters' perceptions of political issues and predisposing them to favor a left or right ideological perspective. In turn, this early deviant appearance of a partisan value cleavage in Japan sheds light on the causes and timing of the later rise of a nearly identical value cleavage in other advanced industrial democracies.

Eleven ■ The Changing Japanese Voter
and the 1989 and 1990 Elections

SCOTT C. FLANAGAN

Having been presented our analysis and model of Japanese voting behavior, the reader may now ask how enduring these parameters and patterns of behavior are likely to be. This question demands all the more urgent a response in light of the July 23, 1989, upper house and February 18, 1990, lower house elections in Japan. These election results would seem to challenge our emphasis in chapter 10 and elsewhere on the stability of electoral outcomes in Japan over the last two decades. Does the 1989 House of Councillors (HC) election represent a turning point, bringing to an end two decades of stability and signaling the beginning of a new period of realignment? If so, will these changes alter or invalidate some aspects of our model? This chapter will begin by reviewing our findings to see what light they shed on how voting behavior is changing in Japan. We will then apply the insights derived from this review of the changing and enduring, stabilizing and destabilizing aspects of voting behavior to explain the divergent outcomes in Japan's two most recent general elections. The marked contrast in outcomes between these two elections, which were held a mere seven months apart, will further challenge our analysis and redirect our attention to the theme, raised in chapter 1, of the juxtaposition of elements of stability and volatility in Japanese voting behavior.

The second of these two elections, the 1990 House of Representatives (HR) election, seems to reaffirm the pattern of stability in party vote shares that set in during the 1970s. Even during the LDP's first two decades in power, when it was continuously losing support at the polls, the interelection volatility rates in its vote shares were very low. Thus, if we average the change in the LDP vote share between each pair of succeeding elections across the six HR elections from the late 1950s to the early 1970s, we find a mean interelection volatility rate of 2.2 percentage points. Beginning in the mid-1970s when the LDP vote decline

I would like to express my thanks to Joji Watanuki, Bradley Richardson, and Ichiro Miyake for supplying much of the data on which this analysis was based and for their useful comments on earlier versions of this chapter.

leveled off, we entered a period of greater long-term stability in the party vote distribution but somewhat higher levels of fluctuation from election to election. Across the six HR elections from the early 1970s up through the 1986 election, the corresponding volatility rate was 3.4. By Western standards, this is still a fairly low rate of shift in popular support. For example, the Republican Party's volatility rate in its vote share across successive American presidential races between 1968 and 1988 was 9.1.[1] In the 1990 HR election the LDP vote fell by nearly 3.3 percent below its 1986 level, placing that decline slightly under the party's average interelection volatility rate over the last two decades. Moreover, as shown in table 11.1, the ruling party's 46 percent share of the vote in 1990 placed it squarely in the middle between its 44 percent average over the three HR elections in the 1970s and its 48 percent average over the three elections in the 1980s.

This pattern of apparent continued stability, however, is sharply challenged by the 1989 upper house election results. On the surface, at least, the 1989 House of Councillors election appears to present a major departure from previous voting patterns. Half of the upper house seats are elected every three years, with fifty seats selected by a vote cast for a party and distributed on a proportional representation (PR) basis, and seventy-six seats elected by a second vote cast for local candidates in forty-seven districts. As shown in table 11.1, over the last three decades, the LDP has been gradually losing ground in the PR or national constituency race and more or less holding its own in the local constituency race.[2] The ruling party's precipitous decline in the 1989 HC election, gaining only 27 percent of the vote compared to 35 percent for the JSP in the PR race and 31 percent compared to a combined JSP and Rengo vote of 33 percent in the local district races, represents a dramatic divergence from past voting patterns.[3]

1. The American presidential elections are of course more volatile than the U.S. congressional elections. Even in the case of the U.S. House of Representatives elections, however, the comparable Republican Party volatility rate for presidential election years between 1964 and 1984 was still 4.5. These rates were computed from data reported in the United States Statistical Abstracts.

2. The districts in the local constituency race are coterminous with Japan's forty-seven prefectures, with twenty-six electing one seat, fifteen two seats, four filling three seats and two choosing four seats every three years. Prior to 1983 the voter's other ballot was cast for one of the candidates running in a single countrywide national constituency, with the top fifty vote-getters declared winners. Beginning in 1983 the national constituency was changed to a PR constituency with voters casting their ballots for parties and seats distributed among the party lists on a proportional representation basis.

3. As substantial as these LDP losses in its party vote shares were, they were not even half as great as the party's seat losses. The HC electoral system that has protected the ruling party from an erosion of popular support for years finally turned on the party. The party's share of the contested seats fell from 59 percent in the 1986 election to only 30 percent in 1989. The largest losses were in

Table 11.1 Average Popular Vote Shares by Party in Upper (HC) and Lower (HR) House Elections by Time Period (In Percentages)

	1950s	1960s	1970s	1980s	1989/90
LDP					
HC nat/PR race[a]	40	47	42	39	27
HC local districts	50	45	41	44	31
N of elections	(2)	(3)	(3)	(3)	(1)
Lower house	61	52	44	48	46
N of elections	(2)	(4)	(3)	(3)	(1)
JSP					
HC nat/PR RACE	28	23	18	16	35
HC local districts	36	32	28	23	33[b]
Lower house	31	26	21	19	24
Minor parties (DSP, CGP, JCP)					
HC nat/PR race	2	23	28	29	23
HC local districts	4	18	23	22	17
Lower house	2	16	27	26	21
Other/independents					
HC nat/PR race	29	7	12	16	15
HC local districts	10	5	8	11	19
Lower house	6	5	8	8	9

Notes: The numbers in parentheses refer to the number of elections in the decade over which the party vote was averaged. We begin with 1955, so only two HC and HR elections are included in that decade average. The 1980s HC election averages include only the three elections of 1980, 1983, and 1986. The minor party vote includes only votes for the DSP, CGP, or JCP; votes for other minor parties are included in the other/independent category.

[a] Beginning with the 1983 election, the National Constituency race was changed from individual candidate voting in a single nationwide district to party voting using a proportional representation method of allocating seats.

[b] The JSP 1989 HC local district vote includes the vote for Rengo candidates.

---

the local constituency races, and, indeed, the party's excessive seat losses were almost entirely attributable to the more rural twenty-six one-seat prefectural districts, where the party fell from twenty-five seats won out of the twenty-six in 1986 to only three seats in 1989. The combination of the decline in LDP support combined with the emergence of virtually all-opposition party coalitions behind Rengo or JSP candidates shifted the balance just enough to elect opposition candidates in virtually all of these winner-take-all districts.

Rengo is the Japan Trade Union Confederation (Nihon Rodokumiai Sorengokai) that largely succeeded in unifying the private-sector unions in 1987 and incorporating the public-sector unions by the end of 1989 (see chapter 2).

Once again, looking at interelection volatility rates in the LDP percentage share of the vote, we find average rates of 1.8 for the national constituency and 2.8 for the local constituency races across the six HC elections from the late 1950s to the early 1970s. During the period of greater long-term stability but higher short-term fluctuations, beginning in the mid-1970s up through the 1986 election, we find average volatility rates of 6.5 and 1.6, respectively, across the five national (PR) and local constituency contests. The higher levels of volatility in the national or PR constituency races suggests that this race is more susceptible to short-term ups and downs in national party images. In contrast, we could argue that the greater closeness of the candidates to the voters in the local races has somewhat insulated them from short-term changes in popular perceptions of national issues and parties. In the 1989 election, however, we see for the first time very pronounced short-term influences in both HC races, with the LDP falling 11.3 percentage points below its 1986 vote share in the PR race and 14.4 percentage points in the local constituency contest.

■ The Changing Japanese Voter

How do we explain this outcome? The findings in this book have argued that short-term forces in Japan have been relatively weak and that at least up until the 1989 election, voting behavior in Japan was driven primarily by long-term factors. These long-term factors have anchored the Japanese vote and accounted for the small size of party vote fluctuations between successive elections. Paradoxically, however, these long-term forces also provided the thrust behind a gradual but very substantial "ecological realignment" of the party vote across two decades from the mid-1950s to mid-1970s (see Flanagan, 1980a, 1984). Here the decline of the farming population and the self-employed old middle class relative to blue- and white-collar workers, the decline of solidaristic communities capable of delivering blocs of votes for the ruling party, and changes within the electorate from more traditional to modern values were associated with a long-term decline in the LDP vote of some 20 percentage points over these two decades. Herein we find one paradox of stability (very small changes from election to election) combined with volatility (major changes over time).

A closer review of our findings demonstrates, however, that the very forces that have been anchoring the vote in Japan have been undergoing subtle changes that themselves have been increasing the potential for a growing volatility in party vote shares. We will look at four interrelated clusters of variables or aspects of our model. The first two are related to sociological explanations of voting behavior and the second two to attitudinal or psychological explanations.

In each case we will highlight how the previously noted trends and changes associated with each of these four sets of variables have been loosening the moorings that have tied the electorate to consistent patterns of vote choice.

Social Structure and Social Context

A key, though not new, finding was that neither the European social cleavage model nor the American socioeconomic status model predicts vote choice in Japan. Rather than a cleavage model, we found a mosaic or matrix of social structure elements that shape vote choice. Instead of religion, class, or social status, it is the intimate living and working environments within which the individual is located that influence electoral decisions. As noted in studies in the United States and elsewhere, these intimate social contexts structure the kinds of people one commonly comes in contact with and hence the partisan influences one is exposed to. We found in chapter 3 that the more precisely we define those environments by adding more structural and contextual variables into the analysis and the more uniformly particular configurations of those variables are associated with exclusively conservative or progressive influences, the more accurately we can predict vote choice.

In the Japanese case, however, these contextual influences have not been left to chance meetings or interactions. Rather, in each case we find important organizational ties that link specific contexts to particular parties. In the case of occupational contexts, strong organizational linkages from party to interest group exist between the LDP and farmers' cooperatives and merchants, retailers, and other trade, service, and manufacturing associations; between the JSP and DSP and the union movement; between the CGP and the Soka Gakkai religious organization, and so forth. Similarly, effective ties appear to be established between certain types of residential settings and the candidates of specific parties, as discussed in chapters 3 and 4. As a result, partisan climates within distinct kinds of occupational and residential contexts are reinforced by explicit organizational ties that link these environments to particular parties.

Two kinds of changes, however, are weakening the power of these social contexts to anchor the vote. First, as shown in chapter 2, occupational mobility has been reducing the size of the self-employed category in Japan, first with the decline of the farm population and more recently with the relative decline of small merchants and manufacturers. As a result, the LDP has had to rely more on nonunion blue- and white-collar workers for support. That support is much more volatile and less dependable because, unlike the party's traditional mainstays of support (the farmers, merchants, and manufacturers), these blue- and white-collar workers are not organizationally linked to the ruling party through interest associations. A similar phenomenon can be found on the left, where declining rates of unionization have forced the JSP, DSP, and JCP to turn increasingly to nonunionized elements of the work force for support. The contracting reach throughout society of these organizational linkages between parties and interest groups is forcing the parties to depend upon voters whose support is not as easily mobilized and therefore is likely to be much less reliable.

Second, the growing scale and complexity of Japanese society are lessening the solidarity and boundedness of Japanese communities. As urbanization has proceeded, we have found, as shown in chapter 3, that higher levels of integration into community networks are necessary in urban areas for residential environments to shape voting choices effectively. Here again an important traditional source of voting stability is being undermined.

Social Networks

We have argued that social networks have functioned as a potent stabilizing force underpinning electoral choices across the postwar period, through both their long-term socialization and reference group effects and their short-term vote mobilization effects. As noted in chapter 4, however, there has been a gradual, long-term shift in the kinds of influences being exerted through social networks in response to growing levels of urbanization, modern values, cognitive mobilization, and political sophistication. We are finding fewer mobilized voters whose electoral decisions are motivated by personal loyalties to candidates or to groups, localities, or local notables. It was the presence of a large proportion of these kinds of mobilized voters that made Japanese voting behavior seem impervious to short-term influences and led to the anomaly of candidates who had been implicated in political scandals being returned to office by their constituents, often with higher levels of support than before their indictments on criminal charges. Even then, the stability of these mobilized voters was conditional, in that it required that the alignments between the parties and the mobilizing local influentials and interest organizations remain unchanged. While shifting alignments by individual local influentials would likely cancel each other out, a shift in support by a major national interest organization could potentially produce a significant change in party fortunes.

This conditional stability has been further qualified by the weakening power of local influentials and interest organizations to marshal and manipulate the voting behavior of their communities and members. There are three factors underlying this declining power of network mobilization efforts. First, as communities become less bounded and more urbanized, their members become exposed to a broader variety of conflicting partisan influences. As the homogeneity of group partisan cues declines, individuals gain more autonomy in deciding which political influences and messages to credit. Second, the rising levels of education, media exposure, and political sophistication in Japanese society are reducing the citizen's dependency on formal and informal groups for voting cues. While social networks remain important sources of political attitudes and preferences, these group-mediated messages are increasingly mixed with other sources of information and remembered experiences and impressions in developing the candidate and party images needed to make personally satisfying electoral decisions.

Finally, the continuing process of value change, as noted most recently in the rise of a new breed of Japanese (the *shinjinrui*) among the younger generation, is weakening the bonds of group loyalty and increasing the difficulty of all groups, organizations, and institutions in enforcing conformity among their members. In this light, the counterintuitive finding, noted in chapters 4 and 9, of higher levels of what we think of as traditional types of influence communication activity in urban, as opposed to rural, settings is probably a reflection of an increased need for higher levels of activity to achieve past levels of conformity. In a similar manner, the candidate's personal support organization (koenkai) emerged in the early postwar period as a response to the weakening power of local bosses, vote brokers, and latent community ties to deliver the vote. Increases in more visible and obtrusive organizational activities, then, may only be a sign of the eroding power of more traditional, latent means of vote mobilization. Of course, these hyperactive campaign efforts to contact voters personally through known or group-affiliated solicitors would not continue if they were no longer effective. Moreover, even if group members are less likely to be mobilized by the traditional norms of loyalty and deference, they may still be swayed by influence communications, especially if they are largely apathetic or have no strong attachments to any party or candidate to direct their voting decisions.

As the Japanese voter has changed by acquiring greater political information and sophistication, so too has the role of social networks, which are less often sources of undigested voting cues and more often sources of ideological socialization and partisan learning. While social networks still play an important role in guiding and narrowing the range of choice, they are increasingly less insulated from short-term forces. Thus, the changes that have been taking place in the structural and contextual aspects of Japanese society as well as the changes in the nature and function of social networks would suggest an erosion of the forces that have anchored the vote and a growing potential for volatility.

Our finding of the weakening power of all our sociological variables to predict vote choice is not unique to Japan. In Western Europe it has been repeatedly shown that the strength of the associations between vote and class, occupation, and other social structure and contextual variables has been declining over the past two to three decades (Dalton et al., 1984; Franklin et al., 1991). Apparently in all the advanced industrial societies, the modernizing forces of urbanization, occupational and geographic mobility, media diffusion, and the like, are taking citizens out of exclusive, insulated community contexts and social networks based on occupation, class, ethnicity, or some other sociological category and moving them into more unbounded, complex, heterogeneous environments in which a greater variety of partisan influences and interests can be found.

These changes are having two effects. One is a weakening of the individual's commitment to and identity with any one social group, thereby eroding the group's influence over the individual. The other is more a measurement problem. Even if the individual were to remain heavily influenced by some one formal or informal group to which he or she belongs, this multiple exposure to conflicting cues makes it more difficult for the researcher to identify the meaningful patterns of influence and estimate their effectiveness, without also knowing on which group the individual most heavily relies. This increased noise may exaggerate somewhat the rate of decline associated with sociological predictors of the vote. Still, even if an individual were to remain dependent on external voting cues, the greater variety of these cues increases the probability of changing one's source of influence, yielding higher levels of volatility. In either case, then, whether the voter is becoming more autonomous from external cues or simply is being influenced by a greater variety of conflicting messages, the power of sociological variables to anchor the vote is diminishing.

Partisanship

If the stabilizing effects of our sociological explanations of the vote in Japan are weakening, we might expect this growing potential for instability to be compensated to some extent by the growing power of our attitudinal or psychological explanations of vote choice. As the decision process becomes more internalized, as the voter develops richer and more enduring images and evaluations of the parties, the partisan voter might be expected increasingly to replace the mobilized voter as the stabilizing force in Japanese election outcomes. There is evidence that party images, if not party identifications, have become increasingly diffused throughout the Japanese electorate (Flanagan, 1984). Partisanship, then, has been on the rise in Japan in the sense that partisan attitudes are becoming deeper and more widespread in response to the stabilization of the party system across the postwar period and the growing levels of political information and sophistication among the electorate.

As noted in chapters 6 and 10, however, partisanship in Japan in all its manifestations does not conform exclusively to the classical Michigan party ID model. Rather, we find that the rise in cognitive partisanship (those who have meaningful information about and reasonably stable images of one or more parties) has not been matched by a concomitant rise in affective partisans (those who have a positive attachment to or identification with one party). The result has been a growing number of negative partisans whose party support is somewhat tentative. These negative partisans introduce another kind of conditional stability into Japanese voting behavior. The voting behavior of negative partisans is stable so long as their party images remain stable. For many Japanese, the image of the LDP has remained fixed across the postwar period as a corrupt, arrogant party, but one that was a competent comptroller of the Japanese economy and a superior alternative to a fumbling and fractious opposition. So long as these remained the dominant party images, stability reigned. The potential for increased volatility, however, has been present for some time.

Value Cleavages, Issues, and the Media

A second major attitudinal candidate that might be seen as playing a stabilizing role in election outcomes would be found in Japan's value cleavages. We have seen that the authoritarian-libertarian value cleavage as conceptualized in chapter 3 has been a consistent line of division across the postwar period, dividing the Japanese population by age and education, by rural versus urban residence, and by small-scale or family enterprises versus modern, unionized large enterprises. These enduring value cleavages have stabilized the vote for two reasons. First, the basic social values that define the A-L cleavage tend to be acquired early in life and to remain largely unchanged throughout one's adult life. Value-induced political change, therefore, tends to come only gradually through intergenerational replacement. Second, these value cleavages defined party and social group alignments in the early postwar period and have been simply reinforcing those alignments ever since. This pattern contrasts sharply with that found in Western Europe, where the rising political salience of value cleavages beginning in the 1960s has been seen as a potent force in realigning European voting patterns, which had been dominated in the early postwar years by class divisions (Inglehart, 1990). While it has been shown elsewhere that the same A-L value cleavage is the politically salient one in both Japan and the West (Flanagan and Lee, 1988, 1990), this cleavage has played an exclusively reinforcing rather than a realigning role in Japan, stabilizing existing electoral patterns.

What further distinguishes the role that this value cleavage has played in Japan and the West is the nature of the issues that have propelled a socially latent value cleavage to the center of the political stage. In the West it has been a New Politics issue agenda, which began to arise only in the 1960s around such issues as peace, the environment, foreign immigration, ethnic and minority rights, abortion, censorship, and gay rights. In the Japanese case the kinds of issues that politicized the A-L cleavage and the timing of their salience have been somewhat different. The peace issue and issues surrounding the rights of protestors were part of the cluster of cultural politics issues that dominated the political scene and defined party alignments in the 1950s, as discussed in chapters 3 and 7. Environmental issues were part of a second set of positions issues focusing on continued economic growth versus welfare and quality-of-life concerns, which accompanied the rise of citizen movements and progressive local administrations in the late 1960s and early 1970s and further reinforced the value cleavage. Most of the other kinds of Western New Politics issues have not as yet become politically salient in Japan.

In Japan, then, during the 1950s and 1960s, value change associated with intergenerational replacement and rising levels of education was reflected in a gradual movement of voter support from the right to the left. Since the early 1970s, continued change along the A-L value continuum has not been manifested in further shifts from right to left in voting patterns for two reasons. First, the ruling party's position on the value-related 1950s and 1960s sets of position issues has moved, reflecting the shifting social consensus resulting from value change. So, for example, the ruling party has to a greater degree come to accept the American-imposed constitution, the limited role of the emperor and the military, and the importance of protecting the environment. Second, with the LDP acceptance of many of the original progressive positions on these issues, their political salience has declined greatly. These issues, then, continue to link values with voting preferences in a largely residual manner by defining the outlines of a generalized establishment/antiestablishment political orientation, one which is further reinforced by the cynicism and protest proclivities of Libertarians.

The void left by the departure of highly salient position issues from the Japanese political stage has been increasingly filled by valence issues.[4] The growing importance of these valence issues is increasing the potential for volatility in Japanese elections for two reasons. First, valence issues have a greater potential to alter party fortunes than do position issues. The emergence of a new position issue in an election typically has mixed effects on a party's share of the vote, especially if the issue cuts across the major issue cleavages that originally defined the party system. In such cases, whichever side of the issue a party takes, it is likely to repel as many old supporters as it attracts new

---

4. As noted in chapter 7, "valence" issues are those that are seen in good/bad, black/white terms. On those issues, the electorate lines up on the positive side of the issue, whereas "position" issues usually divide the electorate along the lines of economic benefits or ideological preferences (Butler and Stokes, 1976).

ones. In contrast, a new valence issue, which aligns the entire electorate on the same side (for example, against corruption), may affect a party's support levels much more strongly, if the party is clearly identified with either the positive or the negative side of the issue. Second, valence issues are inherently short-term in nature, tending to fade rapidly from the voter's mind. Valence issues depend on public outrage and emotion for their salience. Unlike position issues, they tend not to evoke a confrontation between vested interests. It is the confrontation between cherished values and/or economic interests that fuels mobilization and countermobilization efforts on both sides and keeps an issue alive. Lacking this dimension of a perceived personal or group threat, valence issues tend to dissipate with time. As a result, the shift from position to valence issues as the focus of public attention in Japanese elections since the early 1970s has increased the potential for growing swings in party fortunes.

Finally, the emerging role of the media in Japanese elections can be expected to enhance the influence of short-term factors in the future, thereby further increasing electoral volatility. As noted in chapter 8, the media have already demonstrated the power to set the issue agenda by projecting valence issues to the center of the political stage. In some cases, as with the Lockheed and Recruit scandals, the media has been able to hold these issues in focus in the public eye for up to one year, until their brief command of the limelight culminates with a single election outcome, following which they quickly fade. The ability of the media to shape candidate images has also been noted. With the growing trend toward the relaxation of restrictions on candidate access to the electronic media in Japan, we can anticipate, following Western experience, that television will enhance the impact of candidate images on election outcomes, beginning with national party leaders. There are already clear signs that a Nakasone or a Kaifu at the height of his popularity as prime minister can raise levels of support for the ruling party, while a Takeshita or Uno at the depths of his public approval can lower party support levels. Both the shifts in the types of issues that are salient and the growing role of the media, therefore, are increasing the influence of short-ter factors on the voter's choice.

■ Explaining Specific Elections: The 1989 and 1990 Outcomes

The model of Japanese voting behavior presented in this book has been based squarely on the analysis of survey data. In the following examination of the 1989 and 1990 elections, we will bring into our discussion other modes of analysis that provide different kinds of insights than those that can be derived simply from survey research—specifically, analysis of aggregate voting data and a more descriptive presentation of the issues, figures, and events surrounding these two elections. These latter modes of analysis are the ones that typically dominate journalistic accounts of election results and heretofore virtually all the English-language treatments of specific election outcomes in Japan. This exercise is designed to demonstrate how much richer and more penetrating these descriptive analyses can be when they are blended with an understanding of the basic parameters of Japanese voting behavior as set forth in this book. Indeed, a thorough grounding in a behavioral model of a nation's voting behavior will yield more solid interpretations of specific outcomes as well as long-term trends.

If we treat the psychological and sociological explanations of changing voting patterns presented above as two sides or aspects of our voting model, we will find that each provides a different but reinforcing explanation of the 1989 and 1990 election outcomes. To oversimplify our argument for the moment, we could depict our distinct psychological and sociological variables as affecting different segments of the Japanese electorate. For example, voters whose choice is primarily a function of our key psychological variable—partisanship—tend to be younger, male, big-city dwellers, blue- and white-collar workers who are largely unintegrated into their community or other social networks. This first electorate is in many ways like the American one, consisting of voters who respond to national issues and to images of the parties and their leaders conveyed through the mass media. The metropolitan electorate is also very competitive and fairly volatile, with the vote often distributed fairly equally among five parties, with the LDP receiving about a 20 percent share.

In contrast, those whose vote choice is motivated primarily by our key sociological variable—social networks—tend to be older, female, and rural or small-city residents who work in farming, retailing, or other family or small-scale enterprise and who are well integrated into community and/or occupationally related networks. In this second electorate, voting often resembles older American city machine models. Politicians rely on their own support associations to get out the vote, backed up by local farmers and merchant organizations. Labor unions mobilize school teachers, civil servants, and other public and private sector workers. These small city and rural constituencies make up the ruling party's "conservative kingdom," with the LDP often able to command two-thirds of the vote or more. The major opposition here comes from the JSP (especially in the prefectural capitals where public employees are concentrated), while the other opposition parties typically garner little support.[5]

5. These observations on the duality of the voter types in Japan are drawn from an unpublished 1989 postelection comment by Bradley Richardson on "Japan's Grass Roots Revolt" and from Flanagan, 1980a. It should also be noted that, paradoxically, those younger, urban, more educated

Of course, it is a gross oversimplification to depict the Japanese electorate as divided into two different types, each of which responds to a distinct set of influences. As our analysis has shown, multiple factors influence the electoral decisions of most voters, and, indeed, many of the variables we have identified have overlapping or reinforcing effects. Thus, as noted above, social networks are increasingly playing a role in shaping partisan images rather than simply mobilizing largely uninformed voters to cast their votes in line with the suggestions of some opinion leader or as an expression of group loyalty. Nevertheless, it should be pointed out that there has been a growing gap between rural and urban voting behavior across the postwar period. The occupational mobility, weakening community bonds, and value change associated with the ecological realignment discussed above, which shifted the vote sharply away from the ruling to the opposition parties across the 1950s and 1960s, were felt mainly in the urban areas. Most rural areas remained much less affected than the rest of the country, with many of those in the countryside remaining in the same houses on the same farms in the same small towns and villages in the same increasingly overrepresented rural districts. Therefore, not only may it be useful to think of these two distinct types of electorates as ideal types for heuristic purposes, but we also find that the distinction has some meaningful geographic and occupational parameters. In any case we will organize our explanation of the causes underlying the remarkable voting shifts in the 1989 upper house election around a discussion of the effects of our two sets of variables on these two types of electorates.

These distinctions also highlight some of the more singular aspects of Japanese voting behavior. Among our psychological and sociological sets of variables, party images and social networks have been singled out for special emphasis precisely because these variables point to some of the behavioral tendencies that distinguish Japanese and Western voting patterns. Clearly one of the major theoretical contributions of our study has been the identification and description of the two deviant, off-diagonal types of partisans—the negative partisans who are high on the cognitive but low on the affective dimension of

---

employees in our first constituency that rely more heavily on partisanship in making their voting decisions do not necessarily emerge as stronger partisans than the older, rural, less educated, and self-employed that constitute our second type, who rely more on social networks. In the early postwar period the first constituency tended to be more politicized and partisan, the second constituency more apathetic and nonpartisan. Over time, however, there has been a trend from partisanship to independence in the first constituency and from apathy to partisanship in the second (Flanagan, 1984). While many of the first type of more sophisticated and cynical voters do not have a positive affective attachment to a party (and hence often do not emerge as party identifiers), they do have more developed party images that guide their voting decisions. Conversely, while party attachments are increasingly developing among the more apathetic and less informed second type, these attachments in many cases continue to depend heavily on reinforcements from one's social networks.

partisanship, and the uninformed partisans who are high on the affective but low on the cognitive dimension. So while we do find large numbers of loyal partisans in Japan who behave as the Michigan model prescribes, we also find unusually high proportions of our two deviant types, a finding which heightens the importance of party images and social networks in the explanation of Japanese voting behavior.

We can summarize the lessons to be drawn from the above discussion of the changing Japanese voter as follows. Both the sociological and psychological explanations point to an unambiguous, gradual trend toward increasing levels of volatility. The sociological variables have been seen as exerting a declining ability to anchor the vote, while the psychological variables highlight the increasing power of short-term influences. As previously noted, signs of increasing levels of volatility have been visible since the mid-1970s. These long-term trends by themselves, however, could not explain the dramatic surge in volatility associated with the 1989 and 1990 election outcomes.

To explain those unusually sharp fluctuations in party vote shares, we must turn to another paradox of stability combined with volatility in Japanese voting behavior. We have noted that the factors that anchor the vote of both the negative partisans and the mobilized voters (who are either uninformed partisans or nonpartisans) in each case provide them with only a conditional stability that masks a potential for great volatility. Negative partisans are stable in their voting behavior only so long as the relative attractiveness or unattractiveness of their party images remains unchanged or no new, more appealing parties appear. Mobilized voters tend to be nested in stable social networks that activate them to turn out at high levels and vote for the same party in election after election. Their lack of political knowledge and sophistication only serves to further insulate them from short-term influences that might induce defections from their habitual pattern of party support. At the same time, however, their relatively weak internalized evaluations and motivations make them less resistant to change should their formal organizations or community networks switch party allegiances. Thus, both changing party images and shifting party/interest group alignments may potentially upset the apparent stability we find in the levels of party support in Japan.

We have already seen evidence of this kind of conditional stability at work. In chapter 5 we witnessed the striking frailty of partisan attachments in Japan for those voters who had experienced changes in occupational or geographic mobility or in the partisan climates of their adult social networks. As we shall see, the 1989 upper house election provided dramatic proof of the conditional stability of the voting preferences of many Japanese, as changes in both mass perceptions of party images and organizational mobilization efforts on behalf of the ruling party combined to hand the ruling party its first sound defeat in a postwar election.

Party Images, Valence Issues, and the 1989 Election Results
We will begin our analysis of the 1989 election from the perspective of the three major issues that dominated the campaign and their effect on the ruling party's popular image. The impact of these issues was heightened by the fact that all three can be characterized as "valence" rather than "position" issues. In the summer of 1989 the LDP was identified with the negative side of all three valence issues, and this unusual convergence of a set of unrelated events and their reinforcing effects produced perhaps Japan's first "image election," in which short-term influences exerted a profound impact on the election outcome.

The first of these issues was an unpopular new tax that the ruling party had promised not to enact during the 1986 election campaigns and then enacted anyway in December 1988, over the vociferous protests of the opposition parties. The manner in which the measure was passed in the Diet, with the LDP resorting to "forced vote" tactics and unilateral actions in the face of an opposition boycott, may have resurrected images of the 1950s-style confrontational politics, when the powerful and arrogant conservative forces ran roughshod over the opposition. This sequence of events may have convinced some voters that the ruling party could not be trusted to act democratically when given so large a majority in the Diet. In any case, the results of a Kyodo Tsushin postelection poll demonstrate that the tax issue dominated voters' concerns, with 65 percent citing that issue as the most important reason for the LDP defeat and 82 percent identifying the issue as one of the two most important issues for the next election (*Mainichi Shimbun*, 8/25/89).

What seems to have heightened the public's intolerance for this new tax was the image of LDP Dietmen forcing new burdens on the people while at the same time illegally, or at least unscrupulously, receiving large sums of money under the table. This brings us to the second valence issue, the issue of political morality. A major corruption scandal had raged for nearly an entire year prior to the election in the form of the Recruit scandal, which forced the resignation of Prime Minister Takeshita two months before the voting day.[6] Corruption scan-

6. The rapidly rising Recruit conglomerate (in job placement, communications, real estate, and financing) and its president, Hiromasa Ezoe, tried to buy influence with large numbers of politicians and bureaucrats by channeling sizable sums of money to them through unethical but not necessarily illegal means. Ultimately over eighty politicians, bureaucrats, businessmen, and other figures were implicated in the scandal; forty-three of them eventually were forced to resign from some position they held because of the public uproar, but only two of the many politicians involved and four of their aides were ever indicted. The small number of indictments and even fewer

dals are not new to Japan, but in the past the LDP has always been able to deflect much of the negative fallout of a scandal by simply rotating their personnel and replacing tainted leaders with fresh leaders. In this case virtually all the party's prominent leaders were implicated in some way. As Hans Baerwald (1989:835) has aptly put it, "lack of involvement in the scandal was not so much a reflection of probity as a lack of political influence."

The negative ramifications of the Recruit scandal for the ruling party's image, however, went beyond the morality issue and raised an unstated competency issue. In the past the LDP had always looked supremely capable and composed. The Recruit scandal threw the party into confusion, and the difficulty the party had in coming up with a successor and the successor's relatively low previous status in the party did not inspire confidence. It can be argued that the competency issue has played a major role in keeping the ruling party in power over the last two decades. The LDP has been seen as the "not so good but preferred party"—not so good because of its perceived arrogance, unresponsiveness, and corruption, but nevertheless preferred because of its identification with the Japanese economic miracle, growing affluence, and the effective management and continued expansion of the economy. In the aftermath of the Recruit scandal, the perceived competency gap between the LDP and its opposition decreased significantly.

The Recruit scandal and the subsequent succession controversy within the ruling party also focused attention on the fundamental value cleavage that lies at the heart of Japanese politics. As Shinsaku Kohei (1989) has noted, Japan has a village or mura-style politics and modern-style institutions. The former is based on communal, group-centered, particularistic, consensual norms and hierarchic, vertical personal relations and the latter on individualistic, universalistic, and majoritarian norms and horizontal, egalitarian relations. The incompatibilities between these two competing value systems have given rise to many of the problems in Japanese politics—from big money elections and rampant influence peddling to behind-the-scenes decision making and the LDP's exclusivistic, unresponsive management style.

Many critics speak of the structural nature of political corruption in Japan, meaning that corruption in Japan is not a sign of personal moral failings but rather it is built into the system so that a politician's very survival requires, for example, a heavy dependency on large corporations and the exchange of favors for cash. As a result, despite repeated calls to reform the ruling party and politics in general—by dissolving party factions, introducing primary elec-

---

convictions expected results from the fact that under Japanese law receiving large donations is not necessarily illegal, unless it can be shown that these gifts influenced a public official's decision or resulted in some favored treatment (Takeuchi, 1989; Sato, 1989; Ibayashi, 1989).

tions, or changing campaign finance laws or the electoral system—all seem to come to naught because ultimately LDP leaders are reluctant to tamper fundamentally with the system that got them to the top of Japan's political world. Following Takeshita's resignation, the public witnessed the floundering of senior statesman Masayoshi Ito's candidacy for prime minister (presumably because of the leadership's resistance to his reform plans) and the handpicking of the relatively unknown Sosuke Uno for the post through secretive negotiations among party faction leaders. These intraparty maneuvers did nothing to convince the Japanese electorate that the party was seriously prepared to clean house.[7]

Finally, no sooner did Sosuke Uno rise to the prime ministership than he became involved in a scandal involving sex for pay with a series of geisha and mistresses. The Japanese have always tolerated this kind of activity in the past, at least as long as it remained discreet, and so it may be that the public uproar over this issue was largely a response to the national embarrassment of their leader's dirty linen being aired in the international media. Nevertheless, some Japanese women seemed to have been mobilized by this issue, and some observers have pointed to the great public popularity of Takako Doi, the female chairperson of the JSP, and the unusually large number of women elected (twenty-two, only two of whom were LDP candidates) to argue that a gender gap emerged in this election over the unstated issue of the treatment of women in Japan's male-dominated society. As we shall see, the gender gap argument has been overdrawn. What is clear, however, is that the heightened salience of these competence, corruption, and morality issues had a negative impact on the ruling party.

The third valence issue is a rather paradoxical one in that it appears at first glance to be a position issue. The LDP, after many protracted and heated negotiations, finally bowed to American pressure and agreed in May 1988 to the complete liberalization of beef and citrus import restrictions over a three-year period, leading to the assumption that the importation of rice would soon follow (*Asia 1990 Yearbook*). Thus the LDP seemed for the first time to be

7. Some observers have recently argued that the party's faction system, often a target of public criticism, has actually proven to be one of the party's great strengths by providing for meaningful transfers of power and policy direction. These intraparty turnovers substitute for turnover between parties and have often rescued and rejuvenated the ruling party in crisis situations—as when Ikeda replaced Kishi in 1960 and led the nation from crisis and confrontation to stability and prosperity, or when the scandal-plagued Tanaka administration was replaced by the reform-minded Miki in 1974. As faction leaders these LDP politicians came to the prime ministership with national visibility, a proven track record, established reputation, known policy preferences, and an independent power base within the party. In this case, however, Uno had none of these qualifications and hence remained Takeshita's puppet and was unable to provide the party with fresh beginnings (Shinohara, 1989).

abandoning its staunch defense of the interests of farmers, its traditional mainstay of support. The Socialists seized this opportunity to declare themselves to be the new champions of farmers' interests by campaigning against the liberalization of the Japanese agricultural market, resulting in a perceived reversal of party positions on farm issues. In most highly developed, urbanized societies, the LDP's perceived shift in position might be expected to gain a party more new support from urban consumers who would benefit from the resultant drop in food prices than losses from a relatively small farm population. In Japan, however, consumer interests have never been well articulated or represented. Most Japanese seem to be resigned to high food prices, feeling that Japan's national interest and perhaps even survival require no further erosion of the Japanese farmer's ability to feed the nation. Instead of precipitating a debate between opposing interests, the farm issue instead seems to have touched a nationalist nerve in the context of the growing sensitivity of many Japanese to the perceived bullying tactics of the United States on issues surrounding their bilateral trade.[8] In this sense, the farm issue made the LDP look weak, reactive, and unable adequately to defend Japan's national interests in the face of increasingly punitive American demands. Here again this third issue had a diffuse effect on increasing the negative content of the ruling party's image in the popular mind.

As public opinion polls demonstrate, these three issues of the consumption tax, morality and related reform issues, and agricultural policy dominated voters' concerns in the 1989 upper house election (*Mainichi Shimbun*, 8/25/89). Moreover, while the tax issue appears to have been the primary focus of the voters' policy displeasure with the ruling party, the manner in which the tax was passed along with the broader ramifications of the other two issues discussed above may have done more to darken the LDP's public image and heighten the salience of the negative aspects of the party's prolonged rule in the voters' minds than simply their natural interest in reducing their tax burden.

Each of these valence issues, then, was tied up with the emotional baggage of decades of postwar politics, and each cast long shadows on the popular evaluations of the regime's performance. These evaluations have become increasingly central to voters' decisions, because, as noted above and elsewhere

8. One sign of this rising popular sentiment for a more assertive nationalism in Japan's dealings with the United States and other foreign countries can be found in the 1989 book by Akio Morita and Shintaro Ishihara, *A Japan That Can Say No* (to the United States), which has caused quite a stir both inside and out of Japan. This nationalistic note was also sounded in the resolutions of several prefectural farmers' organizations, as seen in the following quote, which sounds the antiforeign and anti–big business themes reminiscent of rural sentiments in the 1930s that fueled ultranationalism: "We entertain misgivings towards the implementation of an agricultural policy that accepts whatever America says and which is led by financial circles" (*Asahi Shimbun*, 4/7/89).

(Kohei, 1989), the issue polarization that characterized Japanese politics in the 1950s and 1960s and locked the electorate into progressive and conservative political camps has been replaced by an issueless politics in the 1970s and 1980s. Japanese politics have become issueless in the sense that the political debate has shifted from position issues to valence issues, which tend to be short-lived and fail to divide the electorate in meaningful ways. This shift has transformed electoral decisions into a referendum on the quality of the incumbent regime's performance. What is ironic about this shift in the type of issues that command public attention is that it is still the low salience, 1950s cultural politics issues that best predict the vote. In contrast, the newer valence issues are largely uncorrelated with vote choice because they are one-sided issues. Nevertheless, these valence issues have the biggest effect on altering the voting results from one election to the next. Clearly this change in the type of issues that dominate Japanese campaigns has heightened the importance of party images for election outcomes and increased the potential for electoral volatility.

As this discussion of the issues reveals, a whole host of short-term factors emerged in the 1989 upper house election to undermine the prior stability of party images. The consequence of this shift in the balance of positive/negative party images was to drive voters temporarily from the LDP. The prime beneficiary of this movement has been the Socialist Party, partly because of the positive and "clean" image of Chairwoman Doi at that time and partly because of the relatively dimmed images of the other opposition parties, because of the implication of the DSP and CGP leaderships in the Recruit scandal and the tarnished image of communism and the JCP owing to the recent Tiananmen Square massacre. Chairwoman Doi's popular image as a sincere, pragmatic, and forceful champion of the average citizen's livelihood seems to have gone far in rescuing the JSP from its public perception as an outdated Marxist party and in improving its support in the polls.[9] This is another sign of the growing impact of party leaders' media images on their party's popularity.

If this was an "image election" driven by events played up in the media with the outcome determined primarily by relative shifts in positive/negative party images, then we should expect a uniform national shift in party fortunes affect-

9. Public support for the JSP, which averaged 13 percent in the eight *Mainichi* polls between May 1986 and September 1988, rose steadily thereafter, peaking at 25 percent in June 1989 (*Mainichi Shimbun*, 1/26/90). It should be pointed out that levels of party support vary systematically among polling organizations owing to differences in question wording and polling procedures. The differences are typically a function of the levels of no party, independent, DK and NA responses. Thus, *Yomiuri* polls on the level of LDP support for the preceding year up through September 1988 were averaging 49 percent, roughly seven percentage points above the *Mainichi* polls reported for the same period. Similarly, preelection support levels of the JSP peaked at 31 percent in the *Yomiuri* polls rather than 25 percent as reported by the *Mainichi* polls.

ing almost all groups and areas to the same degree throughout the nation. As Butler and Stokes (1976) point out, what we should find is not equivalent declines in the number of LDP voters across groups but rather equivalent proportions or rates of decline in support for the party. Groups that normally support the ruling party in higher numbers have more potential defectors. If the effect is the same on all groups, then the percentage defecting should be the same.

We have tested this proposition in table 11.2 by comparing the percentages that voted for the LDP in the upper house PR constituency races as reported in the Akarui Senkyo Suishin Kyokai (ASSK) nationwide surveys conducted immediately after the 1986 and 1989 elections. The percentages saying that they voted for the LDP have been broken down by sex, age, education, occupation, and unionization using the ASSK's standard categories. The defection rate in reported levels of voting LDP across the two elections presented in the table was computed by subtracting the percent voting LDP in 1986 from the percent in 1989 and dividing by the 1986 percentages.

Several caveats should be noted in interpreting these results. First, the PR constituency race was used because in that case the voting stimulus is party rather than candidate and thus the results should more clearly reflect changes in party images; when the same analysis was repeated for the local constituency race, however, an identical pattern with only slightly more variation was found. Second, the age classifications will exaggerate the rate of defection somewhat, because the age cohorts shift with the passage of time, dropping older respondents who are more likely to vote LDP and replacing them with younger respondents who support the LDP at lower rates. Nevertheless, the expected pattern is found, with volatility decreasing with age. Age, then, is an expected exception to our uniform national shift hypothesis, because we know that younger voters are less stable that older voters in their voting behavior and more influenced by short-term factors.

Age aside, however, what is striking is the uniformity of the defection rates across the sex, education, occupation, and union categories. With only the exceptions of unionized and blue-collar workers, all other categories conform to a very narrow range of a 36–38 percent rate of defection. While farmers, merchants, and those with low education typically support the LDP at much higher levels, they were no more likely to defect than white-collar or sales and service workers, housewives, or the highly educated. A final caveat in interpreting this data is to note that postelection surveys typically exaggerate voting swings owing to a bandwagon effect. Some voters report a vote in line with the election outcome rather than their real behavior, a tendency which is particularly likely among the substantial proportion of nonvoters who say they voted. The actual overall rate of defection from the LDP in the PR constituency races

Table 11.2   LDP Vote and Rate of Decline across the 1986 and 1989
Upper House PR Races by Demographic Attributes

	N of Cases (1989)	Percentage Reporting LDP Vote		Defection Rate (% Change)
		1986	1989	
Sex				
Male	(928)	46.9	28.9	−38
Female	(987)	44.2	27.6	−38
Age				
20–29	(178)	34.2	17.4	−49
30–39	(332)	34.1	19.0	−44
40–49	(441)	38.2	22.7	−41
50–59	(444)	51.3	30.9	−40
60 and over	(520)	63.8	40.2	−37
Education				
Compulsory	(599)	55.3	34.4	−38
High school	(928)	42.8	26.9	−37
Higher education	(355)	33.2	20.8	−37
Occupation				
Farmers[a]	(208)	80.8	50.0	−38
Merchants and Manufacturers[a]	(270)	56.4	35.9	−36
White-collar	(285)	27.9	17.2	−38
Sales/service	(149)	30.8	19.5	−27
Blue-collar	(232)	40.8	17.2	−58
Housewives	(446)	39.6	24.9	−37
Other/unemployed	(259)	52.4	32.8	−37
Unionization				
Union	(223)	20.6	9.4	−54
Nonunion	(482)	40.0	24.3	−39

Notes: The table was computed from cross-tabulations reported in the ASSK's election surveys (Akarui Senkyo Suishin Kyokai, 1986, 1989) conducted immediately after the 1986 and 1989 Upper House elections with 2,026 and 1,915 respondents, respectively. To simplify the table while still affording the reader a sense of the relative distribution of cases across categories, the *N*s are reported for only the 1989 survey. This distribution pattern was very similar for the 1986 survey. Two occupational categories, students and managers, were dropped from the table due to the very small number of cases in both categories.

[a] The farmer and merchant categories include family workers.

between 1986 and 1989 was 29 percent. Notwithstanding these caveats, what is compelling about the findings in table 11.2 is the uniformity of the defection rates across virtually all groups in Japanese society.

The explanation of the 1989 HC election result derived from an analysis of our psychological variables would be that a set of valence issues and the media images of the parties and their leaders combined to alter temporarily the relative positive and negative balance of the LDP and JSP images. Given the high proportions of negative partisans found in Japan, that temporary shift in the relative attractiveness of party images was sufficient to induce widespread short-term defections from the LDP that seem to have affected every geographic region and demographic category. One postelection survey found that 30 percent of the voters who said they supported the LDP defected in the 1989 HC election. These are unusually high levels, in that voting defections in Japan in the past have more typically been masked by simultaneous changes in party support. While defections affected all corners and strata in Japanese society, they did not effect all kinds of people equally. The same postelection survey found that the LDP defectors tended to be more concerned with the issues, more dissatisfied with politics, and more ideologically liberal than loyal LDP supporters[10]

More than anything else, it would seem to be the heightened negative images of and dissatisfaction with politics that precipitated the LDP's electoral demise. In comparative perspective, levels of dissatisfaction with politics have always been quite high in Japan. The NHK time series data on the question of general satisfaction with the state of politics in Japan reveal that from 1982 into 1984, when the Tanaka bribery trial and related issues were on the public mind, levels on this item averaged 60 percent dissatisfied and 31 percent satisfied. During the period of Nakasone's high popularity as prime minister from mid-1984 to mid-1986, some improvement was seen with an average of 51 percent dissatisfied and 46 percent satisfied. From 1987 into the fall of 1988 the trend reversed, with an average of 56 percent dissatisfied and 37 percent satisfied. In July of 1989, however, dissatisfaction levels reached record highs, with 76 percent dissatisfied and only 20 percent satisfied (Yoron Chosa Reports, 1989). The upper house vote, then, was more of a vote against the LDP than a vote for the opposition. In this referendum on the LDP's performance, the LDP was found wanting.

Social Networks and the 1989 Election Results

We might be tempted to conclude our analysis on this note, arguing that shifts in party images reflected in the national media by themselves provide a

10. These findings are based on Ichiro Miyake's May 1990 preliminary report of his analysis of the 1989 nationwide Akarui Senkyo Suishin Kyokai HC election survey. See also Miyake, 1991.

satisfactory explanation of the election outcome. Yet this would ignore the sociological explanations and our second key variable, social networks. Did social networks affect the outcome or was this only an image election?

Informal social network influences are always at work, diffusing and interpreting media reactions to national political events. There are also several ways, however, in which we can detect an organizational or mobilization effect of social networks in this election. The first indirect piece of evidence comes from table 11.2. The unusually high levels of defection from unionized blue-collar workers suggest that the efforts of Rengo to unify the private sector of the labor movement and the appearance of Rengo-backed candidates for the first time in this election may have mobilized new supporters. That is, a number of workers who had previously voted LDP in a context in which their local unions or union federation had been politically neutral may have responded to Rengo mobilization efforts and defected.

This indirect evidence of a mobilized group defection raises the question as to whether there were other groups with unusually strong motivations to defect. This leads us to a consideration of the other side of the three valence issues discussed above, the fact that each of them most strongly antagonized one particular group—the morality issue raised by the Uno affair angered women, the tax fell hardest on the large class of small merchants and retailers who had to collect it, and the agricultural issue was clearly aimed against farm interests. Is there any evidence of an organized defection among these groups? In the case of women, an organized defection is unlikely, simply because the women's movement is very weak and largely unorganized in Japan. Women have tended to be much less politically involved in Japan than men and have been easy targets of community vote mobilization efforts in the past. In survey interviews, they have tended to report slightly lower levels of voting support for the LDP consistently across elections, only because of their lower response levels for all party options (higher DK/NA). While social attitudes regarding women's roles are changing in Japan, as seen most remarkably in the unprecedented number of successful women candidates, there is no evidence that a gender gap in voting decisions emerged in this election. This is clearly the conclusion to be drawn from the data in table 11.2, and there is no other hard evidence presently available to persuade us otherwise.

In the case of farmers and merchants, there is ample journalistic evidence that such organizationally mobilized defections did take place. The revolt began in Iwate prefecture's rice-growing districts in late February and had spread to ten other rural prefectures by mid-March. By mid-April a parallel movement had begun among merchants and small businessmen angered by the consumption tax. The official actions of these local defecting organizations included renouncing their party affiliation, endorsing unaffiliated conservative or independent candidates, urging abstentions from voting or support for the opposition party candidates, and refusing to send donations or representatives to LDP candidate support associations (*Tokyo Shimbun,* 3/17/89; *Yomiuri Shimbun,* 3/25/89; *Nihon Keizai Shimbun,* 4/23/89; *Asahi Shimbun,* 4/7/89, 4/26/89, 5/2/89). Most of this activity, however, should be characterized as denying support to the LDP rather than transferring support to some other party. This of course is sensational stuff, which the media like to play up. So while it is impossible to tell how widespread it was or to quantify this anecdotal evidence in any way, the sheer quantity of these reports suggests that important defections were taking place among the leaderships of local farmers' and merchants' associations and that these defections should have had some discernible effect on the voting outcome.

How can we square this evidence with the table 11.2 evidence suggesting that farmers and merchants were no more likely to defect from the LDP than any other group. Two kinds of evidence can be presented, at least for the case of the geographically concentrated farmers. The first of these takes us back to the Butler and Stokes (1976) argument, which is actually more complex than identified above. They further argue that, in the case of geographically concentrated partisan strongholds, a proportional national swing away from the locally preferred party occasioned by national influences should be at least partially offset by a "homing effect" leading previous defectors back to the party fold. This is in effect a social-network or social-context argument, which suggests that the dominant partisan preference of a locality should disproportionately lead residents back toward that area's traditionally preferred party. The fact that there is no evidence of this kind of partially offsetting local effect among farmers in table 11.2 suggests that something else was going on at the local level to lead voters away from the ruling party.

In addition to this indirect piece of evidence of a social network effect, we can find more direct support for such an effect by comparing the survey data in table 11.2 with the actual voting results presented in table 11.3. As survey data, the evidence in table 11.2 reports group proportions of voting support only at the attitudinal level, not the behavioral level. In chapter 6 we learned that the uninformed partisans, who have only low levels of political awareness and are only nominally attached to any political party, are especially prone to shifts back and forth in survey responses from nonsupport to support for one particular party. The voting choices of these "partisans" is often found to be more stable than their reported partisanship, because they are nested in stable social networks that are able to stimulate habitual patterns of support for the party, despite the voter's wavering sense of party affiliation. While the increased negativity of the LDP image in 1989 was sufficient to push many of these uninformed partisans back to a "no party/DK" response, how they actually behaved in the election was more likely to be a function of the kinds of influences that prevailed within their mobilizing networks.

While the image effect was felt uniformly throughout the country, the mobilization effect could vary tremendously across regions and occupation categories depending on the stance a particular local organization took. Most dramatic, some farmers' and merchants' organizations could have elected to mobilize short-term defections from the LDP as a protest vote. Given the major losses the LDP suffered, particularly in rural areas, some mobilized defections undoubtedly took place, if not by formal organization endorsements then at least as a result of informal voting cues.

A less inflammatory and still most effective means of "protest," however, would be simply to mount weaker efforts to get out the vote than usual, leading to an increase in abstentions among the party's traditional supporters. Indeed, it seems likely that many farmers' and merchants' organizations would choose to do nothing and encourage abstentions rather than work for another party. These groups know that they have no better friend than the LDP. They refuse to be taken for granted, however and the way that they can exercise leverage on the ruling party and punish it for ignoring their most vital interests is by sitting out an election and watching the party's fortunes suffer. The comment of one nationwide commerce and industry organization staff member prior to the election may represent the feelings of many leaders in these interest groups. He was anonymously quoted as saying, "I still think that in the end it is the LDP on which we can rely. However, in the coming election, I think I may abstain from voting" (*Asahi Shimbun,* 5/2/89). Abstention at the leadership level suggests more than just a few merchants' association or agricultural coop officials not showing up at the polls. Rather, it means that their typical role as vote mobilizers in the LDP campaign would go unperformed. What we potentially have here, then, is de facto "mobilized abstentions" that rippled throughout these leaders' communities.

Table 11.3 presents the voting distributions including abstentions across the last three upper house local constituency races. The results are presented by district type and represent averages of the percentage distributions for each prefecture in the group. We have then the typical or average voting distribution for each type of prefecture—the twenty-six one-seat districts, the fifteen two-seat districts, and the six three-to-four-seat districts. Over the last two decades there has been substantially greater volatility in the rates of voting abstentions in upper house elections compared with the 1950s and 1960s, as these contests have taken on more the character of a vote of confidence in the ruling party rather than a contest between ideologically polarized camps.

We see in table 11.3 that overall the fluctuations in the abstention rate are

Table 11.3   Party Vote Distributions in Recent Upper House Local Races
by District Size (In Percentages)

Election Year	LDP	Abstainers	Other	JSP	JCP
Average vote distribution across 26 one-seat districts					
1983	32	41	2	20	5
1986	43	28	1	21	7
1989	29	33	0	34	4
Average vote distribution across 15 two-seat districts					
1983	30	44	17	4	5
1986	38	32	19	5	6
1989	26	39	26	4	5
Average vote distribution across 6 three-to-four-seat districts					
1983	18	46	19	10	7
1986	21	35	21	13	10
1989	16	38	18	20	8

Note: The table presents the distribution of the vote including abstainers by district size. To determine the typical pattern for each district type, the vote percentage distributions for each district in each of the three district size groupings were averaged. The table is based on district-by-district data reported in the August 5, 1989, issue of the *Asahi Shimbun Weekly* AERA.

quite comparable to the fluctuations in the support for the LDP. In 1986 in the context of a double election and a rising crest in popularity for Prime Minister Nakasone and the LDP, many more voters were drawn to the polls than in the previous election and most of those additional votes went to the LDP. In 1989, abstentions rose again and support for the LDP fell even faster. While many previous LDP supporters undoubtedly switched their support to the Socialists, perhaps as a short-term protest vote, it may also be that larger numbers of new abstentions among LDP supporters were partially offset by higher numbers of marginal progressive supporters who were mobilized to return to the polls in this election by the appearance of the Rengo and the improved JSP image. We might argue that the data hide a pattern of shifting abstention rates among marginal conservative and progressive voters. When the image of an opposition party improves and its chances of winning seem enhanced, its supporters will be more motivated to go out to the polls. Conversely, when LDP supporters become disillusioned with their party, they will be less likely to go out to the polls, particularly when they are not mobilized to do so.[11]

11. There have been a number of studies on the theme of stability/instability in Japanese elections and the role of abstentions based on the analysis of aggregate data, including Richardson, 1977; Ishikawa, 1978, 1984; Flanagan, 1980b; Campbell, 1987; and Reed, 1990.

It is likely, then, that the greatest source of interelection volatility in recent years has been the result of differential fluctuations in voting and nonvoting among marginal conservative and progressive supporters rather than movement back and forth from the right to left. In the past, panel studies have verified this pattern of greater shifting from support to nonsupport than from party to party. While we do not have the panel data at our disposal to test that proposition here, we would expect that the higher negativity associated with the ruling party's image in this election spurred a higher anti-LDP protest vote than usual, as the evidence on the remarkably high levels of LDP defections cited above suggests. At the same time, it is also likely that this vote switching did not by any means account for the LDP's entire 11 and 14 percentage point drops in the total vote in the two upper house races between 1986 and 1989. Rather, a substantial proportion of these losses are probably the product of this pattern of differential left/right mobilization and abstentions.

Since the twenty-six one-seat prefectures are predominantly rural and the six three-to-four-seat districts largely metropolitan, we have a weak urban-rural measure that can be used to identify the relative concentrations of farmers. This data can be employed to test whether rates of defection in the actual vote for the LDP were greater in rural prefectures than urban. When we normalize the LDP's vote percentages by excluding abstainers and compute its rate of defection between the 1986 and 1989 elections, we find that this rate drops from 28 percent for the one-seat districts to 25 percent for the two-seat districts and to 22 percent for the three-to-four-seat districts. This evidence suggests that there were important mobilization and demobilization effects in the 1989 election that induced some traditional LDP supporters in rural areas to switch their vote to other parties and others to abstain from voting.

Our two sets of variables, therefore, the psychological and sociological, provide two distinct but reinforcing explanations of the LDP defeat in the 1989 HC elections. Each provides us with a different view or model of Japanese voting behavior. The psychological explanations suggest a nationalized, partisan evaluation model, contrasting the destabilizing effects of valence issues and the shifting images of parties and party leaders with the stabilizing effects of value cleavages, residual and latent position issues, and party loyalties. The sociological explanations suggest a localized mobilization effects model, contrasting the stabilizing effects of enduring social contexts and social networks with the destabilizing effects of shifting or weakening party/group alignments, the demobilization of campaign efforts, and the declining reach of social network influences in the face of growing social mobility, complexity, and political sophistication.

As we have suggested, these models can be viewed as differentially motivating the behavior of two distinct electorates defined by region and occupation—one composed of metropolitan blue- and white-collar workers in large enterprises and the comprising other rural and small city farmers, small merchants and manufacturers, and workers in small enterprises. Of course, both sets of influences are at work in all sectors and strata of Japanese society, so the distinction here is one of degrees of variation in the relative importance of each set of variables in explaining the vote of one type of constituency or another. Empirical evidence of variation between variable types in their predictive power was presented in figures 3.3 and 3.4, which show the urban-rural differences in the influence of issues versus occupational context on vote choice. To sum up our argument, the distinctions we have made between sets of variables, voting models, and types of constituencies provide us with two distinct explanations for the dramatic defeat of the ruling party in the 1989 HC election: 1) negative partisans defected from the LDP in droves in response to shifts in the images of parties and party leaders; and 2) the apathetic nonpartisans and uninformed partisans, who had been habitually mobilized to vote LDP, either abstained or defected as a result of their demobilization or countermobilization.

The 1990 Lower House Election

Does the 1989 upper house election signal a major turning point in Japanese politics and voting behavior? Following that election, some observers seized on the results to claim that Japanese voters would no longer tolerate the corruption and immorality of the past, that women voters and their concerns have become an important new force in Japanese elections, and that the policy demands of the people can no longer be ignored by an arrogant and insulated, perpetually ruling party. These kinds of exaggerated claims often accompany the attempts of superficial descriptive accounts to explain large shifts in single election outcomes. While certainly signs of change can be found, it appears that the 1989 election result emerged from a coincidental confluence of unrelated events, which combined to alienate several of the ruling party's traditional constituencies temporarily and momentarily alter the relative negativity of party images. The ruling party's plunging image was only further discredited by the party's unbelievable ineptness in handling the issues of the day.[12] Clearly, this election was more lost by the LDP than won by the Socialists.

12. The Japanese media had a field day with LDP politicians' repeated foot-in-mouth statements, which only served further to tarnish the ruling party's image. For example, Agricultural Minister Hisao Horinouchi was quoted as saying, "Women are useless in politics," while Home Affairs Minister Shigenobu Sakano stated in response to complaints about the cumbersome aspects of the new tax that "a 4 percent consumption tax would be easier to calculate than a 3 percent tax," suggesting that the government might be intending to raise the tax even further. Meanwhile, another LDP Dietmember commented that the ruling party would have to maintain subsidies for the farmers because they were too stupid to do any other kind of work.

Even immediately after the election almost no one was predicting that the LDP would do as badly in a lower house election, even if voting preferences remained unchanged. Differences in the electoral systems between the two houses make this unlikely. Two-fifths of the upper house seats are filled on a proportional representation basis and the election districts are larger, increasing the distance between voters and candidates and the relative importance of party versus candidate in the voter's decision. The smaller lower house districts augment the feasibility and effectiveness of the "personal connections and favors" style of campaigning that exploits social networks and traditionally gives the advantage to LDP candidates, who are better positioned to deliver benefits to their constituents. In addition, more parties compete in the upper rather than the lower house elections, further draining votes away from the ruling party. Finally, for those that voted against the ruling party as a protest vote, the upper house election was a safe arena in which to express their displeasure, because a loss in the upper house does not threaten the LDP's control of the government. These protest voters clearly began having second thoughts when it came to the February 1990 lower house election, since a loss in that election would have meant turning power over to the opposition parties.

Beyond these electoral system differences, however, our analysis above would lead to the prediction that LDP fortunes would almost inevitably rebound somewhat in the 1990 lower house election. Indeed, the sources and causes of the LDP defections in 1989 would suggest that they were not sustainable, at least not to the degree experienced in the upper house election. This becomes clear when we revisit our party image and social network explanations in the context of the 1990 campaign.

It was, after all, the unusual combination of three major and largely unrelated valence issues—all of which heightened the negativity of the ruling party's image and peaked at the time of the 1989 election—that induced a popular swing away from the LDP. As we have noted, however, valence issues are inherently short-term in nature and tend to fade, often within a few short months, as public emotions and attention subside. For example, during the seven months between the 1989 and 1990 elections, the effects of the Recruit scandal on voter attitudes had largely fizzled out. As a result, all but two of the sixteen candidates tainted by the scandal were reelected, including former prime ministers Nakasone, Takeshita, and Uno, LDP faction leaders Abe and Miyazawa, and one of the two indicted candidates. Moreover, the obstacles to leadership that involvement in the scandal previously imposed, requiring resignations from public or party offices and even from the party itself, were now declared null and void, as the victorious candidates claimed that their reelection constituted not simply a public vindication but a purification rite that restored their reputations and rejuvenated their ambitions.

It could be argued that the shift in the relative attractiveness of the LDP and JSP images that impacted so heavily on the 1989 election results provided the JSP with a great opportunity. Having gained the national spotlight, if the party had been able to inspire confidence and act like a real contender, a somewhat coincidental result in the 1989 election could have become the basis for a new reality, with the JSP shedding its ideological baggage, embracing popular stands, and gaining legitimacy. In other words, the shift in the relative attractiveness of the major parties' images might have been sustained if the temporarily increased negativity of the LDP image was reinforced by positive gains in the popular image of the JSP.

Despite Chairwoman Doi's pragmatism and popularity, however, it was perhaps too much to expect that the Socialists could overcome overnight all of their past problems that have been responsible for their steady electoral decline up to 1989. Instead, now it became the Socialists' turn to look bad as *a*) a Pachinko scandal emerged involving Socialist Dietmen, and their evasive responses made the JSP look no different from the LDP;[13] *b*) one JSP Dietman proved that Socialists could be just as arrogant as their LDP counterparts by forcing an express train to make an unscheduled stop at a town where he was scheduled to speak; and *c*) the opportunism and bankruptcy of JSP policies became apparent when the Socialists voted both to repeal the consumption tax and to postpone any vote on a replacement tax until after the coming lower house election. More fundamental, Doi's efforts to soften the party's Marxist principles met with only limited success in the face of the intractable opposition of the party's leftist caucus. As a result, the JSP remained unable to smooth over its policy differences on defense, foreign relations, and other issues with the moderate center parties, thereby frustrating attempts to construct an opposition party coalition alternative to continued LDP rule or a cooperative election strategy. Instead, the JSP appeared to be wedded to obsolete policies and mired down in factional feuding, as seen in former JSP Chairman Masashi Ishibashi's public attack on Doi's leadership as "fascist" (*Asia 1990 Yearbook; Japan Times Weekly*, 2/12/90; *Daily Yomiuri*, 2/20/90).

For its part the ruling party took a number of steps to repair its damaged image. While it did not seriously confront the corruption issue, it was more successful in finding a leader who could project a more positive image for the party. Following the election, Uno was replaced as prime minister by Toshiki

13. It was not simply the improprieties of donations from the pachinko industry to the JSP, but the media claim that the party's relations with the largely Korean-owned industry were part of a broader network of connections with the North Korean government. The JSP is the only Japanese party that recognizes the North Korean regime, and this media association of the Socialists with communism, at a time when communism is in disfavor and retreat, did nothing to improve the public image of the party (*Asia 1990 Yearbook*).

Kaifu, a clean, youthful, eloquent, and witty member of a small reform-minded faction. Like Nakasone, who served as prime minister from 1982–87, Kaifu represents a new breed of Japanese leader who is more at home with and effective in the media. Also like Nakasone, Kaifu's growing public popularity helped improve the party's support at the polls. Indeed, the support for Kaifu's cabinet had risen to 43 percent in a February preelection poll and, by Japanese standards, to a very high 53 percent in a March postelection poll (*Yomiuri Shimbun*, 2/16/90, 3/15/90).[14] The party made a number of other cosmetic changes, including the selection of relatively young men for LDP secretary general and a few other posts and, for the first time ever, the appointment of two women to cabinet positions, including the highly visible post of chief cabinet secretary.

In addition to these efforts to diffuse the reform and gender issues, the LDP took measures to appease public displeasure over the consumption tax. In view of the declining public criticism of the tax, it would appear that by February 1990 either the public was becoming more resigned and accustomed to paying the tax or at least felt that the announced LDP plan to revise it rang more true than the JSP position of abolishing it before agreeing on a replacement tax. Indeed, an Asahi preelection poll reported that more people had come to prefer the LDP modification measure to the complete repeal of the tax by a 45 to 40 percent margin (*Asahi Shimbun*, 1/29/90). Finally, on the farm issue, the LDP took a stiffer stand on import negotiations with the United States, declared that not one grain of foreign rice would be imported, and rescinded an expected cut in rice subsidies (*Daily Yomiuri*, 2/20/90; *Japan Times Weekly*, 2/5/90).

From an outsider's perspective the focus of the campaign rhetoric seemed to miss the mark. The Socialists stubbornly clung to the three issues that had carried them to success in the upper house election, hammering especially hard on the tax issue, despite media criticism that the JSP was relying once again on its traditional posture of pure opposition to LDP policies without offering any fresh programs or new visions for Japan. For its part, the ruling party emphasized its role as the champion of a free market economy, democracy, and political stability, arguing that it would be regressive for Japan to turn to socialism at a time when Eastern Europe was abandoning it as a failed system. Much of the LDP campaign rhetoric seemed designed to raise fears that a JSP victory would bring political instability and economic ruin. Leaders of the LDP

14. Kaifu won this popularity despite repeated rumors that he was only Takeshita's puppet and that his weak position within the party would prevent any serious reform efforts and insure his short tenure in office following the lower house election. Yet the fact that he was able to show signs of leadership and withstand attacks from within the party increased his popularity in the early months following the election.

continually stressed the points that the JSP still calls for a "socialist revolution" in its platform, that its lack of experience would send Japan into an "economic hell," and that its call to revise or abolish the U.S.-Japan Security Treaty would wreck this important bilateral relationship at a time when delicate negotiations were required to ensure continued favorable trade patterns. A largely missing issue concerns the fact that Japan has a first-rate economy and a third-rate standard of living, with land prices averaging twenty-five times higher in Japan than the United States and consumer prices for basic commodities two or three times higher. While the ruling party did announce a package of monopoly controls over domestic business aimed at combating high consumer prices, these measures seemed designed more to placate Japan's trading partners than consumer demand. Judging from the opinion polls, the Japanese public seems willing to largely discount its continuing lag in living standards so long as the trend toward a stronger economy and greater affluence continues (*Christian Science Monitor*, 2/16/90; *Chicago Tribune*, 2/18/90; *Daily Yomiuri*, 2/20/90; *Japan Times Weekly*, 2/5/90).

When we add up the Socialists' dimming image, the dissipation of the valence issues and with them anti-LDP feeling, continued economic prosperity, and the Japanese electorate's basic conservatism and distaste for abrupt change, we can see that the stage was set for an LDP resurgence. This shift was clearly anticipated by the regular monthly polls on party support. In one example of these, the *Yomiuri Shimbun* series, we find that the legacy of the popularity of Nakasone, during his last two years of tenure as prime minister, was unusually high levels of public support for the ruling party, averaging slightly above 50 percent. These levels continued through the early months of the Takeshita cabinet, and then for the monthly polls from March to October 1988 they averaged slightly above 48 percent. In November 1988 a steady decline in LDP support set in, reaching a low point of 26 percent in May 1989. This trend had already begun to reverse by the time of the July upper house election, and LDP support rose steadily thereafter, reaching 35 percent by August, 45 percent in the preelection February 1990 poll, and 49 percent in the March postelection poll. Conversely, the Socialists' support fell from a high of nearly 31 percent in the *Yomiuri*'s preelection July 1989 poll to 21 percent in its preelection February 1990 poll.

As shown in table 11.1, the February preelection survey results were fairly close to the LDP and JSP actual voting percentages of 46 and 24 percent, respectively. This lower house election represented a tremendous victory for the ruling party, winning 275 seats outright, which quickly rose to 286 as 11 conservative independents immediately joined the party after the election. This was well above the 257 needed for a simple majority or the 271 needed for a stable majority (controlling the chairmanships of all HR committees), but not as dominating as the 304 official and nominally independent seats the party won in 1986. The JSP also advanced over its 1986 totals, rising from 17 to 24 percent of the vote and 85 to 136 seats, representing the Socialists' best outing since 1967. Most of the Socialist gains, however, seem to have come at the expense of the other, small opposition parties.

Our analysis of the 1990 lower house election in terms of shifting issue salience and party image would not be complete if we did not also consider the role of our second set of variables and the explanation they provide. Just as an LDP resurgence was implicit in the psychological explanation of the causes of their 1989 defeat, so too does the sociological explanation, with its focus on social network influences and mobilization efforts, suggest that an LDP comeback was virtually inevitable. Mobilization inactivity and voting abstentions are not sustainable strategies. They are one-shot weapons designed to punish and shock in order to better position an interest to drive its best bargain with the ruling party. In reality, there is no other party or coalition of parties to which farmers and small businessmen can reliably turn. The upper house election result did in fact rally the LDP behind farmers and small retail interests, with the party taking steps to placate and reward both groups.

These policy measures at the national level were reinforced by long-standing ties between LDP candidates and local communities and leaders and by unusually active campaigns by desperate LDP candidates.[15] Once again the grease that revitalized these LDP mobilization networks was lavish campaign spending. It was estimated that LDP spending during the fifteen-day campaign reached record levels of $1.5 billion (U.S.) or $4.4 million per candidate. When we consider that very little of this was spent on the media or on advertisements, the impact of this spending on interpersonal mobilization efforts becomes apparent. In addition to the usual reports of heavy spending on food, drink, and trips for supporters, we find an interesting use of large telephone banks of one hundred or more in each of a candidate's campaign offices making tens of thousands of calls during the last two days of the campaign. While this seems to be approaching the anonymous canvassing techniques found in the United States, it appears that the centralization of these efforts was made possible by close relationships between LDP candidates and particular companies, and the use of employee lists for these large, parent companies and their many subcontractors to identify and contact voters. At the same time LDP

15. It was reported that many of the party's top figures who traditionally had more or less safe seats were running for their lives. For example, Nakasone campaigned nearly full time for six months prior to the election, attending every public meeting, school reunion, or community activity we could find (*Asiaweek*, 3/2/90).

Secretary-General Ichiro Ozawa and other party leaders were twisting the arms of big business to make massive donations to the party, threatening that the country would be turned over to "incompetent socialists" if they did not come through. In the case of specific industries that had benefited from recent LDP policy measures, such as construction, securities, autos, and electronics, these approaches sometimes included veiled threats that their benefits might be retracted if they did not make "special donations." As a result, only the most blatant, public fund-raising practices were curtailed, that is, those publicized by the Recruit scandal, such as the raising of $7–8 million in one night by selling large numbers of expensive dinner party tickets to companies (*Asahi Shimbun*, 2/17/90; *Economist*, 2/3/90, 2/24/90; *Asiaweek*, 3/2/90; *New York Times*, 2/29/90).

These vote mobilization efforts were rewarded by a return to the polls of many of the LDP supporters who had sat out the 1989 election. This is apparent from an analysis of election turn-out rates. Typically fewer voters turn out for the upper house contests, but the average turn-out rates in HC elections by decade for the 1960s, 1970s, and 1980s through 1986 hovered within a narrow range of 67–68 percent. Even for an upper house election, then, the 1989 HC rate of 65 percent represented a low participation level. Conversely, the average lower house turn-out rates across the same three decades clustered even more tightly in the 71.3 to 71.8 percent range. From this perspective the 1983 HR turn-out rate of 67.9 was below average, the 1986 double election rate of 71.4 was average, and the 1990 rate of 73.3 was well above average, even without the additional stimulation of a double election. Looking more closely, if we select the three most urban prefectures (Tokyo, Kanagawa, and Osaka) having around 1 percent of their work force engaged in agriculture or fishing in 1985, we find a rise in their turn-out rates between the 1983 and 1990 HR elections of from 60 to 65 percent, very near the average gain for the whole nation. If we select the seven most rural prefectures, however, all having farming populations of over 20 percent of the work force, we find that their turn-out rates rose from 73 to 80 percent, an above-average increase in an area with already high voting levels (*Yomiuri Shimbun*, 2/19/90; *Japan Statistical Yearbooks*). Another useful comparison is that between the numbers of 1989 and 1990 voters. Over ten million more voters turned out for the 1990 election, a gain of almost 18 percent over the number of voters in 1989. This is only slightly larger than the differences in the numbers of voters in the 1983 versus 1990 HR elections (nine million). These data point to the potential for abstention versus mobilization strategies to change the size and composition of the voting public.

Other evidence of the farmers' return to the LDP fold comes from public opinion data on party support by occupation from HR preelection 1986 and 1990 surveys reported in the *Asahi Shimbun* (2/26/90). Here we find support for the LDP falling only from 74 to 72 percent across the two elections, yielding a rate of defection of only 3 percent, which was substantially lower than that for any other occupational category and much lower than the 38 percent figure reported for farmers for the HC elections in table 11.2. As expected, all occupational categories reflected lower declines in LDP support than was true for the upper house election, with the largest defection rate for the HR elections being a 24 percent decline for sales workers.

■ Changing Voters and Unchanging Outcomes

We have argued that the Japanese voter is changing in ways that are increasing the potential for volatility in election outcomes. Our psychological variables have identified the tentative or conditional manner in which the vote of the negative partisans is anchored. As we have noted, negative partisans lack an affective tie to a party and hence are unusually susceptible to shifting party images. The high and apparently growing proportions of negative partisans that we find in Japan are increasing the role of the media, valence issues, and other short-term forces in influencing election outcomes by reshaping the popular images of parties and party leaders.

Our sociological variables point to the contracting power and reach of social contexts and networks in mobilizing and guiding voting decisions in the face of the growing mobility, heterogeneity, and sophistication of the Japanese electorate. Moreover, not only are the ruling party's traditional bastions of support—the farmers and the self-employed old middle class—shrinking in size, but international forces are conspiring to force the LDP to abandon its support for the special privileges and protection these groups have enjoyed in Japanese society in the form of farm subsidies, an archaic and inefficient distribution system that supports many redundant workers, and legal restrictions against the spread of large discount retailers. As the government finds itself pushed to retreat on these group benefits, the party/interest group alignments that have formed the basis of the LDP's vote-mobilization efforts are likely to weaken further. While we are not predicting a realignment, it is nevertheless quite possible that the demobilization/countermobilization phenomenon associated with the 1989 HC election will prove not to have been a unique event.

If we can confidently predict that the growing levels of volatility associated with Japanese elections over the past two decades are here to stay, will this finally bring an end to the LDP's phenomenal string of HR victories over the past thirty-five years. Although many would claim that turnover is necessary to root out the corruption and unresponsiveness associated with one-party rule, we are much less sanguine about the prospects of a real turnover of power in Japan in the foreseeable future. While the 1989 upper house election draws our attention to the potential for substantial change in party support patterns within the Japanese electorate, the 1990 lower house election exemplifies the electorate's apprehension regarding change. Ultimately, the LDP cannot lose because the opposition cannot win. Not only did the opposition parties fail to agree on a coalition platform and structure but the only likely parties in such a coalition— the JSP, DSP, CGP, and SDF—put up between them just 257 candidates. This was only the barest possible simple majority of the seats, so unless every one of them had won they would not have been able to form a government.[16] More fundamental, the opposition could not win because the public does not trust them to run the government. Even directly after the JSP's smashing victory in the 1989 upper house election, only 13 percent of the electorate felt power should be given to the opposition parties, only 16 percent wanted the opposition parties to gain a majority in the next lower house election, and only 14 percent wanted some combination of opposition parties to gain power (*Mainichi Shimbun,* 8/25/89).

Herein we find the dilemma of the Japanese voter. He or she is unhappy with the ruling party but unwilling to see the opposition gain power. This dilemma transforms Japanese elections into an "empty choice." The goal of the Japanese voter then becomes one of returning the LDP to office with the smallest possible margin of victory to force the party to pay more attention to public demands and clean up its act. This creates a pendulum effect whereby if the party comes close to losing its majority, as happened in 1979 and 1983, some protest voters return to the LDP fold in the next election, giving the ruling party a more comfortable margin of victory, as happened in 1980 and 1986. In this most recent case, after punishing the ruling party in the 1989 upper house election, the electorate stepped back from the brink of entrusting the nation's economy to a quarrelsome coalition of opposition parties and swung its support back to the LDP.

There are, however, increasing signs that the Japanese electorate wants to see some kind of political change. For example, the same August 1989 poll found that the Japanese public is moving closer to the idea of preferring some kind of coalition government to place limits on the ruling party's power. Thus, 58 percent desired an electoral outcome with a close power balance between the LDP and all opposition parties, and 59 percent wanted the LDP to share power with one or more of the opposition parties (*Mainichi Shimbun,* 8/25/89). De-

16. This problem is seen particularly clearly in the case of the JSP and Chairwoman Doi's failure to raise her party's number of candidates from 130 in the 1986 election to even 180, having to settle for 149. With Japan's 130 three-to-five member districts, putting up more than 130 candidates pits two JSP candidates against each other in some districts, thereby threatening the defeat of both.

spite the LDP's subsequent resurgence in the polls, these sentiments had not changed by the time of the February 1990 election. A January preelection survey found that, excluding missing cases, only 20 percent wanted the LDP to form a single-party government, 47 percent desired an LDP-led coalition government that would include either the center parties or the JSP, and only 33 percent wanted some sort of opposition party government excluding the LDP (*Asahi Shimbun*, 1/29/90). The electorate has also discovered a new weapon for forcing closer cooperation between the governing and opposition parties by awarding an opposition coalition a majority of the seats in the upper house, thereby requiring some formal or de facto coalition government for the passage of government bills.

It still seems to be true that the more dissatisfied one is with politics in Japan, the more likely one is to vote for the opposition. For example, an *Asahi* postelection poll found that 79 percent of those voting JSP in the 1990 lower house election were dissatisfied with politics, compared to only 54 percent of those voting LDP (*Asahi Shimbun*, 2/26/90). Even among those who voted for the ruling party, however, we find high levels of dissatisfaction. Apparently a more subtle way of registering this dissatisfaction without changing parties is by selectively punishing certain LDP candidates. Several architects of Japan's farm policy, Tatsuo Sasayama, and former Agricultural Minister Hisao Horinouchi went down to defeat, as did the author of the hated consumption tax, Sasanori Yamanaka. Many voters seem to have shifted their support to younger, new faces. In fact, over 25 percent of the successful candidates were first-time winners, a fairly high percentage in Japanese elections where the power of incumbency is very strong.[17]

Meaningful change, however, is not likely to come to Japanese politics until an alternation of parties in power becomes possible, either through a breakup of the LDP into two conservative parties or the growth of a single large opposition party. The first steps toward that latter goal can be seen in the unification of the labor movement behind Rengo and the gains for the JSP in the 1989 and 1990 elections. But at this writing a real turnover in power remains a long way off. Until such a fundamental realignment in the party system and party support

17. Increasingly in Japan, political careers are made through dynastic succession, with sons or other relatives inheriting a politician's support association network and campaign machine. In fact, among the successful LDP candidates in the 1990 election, an estimated half were close kin of past or present party members. Inheriting a successful machine helps the candidate to overcome the high network-building start-up costs associated with establishing a support organization in one's district. Constituents can benefit from the candidate's powerful inherited connections in Tokyo. In his inaugural 1990 lower house campaign Shunichi Suzuki, son of former prime minister Zenko Suzuki, who was returned sixteen times by his district, told his supporters, "My father has built a human network inside the national government. By preserving the network, I hope to be helpful to you" (*Washington Post*, 2/17/90; *Christian Science Monitor*, 2/16/90).

patterns is realized, we are likely to continue to find large proportions of both negative partisans, who extend only a conditional support for their chosen party, and mobilized voters. Moreover, while we have suggested that the diffusion of education and political information is reducing the numbers of uninformed mobilized voters, the personally obligated type of mobilized voter discussed in chapter 4 may not be on the decline. Indeed, the relatively high affective detachment from politics we find in Japan increases the likelihood that votes may be mobilized on the basis of personal loyalties. Until Japanese elections become more than an empty choice, voting as a favor to someone may seem as good a reason as any.

■ References

Abramowitz, Alan I. (1980) "The United States: Political Culture under Stress," pp. 177–211 in Gabriel Almond and Sidney Verba, eds., *The Civic Culture Revisited*. Boston: Little, Brown.

Abramson, Paul R. (1971) "Social Class and Political Change in Western Europe: A Cross-National Longitudinal Analysis." *Comparative Political Studies* 4:131–56.

Adams, William C. (1984) "Media Power in Presidential Elections: An Exploratory Analysis, 1960–1980, pp. 175–85 in Doris A Graber, ed., *Media Power in Politics*. Washington, D.C.: Congressional Quarterly.

AERA Staff and Masumi Ishikawa. (1989) "Nihon no Senkyo." *Asahi Shimbun Weekly AERA* 33 (August 5), pp. 13–18.

Akarui Senkyo Suishin Kyokai. (1977) *Dai 34 kai Shugiin Giin Sosenkyo no Jittai*. Tokyo: Akarui Senkyo Suishin Kyokai.

———. (1979). *Chiho Senkyo no Jittai*. Tokyo.

———. (1980a) *Dai 35 kai Shugiin Giin Sosenkyo no Jittai*. Tokyo.

———. (1980b) *Dai 36 kai Shugiin Giin Sosenkyo no Jittai; Dai 12 kai Sangiin Giin Tsujo Senkyo no Jittai*. Tokyo.

———. (1986) *Dai 38 kai Shugiin Giin Sosenkyo; Dai 14 kai Sangiin Giin Sosenkyo no Jittai*. Tokyo.

———. (1989) *Dai 15 kai Sangiin Giin Sosenkyo no Jittai*. Tokyo.

Akuto, Hiroshi. (1970) *Imeji no Shinrigaku*. Tokyo: Ushio Shuppansha.

———. (1975) "Seitoshiji to Raifu sutairu no Kanren," in Nihonjin Kenkyukai, ed., *Nihonjin Kenkyu No. 2: Tokushu Seitoshijibetsu Nihonjin Shudan*. Tokyo: Shiseido.

Alford, Robert R. (1963) *Party and Society: The Anglo-American Societies*. Chicago: Rand McNally.

Allinson, Gary D. (1975) *Japanese Urbanism: Industry and Politics in Kariya, 1872–1972*. Berkeley: University of California Press.

———. (1979) *Suburban Tokyo: A Comparative Study in Politics and Social Change*. Berkeley: The University of California Press.

———. (1980) "Opposition in the Suburbs," pp. 95–130 in Kurt Steiner, Ellis S.. Krauss, and Scott C. Flanagan, eds., *Political Opposition and Local Politics in Japan*. Princeton: Princeton University Press.

Almond, Gabriel A., and Sidney Verba. (1963) *The Civic Culture*. Princeton: Princeton University Press.

Almond, Gabriel A., and G. Bingham Powell, Jr. (1966) *Comparative Politics: A Developmental Approach*. Boston: Little, Brown.

Asahi Shimbunsha. (1976) *Nihonjin no Seiji Ishiki: Asahi Shimbun Yoron Chosa no Sanjunen*. Tokyo: Asahi Shimbunsha.

———. (1982) *Asahi Nenkan-Bekkan 1982*. Tokyo: Asahi Shimbunsha.

———. (1987) *Asahi Nenkan 1986*. Tokyo: Asahi Shimbunsha.

Asher, Herbert. (1982) "Voting Behavior Research in the 1980s: An Examination of Some Old and New Problem Areas." Paper presented at the annual meeting of the American Political Science Association.

Asia 1990 Yearbook. (1990) Far Eastern Economic Review. Hongkong: Review Publishing Co.

Austin, Lewis. (1975) *Saints and Samurai: The Political Culture of the American and Japanese Elites*. New Haven: Yale University Press.

Baerwald, Hans. (1976) "Lockheed and Japanese Politics." *Asian Survey* 16: 817–29.

———. (1989) "Japan's House of Councillors Election: A Mini-Revolution?" *Asian Survey* 29:833–41.

Baker, Kendall L., Russell J. Dalton, and Kai Hildebrandt. (1981) *Germany Transformed: Political Culture and the New Politics*. Cambridge: Harvard University Press.

Barnes, Samuel H. (1971) "Left, Right and the Italian Voter." *Comparative Political Studies* 4:157–76.

Barnes, Samuel H., and Roy Pierce. (1971) "Public Opinion and Political Preferences in France and Italy." *Midwest Journal of Political Science* 15:643–60.

Barnes, Samuel H., and Max Kaase, eds. (1979) *Political Action: Mass Participation in Five Western Democracies*. Beverly Hills: Sage.

Beardsley, Richard K., John W. Hall, and Robert E. Ward. (1959) *Village Japan*. Chicago: University of Chicago Press.

———. (1965) *Twelve Doors to Japan*. New York: McGraw Hill.

Becker, Lee B., Maxwell E. McCombs, and Jack M. McLeod. (1975) "The Development of Political Cgnitions," in Steven H. Chaffee, ed., *Political Communication: Issues and Strategies for Research*. Beverly Hills: Sage.

Bell, Daniel. (1976) *The Cultural Contradictions of Capitalism*. New York: Basic Books.

Berelson, Bernard R., Paul F. Lazarsfeld, and William N. McPhee. (1954) *Voting: A Study of Opinion Formation in a Presidential Campaign*. Chicago: University of Chicago Press.

Binkley, Wilfred E. (1958) *American Political Parties Their Natural History*. New York: Alfred Knopf.

Borre, Ole, and Daniel Katz. (1973) "Party Identification and Its Motivational Base in a Multi-Party System: A Study of the Danish General Election of 1971." *Scandinavian Political Studies* 8:69–111.

Brody, Richard A. (1977) "Stability and Change in Party Identification: Presidential to

Off-Years." Paper presented at the annual meeting of the American Political Science Association.

Brody, Richard A., and Benjamin Page. (1972) "Comment: The Assessment of Policy Voting." *American Political Science Review* 66:450–58.

Budge, Ian. (1982) "Strategies, Issues, and Votes: British General Elections, 1950– 197." *Comparative Political Studies* 15:171–96.

Budge, Ian, Ivor Crewe, and Dennis Farlie. (1976) *Party Identification and Beyond: Representations of Voting and Party Competition.* London: John Wiley.

Bunka Cho. (1981) *Shukyo Nenkan Showa 56 nenban.* Tokyo: Bunka cho.

Butler, David, and Donald Stokes. (1969) *Political Change in Britain: Forces Shaping Electoral Choice.* New York: St. Martin's. Rev. ed. New York: St. Martin's, 1976.

Cameron, David. (1972–73) "Stability and Change in Patterns of French Partisanship." *Public Opinion Quarterly* 36:19–30.

Campbell, Angus. (1966) "A Classification of Presidential Elections," pp. 63–77 in Angus Campbell, Philip E. Converse, Warren E. Miller, and Donald E. Stokes, *Elections and the Political Order.* New York: John Wiley.

Campbell, Angus, Gerald Gurin, and Warren E. Miller. (1954) *The Voter Decides.* Evanston: Row, Peterson.

Campbell, Angus, Philip E. Converse, Warren E. Miller, and Donald E. Stokes. (1960) *The American Voter.* New York: John Wiley.

Campbell, Angus, and Henry Valen. (1961) "Party Identification in Norway and the United States." *Public Opinion Quarterly* 25:245–68. Reprint, pp. 245–68 in Campbell et al., *Elections and the Political Order,* 1966.

Campbell, John C. (1987) "Reinvigoration of Traditional Support Patterns: The Eleven General Elections, 1958–1986." Paper presented at the annual meeting of the Association of Asian Studies, Boston, April 10–12.

Carmines, Edward G., and James A. Stimson. (1980) "The Two Faces of Issue Voting." *American Political Science Review* 74:78–91.

Chaffee, S. H., Ward, L. S., and Tipton, L. P. (1970) "Mass Communication and Political Socialization" *Journalism Quarterly* 47:647–50.

Cohen, B. C. (1963) *The Press, the Public, and Foreign Policy.* Princeton: Princeton University Press.

Conover, Pamela J., and Stanley Feldman. (1984) "How People Organize the Political World: A Schematic Model." *American Journal of Political Science* 28:95– 126.

Converse, Philip E. (1966) "The Concept of a Normal Vote," pp. 9–39 in Angus Campbell et al., *Elections and the Political Order.*

———. (1969) "Of Time and Partisan Stability." *Comparative Political Studies* 2:139– 57.

———. (1975) "Public Opinion and Voting Behavior," pp. 75–169 in Fred Greenstein and Nelson Polsby, eds., *Nongovernmental Politics,* vol. 4 of *Handbook of Political Science.* Reading, Mass: Addison-Wesley.

———. (1976) *Dynamics of Party Support.* Beverly Hills: Sage.

Converse, Philip E., and Georges Dupeux. (1962) "Politicization of the Electorate in France and the United States." *Public Opinion Quarterly* 26:269–91.

Converse, Philip E., and Gregory Markus. (1979) "Plus ça change . . . : The New CPS Election Study Panel." *American Political Science Review* 73:32–49.

Crewe, Ivor. (1976) "Party Identification Theory and Political Change in Britain," pp. 33–62 in Ian Budge, Ivor Crewe, and Dennis Farlie, *Party Identification and Beyond.* New York: Wiley.

Crewe, Ivor, and David Denver. (1985) *Electoral Change in Western Democracies: Patterns and Sources of Electoral Volatility.* New York: St. Martin's.

Curtis, Gerald L. (1971) *Election Campaigning Japanese Style.* New York: Columbia University Press.

———. (1983) "Social Patterns in the Political Arena," pp. 20–37 in Michael W. D. McMullen, ed., *Japan in the 1980s II: Papers on International Studies,* no. 6. Atlanta: Southern Center for International Studies.

———. (1988) *The Japanese Way of Politics.* New York: Columbia University Press.

Daalder, Hans. (1966) "The Netherlands: Opposition in a Segmented Society," pp. 188–236 in Robert A. Dahl, ed., *Political Opposition in Western Democracies.* New Haven: Yale University Press.

Dalton, Russell J., Scott C. Flanagan, and Paul A. Beck, eds. (1984) *Electoral Change in Advanced Industrial Democracies: Realignment or Dealignment?* Princeton: Princeton University Press.

Dennis, Jack. (1975) "Trends in Support for the American Party System." *British Journal of Political Science* 5:187–230.

———. (1981) "Some Properties of Partisanship." Paper presented at the annual meeting of the American Political Science Association, New York.

Dobson, Douglas, and Douglas St. Angelo. (1975) "Party Identification and the Floating Vote: Some Dynamics." *American Political Science Review* 69:481–90.

Doi, Takeo. (1973) *The Anatomy of Dependence.* Tokyo: Kodansha International.

Donovan, Maureen. (1981) "The Media in Japan," pp. 258–68 in Bradley M. Richardson and Taizo Ueda, eds., *Business and Society in Japan.* New York: Praeger.

Dore, Ronald P. (1956) "Japanese Election Candidates in 1955." *Pacific Affairs* 40:443–67.

———. (1958) *City Life in Japan.* Berkeley: University of California Press.

———. (1959) *Land Reform in Japan.* London: Oxford University Press.

———. (1978) *Shinohata: A Portrait of a Japanese Village.* New York: Pantheon Books.

Easton, D., and J. Dennis. (1969) *Children in the Political System: Origins of Political Legitimacy.* New York: McGraw-Hill.

Efron, E. (1973) *The News Twisters.* Los Angeles: Nash.

Eldersveld, Samuel J. (1973) "Party Identification in India in Comparative Perspective." *Comparative Political Studies* 7:271–95.

Eldersveld, Samuel J., and Akira Kubota. (1973) "Party Identification in India and

Japan—In the Context of Western Theory and Research." Paper presented at the annual meeting of the Canadian Political Science Association.

Erbring, Lutz, Edie Goldenberg, and Arthur Miller. (1980) "Front Page News, Real World Cues: A New Look at Agenda Setting in the Media." *American Journal of Political Science* 24:16–49.

Esping-Anderson, G., and W. Korpi. (1987) "From Poor Relief Towards Institutional Welfare States: The Development of Scandinavian Social Policy," in R. Erikson., ed. *The Scandinavian Model: The Welfare States and Welfare Research*. New York: M. E. Sharpe.

Eulau, Heinz, and Lawrence Rothenberg. (1986) "Life Space and Social Networks as Political Contexts." *Political Behavior* 8:130–57.

Falconeri, G. R. (1976) "The Impact of Rapid Urban Change on Neighborhood Solidarity," in James White and Frank Munger, eds., *Social Change and Community Politics in Urban Japan*. Chapel Hill: University of North Carolina Institute for Research in Social Science.

Fiorina, Morris P. (1981) *Retrospective Voting in American National Elections*. New Haven: Yale University Press.

Fiske, Susan T., and Donald R. Kinder. (1981) "Involvement, Expertise, and Schema Use: Evidence from Political Cognition," pp. 171–90 in Nancy Cantor and John F. Kihlstrom, eds., *Personality, Cognition, and Social Interaction*. Hillsdale, N.J.: Lawrence Erlbaum.

Fiske, Susan T., and Shelley E. Taylor. (1984) *Social Cognition*. New York: Random House.

Flanagan, Scott C. (1968) "Voting Behavior in Japan: The Persistence of Traditional Patterns." *Comparative Political Studies* 1: 391–412.

———. (1978) "The Genesis of Variant Political Cultures: The Origins of Contemporary Citizen Orientations in Japan, America, Britain and Italy," pp. 129–65 in Sidney Verba and Lucian Pye, eds., *The Citizen and Politics: A Comparative Analysis*. Stamford, Conn.: Greylock.

———. (1979) "Value Change and Partisan Change in Japan: The Silent Revolution Revisited." *Comparative Politics* 11:253–78.

———. (1980a) "Electoral Change in Japan: An Overview," pp. 35–54 in Kurt Steiner, Ellis S. Krauss, and Scott C. Flanagan, eds., *Political Opposition and Local Politics in Japan*. Princeton: Princeton University Press.

———. (1980b) "National and Local Voting Trends: Cross-Level Linkages and Correlates of Change," pp. 131–84 in Steiner, et al., *Political Opposition and Local Politics in Japan*.

———. (1980c) "Value Cleavages, Economic Cleavages and the Japanese Voter." *American Journal of Political Science* 24:177–206.

———. (1982) "Changing Values in Advanced Industrial Societies." *Comparative Political Studies* 14:403–44.

———. (1984) "Electoral Change in Japan: A Study of Secular Realignment," pp. 159–

204 in Dalton, et al., *Electoral Change in Advanced Industrial Democracies: Realignment or Dealignment?*

―――. (1986) "The Role of the Media in the Transformation of the Japanese Political Culture." Paper presented at the Conference on Communication, Politics, and Culture in East Asia, University of Minnesota, Minneapolis.

―――. (1987) "Value Change in Industrial Societies." *American Political Science Review* 81:1303–19.

Flanagan, Scott C., and Aierie Lee. (1988) "Explaining Value Change and Its Political Implications in Eleven Advanced Industrial Democracies." Paper presented at the Fourteenth World Congress of the International Political Science Association, Washington, D.C.

―――. (1990) "The Causes and Socio-Political Implications of Value Change in the Advanced Industrial Democracies." Paper presented at the annual meeting of the Midwest Political Science Association, Chicago.

Flanagan, Scott C., and Bradley Richardson. (1977) *Japanese Electoral Behavior: Social Cleavages, Social Networks and Partisanship.* Sage Contemporary Political Sociology Series, no. 06–024. London: Sage.

Flanagan, Scott C., and Michael D. McDonald. (1979) "Party Identification as a Cross-National Concept: A Comparison of Japanese and American Identifiers." Paper presented at the annual meeting of the American Political Science Association, Washington D.C.

Flanagan, Scott C., and Steven Renten. (1981) "Social Networks and Political Participation in Japan." Paper presented at the annual meeting of the American Political Science Association, New York.

Flanagan, Scott C., and James S. Marshall. (1987) "Japan's Persisting Cultural Politics: Value Cleavages and Partisanship in the 1980's." Paper presented at the annual meeting of the American Political Science Association, Chicago.

Franklin, Mark, ed. (1991) *Social Structure and Party Choice.* New York: Cambridge University Press.

Fuchs, Lawrence H. (1955) "American Jews and the Presidential Vote." *American Political Science Review* 49:385–401.

Fukutake, Tadashi. (1967) *Japanese Rural Society.* Reprint. Ithaca: Cornell University Press, 1972.

George, Alexander. (1980) *Presidential Decisionmaking in Foreign Policy.* Boulder, Colo.: Westview Press.

Goldthorpe, J. H. (1968) *The Affluent Worker: Political Attitudes and Behavior.* Cambridge: Cambridge University Press.

Goot, Murray. (1972) "Party Identification and Party Stability." *British Journal of Political Science* 2:121–25.

Graber, Doris. (1980) *Mass Media and American Politics.* Washington, D.C.: Congressional Quarterly.

―――. (1984) *Processing the News: How People Tame the Information Tide.* New York: Longman.

Graetz, Brian, and Ian McAllister. (1987) "Party Leaders and Electoral Outcomes in Britain, 1974–83." *Comparative Political Studies* 4:484–507.

Hamilton, Richard. (1967) *Affluence and the French Worker.* Princeton: Princeton University Press.

Hayashi, Chikio. (1985) "Recent Theoretical and Methodological Developments in Multidimensional Scaling and Its Related Methods in Japan." *Behaviormetrika* 18:67–79.

———. (1988a) "New Developments in Mutidimensional Data Analysis," pp. 3–11 in *Recent Developments in Clustering and Data Analysis.* New York: Academic Press.

———. (1988b) "Principles and Strategy of Data Analysis." *Journal of the University of the Air* 6:113–19.

———. (1989) "Multiway Data Matrices and Methods of Quantification of Qualitative Data as a Strategy of Data Analysis," pp. 131–42 in R. Coppi and S. Bolasco, eds., *Multiway Data Analysis.* Amsterdam: Elsevier Science Publishers.

Hayashi, Chikio, and Tatsuzo Suzuki. (1984) "Changes in Belief Systems, Quality of Life Issues and Social Conditions over 25 Years in Post-War Japan." *Annals of the Institute of Statistical Mathematics* 36:135–61.

Hazelrigg, Lawrence E. (1970) "Religious and Class Bases of Conflict in Italy." *American Journal of Sociology* 75:496–511.

Heath, Anthony, Roger Jowell, and John Curtice. (1985) *How Britain Votes.* London: Pergamon Press.

Heath, Anthony, and Sarah K. McDonald. (1988) "The Demise of Party Identification Theory?" *Electoral Studies* 7:95–107.

Heradstveit, Daniel. (1979) *The Arab-Isreali Conflict: Psychological Obstacles to Peace.* Oslo: Universitetsforlaget.

Holland, Paul W., and Samuel Leinhardt. (1970) "A Method for Detecting Structure in Sociometric Data." *American Journal of Sociology* 70:492–513.

Horie, Fukashi, and Yoko Kidokoro (1978) "Sosenkyo ni okeru shimbun hodo no naiyo bunseki." *Shimbun Kenkyu* 319:65–71.

Hovland, C. I., A. Lumsdaine, and F. Sheffield. (1950) *Experiments in Mass Communication.* Princeton: Princeton University Press.

Howell, Susan E. (1981) "Short-term Forces and Changing Partisanship." *Political Behavior* 3:163–80.

Huckfeldt, Robert. (1986) *Politics in Context: Assimilation and Conflict in Urban Neighborhoods.* New York: Agathon Press.

Huckfeldt, Robert, and John Sprague (1987) "Networks in Context: The Social Flow of Political Information." *American Political Science Review* 81:1197–1216.

———. (1990) "Social Order and Political Chaos: The Structural Setting of Political Information," pp. 23–58 in John A. Ferejohn and James H. Kuklinski, eds., *Information and Democratic Processes.* Urbana: University of Illinois Press.

Hyman, Herbert. (1959) *Political Socialization.* Glencoe, Ill.: Free Press.

Ibayashi, Tsugio. (1989) "Political Corruption and the Business Establishment." *Japan Echo* 16:47–50.

ICPSR. (1972) *1967 Japanese National Election Study Codebook.*

Iga, Mamoru, and Morton Auerbach. (1977) "Political Corruption and Social Structure in Japan." *Asian Survey* 17:556–64.

Ike, Nobutaka. (1972) *Japanese Politics: Patron-Client Democracy.* New York: Alfred A. Knopf.

———. (1973) "Economic Growth and Intergenerational Change in Japan." *American Political Science Review* 67:1194–1203.

———. (1978) *A Theory of Japanese Democracy.* Boulder, Colo.: Westview Press.

Ikeuchi, Hajime. (1960) "Seiji Ishiki ni Taisuru Shakai shinrigaku teki Sekkin." *Nihon Shakai Shinrigaku Nenpo* 1.

Ikeuchi, Hajime, ed. (1974) *Shimin Ishiki no Kenkyu.* Tokyo: Tokyo University Press.

Inglehart, Ronald. (1971) "The Silent Revolution in Europe: Intergenerational Change in Post-Industrial Societies." *American Political Science Review* 65:991–1017.

———. (1977) *The Silent Revolution: Changing Values and Political Styles among Western Publics.* Princeton: Princeton University Press.

———. (1979) "Value Priorities and Socioeconomic Change," pp. 305–42 in Samuel H. Barnes, Max Kaase, eds., *Political Action: Mass Participation in Five Western Democracies.*

———. (1987) "Value Change in Industrial Societies." *American Political Science Review* 81:1289–1303.

———. (1990) *Culture Shift in Advanced Industrial Society.* Princeton: Princeton University Press.

Inglehart, Ronald, and Hans Klingemann. (1976) "Party Identification, Ideological Preference and the Left-Right Dimension among Western Mass Publics," pp. 243–73 in Ian Budge et al., *Party Identification and Beyond.*

Inkeles, Alex, and David H. Smith. (1974) *Becoming Modern: Individual Change in Six Developing Countries.* Cambridge: Harvard University Press.

Ishida, Takeshi. (1961) *Gendai Soshiki Ron.* Tokyo: Iwanami Shoten.

Ishikawa, Masumi. (1978) *Sengo Seiji Kozo shi.* Tokyo: Hyoronsha.

———. (1984) *Deta Sengo Seiji shi.* Tokyo: Iwanami Shinsho.

Iwase, Youri. (1977) "Seito Shiji Taido no Keisei to Kazoku no Yakuwari." *Hyoron Shakaikagaku* 12:15–48.

Iyengar, Shanto, Mark Peters, and Donald Kinder. (1982) "Experimental Demonstrations of the 'Not-so-Minimal' Consequences of Television News Programs." *American Political Science Review* 76:848–58.

Jackson, John E. (1975) "Issues, Party Choices and Presidential Votes." *American Journal of Political Science* 19:161–85.

Janis, Irving L. (1982) *Groupthink.* Boston: Houghton Mifflin.

Japan Statistical Yearbook. Office of the Prime Minister, Bureau of Statistics. Tokyo: Japan Statistical Association.

Jennings, M. Kent, and Richard G. Niemi. (1968) "The Transmission of Political Values from Parent to Child." *American Political Science Review* 62:169–84.

Jichisho Senkyobu. (1966) *Sangiin Tsujo Senkyo no Jittai.*

————. (1987) *Dai 38 kai Shugiin Giin Sosenkyo, Saibansho Saibankan Kokumin Shinsa Kekka Shirabe*. Tokyo: Jichisho.

Jiji Tsushinsha. (1981) *Sengo Nihon no Seito to Naikaku: Jiji Yoron Chosa ni yoru Bunseki*. Tokyo: Jiji Tsushinsha.

Kaase, Max. (1970) "Determinanten des Wahlverhaltens bei der Bundestagswahl 1969." *Politische Vierteljahresschrift* 11:46–110.

Kaga, Osamu. (1975) "Chuo shi o toshite mita Shimbun no Shakai Sayo ni tsuite— Kankyo Mondai to Yoron Keisei e no Sayo ni Kansuru Kosatsu." *Gakko Hoken Kenkyu* 17:487–97.

Katz, Richard S. (1979) "The Dimensionality of Party Identification: Cross-National Perspectives." *Comparative Politics* 11:147–64.

Kelley, Jonathan, Ian McAllister, and Anthony Mughan. (1985) "The Decline of Class Revisited: Class and Party in England, 1964–1979." *American Political Science Review* 79:719–37.

Kelman, Herbert C. (1961) "Processes of Opinion Change." *Public Opinion Quarterly* 25:57–78.

Kiefer, Christie W. (1976) "Leadership, Sociability and Social Change in a White Collar Danchi," pp. 15–30 in J. White and F. Munger, eds., *Social Change and Community Politics in Japan*. Chapel Hill: University of North Carolina Institute for Research in Social Science.

Kim, Young C. (1981) *Japanese Journalists and Their World*. Charlottesville: University Press of Virginia.

Klapper, Joseph T. (1960) *The Effects of Mass Communication*. New York: Free Press.

Klingemann, Hans D. (1972) "Testing the Left-Right Continuum on a Sample of German Voters." *Comparative Political Studies* 5:93–106.

————. (1973) "Issue-Kompetenz und Wahlentscheidung: Die Einstellung zu wertbezogenen politischen Problemen im Zeitvergleich." *Politische Vierteljahresschrift* 14:227–56.

Klingemann, Hans D., and Franz U. Pappi. (1970) "The 1969 Bundestag Election in the Federal Republic of Germany." *Comparative Politics* 2:523–48.

Klingemann, Hans D., and Charles Taylor. (1978) "Partisanship, Candidates and Issues: Attitudinal Components of the Vote in West German Federal Elections," pp. 97–136 in Max Kaase and Klaus von Beyme, eds., *German Political Studies: Elections and Parties*. London: Sage.

Kohei, Shinsaku. (1972) "Political Behavior of the Japanese People." Unpublished report, NHK Hoso Yoron Chosajo.

————. (1974) "Taisei Sentaku no Seiji Ishiki.." *Bunken Geppo* (NHK) 24, no. 282:1–20.

————. (1979) *Tenkanki no Seiji Ishiki*. Tokyo: Keio Tsushin.

————. (1989) "Changing Values in Japanese Politics." *Japan Echo* 16:23–29.

Kojima, Kazuto. (1982) "Gendai Seinen no Seijiteki Mukanshin no Keisei."

Kojima, Kazuto, and Toyoko Akiyama. (1973) "Generation Gap in Contemporary Japan." *Studies of Broadcasting* (NHK Annual), pp. 191–216.

Komei Senkyo Renmei. (1970) *Dai 32 kai Shugiin Giin Sosenkyo no Jittai*. Tokyo: Komei Senkyo Renmei.

———. (1973) *Dai 33 kai Shugiin Giin Sosenkyo no Jittai*. Tokyo: Komei Senkyo Renmei.

Krauss, Ellis S. (1986) "Creating the News at NHK: Organizational Process and Television News in Japan." Paper presented at the annual meeting of the Association for Asian Studies, Chicago.

Krauss, Ellis S., and James M. Fendrich. (1980) "Political Socialization of U.S. and Japanese Adults: The Impact of Adult Roles on College Leftism." *Comparative Political Studies* 13:3–32.

Kubota, Akira. (1974) "Party Identification and Social Cleavage in Japan." Paper delivered at the annual meeting of the American Political Science Association.

Kubota, Akira, and Robert E. Ward. (1970) "Family Influence and Political Socialization in Japan: Some Preliminary Findings in Comparative Perspective." *Comparative Political Studies* 3:140–75.

Lang, Kurt, and Gladys Engel Lang. (1959) "The Mass Media and Voting," in Eugene Burdick and Arthur Brodbeck, eds., *American Voting Behavior*. Glencoe, Ill.: Free Press.

Langton, Kenneth P., and Ronald Rapoport. (1975) "Social Structure, Social Context and Partisan Mobilization: Urban Workers in Chile." *Comparative Political Studies* 8:318–44.

Larson, Charles. (1973) *Persuasion, Reception and Responsibility*. Belmont, Calif.: Wadsworth.

Lau, Richard R. (1986) "Political Schemata, Candidate Evaluations and Voting Behavior," In Richard R. Lau and David O. Sears, eds., *Political Cognition*. Hillsdale, N.J.: Lawrence Erlbaum Associates.

Lazarsfeld, Paul, Bernard Berelson, and Hazel Gaudet. (1944) *The People's Choice: How the Voter Makes Up His Mind in a Presidential Campaign*. New York: Columbia University Press.

Lebra, Takie Sugiyama. (1976) *Japanese Patterns of Behavior*. Honolulu: University Press of Hawaii.

LeDuc, Lawrence. (1981) "The Dynamic Properties of Party Identification: A Four Nation Comparison." *European Journal of Political Research* 9:257–68.

Leghorn, Rex Yamamoto, and Tatsuzo Suzuki. (1985) "Age, Sex and Cohort: Explicating Social Change in Post-War Japan." *Behaviormetrika* 18:1–16.

Liepelt, Klaus. (1971) "The Infrastructure of Party Support in Germany and Austria," pp. 183–202 in Mattei Dogan and Richard Rose, eds., *European Politics*. Boston: Little, Brown.

Lijphart, Arend. (1968) *The Politics of Accommodation: Pluralism and Democracy in the Netherlands*. Berkeley: University of California Press.

———. (1979) "Religious vs. Linguistic vs. Class Voting: The Crucial Experiment of Comparing Belgium, Canada, South Africa and Switzerland." *American Political Science Review* 73:442–58.

Lipset, Seymour Martin. (1960) *Political Man: The Social Bases of Politics*. New York: Doubleday. Reprint. Johns Hopkins University Press, 1981.

Lipset, Seymour Martin, and Stein Rokkan, eds. (1967) *Party Systems and Voting Alignments: Cross-National Perspectives*. New York: Free Press.

Lodge, Milton G., and Ruth Hamill. (1986) "A Partisan Schema for Political Information Processing." *American Political Science Review* 80:505–20.

Lopreato, Joseph. (1971) "Social Mobility and Political Outlooks in Italy," pp. 202–12 in Dogan and Rose, eds., *European Politics*. Boston: Little, Brown.

Lorwin, Val R. (1966) "Belgium: Religion, Class and Language in National Politics," pp. 147–87 in Robert A. Dahl, ed., *Political Oppositions in Western Democracies*. New Haven: Yale University Press.

McClosky, Herbert, and Harold E. Dahlgren. (1959) "Primary Group Influence on Party Loyalty." *American Political Science Review* 53:757–76.

McClure, Robert D., and Thomas E. Patterson. (1974) "Television News and Political Advertising: The Impact of Exposure on Voter Beliefs." *Communication Research* 1:3–31.

McCombs, Maxwell E., and Donald L. Shaw. (1972) "The Agenda-Setting Function of Mass Media." *Public Opinion Quarterly* 36:176–87.

McGuire, William J. (1968) "The Nature of Attitudes and Attitude Change," pp. 136–272 in Gardner Lindzey, ed., *Handbook in Social Psychology*. Reading, Mass.: Addison, Wesley. Reprint. Random House, 1985.

MacKuen, Michael Bruce, and Steven Lane Coombs. (1981) *More than News: Media Power in Public Affairs*. Beverly Hills: Sage.

Maeda, Toshikazu. (1978) "Kodokushi to Seiji Ishiki." *Hogaku Kenkyu,* Keio Daigaku, 51:815–42.

Maggiotto, Michael A., and James E. Piereson. (1977) "Partisan Identification and Electoral Choice: The Hostility Hypothesis." *American Journal of Political Science* 21:645–767.

Manheim, Jarol B. (1976) "Can Democracy Survive Television?" *Journal of Communication* 26:84–90.

Mann, Thomas E., and Raymond E. Wolfinger. (1980) "Candidates and Parties in Congressional Elections." *American Political Science Review* 74:617–32.

Markus, Gregory B., and Philip E. Converse. (1979) "A Dynamic Simultaneous Equation Model of Electoral Choice." *American Political Science Review* 73:1055–70.

Maruyama, Masao. (1963) *Thought and Behavior in Modern Japan*. London: Oxford University Press.

Massey, Joseph A. (1976) *Youth and Politics in Japan*. Lexington, Mass.: D. C. Heath.

Masuda, Hiroshi. (1979) *Nihon Gaiko no Kadai to Kakuto no Seisaku*. Tokyo: Keio Tsushin.

Masumi, Junnosuke. (1966–80) *Nihon Seito Shiron*. 7 vols. Tokyo: Todai Shuppankai.

Matthews, Donald R., and James W. Prothro. (1966) *Negroes and The New Southern Politics*. New York: Harcourt, Brace and World.

Miller, Arthur H., Martin P. Wattenberg, and Oksana Malanchuk. (1986) "Schematic

Assessments of Presidential Candidates." *American Political Science Review* 80:521–40.

Miller, Warren E., and Philip Stouthard. (1975) "Confessional Attachment and Electoral Behavior in the Netherlands." *European Journal of Political Research* 3:219–58.

Miller, William. (1978) "Social Class and Party Choice in England: A New Analysis." *British Journal of Political Science* 8:257–84.

Mitani, Taiichiro. (1977) *Nihon Seitoseiji no Keisei—Hara Kei no Seijishido no Tenkai*. Tokyo: Todai Shuppankai.

Miyake, Ichiro. (1970) "Seiji Ishiki to Tohyo Kodo," pp. 235–95 in Ritsuo Akimoto and Hideo Uchiyama, eds., *Gendai Shakai to Seiji Taikei*. Tokyo: Jichosha.

———. (1971) "Seito Shiji no Ryudosei to Anteisei," in Nihon Seiji Gakkai, ed., *Nenpo Seijigaku 1970*. Tokyo: Iwanami Shoten.

———. (1979) "Yukensha Kozo no Hendo to Senkyo," pp. 259–302 in Nihon Seiji Gakkai, ed., *55 Nen Taisei no Keisei to Hokai*. Tokyo: Iwanami Shoten.

———. (1982) "Trust in Government and Political Cleavages: A Cross-National Comparison." *Doshisha Law Review* 171:802–84; 172:971–1064.

———. (1983a) "Seito Shiji Kyodo no Shocho." *Doshisha Hogaku* 179:1–53.

———. (1983b) "Surge and Decline in the Strength of Partisanship." *Doshisha Law Review* 177:1–43.

———. (1985) *Seito Shiji no Bunseki*. Tokyo: Sobunsha.

———. (1989) *Tohyo Kodo*. Tokyo: Tokyo Daigaku Shuppankai.

———. (1991) "Jiminto Shiji no Hendo to Itsudatsu Tohyo." *Kobe Hogaku Zasshi*.

Miyake, Ichiro, Tomio Kinoshita, and Juichi Aiba. (1967) *Kotonaru Reberu no Senkyo ni Okeru Tohyo Kodo no Kenkyu*. Tokyo: Sobunsha.

Mughan, Anthony. (1989) Candidate-Oriented Voting in Parliamentary Systems: Australia and Great Britain. Unpublished paper.

Murakami, Shigeyoshi. (1971) *Gendai Nihon no Shukyo Mondai*. Tokyo: Asahi Shimbunsha.

Murakami, Yasusuke. (1982) "The Age of New Middle Mass Politics: The Case of Japan." *Journal of Japanese Studies* 8:29–72.

Naganuma, Iwane. (1983) *Chiho Seijika*. Tokyo: Banseisha.

Nakamura, Hajime. (1964) *Ways of Thinking of Eastern Peoples*. Honolulu: University Press of Hawaii.

Nakamura, Takafusa. (1971) *Senzenki Nihon Keizai Seicho no Bunseki*. Tokyo: Iwanami Shoten.

Nakane, Chie. (1970) *Japanese Society*. Berkeley: University of California Press.

Newcomb, Theodore M. (1957) *Personality and Social Change: Attitude Formation in a Student Community*. New York: Dryden.

NHK-HYC (Nihon Hoso Kyokai Hoso Yoron Chosa jo). (1975) *Nihonjin no Ishiki:* NHK Yoron Chosa. Tokyo: Shiseido.

———. (1979, 1985) *Gendai Nihonjin no Ishiki Kozo*, vols. 1 and 2. Tokyo: Nippon Hoso Shuppan Kyokai.

Nie, Norman H., and Kristi Andersen. (1974) "Mass Belief Systems Revisited: Political Change and Attitude Structure." *Journal of Politics* 36:541–91.

Nie, Norman H., Sidney Verba, and John R. Petrocik. (1976) *The Changing American Voter*. Cambridge: Harvard University Press.

Niemi, Richard G. (1974) *How Family Members Perceive Each Other*. New Haven: Yale University Press.

Niemi, Richard G., and Herbert F. Weisberg, eds. (1976) *Controversies in American Voting Behavior*. San Francisco: W. H. Freeman.

Nisbett, Richard, and Lee Ross. (1980) *Human Inference: Strategies and Shortcomings of Social Judgment*. Englewood Cliffs, N.J.: Prentice-Hall.

Nishihira, Naoki. (1964) "A Study of the Social Attitudes of the Present-Day Japanese Youth." *Psychologia* (Department of Psychology, Kyoto University) 7:192–98.

Nishihira, Shigeki. (1972) *Nihon no Senkyo*. Tokyo: Shiseido.

———. (1980) "Yoron Chosa ni miru Dojidai shi (3)." *Jiyu*, November.

———. (1981) "Yoron Chosa ni miru Dojidai shi (5)." *Jiyu*, January.

Norbeck, Edward. (1961) "Postwar Cultural Change and Continuity in Northeastern Japan." *American Anthropologist* 63:297–321.

Norpoth, Helmut. (1977) "Kanzlerkandidaten." *Politische Vierteljahresschrift* 18:551–72.

———. (1978) "Party Identification in Germany: Tracing an Elusive Concept." *Comparative Political Studies* 8:36–61.

Norpoth, Helmut, and Kendall Baker. (1980) "Mass Media Use and Electoral Choice in West Germany." *Comparative Politics* 13:1–14.

Oita Ken Senkyo Kanri Iinkai. (1962) "Senkyo no Jittai: Yoron Chosa no Kekka Gaiyo." Unpublished report, Oita Ken Senkyo Kanri Iinkai.

Okamura, Tadao. (1968) "The Child's Changing Image of the Prime Minister." *Developing Economies* 6:566–86.

Page, Benjamin I., and Calvin C. Jones. (1979) "Reciprocal Effects of Policy Preferences, Party Loyalties and the Vote." *American Political Science Review* 73:1071–89.

Parsons, Talcott. (1951) *The Social System*. New York: Free Press.

Passin, Herbert H. (1975) "Changing Values: Work and Growth in Japan." *Asian Survey* 15:821–50.

Passin, Herbert H., ed. (1979) *A Season of Voting: The Japanese Elections of 1976 and 1977*. Washington, D.C.: American Enterprise Institute for Public Policy Research.

Pempel, T. J. (1982) *Policy and Politics in Japan*. Philadelphia: Temple University Press.

Percheron, Annick, and M. Kent Jennings. (1981) "Political Continuities in French Families." *Comparative Politics* 13:421–36.

Pharr, Susan J. (1981) *Political Women in Japan*. Berkeley: University of California Press.

Pomper, Gerald. (1972) "From Confusion to Clarity: Issues and American Voters, 1956–68." *American Political Science Review* 66: 415–28.

Przeworski, Adam, and Glaucio Soares. (1971) "Theories in Search of a Curve: A Contextual Interpretation of Left Vote." *American Political Science Review* 65:51–68.

Putnam, Robert D. (1966) "Political Attitudes and the Local Community." *American Political Science Review* 60: 640–54.

Pye, Lucien W. (1966) *Aspects of Political Development*. Boston: Little, Brown.

Rabinowitz, George, James W. Prothro, and William Jacoby. (1982) "Salience as a Factor in the Impact of Issues on Candidate Evaluation." *Journal of Politics* 44:41–63.

Radtke, Gunther. (1972) "Gibt es in der Bundesrepublik eine Parteiidentifikation?" *Verfassung und Verfassungswirklichkeit* 6:68–91.

Reed, Steven R. (1988) "The People Speak: The Influence of Elections on Japanese Politics, 1949–55," *Journal of Japanese Studies* 14 (Summer).

———. (1990) "The 1990 General Election: Explaining the Historic Socialist Victory." Paper presented at the biannual meeting of the Southern Regional Japan Studies Seminar. Atlanta.

Reich, Charles A. (1970) *The Greening of America*. New York: Bantam Books.

Repass, David E. (1971) "Issue Salience and Party Choice." *American Political Science Review* 65:389–400.

Richardson, Bradley M. (1966) "Voting Behavior and Political Participation in Japan." Ph.D. diss. University of California, Berkeley.

———. (1967a) "A Japanese House of Councillors Election: Support Mobilization and Political Recruitment." *Modern Asian Studies* 1:393–96.

———. (1967b) "Japanese Local Politics: Support Mobilization and Leadership Styles." *Asian Survey* 7:860–75.

———. (1974) *The Political Culture of Japan*. Berkeley: University of California Press.

———. (1975) "Party Loyalties and Party Salience in Japan." *Comparative Political Studies* 8:32–57.

———. (1977) "Stability and Change in Japanese Voting Behavior, 1958–72." *Journal of Asian Studies* 36:675–93.

———. (1986) "Japan's Habitual Voters: Partisanship on the Emotional Periphery." *Comparative Political Studies* 19:356–84.

———. (1987) "Candidate, Constituency Campaign, and Party in Japanese Parliamentary Election Voting." Unpublished manuscript.

———. (1988) "Constituency Candidates vs. Parties in Japanese Voting Behavior." *American Political Science Review* 82:695–718

———. (1991) "European Party Loyalties Revisited." *American Political Science Review*, Sept.

Richardson, Bradley M., and Scott C. Flanagan. (1984) *Politics in Japan*. Boston: Little, Brown.

Robinson, John P. (1972) "Mass Communication and Information Diffusion," pp. 71–93 in F. G. Kline and P. J. Tichenor, eds., *Current Perspectives in Mass Communication Research*. Beverly Hills: Sage.

————. (1974) "The Press as King-Maker." *Journalism Quarterly* 51:587–94.

Rochon, Thomas. (1981) "Electoral Systems and the Basis of the Vote: The Case of Japan," pp. 1–24 in John Creighton Campbell, ed., *Parties, Candidates and Voters in Japan: Six Quantitative Studies*, vol. 2. Ann Arbor: Michigan Papers in Japanese Studies.

Rose, Richard. (1968) "Class and Party Divisions: Britain as a Test Case." *Sociology* 2:129–62.

————. (1982) "From Simple Determinism to Interactive Models of Voting: Britain as an Example." *Comparative Political Studies* 15:145–70.

Rose, Richard, ed. (1974) *Electoral Behavior: A Comparative Handbook*. New York: Free Press.

Rose, Richard, and Derek Urwin. (1969) "Social Cohesion, Political Parties and Strains in Regimes." *Comparative Political Studies* 2:7–67.

Rose, Richard, and Guy Peters. (1978) *Can Government Go Bankrupt?* New York: Basic Books.

Rose, Richard, and Ian McAllister. (1986) *Voters Begin to Choose: From Closed-Class to Open Elections in Britain*. London: Sage.

Rossi, Peter H. (1959) "Four Landmarks in Voting Research," pp. 5–54 in Eugene Burdick and A. J. Brodbeck, eds., *American Voting Behavior*. Glencoe, Ill.: Free Press.

Roszak, Theodore. (1969) *The Making of a Counter Culture*. New York: Doubleday.

Rusk, Jerrold, and Ole Borre. (1974) "The Changing Party Space in Danish Voter Perceptions, 1971–73." *European Journal of Political Research* 2:329–62.

Sani, Giacomo. (1974a) "Determinants of Party Preference in Italy: Toward the Integration of Complementary Models." *American Journal of Political Science* 15:315–29.

Sani, Giacomo. (1974b) "A Test of the Least-Distance Model of Voting Choice: Italy 1972." *Comparative Political Studies* 7:193–298.

Sartori, Giovanni. (1969) "The Sociology of Parties: A Critical View," pp. 1–25 in Otto Stammer, ed., *Party Systems, Party Organizations and the Politics of the New Masses*. Berlin: Institut für politische Wissenschaft an der Freien Universität Berlin.

Sato, Seizaburo. (1989) "The Recruit Affair: Criticizing the Critics." *Japan Echo* 16:40–46.

Scalapino, Robert A., and Junnosuke Masumi. (1962) *Parties and Politics in Contemporary Japan*. Berkeley: University of California Press.

Sears, David O., and Jonathan L. Freedman. (1967) "Selective Exposure to Information: A Critical Review." *Public Opinion Quarterly* 31:194–213.

Segal, David R., and Marshall W. Meyer. (1974) "The Social Context of Political Partisanship," pp. 217–32 in Mattei Dogan and Stein Rokkan, eds., *Social Ecology*. Cambridge: M.I.T. Press.

Seiji Koho Senta. (1977) *Seiji Handobukku*. Tokyo. Seiji Koho Senta.

Shaw, Donald, and Maxwell McCombs. (1977) *The Emergence of American Political Issues: The Agenda Setting Function of the Press*. St. Paul: West.

Sheingold, Carl A. (1973) "Social Networks and Voting: The Resurrection of a Research Agenda." *American Sociological Review* 38:712–20.

Shell, Kurt L. (1969) "The Socialist Party in Austria—A Party of Integration?" in Kurt L. Shell, ed., *The Democratic Political Process*. Waltham, Mass.: Blaisdell.

Shimane Ken Senkyo Kanri Iinkai. (1960) *Shimane Ken ni Okeru Seiji Ishiki to Tohyo Kodo*.

Shinohara, Hajime. (1970) "Kokumin no 'Shiru Kenri' to Shimbun," *Shimbun Kenkyu* 227:7–14.

———. (1989) "The Day the Mountains Moved." *Japan Echo* 16:14–22.

Shiratori, Rei. (1972) *Yoron, Senkyo, Seiji*. Tokyo: Nihon Keizai Shimbun.

Siegfried, Andre. (1913) *Tableau politique de la France de l'ouest sous la Troisième République*. Paris: Libraire Armand Colin.

Smith, Anthony. (1981) "Mass Communications," pp. 173–95 in David Butler, Howard R. Penniman, and Austin Ranney, eds., *Democracy at the Polls*. Washington, D.C.: American Enterprise Institute.

Steiner, Kurt. (1956) "The Japanese Village and Its Government." *Far Eastern Quarterly* 12:175–90.

———. (1965) *Local Government in Japan*. Stanford: Stanford University Press.

Stephens, John D. (1981) "The Changing Swedish Electorate: Class Voting, Contextual Effects, and Voter Volatility." *Comparative Political Studies* 14:163–204.

Studlar, Donley T., and Susan Welch. (1981) "Mass Attitudes on Issues in Britain." *Comparative Political Studies* 14:327–55.

Takahashi, Akiyoshi. (1977) "Jiminto no Noson Shihai," in Rei Shiratori, ed., *Hoshutaisei*, vol. 1. Tokyo: Toyo Keizai Shimposha.

Takayama, Yoshiyuki. (1980) *Fubyodo no Keizai Bunseki*. Tokyo: Toyo Keizai Shimposha.

Takeuchi, Yasuo. (1989) "Recruit in Review," *Japan Echo* 16:38–39.

Tanaka, Zenichiro. (1977) "Hoshushihai Anteiki (Dai 29, 30, 31 kai Sosenkyo)," in Masao Soma, ed., *Kokusei Senkyo to Seito Shiji*. Tokyo: Seiji Koho Senta.

Tannenbaum, P., B. Greenberg, and F. Silverman. (1962) "Candidate Images," in S. Kraus, ed., *The Great Debates*. Bloomington: Indiana University Press.

Tarrow, Sidney. (1971) "The Urban-Rural Cleavage in Political Involvement: The Case of France." *American Political Science Review* 65:341–57.

Thayer, Nathaniel B. (1969) *How the Conservatives Rule Japan*. Princeton: Princeton University Press.

Thomassen, Jacques. (1976) "Party Identification as a Cross-National Concept: Its Meaning in the Netherlands," pp.63–80 in Ian Budge et al., *Party Identification and Beyond*.

Tichenor, Philip J., George A. Donohue, and Clarice A. Olien. (1970) "Mass Media Flow and Differential Growth in Knowledge." *Public Opinion Quarterly* 34:159–70.

Tingsten, Herbert. (1963) *Political Behavior: Studies in Election Statistics*. Trans. Vilgot Hammarling. Totowa, N.J.: Bedminster.

Toffler, Alvin. (1980) *The Third Wave*. New York: Bantam Books.

Tominaga, Ken'ichi. (1979) *Nihon Shakai no Kaiso Kozo*.Tokyo: Todai Shuppankai.

Tominomori, Eiji. (1977) *Sengo Hoshuto Shi*. Tokyo: Nihonhyoronsha.

Torgerson, Warren S. (1958) *Theory and Methods of Scaling*. New York: John Wiley and Sons.

Trenaman, J., and D. McQuail. (1961) *Television and the Political Image*. London: Methuen.

Trilling, Richard J. (1976) *Party Image and Electoral Behavior*. New York: John Wiley.

TSK-KCI (Tokei Suri Kenkyujo Kokuminsei Chosa Iinkai). (1961, 1970, 1975, and 1982) *Nipponjin no kokuminsei,* vols. 1–4. Tokyo: Shiseido.

———. (1979) *A Study of the Japanese National Character: The Sixth Nationwide Survey, 1978*. Tokyo: Tokei Suri Kenkyujo Report, general series, no. 46, March.

———. (1984) *Kokuminsei no Kenkyu dai 7 kai Zenkoku Chosa: 1983 nen Zenkoku Chosa*. Tokyo: TSK Kenkyu Report, no. 60, November.

———. (1985) *Kokuminsei Chosa no Kohoto Bunseki: dai 3 han*. Tokyo: TSK Kenkyu Report, no. 62, March.

———. (1989) *Kokuminsei no Kenkyu dai 8 kai Zenkoku Chosa: 1988 nen Zenkoku Chosa*. Tokyo: TSK Kenkyu Report No. 69 (November).

Verba, Sidney, and Norman H. Nie. (1972) *Participation in America: Political Democracy and Social Equality*. New York: Harper and Row.

———. (1975) "Political Participation," pp. 1–74 in Fred Greenstein and Nelson Polsby, *Nongovernmental Politics* vol. 4 of *Handbook of Political Science*. Reading, Mass.: Addison-Wesley.

Verba, Sidney, Norman H. Nie, and Jae-on Kim. (1978) *Participation and Political Equality: A Seven Nation Comparison* New York: Cambridge University Press.

Wagner, Joseph. (1983) "Media Do Make a Difference: The Differential Impact of Mass Media in the 1976 Presidential Race." *American Journal of Political Science* 27:407–30.

Wakata, Kyoji. (1986) "Electoral Mobilization in Kansai and California." *Kansai University Review of Law and Politics* 7:31–104.

Ward, Robert E. (1951) "The Socio-Political Role of the Buraku (Hamlet) in Japan." *American Political Science Review* 45:1025–40.

———. (1960) "Urban-Rural Differences and the Process of Political Modernization in Japan." *Economic Development and Cultural Change* 9:135–65.

Watanuki, Joji. (1967a) "Daitoshi Jumin no Seiji Ishiki," *Nihon Rodo Kyokai Zasshi* 94:11–23.

———. (1967b) "Patterns of Politics in Present-Day Japan," pp. 447–66 in Seymour Martin Lipset and Stein Rokkan, eds., *Party Systems and Voter Alignments*. New York: Free Press.

———. (1977) "Tradition and Modernity in Voting Behavior in the 1950s," pp. 77–100 in Joji Watanuki, *Politics in Postwar Japanese Society*. Tokyo: University of Tokyo Press.

———. (1990) "Welfare Policy, Welfare Society, and Welfare State: The Case of Japan." *Journal of International Studies* (Sophia University) 24:17–29.

Watanuki, Joji, Ichiro Miyake, Takashi Inoguchi, and Ikuo Kabashima. (1986) *Nihonjin no Senkyo Kodo*. Tokyo: Tokyo Daigaku Shuppankai.

Wattenberg, Martin. (1981) "The Decline of Political Partisanship in the United States: Negativity or Neutrality?" *American Political Science Review* 75:941–50.

Weatherford, M. Stephen. (1982) "Interpersonal Networks and Political Behavior." *American Journal of Political Science* 26:117–43.

Weisberg, Herbert F. (1980) "A Multidimensional Conceptualization of Party Identification." *Political Behavior* 2:33–60.

———. (1982) "Party Evaluation: A Theory of Separate Effect." Paper presented at the annual meeting of the Midwest Political Science Association, Chicago.

West, S. G., S. P. Gunn, and P. Chernicky. (1975) "Ubiquitous Watergate: An Attributional Analysis." *Journal of Personality and Social Psychology* 32:55–65.

White, Harrison C., Scott A. Boorman, and Ronald L. Breiger. (1976) "Social Structure from Multiple Networks: Block Models of Roles and Position." *American Journal of Sociology* 81:730–80.

White, James W. (1976) "The Metropolitan Voter: Causal Patterns in Electoral Behavior in Tokyo." Paper presented at the Conference on Local Political Opposition in Japan, Wrightsville Beach, N.C.

———. (1982) *Migration in Metropolitan Japan*. Berkeley: Institute of East Asian Studies, University of California, Berkeley.

Winham, George, and Robert Cunningham. (1970) "Party Leader Images in the 1968 Federal Election." *Canadian Journal of Political Science* 3:31–55.

Yamamoto, Tsuyoshi. (1978) *Nik Kan Kankei*. Tokyo: Kyoikusha.

Yanai, Michio. (1972a) "Tokyo to Chiji Senkyo ni okeru Imeii Kiyanpein." *Bulletin of the Faculty of Humanities* (Sekei University) 8:53–82.

———. (1972b) "Tokyo to Chiji Senkyo ni okeru Masu Meidia no Taio." *Shimbungaku Hyoron* 21:36–54.

Yasuda, Saburo, ed. (1973) *Gendai Nihon no Kaikyu Ishiki*. Tokyo: Yuhikaku.

Yoron Chosa Reports. (1989) *Hoso Bunka to Chosa* (January). Tokyo: NHK Hoso Yoron Chosa Kenkyusho.

Yoshihara, Tsuneo, and Osamu Nishi. (1979) *Nihon no Anzenhosho to Kakuto no Boeiseisaku*. Tokyo: Kyoikusha.

Zohlnhofer, Werner. (1969) "Party Identification in the Federal Republic of Germany and the United States," pp. 148–58 in Kurt Shell, ed., *The Democratic Political Process*. Waltham, Mass.: Blaisdell.

■ Index